THE POSTCARD PRICE GUIDE

A Comprehensive Reference

TH EDITION

J. L. Mashburn

Thousands of Prices, Representing Millions of Cards

COLONIAL HOUSE
Enka, North Carolina 28728 USA

Publisher: J. L. Mashburn
Editor: Emma Mashburn

Cover and Interior Design: Colonial House Publishers
Electronic Page Assembly: Colonial House Publishers

A Colonial House Production

Printed in the United States of America

Fourth Edition

10 9 8 7 6 5 4 3

Library of Congress Cataloging-in-Publication Data

Mashburn, J. L. (Joseph Lee)
    The postcard price guide: a comprehensive reference / J. L. Mashburn. -- 4th ed.
        p. cm.
    "Thousands of prices, representing millions of cards."
    Includes index.
    ISBN 1-885940-08-4 (pbk.)
        1. Postcards–Collectors and collecting–United States–Catalogs. 2.
    Postcards–History–20th century--Catalogs. I. Title.

NC1872 .M37 2001
741.6'83'0973075--dc21   00-065785
                                                                  CIP

The author and publisher have made every effort in the preparation of this book to ensure the accuracy of the information. However, the information in this book is sold without warranty, either express or implied. Neither the author nor Colonial House will be liable for any damages caused or alleged to be caused directly, indirectly, incidentally, or consequentially by the information in this book.

AN IMPORTANT NOTICE TO
THE READERS OF THIS PRICE GUIDE:

The comprehensive nature of compiling data and prices on the thousands of cards, sets and series in this publication gives many probabilities for error. Although all information has been compiled from reliable sources, experienced collectors and dealers, some data may still be questionable. The author and publisher will not be held responsible for any losses that might occur in the purchase or sale of cards because of the information contained herein.

The author will be most pleased to receive notice of errors so that they may be corrected in future editions. Contact: J. L. Mashburn, Colonial House, Box 609, Enka NC 28728 USA.

This book and other Mashburn price guides are available worldwide on the Internet at Colonial House Website: http://www.postcard-books.com

---

On the cover: P.F.B. Series 3903, "Cake Walk"

Contents

ACKNOWLEDGMENTS

Appreciation is extended to the following contributors who have given their time and effort by creating, revising or verifying listings and checklists, lending cards for scanning, and for help with countless valuations.

It takes many willing hands and minds to make a book of this size and very comprehensive nature. Without the tremendous input and support from knowledgeable collectors and dealers wanting to make our hobby the best it can be, it would have been an impossible task. Special thanks are given to **John and Sandy Millns, Shirley and Dale Hendricks, Sixto Campana, Russell Hughes** and **Andreas Brown** for their continued support in supplying beautiful cards from their collections for scanning and for additions to checklists. The numerous images they have supplied have helped decorate these pages and have provided a broad insight to collectors showing what is actually available in the **wonderful world of postcards**!

Special thanks also to **Jane Morrison** and **Naomi Welch** for important additions to the Harrison Fisher checklists; to **George Parola** for additions and editing of the Bessie Gutmann and Meta Grimball listings; to **Gordon Gesner** for continuous updating of Philip Boileau's cards; to **Martin Shapiro** for his outstanding contributions concerning cards and checklists of *Wiener Werkstätte, Mucha, Bauhaus,* and other quality cards; to **Fred Kahn** for his tremendous help in providing reports on U.S. market conditions and values, as well as many cards for scanning.

A very special thanks also to **Dr. Antonio and Pia Dell'Aquila** of Bari, Italy for allowing us to update our checklist of Raphael Kirchner using various listings and values from their wonderful book, *Raphael Kirchner and His Postcards,* and to Munich's **Detlef Hilmer** and his fine staff, for allowing me the run of his world famous postcard shop on my visits each year. If ever there was a postcard heaven for me...this is it!

Thanks also to **Alyce Thorson, Audrey Buffington, Lee** and **Shirley Cox, Marilyn Brust, Elaine Taylor, Vernon Ham, Dr. Dennis Hart, Don Preziosi, George Gibbs, Stan Davidson, Pete Brown**, **Steve** and **William Poteet, Norm Platnick, Ben Hawes, Dan DePalma, Rick Crocker, John Monroe, Doug Alford, Richard North, Joseph Epler, Elizabeth West, Kathy Danielson,** Finland's **Kosti Kallio, and England's Brian Smith, Brian Hordle** and **Di,** who continue to supply valuable information on new additions and cards for scanning; to the hundreds of collectors and dealers who have called or written to express their approval and acceptance of our labor; and most of all to Emma.

Introduction

STILL A THRIVING HOBBY!

It has been over three years since the Third Edition of *The Postcard Price Guide* was released. During that time, interest in postcard collecting has continued to grow and prosper. The advent of the Internet, in combination with eBay and other auctions, has literally made it possible (and with ease) for U.S. dealers and collectors to bid or buy from other collectors and dealers from all over the world. With the new computer technology available, postcards may be scanned quickly and most beautifully, and the images can be sent on "approval" by E-mail and can be downloaded by collectors worldwide in a matter of minutes. This saves time, mailing and postage costs, as well as all the wear and tear on cards that are sent the normal "approval" way.

Many new and very avid collectors, both young and old, have entered the hobby with much enthusiasm to pursue their favorite specialties. Creating much additional interest and helpful information is a wonderful new book, *The American and European Postcards of Harrison Fisher Illustrator,* by Naomi Welch. Also, an upcoming release that will greatly impact the market is the book, *Samuel L. Schmucker: The Discovery of His Lost Art,* by Jack and Susan Davis. It concerns the original artwork of S.L. Schmucker which was used for his extremely rare postcards by Detroit Publishing Co. These two reference books, plus our own new titles, *The Sports Postcard Price Guide* and *Black Postcards Price Guide, 2nd Edition,* will be of great help to all postcard enthusiasts.

According to U.S. dealers, the most revered and highly sought-after cards at the present time are those of small town views and real photos of all types, motifs, and eras. However, they also say that these cards have become very scarce and almost impossible to replace for inventory. In the artist-signed market, which has greatly improved, the leaders are Art Deco and rarer cards of beautiful ladies, children and all fantasy types, including Santas, Halloween, dressed animals, golliwoggs, etc.

In this edition, readers will see many changes of values since the Third Edition. This is especially true of the most popular types, various motifs of highest quality, and those in superior condition. However, many groups have not prospered and values have remained the same, or have gone somewhat lower in some instances. There are times when various groups have a dormant period, but good quality cards in best condition will soon return to their former popularity.

–J. L. Mashburn

HOW TO USE THIS PRICE GUIDE

This price guide has been uniquely designed to serve the needs of both the beginning and advanced collector, as well as the established postcard dealer. Our attempt to provide a comprehensive guide to postcards dating from the 1890's through the 1960's makes it possible for even the novice collector to consult it with confidence and ease in finding each particular listing. The following important explanations summarize general practices that will help in getting the most benefits from its use.

CATEGORICAL ARRANGEMENT

Cards are arranged by category, and each category is listed in the Table of Contents. All **artist-drawn** cards are listed under a particular type or theme and have three categorical listings: **Artist-Signed, Publishers, and Anonymous.** **Artists** are listed in alphabetical order in each category and the artist's nationality is listed (if known), as are the publishers if the cards are unsigned.

Publisher listings are usually those of (1) **artist-drawn** cards or, (2) **topical** cards, that do not show the artist's signature. All of these are also listed alphabetically and may include individual listings of some of the most prominent cards, the ones most popular to collectors, and their values. Otherwise, the **prices listed are for generalized cards in the particular topic or theme.**

LISTINGS

Listings may be identified as follows:
1. **SECTION** (Artist-Signed, Fantasy, etc.).
2. **TOPIC** (Beautiful Women, Cats, Dogs, etc.).
3. **ARTIST** (Listed in Bold Capital Letters) when available.
4. **PUBLISHER** (Listed in Bold, Lower Case Letters).
5. **NAME OF SERIES; OR SERIES NUMBER.**
6. **NUMBER OF CARDS IN SET OR SERIES** (In Parentheses) when available.
7. **CAPTION OR TITLE OF CARD** (Enclosed in Quotation Marks).
8. **PRICE RANGE OF 1 CARD IN VERY GOOD CONDITION**
9. **PRICE RANGE OF 1 CARD IN EXCELLENT CONDITION**

Example:

1. **ARTIST-SIGNED**
2. **BEAUTIFUL WOMEN**
3. **HARRISON FISHER**
4. **Reinthal & Newman**
5. **101 Series**
6. (12)
7. "American Beauties"
8. $12 - 15
9. $15 - 20

CONDITION AND GRADING OF POSTCARDS

The condition of a postcard, as with old coins, stamps, books, etc., is an extremely important factor in pricing it for the collector, the dealer, and for those having found cards to sell. Damaged, worn, creased, or dirty cards –cards in less than Very Good condition–are almost uncollectible unless they are to be used as a space filler until a better one is found. **Collectors should never buy a damaged card if they expect to sell it later on.**

It is necessary that some sort of card grading standard be used so that buyer and seller may come to an informed agreement on the value of a card. Two different collectible conditions, **Very Good** and **Excellent,** are used in **THE POST CARD PRICE GUIDE**. There are, of course, higher and lower grades, but these will be most normally seen and most normally quoted for postcards sold throughout the hobby. The standard grading system adapted by most dealers and by the leading postcard hobby publications in the field, "Barr's Post Card News" and "Post Card Collector," is listed below with their permission:

M–MINT. A perfect card just as it comes from the printing press. No marks, or creases, and no writing or postmarks. A clean and fresh card. Cards of this grade are seldom seen.

NM–NEAR MINT. Like Mint but with very light aging or very slight discoloration from being in an album for many years. Not as sharp or crisp.

EX–EXCELLENT. Like mint in appearance with no bends or creases, or rounded or blunt corners. May be postally used or unused and may have writing and postmark only on the address side. A clean, fresh card on the picture side.

VG–VERY GOOD. Corners may be just a bit blunt or rounded. Almost undetectable crease or bend that does not detract from overall appearance of the picture side. May have writing or postal use on address side. A very collectible card.

G–GOOD. Corners may be lightly blunt/rounded with noticeable bends or creases. May be postally used or have writing on address side. Less than VG.

FR–FAIR. Card is intact. Excess soil, stains, creases, writing, or cancellation may affect picture. Could be a scarce card that is difficult to find in any condition.

Postcard dealers always want better condition cards that have no defects. Collectors should keep this in mind if they have cards to sell. Therefore, anyone building a collection should maintain a standard for condition and stick to it. Even if the asking price is a little higher when a card is purchased, it will be worth the cost when it is resold.

VALUATIONS

The postcard values quoted in this publication represent the current retail market. They were compiled with assistance from some of the leading dealers in the U.S., dealer pricing at shows, personal dealer communications, from the author's personal purchasing worldwide, from his approval sales, and from his active day-to-day involvement in the postcard field.

Some values were also compiled from observations of listings in auctions, auction catalogs (U.S., Europe, and Great Britain), prices realized and fixed price sales in the fine hobby publications, *Barr's Post Card News* and *Postcard Collector*, and other related publications. **In most instances, listings of high and low values were taken for each observation, and these were averaged to obtain the "Very Good" and "Excellent" prices quoted. It must be stressed that this price guide and reference work is intended to serve only as an aid in evaluating postcards. It should not be used otherwise. As we all know, actual market conditions change constantly, and prices may fluctuate.** The trend for postcards seems to always be to the upside.

Price ranges for cards in **Very Good** and **Excellent** conditions are found at the end of each listing. Values for cards in less than VG condition would be much lower, while those grading above EX might command relatively higher prices.

Without exception, prices quoted are for **one** card, whether it be a single entity or one card in a complete set or series. Note that after many entries a number is enclosed in parentheses; e.g., (6). This number indicates the total number of cards in a set or in a series. The price listed is for one card in the set and must be multiplied by this number to determine the value of a complete set.

WHY PRICE RANGES ARE QUOTED

For cards graded both **Very Good** and **Excellent**, price ranges are quoted for four major reasons. Any one, or more, of the following can determine the difference in the high or low prices in each of the listing ranges.

1. Prices vary in different geographical areas across the United States. At this time, they are somewhat higher on the Pacific coast and other western states. They tend to be a little lower in the East and somewhere in-between in

the central and Midwestern states. For instance, a card with a price range of $6.00-8.00 might sell for $6.00 in the East, $7.00 in the Mid-West and $8.00 in the Far West.

2. Dealer price valuations also vary. Those who continually set up at postcard shows seem to have a better feel for prices and know which cards are selling well and, therefore, can adjust their prices accordingly. Dealers who sell only by mail, or by mail auction, tend to price their cards (or list estimated values in their auctions) just a bit higher. They usually are able to get these prices because of a wider collector market base obtained by the large number of subscribers served by the nationally distributed postcard auction publications. The publications also reach collectors who are unable to attend shows.

Prices of cards that have been sent on approval are normally higher than at postcard shows, etc., because the dealer has spent more time in selecting and handling and is most likely working from a customer "want list."

3. Cards that are in great demand, or "hot" topics, also have wider price ranges; as collector interests rise there is a greater disparity in values because of supply and demand. If a dealer has only a small number of big demand cards he will almost automatically elevate his prices. Those who have a large supply will probably not go as high.

4. Card appearance and the subject in a set or series can also cause a variance in the price range. Printing quality, more beautiful and varied colors, and sharpness of the image may make a particular card much more desirable and, therefore, it will command a higher price.

Cards that have a wide price range usually are those that are presently the "most wanted" and best sellers. Dealers, most often, will only offer a small discount when selling these because they know there is a good market for them. Cards listed with a narrow price range are usually those that have been "hot" but have settled down and established a more competitive trading range. Dealer discounting on these slow-movers tends to be much more prevalent than those in the wide price ranges.

GUIDELINES FOR BUYING AND SELLING CARDS

As noted above, the prices listed in this price guide are retail prices–prices that a collector can expect to pay when buying a card from a dealer. It is up to the collectors to bargain for any available discount from the dealer.

The wholesale price is the price which a collector can expect from a dealer when selling cards. This price will be significantly lower than the retail price. Most dealers try to operate on a 100% mark-up and will normally pay around 50% of a card's low retail value. On some high-demand cards, he might pay up to 60% or 75% if he wants them badly enough.

Dealers are always interested in purchasing collections and accumulations of cards. They are primarily interested in those that were issued before 1915, but may be induced to take those issued afterwards if they are clean and in good condition.

Collections: Normally, collections are a specialized group or groups of cards that a person has built over the years. They will be in nice condition, without any damage, and may contain some rarities or high-demand cards. If the collection is a group of views from your home town or state it would be to your advantage to sell them to a collector or dealer near you. You might place an ad in your daily paper; you will be surprised at the interest it creates. Set your price a little high; you can always come down.

You might also dispose of your collection by writing to the dealers who advertise in *Barr's Post Card News*, 70 South 6th St., Lansing, IA 52151 or *Postcard Collector*, P.O. Box 1050, Dubuque, IA 52004. Other publications that have postcard sections are *Collectors News*, P. O. Box 156, Grundy Center, IA 50638-0156, *Paper Collectors' Market Place*, P. O. Box 128, Scandinavia, WI 54977, and *The Antique Trader*, P. O. Box 1050, Dubuque, IA 52004. Write to any of these publications and ask for information on subscriptions or sample copies.

Accumulations: Accumulations are usually groups of many different kinds, many different eras, and many different topics ... with the good usually mixed in with the bad. If you have a large accumulation that you wish to sell, your best bet is to contact a dealer as noted above. You may expect only 20% to 30% of value on a group such as this. Many low demand cards are non-sellers and are worthless to a dealer, but he may take them if there are some good cards in the accumulation.

Buying: Without doubt, the best way to buy postcards is to attend a show where there is a large group of dealers. Compare prices among dealers on cards that are of interest to you, and return to those who have the best cards at the lowest price for your purchases.

Buy from a dealer in your area if there is one. A good dealer will help you with your collection by searching for cards you need or want. If none are available, many dealers listed in *Barr's Post Card News* and *Postcard Collector* run auctions or will send cards on approval. Also, you might try joining a postcard club. It is possible to find an excellent choice of cards at these meetings because attendees bring material that they know is of interest to their fellow members.

It is also possible to find cards at Antique Shows, Flea Markets and Antique Shops. You can, however, waste a lot of time and never find suitable cards. It is best to go direct to the source, and that would be a postcard dealer or auctioneer. Here you can almost always find cards that interest you.

IDENTIFYING THE AGE OF POSTCARDS

The dating of postcards for year or era of issue can be accurately determined if the card is studied for identity points. Research has already been done by earlier historians and guidelines have been put into place. There were seven different eras and each has distinguishing points to help establish its respective identity. The following helps determine the era of cards in question:

PIONEER ERA (1893-1898)

The Pioneer Era began when picture postcards were placed on sale by vendors and exhibitors at the Columbian Exposition in Chicago, May, 1893. These were very popular and proved to be a great success. The profitable and lasting future of the postcard was greatly enhanced. These cards are relatively scarce. They can be identified by combinations of the following:

- All have undivided backs.
- None show the "Authorized by Act of Congress" byline.
- Postal cards will have the Grant or Jefferson head stamp.
- Most, but not all, will be multiple view cards.
- The words "Souvenir of ..." or "Greetings from ..." will appear on many.
- Postage rate, if listed, is 2 cents.
- The most common titles will be "Souvenir Card" or "Mail Card."
- Appeared mostly in the big Eastern cities.

PRIVATE MAILING CARD ERA (1898-1901)

On May 19, 1898, the government gave private printers permission to print and sell postcards. The cards were all issued with the inscription "Private Mailing Card," and today they are referred to as PMC's. It is very easy to identify these because of the inscription. Many of the early Pioneer views were reprinted as Private Mailing Cards.

UNDIVIDED BACK ERA (1901-1907)

On December 24, 1901, permission was given to use the wording "Post Card" on backs of privately printed cards. All cards during this era had undivided backs and only the address was to appear on the back. The message, therefore, had to be written on the front (picture side) of the card. For this reason, there is writing on the face of many cards; this is becoming more acceptable on cards of this era.

DIVIDED BACK ERA (1907-1915)

This era came into being on March 1, 1907. The divided back made it possible for both the address and message to be on the back of the card. This prevented the face of the card from being written on and proved to be a boon for collectors. Normally, the colors or images filled the entire card with no white border.

WHITE BORDER ERA (1915-1930)

The so-called White Border Era brought an end to the postcard "golden age" era. It ended with the start of the first World War when imports from Germany ceased and U.S. publishers began printing postcards to fill the void. Thy were very poor quality and many were reprints of earlier Divided Back Era cards which are easily distinguished by the white border around the image.

LINEN ERA (1930-1945)

Improvements in American printing technology brought improved card quality. Publishers began using a linen-like paper containing a high rag content but, in most instances, used very cheap inks. Until recently, these cards were considered very cheap by collectors. Now they are very popular with collectors of Roadside America, Blacks, Comics, and Advertising.

PHOTOCHROME ERA (1939 to present day)

"Modern Chromes," as they are now called, were first introduced in 1939. Publishers, such as **Mike Roberts, Dexter Press, Curt Teich,** and **Plastichrome**, began producing cards that had very beautiful chrome colors and were very appealing to collectors. The growth of this group has been spectacular in recent years, so much so that there are now many postcard dealers who specialize only in chromes.

REAL PHOTO POSTCARDS (1900 to present day)

Real Photo cards were in use as early as 1900 and it is often difficult to date them unless postmarked or dated by a photographer. The stamp box will usually show the printing process; e.g., AZO, EKC, KODAK, VELOX, and KRUXO. (See Process Dating Table at the end of "Real Photos.") Careful study of photo cards is essential to make sure they have not been reproduced.

ART DECO ERA (1910 to early 1930's)

Beautiful **Colors!** Beautiful strong, deep, vibrant **Colors!** This wording only partially describes the new Art Deco movement that began around 1910– just as the Art Nouveau era was ebbing–and continued into the early 1930's. Due to the great influx of Art Deco postcards to the U.S., there has been a great demand for them in recent years as more and more American collectors discover their beauty.

ART NOUVEAU (1898-1910)

Art Nouveau postcards had their beginning at the turn of the century in Europe. Primarily, the movement began in Paris–where the great poster artists congregated–and in Vienna. This new expression of decorative art was the rage of the era, and the posters and magazines such as "*Jugend,*" " *Simplicissimus,*" "*Le Rire,*" "*Le Plume,*" and "*The Poster,*" were used as a means to transmit this expression to the art lovers of the world.

Values of some of these cards have reached unbelievable heights, as can be witnessed by the prices revealed in this book. As values of the better known artists such as Mucha, Kirchner and Toulouse-Lautrec spiral ever upward, they also bring values of the lesser publicized artist up with them.

2

Artist-Signed

What is an artist-signed postcard? It is the original work of an artist, bearing his initials or signature, photographed, colored to represent the original, and then printed into postcard form. The Artist-Signed postcard is overwhelmingly the favorite single type to collect in the entire postcard field. Some may collect views of their home town, transportation or real photos, but almost all collectors search for those of the painted form. Whether they be the beautiful ladies of Fisher or Boileau, or the lovely children of Brundage and Clapsaddle, the artist-signed postcard is the shining star. The beauty and elegance of several cards, or a group or set of cards by a great artist, provide the collector with the desire to eventually possess them.

Since Artist-Signed issues continue to be so extremely popular, we have made every attempt to list as many of the major and minor artists in the U.S. in all fields. Also, listing of major and minor foreign artists and their works in the important topics of Art Deco, Art Nouveau, Fantasy, Fantasy Nudes, Color Nudes, Nursery Rhymes, Fairy Tales, Animals, French Fashion, and others is a must. Since the great influx of foreign cards to the U.S. market, today's collectors and dealers desire information and values of this highly collectible material.

BEAUTIFUL LADIES

	VG	EX
A.G.		
James Henderson & Sons		
Series B5 "The Sports Girls"		
2538 "The Tennis Girl"	$ 20 - 25	$ 25 - 28
"The Golf Girl"	25 - 28	28 - 32
Others	8 - 10	10 - 12
ABIELLE, JACK (FR)		
Lady/Flower Series	40 - 45	45 - 50
Year Dates Series	40 - 50	50 - 60
Art Nouveau Series	60 - 70	70 - 90

Jack Abielle, Art Nouveau Series, 1898

ADRIAN-DUSSEK, EDUARD (See Nudes)		
ALBERTARELLI, R. (IT)	12 - 15	15 - 18
Art Deco	15 - 20	20 - 25
ALEXANDRE (FR) Erotic	15 - 18	18 - 22
ALFRED, JAMES D. (US)		
Gray Lithograph Co.		
P.C. 1 through P.C. 9	6 - 8	8 - 10
ANDERSON, KARL (US)		
Armour & Co. (Both U.S. & Germany Issues)		
The American Girl Series (B&W)		
"The Karl Anderson Girl" (US)	12 - 15	15 - 18
"The Karl Anderson Girl" (GER)	15 - 18	18 - 22
ANICHINI, EZIO (IT) Art Deco and Glamour		
Art Deco	20 - 25	25 - 35
"Fairies" Series	18 - 22	22 - 26
Glamour	15 - 18	18 - 22
Dancer Series	22 - 25	25 - 28
Silhouette Series 458	15 - 18	18 - 22
Exotic Bird Series	15 - 18	18 - 22
ANI-TAH (GER)	10 - 12	12 - 15
ANLURY (Art Deco and Glamour)		
Series 2590	12 - 15	15 - 20
C.C.M.		
No No. Deco Lovers	12 - 15	15 - 20
ANTHONY, MARIA (US)	8 - 10	10 - 12
Tennis Girl	20 - 25	25 - 28
ARMSTRONG, ROLF (US)		
K. Co. Inc., N.Y.		
Water Color Series 101 - 112		
102 Blonde hair, blue collar	15 - 20	20 - 25
108 Reddish-brown hair, white collar	15 - 20	20 - 25

Artelius, Axel Eliassons
Series E, "God Jul"

Artis, SSS, Paris
Deco Series 17

109 Dark brown hair, with locket	15 - 20	20 - 25
ARTELIUS		
Axel Eliassons		
Series E "God Jul"	25 - 30	30 - 35
ARTHUR, JAMES (US)		
Osborne Calendar Co.		
Ladies, Calendar Postcards, Vignettes, 1908		
1 "New Years Greeting"	20 - 25	25 - 30
3 "The Matinee Girl"	20 - 25	25 - 30
4 "The Easter Hat"	25 - 30	30 - 35
5 "In from the Fields"	25 - 30	30 - 35
6 "Vacation Days"	25 - 30	30 - 35
8 "Afternoon Tea"	25 - 30	30 - 35
9 "The Girl in Red"	25 - 30	30 - 35
10 "Yellow Roses"	25 - 30	30 - 35
11 "Chrysanthemums"	25 - 30	30 - 35
12 "Early Snow"	25 - 30	30 - 35
Ladies on Calendar Postcards, 1908		
"A New Years Caller"	20 - 25	25 - 30
"Five O'Clock Tea"	20 - 25	25 - 30
"The Girl in Pink"	20 - 25	25 - 30
"Gossips"	20 - 25	25 - 30
"Midsummer Days"	20 - 25	25 - 30
"The Widow"	20 - 25	25 - 30
"Waiting for Her Carriage"	20 - 25	25 - 30

Ladies on Calendar Postcards, 1910	20 - 25	25 - 30
Ladies on Calendar, Vignettes (12) (900-911)	20 - 25	25 - 30
ARTIS (FR) Glamour	20 - 25	25 - 35
Art Deco		
S.S.S., Paris		
Series 17 (6) Hand Colored	40 - 45	45 - 55
ASLAN, ALAIN (FR)	10 - 12	12 - 15
ASTI, ANGELO (IT)		
Braun & Co., Paris (Sepia) (6) Semi-nudes		
5255 "Volupte"	18 - 22	22 - 26
Others	18 - 22	22 - 26
H&S Color Nudes	22 - 25	25 - 28
International Art (Uns.) (6) Small images	8 - 10	10 - 12
Rotograph Co., N.Y.		
Series T. 5268		
"Beatrice," "Gladys," "Irene"	12 - 15	15 - 20
"Juliet," "Marguerite," "Rosalind"	12 - 15	15 - 20
Salon 1897 (Nudes)		
"Songeuse"	20 - 25	25 - 30
Others	20 - 25	25 - 30
T.S.N. (Theo. Stroefer, Nürnberg)		
Series 505 (6)	10 - 12	12 - 15
Series 508 (8) No Captions	10 - 12	12 - 15
Semi-Nude Real Photo Series		
"Epanouissment"	18 - 22	22 - 26
"Fantasie"	18 - 22	22 - 26
"Solitude"	18 - 22	22 - 26
"Volupte"	18 - 22	22 - 26
Raphael Tuck		
Connoisseur Series 2731 (6)		
"Beatrice," "Gladys," "Irene"	12 - 15	15 - 22
"Juliet," "Marguerite," "Rosalind"	12 - 15	15 - 22
Connoisseur Series 2743 (6)		
"Helena," "Madeline," "Muriel"	12 - 15	15 - 22
"Phyllis," "Portia," "Sylvia"	12 - 15	15 - 22
Series 6295 (6)	12 - 15	15 - 22
"Volupte"	18 - 22	22 - 26
Valentine's Series (Uns.)	10 - 12	12 - 15
Russian Real Photo		
558	15 - 18	18 - 22
Russian Real Photo Nudes		
432	15 - 20	20 - 28
435	15 - 20	20 - 28
826 Same as "Volupte"	15 - 20	20 - 28
Job - Advertising Calendar, 1899	80 - 90	90 - 100
Polish/French Backs		
Nakl. B-ei Rzepkowicz Semi-Nudes (RP)	12 - 15	15 - 22
Anonymous Bi-Lingual Backs (RP)		
A.6	10 - 12	12 - 15
Anonymous French Back Semi-Nudes (RP)		
Tinted	15 - 20	20 - 28

Untinted	12 - 15	15 - 20
AVELINE, F.		
Italy		
Girl with huge red bow on hat	6 - 9	9 - 12
Lindberg'in Kirjap. Oy., Helsinki Series	6 - 9	9 - 12
Others	6 - 9	9 - 12
AXENTOWICZ, T. (PO)		
Czerneckiego Wieliczka		
Heads and full-length	10 - 12	12 - 16
Fantasy	12 - 15	15 - 20
Nudes-Semi-Nudes (See Color Nudes)		
AZZONI, N. (IT) Art Deco and Glamour		
Series 517 (6)	15 - 20	20 - 25
Others	12 - 15	15 - 20
B.G. (Art Nouveau and Glamour)	45 - 50	50 - 55
B.W. See B. Wennerberg		
BACHRICH, M. (GER) (Art Deco and Glamour)		
Ladies/Fashion	12 - 15	15 - 20
Ladies/Sports	15 - 20	20 - 25
Dance Series 102	12 - 15	15 - 20
BAER, GILL (FR) Glamour	12 - 15	15 - 20
BAILEY, S. C. (US)		
Carlton Pub. Co.		
Series 674	6 - 8	8 - 10
Series 689	8 - 10	10 - 12
BAKST, LEON (RUS)		
St. Eugenie Red Cross Society		
Secession Exhibition	125 - 150	150 - 175
Girls of Ballet Puppets & Ladies (10)	70 - 80	80 - 100
+ the 2 Men in the full series = (12)	60 - 70	70 - 80
Others	40 - 50	50 - 60
BALESTRIERI, L. (IT)		
Art Deco	15 - 18	18 - 22
BALFOUR-KER, WILLIAM (US) Romantic	8 - 10	10 - 12
BALL, H. LaPRIAK (US)	3 - 4	4 - 5
BALLETTI, P. (IT) Art Deco and Glamour		
Ladies/Fashion	12 - 15	15 - 20
BALOTINI (IT)		
Ladies & Dogs Series 312	12 - 15	15 - 20
Art Deco	10 - 12	12 - 15
BANERAS, A. (SP)	8 - 10	10 - 12
154 Tennis	18 - 22	22 - 26
BARBARA, S. Art Nouveau	22 - 25	25 - 30
BARBER, COURT (US)		
B.K.W.I.		
Series 861 (12)	10 - 15	15 - 18
Series 686 (6)	10 - 15	15 - 18
Series 1200	10 - 12	12 - 16
Others	8 - 10	10 - 12
Minerva		
Series 683 (Head Studies)	10 - 15	15 - 18

L. Bakst, St. Eugenie Red Cross
La Fee de Poupee Dolls, 6

L. Barribal, Novitas, #15645
No Caption

J. St. Co., Germany		
113 "Good Natured"	8 - 10	10 - 15
116 "Tempting Eyes"	8 - 10	10 - 15
118 "Lissie"	8 - 10	10 - 15
140 "Are you offended?"	8 - 10	10 - 15
J.W. & Co. Series	6 - 8	8 -10
R.H.B		
Series 688 Head Studies		
Pretty girl in big hat No Caption	12 - 15	15 - 18
S.W.S.B.		
Series 616, 1236	10 - 12	12 - 15
Others	6 - 8	8 - 10
"Beauties"	8 - 10	10 - 12
1228 "Following the Race"	8 - 10	10 - 12
1400 "Five O'Clock Tea"	8 - 10	10 - 12
1403 "Sixteen Years"	10 - 12	12 - 15
1405 "Over the Books"	8 - 10	10 - 12
Ladies & Dogs	10 - 12	12 - 16
Ladies & Horses		
"Miss Knickerbocker"	12 - 15	15 - 20
"In Summer Days"	12 - 15	15 - 20
"Thoroughbreds"	12 - 15	15 - 20
2022 "Ready to Ride"	10 - 12	12 - 15
Anonymous Series 2023, 2024	8 - 10	10 - 12
BARBER, C.W. (US)		
B.K.W.I., Vienna		
Series 861 (12)	15 - 18	18 - 22

Series 2128 (8)	15 - 18	18 - 22
Carlton Publishing Co. (6 cards per set)		
Series 549, 660, 661	12 - 15	15 - 20
Series 676, 677, 678, 687, 688	12 - 15	15 - 20
Series 704 (6)	12 - 15	15 - 20
"Lawn Tennis"	18 - 22	22 - 26
Series 709, 716, 735, 739 (10)	12 - 15	15 - 20
Series 861	8 - 10	10 - 15
S.W.S.B., Berlin		
Series 1236		
"Motor Lady"	12 - 15	15 - 20
Others	12 - 15	15 - 18
BARRIBAL, L. (GB)		
Alphasia Publishing Co.		
1207	15 - 20	20 - 25
B.K.W.I.		
Series XIX (Fashion)	15 - 20	20 - 25
Series 860 (Fashion)	15 - 20	20 - 25
H.N. & N.		
15645 Girl in Furs	18 - 22	22 - 26
James Henderson & Sons		
Series C4		
2605 "Pretty Polly"	15 - 18	18 - 22
Series C6 (6)		
2650 "In the Clouds"	18 - 22	22 - 25
Barribal Heads		
2. **"Scotch"**	18 - 22	22 - 26
Inter-Art Pub. Co. Series 3292	15 - 18	18 - 22
Artisque Series	12 - 15	15 - 20
"For the Glory of the Empire"		
Golf Girl	35 - 40	40 - 50
Tennis Girl	25 - 30	30 - 35
Ladies & Horses		
Artisque		
Series 2234 (6) **and Series 2236** (6)	15 - 20	20 - 25
Series 15644 (Heads)	15 - 20	20 - 25
M.K.B.		
Series 2205 (6)	12 - 15	15 - 18
M. Munk, Vienna		
Series 882 (Heads)	15 - 20	20 - 25
Novitas, Germany		
Series 15648 (6) No captions	15 - 18	18 - 22
Series 15464 (6)		
"Mystic Beauty"	15 - 18	18 - 22
"True Blue"	15 - 18	18 - 22
"Wearin' of the Green"	15 - 18	18 - 22
"Yours Darling"	15 - 18	18 - 22
Series 15644, 15645 No captions (6)	12 - 15	15 - 18
Valentine Co.		
"Flags of Nation" Series		
"Great Britain"	15 - 20	20 - 26

"Japan"	15 - 20	20 - 26
"Scotland"	15 - 20	20 - 26
"Ireland"	15 - 20	20 - 26
"Germany"	15 - 20	20 - 26
"Russia"	15 - 20	20 - 26
Lindberg's Tryokeria Series (8)	20 - 22	22 - 26
Lindberg'in Kirjap. O.Y., Helsinki (6)	20 - 22	22 - 26
Ladies & Dogs	15 - 20	20 - 25
Ladies/Tennis	22 - 26	26 - 30
Ladies/Golf	26 - 30	30 - 40
BARBIER, RENE (FR) Fashion	15 - 18	18 - 22
BARCHI (IT) Glamour	10 - 15	15 - 20
BARISON, G. (IT) Glamour	10 - 12	12 - 15
BARRICK		
Paul Heckscher		
Series 1039 (6)	10 - 12	12 - 15
BASCH, ARPAD (HUN)		
Art Nouveau and Glamour		
Series 761 (6)	120 - 130	130 - 150
Series 769 (6)	200 - 225	225 - 250
Series 785 (6)	80 - 90	90 - 100
National Ladies (10)	120 - 130	130 - 140
"1900 Grand Femme" (6)	150 - 175	200 - 250
BEGOND, M. (BEL)	10 - 12	12 - 15
BENDA, WLADYSLAW T. (W.T.)		
"Rosamond"	8 - 10	10 - 12
"Reverie"	8 - 10	10 - 12
BENITO, EDUARDO (SP) Fashion	10 - 12	12 - 15
BENNETT, R. (US) (Listed as Pennell in 2nd Edition)		
M. Munk, Vienna		
Series 578 Love-Marriage Series (6)		
A "Im Restaurant"	10 - 12	12 - 15
Series 640 (6) No Captions	12 - 15	15 - 18
Series 702 Sporting Girls	18 - 22	22 - 26
Series 913 Sporting Girls (6)	18 - 22	22 - 26
Series 1114 Same as Series 913 (6)	18 - 22	22 - 26
Novitas (N in Star)		
Series 15324 Beautiful Ladies (6)	12 - 15	15 - 18
FINLAND		
30/25 Series Same as **Series 913** above	15 - 18	18 - 22
BENOIS, A. (RUS) Ballet	30 - 40	40 - 50
BERTHON, PAUL (Art Nouveau)	120 - 130	130 - 150
BENTIVOGLIO (Art Deco and Glamour) (IT)		
Degami		
Series 2221 Lady with Borzoi, etc. Dogs	50 - 60	60 - 70
Series 2161 Lovers in Boats	30 - 40	40 - 50
Other Deco series with Ladies	30 - 40	40 - 50
Pierrots	35 - 45	45 - 55
BERGER, FRITZI (AUS) See Wiener Werkstätte		
Glamour	25 - 30	30 - 40

R. Bennett, M. Munk, #640
No Caption

Bentivoglio, Degami
Series 2221

BERTIGLIA, AURELIO (IT)
  Art Deco and Glamour
  Rev. Stampa; Dell, Anna & Gasparini

Ladies/Heads	12 - 15	15 - 20
Ladies/Fashion	12 - 15	15 - 20
Ladies/Animals	15 - 18	18 - 22
Golf	25 - 30	30 - 35
Tennis	22 - 25	25 - 30
Pierrots (Harlequins)	22 - 25	25 - 30
Ladies/Pierrots	22 - 25	25 - 30
Ethnic/Blacks	15 - 20	20 - 25
Series 163 Big Hats	15 - 18	18 - 20
Series 241 Semi-Nudes	20 - 25	25 - 30
Series 224 Lovers Kissing	10 - 12	12 - 15
Series 2062 Couples	8 - 10	10 - 12

  Ladies & Dogs

Series 163 (6)	12 - 15	15 - 20

  Ladies & Horses

Series 227 (6)	10 - 15	15 - 20
Series 2132 (6)	10 - 15	15 - 20
Series 2151 (6)	10 - 15	15 - 20

BETTINELLI, MARIO (IT)
  Art Deco and Glamour

Series 884	15 - 18	18 - 22
Others	8 - 10	10 - 12

BETTS, ANNA (US) Couples, Romantic   6 - 8   8 - 10

Card #61-3

Card #61-4

Card #61-1

Card #61-2

Card #61-5

Card #61-6

SIX-CARD SET BY ARTIST E.B. (E. BIGLIARDI)
SERIES 61, PUBLISHED BY REV. STAMPA

BIANCHI, ALBERTO (IT)
  Art Deco and Glamour
  Anonymous

No No. **Dancing Ladies** (6)	22 - 25	25 - 30
No No. **Ladies Outdoors** (6)	15 - 18	18 - 22

  Rev. Stampa and P.A.R.

Series 2024, 2041 Walking (6)	10 - 12	12 - 15
Series 2154 High Fashion, playing cards (6)	15 - 20	20 - 25
Ladies/Heads	12 - 15	15 - 20
Ladies/Fashion	12 - 15	15 - 20
Ladies/Animals	15 - 18	18 - 22
Series 183 (6)	12 - 15	15 - 20

Birger, Axel Eliassons
Art Deco Christmas Lady

Birger, Axel Eliassons
"Gott Nytt Ar"

Ladies/Golf	20 - 25	25 - 35
Ladies/Tennis	15 - 20	20 - 25
Ladies/Dogs/Horses		
Series 483 (6)	12 - 15	15 - 20
Series 2020 (6)	12 - 15	15 - 20
BIANCO, T. (IT) Glamour	10 - 12	12 - 15
BIELETTO, T. (IT)	5 - 8	8 - 12
BIGLIARDI, E. or (EB) (IT)		
Glamour, Mode		
Rev. Stampa Series 61 (6)	15 - 20	20 - 25
BILIBIN, IVAN (RUS) Art Nouveau	60 - 75	75 - 125
BIRGER (SWE) (Art Deco) 1930s		
Axel Eliassons		
Christmas Lady	30 - 40	40 - 50
Others	35 - 40	40 - 45
BIRI, S. (IT) Art Deco and Glamour		
Ladies/Pierrots	18 - 22	22 - 25
Others	12 - 15	15 - 18
BLACHE, M.T. (IT)		
Chatenay		
Tennis Mode Series (6)	25 - 30	30 - 35
BLOCH, ANDRES (NO)	12 - 15	15 - 18
BLUMENTHAL, M. L. (US)	4 - 5	5 -8
BOARD, LESLIE (AUST)	10 - 12	12 - 15
BOCCASILE, GINO (Art Deco)	50 - 75	75 - 100
BODAREVSKY, N.K. (RUS)	12 - 15	15 - 20

BOILEAU, PHILIP (Canada-US)

Many say that ladies by Philip Boileau are the most beautiful of early great painters and illustrators. His works, as with Harrison Fisher, are popular not only in the U.S. but throughout the world. Boileau was born in Canada but finally settled in New York where he became one of the most prolific painters of beauties of the era.

Most of his images on postcards, painted during the "postcard craze" years of 1905-1918, were published in the U.S. by the New York firm of Reinthal & Newman. Other principal publishers were Osborne Calendar Co., who did the very rare Boileau calendar cards, National Art Co. with their advertising cards, and The Taylor, Platt Co. who did the Valentine head issues and the scarce flower-decorated cards of the heads in different form.

Advertising cards by Flood & Conklin, Soapine Mfg. Co., S.E. Perlberg Tailors, and others are in very short supply and command high prices when they do surface.

British, European, Finnish, and Russian publishers issued Boileau cards which are very elusive and also command high prices. The Tuck Connoisseur Series 2819 and German K N G Schöne Frauen, along with the KOY Finnish Series, are among those sought after by collectors worldwide. Several new Russian cards have also surfaced, and this has caused added interest in works of this premier artist.

With the exception of higher valued issues such as the Osborne Calendar cards and the Finnish and Russian issues, Boileau cards have been in a neutral position.

Note: See address of Philip Boileau Society in our Index under Periodicals.

AMERICAN PUBLISHERS
Reinthal & Newman

No No. "A Mischiefmaker"	20 - 25	25 - 30
No No. "A Passing Shadow"	20 - 25	25 - 30
No No. "Little Lady Demure"	20 - 25	25 - 30
No No. "Once Upon A Time____"	20 - 25	25 - 30
No No. "Spring Song"	20 - 25	25 - 30
Series 94*		
"At the Opera"	20 - 25	25 - 30
"Peggy"	20 - 25	25 - 30
"School days"	20 - 25	25 - 30
"Sweethearts"	20 - 25	25 - 30
"Thinking of You"	20 - 25	25 - 30
"Twins"	20 - 25	25 - 30
* Card with Series No. on back, add $5.		
Series 95 * **		
"A Mischiefmaker"	20 - 25	25 - 28
"Anticipation"	20 - 25	25 - 28
"Forever"	20 - 25	25 - 28
"Little Lady Demure"	20 - 25	25 - 28
"My Chauffeur"	20 - 25	25 - 28
"Nocturne"	20 - 25	25 - 28
"Passing Shadow"	20 - 22	22 - 26
"Spring Song"	20 - 25	25 - 28
"To-day?"	18 - 22	22 - 25
"Tomorrow.."	20 - 22	22 - 26
"Winter Whispers..."	15 - 18	18 - 22

"Yesterday!"	15 - 20	20 - 25

* Cards with Series No. on back, add $5.
** Cards distr. by Chas. H. Hauff, add $5.

Series 109*

"Evening and You"	20 - 25	25 - 35
"Girl in Black"	20 - 25	25 - 35
"Her Soul With Purity Possessed"	20 - 25	25 - 35
"In Maiden Meditation"	22 - 27	27 - 32
"June, Blessed June"	20 - 25	25 - 30
"My Moonbeam"	22 - 27	27 - 32
"My One Rose"	20 - 25	25 - 30
"Ready for Mischief"	20 - 25	25 - 30
"The Secret of the Flowers"	25 - 30	30 - 35
"True as the Blue Above"	25 - 30	30 - 35
"Twixt Doubt and Hope"	25 - 30	30 - 35
"Waiting for You"	22 - 25	25 - 28
"With Care for None"	22 - 25	25 - 30

* Cards with Series No. on back, add $5.

200 Series

204 "Rings on Her Fingers"	18 - 22	22 - 25
205 "Question"	18 - 22	22 - 25
205 "Chrysanthemums"	18 - 22	22 - 25
206 "The Enchantress"	18 - 22	22 - 25
207 "A Hundred Years Ago"	18 - 22	22 - 25
208 "Miss America"	20 - 25	25 - 30
209 "Youth"	15 - 18	18 - 22
210 "Joyful Calm"	20 - 25	25 - 28
211 "Chums"	15 - 18	18 - 22
212 "Sweet Lips of Coral Hue"	15 - 18	18 - 22
213 "His First Love"	15 - 20	20 - 25
214 "For Him"	15 - 18	18 - 22
215 "I Wonder"	15 - 18	18 - 22
282 "Ready for the Meeting"	18 - 22	22 - 26
283 "Miss Pat"	18 - 22	22 - 26
284 "Old Home Farewell"	15 - 18	18 - 22
285 "A Serious Thought"	15 - 18	18 - 22
286 "I Don't Care"	15 - 18	18 - 22
287 "The Eyes Say No, The Lips Say Yes"	18 - 22	22 - 26
294 "Blue Ribbons"	22 - 26	26 - 32
295 "A Little Devil" ("Good Little Rogue")	15 - 20	20 - 25
296 "Once Upon A Time"	10 - 15	15 - 20
297 "My Big Brother"	10 - 15	15 - 20
298 "My Boy"	10 - 15	15 - 20
299 "Baby Mine"	20 - 25	25 - 28

Water Color Series 369-380*

369 "Vanity"	25 - 30	30 - 40
370 "Haughtiness"	25 - 30	30 - 40
371 "Purity"	25 - 30	30 - 40
372 "Loneliness"	30 - 35	35 - 45
373 "Happiness"	25 - 30	30 - 40
374 "Queenliness"	25 - 30	30 - 40

Philip Boileau, R&N 375
"Whisperings of Love"

Philip Boileau, R&N 376
"Fairy Tales"

Philip Boileau, R&N 379
"Lullabye"

375 "Whisperings of Love" (Annunciation)	30 - 35	35 - 45
376 "Fairy Tales" (Girlhood)	30 - 35	35 - 45
377 "The Parting of the Ways" (Maidenhood)	30 - 35	35 - 45
378 "Here Comes Daddy"	25 - 30	30 - 40
379 "Lullabye" (Motherhood)		
With white blanket	30 - 35	35 - 40
With blue blanket	30 - 35	35 - 45
With pink blanket	30 - 35	35 - 45
380 "Don't Wake the Baby"	25 - 30	30 - 35
* Cards without Sub-title, add $5.		
445 Series* (Dist. by Charles Hauff)		
1 "Spring Song"	25 - 30	30 - 35
2 "To-day?"	25 - 30	30 - 35
3 "Tomorrow.."	25 - 30	30 - 35
4 "Forever"	25 - 30	30 - 35
5 "My Chauffeur..."	25 - 30	30 - 35
6 "Nocturne"	25 - 30	30 - 35
* With German caption, add $5.		
474 Series * * (Dist. by Charles Hauff)	25 - 30	30 - 35
1 "Spring Song"	25 - 30	30 - 35
2 "A Passing Shadow"	25 - 30	30 - 35
3 "Mischiefmaker" (also "A Mischief Maker")	25 - 30	30 - 40
4 "Anticipating"	25 - 28	28 - 32
5 "Yesterday"	25 - 28	28 - 32
6 "Little Lady Demure"	25 - 28	28 - 32
* With German caption, add $5.		
**Cards are more rare than Series 95.		
700 Series*		
750 "Be Prepared"	20 - 25	25 - 30
751 "Absence Cannot Hearts Divide"	20 - 25	25 - 28
752 "A Neutral"	20 - 25	25 - 28
753 "The Chrysalis"	18 - 22	22 - 26
754 "Pensive"	18 - 22	22 - 26
755 "The Girl of the Golden West"	18 - 22	22 - 26

Philip Boileau, R&N 820
"Devotion"

Philip Boileau, R&N 823
"Priscilla"

P. Boileau, Wildt & Kray
Series 1419, "Tomorrow..."

756 "Pebbles on the Beach"	20 - 25	25 - 30
757 "Snowbirds"	20 - 25	25 - 30
758 "One Kind Act a Day"	20 - 25	25 - 28
759 "The Flirt"	20 - 25	25 - 28
760 "In Confidence"	20 - 25	25 - 28
761 "The Coming Storm"	20 - 25	25 - 28

* With German caption, add $5.

800 Series

820 "Devotion"	35 - 40	40 - 45
821 "Golden Dreams"	35 - 40	40 - 45
822 "Every Breeze Carries My Thoughts..."	35 - 40	40 - 45
823 "Priscilla"	35 - 40	40 - 45
824 "Fruit of the Vine"	30 - 35	35 - 40
825 "Butterfly"	35 - 40	40 - 45
826 "When Dreams Come True" *	20 - 25	25 - 28
827 "Sister's First Love" *	20 - 25	25 - 28
828 "The Little Neighbors" *	20 - 25	25 - 28
829 "Peach Blossoms" *	25 - 30	30 - 35
830 "When His Ship Comes In" *	20 - 25	25 - 28
831 "Need a Lassie Cry" *	20 - 25	25 - 28

* With German caption, add $5.

Water Color Series 936-941

936 "A Bit of Heaven"	30 - 35	35 - 40
937 "Chic"	30 - 35	35 - 40
938 "Have a Care" (also "Hav a Care")	30 - 35	35 - 40
939 "Just a Wearying for You"	30 - 35	35 - 38
940 "Sunshine"	30 - 35	35 - 38
941 "Sincerely Yours"	30 - 35	35 - 38

2000 Series

2052 "Thinking of You"	25 - 30	30 - 35
2063 "Chums"	25 - 30	30 - 35
2064 "His First Love"	20 - 25	25 - 28
2065 "Question"	18 - 22	22 - 26
2066 "From Him"	18 - 22	22 - 26

2067 "The Enchantress"	18 - 22	22 - 26
2068 "Joyful Calm"	18 - 22	22 - 26
Others in Series	18 - 22	22 - 26
Unnumbered Series		
"The Dreamy Hour"	25 - 30	30 - 38
"Out for Fun"	25 - 30	30 - 38

Reinthal & Newman Copyright
Distributed by **Novitas**. (N in Star logo) (12) *

"A Mischiefmaker"	35 - 40	40 - 45
"A Passing Shadow"	35 - 40	40 - 45
"Anticipating"	35 - 40	40 - 45
"Forever"	35 - 40	40 - 45
"Little Lady Demure"	35 - 40	40 - 45
"My Chauffeur..."	35 - 40	40 - 45
"Nocturne"	35 - 40	40 - 45
"Spring Song"	35 - 40	40 - 45
"To-Day?"	35 - 40	40 - 45
"Tomorrow.."	35 - 40	40 - 45
"Winter Whispers..."	35 - 40	40 - 45
"Yesterday!"	35 - 40	40 - 45

 *   See Wildt & Kray below.

Reinthal & Newman, N.Y.

Distributed by J. Beagles & Co., London *	25 - 30	30 - 35
"Little Lady Demure"	25 - 30	30 - 35
"Nocturne"	25 - 30	30 - 35
"Winter Whispers"	25 - 30	30 - 35
Others	25 - 30	30 - 35

 * Probably 12 in series - same as Novitas and
Wildt & Kray

Reinthal & Newman, New York
Distributed by Charles H. Hauff, London

"Forever"	25 - 30	30 - 35
"Music"	25 - 30	30 - 35
"Peggy"	25 - 30	30 - 35
"Out for Fun"	25 - 30	30 - 35
"Winter Whispers"	25 - 30	30 - 35

Reinthal & Newman, New York
Distributed by Wildt & Kray, London
  Series 1419 (12) **Same as Novitas**

"A Mischiefmaker"	30 - 35	35 - 40
"A Passing Shadow"	30 - 35	35 - 40
"Anticipation"	30 - 35	35 - 40
"Forever"	30 - 35	35 - 40
"Little Lady Demure"	30 - 35	35 - 40
"My Chauffeur..."	30 - 35	35 - 40
"Nocturne"	30 - 35	35 - 40
"Spring Song"	30 - 35	35 - 40
"To-day?"	30 - 35	35 - 40
"Tomorrow..."	30 - 35	35 - 40
"Winter Whispers"	30 - 35	35 - 40
"Yesterday!"	30 - 35	35 - 40

Philip Boileau, Taylor, Platt & Co.
"Chrysanthemums"

Philip Boileau, A.V.N. Jones & Co.
#231, "Summer"

Reinthal & Newman
Distributed by Curt Teich (C.T. American Art)

"At the Opera"	55 - 65	65 - 85
3525 "Autumn"	250 - 300	350 - 400
3625 "Chrysanthemums"	300 - 350	350 - 400
------- "Carnations"	300 - 350	350 - 400
Others	300 - 350	350 - 400

   * The Osborne Calendar Cards are the rarest U.S. series.

S. E. Perlberg Co., Tailors (Ad on Back)

"My Moonbeam"	100 - 125	125 - 140
"My One Rose"	100 - 125	125 - 140
"Secret of the Flowers"	100 - 125	125 - 140
"True as the Blue Above"	100 - 125	125 - 140
"Twixt Doubt and Hope"	100 - 125	125 - 140

C. N. Snyder Art

"Spring Song"	90 - 110	110 - 130
Soapine Advertising	90 - 110	110 - 130

Sparks Tailoring (Ad on Back) by **R&N**

"Tomorrow"	90 - 110	110 - 130

Taylor, Platt*

"Chrysanthemums"	80 - 90	90 - 110
"Poppies"	80 - 90	90 - 110
"Violets"	80 - 90	90 - 110
"Wild Roses"	80 - 90	90 - 110

  *   12 cards issued; only 4 have surfaced.

Will's Embassy Pipe Tobacco Mixtures
"Nocturne"	100 - 125	125 - 150

Worthmore Tay Tailors, Chicago
"Ready for Mischief"	100 - 125	125 - 150

Unsigned, Unknown U.S. Publisher *
"Au Revoir"	30 - 35	35 - 45
"Chrysanthemums" **	30 - 35	35 - 45
(To My Sweetheart)		
"Day Dreams"	30 - 35	35 - 40
"Debutantes"	30 - 35	35 - 40
"Devotion"	30 - 35	35 - 40
"Poppies"	30 - 35	35 - 40
(A Greeting from St. Valentine)		
(A Token of Love) 2 types exist.	25 - 30	30 - 35
"Violets"	25 - 30	30 - 35
(A Gift of Love)		
"Wild Roses"	25 - 30	30 - 35
(To My Valentine)		
* Others may exist.	25 - 30	30 - 35
** Embossed and non-embossed varieties exist; possibly in all four cards.		

Wolf & Co.
"Fancy Free" (Silk) Very Rare!	400 - 450	450 - 500

FOREIGN PUBLISHERS

A.V.N. Jones & Co., London
"Quite Ready"	150 - 175	175 - 200

Distributed by **B.K.W.I.**, Vienna
Series 500
"Spring"	150 - 175	175 - 200
"Summer"	150 - 175	175 - 200
"Fall"	150 - 175	175 - 200
"Winter"	150 - 175	175 - 200

Apollon Sophia, Bulgaria
"My Big Brother" (No. 21)	50 - 60	60 - 75

B.K.W.I., German*
"Ready for Mischief"	150 - 175	175 - 200
"June, Blessed June"	150 - 175	175 - 200
* Die-cuts on headbands, necklaces, foil inside.		
Others that exist without die-cut holes.	100 - 125	125 - 150

Diefenthal, Amsterdam (Sepia)
"A Hundred Years Ago"	110 - 120	120 - 130
"C'est Moi"	110 - 125	125 - 135
"The Enchantress"	110 - 125	125 - 135
"His First Love"	110 - 125	125 - 135
"Question"	110 - 125	125 - 135

A.P. Co., Finland
"His First Love"	125 - 135	135 - 150

K. K. OY, 1/20 Series, Finland (No Captions)
"Baby Mine"	150 - 175	175 - 200

Philip Boileau, K. K. Oy.	*P. Boileau, Pub. at Polyphot*	*Philip Boileau, H&S*
N:o 1/20	*New Discovery! Same as*	*No Caption*
"Sister's First Love"	*"Parting of the Ways"*	*New Discovery!*

"Sister's First Love"	150 - 175	175 - 200
"Snowbirds"	150 - 175	175 - 200
"Here Comes Daddy" (Light Pastels)	175 - 200	200 - 225
K.K. Oy. - **KFP-K. Oy.**, Finland		
No Captions		
"Snowbirds"	175 - 200	200 - 225
"Sister's First Love" (827)	175 - 200	200 - 225
N:O Numbered Series, Finland (No Captions)		
N:O 14 "Purity"	175 - 200	200 - 225
Publisher at Polyphot, Finland – **New Discovery!**		
Same as Series 377, "The Parting of the Ways"	150 - 200	200 - 250
Untitled Series, No Publisher, Finland		
(With "Stamp Here" in Stamp Box)		
"From Him"	125 - 150	150 - 175
"His First Love"	125 - 150	150 - 175
"Question"	125 - 150	150 - 175
"Sweet Lips of Coral Hue"	125 - 150	150 - 175
AWE, Russian/Polish Back Real Photo	125 - 150	150 - 175
No No. or Caption	175 - 200	200 - 230
38 No Caption	175 - 200	200 - 230
H & S, Germany (No Captions)		
"Au Revoir"	120 - 140	140 - 160
"At Home" (White Border)	125 - 145	145 - 165
"Fancy Free" (White Border)	125 - 145	145 - 165
"Paying a Call" (White Border)	125 - 145	145 - 165
"Paying a Call" (No border, rev. image)	125 - 145	145 - 165
"I am Late" (Unsigned; blue rev. image)	125 - 145	145 - 165
Embossed Series		
Head & Bust in Gold, chained circle	150 - 175	175 - 200
KNG, Germany (No Captions)		
Schöne Frauen Series 8010		
"I am Late" (No border)	125 - 150	150 - 170

| *Philip Boileau, R. Tuck*
Series 2819, "At Home" | *Philip Boileau, R. Tuck*
Series 2819, "I Am Late" | *Philip Boileau, R. Tuck*
Ser. 2819, "Paying A Call" |

"Paying a Call" (No border)	125 - 150	150 - 175
"Summer Breezes" (No border)	125 - 150	150 - 175
"Fancy Free"	125 - 150	150 - 175
"Au Revoir"	125 - 150	150 - 175
"At Home"	125 - 150	150 - 175
Schöne Frauen Series 8011		
"I am Late" (White border)	100 - 110	110 - 130
"Fancy Free"	110 - 130	130 - 150
"Paying a Call" (White border)	100 - 110	110 - 130
"Summer Breezes" (White border)	100 - 110	110 - 130
Schöne Frauen Series 8012		
"I am Late" (rev. image, uns., untitled)	100 - 110	110 - 130
"Fancy Free"	100 - 110	110 - 130
Schöne Frauen Series 8013		
"I am Late" (reversed image, uns.)	100 - 110	110 - 130
"Paying a Call" (reversed image, uns.)	100 - 110	110 - 130
"Summer Breezes" (blue rev. image)	100 - 125	125 - 150
MEU, Germany Publisher Logo on Back		
Untitled, Woman/Dark Hat, Dated 1905	100 - 110	110 - 120
Albert Schweitzer, Germany	80 - 90	90 - 100
H. S. Speelman, Netherlands		
"Eva" (Same as "Peggy")	100 - 110	110 - 125
"Peggy"	100 - 110	110 - 125
Raphael Tuck, London		
Connoisseur Series 2819		
"At Home"	190 - 210	210 - 230
"Au Revoir"	175 - 200	200 - 225
"Fancy Free"	190 - 210	210 - 230
"I am Late"	175 - 200	200 - 225
"Paying a Call"	175 - 200	200 - 225
"Summer Breezes"	175 - 200	200 - 225
Series 2811 (New Find!) (6?)		
"Ethel" Same as "Paying a Call"	200 - 250	250 - 300
Others	200 - 250	250 - 300

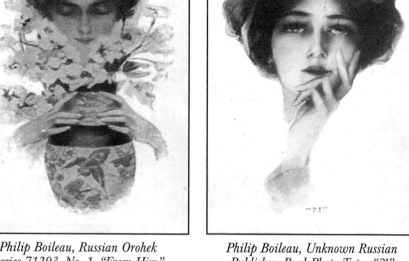

*Philip Boileau, Russian Orohek
Series 71293, No. 1, "From Him"*

*Philip Boileau, Unknown Russian
Publisher, Real-Photo Type, "?!"*

Uitg de Muinck & Co., Amsterdam
  "His First Love" — 90 - 100   100 - 110
Weinthal Co., Rotterdam — 90 - 100   100 - 120
Friedrich O. Wolter, Berlin
  1058 - "Studie" — 75 - 85   85 - 100

RUSSIAN PUBLISHERS

AWE - Russian/Polish Back
  Real Photo Series (No Captions)
    "Joyful Calm" — 200 - 225   225 - 250
    "Miss America" — 200 - 225   225 - 250

"OROHEK" - Russian/English Back *
  Series 66391 5000 (Total Run)
    4 "Question" — 175 - 200   200 - 225
    5 "Rings on her fingers" — 175 - 200   200 - 225
  Series 71293 - 3000 (Total Run)
    1 "From Him" — 175 - 200   200 - 225
    4 "Question" — 175 - 200   200 - 225
    13 "Sweet Lips of Coral Hue" — 175 - 200   200 - 225
    ?   "His First Love" — 175 - 200   200 - 225

* Appears to be same series as Finnish with "Stamp
Here" but without captions; heavier card stock.

"Rishar" (Richard and Phillips) — 150 - 175   175 - 200
  104   "Winter" — 150 - 175   175 - 200
  105   "Spring" — 150 - 175   175 - 200
  106   "Autumn" — 150 - 175   175 - 200
  107   "Summer" — 150 - 175   175 - 200

108	"Poppies"	175 - 200	200 - 225
109	"Wild Roses"	175 - 200	200 - 225
110	"Violets"	175 - 200	200 - 225
111	"Chrysanthemums"	175 - 200	200 - 225
112	No Caption Purple-wine hat and scarf.	175 - 200	200 - 225
113			
114	"Warum?" (Why?)	175 - 200	200 - 225
116			

Unknown Russian Publisher
Real-Photo Type, Russian-Polish back

"? !"	125 - 150	150 - 175
"The Enchantress"	125 - 150	150 - 175
"I Don't Care"	125 - 150	150 - 175
"301" (Sweet Lips of Coral Hue)	125 - 150	150 - 175

Unknown Russian Publisher

"Autumn"	125 - 150	150 - 175

Unknown Russian Publisher (Sepia)

No Caption "Joyful Calm"	125 - 150	150 - 175

Unknown Russian Publisher

5	"Rings on Her Fingers" (Unsigned)	125 - 150	150 - 175
18	"A Brotherly Kiss" (Pebble grain paper)	125 - 150	150 - 175

Unknown Russian Publisher

N:O 3	125 - 150	150 - 175

UNKNOWN PUBLISHERS
  Series 682 (6)

682-1 "Anticipation"	50 - 60	60 - 80
682-2 "True as the Blue Above"	50 - 60	60 - 80
682-3 "In Maiden Meditation" *	50 - 60	60 - 80
682-4 Unknown	175 - 200	200 - 225
682-5 "The Twins"	50 - 60	60 - 80
682-6 "The Girl in Black"	50 - 60	60 - 80

  *   Also with no caption)
    Unsigned

"Miss America"	50 - 75	75 - 100
"Miss America" (signed, 1910, blue ink)	50 - 75	75 - 100
"Rings on Her Fingers"	50 - 75	75 - 100

  Unknown Publisher (Probably Dutch)   **Series R**

R.236 "Miss America"	50 - 75	75 - 100
R.238 "His First Love"	50 - 75	75 - 100
R.239 "Chums"	50 - 75	75 - 100

BOLETTA	6 - 8	8 - 10
BOMPARD, LUIGI (IT) Glamour	12 - 15	15 - 20
BOMPARD, SERGIO (IT)		

  Art Deco and Glamour
  Artistica Riservata,

Series 472, 513 (6)	15 - 20	20 - 25

  Degami

Series 434 Classic Glamour Ladies (6)	15 - 20	20 - 25
Series 639 With Animals	15 - 18	18 - 22

  Rev. Stampa; Dell, Anna & Gasparini

Series 208, 431, 508, 931 Fashion (6)	12 - 15	15 - 20

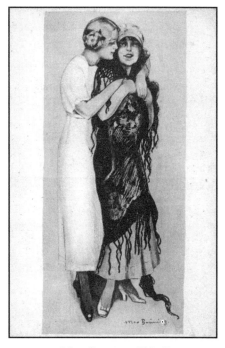

S. Bompard, Rev. Stampa
Fan Lady Series, #434

Max Bruning, 100c/6
No Caption

Series 461 Doing Nails, Fashion (6)	12 - 15	15 - 18
Series 464, 467, 439 Heads (6)	15 - 18	18 - 22
Series 474 Semi-Nudes (6)	20 - 25	25 - 30
Series 534, 914, 955, 476 Heads (6)	10 - 12	12 - 15
Series 407, 472, 496 High Fashion (6)	12 - 15	15 - 20
Series 506, 985 High Fashion (6)	12 - 15	15 - 20
Series 401, 430, 449, 555 High Fashion (6)	15 - 20	20 - 25
Series 971, 972, 987 High Fashion (6)	15 - 20	20 - 25
Series 321, 940, 951 High Fashion (6)	15 - 20	20 - 25
Series 907, 950, 956 Fashion (6)	15 - 18	18 - 22
Series 948 Sitting, Fashion (6)	15 - 18	18 - 22
Series 986 With Doll (6)	20 - 22	22 - 25
Series 456 With Hats (6)	15 - 18	18 - 22
Series 994 Woman/Child, Snowing (6)	12 - 14	14 - 16
Series 458, 498 Lovers Hugging	10 - 12	12 - 15
Series 498, 609 Lovers Talking	10 - 12	12 - 15
Series 448, 988 Lovers Hugging	12 - 14	14 - 16
Series 433 Small Image-Kissing	8 - 10	10 - 12
Series 462 Taking His Pulse (6)	12 - 15	15 - 18
Series 960 Fixing His Tie (6)	10 - 12	12 - 15
Golf	20 - 25	25 - 35
Tennis	15 - 20	20 - 30
Erotic and Semi-Nude	20 - 25	25 - 30
Ladies & Dogs		
Rev. Stampa; Dell, Anna & Gasparini		
Series 11, 17 (6)	15 - 20	20 - 25

Series 343 (6)	12 - 15	15 - 20
Series 457 (6)	15 - 18	18 - 22
Series 461 (6)	12 - 15	15 - 18
Series 637 (6) With Puppies	12 - 15	15 - 18
Ladies & Horses		
Series 343 (6)	15 - 20	20 - 25
Series 457 (6)	15 - 18	18 - 22
Series 641, 931, 556 (6)	12 - 15	15 - 20
Harlequins (Pierrot)	22 - 25	25 - 28
BONNATTA, L. (IT)	12 - 15	15 - 20
BONORA (IT) Art Deco and Glamour		
Ladies	15 - 18	18 - 22
Harlequins (Pierrot)	20 - 25	25 - 30
Greetings (Easter, etc.)	10 - 12	12 - 15
BORGONI, M. (IT)	8 - 10	10 - 15
BORRMEISTER, R. (GER)		
Ladies & Horses	10 - 12	12 - 15
BOTTARO, E. (IT)		
Art Deco and Glamour		
Series 135, Ladies 1900's	20 - 25	25 - 30
Series 123, Bathers 1900's	25 - 30	30 - 35
Others 1920's	12 - 15	15 - 18
BOTTOMLEY, G.	8 - 10	10 - 12
BOUTET, HENRI (FR) (Art Nouveau)	25 - 30	30 - 35
Charming Ladies	15 - 20	20 - 25
Collection des Cent. No 8	300 - 325	325 - 350
BRADLEY, W. H. (US) (Art Nouveau)	150 - 200	200 - 250
BRAUN, R.L. (GER)	10 - 12	12 - 15
BRAUN, W. H. (AUS)	15 - 18	18 - 22
BREDT, F. M. (GER)	5 - 6	6 - 9
BREHM, GEORGE (US)	5 - 6	6 - 9
BRILL, GEORGE (US) Sporting Girl Series	10 - 12	12 - 15
BRISLEY, ETHEL. C. (GB)	6 - 8	8 - 10
BROCK, A. (GER)	5 - 6	6 - 8
BROWN, J. FRANCIS (US)	4 - 5	5 - 6
BROWN, MAYNARD (US)	3 - 4	4 - 6
BRUNELLESCHI, UMBERTO (IT)		
Art Deco & Glamour		
Silhouettes	150 - 175	175 - 200
Advertising, "La Tradotta" Series (6)	100 - 110	110 - 120
R et Cie, France		
"Femmes 1920" Series 31 (6)	150 - 175	175 - 200
Art Nouveau	70 - 80	80 - 100
BRUNING, MAX (GER) (Sepia)	8 - 10	10 - 15
Erotic and Sports	12 - 15	15 - 25
BRYANT, JACK (US)	6 - 8	8 - 10
BRYSON, ROBERT (US)		
S.S. Porter, Chicago		
143 "Secrets"	5 - 8	8 - 12
BUHNE, BUNTE		
Deco Silhouette Series 225-228	15 - 20	20 - 25

Unsigned A. Busi, Rev. Stampa
#4070-2 – No Caption

A. Busi, Rev. Stampa
Series 24-4– No Caption

BULKELEY	5 - 6	6 - 9
BUKOVAC, PROF. V. (PO)	4 - 5	5 - 7
BULAS, J. (PO)	8 - 10	10 - 12
BUNNY	8 - 10	10 - 12
Tennis	22 - 25	25 - 28
BUSI, ADOLFO (IT) Art Deco and Glamour		
Degami		
Series 1017 Pierrots (Harlequins) & Ladies (6)	28 - 32	32 - 36
Series 1036 Ladies in Spanish Dress (6)	22 - 25	25 - 28
Series 1086 Pierrots, Lady, Child (6)	25 - 28	28 - 32
Series 2000 Ladies/Fountains (6)	22 - 25	25 - 28
Series 2074 Pierrots & Ladies (6)	28 - 32	32 - 36
Series 2107 Deco Ladies (6)	22 - 25	25 - 28
Series 2111 Deco Ladies (6)	25 - 28	28 - 32
Series 3059 Large image Ladies	22 - 25	25 - 28
Series 3545 Fantasy headwear (6)	25 - 28	28 - 32
Dell, Anna & Gasparini		
Series 100 Fantasy (6)	25 - 30	30 - 35
Series 110 Girls with kewpie-type doll (6)	18 - 22	22 - 26
Series 112 Diabolo, etc. (6)	25 - 28	28 - 32
Series 126 Girls/Fruit (6)	15 - 18	18 - 22
Series 153 Pajamas (6)	22 - 26	26 - 30
Series 170, 533 Ladies & Horses (6)	18 - 22	22 - 26
Series 193, 1020 Fashion (6)	18 - 20	20 - 25
Series 437 Gypsy Type (6)	15 - 18	18 - 22
Series 558 Couples on Sled (6)	15 - 20	20 - 25

Series 575 Lovers in Moonlight (6)	22 - 25	25 - 30
Series 615 Couples/Autos (6)	22 - 25	25 - 30
Series 628 Scarves/Heads (6)	25 - 30	30 - 35
Series 651 Bathing Girls (6)	22 - 25	25 - 30
Series 687, 1087 Ladies and Horses (6)	22 - 25	25 - 28
Series 3038, 3540, 3555 (6)	15 - 20	20 - 25
Any Golf	25 - 35	35 - 45
Any Tennis	22 - 25	25 - 35
Ricordi, Milan		
Ladies Series	25 - 28	28 - 32
Rev. Stampa		
Series 24 (6)	22 - 25	25 - 30
Series 4070 Heads	25 - 30	30 - 35
Ross-Monopol		
Pierrots (Harlequins)	25 - 30	30 - 35
Ladies & Dogs	18 - 22	22 - 25
Stengel & Co. (Signed AB)		
Series 520 Bathers - Lovers type	22 - 25	25 - 30
C.E.I.C.		
Series 157 (6) Ladies and Horses	18 - 22	22 - 26
Series 159	15 - 20	20 - 25
Anonymous		
Series 30 Ladies with dogs, etc. (6)	25 - 28	28 - 32
Und-Backs Series Pierrot & Lady (?)	28 - 32	32 - 36
BUSSIERE, G. (Art Nouveau)	35 - 40	40 - 50
BUTCHER, ARTHUR (GB)		
Inter-Art Company		
Series 956 "Red Cross Angel"	15 - 18	18 - 22
Series 1098	8 - 10	10 - 12
Series 1234 **Song Series**	8 - 10	10 - 12
Series 2510	6 - 8	8 - 10
Comique Series - **"Leap Year"**	15 - 18	18 - 22
United Six Girls Series		
"Belgium" "Japan"	10 - 12	12 - 15
"Britain" "Russia"	10 - 12	12 - 15
"France" "Serbia"	10 - 12	12 - 15
"Artisque" Series 1509 (6)	8 - 10	10 - 12
A.R.i.B. Series 1963 (6)	8 - 10	10 - 12
CADORIN, G. (IT)		
Ladies/Fashion	10 - 12	12 - 15
CALDERARA, C. (IT) Glamour	12 - 15	15 - 20
CALDONA (IT) Art Deco	12 - 15	15 - 20
CAPIELLO, L. Art Nouveau	200 - 250	250 - 300
CAPUANO, M. (IT) Glamour	12 - 15	15 - 18
CARRERE, RENE (FR) Glamour	18 - 22	22 - 30
CARSON, T. Art Nouveau	25 - 30	30 - 35
CASPARI, W. (GER)	12 - 15	15 - 18
CASTAN, A. (FR) Fashion	15 - 18	18 - 22
CASTELLI, V. (IT) Art Deco (See Children)	12 - 15	15 - 20
CASWELL, E. C. (US)	6 - 8	8 - 10
CAUVY, L. (FR) Art Nouveau	40 - 50	50 - 65

CELEBRI (IT) Art Deco	10 - 12	12 - 15
CENNI, E. (IT) Art Deco	12 - 15	15 - 20
CHAMBERS, C.E. (US)	6 - 8	8 - 10
CHARLET, J.A. (BE) Glamour		
Delta Series 4	15 - 22	22 - 30
CHERET, JULES Art Nouveau	200 - 300	300 - 500
CHERUBINI, M. (IT) Art Deco		
Rev. Stampa		
Series 790 National Ladies	15 - 20	20 - 25
Series 423, 977 Off-Shoulder Fash. (6)	15 - 20	20 - 25
Series 997 With Cupids (6)	15 - 20	20 - 25
Series 408 In Bubbles (6)	15 - 20	20 - 30
Series 887, 959 Beauties (6)	15 - 20	20 - 25
French Glamour	20 - 25	25 - 30
CHIOSTRI, SOFIA (Also FOFI) (IT) See Children		
Art Deco and Glamour		
Ballerini & Fratini		
All Series contain 4 cards		
Series 166 Deco Fashion	38 - 42	42 - 48
Series 167 Pierrot	45 - 48	48 - 52
Series 178 Easter Pierrot	30 - 35	35 - 40
Series 180 Oval Woman/Pierrot	30 - 35	35 - 40
Series 181 Bathers	25 - 30	30 - 40
Series 183 Easter Lovers	35 - 40	40 - 45
Series 184 Japanese Geisha Girls	25 - 30	30 - 40
Series 187 Christmas Ladies	35 - 40	40 - 45
Series 197, 212 Ladies/Pierrot	40 - 50	50 - 60
Series 200, 201 Easter Ladies	30 - 35	35 - 45
Series 202, 203, 214 Ladies, Flowers	30 - 35	35 - 38
Series 211 Harem Girls	40 - 45	45 - 55
Series 218 Early Ladies/Men	35 - 40	40 - 50
Series 220 Santas/Father New Year	35 - 40	40 - 50
Black-Robed Santas	50 - 60	60 - 75
Series 224 Ladies/Men	35 - 40	40 - 45
Series 225 Man and Lady Pierrots	40 - 45	45 - 55
Series 228 Lady & Pierrot	35 - 40	40 - 45
Series 230, 231, 233 Easter Ladies/Men/Children	30 - 35	35 - 40
Series 236 Ladies in Springtime	30 - 35	35 - 40
Series 237, 252 Ladies with Cupid	40 - 45	45 - 50
Series 238 Mermaids	50 - 60	60 - 75
Series 240 Fantasy Flower Ladies	40 - 45	45 - 55
Series 241 "Il Destino" Series	45 - 50	50 - 55
Series 243 Fortune Teller	30 - 40	40 - 45
Series 244 Very Colorful Pierrots	45 - 50	50 - 55
Series 251 Christmas Lovers	40 - 45	45 - 50
Series 257 Pierrot	35 - 40	40 - 50
Series 258 Birthstone Series	50 - 55	55 - 65
Series 259 Gem Series	45 - 50	50 - 55
Series 248, 268, 294, 301 Christmas Ladies	30 - 35	35 - 38
Series 290 Japanese Geisha Girls	35 - 38	38 - 45
Series 295 Colorful Christmas Ladies	40 - 45	45 - 50

S. Chiostri, B&F 373

S. Chiostri, B&F 290

S. Chiostri, B&F 211

Fofi (Chiostri), B&F 163

S. Chiostri, B&F 212

S. Chiostri, B&F 304

S. Chiostri, B&F 350

S. Chiostri, B&F 209

S. Chiostri, B&F 258

Series 300 Lady & Men Christmas Pierrots	40 - 45	45 - 50
Series 302 Winter Sports Lovers-Cupid	30 - 35	35 - 38
Series 304 Fairies-Pierrot Series	40 - 45	45 - 55
Series 305 Pierrot-Mask Series	35 - 40	40 - 45
Series 308 Easter Lovers	18 - 22	22 - 25
Series 309 High Class Easter Ladies	35 - 40	40 - 45
Series 311 Easter Lovers	25 - 30	30 - 40
Series 313, 316 Easter Ladies with Animals	35 - 40	40 - 50
Series 317 Mermaids	50 - 60	60 - 70
Series 318 Japanese Geisha Girls	35 - 38	38 - 42
Series 320 Lady with Wild Animals	40 - 45	45 - 55
Series 348 Lady with Cupid, Flowers	35 - 38	38 - 42
Series 350 Fantasy Ladies in Swimsuits	50 - 55	55 - 65
Series 354 Russian Harem Girls	35 - 40	40 - 45
Series 357 Pierrot-Ladies	30 - 35	35 - 40
Series 358 Girls with Umbrella	40 - 45	45 - 40
Series 359 Ladies-Bird of Paradise	45 - 50	50 - 55
Series 363 Pierrot/Ladies; Lovers	30 - 35	35 - 45
Series 387 Ladies & Flowers	30 - 35	35 - 40
Series 388 Classical Japanese Ladies	40 - 45	45 - 50
Series 426 Russian Lovers	30 - 35	35 - 38
Other Pierrots (Harlequins)	35 - 40	40 - 50
Others, Colored Background	25 - 30	30 - 40
Others, Seasons Greetings	12 - 15	15 - 20
Comics, Flowers & Fruits in Deco Style	15 - 18	18 - 22
Signed FOFI (Pen name of Sofia Chiostri)		
Ballerini & Fratini		
Series 164 French Dressed Couples	20 - 25	25 - 35
Series 165 Lady & Pierrot	35 - 40	40 - 45
W.O.		
Series 663 Russian Lovers (Uns.)	25 - 30	30 - 40
CHRISTIANSEN, HANS (Art Nouveau)		
"Pari" Series, High Fashion Ladies	175 - 200	200 - 225
"Twentieth Century Women"	140 - 150	150 - 160
Darmstadt Expo, 1902		
Lady Vignettes (6)	175 - 200	200 - 225

CHRISTY, F. EARL (US)

F. Earl Christy was one of the leading artists who depicted the total beauty of the American girl, especially of the college and university varieties. Most of his early works were in this category, as he helped start the tradition of glorifying the beauties of the era. He pictured them as high classed, always beautifully dressed, and seemingly in complete command of the situation. These were the girls who attended football games, played golf and tennis, rode in new automobiles, and were gifted with musical talent. His was the *All-American Girl.*

His first College Girl series was published by the U.S.S. Postcard Co. in 1905. This series revealed an artist with promising talents, and he went on to design many of the "College Girl" series for numerous publishers. Among his most popular works were Tuck's College Queens and Kings.

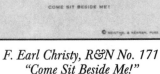

F. Earl Christy, R&N No. 171
"Come Sit Beside Me!"

F. Earl Christy, R&N No. 627
"A Sandwitch"

After the college/university girl fad had run its course, Christy used his talents to paint beautiful ladies and man/woman lover types. The Reinthal & Newman Co. of New York was his major publisher; however, he did many fine sets for the Knapp Co., Edward Gross, and others. His images were also published and distributed in Europe and Scandinavia.

Earl Christy's cards, with the exception of high-flying College Queens and Kings series and other College Girl Series, have elevated only slightly since our third edition. The works of this talented artist should be a favorite of any who collect American artist-signed beautiful ladies.

Reinthal & Newman, N.Y.
No Number Series
"Love"	15 - 18	18 - 22
"A Sandwich"	15 - 20	20 - 25
"Be With You in a Minute"	10 - 12	12 - 15
"Always Winning"	15 - 18	18 - 22
"Love Dreams"	12 - 15	15 - 18
"Lovingly Yours"	12 - 15	15 - 18
"Swimming"	12 - 15	15 - 18

"A Sweet Surrender" Series
168	"A Sweet Surrender"	12 - 15	15 - 18
169	"The Pilot"	15 - 18	18 - 22
170	"My Love is Like a Red, Red Rose"	15 - 18	18 - 22
171	"Come Sit Beside Me"	18 - 22	22 - 26
172	"Come With Me"	15 - 18	18 - 22
173	"Love All"	22 - 25	25 - 30

"The Siren" Series

228	"Masks Off!"	18 - 22	22 - 26
229	"Lovingly Yours"	18 - 22	22 - 26
230	"Be With You in a Minute"	15 - 18	18 - 22
231	"The Rose Maid"	18 - 22	22 - 26
232	"The Siren"	18 - 22	22 - 26
233	"Roses are Always in Season"	18 - 22	22 - 26

"The Path of Love" Series

276	"The Love Song"	12 - 15	15 - 20
277	"Love Dreams"	15 - 18	18 - 22
278	"The Love Story"	15 - 18	18 - 22
279	"The Love Match"	15 - 18	18 - 22
280	"The Love Waltz"	15 - 18	18 - 22
281	"Love"	15 - 18	18 - 22

Water Color Series

363	"A Bit of Tea & Gossip"	15 - 18	18 - 22
364	"The Sweetest of All"	15 - 18	18 - 22
365	"For the Wedding Chest"	15 - 18	18 - 22
366	"The Message of Love"	15 - 18	18 - 22
367	"The Day's Work"	20 - 25	25 - 28
368	"A Finishing Touch"	15 - 18	18 - 22

Series 428-433

428	"What Shall I Answer?"	12 - 15	15 - 18
429	"I'm Waiting for You"	12 - 15	15 - 18
430	"Tender Memories"	12 - 15	15 - 18
431	"A Message of Love"	12 - 15	15 - 18
432	"On the Bridal Path"	12 - 15	15 - 18
433	"Always Winning"	25 - 28	28 - 32

Series 618-623

618	"The Girl I Like"	15 - 18	18 - 22
619	"The Girl I Like to Chat With"	15 - 18	18 - 22
620	"The Girl I Like to Walk With"	15 - 18	18 - 22
621	"The Girl I Like to Flirt With"	15 - 18	18 - 22
622	"The Girl I Like to Play With"	18 - 22	22 - 25
623	"The Girl I Like to Sing With"	15 - 18	18 - 22

Series 624-629

624	"By Appointment"	15 - 18	18 - 22
625	"As Promised"	15 - 18	18 - 22
626	"What Shall I Say?"	15 - 18	18 - 22
627	"A Sandwitch"	22 - 25	25 - 30
628	"With Fond Love"	15 - 18	18 - 22
629	"Nearest Her Heart"	15 - 18	18 - 22

Water Color Series 942-947

		15 - 18	18 - 22
942	"Protected"	18 - 22	22 - 26
943	"Someone is Thinking of You"	18 - 22	22 - 26
944	"Are You There?"	15 - 18	18 - 22
945	"Love, Here is My Heart"	15 - 18	18 - 22
946	"Worth Waiting For"	15 - 18	18 - 22
947	"Not Forgotten"	20 - 25	25 - 28

ENGLISH REPRINTS

2106	"On the Bridal Path"	15 - 20	20 - 25

F. Earl Christy, R&N 620
"The Girl I Like to Walk With"

F. Earl Christy, FAS 198
No Caption

2107	"Tender Memories"	15 - 20	20 - 25
2109	"Nearest Her Heart"	15 - 20	20 - 25
FAS (F.A. Schneider)			
197	Horseback Riding	15 - 20	20 - 26
198	Skates	20 - 25	25 - 28
199	Tennis	25 - 28	28 - 32
200	Golf	35 - 38	38 - 42
201	In an Auto	18 - 22	22 - 26
202	"What the Waves are Saying"	18 - 22	22 - 26
203	Daisies	18 - 22	22 - 26
Edward Gross Co.			
Series 3			
	"Black Eyed Susan"	12 - 15	15 - 20
	"Gold is not All"	18 - 22	22 - 25
	"Her Pilot"	18 - 22	22 - 25
	"In Deep Water"	18 - 22	22 - 25
	"Oldest Trust Co."	12 - 15	15 - 20
	"World Before Them"	18 - 22	22 - 26
Knapp Co., N.Y. W. M. Sanford			
Paul Heckscher Import			
Series 304			
1	"Annie Laurie"	15 - 18	18 - 20
2	"The Lost Chord"	15 - 18	18 - 20
3	"Louisiana Lou"	15 - 18	18 - 20
4	"The Rosary"	15 - 18	18 - 20

5 "The Largo"	15 - 18	18 - 20
6 "Love's Old Sweet Song"	15 - 18	18 - 20
7 "Daughter of the Regiment"	15 - 18	18 - 20
8 "Good Night, Beloved"	15 - 18	18 - 20
9 "The Gypsy Maid"	15 - 18	18 - 20
10 "Maryland, My Maryland"	15 - 18	18 - 20
11 "Home, Sweet Home"	15 - 18	18 - 20
12 "Wish I Was in Dixie"	15 - 18	18 - 20

Paul Heckscher Import – W. M. Sanford
Miniature Image Series 304
(Same as above but with different Numbers)

371 "Annie Laurie"	12 - 15	15 - 18
381 "The Lost Chord"	12 - 15	15 - 18
391 "Louisiana Lou"	12 - 15	15 - 18
401 "The Rosary"	12 - 15	15 - 18
411 "The Largo"	12 - 15	15 - 18
421 "Love's Old Sweet Song"	12 - 15	15 - 18
431 "Daughter of the Regiment"	12 - 15	15 - 18
441 "Good Night, Beloved"	12 - 15	15 - 18
451 "The Gypsy Maid"	12 - 15	15 - 18
461 "Maryland, My Maryland"	12 - 15	15 - 18
471 "Home, Sweet Home"	12 - 15	15 - 18
481 "Wish I Was in Dixie"	12 - 15	15 - 18

Series 1025

1025-3 "I'm Ready"	12 - 15	15 - 20

Knapp Co.

103 Girl in Sailor Blouse and Hat	15 - 18	18 - 22
105 Girl with Lace Collar	15 - 18	18 - 22
114 Girl in Sailor Blouse	15 - 18	18 - 22
115 Beauty, with Pearl Necklace	18 - 22	22 - 26
116 Sweet Girl with Long Curl	15 - 18	18 - 22
119 Blonde Girl with Black Pearls	15 - 18	18 - 22
124 "Prudence"	15 - 18	18 - 22
169 "Let's Go"	15 - 18	18 - 22
176 "Skipper's Mate"	15 - 18	18 - 22
215 "Beauty"	15 - 18	18 - 22
219 "Anna Belle"	15 - 18	18 - 22

Note: There may be several cards missing from Nos.
103 through No. 219 that have not surfaced.

Knapp Co.
H. Import Series 318

"The Best of Chums"	15 - 18	18 - 22
"Blossoming Affection"	15 - 18	18 - 22
"Good-bye Summer"	15 - 18	18 - 22
"The Springtime of Friendship"	15 - 18	18 - 22

Knapp Co.
H. Import
Series 319

"Embracing the Opportunity"	15 - 18	18 - 22
"In Sweet Accord"	15 - 18	18 - 22
"The Message of the Rose"	15 - 18	18 - 22
"Tempting Fate"	15 - 18	18 - 22

F. Earl Christy, K. Co. 103
No Caption

F. Earl Christy, K. Co. 115
No Caption

Knapp Co. by Sanford
  Calendar Card, 1916

"I Wish I Was in Dixie"	18 - 22	22 - 26
Others	18 - 22	22 - 26

Julius Bien, 1907
  College Series 95
  Girl and Boy on Football

950 "Yale"	20 - 25	25 - 30
951 "Harvard"	20 - 25	25 - 30
952 "Columbia"	20 - 25	25 - 30
953 "Penn"	20 - 25	25 - 30
954 "Princeton"	20 - 25	25 - 30
955 "Cornell"	20 - 25	25 - 30

Atkinson News Agency

"Tilton Seminary"	30 - 35	35 - 40

Chapman, N.Y., 1910

1032 "A Brisk Walk"	15 - 18	18 - 22
1034 "Waiting Their Turn"	15 - 18	18 - 22
1039 "At the Horse Show"	15 - 18	18 - 22

William B. Christy (His Father)
  Unnumbered Series

"Harvard," "Michigan," "Penn,"	18 - 22	22 - 26
"Princeton," "Yale"	18 - 22	22 - 26

EAS (Ea. Schwerd Teger)
  Girl on Brick Wall Series

"Columbia," "Cornell," "Harvard"	18 - 22	22 - 26

F. Earl Christy, H. Heininger
37, "Among the Roses"

F. Earl Christy, H. Heininger
39, "On A High Horse"

"Penn," "Princeton," "Yale"	18 - 22	22 - 26
Henry Heininger Co., NY		
Caption and Verse Series Water Colors		
37 "Among the Roses"	20 - 22	22 - 26
39 "On a High Horse"	20 - 22	22 - 26
40 "What The Waves Are Saying"	20 - 22	22 - 26
44 "In an Auto" (Same as **FAS** 201)	20 - 22	22 - 26
45 "Daisies"	20 - 22	22 - 26
Illustrated Postal Card & Novelty Co.		
Series 133*		
1 "Cornell"	20 - 25	25 - 28
2 "Harvard"	20 - 25	25 - 28
3 "Yale"	20 - 25	25 - 28
4 "Penn"	20 - 25	25 - 28
5 "Princeton"	20 - 25	25 - 28
6 "Columbia"	20 - 25	25 - 28
* With Silk Applique Dress, add $10-15.		
Series 150*		
1 "Cornell"	20 - 25	25 - 28
2 "Harvard"	20 - 25	25 - 30
3 "Yale"	20 - 25	25 - 30
4 "Penn"	20 - 25	25 - 30
5 "Princeton"	20 - 25	25 - 30
6 "Columbia"	20 - 25	25 - 30

* With Silk Applique Dress, add $10-15.
  Note: Nos. are on backs of some cards.

Series 160, 1907

160-1	"A Drama"	18 - 22	22 - 26
160-2	"A Critical Moment"	18 - 22	22 - 26
160-3	"The World was Made ..."	18 - 22	22 - 26
160-4	"An Attractive Parasol"	18 - 22	22 - 26
160-5	"Getting Acquainted"	18 - 22	22 - 26
160-6		18 - 22	22 - 26

"Sports" Series

552D	Swinging	8 - 10	10 - 12
554	Bowling	12 - 15	15 - 18
557	Rowing	8 - 10	10 - 12
562	Swimming	8 - 10	10 - 12
567	Driving Old Car	8 - 10	10 - 12
569	Four Princeton Girls in Auto	8 - 10	10 - 12
572	Golf	15 - 18	18 - 22
574	Princeton Belles in Old Car	8 - 10	10 - 12
577	Buggy	8 - 10	10 - 12
582	Three Yale Girls in Auto	8 - 10	10 - 12
584	Tennis	15 - 18	18 - 22

Ill. P.C. & Novelty Co.

Series 5006

3	"Swinging"	8 - 10	10 - 12
7	Golf Girl	15 - 18	18 - 22
8	Horse & Buggy	6 - 8	8 - 10
9	Old Car-Harvard	8 - 10	10 - 12
10	Old Car-Yale	8 - 10	10 - 12
11	Old Car-Princeton	8 - 10	10 - 12
12	Old Car-Penn	8 - 10	10 - 12

Platinachrome, 1907

Girl/Pennant form Letter, College Yell

"Chicago," "Columbia," "Cornell," "Harvard"	22 - 25	25 - 28
"Michigan," "Penn," "Princeton," "Yale"	22 - 25	25 - 28

Platinachrome, © 1905 F. Earl Christy

No Numbers or Captions

Two Women in a Car	10 - 12	12 - 15
Woman Golfing	15 - 18	18 - 22
Woman Bowling	10 - 12	12 - 15
Woman-Ice Hockey	12 - 15	15 - 18

P. Sander, N.Y., 1907 (Ill. P.C. Co.)

Series 198

1	"Is a Caddie always necessary"	20 - 25	25 - 30
2	"Is horseback riding..."	10 - 12	12 - 15
3	"Trying to make a hit"	12 - 15	15 - 18
4	"A Good Racquet for Two"	18 - 22	22 - 26
5	"Out for a catch"	12 - 15	15 - 18
6	"Hockey is not the only game"	12 - 15	15 - 18

P. Sander, N.Y., 1908

Series 246 Large Hats* (6)

1	Full Photo	6 - 8	8 - 12
2	1910 Calendar	10 - 12	12 - 15
3	Christmas, Silver	8 - 10	10 - 12
4	Christmas, Gold	8 - 10	10 - 12
5	Woman in Easter Egg	8 - 10	10 - 12

6 Valentine	8 - 10	10 - 12
* Full card is signed; others cropped & uns.		
Note: There are 6 different cards of each image!		
Series 304-A (6) Signed, 1908		
1 Full Card	8 - 10	10 - 12
2 Birthday, White	8 - 10	10 - 12
3 Birthday, Gold	8 - 10	10 - 12
4 Birthday, Silver	8 - 10	10 - 12
5 Woman in Egg	8 - 10	10 - 12
6 Valentine, Checkered	8 - 10	10 - 12
7 Valentine, Gold	8 - 10	10 - 12
8 Horse Shoe, Birthday, White	8 - 10	10 - 12
9 Horse Shoe, Birthday, Gold	8 - 10	10 - 12
10 Horse Shoe, Birthday, Silver	8 - 10	10 - 12
Note: 10 different cards of each image!		
Anonymous P. Sander Series 383		
Lady, big hat...in big egg "Easter Greetings"	8 - 10	10 - 12
W. H. Sanford Series 371		
"Goodbye Summer"	12 - 15	15 - 18
"Tempting Fate"	12 - 15	15 - 18
Stecher Litho Co., N.Y.		
Series 618, Valentines		
A "To My Sweetheart"	8 - 10	10 - 12
B "Valentine Thoughts" (Unsigned)	8 - 10	10 - 12
C "To My Valentine" (Unsigned)	8 - 10	10 - 12
D "A Valentine Greeting"	8 - 10	10 - 12
F "A Valentine Greeting"	8 - 10	10 - 12
Souvenir Postcard Co., © 1907 **E. Christy**		
Girl and Football Player with Banner		
1 "Michigan"	25 - 28	28 - 32
2 "Chicago"	25 - 28	28 - 32
3 "Princeton"	25 - 28	28 - 32
4 "Penn"	25 - 28	28 - 32
5 "Cornell"	25 - 28	28 - 32
6 "Yale"	25 - 28	28 - 32
7 "Harvard"	25 - 28	28 - 32
8 "Columbia"	25 - 28	28 - 32
Raphael Tuck & Sons		
University Girl Series 2453 (6)		
"Georgetown," "Oberlin College"	22 - 25	25 - 30
"Syracuse," "West Point"	22 - 25	25 - 30
"Tennessee," "U.S. Naval Academy"	22 - 25	25 - 30
Series 2590 (6)		
"Ames," Iowa State	25 - 28	28 - 32
"U. of Arkansas"	25 - 28	28 - 32
"Iowa"	25 - 28	28 - 32
"Kentucky"	25 - 28	28 - 32
"Penn State,"	25 - 28	28 - 32
"Valparaiso U."	25 - 28	28 - 32
Series 2593 (4)		
"Bucknell," "Colby"	25 - 28	28 - 32
"U. of Maine," "U. of Notre Dame"	25 - 28	28 - 32
University Girl Series 2625 (6)		
"Columbia," "Cornell," "Harvard"	20 - 25	25 - 30

F. Earl Christy, R. Tuck
Queens Series 2767, "Pennsylvania"

F. Earl Christy, R. Tuck
Kings Series 2766, "Columbia"

"Penn," "Princeton," "Yale"	20 - 25	25 - 30
Series 2626 (6)		
"U. of Chicago," "U. of Illinois"	20 - 25	25 - 30
"Indiana U.," "U. of Michigan"	20 - 25	25 - 30
"U. of Minnesota," "U. of Wisconsin"	20 - 25	25 - 30
Series 2627 (6)		
"Brown U.," "McGill College"	20 - 25	25 - 30
"Tulane of La." "Vanderbilt U."	20 - 25	25 - 30
"U. of Virginia," "Williston Seminary"	20 - 25	25 - 30
Series 2678 (1)		
"Milliken"	30 - 35	35 - 40
Series 2717 (1)		
"Mary Baldwin Seminary"	35 - 40	40 - 45
Series 2766 College Kings (4)		
"Columbia," "Cornell"	90 - 100	100 - 120
"Chicago," "Michigan"	90 - 100	100 - 120
Series 2767 College Queens (4)		
"Yale," "Penn," "Harvard," "Princeton"	90 - 100	100 - 120
"Good Luck" Series 2769 (4)		
"Not only for today..."	12 - 15	15 - 20
"Good luck attend you..."	12 - 15	15 - 20
"Good wishes greet you..."	12 - 15	15 - 20
"May Fortune spin..."	12 - 15	15 - 20
Series 2794 (1)		
"Williston" **(Very Rare!)**	100 - 125	125 - 150

Ullman Mfg. Co. (4)
College Girls, Copyright 1905

569 "Princeton"	15 - 20	20 - 25
574 "Penn"	15 - 20	20 - 25
575 "Harvard"	15 - 20	20 - 25
582 "Yale"	15 - 20	20 - 25

College Girls
Series 24, © 1905 (Uns.)

1498 "Penn"	15 - 20	20 - 25
1499 "Columbia"	15 - 20	20 - 25
1512 "Yale"	15 - 20	20 - 25
1513 "Harvard"	15 - 20	20 - 25
1514 "Leland Stanford"	15 - 20	20 - 25
1515 "Cornell"	15 - 20	20 - 25
1516 "Princeton"	15 - 20	20 - 25
1517 "Chicago"	15 - 20	20 - 25

College Football Players
Series 24, © 1905 (Unsigned)

1464 "Harvard"	20 - 25	25 - 30
1465 "Princeton"	20 - 25	25 - 30
1466 "Penn"	20 - 25	25 - 30
1467 "Yale"	20 - 25	25 - 30
1518 "Columbia"	20 - 25	25 - 30
1519 "Leland Stanford"	20 - 25	25 - 30
1520 "Chicago"	20 - 25	25 - 30
1521 "Cornell"	20 - 25	25 - 30

Ullman Mfg. Co., 1907
Girl in Big College Letter Series (8)

1990 "Chicago"	20 - 25	25 - 30
1991 "Cornell"	20 - 25	25 - 30
1992 "Michigan"	20 - 25	25 - 30
1993 "Columbia"	20 - 25	25 - 30
1994 "Penn"	20 - 25	25 - 30
1995 "Yale"	20 - 25	25 - 30
1996 "Princeton"	20 - 25	25 - 30
1997 "Harvard"	20 - 25	25 - 30

Ullman Mfg. Co., 1905, N.Y.

501 "Golf"	12 - 15	15 - 18
506 "A Pleasant Ride"	4 - 6	6 - 8
507 "In Fair Japan"	4 - 6	6 - 8
1583 "The Graduate"	8 - 10	10 - 12
1583 Var. of "The Graduate" (with verse)	12 - 15	15 - 18
Series 93	8 - 10	10 - 12

U.S.S.P.C. Co. 1905 College Seal Series

1 "Penn"	20 - 25	25 - 28
2 "Princeton"	20 - 25	25 - 28
3 "Harvard" (also leather) *	20 - 25	25 - 28
4 "Yale"	20 - 25	25 - 28
5 "Michigan"	20 - 25	25 - 28
6 "Chicago"	20 - 25	25 - 28
7 "Columbia"	20 - 25	25 - 28
8 "Cornell"	20 - 25	25 - 28

* Add $5-10 for leather cards.

Valentine & Sons
  "Artotype" Series, No Numbers
    "Columbia"   15 - 18   18 - 22
    "Penn," "Princeton"   15 - 18   18 - 22
Friedman-Shelby Shoe Co.
  Big Hat Series
    Shoe Style 3324   25 - 30   30 - 35
    Shoe Style 3332   25 - 30   30 - 35
    The Style 3151   25 - 30   30 - 35
    Red Goose School Shoes   25 - 30   30 - 35
    Shoe Style 3339   25 - 30   30 - 35
Greenfield's Delatour Chocolates, 1911
    Girl W/Big Hat, Walks Right   25 - 30   30 - 40
Bulls-Eye Overalls   25 - 30   30 - 35
UNKNOWN
  © 1910 F. Earl Christy
    Bust of woman w/nosegay & big hat   8 - 10   10 - 12
    Blue dress and pink flowers   8 - 10   10 - 12
    Blue hat and red flowers   8 - 10   10 - 12
    Orange hat and yellow flowers   8 - 10   10 - 12
  Water Colors
    650-5 "Embracing the Opportunity"   12 - 15   15 - 18
    656-5 "In Sweet Accord"   12 - 15   15 - 18
    657-5 "Vacation Days"   12 - 15   15 - 18
FINNISH ISSUES
Pain. Karjalan Kirjap. Oy, Viipuri
  N:0 12   Unsigned, no caption.
    Same as R&N 173, "Love All" Tennis   30 - 35   35 - 38
  N:0 6   Signed, no caption.
    Girl in white, w/big red umbrella   30 - 35   35 - 38
No Identification Series
  Unsigned, no caption. Same as
  R&N 365, "For the Wedding Chest"   25 - 30   30 - 35
W. & G. American Series N:o 7001/1-35
  Girl with long stemmed roses.   30 - 35   35 - 38
CHRISTY, HOWARD CHANDLER
  Moffat, Yard, & Co., N.Y., 1905
    "The Christy Post Card"
      1 "Arbutus" (B&W)   8 - 10   10 - 12
      2 "At the Opera"   10 - 12   12 - 15
      3 "A City Girl" (B&W)   10 - 12   12 - 15
        Also in partial color.   12 - 15   15 - 18
      4 "The Dance"   10 - 12   12 - 15
      5 "The Debutante"   12 - 15   15 - 18
      6 "Encore"   10 - 12   12 - 15
      7 "Mistletoe" (B&W)   8 - 10   10 - 12
        Also in partial color.   10 - 12   12 - 15
      8 "A Moment of Reflection"   10 - 12   12 - 15
      9 "Reverie" (B&W)   8 - 10   10 - 12
      10 "A Suburban Girl" (B&W)   10 - 12   12 - 15
      11 "The Summer Girl" (B&W)   10 - 12   12 - 15
      12 "Violets" (B&W)   10 - 12   12 - 15
        Also in partial color.   12 - 15   15 - 18

13 "Waiting"	10 - 12	12 - 15
14 "Water Lilies" (B&W)	10 - 12	12 - 15
15 "The Winter Girl" (B&W)	10 - 12	12 - 15
Unnumbered Series, 1908		
"The American Queen"	10 - 12	12 - 15
"American Beauties"	10 - 12	12 - 15
"At the Theater"	10 - 12	12 - 15
"Canoe Mates"	10 - 12	12 - 15
"Drifting"	10 - 12	12 - 15
"Excess Baggage"	10 - 12	12 - 15
"A Fisherman's Luck"	12 - 15	15 - 18
"The Golf Girl"	20 - 25	25 - 28
"Lilies"	10 - 12	12 - 15
"On the Beach"	10 - 12	12 - 14
"Sailing Close"	10 - 12	12 - 15
"A Summer Girl"	12 - 15	15 - 18
"Teasing"	10 - 12	12 - 15
"A Winning Hand"	12 - 15	15 - 18
"The Heart of America"	12 - 15	15 - 18
Edward Gross, New York		
Series 3, 1909		
"Black-Eyed Susan"	15 - 18	18 - 22
"Gold is Not All"	15 - 18	18 - 22
"Her Pilot"	15 - 18	18 - 22
"In Deep Water"	15 - 18	18 - 22
"Miss Demure"	15 - 18	18 - 22
"The Oldest Trust Company"	12 - 15	15 - 18
"A Plea For Arbitration"	12 - 15	15 - 18
"The Sweet Girl Graduate"	15 - 18	18 - 22
"The Teasing Girl"	15 - 18	18 - 22
Series 4, 1910		
"Au Revoir"	12 - 15	15 - 18
"Congratulations"	12 - 15	15 - 18
"The Heart of America"	15 - 18	18 - 22
"Her Gift"	15 - 18	18 - 22
"Honeymoon"	15 - 18	18 - 22
"Into the Future"	15 - 18	18 - 22
"Life's Beginning"	15 - 18	18 - 22
"Love Spats"	15 - 18	18 - 22
"Mistletoe"	15 - 18	18 - 22
"Overpowering Beauty"	15 - 18	18 - 22
"A Rose on the Lips"	15 - 18	18 - 22
Series of 6		
"A Fisherman's Luck"	12 - 15	15 - 18
"The American Queen"	12 - 15	15 - 18
"Teasing"	12 - 15	15 - 18
"The World Before Them"	12 - 15	15 - 18
Scribner's Series of 8	10 - 12	12 - 15
Armour & Co., Chicago, 1901 Ad Card		
"The Howard Chandler Christy Girl" (B&W)	15 - 20	20 - 25
Same, by German Publisher (B&W)	20 - 25	25 - 30
A & V, Jamestown Expo., 1907		
"The Army Girl"	225 - 250	250 - 275
"The Navy Girl"	225 - 250	250 - 275

H. C. Christy, Moffat, Yard & Co.
"The Heart of America"

Haskell Coffin, R. C. Co., N.Y.
Series 205, "An American Queen"

H. Choate & Co.
  Djer-Kiss Rouge & Face Power Compacts
  "American Brunette"   25 - 30   30 - 35
Curt Teich & Co.
  "Boy Scout Jamboree" (Linen, 1937)   10 - 15   15 - 18
T.P. & Co.   10 - 12   12 - 15
Judge Co., N.Y., Series 751
  "You Have a Wonderful Future!"   12 - 15   15 - 18
  "Going Away" (Unsigned)   12 - 15   15 - 20
FOREIGN
Novitas   Series 21655
  "City Girl," "Drifting"   12 - 15   15 - 20
  "Reverie," "A Summer Girl"   12 - 15   15 - 20
  "Violets" "The World Before Them"   12 - 15   15 - 20
  Series 21657 (6)   12 - 15   15 - 18
Pain. Karjalan Kirjap. Oy, Viipuri
  N:O 2 Three Bathing Girls   22 - 25   25 - 28
CLAY, JOHN C. (US)
  Detroit Pub. Co.   10 - 12   12 - 15
  Rotograph Co.
    Water Color Series 160-172
    "Garden of Love" Ser. (12) Head in Flowers   30 - 35   35 - 38
  Armour & Co., Advertising Card
    "The John C. Clay Girl" (B&W)   12 - 15   15 - 18
    Same, by German Publisher (B&W)   15 - 18   18 - 22

CLIRIO, L. (IT) Art Deco
Degami
    Series 29   15 - 18   18 - 22
    Series 30 Couples   12 - 15   15 - 20

COFFIN, HASKELL (US)
R. C. Co., N.Y.

Series 205		
"A Modern Eve"	20 - 25	25 - 28
"An American Queen"	20 - 25	25 - 28
"The Glory of Autumn"	20 - 25	25 - 28
"The Lure of the Poppies"	20 - 25	25 - 28
"Miss Jack Frost"	20 - 22	22 - 25
"Motherhood"	20 - 25	25 - 28
"Queen of the Court"	25 - 30	30 - 35
"The Spring Maid"	20 - 25	25 - 28
"Vanity Fair"	20 - 25	25 - 28
"Winter's Charm"	20 - 25	25 - 28

K. Co. Inc., N.Y.

Water Color Series		
152 "Motherhood"	18 - 22	22 - 26
215 "Beauty"	18 - 22	22 - 26
216 "Sally"	18 - 22	22 - 26
217 "Ruth"	18 - 22	22 - 26
218 "Billy"	18 - 22	22 - 26

Photo Color Graph Co. (PCG Co.)

Series 205 "Art Studies" (10)		
1 "Bohemia"	15 - 18	18 - 22
2 "Senorita"	15 - 18	18 - 22
3 "Sweet Sixteen"	18 - 22	22 - 26
4 "The Final Touch"	15 - 18	18 - 22
5 "Her First Love Letter"	15 - 20	20 - 25
6 "Girl From the Golden West"	15 - 20	20 - 25
7 "June Roses"	15 - 20	20 - 25
8 "Pride of the Orient"	15 - 20	20 - 25
9 "News from the Sunny South"	15 - 20	20 - 25

"Flower & Figure Subjects"

Series 280, with verse (12)		
1 Iris	15 - 20	20 - 25
2 Violet	15 - 20	20 - 25
3 Poppies	15 - 20	20 - 25
4 Narcissus	15 - 20	20 - 25
5 Goldenrod	15 - 20	20 - 25
6 Daffodils	15 - 20	20 - 25
7 Hollyhock	15 - 20	20 - 25
8 Water Lily	15 - 20	20 - 25
9 Nasturtium	15 - 20	20 - 25
10 Rose	15 - 20	20 - 25
11 Sweet Pea	15 - 20	20 - 25
12 Morning Glory	15 - 20	20 - 25
Fantasy Women Series, Semi-Nude	18 - 22	22 - 26
"Celia"	18 - 22	22 - 26
Others	18 - 22	22 - 26

A. R. & C.i.B. Co. (R.C. Co.)

417 "An American Queen"	20 - 25	25 - 30

E. Colombo, Rev. Stampa
Series 407, No Caption

E. Colombo, Rev. Stampa
Series 443-2, No Caption

E. Colombo, Rev. Stampa
Cupid Series 936-3

"A Modern Eve," "The Glory of Autumn"	20 - 25	25 - 30
"The Joy of the Hunt," "Miss Jack Frost"	20 - 25	25 - 30
"Ruth," "Winter's Charm," "Vanity Fair"	20 - 25	25 - 30
536 "The Heyday of Youth"	20 - 25	25 - 30
H & S Co.		
1551 D3 "A New York Belle"	15 - 20	20 - 25
1551 D6 "Thoughtful"	15 - 20	20 - 25
Others with Captions	15 - 20	20 - 25
Others, No Captions	15 - 18	18 - 22
Novitas		
Series 15670		
1. Girl in white, yellow bow, big straw hat	18 - 22	22 - 26
Advertising Cards		
Blue Bell Brand Candies (2)	22 - 25	25 - 35
ESK Co.		
02 Girl with Big Slouch Hat, No Caption	15 - 20	20 - 25
Hires Root Beer Girl	30 - 35	35 - 45
COLIN, PAUL	50 - 75	75 - 100
COLLINS, G.T. (GB)	10 - 12	12 - 15
COLOMBO, E. (IT) Art Deco and Glamour		
Dell, Anna & Gasparini; Rev. Stampa		
407 Women with Horses	20 - 25	25 - 30
416 Couples, with Umbrella (6)	12 - 15	15 - 18
436, 451, 453 Hats (6)	15 - 18	18 - 22
228, 445, 560 High Fashion (6)	20 - 22	22 - 25
443, 522 High Fashion (6)	22 - 25	25 - 28
360, 419, 981 High Fashion	18 - 22	22 - 25
Series 178, 539, 925 High Fashion	22 - 25	25 - 28
Series 948 "Egyptian" (6)	15 - 18	18 - 20
Series 459 Heads (6)	14 - 16	16 - 18
Series 478 Dancers (6)	18 - 20	20 - 22
Series 936 Cupid Series (6)	20 - 25	25 - 28
Golf	25 - 28	28 - 32
Tennis	18 - 22	22 - 25
Harlequins (Pierrot)	22 - 25	25 - 28

T. Corbella
Degami, Series 2258

T. Corbella
Degami, Series 895

Colonial-Style Deco Ladies, Lovers	12 - 15	15 - 18
Ladies & Dogs		
Series 330 (6)	12 - 14	14 - 18
Series 530, 894, 1165, 1763 (6)	15 - 16	16 - 20
Series 1494 (6)	10 - 12	12 - 16
Ladies & Horses		
Series 202 (6)	12 - 15	15 - 18
Series 488, 813, 1676, 1869 (6)	15 - 18	18 - 22
G.P.M. Series 539 (6) Glamour	12 - 15	15 - 20
COMBAZ, GISBERT (BEL) Art Nouveau		
Dietrich, Brussels		
"Elements" Series (12)	140 - 150	150 - 175
"Proverbs" Series (12)	140 - 150	150 - 175
"The Fishermen" Series (12)	150 - 175	175 - 200
"Sins" Series (12)	150 - 175	175 - 200
COPPING, H.	4 - 6	6 - 8
CORBELLA, TITO (IT) Art Deco & Glamour		
Dell, Anna & Gasparini; Rev. Stampa		
Miss Edith Cavell Death-Head Series	20 - 25	25 - 30
Series 127-M Small Images (6)	10 - 12	12 - 15
Series 162-M Small Image, Lovers (6)	8 - 10	10 - 12
Series 162, 355 (6)	14 - 16	16 - 20
Series 160, 203 High Fashion (6)	18 - 22	22 - 25
Series 225M Small image lovers	10 - 12	12 - 15
Series 281-M Lady/Spider & Webs Series (6)	25 - 30	30 - 36
Series 317 Beautifully dressed Ladies (6)	25 - 28	28 - 32
Series 408 Fans (6)	12 - 15	15 - 20

Series Chair and Fans (6)	15 - 18	18 - 22
Series 233, 356, 546, 718 Heads (6)	18 - 22	22 - 26
Series 130, 203, 763 High Fashion (6)	22 - 25	25 - 28
Series 282, 316, 317 Fashion (6)	12 - 15	15 - 20
Series 118, 324 Hats (6)	12 - 15	15 - 20
Series 357 Bear-Cupids (6)	14 - 16	16 - 20
Series 344, 356, 467 High Fashion (6)	20 - 25	25 - 28
Series 102, 232, 267, 236, 516 (6)	18 - 22	22 - 26
Series 162, 234, 269 Lovers-Kissing (6)	10 - 12	12 - 15
Series 225, 367, 531 Lovers-Kissing (6)	10 - 12	12 - 15
Harlequins (Pierrot)	20 - 25	25 - 28
Degami		
Series 319, 868, 1011, 1049 (6)	18 - 22	22 - 26
Series 743 Lady Pierrot Heads (6)	25 - 30	30 - 35
Series 790, 895, 1019 (4) Pierrot	20 - 25	25 - 30
Series 797, 2087, 3026 (4) Pierrot & Lady	25 - 30	30 - 35
Series 2249 "Gypsy" (6)	10 - 12	12 - 15
Series 1022, 2250 In Oval (6)	10 - 15	15 - 18
Series 2066 Fashionable Deco Ladies	25 - 28	28 - 32
Series 1016, 2071 Pierrot and lady (4) (Uns.)	25 - 28	28 - 32
Series 2072, 2158, 2160, 2287, 3033 (6)	15 - 18	18 - 22
Series 2112, 2158 Colorful Lovers (6)	15 - 18	18 - 22
Series 2143, 2214, 3098 (6)	15 - 18	18 - 22
Series 2224 Highly Decorated w/Lovers (4)	18 - 22	22 - 26
Series 2228 Lovers in Viennese gondolas (6)	25 - 28	28 - 32
Series 2229 Colonial Style (6)	15 - 18	18 - 22
Series 3016, 3027, 3055, 3056, 3123, 3560 (6)	15 - 18	18 - 22
Series 1088, 3563 Ladies in springtime	18 - 22	22 - 26
Series 3588 Ladies in beautiful gowns (6)	20 - 25	25 - 30
Series 3136 Post-Woman Series (6)	15 - 18	18 - 22
Series 617, 832 Lovers-Kissing (6)	10 - 12	12 - 15
Series 2283 (6) Not Deco	10 - 12	12 - 15
Golf	30 - 35	35 - 40
Tennis	25 - 30	30 - 35
Erotic/Semi-Nudes	25 - 28	28 - 32
Harlequins (Pierrot)	25 - 30	30 - 35
GPM **"Ultra" Series 2116** (Unsigned) (6)	15 - 18	18 - 22
LADIES WITH DOGS, HORSES		
Rev. Stampa; Dell, Anna & Gasparini, Degami		
Series 117, 230 (6)	15 - 20	20 - 25
Series 233, 237, 316, 330 (6)	15 - 20	20 - 25
Series 335, 464, 624 (6)	20 - 25	25 - 28
Series 516, 532, 578 (6)	20 - 25	25 - 28
Series 530, 1085 (6)	20 - 25	25 - 28
Degami		
Series 636, 2224, 2258 (6)	22 - 25	25 - 30
Series 4646 (6)	15 - 20	20 - 25
COSTANZA, G. (IT)		
Ladies	12 - 15	15 - 20
Comics/Erotic	18 - 22	22 - 26
CRAMER, RIE (NETH)	15 - 18	18 - 22
W. de Haan, Utrecht		
Months of the Year (12)		
January "The New Year"	30 - 35	35 - 40

J. B. Crandall, K. Co. Inc.
"Claire" (Watercolor)

Cyranicus, Anon. Italian
Pub., Ser. 165, Card #5

Cyranicus, Rev. Stampa
Series 204

February "Carnival"	40 - 50	50 - 60
March "Wind"	30 - 35	35 - 40
April "The Birds"	30 - 35	35 - 40
May "The Bride"	30 - 35	35 - 40
June "Roses"	30 - 35	35 - 40
July "Waves"	30 - 35	35 - 40
August "Field Flowers"	30 - 35	35 - 40
September "Apples"	30 - 35	35 - 40
October "Falling Leaves"	30 - 35	35 - 40
November "The Witch"	40 - 50	50 - 60
December "Christmas"	50 - 75	75 - 100
Series 139 Art Deco		
"Romeo et Juliette"	20 - 25	25 - 30
CRANDALL, JOHN BRADSHAW (US)		
K. Co. Inc., N.Y.		
Watercolors		
No No. "A Romany Lass" (Uns.)	15 - 18	18 - 22
"Claire"	15 - 18	18 - 22
113 "Tad"	15 - 18	18 - 22
Also with no caption	15 - 18	18 - 22
118 Girl in white sunbonnet	15 - 18	18 - 22
12 "Toots"	15 - 18	18 - 22
122 Girl wearing red cap	15 - 18	18 - 22
137 "The Bohemian Girl"	15 - 18	18 - 22
170 "The Pace Maker"	15 - 18	18 - 22
CREMIEUX, ED. (FR) French Glamour		
Delta		
Series 27	20 - 25	25 - 30
Series 44	25 - 28	28 - 32
CROTTA (IT)		
Rev. Stampa		
Series 3029 Lovers Kissing (6)	8 - 10	10 - 15
CYRANICUS (IT)		
Anonymous		
Series 165, 204 (6) Glamourous Heads, Hats	20 - 25	25 - 28

Ladies/Heads	15 - 18	18 - 22
Ladies/Fashion	15 - 18	18 - 22
Ladies/Animals	15 - 20	20 - 25
Golf	25 - 28	28 - 35
Tennis	22 - 25	25 - 30
Ladies & Horses		
Series 150 (6)	15 - 20	20 - 25
Series 430 (6)	15 - 20	20 - 25
Raphael Tuck (Uns.)		
"Art" Series 2524 (6)	90 - 100	100 - 110
"Art" Series 2525 (6)	80 - 90	90 - 100
DAVIS, STANLEY (US)	8 - 10	10 - 12
DAY, FRANCES (US)	4 - 5	5 - 8
DEDINA, JAN (PO)	10 - 12	12 - 15
DE FEURE, GEORGES Art Nouveau	25 - 35	35 - 45
DE MARZO (Art Deco)	22 - 25	25 - 35
DENNISON (US)	3 - 4	4 - 6
DERNINI, D. (IT) Art Deco		
Ladies	15 - 20	20 - 25
DERRANTI, D. (IT) Art Deco		
"Elite" Series 2568	25 - 30	30 - 35
DESCH, FRANK (US)		
Knapp Co. (K Co., N.Y.) *		
H. Import Series 300		
"Laura"	20 - 25	25 - 28
Series 303 Watercolors		
2 "Stella"	20 - 25	25 - 30
3 "Violet"	20 - 25	25 - 30
4 "Elouise"	20 - 25	25 - 30
5 "Grace"	20 - 25	25 - 30
6 "Ida"	20 - 25	25 - 30
7 "Isabel"	20 - 25	25 - 30
8 "Eleanor"	20 - 25	25 - 30
9 "Lillian"	20 - 25	25 - 30
10 "Laura"	20 - 25	25 - 30

* H. Import and Paul Heckscher distributed
Series 303 with same images but with
different numbers. H. Import and Heckscher
are the same company.

Series 308 (8) Watercolors		
2 "Phoebe"	18 - 22	22 - 26
Others	18 - 22	22 - 26
Series 309 (**H. Import**) Watercolors		
1 "Katharine"	20 - 25	25 - 28
2 "Virginia"	20 - 25	25 - 28
3 "Olivia"	20 - 25	25 - 28
4 "Diana"	20 - 25	25 - 28
5 "Annette"	20 - 25	25 - 28
6 "Florence"	20 - 25	25 - 28
Others		
Series 336 (**H. Import**) No Captions		
Same as "There He Goes"	18 - 22	22 - 26
Girl with binoculars	18 - 22	22 - 26
Girl with hunting rifle	20 - 25	25 - 30

Frank H. Desch, The Knapp Co.
Series 309-3, "Olivia"

Frank H. Desch, The Knapp Co.
Series 309-6, "Florence"

Series 337 (**H. Import**)

Same as "Diana"	15 - 20	20 - 25

Series 1025 (**Paul Heckscher**) Watercolors

1 "There He Goes"	15 - 20	20 - 25
2 "Here They Come"	18 - 22	22 - 26
Others	15 - 20	20 - 25

Series 1027 (**Paul Heckscher**) Watercolors

1 "Katharine"	20 - 25	25 - 28
2 "Virginia"	20 - 25	25 - 28
3 "Olivia"	20 - 25	25 - 28
4 "Diana'	20 - 25	25 - 28
5 "Annette"	20 - 25	25 - 28
6 "Florence"	20 - 25	25 - 28
Others		
Series 50	10 - 12	12 - 15
Others	12 - 15	15 - 18

Knapp Co., Calendars * **

Some are calendars, others calendar types

515-4 "Annette" May, 1913	18 - 22	22 - 28

Series 6 (12)

502-3 "Stella"	18 - 22	22 - 28
50N-3 "Laura"	18 - 22	22 - 28
9403 "Flora"	18 - 22	22 - 28
9423 "Violet"	18 - 22	22 - 28
9443 "Grace"	18 - 22	22 - 28
9453 "Rosina"	18 - 22	22 - 28

9473 "Isabel"	18 - 22	22 - 28
9483 "Eleanor"	18 - 22	22 - 28
9493 "Lillian"	18 - 22	22 - 28
9503 "Laura"	18 - 22	22 - 28
9513 "Felicia"	18 - 22	22 - 28
69453 "Rosina"	18 - 22	22 - 28
69513 "Felicia"	18 - 22	22 - 28
No No. "Stella" Ad for Montgomery Ward	25 - 30	30 - 40
* Add $5-8 for Calendars		
** Add $1-15 for Advertising Calendars		
McGowan-Silsbee Litho		
No caption (Grace)	15 - 18	18 - 22
Novitas (N in Star)		
No caption Girl wearing Green Dress	15 - 18	18 - 22
Advertisement		
Djer-Kiss Rouge (non-postcard back)		
"Titan Type"	20 - 25	25 - 30
Others	20 - 25	25 - 30
DEWEY, ALFRED (U.S.)		
Frederickson & Co. *		
Romantic Baseball Series 22 (12)		
1 "Play Ball"	12 - 15	15 - 18
2 "Waiting for a good one"	12 - 15	15 - 18
3 "A Hit!" (Rare!)	30 - 35	35 - 38
4 "A Sacrifice"	12 - 15	15 - 18
5 "A Single"	12 - 15	15 - 18
6 "A Double Play"	12 - 15	15 - 18
7 "Two Singles"	12 - 15	15 - 18
8 "Caught Stealing"	12 - 15	15 - 18
9 "A Costly Error"	12 - 15	15 - 18
10 "The Winning Drive"	12 - 15	15 - 18
11 "A Shut Out"	12 - 15	15 - 18
12 "The Score - One to Nothing"	12 - 15	15 - 18
Boston Sunday Post (Date of Paper) (6)		
6-18-1911 "A Sacrifice"	10 - 12	12 - 15
5-28-1911 "A Single"	10 - 12	12 - 15
5-21-1911 "A Double Play"	10 - 12	12 - 15
6-4-1911 "Caught Stealing"	10 - 12	12 - 15
6-25-1911 "A Costly Error"	10 - 12	12 - 15
6-11-1911 "A Shut-Out"	10 - 12	12 - 15
Reinthal & Newman		
"Weather Forecast" Series 221 (12)	7 - 8	8 - 10
"Eventful Hours" Series 270-275	8 - 10	10 - 12
"Mother & Child" Series 450-455	7 - 8	8 - 10
"Love Signal" Series 456-461	7 - 8	8 - 10
"Moon" Series 462-467	8 - 10	10 - 12
"Smoke" Series 668-673	8 - 10	10 - 12
"Love & Nature" Series 807-812	7 - 8	8 - 10
DeYONCH, JOHN (US)	5 - 8	8 - 10
DIEFENBACH, K.	8 - 10	10 - 15
DIETZE (Ladies & Dogs)		
Series 6026	10 - 15	15 - 18
DIHLEN, CHARLES WEBER (US)	5 - 6	6 - 8
DILLON, C. B. (US)	6 - 8	8 - 10

E. Docker, Rafael Neuber
Modern Series 29

E. Docker, Rafael Neuber
Modern Series 29

F. B. Doubek, F. A. Ackermann
"Historic Ladies" Series, #581

DITZLER, H. (US)
  Gibson Art - Water Color Series of Ladies | 6 - 8 | 8 - 10

DITZLER, H. (US)		
Gibson Art - Water Color Series of Ladies	6 - 8	8 - 10
DOBROWOLSKI, A. (PO)		
MJK		
Seasons Series 282 (4)	10 - 12	12 - 15
DOCKER, E. (AUS) Art Nouveau		
Raphael Neuber, Vienna,		
Head Series 26 (6)	75 - 85	85 - 100
Schwere Wahl Series 28 (6)	75 - 85	85 - 100
Modern Series 29 (6)	80 - 90	90 - 110
DOMERGE, JEAN-GABRIEL (FR)		
A.N., Paris Real Photos of nude paintings		
6465 "Josephine Baker"	125 - 150	150 - 175
6466 "The Parasol" (resembles Baker but ??)	40 - 50	50 - 60
6473 "Josephine Baker"	125 - 150	150 - 175
Others not Josephine Baker	15 - 20	20 - 25
DONADINI, JR. (IT)		
Series 1471 (6) Lovers-Cupid Series	8 - 10	10 - 12
Alfred Schweizer		
Military Heads	18 - 22	22 - 25
DOUBEK, F.		
Ackermann Co.		
"Historic Ladies" Series (Many)	12 - 15	15 - 20
EMM		
557 "Uberleg Dir's" Bathing Beauty	12 - 15	15 - 18
585 "Schmetterling"	10 - 12	12 - 15

M. Dudovich, Degami, 1044
No Caption

Frederick Duncan, K. Co., 128
"Reflecting"

O.G.Z.-L

Lover Series 448-453 (6)	6 - 8	8 - 10
DOUKY (FR)		
Fantasy Fashions	15 - 20	20 - 25
E.D.F., Paris		
Series 505 Big Skirt (6)	15 - 20	20 - 25
Others	12 - 15	15 - 20
DRESSLER, A. E. (US)	6 - 8	8 - 10
DUDOVICH, M. (IT) Art Deco		
Degami		
1044 Lady with Petals	25 - 30	30 - 35
"Eureka" Series IV (6)	12 - 15	15 - 20
Early Art Deco Series	75 - 100	100 - 150
Lovers Series (in car; picnic)	30 - 35	35 - 38
Others	12 - 15	15 - 20
DuFRESNE, PAUL	4 - 6	6 - 8
DUHRKOOP, R.u.M (CZ)		
Glamourous Ladies	10 - 12	12 - 15
DUNCAN, FREDERICK (US)		
K. Co. Inc., N.Y. Watercolors		
125 "Dorothy"	18 - 22	22 - 26
126 "Meditating"	18 - 22	22 - 26
128 "Reflecting"	18 - 22	22 - 26
129 "Gloria"	18 - 22	22 - 26
130 "Posing"	18 - 22	22 - 26
131 "Beautifying"	18 - 22	22 - 26
132 "Dreaming"	18 - 22	22 - 26

134 "Helene"	18 - 22	22 - 26
135 "Patricia"	18 - 22	22 - 26
136 "Florella"	18 - 22	22 - 26
137 "The Bohemian Girl"	18 - 22	22 - 26
138 "Florence"	18 - 22	22 - 26
139 "Pleading"	18 - 22	22 - 26
140 "Muriel"	18 - 22	22 - 26
141 "Shopping"	18 - 22	22 - 26
142 "Marjorie"	18 - 22	22 - 26
143 "Kathleen"	18 - 22	22 - 26
144 "Watching"	18 - 22	22 - 26
173 "Motoring"	18 - 22	22 - 26
174 "Riding"	18 - 22	22 - 26
175 "Phoebe"	18 - 22	22 - 26
178 "Swimming"	18 - 22	22 - 26

M. & B. (Meissner & Buch)
Series 1415 (6)

On Train - His Hat	15 - 18	18 - 22
Others	12 - 15	15 - 18

Reinthal & Newman
930-935 Series Watercolors

930 "She's My Daisy"	12 - 15	15 - 20
931 "A Reserved Seat"	15 - 18	18 - 22
932 "For You a Rose"	12 - 15	15 - 20
933 "So Near, Yet so Far"	12 - 15	15 - 20
934 "The Call of the Country"	15 - 18	18 - 22
935 "Won't You Come Back"	12 - 15	15 - 20

EB (IT) (See E. Bigliardi)
Rev. Stampa

Series 61 (6) (Glamour - Mode)	15 - 18	18 - 22

EDY (FR)
J. Picot, Paris

No No. The Nurse (Hand Painted)	15 - 20	20 - 25

ELLETTI (IT) Art Deco
Celesque Series National Ladies

	15 - 20	20 - 25

ELLIOTT, KATHRYN (US)

Gartner & Bender Issues	6 - 8	8 - 10
G.P.M. **1985-1990 Deco Birthday Series**	12 - 15	15 - 18

ELLKA, G. (AUS)
M. Munk, Vienna (Chromolithographs)

Series 443 Head Studies (6)	15 - 20	20 - 25

ERTE (FR) Modern

"Stolen Kiss" (Serigraph)	4 - 5	5 - 8
"Folies Bergeres"	4 - 5	5 - 8

FABIANO (FR) Art Deco and Glamour

Delta Series 5, 32, 59, 63	15 - 20	20 - 25
Series 7, 11, 15	18 - 22	22 - 30

M.L.E., Paris Series 63 At the Beach

	10 - 12	12 - 15

FAINI (IT)

	10 - 12	12 - 14

FARINI, MAY L. (US)

Black & White Issues	5 - 6	6 - 8
With "Feliz Dia" Caption - Lady/Dog	6 - 8	8 - 10
Tennis Girl	12 - 15	15 - 18
Color Issues	10 - 12	12 - 16

Elsie Catherine Fidler
E. Gross, 47

Pearle Eugenia Fidler
E. Gross, Poster #42

Alice Louella Fidler
E. Gross, Poster #40

FERRARIS, A.V. (HUN)	8 - 10	10 - 12
FIDLER, ALICE LUELLA (US) *	12 - 15	15 - 20
(Also Alice Fidler Person)		
Edward Gross Poster Series	15 - 18	18 - 22
FIDLER, PEARLE EUGENIA (US) *	12 - 15	15 - 20
(Also Pearle Fidler LeMunyan)		
Edward Gross Poster Series	15 - 18	18 - 22
FIDLER, ELSIE CATHERINE (US) *	12 - 15	15 - 20
* All Fidler Works by **E. Gross & Ullman Mfg.**		
FINNEMORE, J.	5 - 6	6 - 7
FISCHER, C. (US)	6 - 8	8 - 10
FISCHER, PAUL (DEN)		
Arthur Schurer	8 - 10	10 - 12
Tennis	12 - 15	15 - 20
FISHER, BILL		
John Neury-Geneva		
Romantic Couples, ladies	6 - 8	8 - 10
FISHER, H. (Not Harrison)		
Rev. Stampa		
Series 326 (6)	8 - 10	10 - 12

FISHER, HARRISON (US)

Harrison Fisher was one of the most prolific of all American illustrators, and his postcards of beautiful ladies are collected by more people than any other artist. His works of glamorous women of the era are desired by collectors throughout the world. Values tend to rise yearly as new discoveries inspire all who collect them.

In 1905, The Detroit Publishing Company published a small group of Fisher cards from what were originally illustrations for stories in the old *LIFE* magazine. They were numbered in the 14,000 series and were printed in sepia and black and white.

The New York firm of Reinthal & Newman was the principal publisher and distributor of Fisher postcards. They produced many varied series, ranging from the No-Numbered, the 100's, and on through the rare and final 900 series, and then did the American and English reprints in the 1000 and 2000 series.

The crowning glory for collectors of Fisher cards came in the late 1980's when groups of foreign published images, many of which had been pirated, began to appear on the American scene. A whole new world was opened to Fisher collectors who now realized that there were many more images of his beautiful ladies.

A tremendous new book and price guide by collector Naomi Welch, *American & European Postcards of Harrison Fisher Illustrator*, was released in 1999. This fine work not only lists and values practically all of the Fisher cards you see listed in this publication, but most are shown in beautiful color. It has publisher information, backs of cards, series, and numbers of cards ...this book has it all and is a must for Fisher enthusiasts. See particulars in Bibliography Section in the Appendix.

Albertype Co.
    Indian Maid - Painted on Sandstone Rock

Tassajarla Hot Springs, California	150 - 200	200 - 250
Daley-Soeger Co.		
Indian Maid, as above	150 - 200	200 - 250
Detroit Publishing Co.*		
14028 "I don't see..."	20 - 25	25 - 28
14036 "An Important..."	20 - 25	25 - 28
14037 "So you don't Kiss..."	20 - 25	25 - 28
14038 "Between Themselves..."	20 - 25	25 - 28
14039 "Can you give your Answer?"	20 - 25	25 - 28
14040 "I suppose you Lost..."	20 - 25	25 - 28
14041 "It's just Horrid..."	20 - 25	25 - 28
14042 "Wasn't There..."	20 - 25	25 - 28
14043 "And shall we Never..."	20 - 25	25 - 28
14044 "I fear there is no Hope"	20 - 25	25 - 28

    * 2 Diff. Varieties: Information at top or bottom.

Book Adv. Cards (G&D, Dodd-Mead, etc.)

Double-folded Cards, Entire Card *	200 - 250	250 - 300
With Reply Section Missing		
"54–40 or Fight"	150 - 175	175 - 200
"The Bill Toppers"	150 - 175	175 - 200
"Francezka"	150 - 175	175 - 200
"The Goose Girl" *	250 - 275	275 - 300
"Half A Rogue"	150 - 175	175 - 200
"The Hungry Heart"	150 - 175	175 - 200
"Jane Cable"	100 - 125	125 - 150
"Jewel Weed"	150 - 175	175 - 200
"The Man From Brodney's"	150 - 175	175 - 200
"My Commencement"	150 - 175	175 - 200
"My Lady of Cleeve"	150 - 175	175 - 200
"Nedra"	100 - 125	125 - 150
"The One Way Out"	150 - 175	175 - 200
"The Stooping Lady"	150 - 175	175 - 200
"A Taste of Paradise"	150 - 175	175 - 200
"The Title Market"	150 - 175	175 - 200
"To My Valentine"	150 - 175	175 - 200
"The Violet Book," by Bettina von Hutten *	250 - 300	300 - 325

    * Add $100.

Armour & Co., U.S. (B&W), Narrow Size	50 - 60	60 - 70
Armour & Co., German (B&W), Narrow	60 - 70	70 - 80
Warren's Featherbone Corsets		
"The Featherbone Girl"	90 - 100	100 - 125

A HARRISON FISHER PICTURE
— I N —
MY COMMENCEMENT

THE HARRISON FISHER GIRL
THE AMERICAN GIRL SERIES POST CARD. COPYRIGHT, ARMOUR & Co., CHICAGO. 1906

*Harrison Fisher, Dodd-Mead Book
Advertisement, "My Commencement"*

*Harrison Fisher, Armour & Co.
"The Harrison Fisher Girl"*

Frank V. Draper Co., Des Moines		
Illustration from *"Jane Cable"*		
"His feeble glance took in her face..."	125 - 150	150 - 175
Klaus Mfg. Co., NY		
K. 405 Advertising Play *"Beverly of		
Graustark"* "Beverly Calhoun"	150 - 175	175 - 200
Metropolitan P.C. Co. (M in Bean Pot)		
"Illustration from *"Jane Cable"*		
No Caption. Old man and sitting girl	125 - 150	150 - 175
Curt Teich (C.T. American Art)		
Illustration from *"Nedra"*		
No Caption. Sailor Girl on ship deck	125 - 150	150 - 175
Illustration from *"Jane Cable"*		
No Caption. Girl and man at table.	125 - 150	150 - 175
Tichnor Bros., Boston		
Illustration from *"Truxton King"*		
126984 No Caption. Man, boy and dog	125 - 150	150 - 175
Zim (H.G. Zimmerman, Chicago)		
Illustration from *"Jane Cable"*		
No Caption. Girl (back view) sits in chair	125 - 150	150 - 175
Anonymous		
Illustration from *"Nedra"* by Dodd-Mead		
"Grace Vernon"	125 - 150	150 - 175
Reinthal & Newman		
Unnumbered Series (some by Chas. Hauff)		
"A Fair Driver"	15 - 20	20 - 25
"All Mine"	15 - 20	20 - 25

"After the Dance"	15 - 20	20 - 25
"American Beauties"	15 - 20	20 - 25
"The Critical Moment"	15 - 20	20 - 25
"The Motor Girl"	18 - 22	22 - 25
"Over the Teacup"	12 - 18	18 - 22
"Ready for the Run"	15 - 20	20 - 25
"Ruth"	15 - 20	20 - 25
"A Tennis Champion"	25 - 30	30 - 40
"The Winter Girl"	15 - 18	18 - 22
With overprinting	18 - 22	22 - 25
"Those Bewitching Eyes"	15 - 20	20 - 25
Series 101 (12)		
"American Beauties" *	20 - 25	25 - 35
"Anticipation" **	15 - 20	20 - 25
"Beauties (with cat) **	15 - 20	20 - 25
"Danger" **	15 - 20	20 - 25
"A Fair Driver" *	15 - 20	20 - 25
"Odd Moments" **	15 - 20	20 - 25
"The Old Miniature" **	15 - 20	20 - 25
"Over the Tea Cup" *	15 - 20	20 - 25
"Reflections"**	15 - 20	20 - 25
"The Study Hour" *	15 - 20	20 - 25
"A Thoroughbred" *	20 - 25	25 - 30
"Those Bewitching Eyes" *	15 - 20	20 - 25
* Sometimes listed as **Series 107**		
** Also by publisher **Charles H. Hauff.**		
Series 102 (6)		
"American Girl in England"	20 - 25	25 - 30
"American Girl in France"	20 - 25	25 - 30
"American Girl in Ireland"	20 - 25	25 - 30
"American Girl in Italy"	20 - 25	25 - 30
"American Girl in Japan"	20 - 25	25 - 30
"American Girl in Netherlands"	20 - 25	25 - 30
103 Series (6)		
"An Hour with Art"	20 - 25	25 - 30
"The Canoe"	20 - 25	25 - 30
"Engagement Days"	20 - 25	25 - 30
"Fisherman's Luck"	25 - 28	28 - 32
"Fore" (Golf)	30 - 35	35 - 45
"Wanted- An Answer"	20 - 25	25 - 30
Series 108 (12)		
"The Ambush"	15 - 20	20 - 25
"An Old Song"	15 - 20	20 - 25
"The Artist"	15 - 20	20 - 25
"The Bride"	20 - 25	25 - 30
"The Debutante"	15 - 20	20 - 25
"Dumb Luck"	20 - 25	25 - 30
"He's Only Joking" (with Cat)	18 - 22	22 - 26
"His Gift"	15 - 20	20 - 25
"The Kiss"	12 - 15	15 - 20
"Lost?"	15 - 20	20 - 25
"Oh! Promise Me"	15 - 20	20 - 25
"Song of the Soul" *	15 - 20	20 - 25
* Same image as "The Artist"		

"Two Up" (Golf)	30 - 35	35 - 45
Series 123 (7)		
"The Canoe"	15 - 20	20 - 25
"The Fudge Party" (possibly of another series		
as it does not have **Series 123** on back)	15 - 20	20 - 25
"In Clover"	15 - 20	20 - 25
"Making Hay"	15 - 20	20 - 25
"A Modern Eve"	15 - 20	20 - 25
"Taking Toll"	15 - 20	20 - 25
"You Will Marry a Dark Man"	15 - 20	20 - 25
Series 180-185		
180 "Well Protected"	20 - 25	25 - 30
181 "The Rose"	20 - 25	25 - 30
182 "Miss Santa Claus"	25 - 30	30 - 40
183 "Miss Knickerbocker"	20 - 25	25 - 30
184 "Following the Race"	20 - 25	25 - 30
185 "Naughty, Naughty!"	20 - 25	25 - 30
186-191 Series "The Greatest Moments		
of a Girl's Life" *		
186 "The Proposal"	25 - 30	30 - 35
187 "The Trousseau"	25 - 30	30 - 35
188 "The Wedding"	25 - 30	30 - 35
189 "The Honeymoon"	25 - 30	30 - 35
190 "The First Evening ..."	25 - 30	30 - 35
191 "Their New Love"	25 - 30	30 - 35
* **The set was also printed as Series 468-473**		
Series 192-203 (12)		
192 "Cherry Ripe"	20 - 25	25 - 30
193 "Undue Haste"	20 - 25	25 - 30
194 "Sweetheart"	20 - 25	25 - 30
195 "Vanity"	20 - 25	25 - 30
196 "Beauties"	20 - 25	25 - 30
197 "Lips for Kisses"	20 - 25	25 - 30
198 "Bewitching Maiden"	20 - 25	25 - 30
199 "Leisure Moments"	20 - 25	25 - 30
200 "And Yet Her Eyes Can Look Wise"	20 - 25	25 - 30
201 "Roses"	20 - 25	25 - 30
202 "In the Toils"	20 - 25	25 - 30
203 "Maid to Worship"	25 - 30	30 - 35
Series 252-257		
252 "Dreaming of You"	20 - 25	25 - 30
253 "Luxury"	20 - 25	25 - 30
254 "Pals" (with Dog)	25 - 30	30 - 35
255 "Homeward Bound"	20 - 25	25 - 30
256 "Preparing to Conquer"	20 - 25	25 - 30
257 "Love Lyrics"	20 - 25	25 - 30
Series 258-263		
258 "Tempting Lips"	20 - 25	25 - 30
259 "Good Night"	20 - 25	25 - 30
260 "Bows Attract Beaus"	20 - 25	25 - 30
261 "Girlie"	20 - 25	25 - 30
262 "Beauty and Value"	20 - 25	25 - 30
263 "A Prairie Belle"	20 - 25	25 - 30

Series 300-305

300	"Auto Kiss"	20 - 25	25 - 30
301	"Sweethearts Asleep"	25 - 30	30 - 35
302	"Behave!"	20 - 25	25 - 30
303	"All Mine!"	20 - 25	25 - 30
304	"Thoroughbreds"	25 - 30	30 - 35
305	"The Laugh is on You!"	20 - 25	25 - 30

Water Color Series 381-392

381	"All's Well"	20 - 25	25 - 30
382	"Two Roses"	20 - 25	25 - 30
383	"Contentment"	20 - 25	25 - 30
384	"Not Yet - But Soon"	20 - 25	25 - 30
385	"Smile Even if it Hurts" (with Bulldog)	28 - 32	32 - 36
386	"Speak!"	20 - 25	25 - 30
387	"Welcome Home"	20 - 25	25 - 30
388	"A Helping Hand"	20 - 25	25 - 30
389	"Undecided"	20 - 25	25 - 30
390	"Well Guarded" (with Dog)	22 - 26	26 - 32
391	"My Lady Waits"	20 - 25	25 - 30
392	"Gathering Honey"	20 - 25	25 - 30

Series 400-423 (24)

400	"Looking Backward"	35 - 40	40 - 45
401	"Art and Beauty"	35 - 40	40 - 45
402	"The Chief Interest"	35 - 40	40 - 45
403	"Passing Fancies"	35 - 40	40 - 45
404	"The Pink of Perfection"	35 - 40	40 - 45
405	"He Won't Bite-" (with Boston Terrier)	40 - 45	45 - 55
406	"Refreshments"	35 - 40	40 - 45
407	"Princess Pat"	35 - 40	40 - 45
408	"Fine Feathers"	35 - 40	40 - 45
409	"Isn't He Sweet?" (with Dog)	40 - 45	45 - 50
410	"Maid at Arms" (Military)	40 - 45	45 - 50
411	"He Cometh Not"	35 - 40	40 - 45
412	"Can't You Speak?" (with Dog)	40 - 45	45 - 50
413	"What Will She Say?"	35 - 40	40 - 45
414	"Music Hath Charm"	35 - 40	40 - 45
415	"Do I Intrude?"	35 - 40	40 - 45
416	"My Queen"	35 - 40	40 - 45
417	"My Lady Drives" (with Dog)	40 - 45	45 - 50
418	"Ready and Waiting"	35 - 40	40 - 45
419	"The Parasol"	35 - 40	40 - 45
420	"Tempting Lips"	35 - 40	40 - 45
421	"Mary"	35 - 40	40 - 45
422	"Courting Attention"	35 - 40	40 - 45
423	"My Pretty Neighbor"	35 - 40	40 - 45

Series 468-473 Refer to Series 186-191
   Same Images and same values

Series 600-617 (18)

600	"A Winter Sport"	35 - 40	40 - 45
601	"Winter Whispers"	35 - 40	40 - 45
602	"A Christmas Him"	35 - 40	40 - 45
603	"A Sprig of Holly"	35 - 40	40 - 45
604	"Snow Birds"	35 - 40	40 - 35
605	"A Christmas Belle"	35 - 40	40 - 45

H. Fisher, R&N, 188
"The Wedding"

H. Fisher, R&N, 302
"Behave!"

H. Fisher, R&N, 389
"Undecided"

H. Fisher, R&N, 409
"Isn't He Sweet?"

H. Fisher, R&N, 603
"A Sprig of Holly"

H. Fisher, R&N, 769
"Drifting"

H. Fisher, R&N, 864
"Winners"

H. Fisher, R&N, 974
"Each Stitch A Prayer"

H. Fisher, R&N, 2046
"Princess Pat"

606	"The Serenade"	35 - 40	40 - 45
607	"The Secret"	35 - 40	40 - 45
608	"Good Morning, Mama"	35 - 40	40 - 45
609	"A Passing Glance"	35 - 40	40 - 45
610	"A Fair Exhibitor" (with Dogs)	40 - 45	45 - 55
611	"Paddling Their Own Canoe"	35 - 40	40 - 45
612	"Tea Time"	35 - 40	40 - 45
613	"The Favorite Pillow"	35 - 40	40 - 45
614	"Don't Worry"	35 - 40	40 - 45
615	"June"	35 - 40	40 - 45
616	"Sketching"	35 - 40	40 - 45
617	"Chocolate"	35 - 40	40 - 45

Water Color Series 700-705
"The Six Senses"

700	"The First Meeting" Sight	35 - 40	40 - 45
701	"Falling in Love" Smell	35 - 40	40 - 45
702	"Making Progress" Taste	35 - 40	40 - 45
703	"Anxious Moments" Hearing	35 - 40	40 - 45
704	"To Love and Cherish" Touch	35 - 40	40 - 45
705	"The Greatest Joy" Common Sense	35 - 40	40 - 45

Series 762-773

762	"Alone at Last"	20 - 25	25 - 30
	with image variation (larger)	20 - 25	25 - 30
763	"Alert" (with Dog)	25 - 30	30 - 35
764	"Close to Shore"	25 - 30	30 - 35
765	"Looks Good to Me"	20 - 25	25 - 30
766	"Passers By"	20 - 25	25 - 30
767	"At the Toilet"	20 - 25	25 - 30
768	"Drifting" *	20 - 25	25 - 30
768	Untitled, Oversize "Her Favorite Him" *	25 - 30	30 - 40
769	"Her Favorite Him" *	20 - 25	25 - 30
770	"The Third Party" *	20 - 25	25 - 30
771	"Inspiration" *	20 - 25	25 - 30
772	"Dangers of the Deep" *	20 - 25	25 - 30
773	"Farewell" *	20 - 25	25 - 30

* Add $10 to prices if German caption. They are usually slightly oversized with Universal copyright.

800 Series

819	"Here's Happiness"	25 - 30	30 - 35

With Cosmopolitan or Star bylines, etc.
Series A 832-837

832	"Wireless"**	30 - 35	35 - 40
833	"Neptune's Daughter" *	30 - 35	35 - 40
834	"Her Game" * (Tennis)	35 - 40	40 - 50
835	"All Mine" * (with Dog)	32 - 35	35 - 38
836	"On Summer Seas" *	30 - 35	35 - 40
837	"Autumn's Beauty" *	30 - 35	35 - 40

* **By Cosmopolitan Magazine**
** **By The Star Co.**

Series B 838-843

838	"The Only Pebble" *	30 - 35	35 - 40
839	"A Love Score" * (Golf)	40 - 45	45 - 55
840	"Spring Business" *	30 - 35	35 - 40
841	"The King of Hearts" **	30 - 35	35 - 40

842	"Fair and Warmer" *	30 - 35	35 - 40
843	"Baby Mine" **	30 - 35	35 - 40

   * **By Cosmopolitan Magazine**
** **By The Star Co.**
Series C 844-849

844	"Compensation" **	35 - 40	40 - 45
845	"Sparring for Time" **	30 - 35	35 - 40
846	"Confidences" **	30 - 35	35 - 40
847	"Her Future" *	30 - 35	35 - 40
848	"Day Dreams" *	30 - 35	35 - 40
849	"Muriel" *	30 - 35	35 - 40

   * **By Cosmopolitan Magazine**
** **By The Star Co.**

856	"Song of the Soul" Same as "The Artist" *	25 - 30	30 - 35

   * **By Reinthal & Newman**
Series D 860-865

860	"By right of Conquest" *	35 - 40	40 - 45
861	"The Evening Hour" *	35 - 40	40 - 45
862	"Caught Napping" *	35 - 40	40 - 45
863	"A Novice" *	35 - 40	40 - 45
864	"Winners" * (with Horse)	35 - 40	40 - 45
865	"A Midsummer Reverie" *	35 - 40	40 - 45

   * **By Cosmopolitan Magazine**
Series E 866-871

866	"When the Leaves Turn" * (with Dog)	35 - 38	38 - 42
867	"Over the Teacup" *	30 - 35	35 - 40
868	"A Ripening Bud" * *	30 - 35	35 - 40
869	"I'm Ready" * (Military)	35 - 38	38 - 42
870	"Reflections" *	30 - 35	35 - 40
871	"Peggy" *	30 - 35	35 - 40

   * **By Cosmopolitan Magazine or Print Dept.**
** **By Good Housekeeping Magazine**
Series F 872-877

872	"Penseroso" * *	30 - 35	35 - 40
873	"The Girl He Left Behind" **	30 - 35	35 - 40
874	"A Spring Blossom" **	30 - 35	35 - 40
875	"A Study in Contentment" **	30 - 35	35 - 40
876	"A Lucky Beggar" * (with Dog)	32 - 36	36 - 42
877	"Roses" *	30 - 35	35 - 40

   * **By Cosmopolitan Magazine**
** **By The Star Co.**
Series 900-979
Reinthal & Newman & Cosmopolitan Mag.
Series H 970-975 (6)

970	"Chums"*	125 - 150	150 - 175
971	"Cynthia" **	125 - 150	150 - 175
972	"A Forest Flower" *	125 - 150	150 - 175
973	"The Dancing Girl" * **	125 - 150	150 - 175
974	"Each Stitch a Prayer" *	150 - 175	175 - 200
975	"The Sailor Maid" **	175 - 200	200 - 225

   * **By Cosmopolitan Magazine & R&N**
** **By International Magazine**
*** **By Puck Magazine & R&N**

Series G 976-979 (4)

976 "My Man" *	175 - 200	200 - 250
977 "My Hero" **	175 - 200	200 - 250
978 "Her Heart's in Service" **	175 - 200	200 - 275
979 "Somewhere in France" **	200 - 250	250 - 300

*   **By Cosmopolitan Magazine**
** **By Cosmopolitan Magazine & R&N**
Series 1000 - 1005 American Reprints by
Reinthal & Newman   Original No. in ( ).

1000 "Drifting" (768)	30 - 35	35 - 40
1001 "Cherry Ripe" (192)	30 - 35	35 - 40
1002 "Beauties" (196) (with Dog)	35 - 40	40 - 45
1003 "Vanity" (195)	30 - 35	35 - 40
1004 "Maid to Worship" (203)	30 - 35	35 - 40
1005 "And Yet Her Eyes Can Look Wise" (200)	30 - 35	35 - 40

2000 Series - English Reprints

2040 "Love Lyrics" (257)	30 - 35	35 - 40
2041 "A Fair Exhibitor" (610)	35 - 40	40 - 45
2042 "Can't You Speak" (412)	35 - 40	40 - 45
2043 "Serenade" (606)	30 - 35	35 - 40
2044 "Undecided" (389)	30 - 35	35 - 40
2045 "Behave!" (302)	30 - 35	35 - 40
2046 "Princess Pat" (407)	35 - 40	40 - 45
2047 "Good Little Indian" (261) "Girlie"	30 - 35	35 - 40
2048 "Chocolate" (617)	30 - 35	35 - 40
2049 "Beauty and Value" (262)	30 - 35	35 - 40
2050 "Contentment" (383)	30 - 35	35 - 40
2051 "Preparing to Conquer" (256)	30 - 35	35 - 40
2053 "The Kiss" (Series 108)	30 - 35	35 - 40
2054 "What to See in America" (none)	35 - 40	40 - 45
2069 "Paddling their own Canoe" (611)	30 - 35	35 - 40
2076 "Good Morning, Mama" (608)	25 - 30	30 - 35
2086 "The Pink of Perfection" (404)	30 - 35	35 - 40
2087 "He Won't Bite–" (405)	35 - 40	40 - 50
2088 "Following the Race" (184)	30 - 35	35 - 40
2089 "The Rose" (181)	30 - 35	35 - 40
2090 "Well Protected" (180)	35 - 40	40 - 45
2091 "Sketching" (616)	30 - 35	35 - 40
2092 "Ready and Waiting" (418)	30 - 35	35 - 40
2093 "The Parasol" (419)	30 - 35	35 - 40
2094 "Courting Attention" (422)	30 - 35	35 - 40
2095 "Mary" (421)	35 - 40	40 - 45
2096 "Refreshments" (406)	35 - 40	40 - 45
2097 "Isn't He Sweet?" (409)	35 - 40	40 - 45
2098 "The Old Miniature" (Series 101)	30 - 35	35 - 40
2099 "Beauties" (Series 101)	35 - 40	40 - 45
2100 "Odd Moments" (Series 101)	30 - 35	35 - 40
2101 "Tea Time" (612)	35 - 40	40 - 45
2102 "Good Night!" (259)	30 - 35	35 - 40
2103 "A Prairie Belle" (263)	30 - 35	35 - 40

Mutoscope Card   W/Postcard Back   *

"Happy Halloween" A masked "Princess Pat" same as R&N #407 & 2046 B&W	1500 - 1750	1750 - 2000

* From the collection of Lee & Shirley Cox.

THE FIND OF THE DECADE!
Unsigned Harrison Fisher, "A Mutoscope Card", "Happy Halloween"

Anonymous
   No No. "On Swing"   Girl on Swing   100 - 125   125 - 150
FOREIGN ISSUES

FINNISH

The numbering system for all series of Finnish cards was taken from "The Super Rare Postcards of Harrison Fisher," by J. L. Mashburn.
All Finnish cards are very rare and extremely elusive. None have the R&N copyright and all are untitled with the exception of **The Real Photo Series**. Cards are titled using names from similar R&N images. Several have not appeared as postcards and are named if a title is known. Three had been entitled by the author until the true titles were found for "**Merry Christmas**" in the **30/25 Series** and for "**Eavesdropping**" in the **W. & G. American Series 7031/1-7** and **Publisher at Polyphot Series**. Note the additions in the Polyphot and W. & G. American Series N:o 7001/36-50 – cards that have never appeared as postcards otherwise.

No 30/25 Series –
   Juusela and Levanen, Helsinki
   S=Signed; US=Unsigned
   3025-1-S "Snowbird" *   225 - 250   250 - 300
   3025-1-US "Snowbird" *   275 - 300   300 - 350
   3025-1-S Variation of "Snowbird" *   275 - 300   300 - 350
   3025-2-S "The Debutante" *   225 - 250   250 - 300
   3025-2-US "The Debutante" *   275 - 300   300 - 350
   3025-3-S "Welcome Home" variety * (387)   200 - 225   225 - 275
   3025-4-S "A Midsummer Reverie" (865)   200 - 225   225 - 275
   3025-4-US "A Midsummer Reverie" (865)   275 - 300   300 - 350
   3025-5-S "Close to Shore" (764(175 - 200   200 - 250
   3025-5-US "Close to Shore" (754)   275 - 300   300 - 350
   3025-6-S "Winners" (864)   175 - 200   200 - 250
   3025-6-US "Winners" (864)   250 - 275   275 - 300
   3025-7-US "My Hero" (977)   175 - 200   200 - 250
   3025-8-S "Winifred" *   150 - 175   175 - 225
   3025-8-US "Winifred" *   200 - 225   225 - 275
   3025-9-S "When the Leaves Turn" (866)   125 - 150   150 - 175
   3025-9-US "When the Leaves Turn" (866)   200 - 225   225 - 275
   3025-10-S "My Man" (976)   175 - 200   200 - 250
   3025-10-US "My Man" (976)   200 - 225   225 - 275
   3025-11-S "King of Hearts" (841)   150 - 175   175 - 225
   3025-11-US "King of Hearts" (841)   175 - 200   200 - 250
   3025-12-S "Not Yet, But Soon" (384)   125 - 150   150 - 175
   3025-12-US "Not Yet, But Soon" (384)   175 - 200   200 - 250
   3025-13-S "Autumn's Beauty" (837)   125 - 150   150 - 200
   3025-13-US "Autumn's Beauty" (837)   200 - 225   225 - 275
   3025-14-S "On Summer Seas" (836)   150 - 175   175 - 200
   3025-14-US "On Summer Seas" (836)   200 - 225   225 - 275
   3025-15-S "Baby Mine" (843)   125 - 150   150 - 200
   3025-15-US "Baby Mine" (843)   175 - 200   200 - 250
   3025-16-US "Muriel" (849)   150 - 175   175 - 225
   3025-17-S "Caught Napping" (862)   125 - 150   150 - 200
   3025-18-S "Beauty and Value" (262 (2049)   150 - 175   175 - 225
   3025-19-S "Day Dreams" (848)   150 - 175   175 - 225
   3025-19-S "Stringing Them" * **   175 - 200   200 - 225

Harrison Fisher, Finnish, 30/25 Series
(Stringing Them)

Harrison Fisher , Finnish, 30/25-1-S
"Snowbird"

3025-19-US "Stringing Them" * **	225 - 250	250 - 300
3025-21-S "All Mine" (303)	150 - 175	175 - 225
3025-21-US "All Mine" (303)	175 - 200	200 - 250
3025-22-S "Two Roses" (382)	150 - 175	175 - 225
3025-23-S "Reflections" (870)	150 - 175	175 - 225
3025-23-US "Reflections" (870)	175 - 200	200 - 250
3025-24-S "Love Lyrics" (257) (2040)	150 - 175	175 - 225
3025-24-US "Love Lyrics" (257) (2040)	150 - 175	175 - 225
3025-25-S "An Idle Hour" *	150 - 175	175 - 225
3025-25-US "An Idle Hour" *	175 - 200	200 - 250

* Has not appeared on an R&N postcard.
** Name from Bowers-Budd-Budd Book,
   "Harrison Fisher"

The N:O Numbered Series

N:O-4-S "Close to Shore" (764)	200 - 250	250 - 300
N:O-5-5 "Playing the Game," (Uns.) *	275 - 300	300 - 325
N:O-7-S "A Novice" (863)	200 - 250	250 - 300
N:O-10-S "Midsummer Reverie," (865)	200 - 250	250 - 300
N:O-11-US "At the Toilet" (767) (Uns.)	200 - 250	250 - 300
N:O-13-S "Welcome Home" (387)	200 - 250	250 - 300

* Appears only on Finnish cards.

W.&G. American Series N:o. 7001/1-35
   Unsigned, no Numbers, no Captions

WG35-1-US "Following the Race," (184)	200 - 225	225 - 250
WG35-2-US "American Beauties" (101)	200 - 225	225 - 250
WG35-3-US "Alert" (763)	200 - 225	225 - 250
WG35-4-US "Yet Some Men Prefer Mountains" *	200 - 250	250 - 275

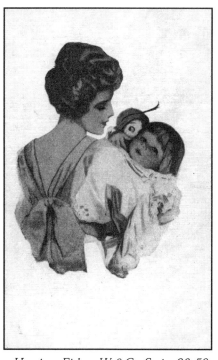

Harrison Fisher, W.&G., Series 36-50
No Caption, New Discovery!!

Harrison Fisher, Finnish Numbered
Series, N:o 4 (Close to Shore)

WG35-5-US "At the Toilet" (767)	200 - 225	225 - 250
* Has not appeared on an R&N postcard.		

W.&G. American Series N:o. 7001/36-50
Unsigned, no Numbers, no Captions

WG50-1-US "A Sprig of Holly" (603)	200 - 225	225 - 250
WG50-2-S "The Favorite Pillow" (613)	200 - 225	225 - 250
WG50-3-US "Girlie" (261)	200 - 225	225 - 250
WG50-4-US Title unknown - Mother-Child *	300 - 350	350 - 400
* This is a new find by the author. Appears only on W.&G. and Polyphot Finnish Series.		

W.&G. American Series No. 7031/1-7
Unsigned, no Numbers, no Captions

WG7-1-US "Their Honeymoon Trip" *	225 - 250	250 - 300
* Has not appeared on an R&N postcard.		

The Publisher at Polyphot Series
Also published by W.&G.
Unsigned, no Numbers, no Captions

PP-5-US "At the Toilet" (767)	150 - 175	175 - 225
PP-1-US "Their Honeymoon Trip"	250 - 275	275 - 300
PP-2-US "A Sprig of Holly" (603)	150 - 175	175 - 225
PP-3-US "Don't Worry" (614)	200 - 225	225 - 250
PP-4-US "Following the Race" (184)	150 - 175	175 - 225
PP-5-US New find - Mother and Child * **	300 - 350	350 - 400

* Not on any R&N postcard; appears only on
  the W.&G. Series 36-50 and this Polyphot Series.
** From the Collection of Kurt McKenzie

Harrison Fisher, Finnish Numbered
Series, N:o 7 (A Novice)

Harrison Fisher, S & K, Kouvola
Reversed Image, Finnish, SKK-3-US

Pain. Karjalan Kirjap. Oy., Viipuri Series

Numbered, Unsigned, no Captions

PKK N:o-5-S "Playing the Game" *	250 - 275	275 - 300
PKK N:o-10-S "A Midsummer Reverie"	200 - 250	250 - 275
PKK N:o-4-S "Close to Shore" (764)	175 - 200	200 - 235
PKK N:o-7-S "A Novice" (863)	175 - 200	200 - 235

* Has not appeared on an R&N postcard.

K.K. Oy N:o 1-20 Series
Publisher is also Pain. Karjalan Kirjap

Signed, no Numbers, no Captions

K.K. 20-1-S "Mistletoe" * **	250 - 275	275 - 325
K.K. 20-2-S "Thoroughbreds" *** (304)	200 - 225	225 - 250

* Has not appeared on an R&N postcard.
** Titled by Author.

*** Also by KYK-KFP	250 - 275	275 - 325

The "No Identification" Series *
S & K, Kouvola *
Unsigned, no Numbers, no Captions

NOP-1-US "Autumn's Beauty" (837)	175 - 200	200 - 250
NOP-2-US "Following the Race" (184)	175 - 200	200 - 250
NOP-3-US "Contentment" (383)	175 - 200	200 - 250
NOP-4-US "The Only Pebble" (838)	175 - 200	200 - 250

* According to Finnish collector Kosti Kallio's
findings, this **"No Identification Series"** was
published by **S & K, Kouvola**, which follows.

The S & K Kouvola Reversed Image Series
  Unsigned, no Numbers, no Captions
  SKK-1-US "Snowbird" *   275 - 300   300 - 350
  SKK-2-US "Winners" (864)   275 - 300   300 - 350
  SKK-3-US "Study in Contentment" (875)   275 - 300   300 - 350
* Appears only on Finnish cards.
The Real Photo Card Series
  5 Additional images have been found.
  S=Signed; US=Uns., * ** Captions
  RP-4-S "A Novice" (863)   125 - 150   150 - 175
  RP-5-S "All's Well" 505 ** (381)   125 - 150   150 - 175
  RP-6-S "Alone at Last" C-68 ** (762)   125 - 150   150 - 175
  RP-1-S "American Beauties," (Series 101)   125 - 150   150 - 175
  RP-2-US "Day Dreams" * (848)   125 - 150   150 - 175
  RP-3-US "Drifting" ** (768)   125 - 150   150 - 175
  RP-7-S "Fair and Warmer" (842)   125 - 150   150 - 175
  RP-8-S "June" ** (615)   125 - 150   150 - 175
  RP-9-US "My Hero" (977)   125 - 150   150 - 175
* Some cards numbered, but not R&N numbers.
The Otto Andersin, Pori Series (Br. & Green)
  Unsigned, no Numbers, no Captions
  OA-1-US "All's Well" (381)   300 - 350   350 - 400
  OA-1-US-MB * "Close To Shore" (764)   300 - 350   350 - 400
  OA-2-US "Drifting" (768)   300 - 350   350 - 400
 * With Multilingual Back.
Untitled Series, No Publisher
  (With "Stamp Here" in Stamp Box)
  There are possibly 25 unnumbered cards
  in this series and at least 4 are known to
  be by Philip Boileau and 20 by Fisher. The
  remaining card has now been identified by
  the author as being by Clarence Underwood.
  There is also a **Russian Set** which we have
  titled **"Orohek"** (publisher). The cards
  have the same captions written on back and
  are numbered up to 25. See Russian section.
  Captions for **"Stamp Here"** are as follows:
  "A Beauty" (404)   150 - 175   175 - 200
  "Be Hove" (302)   150 - 175   175 - 200
  "A Dane" (183)   150 - 175   175 - 200
  "A Prairie Belle" (263)   150 - 175   175 - 200
  "A Rose" (181)   150 - 175   175 - 200
  "Bubbles" (403)   150 - 175   175 - 200
  "Dolly" *   150 - 175   175 - 200
  "Friends" (405)   150 - 175   175 - 200
  "Good Night" (259)   150 - 175   175 - 200
  "Homeward Bound" (255)   150 - 175   175 - 200
  "June" (615)   150 - 175   175 - 200
  "Love Lyrics" (257)   150 - 175   175 - 200
  "On Swing" New Discovery!   175 - 200   200 - 225
  "Preparing to Conquer" (256)   150 - 175   175 - 200
  "Princess Pat" (407)   150 - 175   175 - 200
  "Ready and Waiting" (418)   150 - 175   175 - 200
  "Sport" (184)   150 - 175   175 - 200

ON SWING.

Harrison Fisher, "Stamp Here" Series
New Discovery, "On Swing"

Harrison Fisher, Leningrad Society
Series 52836-10000, No. 6

"To Ball" (Series 108)	150 - 175	175 - 200
"To Walk" White hat, dog in arms (409)	150 - 175	175 - 200
"To Walk" Black hat, brown dog (180)	150 - 175	175 - 200
"Yet Some Men Prefer the Mountains" *	150 - 175	175 - 200
* Does not appear on an R&N postcard.		

ADVERTISING

Maailma Magazine, 1919, of the cover

"The Evening Hour"	250 - 300	300 - 350

RUSSIAN

D. Chromov & M. Bachrach, Moscow
Black & White on pebbled paper

No caption - Same as "Miss Santa Claus"	200 - 250	250 - 300
No caption - Same as "The Rose"	125 - 150	150 - 175

Frolov and Shourek, Moscow

Unknown title	125 - 150	150 - 175
E.K. No. 19 "Maid at Arms" *	150 - 175	175 - 200
* Same back as Frolov and Shourek		

Leningrad Region (Linens)
Total of 4 Duplicate Series with varying
Print Runs. Each card has same numbers.
Series 52836, 10,000 (Total Print Run)
Signed - No Captions

No. 1 "And Yet Her Eyes Can Look Wise"	150 - 175	175 - 200
No. 2 "Leisure Moments"	150 - 175	175 - 200
No. 5 "Springtime"	150 - 175	175 - 200
No. 6 "Those Bewitching Eyes"	150 - 175	175 - 200
No. 54 "Vanity"	150 - 175	175 - 200

No. 60 "Cherry Ripe"	150 - 175	175 - 200
No. 71 "Bewitching Maiden"	150 - 175	175 - 200
No. 72 "Lips for Kisses"	150 - 175	175 - 200

Series 5350, 15,000 (Total Print Run) *
Series 5351, 20,000 (Total Print Run) *
Series 9402, 20,000 (Total Print Run) *
* Values same as for 8 cards in Series 52836

Rishar ("Richard" or "Phillips")
(St. Petersburg or Petrograde) Backs * **

No. 54 "Vanity"	150 - 175	175 - 200
No. 117 "Hexenaugen" (Those Bewitching Eyes)	150 - 175	175 - 200
No. 824 "Made to Worship"	150 - 175	175 - 200
No. 825 "In the Toils"	150 - 175	175 - 200
No. 826 "Leisure Moments"	150 - 175	175 - 200
No. 827 "The American Beauty"	150 - 175	175 - 200
No. 828 "Teacup Time"	150 - 175	175 - 200
No. 829 "And Yet Her Eyes Can Look Wise"	150 - 175	175 - 200
No. 830 "A Faste (Taste) of Paradise"	150 - 175	175 - 200
No. 831 "Spring Time"	150 - 175	175 - 200
No. 832 "Food for Thought"	150 - 175	175 - 200
No. 833 "Lips for Kisses"	150 - 175	175 - 200
No. 834 "Vanity"	150 - 175	175 - 200
No. 835 "Cherry Ripe" Signed	150 - 175	175 - 200
No. 836 "Bewitching Maiden"	150 - 175	175 - 200
No. 837 "Polar Bear"	150 - 175	175 - 200

"May-Time"   Reportedly seen but not verified.
"Food for Thought" Same as above.
Others
* Some cards have captions on front; others on back.
** Fisher's name is misspelled "Fischer."

"Orohek" Russian-English Backs   (25)
  Published in 1927 in Soviet Russia
  Series 71293 - 3000 (Total print run)
  Series 66391 - 5000 (Total print run)
  Duplicates of Series 71293
Paper stock is thicker than normal.

2 "To Walk" (409) "Isn't He Sweet?"	150 - 200	200 - 250
3 "Dolly"	150 - 200	200 - 250
7 "Friends"	150 - 200	200 - 250
9 "Bubbles"	150 - 200	200 - 250
10 "June"	150 - 200	200 - 250
12 "A Dane"	150 - 200	200 - 250
14 "Preparing to Conquer"	150 - 200	200 - 250
15 "To Ball"	150 - 200	200 - 250
17 "A Rose"	150 - 200	200 - 250
19 "Good Night!"	150 - 200	200 - 250
20 "Princess Pat"	150 - 200	200 - 235
21 "Homeward Bound"	150 - 200	200 - 250
22 "Ready and Waiting"	150 - 200	200 - 250
23 "To Walk" (180) "Well Protected"	150 - 200	200 - 250
24 "Sport" (Following the Race)	150 - 200	200 - 250
25 "A Prairie Belle"	150 - 200	200 - 250
"A Beauty"	150 - 200	200 - 250
"Love Lyrics"	150 - 200	200 - 250

Harrison Fisher, D.K. & Co. P. (Listed
"Cermak") 2057, "Voyage de Noce"

Harrison Fisher, MEU
No Caption (Marcia)

"Yet Some Men Prefer Mountains"	150 - 200	200 - 250
"Vanity"	150 - 200	200 - 250
Note: #1, 4, 13 and one other are Boileau's.		
Another image is now known and is by		
Clarence Underwood, #16.		

Russian Backs, Sepia, Signed
Untitled (R&N Numbers)

"Bows Attract Beaus" (260 and 2102)	150 - 175	175 - 200
"Courting Attention" (424 and 2094)	150 - 175	175 - 200
"Fine Feathers" (408)	150 - 175	175 - 200
"From Life" *	175 - 225	225 - 275
"Homeward Bound" (255)	125 - 150	150 - 200
"Isn't He Sweet" (409 and 2097)	125 - 150	150 - 200
"The Kiss" (Series 108 and 2053)	125 - 150	150 - 200
"Maid at Arms" (410)	125 - 150	150 - 200
"Mary" (421 and 2095)	125 - 150	150 - 200
"My Lady Drives" (417)	125 - 150	150 - 200
"My Pretty Neighbor" (423)	125 - 150	150 - 200
"Princess Pat" (407 and 2046)	125 - 150	150 - 200
"Well Protected" (180 and 2090)	125 - 150	150 - 200

* Does not appear on R&N postcard.

Russian-Polish Backs (Hand-tinted)

"Princess Pat" (407 and 2046)	150 - 175	175 - 200
"Sweetheart" (194)	150 - 175	175 - 200

Russian-Polish Real Photo Types
AWE With Russian/Polish Back

"Beauties" (196) (196 and 1002)	175 - 200	200 - 225

"Homeward Bound" (225)	175 - 200	200 - 225
"Luxury" (253)	175 - 200	200 - 225
"Miss Knickerbocker" (183)	175 - 200	200 - 225
"Miss Santa Clause" (182)	175 - 200	200 - 225
"Roses" (201)	175 - 200	200 - 225
"Vanity" (195 and 1003)	175 - 200	200 - 225
"Well Protected" (180 and 2090)	175 - 200	200 - 225
Others		

Russian-French Backs

E.R. No. 12 (B&W) "Beauties"	125 - 150	150 - 175
Flying bird T.M. "The Rose" cheap paper	125 - 150	150 - 175

Russian Real Photo Series   (No. on Front)

3221 "Maid at Arms" (410)	175 - 200	200 - 250
3223 "Princess Pat" (407 and 2046)	175 - 200	200 - 250
3270 "Thoroughbreds" (304)	175 - 200	200 - 250

Anonymous - Blank Backs, (B&W)

"Leisure Moments"	150 - 200	200 - 250

EASTERN EUROPE

Apollon Sophia (Bulgaria)

No. 21 "La Musique" (The Artist)	75 - 90	90 - 125
21 "Title" Same as "A Kiss"	75 - 90	90 - 125

Modern Art, Sofia (Same as above)

No. 024 "A Kiss"	75 - 90	90 - 100
Other Russian	75 - 100	100 - 125
No. 024 "Kuss" (Kiss)	75 - 80	85 - 90
Linen, No. 192 "Cherry Ripe"	125 - 150	150 - 175

D.K. & Co. P. Error card, artist listed "Cermak"
See Finnish Series WG7-1-US (Variation)

2057 "Voyage de Noce" (Honeymoon Trip)	200 - 250	250 - 300

Polish & Ukranian Backs (No Captions)

"A Sprig of Holly" (603)	125 - 150	150 - 200
"A Winter Sport" (600)	125 - 150	150 - 200
"Winter Whispers" (601)	125 - 150	150 - 200

WAE   Probably Polish (Real Photo)

"Well Protected"	125 - 150	150 - 200

EUROPE & GREAT BRITAIN

B.K.W.I., Austria

No No., No Caption ("Naughty, Naughty")	125 - 140	140 - 160

J. Beagles & Co. (Charles H. Hauff)
(R&N backs)

No No. "The Winter Girl"	70 - 80	80 - 90
No No. "A Fair Driver"	70 - 80	80 - 90
No No. "Those Bewitching Eyes"	70 - 80	80 - 90

MEU/Alfred Schweizer, Hamburg
Series 4380

4 "In the Country" *	200 - 225	225 - 250
5 "Final Instructions" *	200 - 225	225 - 250
9 "Beatrice" *	200 - 225	225 - 250
No No. "Marcia" *	200 - 225	225 - 250
No No. "On the Avenue" *	200 - 225	225 - 250
No No. "Rosamond" *	200 - 225	225 - 250
* Image appears on no other postcard.		

Alfred Schweizer

"Santa Claus' First Visit" (J. Henderson Co.)	150 - 175	175 - 200

Gibson Karte No. 1013 (J. Henderson Co.)

"A Critical Moment"	70 - 80	80 - 90

"Vienne" Series 806

"Beatrice"	80 - 90	90 - 100

JTK "Kron-Trier" Series

"A Portrait Sketch"	80 - 90	90 - 100

M.J.S.

"The Kiss" (No Caption) (108 Series)	40 - 50	50 - 60

Muinck & Co., Amsterdam
  Water Color Series (English Captions)

R.185 "The Kiss"	100 - 125	125 - 150
R.188 "Dumb Luck"	120 - 140	140 - 160
R.192 "A Study Hour"	100 - 125	125 - 150
R.217 "The Artist"	100 - 125	125 - 150
R.223 "The Proposal"	100 - 125	125 - 150
R.224 "The Honeymoon"	100 - 125	125 - 150
R.225 "The First Evening in Their..."	100 - 125	125 - 150
R.226 "Their New Love"	100 - 125	125 - 150
R.232 "Lost?"	100 - 125	125 - 150
"His First Love"	100 - 125	125 - 150
"The Dollar Princess, in Holland"	100 - 125	125 - 150

Utigave Louis Diefenthal, Amsterdam

"A Thoroughbred"	100- 120	120 - 140

Friedrich O. Wolter

"Peggy" (871)	60 - 75	75 - 90

FRENCH   Nurse Poster Card

"Affiches De La Grande Guerre," No. 11	450 - 500	550 - 600

F.T. (HUN) Chromolithographic Ladies
  M. Munk, Vienne   Highest Quality

Series 479 (6)	20 - 25	25 - 30
Series 628 (6)	20 - 25	25 - 30
Series 636 (6)	20 - 25	25 - 30

FLAGG, JAMES MONTGOMERY (US)
  Detroit Publishing Co.
  B&W 14000 Series

14011 "The Sweet Magic of Smoke"	10 - 12	12 - 15
14149 "Sir Charles"	10 - 12	12 - 15
14150 "It Certainly Wasn't"	10 - 12	12 - 15
14151 "For Heaven's Sake"	10 - 12	12 - 15
14152 "So Sensible"	10 - 12	12 - 15
14153 "Not Bad to Take"	10 - 12	12 - 15
14154 "Beyond More Conjecture"	10 - 12	12 - 15
14155 "A Cold Proposition"	10 - 12	12 - 15
14156 "If You Get Gay"	10 - 12	12 - 15
14157 "If You're a Perfect Gent"	10 - 12	12 - 15
14158 "Make it Pleasant for Him"	10 - 12	12 - 15

Henderson Litho

501 "Engaged - His Attitude"	8 - 10	10 - 12
2503 "Something on Account"	8 - 10	10 - 12
Golf	18 - 22	22 - 25

Novitas   (Star in circle)

20696 "Etwas a conto!"	12 - 15	15 - 18
20697 "U. A. w. g........!"	12 - 15	15 - 18

*James Montgomery Flagg, Novitas
20696, "Etwas a conto!"*

*James Montgomery Flagg, Novitas
20697, "U. A. w. g.......!"*

Reinthal & Newman

288 "A Club Sandwich"	12 - 15	15 - 20
289 "Putting Out the Flames"	12 - 15	15 - 20
290 "Miss Behaving!"	12 - 15	15 - 20
291 "The Most Exciting Moment"	12 - 15	15 - 20
292 "The Real Love Game"	15 - 20	20 - 25
293 "Dry Goods"	15 - 18	18 - 22

TP & Co., N.Y.
Series 738 (Sepia)

"Trouble Somewhere"	6 - 8	8 - 10

Series 751

"The Hypnotist"	10 - 12	12 - 15
"The Only Way to Eat an Orange"	10 - 12	12 - 15
"Say When"	10 - 12	12 - 15

Series 818

8 "Holding Hands"	10 - 12	12 - 15
10 "In The Hands of the Receiver"	10 - 12	12 - 15

FONTAN, LEO (FR) French Glamour

Series 17, 80	25 - 28	28 - 35
Series 23, 5016	15 - 18	18 - 26
Series 95 Dance Series (Semi-nudes)	20 - 25	25 - 35
FOSTER, F.D. (US)	4 - 5	5 - 6
FRANK, ELLY (GER)	8 - 10	10 - 12

FRANZONI, ROBERTO (IT) Art Deco
Dell, Anna & Gasparini; Uff. Rev. Stampa

Series 44 Heads (6)	15 - 20	20 - 25

Gayac, P. J. Gallais 300
"Dancing Girl"

Charles Dana Gibson
James Henderson & Sons, "Peggy"

Series 78 Hands/Head	12 - 15	15 - 18
Series 4358 Fashion - Windy Day (6)	15 - 18	18 - 20
Ladies/Fashion	12 - 15	15 - 18
Erotic/Semi-Nudes	18 - 20	20 - 22
Golf	22 - 25	25 - 35
Tennis	18 - 20	20 - 22
Ladies & Dogs		
B.K.W.I.		
Series 369 (6)	10 - 12	12 - 15
Series 6309 (6)	12 - 15	15 - 20
P.R.S. **Series 50** (6) High Fashion	20 - 25	25 - 28
FREDILLO (FR) Art Nouveau	25 - 30	30 - 38
FREIXAS, J. (US) (See Halloween)		
Winsch, Copyright	20 - 25	30 - 40
FREYSCHLAG, G.	6 - 8	8 - 10
FRÜNDT, H. (Art Nouveau)	25 - 30	30 - 35
FUCHS, RUD. (GER)	10 - 12	12 - 15
FUKS, PROF. A. (GER)	8 - 10	10 - 12
GALLAIS, P. (FR) French Glamour		
Semi-Nude Series	20 - 25	25 - 30
GAYAC (SP) French Glamour		
P.J. Gallais		
Series 210-?	20 - 25	25 - 30
Series 290-310 Dancing Semi-nudes	25 - 30	30 - 35
GERBAULT, H. (FR) French Glamour		
Series 36	15 - 18	18 - 26

GIBSON, CHARLES DANA (US)
A.H.

"A Fan Out"	15 - 18	18 - 22
"And they call that guy a pitcher"	15 - 18	18 - 22
"Fanned Again"	15 - 18	18 - 22
"Now Watch Cassey..."	15 - 18	18 - 22
"Well, darn his hide..."	15 - 18	18 - 22
"Who's that guy?"	15 - 18	18 - 22

Government Advertising Card

"British American War Relief Fund" Receipt Card	30 - 35	35 - 45

Detroit Publishing Co.
B &W 14000 Series

14000 "Has She a Heart?"	12 - 15	15 - 18
14003 "Their Presence of Mind"	12 - 15	15 - 18
14004 "Melting"	12 - 15	15 - 18
14005 "When Hunting ..."	12 - 15	15 - 18
14006 "Last Days of Summer"	12 - 15	15 - 18
14008 "The Dog"	12 - 15	15 - 18
14009 "Who Cares"	12 - 15	15 - 18
14017 "Good Game for Two" (Golf)	20 - 22	22 - 25
14019 "Here it is Christmas"	12 - 15	15 - 18
14027 "Is a caddy always necessary?" (Golf)	20 - 22	22 - 25
14029 "The Half Orphan"	12 - 15	15 - 18
14046 "Bathing Suits"	12 - 15	15 - 18
14048 "The Half Orphan"	12 - 15	15 - 18
14050 "America Picturesque"	12 - 15	15 - 18
14051 "The Stout Gentleman"	10 - 12	12 - 15
14052 "No Wonder the Sea Serpent ..."	12 - 15	15 - 18
14054 "Stepped On"	10 - 12	12 - 15
14055 "Mr. A Merger Hogg ..."	10 - 12	12 - 15
14057 "Ill Blows the Wind ..."	10 - 12	12 - 15
14059 "Rival Beauties"	12 - 15	15 - 18
14065 "The Gibson Girl"	12 - 15	15 - 18
14066 "Jane"	15 - 18	18 - 22
14067 "Mabel"	15 - 18	18 - 22
14068 "Amy"	15 - 18	18 - 22
14069 "Eleanor"	15 - 18	18 - 22
14070 "Margaret"	15 - 18	18 - 22
14071 "Molly"	15 - 18	18 - 22
14072 "Helen"	15 - 18	18 - 22
14073 "Beatrice"	15 - 18	18 - 22
14074 "The Sporting Girl"	15 - 18	18 - 22
14185 "The Eternal Question"	10 - 12	12 - 15
14186 "Fanned Out"	20 - 25	25 - 30
14187 "Two Strikes and Bases Full"	20 - 25	25 - 30
14192 "The Game Begins"	20 - 25	25 - 30

James Henderson & Sons
"Pictorial Comedy Series" Sepia Heads

"Amy," "Annie," "Clorinda," "Gladys"	10 - 12	12 - 15
"Maude," "Nina," "Peggy," "Beatrice"	10 - 12	12 - 15
"Bertha," "Eileen," "Violet"	10 - 12	12 - 15
Gibson inset among his various images	12 - 15	15 - 18

James Henderson & Sons
Life's Comedy Series (36)

	6 - 8	8 - 10

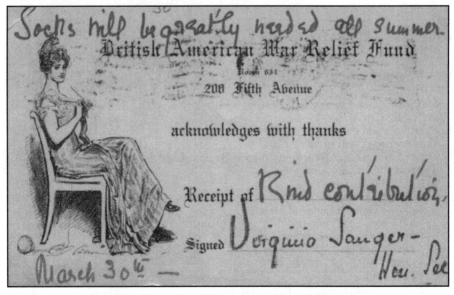

C. D. Gibson, British American War Relief Fund

Golf Images	18 - 22	22 - 26
Schweizer & Co.		
Embossed, Sepia Series		
"The Eternal Question"	10 - 12	12 - 15
Pictorial Comedy Series	10 - 12	12 - 15
Snap-Shots	6 - 8	8 - 10
Golf Images	18 - 22	22 - 26
GEIGER, R. (HUN) Glamour	10 - 12	12 - 15
GERBAULT, HENRI (FR) **Glamour (Also Les Cent)**	15 - 20	20 - 25
GIAMETTI, A. (IT) **Glamour**	15 - 18	18 - 22
GIGLIO	4 - 6	6 - 10
GILBERT, C. ALLEN (US)	8 - 10	10 - 12
Calendar, 1911	12 - 15	15 - 20
Henderson & Sons "Pictorial Comedy" (Sepia)		
No No. "A Heart full of Affection"	10 - 12	12 - 15
99 "Dorothy	10 - 12	12 - 15
Taylor-Platt Issues	12 - 15	15 - 18
A. Schweizer		
"Pictorial Comedy" (Sepia)		
106 "Miranda"	10 - 12	12 - 15
"The Gibson P.C.s" (Color)		
1501 "There is nothing like a good book."	8 - 10	10 - 12
GILLEY (Art Deco)		
Paris Gravure Series 1961, 1971 Semi-Nudes	20 - 25	25 - 30
GILLIS, RENE	12 - 15	15 - 20
GINI, M.		
T.A.M. Series 7618	10 - 12	12 - 15
GIRIS, C. (FR)		
Uff. Rev. Stampa		
Deco Bathing Beauties Series 25	22 - 25	25 - 28
W.E., Paris Series 7044	22 - 25	25 - 28
GNISCHAF, RUAB (GER) Romantic couples	6 - 8	8 - 10

Giris, W.E., Paris
Series 7044, No Caption

D. Gobbi, Majestic No. 2475
No Caption

Playing cards	8 - 10	10 - 15
GOBBI, D. (IT) Art Deco		
Majestic		
Series 2546, Chinese Dragon	15 - 18	18 - 22
Ladies	22 - 25	25 - 28
Gondola/Lovers	18 - 20	20 - 25
Series 1216	12 - 15	15 - 20
Series 2474, 2475 Pierrots/Harlequins/Ladies	20 - 25	25 - 30
Series 2477, 2494	15 - 18	18 - 22
Series 2479	12 - 15	15 - 18
Series 2530, 2556, 2560	20 - 25	25 - 30
Elite		
Series 2631	12 - 15	15 - 18
Series 2550	18 - 20	20 - 22
GODELA, D. (IT)		
Series 272, 296 Head Studies	12 - 15	15 - 20
D.A.G. Series 409 In Oval - Sitting (6)	8 - 10	10 - 12
GOODMAN, MAUDE (Ladies) See Children	15 - 20	20 - 25
GOTTARO	8 - 10	10 - 12
GRAF, MARTE or MG (GER)		
Art Deco & Silhouettes		
Series 733-758	10 - 12	12 - 15
Other Deco Silhouettes	8 - 10	10 - 12
GRANDE (IT) Art Deco and Glamour		
Series 437 (6)	12 - 15	15 - 20
GRASSET, EUGENE (SWI) Art Nouveau	100 - 120	120 - 130
Collection Cinos	125 - 135	135 - 150

Collection des Cent	500 - 550	550 - 600
GREENE, FREDERICK (US)	6 - 8	8 - 10
GREFE, WILL (US)		
M. Munk, Vienna		
Series 526 (6) No captions	12 - 15	15 - 20
Moffat, Yard Co.		
Playing Card Queens		
"Club," "Diamond," "Heart," "Spade"	18 - 22	22 - 26
Moffat, Yard Co. Series 3	10 - 12	12 - 15
Brown & Bigelow		
Advertising Calendars Romantic Couples	12 - 15	15 - 20
GREINER, MAGNUS (US)		
Auburn Publishing Co., Pennant Series	6 - 8	8 - 10
Anonymous German Series 1500	8 - 10	10 - 12
GRIMBALL, M. M. (US) See Children		
Gutmann & Gutmann		
Series 106 "Verdict...Love for life"	18 - 22	22 - 26
GROSS, BELLA (US) **Glamour**	5 - 6	6 - 8
GROSZE, MANNI (IT)		
Art Deco Silhouettes		
Deco Series 2041 Nudes	18 - 22	22 - 25
Others	12 - 15	15 - 20
PFB (In Diamond)		
Series 2042, Nudes	15 - 20	20 - 25
Series 3339, Nudes	15 - 20	20 - 25
Series 2052, Dancing	12 - 15	15 - 18
Others		
GROTT Bathing Girls	8 - 10	10 - 12
GUARINO, ANTHONY	5 - 6	6 - 8
GUARNERI (IT) Art Deco		
Ladies	15 - 18	18 - 22
GUERZONI, G. (IT)		
Art Deco and Glamour		
Ladies/Heads/Fashion	10 - 15	15 - 20
Ladies/Animals	15 - 18	18 - 22
Erotic/Semi-Nudes	15 - 18	18 - 22
Ladies & Dogs	12 - 15	15 - 25
Ladies & Horses	12 - 15	15 - 25
B.K.W.I.		
Series 702 (10)	12 - 15	15 - 20
Series 710 (6)	8 - 10	10 - 12
Series 729 (6)	10 - 12	12 - 15
Rev. Stampa		
Series 1010 (6)	15 - 18	18 - 22
Series 1017 (6) Mother-Daughter	8 - 10	10 - 12
Series 1023, 1025, 1029, 1046 (6)	10 - 12	12 - 15
Series 1030, 1919 (6) Semi-nudes	18 - 22	22 - 25
Anonymous		
Series 716 (6) Colorful Hats	18 - 22	22 - 26
GUIDO (IT) Art Deco	10 - 12	12 - 15
GUILLAUME, ALBERT (FR) Art Nouveau	75 - 100	100 - 125
Collection des Cent No. 22	200 - 225	225 - 250
GUISCHAF, RUAB (GER) Romantic couples	6 - 9	9 - 12

G. Guerzoni
Anon. Publisher, 716-5

Archie Gunn, National Art No. 247
"Clan Lamond"

GUNN, ARCHIE (US)

S. Bergman		
Black & White Series (6)	5 - 6	6 - 8
6317 Tennis Girl	15 - 20	20 - 25
National Art Co.		
13 "Bowling Girl"	12 - 15	15 - 18
14 "Tennis Girl"	15 - 20	20 - 25
15 "Skating Girl"	12 - 15	15 - 18
16 "College Mascot"	8 - 10	10 - 12
"City Belles" Series		
33 "Miss New York"	10 - 12	12 - 15
34 "Miss Philadelphia"	10 - 12	12 - 15
35 "Miss Boston"	10 - 12	12 - 15
36 "Miss Chicago"	10 - 12	12 - 15
37 "Miss Pittsburgh"	10 - 12	12 - 15
38 "Miss Cincinnati"	10 - 12	12 - 15
39 "Miss Toronto"	10 - 12	12 - 15
40 "Miss Washington"	10 - 12	12 - 15
41 "Miss Seashore"	10 - 12	12 - 15
69 "Bride of Niagara"	10 - 12	12 - 15
71 "Miss Milwaukee"	10 - 12	12 - 15
72 "Miss Detroit"	10 - 12	12 - 15
77 "Miss Cleveland"	10 - 12	12 - 15
87 "Miss San Francisco"	10 - 12	12 - 15
90 Untitled	6 - 8	8 - 10
"Clans" Series		
247 "Clan Lamond" (Golf)	25 - 30	30 - 35

249 "McDougald Plaid"	15 - 20	20 - 25
251 "McPherson Plaid"	15 - 20	20 - 25
252 "Gordon Plaid" (Golf)	25 - 30	30 - 35
"College Belle" Series		
147 "College Mascot"	10 - 12	12 - 15
148 Girl in red, pennant and Collie dog	10 - 12	12 - 15
Miscellaneous		
175 "In the Good Old Summertime"	10 - 12	12 - 15
190 "Forget Me Not"	10 - 12	12 - 15
216 "Jack O' Lantern"	10 - 12	12 - 15
218 "Commencement"	10 - 12	12 - 15
"National Belle" Series		
214 "Lady & the Bear"	10 - 12	12 - 15
217 "Devotion"	10 - 12	12 - 15
219 "Yuletide"	10 - 12	12 - 15
220 "Sables"	10 - 12	12 - 15
221 "Ermine"	10 - 12	12 - 15
222 "Driving"	10 - 12	12 - 15
223 "Automobiling"	10 - 12	12 - 15
276 "The Fencer"	10 - 12	12 - 15
277 "On Guard"	10 - 12	12 - 15
Full-Length Santa	12 - 15	15 - 20
Illustrated Postal Card & Novelty Co.		
WWI Army Series 1368 (12)		
"The American Spirit"	6 - 8	8 - 10
"Army, Navy, and Reserves"	6 - 8	8 - 10
"Don't Worry About Me"	6 - 8	8 - 10
"If Wishes Came True"	6 - 8	8 - 10
"Lest We Forget"	6 - 8	8 - 10
"None but the Brave Deserve ..."	6 - 8	8 - 10
"Pals"	6 - 8	8 - 10
"Parting is Such Sweet Sorrow"	6 - 8	8 - 10
"Repairing a Man of War"	6 - 8	8 - 10
"Rosemary! That's for Remembrance"	6 - 8	8 - 10
"Shoulder Arms"	6 - 8	8 - 10
"When the Last Good-byes are Whispered"	6 - 8	8 - 10
WWI Army Series 1371 (12)		
"A Parting Message"	6 - 8	8 - 10
"Hello! I Haven't Heard from You"	6 - 8	8 - 10
"Don't Worry, We're Alright"	6 - 8	8 - 10
"Guardian Spirits"	6 - 8	8 - 10
"Letters are Always Welcome"	6 - 8	8 - 10
"Liberty and Union Now and Forever"	6 - 8	8 - 10
"Pleasant Memories"	6 - 8	8 - 10
"The Rose for Remembrance"	6 - 8	8 - 10
"Sentry Moon"	6 - 8	8 - 10
"Warmth in the Camp and ..."	6 - 8	8 - 10
"We Won't Come Back Till it's Over ..."	6 - 8	8 - 10
"Worthwhile Fighting For ..."	6 - 8	8 - 10
P-H in diamond logo		
Series 1216		
1 "The Belle of the Hunt"	12 - 15	15 - 18
2 "Waiting for a Partner"	22 - 25	25 - 28

J. W. Hammick
Anonymous, Painting Finish

J. Knowles Hare, Paul Heckscher
Series 1010/3, "Beryl"

Same, but without caption	22 - 25	25 - 28
Taylor-Platt		
American Beauty Series (6)	10 - 12	12 - 15
Statler Calendar Cards, 1912 (12)	12 - 15	15 - 20
Anonymous		
Girl Holding Basketball	20 - 25	25 - 30
Girl Wading in Water	12 - 15	15 - 18
Girl at Wheel of Sail Boat	12 - 15	15 - 18
Girl Holding Golf Club	15 - 20	20 - 25
Girl Holding Golf Club, but in Color	25 - 30	30 - 35
Beautiful Lady, Red Bow, Red Dress	8 - 10	10 - 12
Beautiful Lady, Pink Bow, Pink Dress	8 - 10	10 - 12
Beautiful Lady, Bust, Holding 3 Roses	8 - 10	10 - 12
Series 67		
Beautiful ladies, flowers at breast, w/verse	10 - 12	12 - 15
B&W/Sepia, Women, No Captions (3)	5 - 6	6 - 8
Lowney's Chocolates		
Golf Girls Series (6)	20 - 25	25 - 30
GUYMA		
"The Amours of Pierrot" (4)	20 - 22	22 - 25
HAGER, NINI (AUS) Art Nouveau	100 - 125	125 - 150
HAHN (GER)		
A.R. & C. Deco Series 1197 (6)	15 - 18	18 - 22
H.G.R. (Art Nouveau) **Series 316** (6)	25 - 30	30 - 35
HAMMICK, J.W. (GB)		
Photocom "Celesque" Series		
531 "The Motor Girl"	15 - 18	18 - 22

532 "The Society Girl"	15 - 18	18 - 22
533 "The Ball Room Girl"	15 - 18	18 - 22
534 "The Sporting Girl"	15 - 20	20 - 25
535 "The Sea Side Girl"	15 - 18	18 - 22
Anonymous		
Painting Finish	12 - 15	15 - 20
HAMPEL, WALTER (AUS) Art Nouveau	75 - 100	100 - 150
Other	20 - 25	25 - 30
HANNA, THOMAS (US) Couples	6 - 8	8 - 10
HARBOUR, JENNIE (GB)	12 - 15	15 - 20
HARDY, DUDLEY (GB)		
Glamour	10 - 12	12 - 15
Raphael Tuck Series 1502		
Celebrated Posters		
"Egyptian Mail Steamship"	25 - 30	30 - 40
"Liebig Meat Extract"	30 - 35	35 - 45
"The Pearl Girl"	30 - 35	35 - 45
"Royal Naval Tournament"	30 - 35	35 - 45
Hartman Ladies Sports Series	12 - 15	15 - 20
HARDY, HAYWARD (GB) Art Deco		
Ladies	10 - 12	12 - 15
Ladies/Animals	12 - 15	15 - 18
Pierrots/Harlequins	15 - 18	18 - 22
Erotic/Semi-Nudes	15 - 18	18 - 22
HARE, J. KNOWLES (US)		
Empire Art Series 112	8 - 10	10 - 12
Paul Heckscher		
Series 1009 (6) Watercolors		
1 "Eugenie"	15 - 18	18 - 22
2 "Rosamond"	15 - 18	18 - 22
3 "Beryl"	15 - 18	18 - 22
4 "Bernice"	15 - 18	18 - 22
5 "Madeline"	15 - 18	18 - 22
6 "Charmion"	15 - 18	18 - 22
Series 1010 (6)		
3 "Beryl"	15 - 18	18 - 22
5 "Eloise"	15 - 18	18 - 22
6 "Clarice"	15 - 18	18 - 22
Series 1026 (6) No captions	12 - 15	15 - 20
K Co., Inc., N.Y.		
Mother-Child Series Watercolors		
154 "A little bit of heaven"	10 - 12	12 - 15
157 "Happiness"	10 - 12	12 - 15
M&H Fine Woolens	10 - 12	12 - 15
Statler Advertising Cards, 1912 (13)	12 - 14	14 - 16
Anonymous		
Series 226 Girl in oval (6)	10 - 12	12 - 15
HARPER, R. FORD (US)		
Reinthal & Newman Water color Series		
350 "Peg O' My Heart"	15 - 20	20 - 25
351 "My Summer Girl"	15 - 20	20 - 25
352 "Love's Locket"	15 - 20	20 - 25
353 "True Blue"	15 - 20	20 - 25
354 "The Favorite Flower"	15 - 20	20 - 25

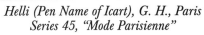

Helli (Pen Name of Icart), G. H., Paris
Series 45, "Mode Parisienne"

Louis Icart, L-E, Paris
"L'Eternel Feminin," Series 48

355 "Miss Innocence"	12 - 15	15 - 20
Gibson Art Co. Issues	10 - 12	12 - 15
P. Heckscher		
Series 1010 2 "Constance"	18 - 22	22 - 26
Series 1013	18 - 22	22 - 26
Series 1025	18 - 22	22 - 26
P. Sander		
Lady Santa Claus (4)	30 - 35	35 - 45
New Year Ladies Series (6)	15 - 18	18 - 22
K.K. OY 1/20 (Finland)		
Girl wearing straw hat, sailor blouse	20 - 25	25 - 30
HART, JOSEF (GR) Art Nouveau	25 - 30	30 - 35
HARRISON (US)	6 - 7	7 - 8
HARTLEIN, W.	4 - 5	5 - 6
HAVILAND, F.	4 - 6	6 - 8
HAYDEN, A.E.	3 - 4	4 - 5
HEINZE, A. Glamour	6 - 8	8 - 10
HELLEU, PAUL (FR) **Ladies of Paris**	20 - 25	25 - 35
HELLI (ICART Pen Name) (FR)		
G.H., Paris		
Series 45 (6) "Mode Parisienne"	70 - 80	80 - 100
Series 53 (6) Ladies	70 - 80	80 - 100
HEROUARD (FR) French Glamour		
Series 55, 300	20 - 25	25 - 35
HERSCHEL, OTTO (AUS)	6 - 8	8 - 10
HERVE, G. (FR)		
Lapina **Series 5064** "Smoker"	10 - 12	12 - 15

HILDER, G. HOWARD

Platinachrome National Girl Series	10 - 12	12 - 15

HILLSON, D. (US)

Girl Series in Red & Black (23)	6 - 8	8 - 10

HOCK, F. (Art Nouveau) · 30 - 35 · 35 - 40

HOFER, A. · 6 - 8 · 8 - 10

HOFFMAN, B.   Glamour · 20 - 25 · 25 - 28

HOFFMANN, JOSEF (Art Nouveau) · 150 - 200 · 200 - 300

"Ver Sacrum" · 1000 - 1500 · 1500 - 2500

HOHENSTEIN, A. (RUS) Art Nouveau

1901 Milano Int. Expo Series · 30 - 35 · 35 - 40

HOLLYER, EVA (GB) · 6 - 8 · 8 - 10

HOLZMAN, A. (GER) · 6 - 8 · 8 - 10

HORN, ANTON (US)

Paul Bendix

120 "Without Love No Life" · 6 - 8 · 8 - 10

HOROWITZ, H.

Raphael Tuck

Series 1 "A Dream of Fair Women" (6) · 10 - 12 · 12 - 15

HORRELL, CHARLES · 4 - 6 · 6 - 8

HORSFALL, MARY (GB) · 10 - 12 · 12 - 15

Ladies & Horses · 12 - 15 · 15 - 18

HUBER, KATHERINE (US) Romantic Couples · 5 - 6 · 6 - 8

HUMPHREY, MAUD (US)

Gray Litho. Co., N.Y. (G. in Diamond)

(All her lady postcards are unsigned.)

P.C. 10 through P.C. 16

Large hat and bust images · 20 - 25 · 25 - 30

P.C. 18, P. C. 20, P.C. 25, P.C. 26 · 18 - 22 · 22 - 26

* P.C. 36, P.C. 37, P.C. 37A, P.C. 38 · 18 - 22 · 22 - 26

P.C. 113, P.C. 133, P.C. 134, · 18 - 22 · 22 - 26

P.C. 135, P.C. 136, P.C. 139, P.C. 141 · 18 - 22 · 22 - 26

* Same images as 130 series except larger

Peroxident Toothpaste

Ads of Beautiful ladies (Uns.) · 25 - 30 · 30 - 35

HUNT, ESTHER (US)

National Art Co.

9-12 Little Chinese Girls · 5 - 6 · 6 - 7

HUNTER, LILLIAN W. (US) · 6 - 8 · 8 - 10

National Art Co.

107 Girl sits in Wreath (Yellow Dress) · 6 - 8 · 8 - 10

109 Wreath Series (Purple Dress) · 6 - 8 · 8 - 10

HUTCHINSON (US)

K Co. Sporting Girls · 8 - 10 · 10 - 15

Tennis · 18 - 22 · 22 - 26

HUTT, HENRY (US)

Detroit Publishing Co.

B&W 14000 Series

14202 "Sincerity" · 10 - 12 · 12 - 15

14203 "Curiosity" · 10 - 12 · 12 - 15

14204 "Tired of Life" · 10 - 12 · 12 - 15

14205 "Expectancy" · 10 - 12 · 12 - 15

14207 "Frivolity" · 10 - 12 · 12 - 15

14208 "Courageous" · 10 - 12 · 12 - 15

14209	"Shy"	10 - 12	12 - 15
14211	"Pleasure"	10 - 12	12 - 15
14212	"Joy"	10 - 12	12 - 15
14213	"Whimsical"	10 - 12	12 - 15

H & S, Germany — 12 - 15 — 15 - 20

ICART, LOUIS (FR) Art Deco, French Glamour *

Italian Gravur

  Series 1785

    Lady & Black Dog — 70 - 90 — 90 - 110

Marque L-E

  Series 48

    "L'Eternal Feminin" (6) — 125 - 150 — 150 - 175

* Also See Artist **Helli, pen name of Icart**

ICHNOWSKI, M. (PO) — 10 - 12 — 12 - 15

IRIBE, PAUL — 150 - 175 — 175 - 200

JANK, ANGELO (GR) Art Nouveau — 25 - 30 — 30 - 35

JANKE, URBAN See Wiener Werkstätte

JANTSY-HORVATH, C. — 5 - 6 — 6 - 10

JANUSZEWSKI, JAN (PO) — 9 - 12 — 12 - 15

JAPHET (Alex Jean Louis Jazet) (FR)

  Costume Series — 25 - 30 — 30 - 35

JARACH, A. (FR) French Glamour

  Delta Series 18, 156, 158 — 18 - 20 — 20 - 25

JAY, CECIL — 5 - 8 — 8 - 10

JEAN (GB) — 5 - 7 — 7 - 9

JIRASEK, A.J. (AUS) — 4 - 5 — 5 - 8

JIRAS, A. (Czech) — 8 - 10 — 10 - 12

JODOLFI (GER) — 6 - 8 — 8 - 10

JOHNSON, J. (US) — 4 - 6 — 6 - 8

JONES, J. (US)

  P. Gordon, 1908

    "Opera Girl" — 6 - 8 — 8 - 10

    "Vacation Girl" (Unsigned) — 6 - 8 — 8 - 10

    College Girl Series — 6 - 7 — 7 - 8

JOSSOT, HENRI (FR) Art Nouveau — 100 - 200 — 200 - 300

JOTTER (Walter H. Young) GB Ladies — 10 - 12 — 12 - 15

JOZSA, KARL (AUS) Art Nouveau

  A. Sockl, Wien

    "Femme au Coeur" — 70 - 80 — 80 - 90

    "Sirens and Circeans" Series (6) — 200 - 250 — 250 - 300

  E.S.D.B., Austria

    "Coeur Dame" Series (6) — 60 - 70 — 70 - 85

  Simon Steffans

    "Smoke Rings" Series (6) — 110 - 115 — 115 - 125

JUNG, MORITZ (CZ) Art Nouveau

  See Wiener Werkstätte

KABY (FR) Fashion — 10 - 12 — 12 - 15

KAINRADL, L. (GR) Art Nouveau — 75 - 100 — 100 - 250

KALHAMMER, G. (AUS) See Wiener Werkstätte

KALOUS, GRET — 6 - 8 — 8 - 10

KALVACH, RUDOLPH (AUS)

  See Wiener Werkstätte

KANDINSKY, W. (RUS)

  Bauhaus Series, 1923 See Bauhaus Section

KASKELINE, F. (GER)		
Deco/Silhouettes	12 - 15	15 - 18
Nudes-Semi-nudes	15 - 18	18 - 22
S.W.S.B.		
Ladies and Horses		
Series 1119	10 - 12	12 - 15
KATINKA (SW) Art Deco	10 - 12	12 - 15
KAVAL, M. (FR) Art Deco		
Lapina, Paris		
Series 5027, 5029, 5030 Hats (6)	12 - 15	15 - 18
Series 5031, 5032 Hats (6)	12 - 15	15 - 18
Series 5034, 5036 Hats (6)	12 - 15	15 - 18
KELLER, A. I. (US)		
Historical Sweethearts Series		
"The Introduction"	4 - 6	6 - 8
"The Wooing of Anne Hathaway"	6 - 8	8 - 10
"The Proposal"	6 - 8	8 - 10
"The Wedding"	6 - 8	8 - 10
KEMPF, TH. (AUS) Art Nouveau		
Series 165 (10)	50 - 60	60 - 70
Series 166 (10)	55 - 60	60 - 65
KENYON, ZULA (US) Glamour	6 - 8	8 - 12
Gerlach-Barklow		
Advertising Calendars – 1910-1914		
Beautiful ladies with flowers	10 - 12	12 - 15
KIEFER, E.H. (GB)		
Bamforth & Co.		
"Could You Be True," "Dear Heart"	8 - 10	10 - 12
"Good Bye," "I'm Growing Fond of You"	8 - 10	10 - 12
"Love a Lassie," "My Chum"	8 - 10	10 - 12
"There's Nobody Like You"	8 - 10	10 - 12
"You Know You're Not Forgotten"	8 - 10	10 - 12
"Waiting For You," "When Dreams Come True"	8 - 10	10 - 12
"When You Feel Dreamy"	8 - 10	10 - 12
"When You Feel Naughty..."	8 - 10	10 - 12
"When You're Traveling..."	8 - 10	10 - 12
"When Your Heart Aches...," "Would You Care"	8 - 10	10 - 12
"Would You Learn to Love Me"	8 - 10	10 - 12
Gray Litho, 1909		
"When you feel drowsy..."	8 - 10	10 - 12
KIENERK, G. (IT) (Art Nouveau)		
"Cocorico"	450 - 500	500 - 600
KIEZKOW (PO) (Art Nouveau)	80 - 90	90 - 100
KIMBALL, ALONZO (US)		
Reinthal & Newman		
Series 122, Lovers (6)	6 - 8	8 - 10
KING, HAMILTON (US)		
Coca Cola Girl (Advertising Card)	1100 - 1200	1200 - 1400
Coca Cola Motor Girl	1300 - 1500	1500 - 1700
E. Gross		
American Girls Series	8 - 10	10 - 12
Bathing Beauties (12)		
"Asbury Park Girl," "Atlantic City Girl"	18 - 22	22 - 26
"Bar Harbor Girl," "Cape May Girl"	18 - 22	22 - 26

"Coney Island Girl," "Long Branch Girl"	18 - 22	22 - 26
"Larchmont Girl," "Manhattan Beach Girl"	18 - 22	22 - 26
"Narragansett Girl" "Newport Girl"	18 - 22	22 - 26
"Palm Beach Girl," "Ocean Grove Girl"	18 - 22	22 - 26

Henry Heininger Co.
Sports Series (6) Watercolors

"After the Ball"	25 - 30	30 - 35
"Beneath the Sun Shade"	18 - 22	22 - 26
"The Fencer" (Uns.)	18 - 22	22 - 26
"In the Swim"	18 - 22	22 - 26
"Lady in Blue"	18 - 22	22 - 26
"On a Skate"	18 - 22	22 - 26

F.A. Schneider
454-459 Series (6) Watercolors

454 "Contented"	12 - 15	15 - 20
455 "Secure"	12 - 15	15 - 20
456 "Graceful"	12 - 15	15 - 20
459 "Stunning"	12 - 15	15 - 20

Raphael Tuck
Series 1605 Gem Glosso

"My Lady Fair"	12 - 15	15 - 20

Brown & Bigelow
Advertising Calendars, 1907 (12)

Beautiful ladies	15 - 18	18 - 26

Armour & Co. See Advertising
KING, JESSIE M. (GB) Art Nouveau
Millar & Lang

Series 122 "The National Series"	70 - 80	80 - 100
KINNEYS, THE (US)	8 - 10	10 - 15

KIRCHNER, RAPHAEL (AUS)

The following check list, which appeared in the 3rd Edition, is in part from the book, *RAPHAEL KIRCHNER AND HIS POSTCARDS,* by Antonio and Pia Dell'Aquila. There were three distinct periods for classifying his works – **The Early Period**, from 1897 through 1899; **The Golden Age**, from 1900 through 1907; and **The Glamour Age,** from 1910 through 1916. Raphael Kirchner died in New York in 1917.

Kirchner's works were extremely popular during his lifetime and many of his sets and series were issued by more than one publisher, making it almost impossible to catalog each one. Therefore, our listing is incomplete, and we recommend that you obtain a copy of the above book for a more complete checklist and other vital publisher information.

RAPHAEL KIRCHNER

Art Nouveau & Art Deco

EARLY PERIOD

Back & Schmitt, Vienna

"A Quatre Feuilles" (Clovers) (6)	175 - 200	200 - 250
"Aus Arkadien" (From Arkadia) (6)	175 - 200	200 - 250
"Fleur de Chemin" (Street Flowers) (10)	175 - 200	200 - 250
"Myths and Legends" (6)	175 - 200	200 - 250

 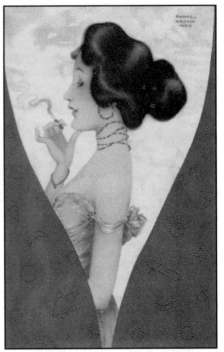

Raphael Kirchner, B.K.W.I.
"Bijoux" (Jewels), Series 538

Raphael Kirchner, B.K.W.I.
"Bijoux" (Jewels), Series 538

Raphael Kirchner, Anonymous
"All Heil" Series D.1 – No Caption

"Music Postcards" (1)	500 - 600	600 - 700
"Radlerei" (Girl Cyclists) (6)	275 - 300	300 - 350
"Wiener Blut" (Viennese Blood) (6)	175 - 200	200 - 250
"Um die Liebe" (To the Love) (7)	175 - 200	200 - 250
J. Gerson, Paris		
"Happy New Year" (10)	150 - 175	175 - 200
Philipp and Kramer		
"Auf Sommerfrische" (On Holiday) (10)	175 - 200	200 - 250
KK, Munich		
"Eisblumen" (Ice Flowers) (10) (Uns.)	175 - 200	200 - 250
Theo. Stroefer, Nürnberg		
"Coeur Dame" (Heart Lady) (10) (Uns.)	100 - 125	125 - 150
Anonymous (Signed R.)		
"Wiener Typen" (Viennese types) (12)	175 - 200	200 - 250

THE GOLDEN AGE

Anonymous		
"All Heil" (Cyclists) (10)	175 - 200	200 - 250
"Au Serail" (In the Harem) (6)	175 - 200	200 - 250
"Christmas" signed w/Paris Ser. 184 (6)	75 - 100	100 - 125
Santa Claus	300 - 350	350 - 400
"Delighted Girls" (4)	400 - 450	450 - 500
"Erika" Heads on Flowers background (6)	100 - 125	125 - 150
"Fruits Douces" (Sweet Fruits) (6)	100 - 125	125 - 150
Also by ESW (Emil Storch, Wien)	100 - 125	125 - 150
"Girls and Eggs" Horizontal (1)	250 - 300	300 - 350
"Girls' Head in Circle, white b.g." (6)	100 - 125	125 - 150
"Hinter den Coulissen"		
(Behind Scenes) (10)	150 - 175	175 - 200
"Portraits of Girls" Gray Border (6)	150 - 175	175 - 200
"Portraits of Viennese Ladies" (6)	100 - 125	125 - 150
E. Arenz, Wien		
"Leda & the Swan" (10)	100 - 125	125 - 150
"Santoy" (Japanese Life) (6)	75 - 100	100 - 125
B.K.W.I. (Bruder Kohn, Wien)		
"Bijoux" (Jewels) Emb. Heads **538** (6)	75 - 100	100 - 125
"Christmas Pictures" Ser. 2049 (10)	150 - 175	175 - 200
J. Beagles & Co.		
"Girls Holding Bunnies" (3)	300 - 325	325 - 350
"COCK" in small shield		
"Girls in Car on White b.g." 4325 (1)	275 - 300	300 - 350
"The Christmas Girls" Ser. 4329 (5)	200 - 225	225 - 250
B. Dondorf, Frankfurt (BD)		
Series 109 "Girls and Eggs, Vertical" (6)	150 - 175	175 - 200
H.M. & Co.		
"Christmas, signed w/Paris" 184 (6)	80 - 100	100 - 125
Santa Claus	300 - 350	350 - 400
K. & B. D.		
"Rauchende Damen" (Women		
Smoking) **Series 4501** (6)	150 - 175	175 - 200
MMP in circle		
Die-cut Hold-to-Light (5)	800 - 900	900 - 1000
"Vitraux d'Art (Stained Gl. Windows) (5)	400 - 450	450 - 500

Raphael Kirchner, E. Storch, Wien
"Vieux Temps ...III" – D.19

Raphael Kirchner, E. Storch, Wien
"Vieux Temps...V" – D.19

Also R. Tuck Series 3051	400 - 450	450 - 500
Meissner & Buch, Leipzig		
"Modern Madchen" Series 1129		
(Modern girls) (6)	100 - 125	125 - 150
M. Munk, Vienna		
"Bronzes d 'Art (Emb.) (10)	100 - 125	125 - 150
"Fleur Au Pied" (10)	125 - 150	150 - 175
"Geisha" Series (10)	65 - 75	75 - 100
"Girls and Eggs" (5) (Uns.)	65 - 75	75 - 100
"Girls with flowers at feet" (10)	150 - 175	175 - 200
"Girls' faces in circle, violet b.g." (10)	150 - 175	175 - 200
Girls with turquoise surrounds (10)	150 - 175	175 - 200
Girls with beige border, Ser. 113 (10)	100 - 125	125 - 150
Girls w/olive green surrounds (10)	150 - 175	175 - 200
Girls with purple surrounds (10)	150 - 175	175 - 200
"Girls' faces, red border" Ser. 115 (10)	200 - 225	225 - 250
"Love Thoughts" (10)	200 - 225	225 - 250
"Maid of Athens" Series 73 (9)	50 - 75	75 - 100
"Mikado" Series (6)	65 - 75	75 - 100
"Les Cigarettes Du Monde" (6)	125 - 150	150 - 175
"La Favorite" (6)	125 - 150	150 - 175
Pascalis, Moss & Co.		
"Girls and Eggs" Yellow signature (6)	100 - 125	125 - 150
"Marionette" Series 4140 (6)	75 - 100	100 - 125
Also by **E. Storch & H.M. & Co.**	75 - 100	100 - 125
"Leda & the Swan" (10) Unsigned	150 - 175	175 - 200
Also by **E. Arnenz, Wien**		

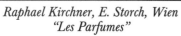

Raphael Kirchner, E. Storch, Wien
"Les Parfumes"

Raphael Kirchner, Marque L-E, No. 22
"Le Gui de Paris"

Edgar Schmidt, Dresden
"Girls Between Green & Brown Borders"

Series 350 (6)	100 - 125	125 - 150

Raphael Tuck

"Flashing Motorists" Series 2709 (6)	100 - 125	125 - 150
"Girls Heads-Christmas Foliage b.g."		
Christmas C.316	400 - 450	450 - 500
"Girls & Pig Heads" Series 1902 (3) B&W	50 - 75	75 - 100
"Girls Surrounded by Hearts, Stars, Etc."		
Series 1190 (B&W) (3)	100 - 125	125 - 150
"Salome" (6) Series 2555 (6)	75 - 100	100 - 125
"Les Sylphides" Series 285 (6)	100 - 125	125 - 150

Raphael Tuck, Paris

"Les Ephemeres" (Mayflies) 375 (6)	200 - 225	225 - 250
Also by **R. Tuck** Series 2642	200 - 225	225 - 250
"Farfadets" (Elves) 286 (6) Sculptures	100 - 125	125 - 150
"Osterautomobil" (Easter autos) 777 (6)	100 - 125	125 - 150
"Reveries" (Dreams) (2)	400 - 450	450 - 500
"Salome" Series 241 (6)	75 - 100	100 - 125
"Sylphides" Series 285 (6)	100 - 125	125 - 150

A. Sockl, Wien

"All Heil" (Bicycle Girls) (10)	200 - 225	225 - 250
"Demi Vierge" (6)	100 - 125	125 - 150

Christoph Reisser's Söhne, Wien

"Couples Between Red Borders" (6)	150 - 175	175 - 200
"Enfants de la Mer" (10)	100 - 125	125 - 150
"Erika" Series 1123 (6)	150 - 175	175 - 200

E. Storch, Wien

"Les Cigarettes du Monde" (Cigarettes from the world) (6)	100 - 125	125 - 150
"La Favorite" (The Favorite) (6)	100 - 125	125 - 150
"Fables" (6)	75 - 100	100 - 125
"Femmes Soleil" (Women in the Sun) (6)	100 - 125	125 - 150
"Fruits Doux" (Sweet Fruits) (6)	100 - 125	125 - 150
"Geisha" Series (10)	50 - 75	75 - 100
"Les Parfumes" (Perfumes) (6)	100 - 125	125 - 150
"Marionettes" (Girls with puppets) (6)	100 - 125	125 - 150
"Mikado" (Japanese Girls) (6)	75 - 100	100 - 125
"Red & White Figures," Small Shields (6)	250 - 300	300 - 350
"Vieux Temps" (Old Times) (6)	150 - 175	175 - 200

Theo. Stroefer, Nürnberg **(T.S.N.)**

"Fleurs d'Amour (Love Flowers) 332 (6)	150 - 175	175 - 200
"Fröliche Ostern" (Happy Easter) 222 (6)	100 - 125	125 - 150
"Girls, Good Luck Charms" 235 (10)	100 - 125	125 - 150
"Girls dominating landscape" 427 (6)	200 - 225	225 - 250
"Greek Girls" Series 71 (16)	50 - 75	75 - 100
"Greek Vierges" Series 99 (12)	100 - 125	125 - 150
"Legendes" Series 311 (6)	150 - 175	175 - 200
"Moderne Madchen" Series 1129 (6)	125 - 150	150 - 175
"Noel!" Series 184 (Christmas) (6)	75 - 100	100 - 125
"Noel!" Series 197 (Christmas) (6)	150 - 175	175 - 200
"Roma" Series 220 (10)	100 - 125	125 - 150
Santa	300 - 350	350 - 400

GLAMOUR AGE

Photographic Postcards

"Kirchner's Erotic Pictures" (B&W + Brown) Signed & Unsigned (20) Some P/**LP**	150 - 175	175 - 200
Lustigen Blatter		
"In den Karten steht's geschrieben" (1)	275 - 300	300 - 350
Novitas, Berlin "Vain Girls" (3)	100 - 125	125 - 150
Marque L-E		
"Pour le Droit et la Libertie"	100 - 125	125 - 150
"For Rights & Freedom" (1)	75 - 100	100 - 125
Puzzle "Pour le Droit et la Libertie" (8)	75 - 100	100 - 125
"Les Peches Capitaux" (7 Deadly Sins) (7)	50 - 60	60 - 75
L-E Glamour Series (32)		
Various 9 - 311	50 - 60	60 - 75
Bruton Galleries		
Delta "Kirchner Girls" (24)	50 - 60	60 - 75
Alphasia Pub. Co. (12)	50 - 60	60 - 75
Reinthal & Newman, N.Y.		
"The Pierrot's Loves" 990-999 (10)	75 - 100	100 - 125

ADVERTISING, ETC.

"Bellage des 'Sect'" (2)	150 - 175	175 - 200
"Byrrh" Tonic (1)	500 - 600	600 - 700
"Gruss von der Hochzeit" (Wedding Wish) (2)	275 - 300	300 - 350
"Int. Exhibition of Paris, 1900" (1)	800 - 900	900 - 1000

"Les Graces" (The Graces) (1)	100 - 125	125 - 150
"Robert Schlesinger, Wien" Viennese		
Footwear Emporium (1)	100 - 125	125 - 150
S.P. (English Silver Ad) (B&W) (Uns.)	100 - 125	125 - 150
"Sirene" Real Photo		
Salon 1904 (1)	100 - 125	125 - 150
"Streeter"		
Streeter & Co. Jewellers (1)	200 - 225	225 - 250
"Union Cartophile Universelle"	350 - 400	400 - 500
KLEE, PAUL See Bauhaus Listing		
KLIMES, FR. (PO)	8 - 10	10 - 15
KNOEFEL		
Novitas Illumination Series		
Series 668 Nudes (4)	20 - 25	25 - 30
Series 20888 Mother/Baby (6)	10 - 12	12 - 15
Series 15661 Ladies/Lamps (6)	15 - 18	18 - 22
Series 15662 With Japanese Lantern (6)	15 - 20	20 - 25
Other Illuminated	12 - 15	15 - 18
M. Munk Illumination		
Series 1992 Japanese Lanterns	15 - 20	20 - 25
KNOX, S. (US)	8 - 10	10 - 12
KÖHLER, MELA (AUS) (See Children Section) *		
Art Nouveau/Art Deco/Fashion		
B.K.W.I. (Bruder Kohn, Wien)		
Series 131 (6) Ladies Fashion	80 - 100	100 - 125
Series 143 (6) Ladies Fashion	80 - 100	100 - 125
Tennis	100 - 125	125 - 150
Series 187 (6) Women Sports	100 - 125	125 - 150
Series 178, 187, 188 (6) Fashionable ladies	80 - 100	100 - 120
Series 201 (6) Fashionable ladies & children	80 - 100	100 - 120
Series 271 (6) Women's Winter Sports	100 - 125	125 - 140
Series 292 (6) Ladies at home	70 - 80	80 - 90
Series 349, 384 (6) Wonderfully dressed ladies	80 - 90	90 - 100
Series 418 (6) Tropical ladies	80 - 90	90 - 100
Series 423 (4) Dance Series		
1 "Blumentanz"	70 - 80	80 - 90
2 "Der Tanz mit den Tulpen"	70 - 80	80 - 90
3 "Schleiertanz"	70 - 80	80 - 90
4 "Der Sprung Zurch die Blumenkette"	70 - 80	80 - 90
Series 477 (6) Ladies w/Exotic Birds	80 - 90	90 - 110
Series 481, 641 (6) Fashionable Hats	80 - 100	100 - 120
Series 620 (6) Fashionable Ladies	80 - 100	100 - 120
Series 621 (6) Fashionable Ladies/Pets	90 - 110	110 - 130
Series 843 (6) Dancers, (Tango, etc.)	100 - 125	125 - 150
Series 641 (6) Ladies with flower bouquets	80 - 100	100 - 110
Series 3089 (6) Christmas Ladies	80 - 100	100 - 120
Series 3090 (6) Christmas, wallpaper b.g.	100 - 125	125 - 150
Series 3121, 3142 (6) Christmas Ladies	75 - 85	85 - 100
Meissner & Buch		
Series 2816		
Fantasy Flower Ladies (6)	110 - 120	120 - 135
M. Munk, Vienne		
Series 1037 (6)	70 - 80	80 - 90
Series 1118 (6)	70 - 80	80 - 90

Mela Köhler, B.K.W.I., 178-1
No Caption

Mela Köhler, B.K.W.I., 271-2
No Caption

Mela Köhler, B.K.W.I., 843-2
"Tango"

Mela Köhler, B.K.W.I., 3089-4
"Frohliche Weihnachten!"

Series 1188 (6) Ladies at leisure, tea, etc.	70 - 80	80 - 90
After 1920	40 - 50	50 - 60
Wenau "Brabant"		
1862 Two girls with time on their hands	80 - 90	90 - 110
1865 Lady with fan and flower bouquet	80 - 90	90 - 110
1867 Lady with little bird	80 - 90	90 - 110
* See Wiener Werkstätte Section		
KOISTER (FR) French Glamour		
Delta Series 71	15 - 20	20 - 25
KOKOSCHKA, OSKAR (AUS) See Wiener Werkstätte		
KONOPA, RUDOLF (AUS) Art Nouveau		
Philipp & Kramer	50 - 70	70 - 90
KOPAL Art Nouveau	30 - 35	35 - 40
KOSA (AUS) Art Nouveau	150 - 165	165 - 175
KOSEL, H.C.		
B.K.W.I. Series 181	10 - 12	12 - 15
KOTAS, V.	6 - 8	8 - 10
KOVIES, K. Art Deco		
D.A.G.		
Series 474-1, 474-3, 474-4 (Skating)	12 - 15	15 - 20
KRATKI, F.	5 - 6	6 - 8
KRAUSZ, J.V. (AUS)	8 - 10	10 - 12
KRENEK, CARL (AUS) See Wiener Werkstätte		
KRENNES, H. (PO)	8 - 10	10 - 15
KUANI, C. COLAN Art Deco		
Ultra - Series 2166 Shoulders (6)	10 - 12	12 - 15
KUCHINKA, JAN (CZ)		
Praha-Podol 150 Erotic Series	25 - 30	30 - 35
H. Co. Semi-Nudes	30 - 35	35 - 40
KUDERNY, F. (AUS)		
M. Munk, Vienna		
Series 606, 634 (6)	12 - 15	15 - 20
Series 841 Semi-Nudes	15 - 20	20 - 25
Series 835 Tiny Men	15 - 18	18 - 22
KULAS, J.V. (GER) Art Nouveau	35 - 40	40 - 45
KUNZLI, MAX	6 - 8	8 - 10
KURT, E. MAISON Art Deco		
P.F.B. (in Diamond)		
Fantasy Doll Series	15 - 20	20 - 25
Fantasy Dance Series (Lesbian Types)	30 - 35	35 - 40
Japanese Series	12 - 15	15 - 18
KUTEW, CHRISTO (PO)	8 - 10	10 - 12
LAFUGIE Series 45	15 - 18	18 - 22
LAMASURE, EDWIN (US)		
Osborne Calendar Co.		
Year 1909 Beautiful Women	15 - 18	18 - 26
LAPORTE (FR) Glamour	10 - 12	12 - 15
LARCOMBE, ETHEL Art Nouveau	25 - 30	30 - 35
LARRONI (IT) Art Deco		
S.W.S.B. Series 6733 Lovers Kissing (6)	8 - 10	10 - 12
LASKOFF, F. (PO) Art Nouveau		
Ricordi		
Ladies Series	75 - 85	85 - 100
LASALLE, JEAN	5 - 8	8 - 10

LAURENS, P.A. (CZ)	8 - 10	10 - 12
LAUDA, RICHARD (DEN) Art Nouveau	60 - 65	65 - 70
LAWRENCE, F. (US)		
Carlton Pub. Co. Series 707 (6)	8 - 10	10 - 12
M.S.i.B. Sporting Series	10 - 15	15 - 18
LE ANDRE, CHARLES (FR)		
"Cocorico" Series	400 - 450	450 - 500
"Collection des Cent" No. 7	200 - 225	225 - 250
"Collection Job" No. 3	60 - 70	70 - 85
LEARNED	5 - 6	8 - 10
LEBISCH, FRANZ (AUS) See Wiener Werkstätte		
LE DUCIS, A. (IT)		
Rev. Stampa		
Series 2039 High Fashion (6)	10 - 15	15 - 18
LeDUEI	10 - 12	12 - 15
LEETE, ALFRED (GB) Romantic	8 - 10	10 - 12
LEFLER, H. (AUS) Romantic couples	6 - 8	8 - 10
LEINWEBER, R. (GER)	6 - 8	8 - 10
LELEE, L. (FR) Art Nouveau		
Collection des Cent.	90 - 100	100 - 125
Other Ladies	15 - 20	20 - 25
LE MONNIER, HENRY (FR) Glamour	25 - 30	30 - 40
LE MUNYAN, PEARLE FIDLER (See Pearle Fidler)		
LENDECKE, OTTO (PO) See Wiener Werkstätte		
LENG, MAX Art Nouveau	20 - 30	30 - 40
LEONEM (FR) French Glamour		
Degami		
Series 1047 Art Deco	22 - 25	25 - 28
Meissner & Buch Series 219	18 - 20	20 - 25
LENZ, M. (AUS) Art Nouveau	40 - 50	50 - 60
LEONNEC, G. (FR) French Glamour	15 - 20	20 - 30
LESKER, H. Art Deco	8 - 10	10 - 12
LESSIEUX, LOUIS (FR) Art Nouveau	35 - 40	40 - 45
Diamonds, Emeralds, etc. Series	25 - 30	30 - 35
LEVIN, MEYER (USA) See Mutoscope Pin-ups		
LHUER, VICTOR	15 - 18	18 - 22
LIBERTS, LUDOLFS (LAT)		
Graphic Arts of Ladies & Costumes		
"Pas des Deux" Series	20 - 25	25 - 30
"Pas des fleures" Series	20 - 25	25 - 30
"Samsons un Dalila" Series	20 - 25	25 - 30
Kostims "Blondai" Opera "Begsan no Seraja"	25 - 30	30 - 35
Kostims baletam "Judite"	20 - 25	25 - 30
Kostims Opera "Salinieki"	20 - 25	25 - 30
LIKARZ-STRAUSS, MARIA (AUS)		
See Wiener Werkstätte		
LINDSELL, L.	8 - 10	10 - 12
LIST, WILHELM (AUS) Art Nouveau		
B.K.W.I.		
Series 130 (6)	70 - 80	80 - 100
Series 1339 (6)	40 - 50	50 - 60
LIVEMONT, P. (BEL) Art Nouveau	200 - 250	250 - 350
LLOYD, T.	4 - 6	6 - 8

Chilton Longley, A. G. & Co.
Series 845-3

Chilton Longley, A. G. & Co.
Series 845-4

LOFFLER, B. (AUS) Art Nouveau		
Wiener Werkstätte	200 - 250	250 - 300
LONGLEY, CHILTON (GB) Art Deco		
A.G. & Co. Ltd.		
Series 422 (6	30 - 35	35 - 40
Series 845 (6)	40 - 50	50 - 75
Series 90 Hats (6)	15 - 18	18 - 22
LORELEY Art Deco	12 - 15	15 - 20
LORENZI, FACIO (IT)	15 - 18	18 - 22
LÖW, FRITZI (AU) **See Wiener Werkstätte**		
LUCIEL Glamour	10 - 12	12 - 15
LUDOVICI, ANTHONY (IT))	12 - 15	15 - 20
LUDSON Series 90 Hats (6)	10 - 12	12 - 14
LYETT Fashion and Glamour	10 - 12	12 - 15
M.M.S.	5 - 6	6 - 8
MSM		
Meissner & Buch	15 - 18	18 - 22
MACDONALD, A. K. (GB) Art Nouveau	40 - 50	50 - 60
MAGRINI, A. (IT) Glamour	12 - 15	15 - 20
MAGRITTE, RENE (BEL)		
Surrealistic Real Photo-types (Cont. size)		
15 "La Solution de Rebus" (1937)	80 - 90	90 - 100
3531 "Der Sommer" (1938)	80 - 90	90 - 100
MAILICK, A. (GER) (See Santas, Angels, Animals)		
G.B.D.		
Series 4244 (6)		
"Am See"	15 - 18	18 - 22

A. Mailick, G.B.D., Series 4244/4
"Am See"

G. Malugani, Rev. Stampa
Series 77, No Caption

Ladies	10 - 12	12 - 15
MAIA (IT)		
Ballerini & Fratini		
Series 407 (6) **Art Deco**	20 - 25	25 - 30
Series 425 6) **Art Deco**	15 - 20	20 - 25
MAISON-KURT, E. (GER) Glamour	10 - 12	12 - 15
MALUGANI, G. (IT)		
Rev. Stampa		
Fashion and Glamour	15 - 18	18 - 22
Series 77	18 - 22	22 - 26
Series 138 (6) Beauties in the Boudoir	20 - 25	25 - 30
Series 148 (6) Sports	12 - 15	15 - 18
4 Tennis	18 - 22	22 - 26
Golf	25 - 30	30 - 40
MANASSE, A. (AUS)	5 - 6	6 - 8
MANNING, FREDERICK S. (US)		
Rev. Stampa		
Series 116 (6) Heads/Hats	12 - 15	15 - 20
Series 117 (6) Portraits	9 - 12	12 - 16
Series 327 (6) Glamour Studies	9 - 12	12 - 16
Others	6 - 8	8 - 10
MANNING, G.		
P.A.R. Series 144 Coat-Hat (6)	10 - 14	14 - 16
MANNING, REG (US)	8 - 10	10 - 12
MG or MANNI GROSZE (GER) (Silhouettes)	12 - 15	15 - 18
Nudes	15 - 20	20 - 26
Others	12 - 15	15 - 18

MANUEL, HENRI (FR) French Glamour

Series 51, 55	20 - 25	25 - 30

MANSELL, VIVIAN (GB)

"National Ladies" Series	10 - 12	12 - 15
Others	8 - 10	10 - 15

MARBACH, MITZI (AUS) (Art Deco)
B.K.W.I.

Series 3091 "Fröhliche Weihnachten!" (6)	25 - 30	30 - 40

MARCO, M.

Raphael Tuck, Series 2763 (Asti-type)	10 - 12	12 - 15

MARCOS JAN (IT)
Anonymous

Lady/Bubbles Fantasy	20 - 25	25 - 28
Series 891 (6) Heads	15 - 18	18 - 22
Others	12 - 15	15 - 20

MARECHAUK, C.

	6 - 8	8 - 10

MARS (FR) (Undb)

Anonymous Bathing Girls (4)	20 - 25	25 - 28

MARSHEL, HARRY

Djer-Kiss Rouge	12 - 15	15 - 18

MARTIN-KAVEL
Lapina

Series 5027-5036	10 - 12	12 - 15
Lapina Nudes	12 - 15	15 - 20

MARTINEAU, ALICE

	6 - 8	8 - 10

MASTROAINI, D. (Italy)

Ladies	8 - 10	10 - 12

MATALONI, G. (Italy) Art Nouveau (Japanese) | 25 - 30 | 30 - 35

MAUZAN, L. A. (Italy) Art Deco & Glamour
Dell, Anna & Gasparini; Rev. Stampa

Series 386, 394 Lovers - Kissing (6)	10 - 12	12 - 15
Series 462, 498 Lovers-by-the-Sea (6)	10 - 12	12 - 15
Series 343, 424 Couples (6)	10 - 12	12 - 15
Series 248 Roman "Lovers" (6)	12 - 14	14 - 16
Series 42 Sport (6)	15 - 18	18 - 22
Tennis	20 - 25	25 - 28
Golf	30 - 35	35 - 45
Series 106, 301, 438 (6)	10 - 12	12 - 15
Series 279, 297 Heads - Green Ring (6)	20 - 22	22 - 25
Series 145, 252 Hat & Scarf (6)	15 - 18	18 - 22
Series 46, 230 Fashion (6)	15 - 18	18 - 22
Series 83 Little Men	12 - 15	15 - 18
Series 250, 174 Walk, Traveling (6)	20 - 22	22 - 25
Series 247, 298 Beauties (6)	20 - 22	22 - 26
Series 53 Man Sits on Giant Shoes (6)	10 - 12	12 - 15
Series 43, 235 Shoulders Up (6)	15 - 18	18 - 22
Series 321, 343, 414 Fashion (6)	15 - 18	18 - 22
Series 8, 14, 80 High Fashion (6)	15 - 20	20 - 25
Series 201, 202, 2050 Walking (6)	10 - 12	12 - 15
Series 126 Waist-Up, in Chair (6)	18 - 22	22 - 25
Series 2, 10 With Cupid (6)	12 - 15	15 - 20
Tennis	20 - 25	25 - 28
Golf	30 - 35	35 - 45
Erotic/Semi-Nudes	22 - 25	25 - 30

Degami
Series 106, 201 (6)	15 - 18	18 - 22
Series 250 (6) Lingerie	15 - 20	20 - 25

G.B.T.
Series 3 (6) Nudes-semi nudes with Cupid	22 - 25	25 - 30

Rev. Stampa – Ladies & Dogs
Ladies & Dogs Series 316, 453, 491 (6)	15 - 20	20 - 25

Ladies & Horses
Series 383 (6)	15 - 20	20 - 25

MAYER, LOU (US)

K. Co., Inc.
207 "Vanity Fair"	10 - 12	12 - 15

Reinthal & Newman
400, 500 Series	8 - 10	10 - 12
Fantasy Series (6) 878-883		
878 "The Pearl in the Oyster"	15 - 18	18 - 22
880 "Pond Lilies"	15 - 18	18 - 22
881 "Grape Shot"	15 - 18	18 - 22
882 "Bric-a-Brac"	15 - 18	18 - 22
883 "Here's Looking at You"	15 - 18	18 - 22
Ullman Mfg. Co. Pretty Girl Series	8 - 10	10 - 12
M.C. Beautiful Fashions	15 - 18	18 - 25
McFALL, J.V. (US)	4 - 5	5 - 8
McLELLAN, CHAS. A. (US)	4 - 5	5 - 8

McMEIN, NEYSA (US)
Novitas Series 15672 Head Studies (6)	12 - 15	15 - 18
Publisher at Polyphot (Finland)	12 - 15	15 - 20
Osh Kosh Pennant Girls (6)	10 - 12	12 - 15

MELASSO
Series 125 Hats (6)	12 - 15	15 - 18
MERCER, JOYCE (GB) Art Nouveau	15 - 18	18 - 22

MESCHINI, GIOVANNI (IT) Art Deco

G.P.M.
Series 113 High Fur Collars, Hats (6)	40 - 45	45 - 55
Series "Ars Nova"	35 - 40	40 - 50
"Ultra" Series		
Series 2197 (Uns) Ladies/Dogs	40 - 45	45 - 55

Ditta A. Guarneri, Milano
Series 2409 Lovers	30 - 35	35 - 45
Series 2411 Ladies/Dogs	40 - 50	50 - 60
Series 2443 Lovers Uns)	30 - 35	35 - 45
Series 2448 (Uns) Ladies/Dogs	40 - 50	50 - 60
Ladies	30 - 35	35 - 45
Harlequins/Pierrot	40 - 45	45 - 50
Lovers	30 - 35	35 - 40
Series 48 Non-Deco Ladies	25 - 30	30 - 35
MCA (Ars Nova) Uns.	35 - 40	40 - 45
MERTZANOFF, ARIS (RUS)	10 - 12	12 - 15

METLOKOVITZ, LEOPOLDO or LM (IT)
Art Nouveau Works	50 - 75	75 - 100
Art Deco	20 - 25	25 - 30
Ladies/Fashion	10 - 12	12 - 14
Bathing Beauties	10 - 12	12 - 15

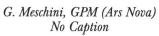

G. Meschini, GPM (Ars Nova)
No Caption

Suzanne Meunier, L-E, Paris
Series 138, "Le Bain de la Parisienne"

Pierrot	25 - 28	28 - 32
Couples	8 - 10	10 - 12
MEUNIER, GEORGES (FR)		
Cinos and Collection des Cent	150 - 200	200 - 250
MEUNIER, HENRI (Belgium) Art Nouveau		
"Four Seasons" (4)	60 - 70	70 - 80
"Les Grandes Femmes" (12)	200 - 250	250 - 300
"Inspiration"	100 - 110	110 - 120
"Zodiac" (12)	100 - 125	125 - 150
MEUNIER, SUZANNE (FR) French Glamour		
Marque L-E		
No. 500-506	20 - 25	25 - 30
Series 11, 20, 22	18 - 22	22 - 26
Series 40 Semi-nude-Wild animals	32 - 35	35 - 40
Series 26, 42, 77	22 - 25	25 - 35
Series 29, 32, 35	20 - 25	25 - 30
Series 24, 52, 56, 74, 99	18 - 22	22 - 26
Series 60, 64, 69, 96, 98, 99, 138	25 - 30	30 - 35
Series 62 Sports	25 - 30	30 - 35
Tennis	30 - 35	35 - 40
Series 79 Ladies wearing hats	20 - 25	25 - 28
Series 96 (Smoking Ladies)	32 - 35	35 - 40
Delta		
Series 90	20 - 22	22 - 26
MIGNOT, VICTOR (BEL) Art Nouveau	30 - 35	35 - 40
MIKI (FR) Art Deco	10 - 12	12 - 15
MILLER, MARION (US)	3 - 4	4 - 6

M. Milliere, L-E, Paris, Series 37-2   *C. Monestier, Rev. Stampa*
"Les Plaisirs permis"   *Series 7512, No Caption*

MILLIERE, MAURICE (FR) French Glamour

L-E, Paris

Series 6, 21, 30	18 - 22	22 - 28
Series 34, 54, 65	25 - 30	30 - 35
Series 37 "Les Plaisirs permis" Soap Bubbles	25 - 30	30 - 35

MITCHELL, SADIE WENDELL (US)

W.G. McFarlane

Fantasy Cupid Series	10 - 12	12 - 15
Valentine Series	8 - 10	10 - 12

"Troilene"   American Girl Series (6)

"The Country Club Girl"	12 - 15	15 - 20
"The Automobile Girl"	10 - 12	12 - 15
"The Summer Girl"	10 - 12	12 - 15
"The Yachting Girl"	10 - 12	12 - 15
"The Society Girl"	10 - 12	12 - 15
"The Bathing Girl"	10 - 12	12 - 15

German-American Art

Christmas & Easter Series	5 - 8	8 - 10

MOLINA, ROBERTO

"Diabolo" Series	10 - 12	12 - 15

MONESTIER, C. (IT) Art Deco

E. G. Falci

Series 27 Girl-Mask, Pierrot	15 - 18	18 - 22
Series 830 Hats (6)	12 - 15	15 - 20
Others	8 - 10	10 - 12

Rev. Stampa

Series S-7512 (6) Busts of Ladies	12 - 15	15 - 20

Koloman Moser, Philipp & Kramer, Series III – "Lady and the Tulips"

Ladies & Dogs Series 36 (6)	12 - 15	15 - 20
MONIER, MAGGY	15 - 18	18 - 22
MONTEDORO (IT) Art Deco		
Rev. Stampa		
Series A (6)	45 - 55	55 - 65
Series B (6)	65 - 70	70 - 75
MORAN, LEON (US) Glamour	5 - 6	6 - 9
MORIN, LOUIS (FR)		
Collection des Cent No. 2b "Volupte"	300 - 325	325 - 350
MOSER, KOLOMAN (AUS) Art Nouveau		
Ackerman	225 - 250	250 - 275
Gerlach & Schenk "Ver Sacum"	1000 - 1500	1500 - 2500
Philipp & Kramer		
Series I - V	200 - 250	250 - 350
MOSTYN, MARJORIE (GB)		
Raphael Tuck		
Series 108 Jewel Girls	12 - 15	15 - 20
Series 11 "Fair of Feature"	12 - 15	15 - 18
Water Color Series 2397 "A Maiden Fair"	10 - 12	12 - 15
MOUTON, Georges (FR)		
Erotic	12 - 15	15 - 18
Others	20 - 25	25 - 30
MOZERT, ZOE (US) See Mutoscope Pin-ups		
MUCHA, ALPHONSE (CZ)		
French Issues		
Home Decor, 1894		
Store ad – extremely rare; no recorded sales.		
Collection Cinos, 1898		
Waverley Cycles Advertising Bicycles		
Last recorded sale in 1998 - around $7,500.		
"Gismonda"	500 - 550	550 - 600

"Samaritaine,"	500 - 550	550 - 600
"La Dame aux Camélias"	500 - 550	550 - 600
"Lorenzaccio"	650 - 700	700 - 750
Cocorico, 1900		
Blue with rooster; horizontal.	650 - 700	700 - 750
Moet et Chandon, 1900		
Menu designs (10)	250 - 300	300 - 350
F. Champenois		
"Cartes Postales Artistiques"		
First Series (C1-12), 1898		
The Seasons (4)	125 - 150	150 - 200
The Flowers (4)	125 - 150	150 - 200
The Ages of Man (4)	200 - 250	250 - 300
Second Series (C13-24), 1899		
Byzantines (2)	125 - 150	150 - 200
The Seasons (4)	125 - 150	150 - 200
The Arts (4)	175 - 200	200 - 225
Zodiac	250 - 300	300 - 350
Rêverie	250 - 300	300 - 350
Third Series (C25-36), 1900	250 - 300	300 - 350
Vignettes (3)	250 - 300	300 - 350
"Salomé"	250 - 300	300 - 350
"L'aube" (Dawn), "Crepuscule" (Dusk)	350 - 400	400 - 450
"Le primevère" (Primrose)	350 - 400	400 - 450
"La Plume" (Quill)	350 - 400	400 - 450
Seasons, vertical (4)	200 - 250	250 - 300
Fourth Series (37-48), 1900	200 - 250	250 - 300
The Months of the Year (12)	150 - 175	175 - 200
Fifth Series (49-60), circa 1901	150 - 175	175 - 200
Sarah Bernhardt - "La Plume"	500 - 525	525 - 550
Austro-Hungarian Benefit Society	550 - 600	600 - 650
Cocorico (with Rooster, vertical)	500 - 550	550 - 600
Cocorico (lady in rectangle)	250 - 275	275 - 300
Cocorico (lady in oval)	250 - 275	275 - 300
Menu for a Banquet	400 - 450	450 - 500
Menus (4)	225 - 250	250 - 300
Design for a Fan	475 - 500	500 - 525
Paris 1900 Exposition	400 - 450	450 - 500
Sixth Series (C61-72), circa 1901	400 - 450	450 - 500
Design for a Menu	325 - 350	350 - 375

Alphonse Mucha, F. Champenois
"Byzantine Head – Blonde"

Alphonse Mucha, F. Champenois
"Byzantine Head – Brunette"

Alphonse Mucha, Collection des Cent, 11B
"Austro-Hungarian Benevolent Society"

Alphonse Mucha, F. Champenois
"Topaz"

Alphonse Mucha, F. Champenois, Paris, "The Water Lilly"
"Souvenir de la Belle Jardiniere – Succursale de Bordeaux"

Cover for the Champenois Catalog	350 - 375	375 - 400
"Papeterie" (Stationery)	325 - 350	350 - 375
Design for a Program (lady with harp)	350 - 375	375 - 400

"Les Moments de la Journée"		
(Times of the Day) (4)	250 - 300	300 - 350
"Printemps" (Spring)	325 - 350	350 - 375
Lady with a Quill	500 - 550	550 - 600
"Nénuphar" (Water Lily)	400 - 450	450 - 500
"Fleur de cerisier" (Cherry Blossom)	400 - 450	450 - 500
Seventh Series (C73-84), circa 1902	400 - 450	450 - 500
Autumn	500 - 550	550 - 600
Lygie	450 - 500	500 - 550
Heather, Sea Holly	450 - 500	500 - 550
Ivy, Laurel	500 - 550	550 - 600
Gemstones (4)	500 - 550	550 - 600
Flowers	650 - 750	750 - 850
Fruits	650 - 750	750 - 850
Collection des Cent., 1901		
No. 11a Peasant Woman	1500 - 2000	2000 - 2500
No. 11b Austro-Hungarian Benevolent		
Society	900 - 1000	1000 - 1200
Lygie, 1901		
B&W – Same design as Champenois Series 7.	750 - 850	850 - 950
La Revue du Bien, circa 1903		
Photographic process	900 - 1000	1000 - 1200
Printed process	900 - 1000	1000 - 1200
Lefèvre-Utile, 1904		
Biscuit advertisement	900 - 1000	1000 - 1200
Collection JOB (Cigarette Papers)		
"Femme Blonde"		
1903, horiz., plant motif background	350 - 375	375 - 400
1905, horiz., "Collection JOB" inscription	200 - 250	250 - 300
1908, horiz., "Bureau de Londres" inscript.	500 - 550	550 - 600
1911, horiz., "Collection JOB,		
Cigarettes JOB" inscription	400 - 450	450 - 500
1914, vertical	800 - 900	900 - 1000
"Femme Brune"		
1905, horiz., "Collection JOB" inscription	200 - 250	250 - 300
1911, horiz., "Collection JOB,		
Cigarettes JOB" inscription	400 - 450	450 - 500
1915, vertical	800 - 900	900 - 1000
Vin Mariani, 1910	1000 - 1200	1200 - 1400
Cognac Bisquit, circa 1908		
Horizontal, color	800 - 900	900 - 1000
(w/cognac manufacturers adv. imprint; one		
recorded sale of $4,100 in 1993.) Also		
comes in B/W in both vertical & horizontal		
format. No recorded sales. Extremely rare.		
Rudolf Friml		
Black & White	1000 - 1200	1200 - 1400
Color	1200 - 1500	1500 - 2000
U.S. Issues		
Joan of Arc (Maude Adams) by Blanchard		
Warner's Rust-Proof Corsets, 1909		
No margin imprint	1000 - 1200	1200 - 1400
Three text paragraph & 4 text in margin	750 - 850	850 - 1000

Sarah Bernhardt American Tour
Four designs: "Gismonda," "Lorenzaccio," "Harriet," and "La Samartine." All in single color but issued in different color combinations and with repertories for three different tours: 1905-6, 1910, and 1916-1917. Extremely rare; prices estimated at $10,000-20,000 each.

Czechoslovakian Issues

Advertisements

Dvacàtý Vek (20th Century), 1902		
magazine cover	250 - 300	300 - 350
Slavia, 1909, insurance company		
Large Border	200 - 250	250 - 300
Small Border	250 - 300	300 - 3350
Krinogen, 1928, herbal hair preservative	400 - 450	450 - 500
The Kiss of Springtime, Fine Arts Society		
of Prague	250 - 300	300 - 350
Vopalka Textiles, attributed.		

Benefit Societies

The Moravian Teachers' Choir, 1911	200 - 250	250 - 300
Bohemian Heart Charity, 1912	250 - 300	300 - 350
Foundation for the Schools of Brno, circa 1912	350 - 400	400 - 450
Kamensky Society, 1920	250 - 300	300 - 350
Y.W.C.A., 1922	350 - 400	400 - 450
For the Blind, 1939	250 - 300	300 - 350

Festivals

Prague Sokol, 1901	350 - 400	400 - 450
Vyskov Exhibition of Agriculture,		
Industry and Ethnology, 1902	250 - 300	300 - 350
Vyskov Exhibition of Agri. & Ind., 1902	400 - 450	450 - 500
Student Festival, 1909	350 - 400	400 - 450
Ivancice Regional Fair, 1912-13	175 - 200	200 - 250
Prague Spring Festival, 1914	175 - 200	200 - 250
Eighth Sokol Festival, 1926	150 - 175	175 - 200
Jubilee Festival, 1928	175 - 200	200 - 250
Fiftieth Anniversary of the Sokol at		
Ivancice, 1937	350 - 400	400 - 450
Czechoslovak Post, 1957; post-mortem.	175 - 200	200 - 250

Frescoes-Prague Municipal Building

Original 1909 Issue by Stenc (mark UP)

General views of the hall (2)	60 - 75	75 - 85
Ceiling circular frescoes (2)	60 - 75	75 - 85
Mural frescoes P/**A. Pesl** (3)	60 - 75	75 - 85
Cardinal virtues (8)	85 - 100	100 - 125

1919 Reissue by Amos Pesl

Cardinal virtues (8)	75 - 85	85 - 100
Others	50 - 60	60 - 75

Other Reissues

Cardinal virtues (8)	75 - 85	85 - 100
Others	50 - 60	60 - 75

The Beatitudes, 1909 (6)

Original 1909 Issue by Stenc (mark UP)	60 - 75	75 - 85
Circa 1919 Reissue by Amos Pesl	50 - 60	60 - 75

A. M. Mucha, A. Pesl, Prague, Mural Frescoe, "SILOU K SVO-BODE, LASKOU K SVORNOSTI!" ("With strength to freedom, with love to unity")

Slav Epic, 1928
Poster Design for the Exhibition of Slav Epic	175 - 200	200 - 250
The Slkav Epic Paintings		
Published by Neubert, brown (6)	45 - 50	50 - 55
Photographic process (7)	50 - 55	55 - 60

Miscellaneous
Barcelona Expo, 1903 - Extremely Rare	Range	10000-15000
"Dance Soirée," 1899	750 - 850	850 - 950
Remembrance of Ivancice, 1909		
Color, large	175 - 200	200 - 250
Black & light brown, regular size	150 - 175	175 - 200
Defense of National Minorities, 1915	750 - 850	850 - 950
"Russia Restituenda," 1922	150 - 175	175 - 200
Reconciliation of Czechs & Slovaks, 1928	350 - 400	400 - 450
Château Emmahof, 1931	400 - 450	450 - 500
Nativity, 1934	175 - 200	200 - 250
Orphan	350 - 400	400 - 450

Other Countries
Barcelona Expo – extremely rare		10000 - 15000
Bergamo Fair, 1900, Italy (2)	2000 - 2500	2500 - 3000
Zodiac, 1905	2000 - 2500	2500 - 3000
Ad for English Clothiers in Germany (B&W)	500 - 600	600 - 700

* Listings for most Mucha cards are from Les Illustrateurs, 1991 Edition, by **Neudin.**

MUGGIANI (IT) Art Deco
Rev. Stampa, Milano
Ladies/Heads/Fashion	15 - 20	20 - 25
Ladies/Animals	20 - 25	25 - 28

MUHLBERG, G. (GER)	8 - 10	10 - 12
MULLER, RICHARD (AUS) Women Studies	8 - 10	10 - 12

G. Nanni, Rev. Stampa   *Ney, Editions Delta*   *Ney, Ed. Delta, Ser. 24/116*
Fan Series 256-6   *Ser. 29/142, "A sa toilette"*   *"Colifichets Galants"*

MURCH, FRANK (US)
  Decorative Poster Co.

Series HC 1-12	12 - 15	15 - 20
MUSSINO (IT) Art Deco	12 - 15	15 - 20
MUTTICH, C.V. (CZ)		
Head Studies	8 - 10	10 - 12
MYER (US)	4 - 5	5 - 6
NP Art Deco	12 - 15	15 - 18
NAILLOD, C.S. (FR) Fashion	15 - 20	20 - 25
NAM, JAQUES (FR)	12 - 15	15 - 20
NANNI, Giovanni (IT) Art Deco		
Rev. Stampa; Dell, Anna & Gasparini		
Series 26-A, 597 Couples Kissing (6)	12 - 15	15 - 18
Series 373 Couples Kissing (6)	12 - 15	15 - 18
Series 255 National Girls (6)	15 - 20	20 - 25
Series 256 Lady/Fan (6)	25 - 28	28 - 32
Series 529 Pajamas, Smoking (6)	20 - 22	22 - 27
Series 21, 206, 253, 256, 304, 378 Hats (6)	18 - 22	22 - 26
Series 162 Hats and Ties (6)	20 - 25	25 - 30
Series 308, 376, 396 Heads (6)	12 - 15	15 - 20
Series 309, 434 (6) Sports	25 - 30	30 - 40
Series 283 Fur Collar Hats (6)	18 - 20	20 - 25
Series 377, 521 Hats, Coats	15 - 18	18 - 22
Series 337 Playing Cards-Hats (6)	18 - 22	22 - 26
Series 372, 505 Heads, High Fash. (6)	20 - 22	22 - 27
Series 480 In Buggy (6)	15 - 18	18 - 22
Series 494 With Hat Boxes (6)	20 - 22	22 - 25
Series 445 Lounging Around (6)	15 - 18	18 - 22
Series 540 Heads (6)	22 - 25	25 - 30
Couples	10 - 12	12 - 15
Ladies/Animals	15 - 20	20 - 25
Pierrot/Harlequins	22 - 25	25 - 30
Soccer Series	22 - 25	25 - 30
Erotic/Semi-Nudes	22 - 25	25 - 30
Tennis	22 - 25	25 - 30

Golf	25 - 30	30 - 35
Ladies & Dogs		
Series 205, 300 (6)	15 - 18	18 - 22
Ladies & Horses		
Series 116, 257 (6)	15 - 18	18 - 22
Series 307, 374 (6)	15 - 18	18 - 22
NASH, ADRIENNE. A. (GB) (Ladies & Dogs)		
Heckscher		
703 "Love Me, Love My Dog"	10 - 12	12 - 15
NAST, THOMAS, JR.		
Tennis "Love Game"	18 - 22	22 - 25
Others	6 - 8	8 - 10
NEFF, GUY	2 - 3	3 - 4
NEWTON, RUTH	4 - 5	5 - 6
NEY (FR) French Glamour		
Editions Delta		
Series 24, 29	20 - 25	25 - 30
NICCO, CARLO (IT) Glamour	15 - 20	20 - 25
NICOLET, G. (FR) Glamour	12 - 15	15 - 20
NICZKY, R.	10 - 12	12 - 15
NIKOLAKI, Z.P. (US)		
Reinthal & Newman Ladies Series	8 - 10	10 - 15
NOE, E.E. (FR) Glamour	8 - 10	10 - 12
NORMAN, S. (US)		
Reinthal & Newman - Series 1000 (6)	8 - 10	10 - 12
1000 "After the Game" Basketball	30 - 35	35 - 40
1001 "A Champion" Tennis	20 - 25	25 - 30
NOURY, GASTON (FR) Art Nouveau	60 - 75	75 - 150
See Mermaids Section		
NYSTROM, JENNY (SW)	10 - 12	12 - 15
OCCHIPINTI, F. (FR)		
Raphael Tuck		
Series 1251 (6) Ladies at the Opera	12 - 15	15 - 20
OGILVIE, L. (GB) Glamour	8 - 10	10 - 12
OPLATEK (Ladies & Horses)	8 - 10	10 - 12
ORIS (Glamour)	8 - 10	10 - 12
ORLANDI, V. (IT)		
T.A.M.		
Series 7612 Couples Hugging (6)	8 - 10	10 - 12
OST, A. (BE) Art Nouveau	20 - 25	25 - 35
PAGNOTTA (IT) Art Deco		
Series 494 High Fashion (6)	10 - 15	15 - 20
PAGONI (IT) Art Deco	12 - 15	15 - 20
PALANTI, G. (IT) Art Deco & Glamour	12 - 15	15 - 20
PANNETT, R.	6 - 8	8 - 10
PATELLA, B. (IT)		
Art Deco	15 - 20	20 - 25
Art Nouveau	35 - 40	40 - 45
PAWLOWSKI, J. (PO)	10 - 12	12 - 15
PELLEGRINI, E. (IT) Lady Winter Sports	12 - 15	15 - 25
PELLON, A.		
Ideal Series (6)	80 - 90	90 - 100

L. Peltier, L-E, Paris
34/164, "Les Pajamas"

A. Penot, L-E, Paris
Series 28/4

Maurice Pepin, Ed. Delta
Series 23-115, "Porte-Bonheur"

PELTIER, L. (FR) French Glamour
Delta

Series 17	25 - 30	30 - 35
Series 28	18 - 20	20 - 22

L-E, Paris

Series 8 "Le mauvais tempa indiscret" (7)	25 - 28	28 - 32
Series 10 "La Parisienne che elie" (7)	25 - 28	28 - 32
Series 14 "Par les Chaleurs" (7)	25 - 30	30 - 35
Series 17 "Les Balcons de la Parisienne" (7)	25 - 30	30 - 35
Series 19, 20, 22, 25, 28 (7)	25 - 28	28 - 32
Series 34 "Les Pajamas" (7)	25 - 30	30 - 35

PENOT, ALBERT (FR) French Glamour   See Nudes
French Glamour
Delta

Series 9 "Tennis Feminin" (7)	30 - 35	35 - 45
Series 10, 12, 16, 25, 28	25 - 28	28 - 32
Series 97, 98, 109	25 - 30	30 - 35
PENTSY	8 - 10	10 - 12

PEPIN, MAURICE (FR) French Glamour
Delta

Series 18, 21, 23 Semi-nudes	25 - 28	28 - 32
Series 16, 30 French Glamour	20 - 25	25 - 30

PERAS, A. (FR) French Glamour

Series 68	15 - 20	20 - 25
PERINI, T. (IT) **Ladies & Horses**	10 - 12	12 - 15
PETER, OTTO (GER) (Glamour)	10 - 12	12 - 15

PETERSON, L. (US)   See Cowboys/Indians

H. H. Tammen – Love & Life Series	6 - 8	8 - 10

PEW, G. L. (US)

Aquarelle Series 109, 2239	6 - 8	8 - 10
E.A.S.B. Series 108, 109	8 - 10	10 - 12
Leubrie & Elkus (L&E)		
Series 2221, 2223 (Heads)	10 - 12	12 - 14

PHILIPPI, ROBERT (AUS) Art Nouveau

B.K.W.I. Cupid Series 3095 (6)	15 - 20	20 - 25

Coles Phillips, Edward Gross
© Life Pub. Co., "Illusion"

Coles Phillips, Edward Gross
Life Pub. Co., "Home Ties"

PHILLIPS, COLES (US)

Coles Phillips' works are the most elusive of the famous U.S. illustrators, and his cards are rarely seen in auctions. The famous Fadeaway Girls, both signed and unsigned, are among the most beautiful ever published. His renderings of ladies for Community Plate are also very popular with advertising collectors. Relatively unknown are his set of six movie stars for C.P. & Company, New York. These also are extremely rare and hard to find.

Cards listed with an asterisk are Fadeaway Girls images.

Life Publishing Co., 1907		
Life Series 1		
"Her Choice"	40 - 45	45 - 55
Life Publishing Co., 1909		
© Coles Phillips Series		
"Arms and the Man" *	50 - 60	60 - 70
"Between You and Me and the Post" *	50 - 60	60 - 70
"Home Ties"*	50 - 60	60 - 70
"Illusion" *	50 - 60	60 - 70
"Inclined to Meet" Series 2 *	50 - 60	60 - 70
"The Sand Witch"	50 - 60	60 - 70
"Such Stuff as Dreams are Made Of"	50 - 60	60 - 70
"What Next?" Series 2	50 - 60	60 - 70
"Which?" Series 2 *	50 - 60	60 - 70
Life Pub. Co., 1910		
"A Call to Arms" *	50 - 60	60 - 75

Coles Phillips, P. F. Volland & Co.
© *Life Pub. Co., "May Christmas Day..."*

Plum, G. H., Paris, Series 27
"Bonne Année"

"All Wool and Face Value" Series 2	50 - 55	55 - 60
"And Out of Mind as Soon as Out of..." Series 2	50 - 55	55 - 60
"Discarding from Strength" Series 2	50 - 55	55 - 60
"Hers"	45 - 50	50 - 60
P.F. Volland & Co., Chicago		
© **by Life Publishing Co.**		
1898 "May Christmas Day Heap Up for You"	50 - 55	55 - 65
409 "The Survival of the Fittest" *	55 - 60	60 - 70
410 "The Latest in Gowns, Good Night" *	55 - 60	60 - 70
411 "Pals" *	55 - 60	60 - 70
412 "Memories" *	55 - 60	60 - 70
414 "Long Distance Makes the Heart Grow..." *	55 - 60	60 - 70
"My Christmas Thoughts ..." *	55 - 60	60 - 70
C.P. Co. Inc., N.Y.		
Movie Star Series (Color)		
"King Baggott," "Francis X. Bushman"	65 - 75	75 - 90
"Alice Joyce," "Blanche Sweet"	65 - 75	75 - 90
"Rosemary Theby," "Lillian Walker"	65 - 75	75 - 90
ADVERTISING		
Community Plate		
R. Stafford Collins, N.Y.	50 - 55	55 - 60
Community Plate		
"The Aristocrat of the Dining Table"	50 - 55	55 - 60
Ad for Brunner Fl. Jeweler	50 - 55	55 - 60
Community Silver		
"A Case of Love at First Sight"	50 - 55	55 - 60

Book Advertisement
　Penn Publishing Co.

"The Dim Lantern," by Temple Bailey	75 - 85	85 - 95
"The Trumpeter Swan," by Temple Bailey	75 - 85	85 - 95
Calendar Cards, With Verse (Uns.)	60 - 70	70 - 85

Ten unsigned Fadeaway Girls have
been attributed to Coles Phillips.

Values of these are:	35 - 40	40 - 50

PIERCE, THOMAS MITCHELL (US)
　Armour & Co. (B&W) *

"The Thomas Mitchell Pierce Girl"	18 - 22	22 - 25
* German Back	22 - 25	25 - 28
PILLARD	5 - 6	6 - 9
PINKAWA, ANTON (JAP) Art Nouveau	25 - 30	30 - 35

PINOCHI (IT) Art Deco

Series 206 Hats (6)	15 - 18	18 - 22
Series 172 Lovers (6)	15 - 18	18 - 22
Others	10 - 12	12 - 15
PIOTROWSKI, A. (PO)	8 - 10	10 - 12
PLANTIKOW	8 - 10	10 - 12
Ladies & Horses	10 - 12	12 - 15
Ladies/Tennis	15 - 20	20 - 25

PLUM (FR)
　G.H., Paris

Big Hats, Mode	12 - 15	15 - 20
Series 27		
Motoring Series, Mode	15 - 18	18 - 22

POWELL, LYMAN (US)
　"Eventful Days" Series

"Graduation Day," "Engagement Day"	10 - 12	12 - 15
"Wedding Day," "Birthday"	10 - 12	12 - 15
Flower Series 783, Fade-A-Way Series	6 - 8	8 - 10

　Granbergs Konst.

Glamour	8 - 10	10 - 12
Ladies/Animals	10 - 12	12 - 15

PRESSLER, GENE (US)

Djer-Kiss Rouge	6 - 8	8 - 10

　F.A.S.
　"Armed Service Girls" Series (6)

403 "Aviator Girl"	15 - 20	20 - 25
406 "Sailor Girl"	15 - 20	20 - 25
409 "Quartermaster Girl"	15 - 20	20 - 25
PSTRAK, J. (HUN)	8 - 10	10 - 12
PUTTKAMER Erotic Lovers Series 8027 (6)	15 - 18	18 - 22

QUINNELL, CECIL W. (GB)
　B.K.W.I.
　Series 258 "The Jewel Girls" (6)

"Emerald," "Pearl," "Ruby," "Sapphire,"	12 - 15	15 - 20
"Topaz," "Turquoise"	12 - 15	15 - 20
"Glad Eye" Series (6)	10 - 12	12 - 15

　Paul Hecksher

Series 1225 (6) – 5 Fishing Lady	25 - 30	30 - 35
RABES, MAX (GER)	8 - 10	10 - 12

Gene Pressler, F.A.S., #406
"Sailor Girl"

Gene Pressler, F.A.S., #409
"Quartermaster Girl"

Lester Ralph, R&N 813
"The Awakening of Love"

Lester Ralph, R&N 816
"For All Eternity"

RALPH, LESTER (US)
Reinthal & Newman
"Dancing" Series 801-806

801 "La Furlana"	18 - 22	22 - 26
802 "The Cortez"	18 - 22	22 - 26
803 "The One Step"	18 - 22	22 - 26
804 "The Half and Half"	18 - 22	22 - 26
805 "The Maxie"	18 - 22	22 - 26
806 "The Tango"	18 - 22	22 - 26

813-818 Series * Love and Marriage Series

813 "The Awakening of Love"	15 - 18	18 - 22
814 "The Stage of Life"	15 - 18	18 - 22
815 "Up in the Clouds"	15 - 18	18 - 22
816 "For All Eternity"	18 - 22	22 - 26
817 "In Proud Possession"	15 - 18	18 - 22
818 "The Home Guard"	15 - 18	18 - 22

* With German Caption add $5.00.

The Knapp Co., N.Y.
Paul Heckscher (Distributed by)
Series 302

1 "Favored by Fortune"	12 - 15	15 - 20
2 "An Offer of Affection"	12 - 15	15 - 20
3 "Weathering it Together"	15 - 20	20 - 25
4 "His Proudest Moment"	12 - 15	15 - 18
5 "Four-In-Hand"	12 - 15	15 - 18
6 "Her First Mate"	12 - 15	15 - 18
7 "Two is Company Enough"	12 - 15	15 - 18
8 "Fast Companions"	12 - 15	15 - 18
9 "Fellow Sports"	15 - 18	18 - 22
10 "Diana of the Shore"	12 - 15	15 - 18

H. Import (Heckscher)
Series 307

1 "Take Me Along"	10 - 12	12 - 15
2 "Feathered Friends"	10 - 12	12 - 15
3 "Wanted - A First Mate"	10 - 12	12 - 15
4 "A Stroll Together"	15 - 18	18 - 22
5 "Heart's Melody"	10 - 12	12 - 15
6 "Speeding Her Up"	15 - 18	18 - 22

H. Import (Heckscher)
Series 308

1 "Confidential Chatter"	10 - 12	12 - 15
2 "A Stroll Together"	15 - 18	18 - 22
3 "A Social Call"	10 - 12	12 - 15
4 "Playmates"	10 - 12	12 - 15
5 "The Wings of the Wind"	10 - 12	12 - 15
6 "A Surprise Party"	12 - 15	15 - 18
7 "Two is Company Enough"	10 - 12	12 - 15
9 "Fellow Sports"	12 - 15	15 - 18

H. Import (Heckscher)
Series 335 No Caption

No No. Driving Red Convertible	15 - 18	18 - 22
1 Same as "Diana of the Shore"	8 - 10	10 - 12
2 Same as "Four in Hand"	10 - 12	12 - 15

3 Same as "Speeding Her Up"	15 - 18	18 - 22
Heckscher Import		
Series 1026		
2 "Feathered Friends"	10 - 12	12 - 15
3 "Wanted - A First Mate"	10 - 12	12 - 15
Calendar Cards With Advertising		
The Knapp Co.		
1913 (12)		
February "The Wings of the Wind"	18 - 22	22 - 26
April "Playmates"	18 - 22	22 - 26
June "A Surprise Party"	18 - 22	22 - 26
September "Speeding Her Up"	18 - 22	22 - 26
October "Confidential Chatter"	18 - 22	22 - 26
December "A Social Call"	18 - 22	22 - 26
Others		
Series 7 * (12)		
9523 "Fast Companions" January	12 - 15	15 - 20
9533 "Weathering it Together" February	12 - 15	15 - 20
9543 "Favored by Fortune" March	12 - 15	15 - 20
9553 "His Proudest Moment" April	12 - 15	15 - 20
9563 "Two is Company Enough" May	12 - 15	15 - 20
9573 "Her First Date" June	12 - 15	15 - 20
9583 "A Challenge from the Sea" July	12 - 15	15 - 20
9593 "A Game in the Surf" August	12 - 15	15 - 20
9603 "Diana of the Shore" September	12 - 15	15 - 20
9613 "Four-in-Hand" October	12 - 15	15 - 20
9623 "Fellow Sports" November	12 - 15	15 - 20
9633 "An Offer of Affection" December	12 - 15	15 - 20
* With advertising - Add $5-$10.		
C.W. Faulkner Series 1314 (6)		
B "Fast Companions"	10 - 12	12 - 15
C "Fellow Sports"	15 - 18	18 - 22
E "Her First Mate"	12 - 15	15 - 18
Series 1315 (6)		
D "Her Proudest Moment"	10 - 12	12 - 15
McGowan-Silsbee Litho Co., N.Y.		
No Captions (B&W)		
Same as "An Offer of Affection"	15 - 20	20 - 25
RAPPINI (IT) Art Deco and Glamour		
Series 2016 With Hand Mirror (6)	10 - 15	15 - 20
Ladies/Heads/Fashion	12 - 15	15 - 20
Ladies/Animals	15 - 18	18 - 22
Ladies/Tennis	18 - 22	22 - 26
Ladies/Golf	25 - 30	30 - 40
Ladies & Horses		
Series 1002 (6)	10 - 15	15 - 20
Series 1092, 2019 (6)	10 - 15	15 - 18
RAUH, LUDWIG (AUS) Art Nouveau	25 - 30	30 - 40
READ, F. W. (US)		
Edward Gross Life Series 1	4 - 5	5 - 6
READING	7 - 8	8 - 10
REED, MARION (US)	3 - 4	4 - 6
REINITZ (FR)		
B.K.W.I.		
Series 340 Large hats (6)	25 - 30	30 - 40

Loris Ricco, Degami
Series 1014

L. Rosa, T.A.M.
Series 7615

Series 366 Mode, with large hats (6)	30 - 35	35 - 40
Series 763 Mode, with large hats (6) (Uns.)	25 - 30	30 - 35
Series 889 Mode, with large hats (6) (Uns.)	25 - 30	30 - 35
RELYEA (US)		
Edward Gross		
Relyea Numbered Series	8 - 10	10 - 12
Relyea - No. 9 Golf	18 - 22	22 - 26
REYNOLDS, FRANK (US)		
Anonymous		
Hat Series		
3701 "Ruth"	5 - 7	7 - 9
3702 "Helen"	5 - 7	7 - 9
3703 "Rose"	5 - 7	7 - 9
3706 "Grace"	5 - 7	7 - 9
Cowgirl Series	7 - 8	8 - 9
REYZNER, M.	6 - 8	8 - 10
REZSO, KISS "Siren Lady" Series 68-73	10 - 15	15 - 20
RICCO, CARLO (IT) Art Deco	15 - 20	20 - 25
RICCO, LORIS (IT) Art Deco		
Ladies	22 - 25	25 - 30
Lovers	15 - 18	18 - 22
Pierrots/Harlequins	25 - 30	30 - 35
ROBERTY, L.		
M. Munk, Vienna		
Bather Series 1124	10 - 12	12 - 15
Fashion Series	15 - 20	20 - 25
RODE, G.		
Rev. Stampa Series 6529 On Chair (6)	12 - 15	15 - 18

Carl Rylander, Alex Eliassons
"God Jul"

Carl Rylander, A&E, Stockholm
No Caption

RODELLA, G.	4 - 6	6 - 8
ROSA, L. (IT)		
T.A.M.		
Glamour Series 7615	10 - 12	12 - 15
ROUSSELET, E.		
Lapina, Paris 889 "The Night Bird"	18 - 22	22 - 26
RUMPEL, F.	6 - 8	8 - 10
RUNDALZEFF, M. (RUS)	6 - 8	8 - 10
RUSSELL, MARY LA F.	5 - 7	7 - 8
RYAN, C. (US)		
Art Nouveau		
A633 "Folly" A634 "Joy"	15 - 18	18 - 22
A635 "Curiosity" A636 "Vanity"	15 - 18	18 - 22
A637 "Harmony" A638 "So Lonesome"	15 - 18	18 - 22
A639 "Love" A640 "Temptation"	15 - 18	18 - 22
673 "Constancy" A674 "Sweet Memories"	15 - 18	18 - 22
675 "Sweet Dreams" 677 "Dreaming of Days..."	15 - 18	18 - 22
679 "May Success Be Thine" 680 "Love's Token"	15 - 18	18 - 22
Winsch Backs		
Non-Art Nouveau, Glamour		
"Blissful Moments, etc."	5 - 6	6 - 8
RYLAND, H. (GB)	8 - 10	10 - 12
RYLANDER, CARL (SWE) Art Deco		
A&E, Stockholm		
Lady with Umbrella	30 - 35	35 - 40
Axel Eliassons **Sports Series**		
B Skiing Lady "God Jul"	35 - 45	45 - 55

Xavier Sager, K.F., Paris
Series 4289

Scattini, SBORGI
Pierrot Series, No Caption

C Skating couple "God Jul"	35 - 45	45 - 55
Christmas Series		
C Lady at fireplace "God Jul"	30 - 40	40 - 45
SACCHETTI, ENRICO (IT)		
E. Polenghi		
Beautiful Ladies	20 - 25	25 - 28
Ladies & Dogs	15 - 20	20 - 25
Others	12 - 15	15 - 18
SAGER, XAVIER (FR)		
French Glamour/Fantasy		
B.M., Paris		
524 "Le Golf"	40 - 50	50 - 60
K.F., Paris		
Series 4289, 4485, 4486 Ladies Fashions	20 - 25	25 - 30
A. Noyer, Paris		
Series 61, 131 Pajamas	15 - 20	20 - 25
Series 84 "Proverbs Americans" (6)	18 - 22	22 - 26
Series 138 Lingerie	22 - 25	25 - 28
Series 147 Semi-Nudes	22 - 25	25 - 30
Series 156 Lesbian Dancers	22 - 27	27 - 35
Series 690 "Peaceful Shells" (6)	18 - 22	22 - 25
Raphael Tuck		
Lady Golfer "Le Golf"	50 - 60	60 - 75
Other Glamour Series	18 - 22	22 - 25
Ladies/Tennis	20 - 22	22 - 27
Ladies/Golf	25 - 30	30 - 40
Erotic/Nudes	20 - 25	25 - 30

ST. JOHN (US)
  National Art

"National Girls" Series	12 - 15	15 - 20
"Foreign Girls" Series	10 - 12	12 - 15
"The Four Seasons"	12 - 15	15 - 18
"State Girl" Series	10 - 12	12 - 15
Montgomery Co., Chicago		
103 "Shopping"	10 - 12	12 - 15
104 "Promenade"	10 - 12	12 - 15
106 "Beauties"	12 - 15	15 - 18
SALMONI, G. (IT) Art Deco	10 - 12	12 - 15
SALVADORI (IT) Art Deco		
Series 168 "The Wolf" Fur (6)	15 - 18	18 - 22
SAMSON, C. W. (GB)		
Valentine & Sons Bathing Girls	10 - 12	12 - 15
SAN MARCO (IT) Art Deco		
P.A.R.		
Series 2037, 2082 Hats	12 - 15	15 - 20
Fantasy Series - Lady/Bubbles	20 - 25	25 - 30
Others	12 - 15	15 - 18
SAND, ADINA (Art Nouveau)	10 - 15	15 - 20
SANTINO, F. (IT) Art Deco		
Rev. Stampa		
Series 131		
Fashion Pose (6)	12 - 15	15 - 20
Ladies & Dogs Series 6783 (6)	12 - 14	14 - 16
Ladies & Horses Series 68 (6)	8 - 10	10 - 12
SCATTINI (IT) Art Deco		
Ladies	20 - 25	25 - 35
SBORGI Pierrots/Harlequins	20 - 25	25 - 35
SCHIELE, EGON (Art Nouveau)	150 - 200	200 - 250
See Wiener Werkstätte Section		
SCHENK (CZ)		
H.P., Praha		
Sporting Series (10)		
Lady Basketball player	25 - 30	30 - 40
SCHIFF, ROBERT (AUS)		
W.R.B. & Co. Series 22-62	8 - 10	10 - 12
SCHILBACH (GER)	8 - 10	10 - 12
SCHLOSSER, R. (GER)	5 - 6	6 - 8

SCHMUCKER, S. L. (US)

    The beautiful works of Samuel L. Schmucker, or SLS initials as seen on the few cards he actually signed, are among the most collectible cards in the hobby. His fantastic fantasy cards by Detroit Publishing Co., are extremely rare, and are favorites of the collecting fraternity. Recent additions to the Raphael Tuck Series 556 of "Long Ago Children," the rare Halloween Series 100, the "Quaint Dutch" series, and the Whitney sets have given collectors even more beauties to pursue.

    Equally outstanding are his works of beautiful ladies and children of Halloween, Christmas, New Year, Valentine's Day, Easter, Thanksgiving and St. Patrick's Day by John Winsch. The workmanship and fine quality of John Winsch set the standard for other publishers. Postcard collectors and historians have also concluded that a group of cards by National Art Company, as well as those of Whitney, are the works of Schmucker, and these are also listed.

According to collector Shirley Hendricks, there are reprint variations of the cards where slight changes were made as promotional efforts by the publishers. This is particularly true in the Valentines, where many silk inserts, booklets, and die-cuts were issued using the original image.

For example, a collector who has the six Winsch copyright 1911 Halloween series of ladies has the basic images from which three other sets were developed...using smaller images, different captions, different borders, or different printing techniques. Since this is true with most all Winsch Holiday Schmucker cards, it makes a very interesting quest to find them all. These variations tend to have a higher value than the originals.

Detroit Publishing Co.

There has been a tremendous and enlightening discovery by Jack and Susan Davis of the original artwork by Schmucker which was used for most cards in the eight series of postcards by Detroit Publishing Co. They have published a newly released book, showing the 88 Schmucker watercolor paintings. Among these are 45 of the total of 52 (all were copyrighted in 1907) that were used in the 8 sets of postcards listed below. The size of the paintings have made it possible to see where many previously unknown hidden signatures of "SLS" were located and also gives true titles of all the cards, plus much more valuable information. Collectors should have a copy of this fine book. See "Bibliography" section in our index for details.

"The Adventures of a Gnome" or "All's well that ends well" Series. (6) *

All images are unsigned.

1 Hummingbird	175 - 200	200 - 250
2 Bee	175 - 200	200 - 250
3 Mouse	175 - 200	200 - 250
4 Frog	175 - 200	200 - 250
5 Beetle	175 - 200	200 - 250
6 Owl	175 - 200	200 - 250

* **Same series with short quotation instead of a one-word title - Value: $1500 - $1650**

"The Butterfly Girls" Series (6)

Five images are unsigned.

"Beauty" Girl in Blue	175 - 225	225 - 275
"Elusoriness" Girl in Yellow	175 - 225	225 - 275
"Fragility" Girl in Blue-Green	175 - 225	225 - 275
"Inconstancy" Girl in Red	175 - 225	225 - 275
"L'Envoi" Girl in Gray	175 - 225	225 - 275
"Sensibility" Girl in Pink (Signed)	175 - 225	225 - 275

"Childhood Days" (6)

All images are unsigned.

I "Baby Days"	200 - 250	250 - 350
II "The Runaways"	200 - 250	250 - 350
III "Playtime"	200 - 250	250 - 350
IV "Among the Flowers"	200 - 250	250 - 350
V "Fairy Tales"	200 - 250	250 - 350
VI "Off to School"	200 - 250	250 - 350

"The Drinkers" Series

All images are signed.

"Champagne"	175 - 225	225 - 275

"Claret"	175 - 225	225 - 275
"Creme de Menthe"	175 - 225	225 - 275
"Manhattan"	175 - 225	225 - 275
"Martini"	175 - 225	225 - 275
"Sherry"	175 - 225	225 - 275

"The International Girls" Series (10)
All images are unsigned.

"England," "France," "Italy"	175 - 225	225 - 275
"Netherlands," "Norway"	175 - 225	225 - 275
"Russia,""Spain"	175 - 225	225 - 275
"Switzerland," "Turkey"	175 - 225	225 - 275
"United States"	200 - 250	250 - 300

I. Baby Days

II. The Runaway

III. Playtime

IV. Among the Flowers

V. Fairy Tales

VI. Off to School

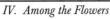

**SAMUEL L. SCHMUCKER — DETROIT PUBLISHING CO.
"CHILDHOOD DAYS" SERIES**

"The Adventures of a Gnome"
Unsigned, "The Hummingbird"

"The Butterfly Girls"
Uns. Girl in Blue, "Beauty"

"The Drinkers"
Signed, "Creme de Menthe"

"The International Girls"
No No., "Italy"

"The Mermaid's Lovers"
Unsigned, "Sea Horse"

"Mottos"
Signed, No. 14661, "Colridge"

This is a scan of an original envelope used by the Detroit Publishing Co. to package the six-card set of "Childhood Days." Other sets were packaged similarly.

Childhood Days

Ah! what would the world be to us
If the children were no more?

Detroit Publishing Co.
Detroit, Mich.

SIX CARDS.

"The Smoker's Dream"
Signed, "Clarice"

Each of the eight sets produced by S. L. Schmucker and published by Detroit Publishing Co. are represented here. The set of "Childhood Days" is on preceding page.

"The Mermaid's Lovers" Series (6)
  Only two cards are signed.

Head of Girl and Fish {Signed left of fish}*	250 - 275	275 - 325
Toad Fish	250 - 275	275 - 325
Japanese Globe Fish	250 - 275	275 - 325
Salmon	250 - 275	275 - 325
Lobster (Signed, upper right corner)	250 - 275	275 - 325
Seahorse	250 - 275	275 - 325

  *** Image named by Nancy Stechschulte in her**
    book, "The Detroit Publishing Co. Postcards"
"Mottoes" Series   (6)
  All images signed except "Youth's Garden"

14659 "Roses" by Rossetti	250 - 300	300 - 350
14660 "Harmony" by Thomas Moore	250 - 300	300 - 350
14661 "Captive" by Coleridge	250 - 300	300 - 350
14662 "Youth's Garden" by Herrick (Uns.)	250 - 300	300 - 350
14663 "Unafraid" by Shakespeare	250 - 300	300 - 350
14664 "Philomeis" by Byron	250 - 300	300 - 350

"The Smoker's Dreams" Series (6)
  All images are signed in edge of smoke.

"Clarice" Cigarette	200 - 225	225 - 275
"Laughing Waters" Indian pipe	200 - 225	225 - 275
"Lucinda" Cigar	200 - 225	225 - 275
"Maude Miller" Corncob pipe	200 - 225	225 - 275
"Molly" Clay pipe	200 - 225	225 - 275
"Virginia" Brier pipe	200 - 225	225 - 275

National Art Company
  WWI Soldier's Letter Series (Unnamed) (10)

"A letter a day keeps the blues away"	175 - 200	200 - 250
"A letter from you looks big as this to me"	175 - 200	200 - 250
"I wasn't so happy last night..."	175 - 200	200 - 225
"Oh! Let this dream come true"	175 - 200	200 - 250
"Three Cheers and Hip Hip Hooray..."	175 - 200	200 - 250
"You'll send me away with a smile..."	175 - 200	200 - 250
"Your letter today was a treat..."	175 - 200	200 - 250
"When of me you sometimes think..."	175 - 200	200 - 250
"When time hangs heavy on my hands..."	175 - 200	200 - 250
"Write"	175 - 200	200 - 250

Raphael Tuck & Sons, Ltd. –- New York
  Series 100 – Halloween Greetings (9)

Girl dressed in sheet, many JOL's		
"Bats and owls and witch-y capers..."	125 - 150	150 - 175
Girl pixie dressed in black, 3 JOL's		
"Hallowe'en Greetings..."	125 - 150	150 - 175
Girl with cape and Japanese lanterns		
"Hallowe'en Wishes"	125 - 150	150 - 175
Girl with mask, 5 big masks behind		
"This maid will mask on Hallowe'en"	125 - 150	150 - 175
Boy with Japanese lanterns, big moon		
"Sing a Song of Hallowe'en"	125 - 150	150 - 175
Girl wears checked dress and JOL man		
"This Maiden Here is Dancing With..."	125 - 150	150 - 175
Girl wears JOL cloak, with JOL on stick		

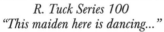

R. Tuck Series 100
"This maiden here is dancing..."

Uns. Schmucker, Whitney Stand-up
"Hallowe'en Greetings to You"

"Were you this maid on Hallowe'en"	125 - 150	150 - 175
Girl dressed as clown, JOL on a stick		
"Witches, Fays and Sprites unseen..."	125 - 150	150 - 175
Boy with flute sits on big JOL		
"When you're away on Hallowe'en"	125 - 150	150 - 175
Series 198 – Birthday Greetings		
"Quaint Dutch" (10)	70 - 80	80 - 90
Series 556 – Christmas Greetings		
"Long Ago Children" (8)	30 - 35	35 - 45
Series 618 – News Years Greetings		
"Joyous" (6)	40 - 45	45 - 50
Series 619 – News Years Greetings		
"Ye Olden Days" (6)	30 - 35	35 - 45
Whitney Co.		
Halloween Greetings (6)	90 - 100	100 - 110
Halloween Stand-ups	100 - 125	125 - 150
New Years Greetings (6)	50 - 60	60 - 75
Christmas Greetings (6)	50 - 60	60 - 75
John Winsch, Copyright		
Christmas Greetings		
Copyright 1910 – Vertical* (4)		
Lady in poinsettia dress and background		
"Christmas Wishes"	25 - 30	30 - 35
Lady in green dress, poinsettia coat		
"Christmas Greeting"	25 - 30	30 - 35

Uns. Schmucker, Winsch Back
No Copyright, "A Merry Christmas"

Uns. Schmucker, Winsch, © 1911
"To Wish You a Happy New Year"

Lady in yellow dress, holly background		
"A Merry Christmas"	25 - 30	30 - 35
Lady in white dress and red jacket		
"A Joyful Christmas"	25 - 30	30 - 35
* Smaller images reprinted in 1915 with		
different captions, Vertical	25 - 30	30 - 40
Copyright 1911 – Vertical (4)		
Girl in red hugs big snowman		
"A Merry Christmas"	50 - 60	60 - 75
Girl in blue with dark red scarf		
"Christmas Greetings"	50 - 60	60 - 70
Girl in green with yellow scarf		
"Merry Christmas"	50 - 60	60 - 70
Girl with red mittens and snowballs		
"A Joyful Christmas"	50 - 60	60 - 70
Winsch Backs, No Copyright (4)		
Glamour blonde with Santa mask		
"A Joyful Christmas"	55 - 60	60 - 65
Blonde lady with ermine fur		
"A Merry Christmas"	50 - 55	55 - 60
Blond lady sleeps, Santa watches		
"A Merry Christmas"	55 - 60	60 - 65
Lady in red setting on gold bell		
"Christmas Greeting"	50 - 55	55 - 60

New Year Greetings
Copyright, 1910 - Vertical (4)

Reprints of 1910 Christmas issue		
with New Year Captions, Vertical	20 - 25	25 - 35
Silks, with no copyright	25 - 30	30 - 45

Copyright, 1910 - Father Time, Vertical (4)

With lady in purple		
"Jan. 1st."	45 - 55	55 - 65
With lady in gold		
"Jan. 1st.	45 - 55	55 - 65
With lady in pink flowered dress		
"Jan. 1st."	45 - 55	55 - 65
With lady in red		
"Jan 1st."	45 - 55	55 - 65

Copyright, 1910 - 1911 Year - Vertical (4)

1911 Baby New Year rides big bell		
"To wish you a Happy New Year"	30 - 35	35 - 40
Stork carrying Baby New Year		
"A Happy New year"	30 - 35	35 - 40
Baby New Year/Father Time		
"Best New Year Wishes"	30 - 35	35 - 40
Baby New Year sits on trunk		
"A Happy New Year to You"	30 - 35	35 - 40

Copyright, 1911 - Vertical* (4)

Girl in red hugs snowman		
"A Happy New Year"	40 - 45	45 - 55
Girl in Blue with dark red scarf		
"With Best New Year Wishes"	40 - 45	45 - 55
Girl in green with yellow scarf		
"A Happy New Year to You"	40 - 45	45 - 55
Girl with red mittens and snowballs		
"To Wish you a Happy New Year"	40 - 45	45 - 55

* Reprints of 1911 Christmas Series as New Year

Valentine's Day Greetings
Copyright, 1910 - **Vertical** (6)

Girl in purple with 2 red heart faces		
"St. Valentine's Greeting"	40 - 45	45 - 55
Side view of blonde, gold halo and hearts		
"My Valentine, think of me"	40 - 45	45 - 55
Red head, large green heart behind		
"I Greet Thee, Valentine"	40 - 45	45 - 55
Red head wearing blue, green heart		
"To my Valentine"	40 - 45	45 - 55
Lady wearing white chiffon hat		
"Be my Valentine"	40 - 45	45 - 55
Blond wearing chiffon scarf		
"A Valentine Message"	40 - 45	45 - 55

Copyright, 1910 - Green Heart, Vertical (4)

Irish lady and Irish cupid		
"Be my Valentine"	35 - 40	40 - 50
Oriental lady and oriental cupid		
"To my Valentine"	35 - 40	40 - 50
Indian maid and Indian cupid		
"A Valentine Message"	35 - 40	40 - 50

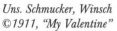

Uns. Schmucker, Winsch
©1911, "My Valentine"

Uns. Schmucker, Winsch
© 1910, "A Happy Easter"

Uns. Schmucker, Winsch Back
No Copyright, "St. Patrick's..."

Spanish Girl and Spanish cupid		
"St. Valentine's Greeting"	35 - 40	40 - 50
Copyright, 1910 - Sports Cupid, Horiz. (4)		
Fishing Cupid		
"To My Valentine"	35 - 40	40 - 45
Football Cupid		
"A Valentine Message"	40 - 50	50 - 60
Golfing Cupid		
"To My Valentine"	45 - 55	55 - 65
Tennis Cupid		
"To My Valentine"	40 - 50	50 - 50
Copyright, 1910 - Vertical (4)		
Blonde holding large red heart		
"My Valentine think of me"	30 - 35	35 - 45
Blonde Sleeping - purple-pink flowers		
"Valentine Greetings"	40 - 45	45 - 55
Blonde lady wearing ermine hat		
"To my Valentine"	30 - 35	35 - 45
Lady in red sitting on flower heart		
"St. Valentine's Greeting"	30 - 35	35 - 45
Copyright, 1911 - Gold Heart, Vertical (4)		
Golf Girl		
"Valentine Greeting"	45 - 55	55 - 65
Fishing Girl		
"To my Valentine"	30 - 40	40 - 50
Football Girl		
"My Valentine"	35 - 45	45 - 55
Tennis Girl		
"Greeting to my Valentine"	35 - 45	45 - 55
Girl in red sweater kicking football		
heart - Very Rare		
"Valentine Greeting"	80 - 90	90 - 100
Winsch Backs, Non-Copyright (6)		
Nurse bandaging a broken heart		
"A Valentine Message"	40 - 45	45 - 55

Side view of blonde with hearts in hair		
"I greet thee Valentine"	40 - 45	45 - 55
Spider web background, w/hearts entangled		
"My Valentine, think of me" Signed SLS	45 - 50	50 - 55
Dark-haired lady, spider web background		
"Be my Valentine"	55 - 60	60 - 65
Blonde lady holds red heart, spider web		
"To my Valentine"	45 - 50	50 - 55
Lady floating in water with hearts		
"St. Valentine's Greeting"	45 - 50	50 - 55

Copyright 1911 – Vertical (4)

Lady in blue holding green umbrella		
"A Prayer to Valentine"	35 - 40	40 - 50
Blonde lady in pink carrying basket		
"Gathering Hearts"	35 - 40	40 - 50
Lady in yellow catching butterfly hearts		
"Your Valentine"	35 - 40	40 - 50
Lady in green playing heart guitar		
"Valentine Plea"	35 - 40	40 - 50

Easter Greetings
Copyright 1910 – Flower Faces, Vertical (6)

4 Ladies' faces in red and pink flowers		
"A Happy Easter"	35 - 40	40 - 50
5 Children's faces in pink flowers		
"Welcome Easter Morning"	35 - 40	40 - 50
4 Ladies' faces in pansies		
"A Joyful Eastertide"	35 - 40	40 - 50
5 Ladies' faces in tulips		
"Best Easter Wishes"	35 - 40	40 - 50
5 Ladies' faces in daffodils		
"Glad Easter Greeting"	35 - 40	40 - 50
5 Ladies' faces in Easter Lilies		
"Easter Greeting"	35 - 40	40 - 50

St. Patrick Day Greetings
Copyright 1911 - Vertical (4)

Pretty lady sitting in shamrock wreath		
"Erin Go Bragh"	35 - 40	40 - 45
Lady sitting atop map of Ireland		
"St. Patrick's Day Greetings"	30 - 35	35 - 40
Lady sitting on Irish hat		
"The Scots man loves..."	30 - 35	35 - 40
Lady at window, Horizontal		
"St. Patrick's Day in the morning"	30 - 35	35 - 40

Copyright 1912 - **Transportation**, Vertical (4)

Man/woman riding shamrock sailboat		
"St Patrick's Day Souvenir"	35 - 40	40 - 45
Man/lady riding in shamrock cart		
"St. Patrick's Day Greeting	35 - 40	40 - 45
Man swinging lady on shamrock swing		
"Erin Go Bragh"	35 - 40	40 - 45
Man/lady riding in shamrock airship		
"St Patrick's Day Greeting"	40 - 45	45 - 50

Copyright 1912 - Named Views, Horiz. (4)

Lady playing harp "Erin Go Bragh"	20 - 25	25 - 30
Lady wearing shamrock hat, with harp "St. Patrick's Day Greetings"	20 - 25	25 - 30
Lady on map of Ireland "St. Patrick's Day Souvenir"	15 - 20	20 - 25
Lady and man dancing "St. Patrick's Day Greetings"	20 - 25	25 - 30

Winsch Backs, No Copyright (9 known)

Lady with pig, wreath behind "Erin Go Bragh"	30 - 35	35 - 40
Lady standing in front of crossed pipes "St. Patrick's Day Souvenir"	30 - 35	35 - 40
Lady sitting on bouquet of shamrocks "St. Patrick's Day"	30 - 35	35 - 40
Lady with pig, wreath behind "Erin Go Bragh"	25 - 30	30 - 35
Lady in shamrock dress, holds big pipe "St. Patrick's Day Greetings"	25 - 30	30 - 35
Lady riding big white pipe "St. Patrick's Day Souvenir"	25 - 30	30 - 35
Lady sitting on big harp, mesh background "Erin Go Bragh"	25 - 30	30 - 35
Lady holds big pipe, mesh background "St. Patrick's Day Greetings"	25 - 30	30 - 35
Lady at the window - Horizontal "The Top of the Mornin' to you..."	25 - 30	30 - 35

Thanksgiving Greetings

Copyright 1910 – Vertical (4)

Kneeling Pilgrim w/basket beside her "A Peaceful Thanksgiving"	20 - 25	25 - 30
Lady holding pumpkins "Hearty Thanksgiving Greetings"	20 - 25	25 - 30
Lady feeding grain to turkey "With Thanksgiving Greeting"	20 - 25	25 - 30
Pilgrim man/woman preparing to eat "Best Wishes for a Happy Thanksgiving"	20 - 25	25 - 30

Copyright 1911 – **Vertical** (8)

Girl in purple picks fruit, turkey "With Thanksgiving Greeting"	15 - 20	20 - 25
Pilgrim lady in field, corn/pumpkins "A Peaceful Thanksgiving"	15 - 20	20 - 25
Pilgrim girl w/turkey, big moon "Hearty Thanksgiving Greeting"	20 - 25	25 - 30
Lady carrying tray with turkey "Best Wishes for a Happy Thanksgiving"	15 - 20	20 - 25
Lady holding armful of wheat "A Peaceful Thanksgiving"	15 - 20	20 - 25
Pilgrim lady, dead turkey "Best Wishes for a Happy Thanksgiving"	15 - 20	20 - 25
Pilgrim lady with basket on arm "A Peaceful Thanksgiving"	15 - 20	20 - 25
Indian maid driving fantasy turkey wagon "A Thanksgiving Bounty be Thine" - Horiz.	20 - 25	25 - 30

Uns. Schmucker, Winsch, © 1913 – "Hallowe'en Night"

Copyright 1912 – Indian Maids, Vertical (6)

Indian in green dress		
"Sincere Thanksgiving Greeting"	25 - 30	30 - 35
Indian holding white turkey		
"All Thanksgiving Bounty be Thine"	20 - 25	25 - 30
Indian walking with turkey		
"Glad Thanksgiving Wishes"	20 - 25	25 - 30
Indian and Pilgrim with turkey		
"Hearty Thanksgiving Greeting"	20 - 25	25 - 30

Copyright 1913 – Vertical (4)

Pilgrim with turkey behind her		
"All Thanksgiving Bounty be Thine"	20 - 25	25 - 30
Pilgrim with turkey platter in front		
"Thanksgiving Greeting"	20 - 25	25 - 30
Pilgrim girl sitting on wishbone		
"A Peaceful Thanksgiving"	20 - 25	25 - 30
Indian girl sits on ear of corn		
"Best Wishes for a Happy Thanksgiving"	20 - 25	25 - 30

Halloween Greetings

Winsch combined the works of S.L. Schmucker and Jason Freixas on a number of variations and reduced designs. On these designs Freixas children are usually shown but Schmucker designs fill the remainder of the card. These bring a premium above those of non-combined issues.

Copyright 1911 – Vertical * (6)

Head & shoulders of blonde, black hood		
"A Happy Hallowe'en"	100 - 120	120 - 140
Lady riding broom, moon behind		
"All Hallowe'en"	100 - 120	120 - 140

Lady in long white hooded robe		
"On Hallowe'en"	100 - 120	120 - 140
Lady in red dress, owl on head		
"Hallowe'en Greeting"	100 - 120	120 - 140
Lady in black evening gown		
"Greetings at Hallowe'en"	100 - 120	120 - 140
Lady asleep, 3 fairies		
"Hallowe'en Time"	100 - 120	120 - 140
* 3 different sets of variations of 1911 series show smaller same design images but with different captions – Range		75 - 160
Copyright 1912 – Vertical* (6)		
Lady witch in front of big cauldron		
"The Hallowe'en Cauldron"	100 - 120	120 - 140
Lady in black, leering moon behind		
"The Hallowe'en Lantern"	100 - 120	120 - 140
Lady in white-hooded cape, JOL's		
"The Magic Hallowe'en"	100 - 120	120 - 140
Lady in red elfin costume		
"The Hallowe'en Witch's Wand"	100 - 120	120 - 140
Lady in white clown suit, owls		
"A Hallowe'en Morning"	100 - 120	120 - 140
Lady in green dress, JOL man		
"A Hallowe'en Wish"	100 - 120	120 - 140
* 4 different sets of variations of 1912 series (one same size images and 3 smaller; 3 are copyrighted; 2 are vertical and 2 are horizontal) – Range		75 - 160
Copyright 1913 "Mask Series" – Horiz.* (4)		
Clown in red and Jack-in-the Box		
" Hallowe'en Surprises"	100 - 125	125 - 150
Witch and clown hold jump rope		
"Hallowe'en Gambols!"	100 - 125	125 - 150
Woman in long white hooded robe		
"Hallowe'en Faces"	100 - 125	125 - 150
Girl in white dress, huge masks		
"Hallowe'en Faces"	100 - 125	125 - 150
* One other set of variation of 1913 series has embossed design, black/gold stars border, different captions and cards are not copyrighted (#4972 on reverse)	120 - 140	140 - 165
Copyright 1913 – Horizontal* (4)		
Girl in white dress with pink dress		
"A Starry Hallowe'en"	100 - 125	125 - 150
Girl in dotted dress sits on pumpkin		
"Hallowe'en Night"	100 - 125	125 - 150
Boy surrounded by big JOL's		
"Hallowe'en Pumpkins"	100 - 125	125 - 150
Girl in white between owl and vegetable		
"Hallowe'en Jollity"	100 - 125	125 - 150
* 4 other sets of variations of 1913 series and all are copyrighted 1913.	110 - 130	130 - 160
SCHROCCHI (IT) Art Deco		
Series 4360 Fashion (6)	12 - 15	15 - 20

SCHMUTZLER, L. (GER) (See Color Nudes)		
Moderne Kunst Series	8 - 10	10 - 12
SCHUBERT, H. (AUS)		
M. Munk, Vienna		
Glamorous Ladies	12 - 15	15 - 18
Ladies & Dogs	12 - 15	15 - 18
Tennis	18 - 22	22 - 26
SCHUTZ, ERIC (AUS) See Fantasy Section		
B.K.W.I.		
Series 128 (6)	15 - 20	20 - 25
Series 163 (6)	15 - 20	20 - 25
"Sommernachtstraus" (Summer Nights Dream)	25 - 28	28 - 32
SCHWETZ, KARL (CZ)		
See Wiener Werkstätte Section		
SHAND, C. Z. (Art Deco)		
Fairy Series	40 - 50	50 - 60
Others	30 - 40	40 - 50
SHARPE, J. T. (GB)		
Carleton Pub. Co.		
Series 703 Hats (6)		
1 "Inspiration"	15 - 20	20 - 25
2 "Disappointed"	15 - 20	20 - 25
3 "Fascinating"	15 - 20	20 - 25
4 "Memories"	15 - 20	20 - 25
6 "Good-Bye"	15 - 20	20 - 25
Other	15 - 20	20 - 25
SHERIE (FR)	6 - 9	9 - 12
SICHEL, N.	5 - 6	6 - 8
SIMM, PROF. FRANZ (GER)	5 - 6	6 - 8
SIMONETTI, A. (IT) Art Deco & Glamour	12 - 15	15 - 20
Ladies & Horses		
Series 41 (6)	15 - 18	18 - 22
Series 90 (6)	15 - 20	20 - 25
SINGER, SUSI (HUN) **See Wiener Werkstätte**		
SITSCHKOFF (RUS)	10 - 12	12 - 15
SOLDINGER, A. (PO)	8 - 10	10 - 12
SOLOMKO, S. (RUS)		
Russian Backs (1901 era) (Sepia)		
Pen drawings, Heads of Beautiful Women (12)	60 - 70	70 - 85
Lapina, Paris		
"Country Series - War 1914-19"	15 - 18	18 - 22
Russian Princess 1600 Series*		
"Queen Azviakovna"	20 - 25	25 - 30
"Wassilisa Mikoülichna"	20 - 25	25 - 30
"Princess Apraksia"	20 - 25	25 - 30
"Princess Warrior Nastasia"	20 - 25	25 - 30
"Princess Mary, The White Swan"	20 - 25	25 - 30
"Princess Zabava Poutiatichna"	20 - 25	25 - 30
"Queen Azviakovna of the East"	20 - 25	25 - 30
* Russian Backs - Add $4-5 each.		
T.S.N. (Theo. Stroefer, Nürnberg) *		
15 "Parisiene"	12 - 15	15 - 18
175 "Phantasy"	16 - 18	18 - 22

C. Z. Shand, Anonymous Publisher
"Winter"

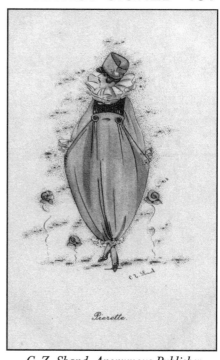

C. Z. Shand, Anonymous Publisher
"Pierette"

J. T. Sharpe, Carlton Publishing Co.
Series No. 703/3, "Fascinating"

S. de Solomko, Lapina, Paris, 1633
"Princess Mary, The White Swan"

Elisabeth Sonrel, Art Nouveau
"Printemps"

Penrhyn Stanlaws, Edward Gross
Stanlaws Series, No. 8, No Caption

"Dream of Icarius"	12 - 15	15 - 18
"Pearl of Creation"	15 - 18	18 - 22
228 "Vanity" (Semi-nude)	15 - 20	20 - 25
"Circe" (Semi-nude)	20 - 25	25 - 28
"The Tale" (Fantasy)	15 - 16	16 - 18
155 "The Blue Bird" (Fantasy)	15 - 20	20 - 25
"Magician Circe" (Semi-nude)	15 - 20	20 - 25
154 "Temptations" (Semi-nude)	18 - 22	22- 26
95 "Glow Worm" (Fantasy)	15 - 18	18 - 22
"Fortune Telling" (Fantasy)	15 - 18	18 - 22
Other **T.S.N.** (Many)	8 - 10	10 - 12
* Russian Backs - Add $4-5 to prices.		
SOMERVILLE, H.	4 - 6	6 - 8
SONREL, ELISABETH (Art Nouveau)		
Seasons Series – "Printemps"	75 - 100	100 - 150
Glamour	18 - 20	20 - 25
SOWERBY, AMY MILLICENT (GB) See Children		
SPOTTI, F. (Ladies & Dogs)		
Rev. Stampa		
Series 158	15 - 18	18 - 22
SPURGIN, FRED (LAT) See Comics	5 - 7	7 - 10
STACHIEWICZ, P. (PO)	10 - 12	12 - 15
STAMM, MAUD	5 - 6	6 - 7
STANLAWS, PENRHYN (US)		
Davidson Bros.		
Series 6079 Women of the Regiment (6)	18 - 22	22 - 25

Edward Gross   Watercolors
   Stanlaws 1-12   No Captions
   One of the most beautiful sets ever!

1 Pink rimmed hat, facing left	20 - 25	25 - 30
2 Green cap, white blouse	20 - 25	25 - 30
3 Queenly beauty with strand of pearls	20 - 25	25 - 30
4 Young girl with blue headband	20 - 25	25 - 30
5 Wide brim hat - beach background	20 - 25	25 - 30
6 Toboggan ski cap, red stripes	20 - 25	25 - 30
7 Large brim hat with roses	20 - 25	25 - 30
8 Large hat, sailor shirt top	20 - 25	25 - 30
9 Wide brim hat with pink plume	20 - 25	25 - 30
10 Yellow hat, blue background	20 - 25	25 - 30
11 Hat tied at chin, with pink roses	20 - 25	25 - 30
12 Fur hat, with fox fur, snow	20 - 25	25 - 30

Knapp Co., N.Y.   Watercolors
   900 Series

"A Midsummer Maid," "After the Matinee"	18 - 22	22 - 26
"Daisies Won't Tell," "Fair as the Lily"	18 - 22	22 - 26
"Fresh as the Morn," "Girl of the Golden West"	18 - 22	22 - 26
"Kissed by the Snow," "The Pink Lady"	18 - 22	22 - 26
"School Days"	18 - 22	22 - 26

K. Co. (**Distributed by A.R. & C.i.B.**) Watercolors
   Series 500   Series 900 Reprints

"A Midsummer Maid," "Daisies Won't Tell"	18 - 22	22 - 26
"Fresh as the Morn," "Girl of the Golden West"	18 - 22	22 - 26
"The Pink Lady"	18 - 22	22 - 26

   Series 544

5 "Among the Blossoms"	15 - 20	20 - 25

   Series 550

"A Midsummer Maid"	15 - 20	20 - 25
"Daisies Won't Tell"	15 - 20	20 - 25
"Fair as the Lily"	15 - 20	20 - 25
"Fresh as the Morn"	15 - 20	20 - 25

   Series 551

"After the Matinee"	15 - 20	20 - 25
"Kissed by the Snow"	15 - 20	20 - 25
"School Days"	15 - 20	20 - 25
"Fair as the Lily"	15 - 20	20 - 25

   Series 1025

4 "The Pink Lady"	20 - 25	25 - 30

Reinthal & Newman
   Military Ladies Series

981 U.S.	18 - 22	22 - 25
982 Serbia	12 - 15	15 - 20
983 Belgium	12 - 15	15 - 20
984 France	12 - 15	15 - 20
985 Italy	12 - 15	15 - 20
986 Greece	12 - 15	15 - 20
987 Great Britain	12 - 15	15 - 20
988 Japan	12 - 15	15 - 20
989 Russia	12 - 15	15 - 20

H. Choate & Co.
   Djer-Kiss Rouge & Face Powder Compacts

"Silver Blonde"	22 - 25	25 - 30

Jean Tam, Marque L-E
Series 67-7

A. Terzi, Rev. Stampa
Series 322/2

STEINLEN, A.T. (SW)		
Art Nouveau		
Better Issues	175 - 200	200 - 500
Others	30 - 35	35 - 45
STENBERG, AINA (SWE) Art Deco	12 - 15	15 - 20
Art Nouveau issues	20 - 25	25 - 30
STOLTE, F. (Ladies & Horses)		
Series 25 (6)	10 - 12	12 - 15
STUCK, FRANZ V. (GER)		
W & G		
"Tilla Durieuz als Circe"	12 - 15	15 - 18
STYKA, TADE		
Lapina, Paris		
181 "Salome"	12 - 15	15 - 20
183 "Cinquecento"	8 - 10	10 - 12
SZANKOWSKI, B.	9 - 12	12 - 15
F.T.		
M. Munk Chromolithos		
Series 479 (6) Glamourous Ladies, Hats	20 - 25	25 - 30
Series 579 (6) Glamourous Ladies, Hats	20 - 25	25 - 30
Series 636 (6) (Unsigned) with Hats	22- 26	26 - 32
TACCHI, E. (IT) Art Deco		
Series 494 High Fashion (6)	10 - 12	12 - 15
TAM, JEAN (France) French Glamour		
Series 39 "The Sammies in Paris" (6)	25 - 28	28 - 32
Series 47, 50, 70, 78, 81	20 - 25	25 - 30
Series 57, 67	25 - 30	30 - 35

TERZI, A. (IT) Art Deco and Glamour

  Rev. Stampa; Dell, Anna & Gasparini

Series 287, 299 Heads (6)	12 - 15	15 - 18
Series 215, 322 Heads/Hats (6)	18 - 22	22 - 26
Series 323 Sitting (6)	12 - 15	15 - 18
Series 360, 486 Fashion (6)	15 - 18	18 - 22
Series 454, 468 Fashion (6)	15 - 18	18 - 22
Series 482 Small Images (6)	8 - 10	10 - 12
Golf	20 - 25	25 - 35
Tennis	15 - 18	18 - 25
Couples	10 - 12	12 - 14
Ladies With Wild Animals	20 - 25	25 - 28
Ladies & Dogs		
Series 341, 349, 399, 457, 482, 973 (6)	15 - 18	18 - 22
Series 976, 559, 969 (6)	15 - 18	18 - 22
Ladies & Horses		
Rev. Stampa Series 320 (6)	15 - 18	18 - 22

TORNROSE, ALEX

Welles Head Series (B&W)	6 - 8	8 - 10
Others	6 - 7	7 - 8

TOULOUSE-LAUTREC, HENRI (France)

"Cabaret Bruant"	800 - 900	900 - 1000
"La Goulue au Moulin Rouge"	1600 - 1800	1800 - 2000
(Card recently sold for $2000)		

TRAVER, C. WARD (U.S.)

  H & S Art Co.

"The Beauty of the Season"	8 - 10	10 - 15
"Sweet Seventeen"	8 - 10	10 - 15

TRAVIS, STUART (U.S.)

T.P. & Co. Series 727 Lovers	5 - 6	6 - 8
Calendar Advert. "Dog Days"	10 - 12	12 - 15

TUHKA, A. (FIN) Art Deco	10 - 12	12 - 15
TURRAIN, E.D. Art Nouveau	25 - 30	30 - 35
TWELVETREES, C.	5 - 6	6 - 9

CLARENCE UNDERWOOD (US)

Clarence Underwood was another of the more important illustrators of magazine covers and magazine fiction who benefitted from the great postcard era. This painter of beautiful ladies did work for Reinthal & Newman of New York, but his most beautiful images were published by the R. Chapman Co. (better known as the R.C. Co., N.Y.). They did the 1400 Series Water Colors of his ladies wearing big, beautiful, and colorful hats. These will always be some of the most beautiful images of the era.

  C.W. Faulkner

Series 5	10 - 12	12 - 15
Series 1010		
1278 "A Symphony of Hearts"	10 - 12	12 - 15
"Their Search for Old China"	10 - 12	12 - 15
National Art		
"Playing Card" Series		
78 "Hearts" Two Men, Two Women	12 - 15	15 - 20
79 "Poker" Five Men	12 - 15	15 - 20

80 "Bridge" Four Women	12 - 15	15 - 20
81 "Euchre" Five Men	12 - 15	15 - 18
Reinthal & Newman		
300 Series Water Colors		
345 "The Flirt"	12 - 15	15 - 20
346 "Pretty Cold"	12 - 15	15 - 20
347 "Her First Vote"	25 - 30	30 - 35
348 "It's Always Fair Weather"	10 - 12	12 - 15
349 "Rain or Shine"	12 - 15	15 - 20
350 "Pleasant Reflections"	12 - 15	15 - 20
Others		
775 "Wanted - An Answer"	20 - 25	25 - 28
776 "Night - A World of Pleasure"	15 - 20	20 - 25
R.C. Co., N.Y.		
Series 1400 Water Colors	20 - 25	25 - 30
1436 "Constance"	20 - 25	25 - 30
1437 "Diana"	20 - 25	25 - 30
1438 "Vivian"	20 - 25	25 - 30
1439 "Phyllis"	20 - 25	25 - 30
1440 "Celestine"	22 - 27	27 - 32
1441 "Rosabella"	22 - 27	27 - 32
1442 "Juliana"	22 - 27	27 - 32
1443 "Victoria" Tennis	30 - 35	35 - 45
1444 "Aurora"	22 - 27	27 - 32
1445 "Sylvia"	22 - 27	27 - 32
1446 "Virginia"	22 - 27	27 - 32
1447 "Doris"	22 - 27	27 - 32
Frederick A. Stokes Co.		
Series 1		
"A Problem of Income"	8 - 10	10 - 12
"Castles in the Smoke"	8 - 10	10 - 12
"For Fear of Sunburn"	8 - 10	10 - 12
"Knight Takes Queen"	8 - 10	10 - 12
Series 2		
"Love Me, Love My Cat"	8 - 10	10 - 12
"Love Me, Love My Dog	8 - 10	10 - 12
"Love Me, Love My Donkey"	8 - 10	10 - 12
"Love Me, Love My Horse"	8 - 10	10 - 12
Series 3		
"When We're Together Fishing"	10 - 12	12 - 15
"When We're Together at Luncheon"	8 - 10	10 - 12
"When We're Together Shooting"	12 - 15	15 - 18
"When We're Together in a Storm"	8 - 10	10 - 12
Series 4		
"Beauty and the Beast"	10 - 12	12 - 15
"The Best of Friends"	8 - 10	10 - 12
"Expectation"	8 - 10	10 - 12
"The Promenade"	8 - 10	10 - 12
Series 5		
"A Lump of Sugar"	10 - 12	12 - 15
"After the Hunt"	10 - 12	12 - 15
"The Red Haired Girl..."	10 - 12	12 - 15

"Three American Beauties"	10 - 12	12 - 15
Series 6		
"Feeding the Swans"	8 - 10	10 - 12
"A Pet in the Park"	8 - 10	10 - 12
"Posing"	10 - 12	12 - 15
"A Witch"	10 - 12	12 - 15
Series 7		
"An Old Melody"	10 - 12	12 - 15
"Over the Teacups"	10 - 12	12 - 15
"The Opera Girl"	10 - 12	12 - 15
"The Violin Girl"	10 - 12	12 - 15
Series 8		
"At the Races"	8 - 10	10 - 12
"Embroidery for Two"	8 - 10	10 - 12
"Out for a Stroll"	8 - 10	10 - 12
"Two Cooks"	8 - 10	10 - 12
Series 14		
"Their First Wedding Gift"	8 - 10	10 - 12
"Their Love of Old Silver"	8 - 10	10 - 12
"Two and an Old Flirt"	8 - 10	10 - 12
"Vain Regrets"	8 - 10	10 - 12
Series 15		
"A Lesson in Motoring"	9 - 12	12 - 15
"A Skipper and Mate"	9 - 12	12 - 15
Series 19		
"The Only Two at Dinner"	9 - 12	12 - 15
"The Only Two at the Game"	9 - 12	12 - 15
"The Only Two at the House Party"	9 - 12	12 - 15
"The Only Two at the Opera"	9 - 12	12 - 15
Series 22		
"The Greatest Thing in the World"	8 - 10	10 - 12
"The Last Waltz"	9 - 12	12 - 15
"Lost?"	9 - 12	12 - 15
"Love on Six Cylinders"	9 - 12	12 - 15
Series 377 Untitled (4) B&W	5 - 6	6 - 8
Taylor, Platt & Co. (T.P. & Co., N.Y.)		
Series 782		
"A Fisherman's Luck"	9 - 12	12 - 15
"A Heart of Diamonds"	9 - 12	12 - 15
"A Modern Siren"	9 - 12	12 - 15
"Daisies Won't Tell"	9 - 12	12 - 15
"The Glories of March"	9 - 12	12 - 15
"His Latest Chauffeur"	9 - 12	12 - 15
"Indicating a Thaw"	9 - 12	12 - 15
"The Magnet"	9 - 12	12 - 15
"Let's Paddle Forever"	9 - 12	12 - 15
"Love Has It's Clouds"	9 - 12	12 - 15
"Stolen Sweets"	9 - 12	12 - 15
"True Love Never Runs Smooth"	9 - 12	12 - 15
Osborne Calendar Co. − Advertising Cards		
1521 "Fancy Work"	30 - 35	35 - 40
1561 "Mary had a Little Lamb"	30 - 35	35 - 40
1571 "The Tongue is Mightier ..."	30 - 35	35 - 40
1601 "The Favorite's Day"	30 - 35	35 - 40

Clarence Underwood, Novitas, 20454
"Liebe auf Eis"

C. Underwood, Finnish With "Stamp
Here" in Stamp Box – "Cherry Ripe"

1621 "Music Hath Charm"	30 - 35	35 - 40
A.R. & C. i.B.		
Series 283 Lovers		
"Des Meeres und der Liebe Wellen"	9 - 12	12 - 15
"Verlobt"	9 - 12	12 - 15
Series 1283 Duplication of Series 283		
"Des Meeres und der Liebe Wellen"	9 - 12	12 - 15
M. Munk, Vienna		
No. No. "Skipper & Mate"	12 - 15	15 - 20
Series 303 (8)		
Beautiful Ladies With Pets–No captions	9 - 12	12 - 15
Series 377, 385, 387, & 388	9 - 12	12 - 15
Ladies & Dogs "My Companion"	9 - 12	12 - 15
Series 524 No Captions	9 - 12	12 - 15
Series 742 * (8)		
"Love Laughs at Winter"	8 - 10	10 - 12
"Love on Wings"	12 - 15	15 - 18
"Under the Mistletoe"	8 - 10	10 - 12
"The Sender of Orchids"	9 - 12	12 - 15
"The Last Waltz"	9 - 12	12 - 15
"The Greatest Thing"	9 - 12	12 - 15
* **Series 742** A,B,C,D,E,F,G & H.		
All same as Series 742 but with German		
captions, add $3.		
Series 832, 834, 834C, 837 & 860 *		
"A Penny for Thought"	9 - 12	12 - 15
"A Problem of Income"	9 - 12	12 - 15

"Cherry Ripe"	12 - 15	15 - 18
"He Loves Me ..."	12 - 15	15 - 18
"How to Know Wildflowers"	12 - 15	15 - 20
"Only a Question of Time"	10 - 12	12 - 15
"The Sweetest Flower that ..."	10 - 12	12 - 15
"Skipper and Mate"	10 - 12	12 - 15
"Love and Six Cylinders"	12 - 15	15 - 18

With German Captions, add $3.

Novitas, Germany (N in Star - in circle logo)
400 Series

445 "Gestand nis"	9 - 12	12 - 15
446 "Hast Du mich lieb?"	9 - 12	12 - 15
447 "Einig"	9 - 12	12 - 15
449 "Zukunftplane"	9 - 12	12 - 15
Others, No Captions	9 - 12	12 - 15

20000 Series

20391 No Caption	9 - 12	12 - 15
20392 No Caption	9 - 12	12 - 15
20451 "Wer Wird Siegen"	9 - 12	12 - 15
20452 "Dem Fluck Entgegen"	9 - 12	12 - 15
20453 No Caption (Lovers of Beauty)	9 - 12	12 - 15
20454 "Liebe Auf Eis"	9 - 12	12 - 15
20455 "Abwesend, Aber Nicht Vergessen"	9 - 12	12 - 15
20456 No Caption	9 - 12	12 - 15
20457 "Zwei Seelen und ein Genankt"	9 - 12	12 - 15
20458 "Zukunpt Straune"	9 - 12	12 - 15
20459 "Glückliche Stunden"	9 - 12	12 - 15
20460 "Glückliche Tagt"	9 - 12	12 - 15

AMSTERDAM
De Muinck & Co., Amsterdam

R. 194 "Cherry Ripe"	18 - 22	22 - 26

FINLAND
W. & G.   (Weilin & Goos)
American Series N:0 7001 1-35

6 Cards with No Captions	18 - 22	22 - 26

Untitled Series, No Publisher, with "Stamp Here"
in Stamp Box. This is the missing 25th card in
the Fisher-Boileau series of 25.

"Cherry Ripe"	40 - 50	50 - 75

RUSSIA
Rishar (Richard or Phillips)

"The Last Waltz Together"	25 - 30	30 - 40
UNIERZYSKI, J. (POL)	6 - 9	9 - 12
UPRKA, JOZA (CZ)	6 - 8	8 - 10

USABAL, LOTTIE (IT)

P.F.B. (in Diamond) **Series 3796** (6)	12 - 15	15 - 18
Ladies & Dogs Series 3968 (6)	12 - 14	14 - 16

E.A.S.B.

Series 111 Lovers under the Mistletoe	8 - 10	10 - 12
Series 103 Lovers Dancing	8 - 12	12 - 16
Series 114, 370 Lovers Dancing	8 - 12	12 - 16

Erkal

Series 301, 308, 315, 367 Hats (6)	8 - 10	10 - 12
Series 303 Smoking Ladies (6)	10 - 12	12 - 15
Series 336 Tennis (6)	22 - 25	25 - 30

Lottie Usabal, R&K "Erkal"
Series 306/4

Lottie Usabal, R&K "Erkal"
Series 363

Series 343 Skiing (6)	10 - 15	15 - 18
Series 318, 356 Lovers (6)	10 - 12	12 - 15
Series 339 On Toboggan Sled (6)	10 - 12	12 - 15
Series 347 Gypsy Heads (6)	8 - 10	10 - 12
Series 330, 337, 357 Dancing/Kissing (6)	8 - 10	10 - 12
Series 1318 Lovers on Couch (6)	10 - 12	12 - 15
G. Kuais		
Series 1393 Hats	8 - 10	10 - 12
Gurner & Simon		
Series 2027 Lovers at the Bar (6)	6 - 8	8 - 10
S. & G.		
Series 694 Couples, Man in Uniform	6 - 8	8 - 10
S.W.S.B.		
Series 128, 1251 Lovers Kissing (6)	8 - 10	10 - 12
Series 1007, 1068, 1256 Couples Dancing (6)	10 - 12	12 - 15
Series 1091, 6380, 6383 Couples Dancing (6)	10 - 12	12 - 15
Series 1070 Lesbian Dancers (6)	22 - 25	25 - 35
Series 1108 Nude in Fur (6)	12 - 15	15 - 20
Series 1122 Courtship-Marriage (6)	12 - 15	15 - 20
Series 1295-1300 Dancing/Blacks (6)	20 - 22	22 - 25
Series 1356 Heads/Smoking (6)	10 - 12	12 - 18
Series 303 "Ladies Smoking" (6)	12 - 15	15 - 18
Series 4668, 4669, 4670 (6)	10 - 12	12 - 15
Series 6447 Lovers/Cupids (6)	10 - 12	12 - 15
Ladies & Dogs		
S.W.S.B.		
Series 1336, 4989 (6)	10 - 12	12 - 15

Series 1336 (6)	10 - 12	12 - 15
Ladies & Horses		
S.W.S.B.		
Series 257, 328, 345, 347, 5568 (6)	10 - 12	12 - 15
Erkal		
Series 306, 307, 320, 335 (6)	10 - 12	12 - 15
S.W.S.B. Women in Uniform	10 - 12	12 - 15
Anonymous		
Series 20468 Couples Dancing	10 - 15	15 - 18
Art Deco		
Erkal		
Series 308 **Ladies/Hats**	10 - 12	12 - 15
Series 324 "Gypsy"	10 - 12	12 - 15
Series 338 Ladies/Hats	10 - 12	12 - 15
Series 363 Fantasy Butterfly Ladies (6)	20 - 25	25 - 35
P.F.B. in Diamond		
Series 6073 Beauties on Pillows (6)	12 - 15	15 - 20
S.&G.S.iB.		
Series 6378, 6379, 6381, 6382 Dancing (6)	10 - 12	12 - 15
Series 6384, 6387, 1071, 1091 Dancing (6)	10 - 12	12 - 15
Series 1058, 1207, 1208,1330, 1333 Dancing (6)	10 - 12	12 - 15
Guner & Simon		
Series 2027 Lovers Kissing	8 - 10	10 - 12
UZLEMBLO, HENRY (PO)	12 - 15	15 - 18
Wyd. Galeria Artystyczna, Kraków, "Zosia"	12 - 15	15 - 18
VALLEE. A. Dancing	12 - 15	15 - 20
VALLET, L. (FR) French Glamour		
Lapina		
Nude "La Douche" Series	25 - 30	30 - 35
Collections des Cent. 63b	150 - 175	175 - 200
VASSALO, A. (IT) Art Deco	12 - 15	15 - 18
VEITH, PROF. E. (AUS)		
B.K.W.I. Series 884B (6)	10 - 12	12 - 15
VENTURA, R.	10 - 12	12 - 15
VERNON, EMILE (US)		
Osborne Calendar Co.		
Year 1909 Beautiful Ladies	15 - 18	18 - 22
VILLON, JACQUES (FR) Art Nouveau		
Collections des Cent.	400 - 500	500 - 800
Gala Henri Monnier	900 - 1000	1000 - 1100
VINCENT, RENE Art Deco Sports	25 - 30	30 - 35
VILLA, A. (IT)	10 - 12	12 - 15
VINNOY (FR) Art Deco	12 - 14	14 - 18
W.Z.		
CBB (Hand-painted)		
Series I (6) Dancing	20 - 25	25 - 28
Series 8 (6) Bathing Beauties	18 - 22	22 - 25
WACHTEL, WILHELM (GER)	8 - 10	10 - 12
WALLACE (US)	8 - 10	10 - 12
Ladies/Horses	10 - 12	12 - 15
WANKE, ALICE (AUS)		
Art Nouveau	50 - 60	60 - 75
M. Munk, Vienne		
Series 452 Fashionable Ladies (6)	40 - 45	45 - 50

W.Z., CBB, Series VIII
No. 6

W.Z., CBB, Series I
No. 6, "Two-Step"

Elinore Weber, NGP
A-1014/5, No Caption

WAPALLOKA (RUS)	6 - 8	8 - 10
WASILKOWSKI, K. (PO)	8 - 10	10 - 12
WASKO, EDWARD G. (PO)	6 - 8	8 - 10
WEBER, ELINORE		
N.G.P.		
A-1014/5	10 - 12	12 - 15
WEBSTER, W.E.	8 - 10	10 - 12
WENNERBERG, B. (SWE) Art Nouveau		
Nurses	12 - 15	15 - 20
War (w/soldiers)	8 - 10	10 - 12
Ladies Fashion	10 - 12	12 - 15
Tennis Series	30 - 35	35 - 40
Black Tennis	45 - 50	50 - 60
Meissner & Buch		
"Lawn Tennis" Ladies Sports	35 - 40	40 - 50
Blacks	45 - 50	50 - 60
WEZEL, A. (AUS)	8 - 10	10 - 12
WFA Ladies & Horses		
Series 204 (6)	10 - 12	12 - 15
WICHERA, R. R. (AUS)		
M. Munk, Vienna		
Series 112, 224, 229, 322, 411, 450 (6)	10 - 12	12 - 15
Series 530, 633, 683, 1101, 1163 (6)	10 - 12	12 - 15
Series 559, 5590 Big Hats (6)	12 - 15	15 - 18
Series 684 Semi-Nudes (6)	15 - 18	18 - 22
WIEDERSEIM, GRACE (also Grace Drayton)		
Armour & Co.		
"American Girl" Series		
"The Wiederseim Girl"	30 - 35	35 - 40
"The Wiederseim Girl" (German Pub.)	35 - 40	45 - 50
WIMBUSH, WINIFRED (GB)		
Raphael Tuck		
Sporting Girls, Series 3603 (6)		
Bathing, Boating, Cricket	15 - 20	20 - 25
Golf	30 - 35	35 - 45

Adelina Zandrino – Rev. Stampa
Series 18-2

Adelina Zandrino – Rev. Stampa
Series 18-4

Skating	30 - 35	35 - 45
Tennis	25 - 30	30 - 40
WITT, MIA Art Deco	15 - 20	20 - 25
WUYTS, A.	4 - 6	6 - 8
YOBBI, L. (IT)	10 - 12	12 - 15
ZABCZINSKY		
C.B.B.		
Series 21-1 Dancing (6)	15 - 18	18 - 22
Series 21-2 Standing (6)	18 - 20	20 - 25
Series 21-3 Dancing (6)	15 - 18	18 - 22
Series 21-4 Dancing (6)	15 - 18	18 - 22
Series 21-5 Dancing (6)	15 - 18	18 - 22
Series 21-6 Dancing (6)	15 - 18	18 - 22
ZABCZOMSLU, W. Art Deco	8 - 10	10 - 12
ZANDRINO, A. (IT) Art Deco		
Series 18 Nude With Wild Animals (6)	20 - 25	25 - 30
Series 17 Fans (6)	12 - 15	15 - 20
Series 23, 24, 30 Fashion (6)	12 - 15	15 - 20
Series 94 Hats (6)	12 - 15	15 - 20
Pierrots	20 - 22	22 - 25
ZASCHE, TH. (GER)	8 - 10	10 - 12
Tennis Lady	15 - 20	20 - 25
ZELECHOWSKI, K. (PO)	8 - 10	10 - 12
ZENISER, JOSEF	6 - 8	8 - 10
ZEUMER, BRUNO (GER)	5 - 6	6 - 8
ZINI, M. Ladies	10 - 12	12 - 15
ZMURKO, FR. (PO) See Color Nudes		
ANCZYC Series	8 - 10	10 - 12
ZOLN, L.		
Anonymous	6 - 8	8 - 10

NATIONALITY OF ARTIST LISTINGS

AUS–Austria; AUST–Australia; BEL–Belgium; BUL–Bulgaria; CAN–Canada; CZ–Czechoslovakia; DEN–Denmark; FIN–Finland; FR–France; GB–Great Britain; GER–Germany; HUN–Hungary; IT–Italy; JAP–Japan; LAT–Latvia; NETH–Netherlands; NOR–Norway; PO–Poland; RUS–Russia; SP–Spain; SWE–Sweden; SWI–Switzerland; US–United States.

BEAUTIFUL CHILDREN

ALANEN, JOSEPH (FIN)
Easter Witch Children	10 - 12	12 - 15
Easter Witches	8 - 10	10 - 12
Miniature Easter Witch Cards	15 - 18	18 - 20

ALDAN (IT) Art Deco　　　8 - 10　　10 - 12
ALDIN, CECIL (GB) Nursery Rhymes　　10 - 12　　12 - 15
ALLEN, DAPHNE (GB)　　5 - 7　　7 - 10
　Nursery Rhymes　　7 - 10　　10 - 12
ALYS, M.　　2 - 3　　3 - 5
ANDERSON, ANNE (GB)　　6 - 9　　9 - 12
ANDERSON, FLORENCE (GB) Fairies　　10 - 12　　12 - 15
ANDERSON, V. C. (US)　　5 - 6　　6 - 8
　Raphael Tuck Series 7 – Leap Year (12)　　8 - 10　　10 - 15
ETA (E. T. ANDREWS)
Early Chromolithographs	25 - 35	35 - 45
B. Dondorf Series 173	25 - 35	35 - 45
Raphael Tuck		
Series 1629 **"Art" Series** (6)	25 - 30	30 - 40
Series 6615 "Brown Eyes and Blue" (6)	25 - 30	30 - 40
Series 8431 "Christmas" Series	25 - 30	30 - 40
Wenau-Delila		
Series 1424 through 1427 (4)	20 - 25	25 - 30

ANTTILA, EVA (FIN)　　6 - 8　　8 - 10
ATTWELL, MABEL LUCIE (GB)
Early Period, Pre-1915	15 - 18	18 - 22
Middle Period, 1915-1930	10 - 15	15 - 18
1930's-1950's Period	5 - 8	8 - 10
Valentine & Sons (See Blacks)		
Series 748 Golliwoggs	20 - 25	25 - 30
Series A561 Golliwoggs	20 - 25	25 - 30
Series A579 Golliwoggs	20 - 25	25 - 28
Suffragette "Where's My Vote"	30 - 35	35 - 45

AVERILL, JOYCE (GB)
　Vivian A. Mansell & Co.
　　Series 1047 National Sailor Boys (6)　　12 - 15　　15 - 18
AVERY, A.E. (US)　　3 - 5　　5 - 6
AZZONI, N. (IT) Art Deco
　Dell, Anna & Gasparini
　　Series 517 (6)　　12 - 15　　15 - 18
BANKS, M. E. (GB)
　Raphael Tuck
　　Dressing Doll Series 1, #3381 (6)
"Dolly Dimple"	150 - 180	180 - 200
"Little Pamela"	150 - 180	180 - 200
"Our Jimmy"	150 - 180	180 - 200
"Pretty Peggy"	150 - 180	180 - 200
"Tommy Lad"	150 - 180	180 - 200

BARBER, C. W. (GB)
　Carleton Publishing Co.
　　Children Studies　　8 - 10　　10 - 12

E. T. Andrews, Raphael Tuck
"Christmas" Series 8431

E. T. Andrews, Wenau (W&N)
#1425, No Caption

Mabel L. Attwell, B.K.W.I. #257/4
Suffragette, "Now! Where's my Vote?"

Mabel L. Attwell, Wolgemuth & Sissner
#2538, "Mir kann keiner!" (1950's)

Series 676 (6)		
Daughter/Mother Series	8 - 10	10 - 12
BARHAM, SYBIL (GB) See Fairies/Fairy Tales		
C. W. Faulkner Series 502, 701, 964 (6)	5 - 7	7 - 10
BARKER, CECILY M. (GB)	6 - 8	8 - 10
BARNES, G. L. See F. Tales/Nursery Rhymes, Cats		
BARRIBAL, L. (GB)	8 - 10	10 - 15
BARROWS, ELIZABETH (GB)	5 - 6	6 - 8
BARTH, K. (GER)		
A.R. & Co.		
Children with Dachshunds, etc.	15 - 18	18 - 22
BARWICK, THOMAS (GB)	5 - 7	7 - 9
BAUMGARTEN, FRITZ or (F.B.) (GER)		
See Fairy Tales/Nursery Rhymes		
Erika		
Series 6390	15 - 18	18 - 22
Meissner & Buch		
Early years to 1920	15 - 20	20 - 25
1920's to 1930		
Colorful Children, Holiday Greetings	15 - 20	20 - 25
Children with Fantasy Theme	18 - 22	22 - 28
Series 2970 First Day of School	18 - 22	22 - 26
Series 2994, 3008, 3044	12 - 15	15 - 20
Series 3238 "Prosit Neuyahr!" (New Year)	15 - 20	20 - 25
Other Publishers - Cellaro, etc.	10 - 12	12 - 15

F. Baumgarten, Meissner & Buch
Series 2027 (1910 Era)

F. Baumgarten, Meissner & Buch
"Godt Nytaar!" (1910 Era)

Uns. F. Baumgarten, Meissner & Buch
Series 2011 (1910 Era)

E. Bem, Lapina, #176 – "Cinderella"
(Russian Caption)

A. Bertiglia, C.C.M., #2607
No Caption

BAYER, CHARLES A.	2 - 3	3 - 5
BEM, E. (RUS)		
Lapina Series	15 - 18	18 - 22
Russian Backs	18 - 22	22 - 26
Russian Alphabet Series	15 - 18	18 - 20
BENJEN (US)	3 - 4	4 - 6
BERTI (FR)	5 - 7	7 - 10
BERTIGLIA, A. (IT) Art Deco		
Series 155 & 1053 Dutch Kids (6)	8 - 10	10 - 12
Series 1010 Playing War (6)	12 - 15	15 - 20
Series 1069 (6)	7 - 8	8 - 10
Series 2114 With Dolls (6)	10 - 12	12 - 16
Series 2428 Making Movies (6)	12 - 15	15 - 20
Series 2444, 2461, 2499 (6)	8 - 10	10 - 12
C.C.M. **Series 2607** (6) Art Deco	12 - 15	15 - 20
BEST, R.J. (US)	3 - 5	5 - 7
BETTS, E.F. (US)	3 - 5	5 - 7
BIRGER (SWE) Art Deco	15 - 20	20 - 30
BISHOP, C. (US)	1 - 2	2 - 3
BLODGETT, BERTHA E. or B.E.B. (US)		
AMP Co.		
Series 209, Easter	6 - 8	8 - 10
Series 410, Christmas	5 - 6	6 - 8
Little Girls/Huge Hats Series	6 - 8	8 - 10
BOMPARD, L. (IT) Art Deco		
Series 379, 454, 497 (6)	8 - 9	9 - 10
Series 523, 567, 906, 993 (6)	8 - 10	10 - 12
BONNE, SIGRID	5 - 6	6 - 7
BONNIE (1940's)	4 - 6	6 - 8
BONORA (IT)		
Boy Scout Series 760	20 - 25	25 - 30
BORELLI, C. ZOE (AUS)		
M. Munk		
Series 539 Children with dolls	12 - 15	15 - 20
Series 918 Children with dolls	12 - 15	15 - 20
BORISS, MARGRET (NETH) (Art Deco)		
Armag Co. Comical children		
Series 0280 Artist Children	8 - 10	10 - 12
Series 0332, 0341 Children playing adults	8 - 10	10 - 12
Series 0322, 0397 Black Children	15 - 18	18 - 22

Series 1927 "Occupations" Series	8 - 12	12 - 14
Others	8 - 10	10 - 12
See Fairy Tales/Nursery Rhymes		
BORRMEISTER, R. (GER)	5 - 6	6 - 9
BOURET, GERMAINE (FR)	8 - 10	10 - 12
BOWDEN, DORIS Nursery Rhymes	8 - 10	10 - 12
BOWLEY, A. L. (GB)		
Early Unsigned Chromolithographs	25 - 30	30 - 35
Raphael Tuck		
Series C218 Christmas Children	20 - 25	25 - 30
Series C1757 Children and Santa	25 - 30	30 - 35
Series C 3781, C3782	20 - 25	25 - 28
Series 6037 Children and Snowman	18 - 22	22 - 26
BOWLEY, MAY (GB)		
Early Unsigned Chromolithographs	20 - 25	25 - 30
Others	15 - 18	18 - 20
BRETT, MOLLY See Fairy Tales/Nursery Rhymes		
BRISLEY, E.C. (GB)		
BRISLEY, NINA (GB)	6 - 8	8 - 10
BROMAN, MELA K. (MELA KÖHLER) (AUS)		
Sago-Konst A.B., Stockholm (1930's)		
Series B41	25 - 30	30 - 35
BRUNDAGE, FRANCES (US)		
A.M.P. Co. (Emb)		
Series 403 Christmas (Uns.)		
Girl in red rides toy stick horse	15 - 18	18 - 22
Others	12 - 15	15 - 18
J. Biau, Spain		
Die-cut of boy with big head (Uns.)	50 - 60	60 - 70
Sam Gabriel		
New Year		
Series 300, 302, 316 (10)	10 - 12	12 - 15
St. Patrick's Day		
Series 140 (10) (Unsigned)	8 - 10	10 - 15
Memorial Day		
Series 150 (10)		
"And summon from the shadowy Past..."	15 - 20	20 - 25
"Brave minds, howe'er at war..."	15 - 20	20 - 25
"By fairy hands their knell..."	15 - 20	20 - 25
"Enough of Merit has each..."	15 - 20	20 - 25
"From every mountain side..." "Peace" at top	15 - 20	20 - 25
"Glory guards with solemn round..."	15 - 20	20 - 25
"How sleep the brave, who sink to rest..."	15 - 20	20 - 25
"In that instant o'er his..."	15 - 20	20 - 25
"One Flag, one Land, one Heart..."	15 - 20	20 - 25
"Would I could duly praise..."	15 - 20	20 - 25
Valentine's Day Series 413 (6)	8 - 10	10 - 15
Halloween		
Series 120, 121 (10)	20 - 22	22 - 30
Series 123 (10)	15 - 18	18 - 22
Series 125 (6)	20 - 23	23 - 28
Series 174 (6) (Uns.)	20 - 25	25 - 30
Series 184 (12) (Uns.)	18 - 22	22 - 26

Uns. Frances Brundage , Theo. Stroefer
Series S675, "Prosit Neujahr!"

Frances Brundage (Unsigned)
Theo. Stroefer, 1896 (adv. on back)

Frances Brundage (Unsigned)
Wezel & Naumann, Series X, No. 9

Frances Brundage (Unsigned)
Wezel & Naumann, Series 67

Frances Brundage (Unsigned)
Wezel & Naumann, Series 41, #5

Thanksgiving
Series 130, 132, 133 (10)	8 - 10	10 - 12
Series 135 (6)	6 - 8	8 - 10
Christmas Series 200, 208, 219	12 - 15	15 - 20
Santas	15 - 20	20 - 25

FOREIGN
B&K
Series 33-3 (Sepia) Ps. 51:12	30 - 40	40 - 50

Raphael Tuck
New Year
Series No. 12 (Uns.)	15 - 20	20 - 25
Series 601 (Uns.)	10 - 12	12 - 15
Series 665 "Little Sunbeam"	30 - 35	35 - 45
Series 1036	12 - 15	15 - 20

Valentine's Day
Series 11 (4) (Uns.)	12 - 15	15 - 18
Series 20, 26 (Uns.)	12 - 15	15 - 18
Series 100, 101 (6) (Uns.)	12 - 15	15 - 18
Blacks (1 in Series 100 and 3 in Series 101)	25 - 28	28 - 32
Series 102 (6)	12 - 15	15 - 20
Blacks (1)	22 - 25	25 - 28
Series 103	12 - 15	15 - 20
Blacks (1)	22 - 25	25 - 28
Series 106 Same as Series 101 and French		
Series 941 w/French captions - all unsigned	12 - 15	15 - 18
Blacks	25 - 28	28 - 32
Series 107 and 117	10 - 12	12 - 15
Blacks	22 - 25	25 - 30
Series 108 Valentine (4)		
Blacks (4)	22 - 25	25 - 30

Unsigned Frances Brundage, B&K, No. 33-3 (Sepia)
Psalm 51:12 In German ("Restore unto me the joy of thy salvation...")

Frances Brundage (Unsigned)
Theo. Stroefer, Series 85, #1

Frances Brundage (Unsigned)
Wezel & Naumann, Series 237

Frances Brundage, Raphael Tuck – "Babydom" Series C40

Series 115 "Little Wooers" Valentines (4)	10 - 12	12 - 15
Blacks (2)	22 - 25	25 - 30
Series 118 (4)	10 - 12	12 - 15
Blacks	25 - 30	30 - 35

Series 165	10 - 12	12 - 15
Blacks (2)	22 - 25	25 - 28
Series 1035	10 - 12	12 - 15
Blacks (2)	22 - 25	25 - 28
Easter Series 1049 (3)	8 - 10	10 - 15
Memorial Day		
Series 173 (12) (Uns.)	12 - 15	15 - 18
Halloween (See Halloween Greetings)		
Christmas		
Series 4 (12)	12 - 15	15 - 20
Series 165 (2)	10 - 12	12 - 15
Blacks (2)	22 - 25	25 - 28
Series 1035 (2)		
Blacks	22 - 25	25 - 28
Series 2723 "Colored Folks" (6)		
"The Christening"	55 - 65	65 - 75
"Church Parade"	55 - 65	65 - 75
"De Proof of de Puddin"	55 - 65	65 - 75
"Don'! Took de las' piece"	55 - 65	65 - 75
"The Village Choir"	55 - 65	65 - 75
Chalk Boards - "You is a Chicken"	55 - 65	65 - 75
Series 2816 The "Connoisseur" Series duplicates		
Series 2723 (6)	55 - 65	65 - 75
Series 4096 "Funny Folks" (8) **		
Blacks (5)		
"A Trial of Patience"	50 - 60	60 - 70
"I'se Just Been Married"	50 - 60	60 - 70
"The Pickaninnies Bedtime"	50 - 60	60 - 70
"Preparing for the Party"	50 - 60	60 - 70
"Tubbing Time in Darkie Land"	50 - 60	60 - 70
White related (3)		
"Double Dutch"	15 - 20	20 - 25
"Gossips"	15 - 20	20 - 25
"The Happy Pair"	15 - 20	20 - 25
* Series was published by Tuck in book form w/duplicate copies. One in color to show how the B&W should be colored. All had P.C. backs and were serrated for mailing purposes.		
** Deduct $15 for B&W issues.		
Series 6616 "Humorous" (Uns.)	15 - 18	18 - 22
Blacks (1) "Git a move on" Black	20 - 25	25 - 30
Raphael Tuck, Paris		
Series 131 (B&W) (6)		
1 Girl leaning on big rock	25 - 30	30 - 35
3 Girl at brook side carrying large urn	25 - 30	30 - 35
Early Foreign Publishers (Chromolithos)		
H & S, Carl Hirsch, W.H.B.,		
Theo. Stroefer (T.S.N.), Wezel &		
Naumann, C. Baum & Anon.		
Large Images	40 - 50	50 - 60
Small Images	30 - 35	35 - 40
BUCHANAN, FRED (GB)	10 - 12	12 - 15
Tennis	22 - 25	25 - 28

Unsigned Adolfo Busi   *G. Caspari, Erika, #1694*   *Unsigned V. Castelli*
Degami, Fantasy Series 667   *"Fröhliche Weinnachten"*   *Degami, Series 2105*

BULL, RENE (GB)	6 - 8	8 - 10
BURD, C. M. (US) (See Advertising)		
Rally Day Series	10 - 12	12 - 15
Birthday Series	8 - 10	10 - 12
BUSI, ADOLFO (IT)		
Degami		
Series 500 (6)	12 - 15	15 - 20
Series 667 (6) Fantasy	15 - 18	18 - 22
Series 677 (6) Christmas Children	12 - 15	15 - 20
Boy Scout Series	16 - 20	20 - 25
BUTCHER, ARTHUR (GB)	5 - 6	6 - 9
CARTER, SYDNEY (GB)		
S. Hildesheimer & Co.		
"Children's Frolics" (6)	10 - 12	12 - 15
"Romps" Series		
"A Morning Drive"	10 - 12	12 - 15
"Battledore"	8 - 10	10 - 12
"Baby's New Ball"	10 - 12	12 - 15
"Gee Up"	10 - 12	12 - 15
"The Military Band"	10 - 12	12 - 15
"Pickaback"	10 - 12	12 - 15
Series 5246 "An Excursion on Bank Holiday"	8 - 10	10 - 12
Series 5188 "Months of the Year" (12)		
114 "March"	15 - 18	18 - 22
CARR, GENE (US)		
Rotograph Co.		
Series 219 (4th of July)	8 - 10	10 - 15
CASPARI, GERTRUD		
Erika		
Little Girl Santa, with witches	25 - 30	30 - 35
Herman A. Peters		
Children with Birds	10 - 15	15 - 20
CASTELLI, V. (IT) Art Deco		
Degami **Series 2105**	15 - 18	18 - 22
Ultra **Series 533** (6)	8 - 10	10 - 15

Sofia Chiostri
Ballerini & Fratini, No. 303

Sofia Chiostri
Ballerini & Fratini, No. 293

C.B.T.	2 - 3	3 - 4
CENNI, E. (IT) Art Deco	6 - 8	8 - 10
CHAMBERLIN (US)		
Campbell "Women's Suffrage"		
310 "Suffrage First"	70 - 80	80 - 100
312 "Let's Pull..." Suffrage	70 - 80	80 - 100
CHIOSTRI, SOFIA (IT) Art Deco		
Ballerini & Fratini		
Series 117, 362 (4) Children Pierrots	18 - 22	22 - 25
Series 176 (4) French-type children	20 - 25	25 - 28
Series 184 (4) Japanese	20 - 25	25 - 30
Series 188, 268, 418 (4)	15 - 20	20 - 25
Series 261 (4) Easter Fantasy	20 - 25	25 - 28
Series 293 (4) Christmas, with toys	25 - 30	30 - 35
Series 303 Dancing, Music	20 - 25	25 - 30
Series 319 (4)	20 - 25	25 - 30
Series 246, 334, 336, 405 (4) Christmas	20 - 25	25 - 30
Series 365 (4)	22 - 25	25 - 30
Series 483 (4) Pfingsten	25 - 30	30 - 35
CLAPSADDLE, ELLEN H. (US)		
International Art. Publishing Co.		
Angels, Cherubs	8 - 10	10 - 13
Animals	4 - 5	5 - 6
Young Ladies, Women	6 - 8	8 - 12
Bells, Florals, Crosses, Sleds, etc.	2 - 4	4 - 5
Good Luck, Thanksgiving	2 - 4	4 - 5
Thanksgiving Children	8 - 10	10 - 15

Ellen H. Clapsaddle, International Art Pub. Co. — "I offer you my heart, my hand..."

Indians	8 - 10	10 - 12
Transportation	2 - 3	3 - 6
Christmas Children	10 - 15	15 - 20
Santas	15 - 20	20 - 25
Easter Children	8 - 10	10 - 15
Valentine Greetings	8 - 10	10 - 15
Valentine Children	6 - 10	10 - 20
Series 941, 942, 944	8 - 12	12 - 16
Series 952, 953	8 - 10	10 - 15
Series 1034, 1081 (Uns.)	6 - 8	8 - 10
Valentine Mechanicals		
Series 16190 (4)		
"To My Valentine"	40 - 50	50 - 60
"St. Valentine's Greeting"	40 - 50	50 - 60
"To My Sweetheart"	40 - 50	50 - 60
"Love's Fond Greeting"	40 - 50	50 - 60
Series 51810	20 - 25	25 - 30
Memorial Day Series 973, 2444, 4397 (6)	15 - 20	20 - 25
Series 2935 (6)	15 - 20	20 - 25
Washington's Birthday		
Series 16208, 16209 (4)	8 - 10	10 - 15
Series 16250 (6)	8 - 10	10 - 15
Series 51896 (6)	8 - 10	10 - 15
Lincoln's Birthday	8 - 10	10 - 15
St. Patrick's Day	10 - 12	12 - 15
Independence Day		
Series 2443, 4398	15 - 20	20 - 25
Halloween (See Halloween Greetings)		
Wolf & Co.		
Large Children images	12 - 15	15 - 22
Small Children images	6 - 8	8 - 10

Unsigned Ellen H. Clapsaddle
Kopal, No. 403

Ellen H. Clapsaddle, Wolf & Co., No. 5
"Merry Christmas"

Later, smaller images	5 - 6	6 - 8
Suffragettes		
"Love Me, Love My Vote"	70 - 80	80 - 90
"Woman's Sphere is in the Home" (106)	50 - 60	60 - 70
Halloween (See Halloween Greetings)		
Foreign Publishers		
Signed issues: Add $5-$10 to above prices.		
Unsigned issues: Add $5-$7 to above prices.		
New discoveries: Add $10-$20.		
CLARK, A. (US)	5 - 6	6 - 7
CLOKE, RENE (GB) See Fairies		
C. W. Faulkner Series (1930's)	12 - 15	15 - 20
Valentine's Series (1930's-40's)	8 - 10	10 - 15
Salmon Bros.		
Series (1930's-40's)	8 - 10	10 - 12
1950's Series	3 - 4	4 - 7
Medici Society Series (1950's-60's)	3 - 4	4 - 7
COLBY, V. (US) (B&W)	2 - 3	3 - 4
COLEMAN, W. S.	6 - 8	8 - 10
COLOMBO, E. (IT)		
A. Guarneri (Milano)		
Series 234, 454, 618 (6)	8 - 10	10 - 15
Series 665 Child With Dog (6)	8 - 10	10 - 16
Series 960, 1764, 1905, 1964 (6)	8 - 10	10 - 15
Series 1968 (6)	10 - 12	12 - 16
Series 2007, 2140, 2141 (6)	8 - 10	10 - 12
Series 2033, 2044, 2181 (6)	10 - 12	12 - 16

E. Colombo
G.P.M., Series 1923

E. Colombo
Rev. Stampa, Series 479

Series 2223 (6)	10 - 12	12 - 16
Series 2252, 2426 (6)	8 - 10	10 - 12
G.P.M.		
Series 1693-2 Tennis	15 - 18	18 - 22
Series 1923	12 - 15	15 - 20
Series 1962-2 Tennis	15 - 18	18 - 22
Series 1964, 1996 (6)	8 - 10	10 - 15
Series 1976 (6) Romeo & Juliette	10 - 12	12 - 16
Ultra		
Series 2039 (6)	8 - 10	10 - 15
Rev. Stampa		
Series 479 Soccer	15 - 18	18 - 22
COOK, A. M.	8 - 10	10 - 12
COOPER, M.B. (GB)	5 - 6	6 - 8
COOPER, PHYLLIS (GB) Art Deco		
Raphael Tuck "Happy Land" Nursery Rhymes		
Series 1, 3463 (6)	22 - 26	26 - 32
W/Golliwoggs	30 - 35	35 - 45
Series 2, 3464 (6)	22 - 26	26 - 32
W/Golliwoggs	30 - 35	35 - 45
Doll-Toy Series (6)	30 - 35	35 - 45
CORBELLA, TITO (IT)		
"Ultra"		
Series 2034, 2035, 2321	8 - 10	10 - 12
Series 2161 Dutch Kids	8 - 10	10 - 12
Series 2182, 2221	10 - 12	12 - 15

P. Cooper, Raphael Tuck, "Happy Land" Series 2, No. 3464 – "O you naughty..."

CORBETT, BERTHA (US)		
J.I. Austen Sunbonnet Children	8 - 10	10 - 15
CORY, F. Y. (US)	5 - 6	6 - 8
COTTOM, C. M.	4 - 6	6 - 8
COWDEREY, K. (GB)	8 - 10	10 - 12
COWHAM, HILDA (GB) (See Fairies)		
C. W. Faulkner		
Series 1601 (6) **"Fairies"**		
"When the Moon Rises," "Up in the Morning..."	18 - 22	22 - 26
Series 1618 (6)	18 - 22	22 - 26
Inter-Art	15 - 18	18 - 22
Raphael Tuck		
Series 6076 "Humorous" (6)	15 - 18	18 - 22
Valentine's	15 - 18	18 - 22
CRAMER, RIE (NE)	12 - 15	15 - 18
Fairy Tales	15 - 18	18 - 22
CURTIS, E. (US)		
McGowen Silsbee Litho, N.Y. (B&W)	6 - 8	8 - 10
Raphael Tuck "Garden Patch" 2		
"Apple" "Peach"	8 - 10	10 - 12
"Beet" "Radish"	8 - 10	10 - 12
"Canteloupe" "Red Pepper"	8 - 10	10 - 12
"Carrot" "Watermelon"	8 - 10	10 - 12
Raphael Tuck		
Series 7 -- Leap Year (12)	8 - 10	10 - 12
"Valentine Maids" Series D12		
PC 1 "School Slates" (12)	6 - 8	8 - 10
PC 3 "Love's Labors" (12)	6 - 8	8 - 10
PC 4 "From Many Lands" (12)	6 - 8	8 - 10
CZEGKA, B. (PO)		
W.R.B. & Co. Series 22 (6)	8 - 10	10 - 12

When the Moon Rises.

Up in the Morning Early.

Hilda Cowham, C. W. Faulkner
Series 1601, "When the Moon Rises"

Hilda Cowham, C. W. Faulkner
Series 1601, "Up in the Morning ..."

DAWSON, MURIEL (GB)	5 - 7	7 - 10
DeGARMES	1 - 2	2 - 3
DEWEES, ETHEL, E.D., EHD (US)		
AMP Co.	6 - 8	8 -10
Ernest Nister		
Series 2543	8 - 10	10 - 15
DEXTER, MARJORIE	4 - 5	5 - 6
DIXON, DOROTHY (US)		
Ullman Mfg. Co.		
Sunbonnet Babies (6)	8 - 10	10 - 14
DRAYTON, GRACE - **(Wiederseim)** (US)		
A.M. Davis Co. (Quality Cards)		
34 "Here's a load of Christmas Wishes..."	20 - 25	25 - 30
"Sing a song of Christmas"	20 - 25	25 - 30
"Though the weather's cold..."	20 - 25	25 - 30
"I told this Little Birdie..."	20 - 25	25 - 30
Baby Girl in Sled	20 - 25	25 - 30
"Pussy in the corner..."	20 - 25	25 - 30
Jack in the Box	20 - 25	25 - 30
Santa Pops up in mechanical version	50 - 60	60 - 70
Others	20 - 25	25 - 30
Series 143 Birthday Months (12)		
"January," "February," "March"	35 - 40	40 - 45
"April sun or April showers"	35 - 40	40 - 45
"May," "June," "July," "August," "September"	35 - 40	40 - 45
"October," "November," "December"	35 - 40	40 - 45

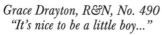

Grace Drayton, R&N, No. 490
"It's nice to be a little boy..."

Grace Drayton, R&N, No No.
"A Button Sewed On By a Maiden ..."

Series 357

"As I pass upon the street..."	30 - 35	35 - 40
"Chubby leg and stubby toe..."	30 - 35	35 - 40
"I rode my cock horse"	30 - 35	35 - 40
"I sent a pretty blue bird"	30 - 35	35 - 40
"I told this little birdie"	30 - 35	35 - 40
"I took my bestest pen in hand"	30 - 35	35 - 40
"Jack in the box is full of glee"	30 - 35	35 - 40
"Pussy in the corner"	30 - 35	35 - 40
B.B., London (Birn Bros.) (6)	20 - 25	25 - 30
Reinthal & Newman, N.Y.		
No No. Dollie: "Dickey has had a accident..."	25 - 30	30 - 35
No No. Eve: "Oh Adam! Wait!..."	25 - 30	30 - 35
No No. "A Button Sewed on..."	25 - 30	30 - 35
306 "A Button Sewed on ..."	25 - 30	30 - 35
307 "Dressy Lady: "What are you crying..."	25 - 30	30 - 35
308 "I'd rather say Hello"	25 - 30	30 - 35
488 "Oh come and be my Lambey dear..."	25 - 30	30 - 35
489 "Oh dear me, what do I see..."	25 - 30	30 - 35
490 "It's nice to be a little boy..."	25 - 30	30 - 35
491 "Little maid neat and sweet..."	25 - 30	30 - 35
492 "Gee up Dobin - tried and true..." (Uns.)	25 - 30	30 - 35
493 The sun is shining warm and sweet..."	25 - 30	30 - 35
495 Teacher & Children	25 - 30	30 - 35
496 "Do you, or don't you?"	25 - 30	30 - 35
497 "I should worry"	25 - 30	30 - 35

498 "I Love to Dance with You"	25 - 30	30 - 35
499 "I think I'd Rather..."	25 - 30	30 - 35
500 "More of All"	25 - 30	30 - 35
502 "Love at first sight" *	30 - 35	35 - 40
503 "The Trousseau" *	30 - 35	35 - 40
504 "The Wedding" *	30 - 35	35 - 40
505 "The Honeymoon" *	30 - 35	35 - 40
506 "First Night in their New Home" *	30 - 35	35 - 40
507 "Their New Love" *	30 - 35	35 - 40
* Easel Cutouts - add $5-10		
Raphael Tuck		
Series 223 (6) (Unsigned)	25 - 30	30 - 35
Series 241 "Bright Eyes" (Uns.) (6)	25 - 30	30 - 35
"I'se Awful Sweet..."	25 - 30	30 - 35
"I'm Your Little Darling Boy..."	25 - 30	30 - 35
"The Boys About Me Rant..."	25 - 30	30 - 35
Others	25 - 30	30 - 35
Series 242 (Unsigned) (6)	25 - 30	30 - 35
Children with Pets	25 - 30	30 - 35
Girl with drum and Teddy Bear	30 - 35	35 - 38
Others	25 - 30	30 - 35
Series 243 "Love Message" (Uns.) (6)	20 - 25	25 - 30
Series 244 "Sweet Bliss" (Uns.) (6)	20 - 25	25 - 30
Series 807 "Halloween"	90 - 100	100 - 120
Series 1002 "Happy Easter" (Uns.) (6)	20 - 25	25 - 28
See Blacks		
Advertising		
"Adam and Eva" A Comedy Play	50 - 60	60 - 70
Minneapolis Tribune		
North American Co. "I'm Kaptin Kiddo"	70 - 80	80 - 100
DUDDLE, JOSEPHINE (GB)	8 - 10	10 - 12
DULK, M. (US)		
Gibson Art		
Series 252 Fantasy Flower Girls, Birthday		
"Daffodil" "Rose"	10 - 12	12 - 15
"Pansy" "Sweet Pea"	10 - 12	12 - 15
"Forget me Not" "Violet"	10 - 12	12 - 15
"Poppy" "Red Rose"	10 - 12	12 - 15
"Pussy Willow" "Tulip"	10 - 12	12 - 15
Valentine Series - Girls (6)	8 - 10	10 - 14
E.H.S. (Ellen H. Saunders) (US)		
M.T. Sheahan, Boston	5 - 7	7 - 9
EBNER, PAULI (GER)		
Early - Signed **PE**	15 - 20	20 - 25
Santas	22 - 25	25 - 30
Santas in Art Deco colored Robes	25 - 30	30 - 40
A.G.B.		
Series 1025 Dancing	15 - 20	20 - 25
Series 2484 Children with toys	20 - 25	25 - 28
B. Dondorf		
Series 1362 "Marriage of the Dolls"	20 - 25	25 - 30
M. Munk, Vienna		
Series 878 Toys	18 - 22	22 - 26
Series 1126 Victorian Children	12 - 15	15 - 20
Series 1129 Birthday	12 - 15	15 - 20

Pauli Ebner, M.D., Series 1101
"Stern-singer"

K. Feiertag, B.K.W.I., Series 27-4
"I kiss your little hand, Madam."

Series 403, 986, 1019 New Year	12 - 15	15 - 20
Series 550, 1136, 1269 New Year	15 - 18	18 - 22
Series 1044 Winter	12 - 14	14 - 16
Series 1158, 1263	12 - 15	15 - 20
Series 1106 Christmas	12 - 15	15 - 20
Series 1227 Christmas, w/Santa	22 - 25	25 - 30
M.D.		
Series 1101 "Stern-Singer" (4)	15 - 20	20 - 25
August Rokol, Vienna or AR		
Series 1428 Birthday	12 - 15	15 - 20
Series 1375, 1440 Toys	15 - 20	20 - 25
Series 1321 "Dolls Marriage"	20 - 25	25 - 30
E.F.D. or ELLEN F. DREW		
M.A.P. Co.	4 - 6	6 - 8
Ernest Nister	8 - 10	10 - 12
EGERTON, LINDA (GB) (See Fantasy)	10 - 12	12 - 15
ELLAM, WILLIAM (GB) See Sports, Blacks	10 - 12	12 - 15
ELLIOTT, KATHRYN (US)	4 - 5	5 - 6
Gibson Art Co. Halloween Series (10)	8 - 10	10 - 12
Art Deco Ladies	15 - 18	18 - 22
ENGLEHARD or **P.O.E.** (GER)	5 - 6	6 - 8
With dogs	8 - 10	10 - 15
ENGELMANN, ANNY (GER) Children and Dolls	8 - 12	12 - 18
F.B. (not Brundage)	5 - 6	6 - 8
F.B. (See Fritz Baumgarten)		
F.S.M. (US)		
Heininger **"Courtship & Marriage"** Series	8 - 10	10 - 12

FEDERLEY, ALEXANDER (FIN)	5 - 7	7 - 10
FEIERTAG, K. (AUS)		
B.K.W.I.	6 - 8	8 - 10
Series 27	15 - 20	20 - 25
Tennis, Golf, Santas	12 - 15	15 - 18
Dachshund Dogs with Children	12 - 15	15 - 20
FIALKOWSKA, WALLY (GER)		
W & S		
Large Children, Comical	12 - 15	15 - 18
Small Children & Babies	8 - 10	10 - 12
Dachshund Dogs with children	15 - 20	20 - 25
Black Children	12 - 15	15 - 22
FOLKARD, CHARLES (GB)		
A & C Black		
Series 91 "Nursery Rhymes & Tales" (6)		
"Beauty and the Beast"	15 - 20	20 - 25
"Cinderella"	15 - 20	20 - 25
"Little Bo Peep"	15 - 20	20 - 25
"Tom, Tom, the Piper's Son"	15 - 20	20 - 25
"Red Riding Hood"	15 - 20	20 - 25
"Sleeping Beauty"	15 - 20	20 - 25
FRANK, E. (GER)	6 - 8	8 - 10
GASSAWAY, KATHARINE (US)		
Julius Bien & Co.		
Series 55, "Full Day" (6)		
550 "Rising Time"	10 - 12	12 - 15
551 "Bath Time"	10 - 12	12 - 15
552 "Study Time"	10 - 12	12 - 15
553 "Play Time"	10 - 12	12 - 15
554 "Dinner Time"	10 - 12	12 - 15
555 "Bed Time"	10 - 12	12 - 15
Series 75 "Courtship" Series (6)		
750 "Rising Time"	10 - 12	12 - 15
751 "The Introduction"	10 - 12	12 - 15
752 "The Proposal"	10 - 12	12 - 15
753 "The Engagement"	10 - 12	12 - 15
754 "The Marriage"	10 - 12	12 - 15
755 "The Honeymoon"	10 - 12	12 - 15
Edward Gross, N.Y.		
"Butterfly" Series	8 - 10	10 - 12
"Ailments of Childhood" Series		
"Hives," "Mumps," "Measels"	10 - 12	12 - 15
D. Hillson	6 - 8	8 - 10
National Art Co.		
169 "This is so sudden"	6 - 8	8 - 10
170 "I Send my Love by Mail"	6 - 8	8 - 10
171 "My heart is All for You"	6 - 8	8 - 10
Raphael Tuck		
Series 113 Bridal, Valentines (6)	6 - 8	8 - 10
Series 130 Easter Series (12)	6 - 7	7 - 8
Series 2495, 9435 "The New Baby" (6)	6 - 8	8 - 10
Blacks	15 - 18	18 - 22
The Rotograph Co. "F. L" precedes numbers		
100 "New York"	8 - 10	10 - 12
101 "Boston"	8 - 10	10 - 12

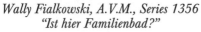

Wally Fialkowski, A.V.M., Series 1356
"Ist hier Familienbad?"

K. Gassaway, R. Tuck, "The New Baby"
Ser. 2, 9435, "Welcome Little Stranger"

102 "Chicago"	8 - 10	10 - 12
103 "St. Louis"	8 - 10	10 - 12
104 "Philadelphia"	8 - 10	10 - 12
105 Black Girl, "I'm scared I'll..."	15 - 18	18 - 22
106 "What are little girls made of..."	8 - 10	10 - 15
107 "What are little boys made of..."	8 - 10	10 - 15
113 "Beware of the Dog"	8 - 10	10 - 12
108-116		
"Age" Series	10 - 12	12 - 15
117 "1 Year"	10 - 12	12 - 15
118 "2 Years"	10 - 12	12 - 15
119 "3 Years"	10 - 12	12 - 15
120 "4 Years"	10 - 12	12 - 15
121 "5 Years"	10 - 12	12 - 15
123 Black girl: "I wish I was in Dixie"	15 - 20	20 - 25
124 Black boy: "Thought I heer'd de boss..."	15 - 20	20 - 25
125-138	6 - 8	8 - 10
139-158 Occupation Series	8 - 10	10 - 12
The Sports images in this series	10 - 12	12 - 15
159-186	6 - 8	8 - 10
193 Black boy: "New Orleans"	15 - 18	18 - 22
171 "My heart is All for You"		
Raphael Tuck		
Series 113 Bridal, Valentines (6)	6 - 8	8 - 10
Series 130 Easter Series (12)	6 - 7	7 - 8
Series 2495 "The New Baby" (6)	6 - 8	8 - 10
Blacks	15 - 18	18 - 22

The Rotograph Co. "F. L." precedes numbers

100 "New York"	8 - 10	10 - 12
101 "Boston"	8 - 10	10 - 12
102 "Chicago"	8 - 10	10 - 12
103 "St. Louis"	8 - 10	10 - 12
104 "Philadelphia"	8 - 10	10 - 12
105 Black Girl, "I'm scared I'll..."	15 - 18	18 - 22
106 "What are little girls made of..."	8 - 10	10 - 15
107 "What are little boys made of..."	8 - 10	10 - 15
113 "Beware of the Dog"	8 - 10	10 - 12
108-116	8 - 10	10 - 12
"Age" Series	10 - 12	12 - 15
117 "1 Year"	10 - 12	12 - 15
118 "2 Years"	10 - 12	12 - 15
119 "3 Years"	10 - 12	12 - 15
120 "4 Years"	10 - 12	12 - 15
121 "5 Years"	10 - 12	12 - 15
123 Black girl: "I wish I was in Dixie"	15 - 20	20 - 25
124 Black boy: "Thought I heer'd de boss..."	15 - 20	20 - 25
125-138	6 - 8	8 - 10
139-158 Occupation Series	8 - 10	10 - 12
Sports images in this series	10 - 12	12 - 15
159-186	6 - 8	8 - 10
193 Black boy: "New Orleans"	15 - 18	18 - 20
214 "Don't cry little girl..."	6 - 8	8 - 10
National Girls		
220 "America"	8 - 10	10 - 12
221 "Ireland"	6 - 8	8 - 10
222 "England"	6 - 8	8 - 10
223 "Germany"	6 - 8	8 - 10
224 "France"	6 - 8	8 - 10
225	6 - 8	8 - 10
226 "Italy"	6 - 8	8 - 10
227 "Sweden"	6 - 8	8 - 10
American Kid Series (6)	6 - 8	8 - 10

GEORGE, MARY ELEANOR (US)

Ernest Nister

1858 "Dear Valentine, you're..."	18 - 22	22 - 26
1862 "Telling the Secret..."	18 - 22	22 - 26
2117 "For my own love"	18 - 22	22 - 26
2182 "The surest way to hit a woman's heart..."	18 - 22	22 - 26
2183 "Choose your Love..."	18 - 22	22 - 26
3119 "You've got me on the string"	18 - 22	22 - 26

GILSON, T. (US)

Black Children Comics	6 - 8	8 - 10
	12 - 15	15 - 20

GOLAY, MARY Flowers, Still Scenes — 3 - 4 / 4 - 6

GOODMAN, MAUDE

Raphael Tuck Series 824-833	15 - 20	20 - 25
Early Chromolithographs	25 - 30	30 - 35

GOLIA, E. (IT) Art Deco

Series 102 Wartime Children	18 - 20	20 - 25

GOVEY, A. (GB)

Humphrey Milford, London

"Dreams and Fairies" Golliwoggs	18 - 22	22 - 25

M. Greiner, International Art Pub.
Series 791, "Hearty Christmas..."

M. M. Grimball, Novitas, 10726
"Kinderdieb"

GRASSETTI (IT) Art Deco	8 - 10	10 - 12
GREINER, MAGNUS (US) See Blacks		
International Art Pub. Co.		
Dutch Children Series 491, 692 (6)	8 - 10	10 - 12
"Molly & the Bear" Series 791	12 - 15	15 - 20
GRIGGS, H. B. (also H.B.G.)		
L & E (Leubrie & Elkus)		
Christmas Series 2224, 2264, 2275	10 - 12	12 - 15
New Year's Series 2225, 2266, 2276	10 - 12	12 - 15
Easter Series 2226, 2254, 2271	10 - 12	12 - 15
Valentine's Day		
Series 2218, 2243, 2244, 2267	12 - 15	15 - 18
Series 2217, 2219, 2248	12 - 15	15 - 18
Blacks	20 - 25	25 - 30
St. Patrick's Day		
Series 2230, 2232, 2253, 2269	9 - 12	12 - 15
Thanksgiving		
Series 2212, 2213, 2233, 2263, 2273	6 - 8	8 - 10
George Washington's Birthday		
Series 2242, 2268	8 - 10	10 - 12
Halloween		
Series 2214, 2216, 2262	15 - 18	18 - 22
Series 2263, 2272	15 - 18	18 - 22
Series 2231, 7010	18 - 22	22 - 26
Birthday		
Series No No., 2232	6 - 8	8 - 10

Anonymous Publisher Series

Series 2215, 7010	12 - 14	14 - 16
GRILLI, S. (IT) Art Deco **Series 1839** (6)	10 - 12	12 - 15

GRIMBALL, Meta M. (US)

Gutmann & Gutmann

203 "Our Flag at the Pole"	30 - 40	40 - 50
210 "The Top of the World"	25 - 30	30 - 35
604 "Fired"	25 - 30	30 - 35
701 "Have Some?"	25 - 30	30 - 35
Same - no number	25 - 30	30 - 35
702 "The Kidnapper"	25 - 30	30 - 35
703 "Some Dog Biscuits Please"	20 - 25	25 - 30
705 "Help"	25 - 30	30 - 35
Same - No Caption	30 - 35	35 - 40
"A Good Catch	20 - 25	25 - 30
"A Welcome Guest"	20 - 25	25 - 30
"And They Say School Days..."	20 - 25	25 - 30
"The Advance Guard"	25 - 30	30 - 35
"The Captive"	25 - 30	30 - 35
"The Champion"	40 - 45	45 - 50
"The Christmas Spirit"	40 - 45	45 - 50
"The Convalescent"	20 - 25	25 - 30
"The Grand Finale"	25 - 30	30 - 35
"Guess Who?"	25 - 30	30 - 35
"He Won't Bite"	25 - 30	30 - 35
"The Loving Cup"	25 - 30	30 - 35
"Love at First Sight"	25 - 30	30 - 35
"Now Don't You Tell"	25 - 30	30 - 35
"Rivals"	25 - 30	30 - 35
"Stolen Sweets"	25 - 30	30 - 35
"Sweethearts"	25 - 30	30 - 35
"Verdict - Love for Life"	25 - 30	30 - 35
"A Call to Arms"	40 - 50	50 - 65
Reinthal & Newman Issues	15 - 20	20 - 25

FOREIGN ISSUES

Novitas (N in star)

Series 542		
1 "Puppchen's neuer Hut" ("Dollie's Bonnet)	35 - 40	40 - 50
Series 10542		
3 "Liebe auf den ersten Blick" (Love at first sight)	35 - 40	40 - 45
Series 10543		
3 "The Introduction"	30 - 35	35 - 40
Series 10726		
"Hunde Mutterchen" Girl with puppies	30 - 35	35 - 40
"Puppenmutterchen's Einkauf"	25 - 30	30 - 40
"Storenfried"	25 - 30	30 - 40
"Kinderdieb" Same as "The Kidnapper"	30 - 35	35 - 40
"Leckerbissen"	25 - 30	30 - 40
Series 10930 (R&N)		
No Caption - Same as "Gossip..."	25 - 30	30 - 40
"Say Das Nicht Noch Mal!"	25 - 30	30 - 35
"Und da sagen sie mir..."	25 - 30	30 - 40
"And They Say School Days..."	20 - 25	25 - 30

Series 10966

"Kinderlieb"	25 - 30	30 - 40
1 "He Won't Bite" (German Caption) Uns.	25 - 30	30 - 40
Also U.S. Caption	20 - 25	25 - 30
5 "The Grand Finale"	30 - 35	35 - 40

Series 20608

4 "The Champion"	40 - 45	45 - 55

Series 21681

"Fired"	25 - 30	30 - 35
"Love at First Sight"		
Others with German Captions	25 - 30	30 - 35

Rishar (Russia) (Phillips or Richard)

330 "Gossip..."	30 - 35	35 - 45
452 Signed MG but labeled H. Gutmann - Little girl rocking cradle	40 - 50	50 - 60
453 "The Grand Finale"	30 - 35	35 - 45

Leningrad Society (Russia)

69 No Caption Little girl rocking cradle	40 - 50	50 - 60

Series 19123 (10,000)

No Caption Boy writing on slate	30 - 35	35 - 40
GROSS, O.	2 - 3	3 -5
GUARINO, ANTHONY	3 - 4	4 - 5
GUASTA (IT) Art Deco	10 - 12	12 - 15

GUTMANN, BESSIE PEASE (US)

Gutmann & Gutmann

No No.

"Autumn"	35 - 40	40 - 45
"Baby's First Christmas"	35 - 40	40 - 50
"Blue Bell"	35 - 40	40 - 45
"Fall"	35 - 40	40 - 45
"Falling Out" S/**Bessie C. Pease**	25 - 30	30 - 35
"Feeling"	25 - 30	30 - 35
"The First Born"	35 - 40	40 - 45
"The First Lesson"	35 - 40	40 - 45
Girl in Hat	35 - 40	40 - 45
"Love at First Sight"	25 - 30	30 - 35
"Love is Blind"	25 - 30	30 - 40
"Making Up" S/**Bessie C. Pease**	25 - 30	30 - 40
"Ragtime"	30 - 35	35 - 40
"S.O.S" (C.Q.D.)	40 - 45	45 - 50
Skater	30 - 35	35 - 45
"Spring"	30 - 35	35 - 40
"Summer"	30 - 35	35 - 40

200 Series - Children

200 "The New Love"	30 - 35	35 - 40
201 "The Lone Fisherman"	30 - 35	35 - 40
211 "The Happy Family"	35 - 40	40 - 45

500 Series - Beautiful Women

500 "Rosebuds"	40 - 45	45 - 50
501 "Senorita"	40 - 45	45 - 50
502 "Waiting"	50 - 55	55 - 60
503 "Daydreams"	40 - 45	45 - 50
504 "Poppies"	40 - 45	45 - 50

505 "I wish you were here"	40 - 45	45 - 50
704 "The Foster Mother"	25 - 30	30 - 35

800 Series – Young Girls

800 "Margaret"	30 - 35	35 - 40
801 "Betty"	30 - 35	35 - 40
802 "Virginia"	30 - 35	35 - 40
803 "Alice"	30 - 35	35 - 40
804 "Lucille"	30 - 35	35 - 40
805 "Dorothy"	30 - 35	35 - 40

900 Series - Babies

900 "Contentment"	35 - 40	40 - 45
901 "Come play with me"	35 - 40	40 - 45
902 "All is Vanity"	35 - 40	40 - 45
903 "His Majesty"	35 - 40	40 - 45
904 "Dessert"	35 - 40	40 - 45

1000 Series - Baby/Mother

1000 "Sunshine"	40 - 45	45 - 50
1001 "I love to be loved by a baby"	40 - 45	45 - 50
1002 "In Slumberland"	40 - 45	45 - 50
1003 "Baby mine"	40 - 45	45 - 50
1004 "The Sweetest Joy"	40 - 45	45 - 50

1100 Series - Young Women

1100 "Repartee"	70 - 75	75 - 85
1101 "Sweeheart"	70 - 75	75 - 85
1102 "Sweet Sixteen"	70 - 75	75 - 85
1103 "Speeding"	50 - 55	55 - 60
1104 "Happy Dreams"	50 - 55	55 - 60

1200 Series - The Five Senses

1200 "Tasting"	30 - 35	35 - 45
1201 "Seeing"	30 - 35	35 - 45
1202 "Smelling"	30 - 35	35 - 45
1203 "Hearing"	30 - 35	35 - 45
1204 "Feeling"	30 - 35	35 - 45

1300 Series - A Woman's Life

1300 "The Baby"	40 - 45	45 - 50
1301 "Off to school"	40 - 45	45 - 50
1302 "The Dubutante"	40 - 45	45 - 50
1303 "The Bride"	40 - 45	45 - 50
1304 "The Mother"	40 - 45	45 - 50

Metamorphic

B505 "Love or Money" S/**B.C.P.**	175 - 200	200 - 225

FOREIGN

The "Alphasia" Publishing Co., London

"The New Love"	50 - 60	60 - 75
Others	50 - 60	60 - 75

W. de Haan, Utrecht

3004 "Het Gezicht" Girl sits at mirror	45 - 50	50 - 55

De Muinck & Co., Amsterdam

54 "Liefde is Blind" (Love is Blind) Sepia	45 - 50	50 - 55

M.J.S., Bulgaria Johnson listed as artist

011 Images in water "Cupid's Reflection"	70 - 80	80 - 90

Uns. B. P. Gutmann, Finnish, 517
"Hauskaa Joulua"

B. P. Gutmann, Leningrad Society, 418
Same as "Delighted"

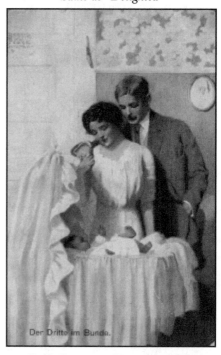

B. P. Gutmann, Novitas, 10931
"Betty" (G. & G. No. 801)

B. P. Gutmann, Novitas, 20557
"Der Dritte im Bunde"

Novitas - N in Circle
No No. Girl with muffler and Holly	60 - 65	65 - 75
Series 542		
4 Little girl sits in big hat box	35 - 40	40 - 45
10357 "Come Play With Me" Baby/butterfly		
10557 "His Majesty"	30 - 35	35 - 40
Series 10930		
"Zwietracht" Same as "Falling Out" (S/**B.C.P.**) *	50 - 55	55 - 60
"Eintracht" Same as "Making Up" (S/**B.C.P.**) *	50 - 55	55 - 60
"Hoppa Hoppa Reiter!" Same as "Strenuous"	45 - 50	50 - 55
* Also without caption	50 - 55	55 - 60
Series 10931		
"Betty" (No. 801)	50 - 55	55 - 60
"Dorothy" (No. 805)	50 - 55	55 - 60
Series 15727		
"Rosebuds"	35 - 40	40 - 50
Series 20360 (6)	35 - 40	40 - 50
Same cards as **G&G 1300 Series**		
"A Woman's Life"	40 - 45	45 - 50
Series 20361 - Sunshine Series	40 - 45	45 - 50
20556 "Das Bild des Zukunftigen" ("Cupid's Reflection")	80 - 90	90 - 100
20557 "Der Dritte im Bunde" ("Tie that binds")	55 - 60	60 - 65
20558 "Aufbruch in der Krieg" Mother on knees kisses boy	50 - 55	55 - 60
20559 "Ihr Liebling" Boy kissing mother	45 - 50	50 - 55
Series 20607		
"Delighted"	40 - 45	45 - 50
"Love at First Sight"	35 - 40	40 - 45
3 "Love is Blind"	35 - 40	40 - 45
Also German caption "Liebe Macht Blind"	40 - 45	45 - 55
4 "The First Lesson"	35 - 40	40 - 45
Also German caption "	40 - 45	45 - 55
6 "Barchen Schlaft" ("The New Love")	35 - 40	40 - 45
Series 20608 (6)		
1 "Music Hath Charm"	40 - 45	45 - 50
3 "Ragtime"	40 - 45	45 - 50
"My Bruzzer has a fever..."	40 - 45	45 - 50
5 "Puppenmutterchen" Girl with many dolls	45 - 50	50 - 60
6 "The Lone Fisherman"	45 - 50	50 - 60
Series 20697 (6)		
Same cards as **G&G 200 Series**	35 - 40	40 - 45
Others		
"All is Vanity"	40 - 50	50 - 55
"Feeling"	35 - 40	40 - 45
"Delighted"	35 - 45	45 - 55
"The Foster Mother"	40 - 50	50 - 60
"Guess Who?" (Unsigned)	35 - 45	45 - 55
"Love is Blind"	35 - 40	40 - 45
"Margaret"	40 - 50	40 - 60
"Stolen Sweets" Unsigned	40 - 50	50 - 60
"Strenuous"	40 - 50	50 - 60
Others	40 - 50	50 - 60
C.Q.D.	40 - 50	50 - 60

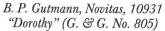

B. P. Gutmann, Novitas, 10931
"Dorothy" (G. & G. No. 805)

Bessie Pease Gutmann
Rishar, No. 1277 ("Good Night")

"S.O.S." Crying baby standing in bed	45 - 50	50 - 60
FINNISH – By Gutmann & Gutmann		
517 Christmas girl with muffler & Christmas gifts.		
Finnish Christmas greeting "Hauskaa Joulua"	100 - 125	125 - 150

RUSSIAN

Rishar (Richard or Phillips) =

(Petrograde or St. Petersburg)

91 "The New Love"	40 - 50	50 - 55
93 "A nice family" Little girl w/many dolls	40 - 50	50 - 55
Also has German and Russian captions	50 - 60	60 - 70
95 "Die Liebe ist blind" Little girl kisses doll		
with broken head. (Love is Blind)	45 - 50	50 - 60
99 "Die Perle" Mermaid in large clam shells	80 - 90	100 - 110
100 "Wasserlilie" Mermaid sits on lily pad	80 - 90	100 - 110
135 "The Intruder" Boy kisses white bunny	45 - 50	50 - 60
136 "The Strenuous Life"	45 - 50	50 - 60
137 "Making Up" Girls with umbrella	45 - 50	50 - 55
138 "Falling Out" Girls with umbrella	45 - 50	50 - 55
150 "Delighted" Boy with rifle and Teddy		
Bear by foot. A takeoff on Teddy Roosevelt.	45 - 50	50 - 55
155 Little Girl with many dolls	50 - 55	55 - 65
414 Listed as H. Gutmann "The First Lesson"	45 - 50	50 - 55
1277 "Good Night" Woman holding candle	65 - 70	70 - 80
Others	45 - 50	50 - 55
Russian/Universal Back		
173 Boy kissing rabbit (The Intruder)	45 - 50	50 - 60

Leningrad Society
Russian/French Back

50 No Caption - Same as "The New Love"	55 - 65	65 - 75
224 No Caption - Same as "Love is Blind"	55 - 65	65 - 75
418 No Caption - Same as "Delighted"	55 - 60	60 - 65
Series 9402 20000 (Print Run)		
Same as "The New Love"	55 - 65	65 - 75
Series 15104 20000 (Print run) Oversized		
248 No Caption - Same as "Feeling"	55 - 60	60 - 65
Other Foreign Publishers & Distributors	40 - 45	45 - 50

ADVERTISING

Brown & Bigelow Calendars (12)
Misspelled artist name - ("Gutman")
Months of the Year (Various Advertisers)

120 "The Defenders" January 1911	80 - 90	90 - 110
121 "Allow Me"	80 - 90	90 - 110
122 "A Little Breezy" March 1910	80 - 90	90 - 110
123 "Which Hand?" August 1909	80 - 90	90 - 110
124 "New Arrivals" May 1910	80 - 90	90 - 110
125 "Easter Boy"	80 - 90	90 - 110
126 "First Aid" July 1910	80 - 90	90 - 110
127 "Vacation" August 1909	80 - 90	90 - 110
128 "School Days"	80 - 90	90 - 110
129 "His First Attempt" October 1909	80 - 90	90 - 110
130 "Who's Afraid" November 1909	80 - 90	90 - 110
131 "Tired Out" December 1909	80 - 90	90 - 110

GUTMANN, BERNHARDT (Bessie's brother-in-law)
Gutmann & Gutmann

B502 "In the Midst of Life..." Metamorphic	90 - 100	100 - 125
B503 "The Breakers" Comical cooks	40 - 50	50 - 60
B504 "Coming events cast their shadows..."	40 - 50	50 - 60
This G&G card was signed by George Blake	20 - 25	25 - 35

Rishar (Phillips or Richard, Russia)

234 "The Poodle-Mobile" (S/**H. GUTMANN**)	90 - 100	100 - 125
HALLOCK, RUTH	5 - 6	6 - 8

HARDY, FLORENCE (GB)
C. W. Faulkner & Co.

Dancing Series 914 (6)	12 - 15	15 - 20
M. Munk, Vienna		
Series 352 (6)	12 - 15	15 - 20
Others	10 - 12	12 - 15
Raphael Tuck		
Series 9694 "Young Hearts" (6)	18 - 22	22 - 25

HAYS, MARGARET G. (US)
Ernest Nister
Big Eyes Series
"Miss Polly Pigtail" Series (6)

2748 Dressed in Pink	25 - 30	30 - 35
2749 Dressed in Green	25 - 30	30 - 35
2750 Dressed in Purple	25 - 30	30 - 35
2751 Dressed in Red	25 - 30	30 - 35
2752 Dressed in Yellow	25 - 30	30 - 35

Florence Hardy, Raphael Tuck
"Young Hearts" Series, No. 9694

Uns. Maud Humphrey, L. R. Conwell
No Caption

2753 Dressed in Blue	25 - 30	30 - 35
Series 3059 Valentine Children	15 - 18	18 - 22
Series 3061 (6) Large Images	15 - 18	18 - 22
Series 3463 Pink hat, roses, white dress	15 - 18	18 - 22
The Rose Co.		
Christmas Series (6)	15 - 17	17 - 20
Anonymous		
Paper Doll Series 3, 6 (6)	75 - 85	85 - 100
HEINMULLER, A.		
International Art Pub. Co.		
Series 1002, Halloween (6)	12 - 15	15 - 20
Series 1003, St. Patrick's Day (6)	6 - 8	8 - 10
Series 1004, Thanksgiving (6)	4 - 5	5 - 6
Series 1620, Valentines (6)	5 - 6	6 - 7
HOLLYER, EVA	6 - 8	8 - 10
HORSFALL, MARY (GB)	4 - 6	6 - 8
HUMMEL (GER)		
Pre-1950	12 - 15	15 - 18
Later Period	5 - 6	6 - 7
HUMPHREY, MAUD (US)		
V. O. Hammon Pub. Co.		
"Children of the Revolution" (all Signed)		
576 "Benjamin Franklin Entering Phila."	125 - 150	150 - 175
577 "Boston Tea Party"	125 - 150	150 - 175
578 "Bunker Hill"	125 - 150	150 - 175
579 "Washington's Courtship"	125 - 150	150 - 175

Total of 12 possible as prints seen in the book,
"*Children of the Revolution*" by Maud Humphrey
and Copyright 1900 by Frederick A. Stokes Co.
contain the 4 listed above. Captions are:

"Martha Washington Pouring Tea" **If so:**	125 - 150	150 - 175
"The Surrender of Cornwallis"	125 - 150	150 - 175
"LaFayette Dancing the Minuet"	125 - 150	150 - 175
"Paul Revere's Ride"	125 - 150	150 - 175
"Betsy Ross"	125 - 150	150 - 175
"Paul Jones"	125 - 150	150 - 175
"Moll Pitcher"	125 - 150	150 - 175
"Washington Crossing the Delaware"	125 - 150	150 - 175
L. R. Conwell Co. (Unsigned)	15 - 18	18 - 22
Anonymous Publisher		
Signed M.H. – "The Four Seasons" (4)	50 - 60	60 - 80
Gray Lithograph Co. (Unsigned)		
43, 44, 45, 46, 47, 48, 49, 50, 54	12 - 15	15 - 20
Rotograph		
Series F457	12 - 15	15 - 20
HUMPHREYS, L. G.	2 - 3	3 - 4
HUTAF, AUGUST (US)		
Ullman Mfg. Co.		
"A Little Odd Fellow"	6 - 8	8 - 10
"A Little Shriner"	6 - 8	8 - 10
Other	6 - 8	8 - 10
Other Publishers	4 - 6	6 - 8
I.M.J. (I.M. JAMES) (GB)		
M. Munk		
Children Series	6 - 8	8 - 10
JACKSON, HELEN (GB) (See Fairy Tales)		
Others	10 - 12	12 - 15
JACOBS, HELEN (GB)		
Henderson & Sons		
"Kiddies" Series K8		
3244, 3246 Child and Golliwogg	30 - 35	35 - 40
Others	10 - 12	12 - 15
K.V.		
LP Co.		
Kewpie-like Children	8 - 10	10 - 12
Black Children (or Mixed)	12 - 15	15 - 20
KASKELINE, FRED		
Silhouette Series 9033 (6)	6 - 8	8 - 10
Others	6 - 7	7 - 8
KEMBLE, E. B. (US) See Blacks		
Comic Children	3 - 4	4 - 5
KENNEDY, A.E. or A.K. (GB) (See Fairy Tales)	5 - 8	8 - 12
KIDD, WILL (US)	3 - 5	5 - 6
KER, MARY SIGSBEE (US)	4 - 5	5 - 6
KING, HAMILTON (US)	8 - 10	10 - 12
KING, JESSIE M. (GB)	10 - 12	12 - 15
KINSELLA, E. P. (GB)		
Langsdorff & Co.		
Series 675 Cricket Series (6)	18 - 22	22 - 26
Series 695 Tennis Series (6)	18 - 22	20 - 26

Helen Jacobs, James Henderson & Sons
Series K-8, No. 3244, "Oh Golly!"

Maison Kurt
AVM, Series 300

Others	12 - 15	15 - 18
KIRK, M. L. (US)		
National Art Co. Birthday Signs (7)	8 - 10	10 - 12
KLEEHAAS (GER) Children with Dogs	12 - 15	15 - 20
KLEMM, LOTTE		
J. Qwifflers	10 - 12	12 - 15
KNOEFEL		
Illuminated Appearance		
Novitas		
Series 664 (6)	8 - 10	10 - 12
Series 656 With Phones (6)	10 - 12	12 - 15
Series 15834, 20887 (Mother/Child) (6)	8 - 10	10 - 12
KÖHLER, MELA (AUS) Art Deco (See Mela Broman)		
B.K.W.I.		
Series 298 (6) Children out of doors	35 - 40	40 - 50
Edart, Wien		
Series 1454 (6) New Year Greetings	30 - 35	35 - 40
M. Munk, Wien		
Series 1187 (6) Christmas Children w/toys	35 - 40	40 - 50
Series 1232 (6) Children playing grown-ups	25 - 35	35 - 45
Sago-Konst A.B., Stockholm (1930's)		
Series B41	25 - 30	30 - 35
Schulverein		
No. 1145 Little Girl/Bunny dance	25 - 35	35 - 45
Frau und Kind Ausstellung (5) **Child w/dolls**	40 - 50	50 - 60
KURT, MAISON (GER)		
AVM **Series 998, 300**	12 - 15	15 - 18

Mela Köhler Broman — Sago-Konst A.B., Series B-41, No. 56

Mela Köhler, Deutscher
Schulverein, Ser. 1145
German Easter Caption

Mela Köhler, Edart, Wien
Series 1454
"Herzliche Neujahrsgrüsse"

Mela Köhler, M. Munk,
Series 1187
No Caption

K.V.i.B.
  Series 100, 1842 Deco Children

LeMAIR, H. WILLEBEEK (GB)
  Augener, Ltd.
    Children's "Pieces of Schumann"

Series 100, 1842 Deco Children	12 - 15	15 - 18
"Catch Me if You Can," "Dreaming"	15 - 18	18 - 22
"Perfect Happiness," "Melody"	15 - 18	18 - 22
"The Merry Peasant," "First Loss"	15 - 18	18 - 22
"The Poor Orphan." "Romance"	15 - 18	18 - 22
"Roundelay," "Sicilienne"	15 - 18	18 - 22
"Soldier's March," "Vintage"	15 - 18	18 - 22

H. Willebeek LeMair, Augener, Ltd. – "Little People" Series, "Evening prayer"

"Baby's Fright," "Dreadfully Busy"	15 - 18	18 - 22
"Fishing Boats," "Greedy"	15 - 18	18 - 22
"Hair Cutting," "Last Year's Frock"	15 - 18	18 - 22
"Out of the Snow," "Preserving Dickey"	15 - 18	18 - 22
"Poor Baby," "Queen of the Birds"	15 - 18	18 - 22
"The Dove's Dinner Time," "The Garden City"	15 - 18	18 - 22
"The Invalid's Birthday"	15 - 18	18 - 22
"Little People" Series "Evening prayer"	15 - 18	18 - 22
LEVI, C. (US)		
Suffragette	20 - 22	22 - 28
Series 210, 3308 "Komical Koons"	12 - 15	15 - 18
LEWIN, F.G. (GB) (See Blacks)		
Bamforth Co.		
Children Comics	6 - 8	8 - 10
LINDEBERG		
Head Studies	8 - 10	10 - 12
LD		
Meissner & Buch	8 - 10	10 - 15
LANDSTROM, B. (Finland) Fairy Tales	6 - 8	8 - 10
MAILICK, A. (German)		
Angels, Children	8 - 10	10 - 15
MAISON-KURT		
Fantasy Bear Set with Girl (4)	15 - 18	18 - 22
MALLET, BEATRICE (GB)		
Raphael Tuck "Cute Kiddies" Oilette Series		
Series 3567, 3568, 3628, 3629 (6)	8 - 10	10 - 12
Others	8 - 10	10 - 12
MARCELLUS, IRENE		
E. Nister		
Series 3215, Child's Head in Pie, Mitten, etc.	15 - 18	18 - 22
Series 736, 737, 1885, 3097	15 - 18	18 - 22
MARGOTSON, H.	6 - 8	8 - 10

L.D., Meissner & Buch
Series 2891
(Beginning School)

Irene Marcellus, E. Nister
Series 3215
"A Happy Christmas..."

Corneille Max, Wohlgemuth
& Sissner, No. 5085
"Musik"

MARSH-LAMBERT, H.G.C. (GB)
  BD
    Child and Teddy Bear ... 10 - 12 ... 12 - 15
    "Wee Willie Winkle" ... 8 - 10 ... 10 - 12
    "Curly Locks" ... 7 - 8 ... 8 - 10
    Series 389, 562 (6) ... 10 - 12 ... 12 - 15
  C. W. Faulkner
    Series 962 (6) ... 10 - 12 ... 12 - 15
MARSHALL, ALICE (GB) ... 8 - 10 ... 10 - 15
MART, L. ... 5 - 6 ... 6 - 7
MARTINEAU, ALICE ... 6 - 8 ... 8 - 10
MAURICE, REG. (GB) Children Cricket ... 15 - 18 ... 18 - 22
MAX, CORNEILLE
  Wohlgemuth & Sissner
    Series 5085 ("Musik," etc.) ... 10 - 12 ... 12 - 16
MAYBANK, THOMAS (See Fairies) ... 8 - 10 ... 10 - 12
McCUTCHEON, JOHN T. (U.S.) ... 6 - 8 ... 8 - 10
MAUZAN, L. A. (Italy) Art Deco
    Series 45 With Dogs ... 10 - 12 ... 12 - 15
    Anonymous "Cendrillon"
M.D.S. (US) See Blacks and Teddy Bears
M.E.P. (see MARGARET EVANS PRICE, MP) (US)
    Others ... 6 - 8 ... 8 - 10
M.M.S. (US)
    G. K. Prince Series 421 ... 6 - 8 ... 8 - 10
M.S.M. (AUS)
    A.V.M. ... 10 - 12 ... 12 - 15
    Meissner & Buch ... 12 - 15 ... 15 - 20
MERCER, JOYCE (GB) ... 12 - 15 ... 15 - 18
MILLER, HILDA T. (GB) See Fairies/Mermaids
MITCHELL, SADIE ... 4 - 5 ... 5 - 6
MORGAN, OLWEN ... 6 - 9 ... 9 - 12
NASH, A. A. (US)
    Heckscher   Series 704 ... 10 - 12 ... 12 - 15

Inter-Art Co.
Series 1745 "Artistique" Patriotic Series	15 - 18	18 - 25

NIXON, K.
See Fairy Tales

NORFINI (IT) Art Deco	8 - 10	10 - 15
NOSWORTHY, FLORENCE E. (GB)	6 - 8	8 - 10

See Fairy Tales

NUMBER, JACK
PFB (in Diamond) German Captions
Series 2068, 2070, 2076 (4)	8 - 10	10 - 12

NYSTROM, JENNY (SW)
B.K.W.I. - New Year Children	15 - 18	18 - 22
Others	10 - 12	12 - 15

See Fairy Tales
NYSTROM, KURT (SW)	6 - 8	8 - 12

O'NEILL, ROSE (US)

One of the most popular of all children artists was Rose O'Neill, who created and drew the lovable Kewpie doll. The Kewpies delighted children and adults during the period after World War I through the Depression of the thirties.

Her first works were for advertising, covers and inside illustrations for some of the leading magazines. All showed the adorable Kewpies collection. The Gibson Art Company published many of O'Neill's designs on postcards for most holiday seasons. Her most popular were probably of Christmas. The Edward Gross Co. did a great set of six large image Kewpies and the Suffrage issues of Campbell Art and National Publishers Suffrage group have become the most famous of all her works. She also did two series of blacks that were published by Raphael Tuck which are extremely scarce and are avidly pursued by many collectors.

Rose O'Neill also did illustrations for advertisements as well as illustrated books. The book signatures sometimes used her married name, Latham.

Campbell Art Co.
"Klever Kards" Folds to form easel; stands up.
Dated 1914 (29)	50 - 55	55 - 60
Dated 1915 (30+)	55 - 60	60 - 65
Miniature Klever Kards (3 x 4.5)	80 - 90	90 - 100

Suffrage Klever Kard
228 "Votes for Women—Do I get your Vote?"	150 - 175	175 - 200

Gibson Art Co. (64 in all)
New Years (9)	30 - 35	35 - 45
Valentine (18)	30 - 35	35 - 45
Easter (13)	30 - 35	35 - 45
Christmas (18)	30 - 35	35 - 45
Miscellaneous types (6)	30 - 35	35 - 45

Edward Gross Co.
Large Image Kewpies (6)
100 "The Kewpie Army"	90 - 100	100 - 120
101 "The Kewpie Carpenter"	90 - 100	100 - 120
102 "This Kewpie wears overshoes"	90 - 100	100 - 120
103 "The Kewpie Cook"	90 - 100	100 - 120
104 "This Kewpie careful of his voice"	90 - 100	100 - 120
105 "The Kewpie Gardener"	90 - 100	100 - 120

Rose O'Neill, Gibson Art
"I wish I were with you under..."

Rose O'Neill, Gibson Art No No.
"Oh, if your chimney..."

National Suffrage Pub. Co.
"Votes for Women - Spirit of '76"	300 - 400	400 - 500
"Votes for our Mothers" (not Kewpies)	450 - 600	600 - 750

Raphael Tuck   Black Comics
Series 2483 "Pickings from Puck" (4)
"One View"	60 - 70	70 - 80
"Better than a Sermon"	60 - 70	70 - 80
"A Brain Worker"	60 - 70	70 - 80
"Ne Plus Ultra"	60 - 70	70 - 80

Series 9411 "High Society in Coontown" (6)
"All that was Necessary"	100 - 110	110 - 120
"Taken"	100 - 110	110 - 120
"A Provisional Finance"	100 - 110	110 - 120
"A Misunderstanding"	100 - 110	110 - 120
"Finis"	100 - 110	110 - 120
"Has Limited Provisioning Capacity"	100 - 110	110 - 120

Series 9412 "Coontown Kids" (6)	80 - 90	90 - 100
Rock Island Line, Advertising	45 - 50	50 - 60
Parker-Bruaner Co. Ice Cream Ad.	100 - 150	150 - 200
OUTCAULT, R. (US)	8 - 10	10 - 12

See Artist-Signed Comics
OUTHWAITE, IDA R. (See Fantasy Fairies & Mermaids)
OVERNELL
Anonymous "I expected a little sister"	10 - 12	12 - 15

OWEN, WILL
Meissner & Buch, No. 1979	10 - 12	12 - 15

Overnell, Anon. Publisher
"I expected a little sister"

Will Owen, Meissner & Buch
Series 1979

Felicien Philipp
Series 335/3

PALMER, PHYLLIS (US)	4 - 6	6 - 8
PARKINSON, ETHEL (GB)		
BC		
Series 745 (6)	8 - 10	10 - 12
BD		
Series 475 (6)	10 - 12	12 - 14
C. W. Faulkner		
Series 951	12 - 14	14 - 16
M. Munk, Vienna		
Series 132, 380, 488 (6)	10 - 12	12 - 15
Series 191, 232, 234, 502, 554 (6)	8 - 10	10 - 12
Series 531 (6)		
Days of the Week (Dutch Children)	12 - 15	15 - 18
Others	8 - 10	10 - 12
PARTLETT, HARRY (**COMICUS**) (GB)	5 - 6	6 - 7
PATEK, AUGUST		
Josef Gerstmayer	15 - 18	18 - 22
PATERSON, VERA (GB)	6 - 7	7 - 8
Golf Series	10 - 15	15 - 20
PEARSE, S. B. (Susan) (GB)		
M. Munk, Vienna		
Series 563, 728 (6)	15 - 18	18 - 22
Series 635, 727 (6) Dolls	20 - 25	25 - 30
Series 679, 712, 713 (6)	12 - 15	15 - 18
Series 758 (6) Dancing	18 - 22	22 - 26
Series 844, 922, 925 (6)	18 - 22	22 - 26
Series 856 (6) With Toys	20 - 25	25 - 30

August Patek
Josef Gerstmayer

Hannes Peterson, H.W.B., Series 3977
"Die besten Glückwünsche zum ..."

Unsigned Susan B. Pearse, M. Munk
Series 635, "Waschtag."

Unsigned Susan B. Pearse, M. Munk
Series 727, "Schlaft, Kindlein, schlaft!"

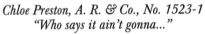

Chloe Preston, A. R. & Co., No. 1523-1
"Who says it ain't gonna..."

Phyllis M. Purser, J. Salmon, Ltd.
No. 5218, "O wonder why the sea..."

Series 862 (6)	12 - 15	15 - 18
PEASE, BESSIE COLLINS (US)		
PETERSEN, HANNES or HP (BEL)	6 - 8	8 - 10
HWB		
Series 3708 In the kitchen	8 - 10	10 - 15
Series 3710, 3716, 3978 First Day of School (6)	12 - 15	15 - 22
Series 3977	8 - 10	10 - 15
Others	8 - 10	10 - 15
PETO, GLADYS (GB)	10 - 12	12 - 15
PHILIPP, FELICIEN	6 - 8	8 - 10
PIATTOLI, G. (IT) Art Deco	8 - 10	10 - 12
PINOCHI, E. (IT) Art Deco	8 - 10	10 - 15
PITTS, JAMES E. or **J.E.P.** (US)	5 - 6	6 - 10
PLUMSTEAD, JOYCE (GB) Fairy Tales	10 - 12	12 - 16
POWELL, LYMAN (US)		
Series 82 (6) Watercolors		
"Baby Sends Love"	8 - 10	10 - 12
"Introducing Baby"	8 - 10	10 - 12
PRESTON, CHLOE (GB) Art Deco		
A. R. & Co.		
Tennis Series 1523 (6)	15 - 20	20 - 25
Cricket Series 1587 (6)	22 - 25	25 - 30
B. R. Co. Series E (Black Background) (6)	12 - 15	15 - 20
Raphael Tuck		
Series 461 (6)	12 - 15	15 - 18
Valentines		
Series 1022 (6)	12 - 15	15 - 18

A. Richardson, "National" Series, #3319
"Oh Yes!!! We are all Scotch."

Agnes Richardson, R. Tuck, "Little Tots"
Series, "I am trying to get them all comfy."

PRICE, MARGARET EVANS   M.E.P & MP (US)
  Stecher Litho Co.

Series 413, 415, 417 Christmas (6)	8 - 10	10 - 12
Series 648, 656, 657, 749, 875 Christmas (6)	8 - 10	10 - 12
Series 517, 628, 821 Valentine's (6)	8 - 10	10 - 12
Series 503, 750, 783 Easter (6)	8 - 10	10 - 12
Series 98 Flower Children (6)	8 - 10	10 - 15
Series 403 St. Patrick's (6)	8 - 10	10 - 15
Girl Scouts	12 - 15	15 - 18
Note: Many of the **Stecher** Series were reprinted in the 40's & 50's.	2 - 3	3 - 5

PURSER, PHYLLIS M.
  J. Salmon, Ltd.

5218, "O wonder why the sea..."	5 - 8	8 - 10

R.R.
  M. Munk, Vienna

Series 1030	8 - 10	10 - 12
RACKHAM, ARTHUR (GB)	12 - 15	15 - 20
RICHARDS, EUGENIE (GB)	6 - 8	8 - 10

RICHARDSON, AGNES (GB)

Charles Hauff No No. Series	12 - 15	15 - 20
C. W. Faulkner		
Series 126, 6126 (6)	15 - 18	18 - 22
M. Munk, Vienna Series 706 (6)	8 - 10	10 - 12
"National" Series 3319 – Golliwoggs	25 - 30	30 - 35
International Art Co.		
1958 "My Love is Like..."	8 - 10	10 - 14

1959 "I'll Take Care of Mummy"	8 - 10	10 - 14
Photo Chrom Co.		
"Celesque" Series		
No No. "Love at First Sight" Blacks	20 - 25	25 - 30
554 "My Curley-Headed Babby"	20 - 25	25 - 30
555 "So Shy"	18 - 22	22 - 26
557 "Well I Never"	18 - 22	22 - 26
558 "I Loves Yo Ma Honey..." Blacks	20 - 25	25 - 30
635 "Twas Ever Thus"	18 - 22	22 - 26
1016 "I've Quite Lost My Heart Down Here"	18 - 22	22 - 26
1425 "Anxious to start"	15 - 18	18 - 22
1426 "When the heart is young"	15 - 18	18 - 22
1427 "Happy Days"	15 - 18	18 - 22
1428 "The Riding Lesson"	15 - 18	18 - 22
1430 "News for Daddy"	15 - 18	18 - 22
1718 "Ma Honey!" Blacks	20 - 25	25 - 30
1720 "A Dusky Cavalier"	20 - 25	25 - 30
Unsigned Series	18 - 22	22 - 26
Raphael Tuck (See Blacks) **Golliwoggs**		
Series 1232 "Rescued" (6)	25 - 30	30 - 40
Series 1262 (6)	25 - 30	30 - 40
Series 1397 (6)	25 - 30	30 - 35
Series C-1420, C-1421, C-1422	15 - 18	18 - 22
Series C3609, 8670 (6)	10 - 12	12 - 15
Card 8470 "I've brought you some..."	25 - 30	30 - 40
Series 9982 "Little Tots" (6)	18 - 22	22 - 25
With Golliwoggs	25 - 30	30 - 40
"Family Cares" Series (6)	20 - 25	25 - 30
With Golliwoggs	25 - 30	30 - 40
Children and Golliwoggs	25 - 30	30 - 40
Valentine & Sons		
Series C2006 (6) Golliwoggs	25 - 30	30 - 40
Others	8 - 10	10 - 12
ROBINSON, ROBERT (US) (See Baseball)		
Edward Gross		
207 Boy fisherman with big trout	15 - 20	20 - 25
ROWLES, L. Art Deco	10 - 12	12 - 15
RUSSELL, MARY LA FENETRA (US)		
Sam Gabriel Co.		
Children	4 - 6	6 - 8
Halloween	9 - 12	12 - 15
Salke		
"Brick Wall" Children	6 - 8	8 - 10
RYLANDER Art Deco		
Alex Eliassons "God Jul!"	20 - 25	25 - 30
SANDFORD, H. DIX (GB) See Blacks	8 - 10	10 - 12
SANFORD, M. (GB) See Blacks	8 - 10	10 - 12
SAUNDERS, E. H. (US)	5 - 6	6 - 8
SCHENKEL, F.		
H.F.A., Dresden		
488 "Puppenmutter"	10 - 12	12 - 15
SELLDIN, HELFRID		
Nordist Konst Series 9010	25 - 35	35 - 45

Rylander, Alex Eliassons
"God Jul!"

Rylander, Alex Eliassons
"God Jul!"

F. Schenkel, H.F.A., Dresden
No. 488, "Puppenmutter"

Helfrid Selldin
Nordist Konst, Series 9010
"Gott Nytt År"

Sgrilli, G.P.M.
Series 1825-2

C. Z. Shand
Anonymous Publisher
"A Kiss for Bo Peep"

SHAND, C. Z.		
Anonymous (10) Art Deco	30 - 40	40 - 50
SHEPHEARD, G.E. (GB)		
M. Munk Series 185 (6) Dutch Children	6 - 8	8 - 10
Raphael Tuck		
Series 9060 Cricket (6)	20 - 25	25 - 30
Series 9375 "A Coming Cricketer" (6)	20 - 25	25 - 30
S.K. Art Deco	8 - 10	10 - 15
SGRILLI (IT) Art Deco	8 - 10	10 - 15
SMITH, JESSIE WILCOX (US)		
Reinthal & Newman		
"Garden" Series 100		
"Among the Poppies," "Five O'Clock Tea"	18 - 22	22 - 25

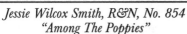

Jessie Wilcox Smith, R&N, No. 854
"Among The Poppies"

Suze, Cathblain and Bartrim
Series 51, French Caption

"The Garden Wall," "The Green Door"	18 - 22	22 - 25
"In the Garden," "The Lily Pool"	18 - 22	22 - 26
SMITH, MAY	6 - 8	8 - 10
SUZE		
Cathblain & Bartrim		
Series 51	8 - 10	10 - 12

AMY MILLICENT SOWERBY

Amy Millicent Sowerby was an English artist and illustrator of many wonderful children's books. Her most famous was Lewis Carroll's *"Alice in Wonderland,"* and afterward Robert Lewis Stevenson's *"A Child's Garden of Verse."* Wonderful illustrations of beautiful children, fairies, fairy tales and nursery rhymes also appeared on picture postcards that were intended for children, and they have become very desirable by all who collect these motifs.

Her cards all have precise detail, the colors are exceptionally bright, and the lithography is excellent. Most of Sowerby's cards were published in England by Henry Frowde and Hodder & Stoughton, Humphrey Milford, and by B. Dondorf in Germany. The American Post Card Co. and Reinthal & Newman, of New York, published several series for U.S. distribution.

I. BEAUTIFUL CHILDREN

B.D. (**B. Dondorf,** Frankfurt) (Art Deco)		
Series 130 (6)		
Little Girl with basket of apples	20 - 25	25 - 30

Amy Millicent Sowerby
B. Dondorf, Series 154

Amy Millicent Sowerby
B. Dondorf, Series 154

Others	20 - 25	25 - 30
Series 154 Victorian Children (6)		
Little girls stand on stools	20 - 25	25 - 30
Girl ties another's shoes	20 - 25	25 - 30
Others	20 - 25	25 - 30
Series 168 (6)		
Girls having tea	20 - 25	25 - 30
Others	20 - 25	25 - 30
Series 169 (6)		
Boy and girl take out washing	18 - 22	22 - 26
Mother-Daughter	18 - 22	22 - 26
Series 170 (6)	20 - 25	25 - 30
C. W. Faulkner & Co.		
Series 568 (6)		
"It was a lover and his lass"	20 - 25	25 - 30
Others	20 - 25	25 - 30
Henry Frowde and Hodder & Stoughton		
"Britain & Her Friends" (6)		
"Belgium," "England"	18 - 22	22 - 26
"France," "Portugal"	18 - 22	22 - 26
"Russia"	18 - 22	22 - 26
"U.S."	20 - 25	25 - 30
"The Children's Day" Series (6)		
"Morning," "Mid-Morning"	20 - 25	25 - 28
"Noon," "Afternoon"	20 - 25	25 - 28
"Evening," "Night"	20 - 25	25 - 28

"Happy Little People" Series (6)
"Union is Strength"	18 - 22	22 - 26
Others	18 - 22	22 - 26

"Little Folk of Many Lands" Series (6)
"England," "Holland," "Italy"	20 - 25	25 - 30
"Negro - North American"	25 - 30	30 - 35
"Russia," "Turkey"	20 - 25	25 - 30

"Little Jewels" Series (6)
"Amethyst," "Emerald," "Pearl," "Ruby"	35 - 40	40 - 45
"Sapphire," "Turquoise"	35 - 40	40 - 45

"Little Patriot" Series (6)
"For the Soldiers"	20 - 22	22 - 26

"Playtime" Series (6)
"Blind Man's Bluff"	25 - 30	30 - 35
"A Three-Legged Race"	25 - 30	30 - 35
"A Tug of War," "Leap Frog"	25 - 30	30 - 35
"See-Saw," "With Bat and Ball"	25 - 30	30 - 35

"Pleasant Days" Series (6)
"My Lady's Chair"	20 - 22	22 - 26

Humphrey Milford, London
"Farmyard Pets" Series (6)
"I know you like some fruit"	15 - 20	20 - 25
Others	15 - 20	20 - 25

"Golden Days" Series (6)

	15 - 20	20 - 25

"Guides and Brownies" Series (6) Scouts
"In Spring a gardening we go..."	20 - 25	25 - 30
Others	20 - 25	25 - 30

"Happy Days" Series (6)
"We've waited long to greet you"	15 - 20	20 - 25
Others	15 - 20	20 - 25

"Happy as Kings" Series (6)

	15 - 20	20 - 25

"Just" Series (6)

	15 - 20	20 - 25

"Old Time Games" Series (6)
"In Days of Old when John was King"	18 - 22	22 - 26
Others	18 - 22	22 - 26

Meissner & Buch
Series 1427 (6)
	18 - 22	22 - 26

Humphrey Milford, London (See Fairy Tales)
Name of Series
"Farmyard Pets" (6)	18 - 22	22 - 26
"Golden Days" (6)	18 - 22	22 - 26
"Guides and Brownies" (6) Scouts	20 - 25	25 - 30
"Happy as Kings" (6)	12 - 15	15 - 20
"Happy Days" (6)	15 - 20	20 - 25

"Just" (6)
"Just in time!"	10 - 15	15 - 20
"Just-too-late!"	10 - 15	15 - 20

"Old Time Games" (6)
"In Days of Old, when John was King..."	15 - 18	18 - 22
Others	15 - 18	18 - 22

Misch & Co.
"Greenaway Girls"
Series 833 (6)
	18 - 22	22 - 26

Reinthal & Newman, N.Y.
  Series 2001 (6)

"Pamela," "Pat," "Peggy"	20 - 25	25 - 30
"Phoebe," "Phyllis," "Priscilla"	20 - 25	25 - 30
"Weather" Series (6) (Charles Hauff)		
"Cloudy," "Cold," "Dry"	20 - 25	25 - 30
"Dull," "Fair," "Wet"	20 - 25	25 - 30

II. FAIRIES

Humphrey Milford, London
  "Bird Children" Series (6)

"Good Gracious Me!..."	25 - 30	30 - 35
"Hark, Mister Owl!..."	25 - 30	30 - 35
"Kingfisher Green..."	25 - 30	30 - 35
"When Robin Sings Above..."	25 - 30	30 - 35
"When the First Star..."	25 - 30	30 - 35
"When the First Swallows..."	25 - 30	30 - 35
"Fairy Frolic" Series (6)		
"This Fay among the berries swings..."	25 - 30	30 - 35
"The Summer Elves"	25 - 30	30 - 35
"This Springtime Fairy Pipes..."	25 - 30	30 - 35
"When Crocuses and Snowdrops Peep..."	25 - 30	30 - 35
"When Winter Comes..."	25 - 30	30 - 35
"Flower Children" Series (6)		
"Day-Lily," "Evening Primrose," "King-Cups"	25 - 30	30 - 35
"Love-in-a-Mist," "Pansies," "Snowdrop"	25 - 30	30 - 35
"Flower Fairies" Series (6)		
"Says Jolly Red-cap in the Tree..."	25 - 30	30 - 35
"This Elf and Field-Mouse Play..."	25 - 30	30 - 35
"Flowers and Wings" Series (6)		
"By Moonlight the Wood Fairies..."	25 - 30	30 - 35
"Daddy Longlegs, Flying Strong..."	25 - 30	30 - 35
"Grasshopper, Grasshopper..."	25 - 30	30 - 35
"Oh Bumble Bee..."	25 - 30	30 - 35
"Says Periwinkle Elf..."	25 - 30	30 - 35
"This Poor Little Elf..."	25 - 30	30 - 35
"Merry Elves" Series (6)		
"At Dawn the Sun..."	22 - 25	25 - 30
"Hedgerow Elves in Roses..."	22 - 25	25 - 30
"This Baby Elf flew..."	22 - 25	25 - 30
"This Elf has found some Grapes..."	22 - 25	25 - 30
"Two Dicky Birds sat..."	22 - 25	25 - 30
"When the Mother Bird..."	22 - 25	25 - 30
"Peter Pan Postcards" Series (6)		
"In the Lost Boys' Cozy Cave..."	22 - 25	25 - 28
"The Lost Boys..."	22 - 25	25 - 28
"Peter Pan is afloat on a nest..."	22 - 25	25 - 28
"To the Velvety Tree Tops..."	22 - 25	25 - 28
"Wendy and Joan and Michael..."	22 - 25	25 - 28
"When Peter Lost his Shadow..."	22 - 25	25 - 28
"Pretty Wings" Series (6)		
"Brimstone" and Caterpillar	25 - 30	30 - 35
"Clifton Blue" and Caterpillar	25 - 30	30 - 35
"Large White" and Caterpillar	25 - 30	30 - 35

"Orange Tip" and Caterpillar	25 - 30	30 - 35
"Peacock" and Caterpillar	25 - 30	30 - 35
"Red Admiral" and Caterpillar	25 - 30	30 - 35
"Sky Fairies" Series (6)		
"This Fairy got up in good time..."	25 - 30	30 - 35
"To See-Saw on a Sunbeam is..."	25 - 30	30 - 35
"Two Sky Fairies are hiding..."	25 - 30	30 - 35
"When Mr. Dustman scatters..."	25 - 30	30 - 35
"Woodland Games" Series (6)		
"Listen Bun. We'll have some fun..."	20 - 25	25 - 30
"Oh come and float on My..."	20 - 25	25 - 30
"The Rules of Fairy Leapfrog..."	20 - 25	25 - 30
"The Elf makes the Squirrels..."	20 - 25	25 - 30
"To swing over Poppies is Nice"	20 - 25	25 - 30
"Two Elves on the Wing..."	20 - 25	25 - 30
"Fairies Friends" Series (6)	22 - 25	25 - 30

III.   FAIRY TALES & NURSERY RHYMES

Humphrey Milford, London

"Favourite Nursery Rhymes" (6)		
"Little-Bo-Peep," "Little-Jack-Horner"	25 - 30	30 - 40
"Little-Miss-Muffet," "Mistress-Mary"	25 - 30	30 - 40
"The-Piper's-Son," "Wee-Willie-Winkle"	25 - 30	30 - 40
"Favourite Nursery Stories" (6)		
"The Babes in the Wood"	25 - 30	30 - 40
"Beauty and the Beast"	25 - 30	30 - 40
"Cinderella," "Goldilocks"	25 - 30	30 - 40
"Jack and the Beanstalk," "Red Riding Hood"	25 - 30	30 - 40
"Storyland Children" (6)		
"Little Boy Blue," "Little-Bo-Peep"	25 - 30	30 - 40
"Little Miss Muffet," "Red Riding Hood"	25 - 30	30 - 40
"Tom, Tom, the Piper's Son"	25 - 30	30 - 40

IV. BEAUTIFUL LADIES

Humphrey Milford, London

"Shakespeare's Heroines" (6)		
"A Maid so Tender, Fair and Happy"	25 - 30	30 - 35
"And She is Fair..."	25 - 30	30 - 35
"The Brightness of Her Cheek..."	25 - 30	30 - 35
"From the East to Western..."	25 - 30	30 - 35
"My Lady Disdain..."	25 - 30	30 - 35
"What's Done is Done" *Macbeth*	25 - 30	30 - 35
SPARK, CHICKY (GER)	8 - 10	10 - 15
SPURGIN, FRED (LAT/GB) See Blacks	6 - 8	8 - 10
STEELE, L.R. (GB) See Fantasy	6 - 8	8 - 10
STENBERG, AINA (SWE)	12 - 15	15 - 18
STOCKS, M. (GB)		
H.K. & Co.		
"Jack in the Box" (Golliwoggs)	15 - 20	20 - 25
SURR, RUTH WELCH (US)	2 - 3	3 - 4
SYMONDS, CONSTANCE (GB)	8 - 10	10 - 15
TARRANT, MARGARET (GB) (See Nursery Rhymes)	6 - 8	8 - 15

A. M. Sowerby, Humphrey Milford
"Fav. Nursery Rhymes" – "Little Bo-Peep"

C. H. Twelvetrees, Edward Gross, No. 39
"All the boys love a little 'spoon'."

TEMPEST, DOUGLAS (GB) (See Blacks)		
Bamforth Co. Comic Kids (30's)	5 - 8	8 - 10
Raphael Tuck Series 3 (6) "Dainty Dimples"	6 - 8	8 - 10
TEMPEST, MARGARET (GB)	4 - 6	6 - 10
TWELVETREES, CHARLES or **C.T.** (US)		
Ullman Mfg. Co.		
"National Cupid" Series 75		
1877 "United States"	20 - 25	25 - 30
1878 "England"	15 - 20	20 - 25
1879 "Ireland"	15 - 18	18 - 22
1880 "Scotland"	15 - 18	18 - 22
1881 "Germany"	15 - 18	18 - 22
1882 "Mexico"	15 - 18	18 - 22
1883 "Holland"	15 - 18	18 - 22
1884 "Spain"	15 - 18	18 - 22
1885 "Canada"	15 - 18	18 - 22
1886 "France"	15 - 18	18 - 22
1887 "China"	15 - 18	18 - 22
1888 "Italy"	15 - 18	18 - 22
Edward Gross, N.Y.		
Comical Kids	6 - 8	8 - 10
39 "All the boys love a little 'spoon'." (Nurse)	15 - 20	20 - 25
Wedding Series	10 - 12	12 - 15
1050 "Infant Series"	5 - 7	7 - 8
"Am I crying..."	5 - 8	8 - 12
"I'm a war baby, but..."	5 - 8	8 - 12

"I'm the family darling..."	5 - 8	8 - 12
"Folks all say..."	5 - 8	8 - 12
"Our baby can't talk..."	5 - 8	8 - 12
"Watch your step..."	5 - 8	8 - 12

National Art

Days of the Week Series	5 - 7	7 - 9
Morning-Noon-Night Series	6 - 8	8 - 10

Reinthal & Newman

716 "I'll get that vote yet!!!"	25 -30	30 - 40

UPTON, FLORENCE K. (GB)

Raphael Tuck

Golliwogg Series   See Fantasy Chapter

VOIGHT, C.A. (US) **See Baseball**

VON HARTMANN, E.	2 - 3	3 - 4

WALL, BERNHARDT C. (US) (See Blacks & Baseball)

Ullman Mfg. Co.

"Overall Boys"

92 "Young America"	8 - 10	10 - 12
93 "Me and Jack"	8 - 10	10 - 12
94 "Leap Frog"	8 - 10	10 - 12
95 "A Rough Rider"	8 - 10	10 - 12

"The Senses"

1716 "Feeling"	10 - 12	12 - 15
1717 "Smelling"	10 - 12	12 - 15
1718 "Tasting"	10 - 12	12 - 15
1719 "Hearing"	10 - 12	12 - 15
1720 "Seeing"	10 - 12	12 - 15

"Nursery Rhymes" Series (Uns.)

1664 "Little Bo Peep"	15 - 20	20 - 25
1665 "To Market, To Market"	15 - 20	20 - 25
1666 "Rain, Rain Go Away"	15 - 20	20 - 25
1667 "See Saw, Marjorie Daw"	15 - 20	20 - 25
1668 "Come, Let's Go to Bed"	15 - 20	20 - 25

Sunbonnet Months of the Year

Unsigned, 1633-1644	8 - 9	9 - 12

Sunbonnet Girls' Days of the Week

Unsigned, 1408-1410, 1491-1494	10 - 12	12 - 16

Sunbonnet Seasons

1901 Spring	10 - 12	12 - 16
1902 Summer	10 - 12	12 - 16
1903 Autumn	10 - 12	12 - 16
1904 Winter	10 - 12	12 - 16

"Mary and Her Lamb" Sunbonnets

1759-1762	8 - 10	10 - 13

Sunbonnet Twins

1645 "Give us this Day..."	10 - 12	12 - 15
1646 "The Star Spangled..."	12 - 15	15 - 18
1647 "Should Auld Acquaintance..."	10 - 12	12 - 15
1649 "Now I Lay Me Down..."	10 - 12	12 - 15
1650 "Be It Ever So Humble..."	10 - 12	12 - 15

Sunbonnet Girls

1765 "6 A.M., Milking Time"	10 - 12	12 - 15
1766 "7 A.M., Breakfast Time"	10 - 12	12 - 15

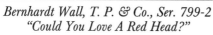

Bernhardt Wall, T. P. & Co., Ser. 799-2
"Could You Love A Red Head?"

Bernhardt Wall, Bergman Co., Ser. 6104
"If My Face Was My Fortune—I'd ..."

1767 "10 A.M., Mowing Time"	10 - 12	12 - 15
1768 "12 N., Noon Time"	10 - 12	12 - 15
1769 "3 P.M., Haying Time"	10 - 12	12 - 15
1770 "6 P.M., Home, Sweet Home"	10 - 12	12 - 15
Sunbonnet Girls Nursery Rhymes		
1664 "Little Bo Peep"	10 - 12	12 - 16
1665 "To Market, to Market"	10 - 12	12 - 16
1666 "Rain, Rain, Go Away"	10 - 12	12 - 16
1667 "See Saw, Marjorie Daw"	10 - 12	12 - 16
1668 "Goosey, Goosey, Gander"	10 - 12	12 - 16
Bergman		
Suffragettes		
"Votes for Women" Series	30 - 40	40 - 50
Unnumbered Sunbonnet Series	8 - 10	10 - 12
Series 6104 Kid Cowboy Series (6)	10 - 15	15 - 18
Schlesinger Bros., N.Y.		
Dutch Kids (6) (B&W)	3 - 4	4 - 5
T.P. & Co. Series 799-2 "Could You Love a Red..."	8 - 10	10 - 12
No Publisher		
Animated Fruit & Vegetable Set		
"Apple" "Cabbage"	8 - 10	10 - 12
"Karat" "Ears"	8 - 10	10 - 12
"Cucumber" "Lemon"	8 - 10	10 - 12
"Melon" "Onion"	8 - 10	10 - 12
"Pair" "Peach"	8 - 10	10 - 12
"Pine" "Potato"	8 - 10	10 - 12
"Pumpkin" "Turnip"	8 - 10	10 - 12

Ida Waugh, Theo Stroefer
Series 1695

Flora White, The Photochrom Co.
"The Post Girl"

WANKE, ALICE (AUS)	8 - 10	10 - 15
WAUGH, IDA		
Theo. Stroefer (**TSN**) (Uns.)		
Series 1695 (6)	30 - 40	40 - 50
Series 1895 (6)	30 - 40	40 - 50
WHEELER, DOROTHY (See Fairy Tales-Nursery Rhymes)		
WHITE, FLORA (See Fairy Tales-Nursery Rhymes)		
The Photochrom Co. "The Post Girl"	10 - 12	12 - 15
W. E. Mach Pub. Co. "Musical Children" (6)	8 - 10	10 - 12
Others	8 - 10	10 - 12
WICHERA, R. R. (AUS)		
M. Munk (B&W)	6 - 8	8 - 10
Color	8 - 10	10 - 12
WIEDERSEIM, GRACE G. (also Grace Drayton) (US)		
Reinthal & Newman		
No Number		
"A button sewed on..."	22 - 26	26 - 32
"Blow"	22 - 26	26 - 32
Bobby: "I brought your birdie..."	22 - 26	26 - 32
Dressy Lady: "What are you crying for...?"	22 - 26	26 - 32
"I think I'd rather..."	22 - 26	26 - 32
"The more I see..."	22 - 26	26 - 32
"Nothing doing"	22 - 26	26 - 32
"You're going to get..."	22 - 26	26 - 32
98 "Nothing doing"	22 - 26	26 - 32
98 "Happy Days"	22 - 26	26 - 32
99 "Where's oo hanky"	22 - 26	26 - 32

110 "What you don't know..."	22 - 26	26 - 32
112 "No Ma'am, we ain't..."	22 - 26	26 - 32
113 "So near & yet so far"	22 - 26	26 - 32
114 "Tis better to have loved and lost..."	22 - 26	26 - 32
115 "Curfew shall not..."	22 - 26	26 - 32
116 "I'm so discouraged..."	22 - 26	26 - 32
117 "Courage"	22 - 26	26 - 32
120 "I hate a spanking..."	22 - 26	26 - 32
121 "Stung!"	22 - 26	26 - 32
174 "Here's How"	22 - 26	26 - 32
175 "Don't wake me up..."	22 - 26	26 - 32
176 "I wish somebody was..."	22 - 26	26 - 32
177 "And what did Mamma's boy do..."	22 - 26	26 - 32
178 "Mr. Moon Man--Turn off your light"	22 - 26	26 - 32
179 "Music Hath Charms"	22 - 26	26 - 32
249 "Gee! But this is..."	22 - 26	26 - 32
250 "Wanted! Somebody..."	22 - 26	26 - 32
308 "I'd rather say Hello..."	22 - 26	26 - 32
310 "All I want is you"	22 - 26	26 - 32
493 Skipping Rope	22 - 26	26 - 32
495 "Why do we place a hyphen..."	22 - 26	26 - 32
496 "Do you or don't you"	22 - 26	26 - 32
500 "More of all"	22 - 26	26 - 32
A. G. Taylor (Orthochrome Series) **(Schweizer)**		
"Help the Poor"	30 - 40	40 - 45
"His First Case"	30 - 40	40 - 45
"I don't think..."	30 - 40	40 - 45
"Two Hearts that beat as one"	30 - 40	40 - 45
"Weary Willy and 'Appy Ann"	30 - 40	40 - 45
Raphael Tuck		
"Bright Eyes" Series (Uns.)	30 - 35	35 - 38
"Sweet Bliss" Series	30 - 35	35 - 38
"It fills my heart..."	30 - 35	35 - 38
"In Arcady"	25 - 30	30 - 35
Series 200 "Cunning Cupids"	40 - 50	50 - 60
Series 223 (6)	30 - 35	35 - 40
Series 242 "Childhood Pets" (Uns.)	25 - 30	30 - 35
Series 243 "Love's Messages" (Uns.)	25 - 30	30 - 35
Series 244 "Masquerade Children" (Uns.)	25 - 30	30 - 35
Halloween Series 807 (Uns.) (4)		
"Hallowe'en. Look in the glass..."	80 - 100	100 - 120
"Jack O'Lantern"	80 - 100	100 - 120
"O-o-o The Witches Brew"	80 - 100	100 - 120
"The Witch!"	80 - 100	100 - 120
Series 2914 "Cunning Cupids"	40 - 50	50 - 60
Armour & Co.		
American Girl Series "The Wiederseim Girl"	30 - 35	35 - 40
Fairman Co.		
"Everything goes wrong when you're away"	20 - 25	25 - 30
C. W. Faulkner		
Series 1281 (Uns.)		
"Dressed in his best"	32 - 35	35 - 40
North American		
"What-che-know- 'bout that"	30 - 35	35 - 40

G. G. Wiederseim, R&N, No. 114
'Tis better to have loved and lost..."

G. G. Wiederseim, Alfred Schweizer
Series 9, "Jilted"

G. G. Wiederseim, R&N, No. 178
"Mr. Moon Man—Turn off your light."

Anonymous
   Series 38 "Days of Week" (Uns.)

Campbell Art Co.	30 - 35	35 - 40
Campbell Soup Co. - Advertising		
Campbell Soup Kids		
Horizontal - (4) (with variations) (1909)	35 - 40	40 - 50
Vertical - (10¢ a can) – (24) * **		
Series 1-12 With **No Series No.** (1912)	125 - 150	150 - 175
Series 1 Numbered 1 through 6 (1912)	120 - 140	140 - 160
Series 2 Numbered 7 through 12 (1912)		
Card 7 with Suffragette jingles (2)	150 - 175	175 - 200
Series 3 Numbered 13 through 18 (1913)	120 - 140	140 - 160
Series 4 Numbered 19 through 24 (1913)	120 - 140	140 - 160

* The 24 images have from 3 to 4 different
jingles on each card...meaning there could be
as many as 80 to 96 different total cards.
** Grace Wiederseim remarried in 1911 so
any of these cards with copyright date after that
would be by Grace Drayton. Nos. 1 through 24
were ©1912-1913.

Swift & Co.		
"Days of the Week" With Ads on Reverse (7)	40 - 45	45 - 55
Alfred Schweizer Co., Hamburg		
No No.		
"I Don't Think!"	35 - 40	40 - 50
Set 10 (Signed)		
Boy pulls girl on sled	35 - 40	40 - 50

Series 8		
"Tit for tat"	35 - 40	40 - 50
Series 9		
Girl walking Poodle	30 - 35	35 - 40
"Jilted"	30 - 35	35 - 40
Series 10596		
Boy/Girl under Mistletoe	30 - 35	35 - 40
"Beware of Dog" Sign	30 - 35	35 - 40
"Chase Me"	30 - 35	35 - 40
"Help the Poor"	30 - 40	40 - 50
"Jilted"	30 - 35	35 - 40
"Time is money"	30 - 35	35 - 40
"Weary Willie and 'Appy Ann"	35 - 40	40 - 50
"You mustn't kiss me!"	30 - 35	35 - 40
Russian Real Photo, No. 279 (Russian Caption)	50 - 60	60 - 75
WILLIAMS, MADGE (GB)	6 - 8	8 - 10
Fairies	10 - 12	12 - 15
WOODWORTH, JULIA (US)	3 - 4	4 - 5
WRIGHT, ALAN (GB) **Fairies**	8 - 10	10 - 12
WUYTS, A. (AUS)	4 - 6	6 - 8

COMICS

ANDERS, O. (GB)	5 - 6	6 - 8
ANDERSON, M. (CYNICUS) (GB)	6 - 8	8 - 10
Golf Comics	15 - 18	18 - 22
ARIS, ERNEST (GB)	5 - 6	6 - 8
BAIRNSFATHER, BRUCE (GB)	6 - 8	8 - 10
F.R. BANKS (US)	3 - 5	5 - 7
"I am missing the Children"	8 - 10	10 - 12
BARNES, G. L. (GB)	3 - 5	5 - 8
BATEMAN, H. M. (GB)	4 - 5	5 - 7
BIGGAR, J. L. (GB)	4 - 5	5 - 8
BIANCO, T. (IT)		
Political Comics	15 - 20	20 - 25
BISHOP, P. (US)	4 - 5	5 - 7
BLACK, W. M. (W.M.B.) (GB)	5 - 6	6 - 8
BLOODGOOD, DON (US) Chromes		
HSC Outhouses	3 - 5	5 - 8
BOULANGER, MAURICE (See Animals)	10 - 12	12 - 15
BRADSHAW, P.V. (GB)	6 - 8	8 - 10
BREGER, DAVID (Linen)		
Graycraft Card Co.		
World War 2 comics (24)	4 - 7	7 - 10
Nyack Art Pictures		
Series 602 "Mr. Breger on Vacation"	8 - 10	10 - 12
BRILL, GEORGE R. (US)	6 - 7	7 - 10
Rose Co.		
"Ginks" Series	8 - 10	10 - 12
Golf - "This is the Life - Your Gink"	10 - 12	12 - 15
BROWNE, TOM (GB)		
Davidson Bros.		
Each Series Contains 6 Cards:		
Series 2507 "Illustrated Sports"	12 - 15	15 - 20

F. R. Banks, Anonymous Publisher
"I am missing the Children"

Don Bloodgood, HSC-32
"Double Trouble"

Tom Browne, Davidson Brothers
Series 2589, "Johnny's Ma goes to a..."

Tom Browne, Davidson Brothers
Series 2638-2, "Pa's Adventures."

"Golf"	22 - 25	25 - 28
Series 2525 "Golf"	20 - 25	25 - 28
Series 2575 "Seaside Comfort"	6 - 8	8 - 10
Series 2578 "Billiards Made Easy"	20 - 25	25 - 28
Series 2585 "Amateur Photographer"	10 - 12	12 - 15
Series 2587 "Cycling"	12 - 15	15 - 20
Series 2589 "Johnny's Ma"	10 - 12	12 - 15
Series 2594 "Kissing"	8 - 10	10 - 12
Series 2596 "Ma's Little Worries"	8 - 10	10 - 12
Golf	22 - 25	25 - 28
Series 2598 "Are We Downhearted..."	5 - 10	10 - 15
Series 2602 "Illustrated Sports"		
Golf	22 - 25	25 - 30
Series 2615 "Love is Blind"	5 - 10	10 - 12
Series 2618 "Baseball III"	20 - 25	25 - 30
Series 2619 "Baseball III"	20 - 25	25 - 30
Series 2627 "Diabolo"	12 - 15	15 - 20
Series 2637 "New Compensation Act"	8 - 10	10 - 12
Series 2638 "Pa's Adventures"	8 - 10	10 - 12
Series 2640 "Spooning by Moonlight"	10 - 12	12 - 15
5 "Spooning on the links"	20 - 25	25 - 28
Series 2642 "Joys of the Ocean"	6 - 8	8 - 10
BUCHANAN, FRED (GB) (See Blacks)	6 - 8	8 - 10
Golf	20 - 25	25 - 30
BULL, RENE (GB)	5 - 6	6 - 8
BUXTON, DUDLEY (GB)	5 - 6	6 - 8

CADY, HARRISON (US)
  Quaddy Plaything Co.
    "QUADDY" Series 10   35 - 40   40 - 45
CARMICHAEL (US)
  S. K. Simon
    Series 200 "You Look Good to Me" (6)   6 - 8   8 - 10
  S.B. Co.
    Series 261 "Would You?" (12)   6 - 8   8 - 10
    Series 262 "If" (12)   6 - 8   8 - 10
  Anonymous
    Series 310 "Why?" (12)   6 - 8   8 - 10
    Series 311 "There are Others" (6)   6 - 8   8 - 10
    Series 315 "Don't Marry" (12)   6 - 8   8 - 10
  T.P. & Co.
    Series 565 "I love my wife, but oh you kid" (12)   6 - 8   8 - 10
    Series 568 "I wish I had a beau" (12)   6 - 8   8 - 10
    Series 620 Playing Card Series (12)   8 - 10   10 - 12
    Series 621 "Your Fortune" (12)   8 - 10   10 - 12
    Series 668 "Anybody here seen Kelly?" (12)   6 - 8   8 - 10
    Series 669 Fish Series (12)   6 - 8   8 - 10
    Series 761 Stork Series (12)   6 - 8   8 - 10
  Bamforth Co.
    Series 262 "If" (12)   5 - 7   7 - 8
CARR, GENE (US)
  Bergman Co.
    Series 2003, 2004, 8515 Easter   6 - 8   8 - 10
  Rotograph Co., N.Y.
    Series 218 Mosquitos (4)   6 - 8   8 - 10
    Series 219 4th of July Series (5)   7 - 10   10 - 15
    St. Patrick's Series 187-192 (6)   6 - 9   9 - 12
    Comic Series 201-213 (12)   6 - 8   8 - 10
CARTER, REG. (GB)
    Early Issues   8 - 10   10 - 14
    Golf Comics   20 - 25   25 - 28
    After 1920 Issues   3 - 4   4 - 7
CARTER, R.C.   5 - 6   6 - 9
CARTER, SYDNEY (GB)   8 - 10   10 - 12
CAVALLY, FRED L. (US) Also See Teddy Bears   2 - 4   4 - 6
CHANDLER, E.   5 - 6   6 - 8
CHRISTIE, G. F. (GB)
    Pre 1920   8 - 10   10 - 14
    Post 1920   4 - 6   6 - 8
COCK, STANLEY   4 - 5   5 - 8
COMICUS (HARRY PARTLETT) (GB)   2 - 3   3 - 5
COLBY, V. (US)   1 - 2   2 - 3
COOK, C. K. (GB)   6 - 8   8 - 12
COWHAM, HILDA (GB)
  Raphael Tuck
    "Write Away" Series 1009   4 - 7   7 - 10
CRANE, D.P.
  Zim Pub. Co.   6 - 9   9 - 12

D. P. Crane, Zim Pub.   *DWIG, Chas. Rose*   *DWIG, Chas. Rose*
"It's No Use Girls"   *Series 22, "I Adore You"*   *Ser. 21, "Dear, You will..."*

CROMBIE, CHARLES (GB)
  Valentine

"Rules of Golf" Series	20 - 25	25 - 30
"The Golf Series"	22 - 25	25 - 30
"Rules of Cricket" Series	18 - 22	22 - 26
"Humors of Fishing" Series	10 - 12	12 - 15
Others	4 - 6	6 - 10

CYNICUS (GB) See M. Anderson

DARLING, JAY (US)	10 - 12	12 - 15
DAVEY, GEORGE (GB)	5 - 6	6 - 8
DENSLOW, W. W. (US) Thanksgiving	10 - 12	12 - 15

  See Teddy Bears
DeWEES, ETHEL H. or E.H.D.
  A.M.P. Co.

"Billy Possum" Political Series (6) Golf	25 - 30	30 - 35
DIRKS, GUS (GB) Comic Insects	8 - 10	10 - 12

DIRKS, R. (GER)
  American Journal Examiner

Katzenjammer Kids	6 - 8	8 - 12

DISNEY, WALT (US)
  Foreign Issues

French, 30's Era	20 - 25	25 - 35
German, 30's Era	20 - 25	25 - 30
Czech., 30's Era	20 - 25	25 - 30
Hungarian, 30's Era	20 - 25	25 - 30
Other 30's Era Issues	15 - 20	20 - 25
Felix the Cat		

DONADINI, JR. (IT) See Blacks)

A-H Motoring Comics (6)	6 - 8	8 - 12

  German-American Novelty Art Co.
    Series 491 Driving Comics (6)

"What is worth doing..."	12 - 15	15 - 18

K. & B. D.
Boating Comics, Series 1660 (6)	10 - 12	12 - 15
Driving Comics, Series 3033 (6)	12 - 15	15 - 18
Driving Comics, Series 202 (6)	10 - 12	12 - 15
Drunk Comics, Series 357 (6)	6 - 8	8 - 10
Lover Comics, Series 362 (6)	8 - 10	10 - 12
Seashore Comics, Series 393 (6)	8 - 10	10 - 12
"Sell Well" Comics Series 14 (6)	6 - 8	8 - 10
Children Comics, Series 201 (6)	6 - 8	8 - 10

Ottmar Ziehr
Mountain Climbing Series 129	10 - 12	12 - 16

Anonymous
Driving Comics, Series 652 (6)	10 - 12	12 - 15
Easter Comics, Series 787 (6)	6 - 8	8 - 10
Farm Life, Series 239 (6)	6 - 8	8 - 10
Men at Seashore Series (6)	8 - 10	10 - 12
Funny Children Head Studies (6)	8 - 10	10 - 15

DUNCAN, HAMISH (GB)	3 - 4	4 - 6

DWIG (C.V. DWIGGINS) (US)

J. Marks
Series 981 "Halloween" (6)	25 - 30	30 - 40

Raphael Tuck
"Cheer Up" Series (24)	6 - 8	8 - 10
"Don't" Series (24)	8 - 10	10 - 12
"Everytime" Series (24)	6 - 8	8 - 10
"Follies" Series (12)	6 - 8	8 - 10
"If" Series (24)	6 - 8	8 - 10
"Ophelia" Series (24)	6 - 8	8 - 10
"Pipe Dreams" Fantasy Series 122 (12)	12 - 15	15 - 20
"Help Wanted" Series (12)	6 - 8	8 - 10
"Never" Series (24)	6 - 8	8 - 10
"Jollies" Series (12)	6 - 8	8 - 10
"School Days" Series (24)	6 - 8	8 - 10
"Smiles" Series (24)	6 - 8	8 - 10
Series 127 "Toasts For Today" (12)	10 - 12	12 - 15
Series 128 "Toasts for Occasions" (12)	8 - 10	10 - 12
"Zodiac" Series (12)	12 - 15	15 - 18

Charles Rose
"Baby" Series (6)	6 - 8	8 - 10
"Figures in Mountains" Series (6)	10 - 12	12 - 15
"Moon" Series 21 (6)	10 - 12	12 - 15
"Moving" Series (6)	8 - 10	10 - 12
"New York" Series (6)	12 - 15	15 - 20
"Oyster Girl" Series (6)	10 - 12	12 - 15
"Sandwich" Series (6)	8 - 10	10 - 12
"Superstition" Series (6)	8 - 10	10 - 12
"What are Wild Waves..." Series 22 (6)	10 - 12	12 - 15
"The Wurst Girl" Series (6)	12 - 15	15 - 20
"The Frankfurter Girl" Series (6)	10 - 12	12 - 15

Fox, Colourpicture Pub., No. 1307
"You and I Both Bud!"

Fox, Colourpicture Pub., No. 1268
"The Pause That Refreshes"

Herman Hanke, Illustrated Postcard Co.
No. 5004-23, "The Masher"

R. Kaplan		
"Fortune Teller" Series (12)	8 - 9	9 - 10
"How Can You Do It?" Series (24)	6 - 7	7 - 8
"Mirror Girl" Series (24)	8 - 10	10 - 12
Sam Gabriel		
"If's & And's" Series (6)	6 - 7	7 - 8
"Leap Year" Series 401 (12)	9 - 10	10 - 12
"Fortune Teller" Series 55 (12)	6 - 8	8 - 10
Edward Gross		
"What's the Use?" Series (6)	6 - 7	7 - 8
Cardinell-Vincent Co. © 1910 Ninon Traver		
Series 101 "Widow's Wisdom" (12)	75 - 80	80 - 100
EARNSHAW, H.C. (GB)	5 - 7	7 - 9
EDWARDS, LIONEL	4 - 6	6 - 8
ELLAM (W.H.) (GB) (See Teddy Bears)		
"Breakfast in Bed" Series	20 - 22	22 - 25
Others	10 - 12	12 - 15
FOX, CRAIG (US) (Linens)	1 - 2	2 - 3
FISHER, BUD (US)		
Mutt and Jeff (Uns.)	12 - 15	15 - 20
FLEURY, H.	4 - 6	6 - 8
FLOHRI (US)		
Rotograph Co.		
Comic Set 2	12 - 15	15 - 20

FOX
  Colourpicture
    1268 "The Pause That Refreshes"   2 - 3   3 - 4
    1307 "You and I Both Bud!"   2 - 3   3 - 4
FULLER, EDMUND G.   5 - 7   7 - 8
GIBBS, MAY   18 - 22   22 - 26
GIBSON, CHARLES DANA (US) (See Artist-Signed)
  Henderson Co. Sepia Comics (36)   5 - 6   6 - 8
  Detroit Publishing   7 - 10   10 - 12
  Golf   18 - 22   22 - 26
GILL, ARTHUR (GB)   4 - 5   5 - 7
GILSON, T. (GB) (See Blacks)   4 - 5   5 - 7
GLADWIN, MAY (GB)   4 - 5   5 - 7
GOLDBERG, RUBE (US)
  Albie the Agent   8 - 10   10 - 12
  Samson Bros.
    Series 212 "The Ancient Order"   6 - 8   8 - 10
    Series 213 "Foolish Questions"   5 - 6   6 - 8
    Dreamland Skating Rink – Advertising   15 - 18   18 - 22
GOODYEAR, ARCHIE   4 - 5   5 - 7
GOTHARD, F. (GB)   4 - 5   5 - 7
GRIGGS, H. B. or HBG
  L & E
    Halloween (See Halloween)
    George Washington Women's Suffrage   80 - 90   90 - 100
    Others   8 - 10   10 - 12
HAMILTON, J.M. (GB)
  Raphael Tuck Series 9461 "Our Caddy" (6)   20 - 25   25 - 30
H.H. (HERMAN HANKE)
  Illustrated Postcard Co.
    Series 5004 (30+)   5 - 8   8 - 12
HAMISH (GB)   4 - 5   5 - 6
HARDY, DUDLEY (GB)   6 - 8   8 - 10
  Davidson Bros.
    Series 3000, 3001, 3002, 3003 (6)   5 - 7   7 - 10
    Series 3004, 3005, 3006, 3007 (6)   5 - 7   7 - 10
    Series 3008, 3009, 3011, 3012 (6)   5 - 7   7 - 10
    Series 3008 Nursery Rhymes (6)   9 - 12   12 - 16
    Series 3013, 3014, 3015 (6)   5 - 7   7 - 10
HASSALL, JOHN (GB)   6 - 8   8 - 10
HATLO, JIMMY (US) (Linen)
  Tichnor Bros. (24+)   6 - 8   8 - 12
HORINA, H.
  Illustrated P.C. Co.   5 - 6   6 - 9
HURST, HAL (US)   4 - 5   5 -7
HUTAF, AUGUST (US) (See Blacks)
  P.C.K. "Advice to Vacationists"   5 - 6   6 - 8
IBBETSON, ERNEST (GB)   6 - 8   8 - 10
KENNEDY, A. E. (GB)   6 - 8   8 - 10

KINSELLA, E. P. (GB) (See Blacks)
  Langsdorff & Co.

Series 695 Comical Children, Tennis (6)	20 - 25	25 - 30
Series 710 Comical Children Golfing (6)	25 - 30	30 - 35

KYD, J.C.C. (GB)
  Raphael Tuck "Dickens Characters"

"The Artful Dodger" – Oliver Twist	8 - 10	10 - 12
"Mrs. Bardell" – Pickwick Papers	8 - 10	10 - 12
"Bikes" – Oliver Twist	8 - 10	10 - 12
"Bumble" – Oliver Twist	8 - 10	10 - 12
"Captain Cuttle" – Dombey & Sons	8 - 10	10 - 12
"Dick Swiveller" – Old Curiosity Shop	8 - 10	10 - 12
"Fat Boy" – Pickwick Papers	8 - 10	10 - 12
"Mr. Jingle" – Pickwick Papers	8 - 10	10 - 12
"The Little Marchioness" – Old Curiosity Shop	8 - 10	10 - 12
"Mr. Micawber" – David Copperfield	8 - 10	10 - 12
"Mr. Pecksniff" – Martin Chuzzlewit	8 - 10	10 - 12
"Mr. Peggotty" – David Copperfield	8 - 10	10 - 12
"Mr. Pickwick" – Pickwick Papers	8 - 10	10 - 12
"Quilp" – Old Curiosity Shop	8 - 10	10 - 12
"Sam Weller" – Pickwick Papers	8 - 10	10 - 12
"Samson Brass" – Old Curiosity Shop	8 - 10	10 - 12
"Mrs. Sarah Gamp" – Martin Chuzzlewit	8 - 10	10 - 12
" Sergeant Buzfuz" – Pickwick Papers	8 - 10	10 - 12
"Toots" – Dombey & Sons	8 - 10	10 - 12
"Trotty Veck" – The Chimes	8 - 10	10 - 12
"Uriah Heep" – David Copperfield	8 - 10	10 - 12
"Mr. Weller" – Pickwick Papers	8 - 10	10 - 12
"Whackford Squeers" – Nicolas Nickleby	8 - 10	10 - 12

LEETE, ALFRED

"London Opinion" Series	8 - 10	10 - 12

LEWIN, F.G. (GB) (See Blacks)	5 - 6	6 - 10
LEVI, C. (US) (See Blacks)	5 - 6	6 - 8

LILLO, R. (US)
  P. Sander

Series 503 (36) 1-36 Superb Cartoons	4 - 7	7 - 12
LUDOVICI, A.	8 - 10	10 - 12

MARTIN, ABE (US)

Illustrated P.C. Co.	5 - 6	6 - 10
"Leap Year"	6 - 8	8 - 10
Other "Leap Year" Issues	6 - 8	8 - 10

  F.L.

"Comical Types" (The Strong Man, etc.)	6 - 8	8 - 10
Others	5 - 6	6 - 8
MASON, GEORGE W.	5 - 6	6 - 7
MAY, PHIL (GB)	6 - 8	8 - 10

  Raphael Tuck

Series 1008 (6) Golf Write-Away Series	20 - 25	25 - 30

R. Lillo, P. Sander
Series 503, "Old but still..."

R. Lillo, P. Sander
Series 503, "Two soles ..."

R. Lillo, P. Sander
Series 503, "Billy Bluff"

Series 1295 (6)	8 - 10	10 - 12
Series 1775 (6) Drunks	6 - 8	8 - 10
McCAY, WINSOR (US)		
Raphael Tuck		
"Little Nemo" Series	25 - 30	30 - 35
McGILL, DONALD (GB) See Blacks		
Pre-1914	6 - 8	8 - 10
Valentine's	6 - 8	8 - 10
Bamforth		
Kid Comics	4 - 6	6 - 8
McMANUS, GEORGE (US)		
"Bringing Up Father" Series	35 - 40	40 - 45
MORELAND, ARTHUR	5 - 6	6 - 8
MORGAN, F. E. (GB)	5 - 8	8 - 10
Golf	15 - 20	20 - 25
MORGAN, F. R.		
Question Series	8 - 10	10 - 12
MUNSON, WALT (Linens) (See Blacks)	1 - 2	2 - 3
WW2 Comics	2 - 3	3 - 6
MYER		
Aurochrome Series	4 - 5	5 - 6
Golf comics	15 - 18	18 - 22
NEILSON, HARRY B. (GB)		
"Toast" Series (Undb)	8 - 10	10 - 12
NEWELL, PETER (US)		
Detroit Publishing Co.		
Series 14169-14178		
"Bigger-than-Weather-Boys"	10 - 12	12 - 15
OPPER, FRED (US)		
American Journal Examiner		
"Happy Hooligan" Series	8 - 10	10 - 12
"Alphonse & Gaston" Series	6 - 8	8 - 10

F. Opper, American Journal Examiner − "You First, My Dear."

"And Her Name Was Maud" Series	6 - 8	8 - 10
Others	5 - 6	6 - 8
Add $3 for Tuck Issues.		

OUTCAULT, R. F. (US)
  American Journal Examiner
  Buster Brown Series (8)

"Look at Santa Claus"	18 - 22	22 - 26
"Oh, See the Sea Serpent"	12 - 15	15 - 20
"Resolved: Nothing Can Stop Us"	10 - 12	12 - 15
"Say! Mary Jane..."	12 - 15	15 - 20
"What Enormous Bill on Legs..."	10 - 12	12 - 15
"Who is Buster Posing?"	15 - 18	18 - 22
"Who is Buster Getting Away From?"	12 - 15	15 - 20
"Who is the Laugh On?"	12 - 15	15 - 20
"A Smooth Bit of Road" (Blacks)	20 - 25	25 - 30
"The Constable"	20 - 25	25 - 30
"All Over"	15 - 20	20 - 25

Bloomingdale Brothers, 1902
  Buster Brown Adv. Series (6) — 70 - 80 — 80 - 90
Bloomingdale Brothers
  Buster Brown Santa Claus Card — 100 - 120 — 120 - 130
Brown Shoe Company, 1909
  Buster Brown Blue Ribbon Shoes
    Months of Year (12) — 20 - 25 — 25 - 30
Burr-McIntosh, 1903
  "Buster Brown and His Bubble" (10) *

"A Quiet Day in Town"	15 - 20	20 - 25
"Hands Up"	15 - 20	20 - 25

"Black or White?" (Blacks)	28 - 32	32 - 35
"Looking for Trouble"	15 - 20	20 - 25
"A Good Bump"	25 - 30	30 - 35
"Over the Bounding Main" (Blacks)	25 - 30	30 - 35
"A Rise in Bear"	15 - 20	20 - 25
"A Smooth Bit of Road" (Blacks)	25 - 30	30 - 35
"The Constable"	15 - 20	20 - 25
"All Over"	15 - 20	20 - 25

* Set also by I.H. Blanchard Co. and by
Souvenir P.C. Co. - Appr. same values.

Kaufmann and Strauss, 1903

Advertising Cards with Imprints of Var. Firms (16+)	12 - 15	15 - 18

J. Ottoman, 1905

Comic Series (40+)	10 - 12	12 - 15

J. Ottoman, 1906

Christmas Card Set (4?) Unsigned	12 - 15	15 - 18

F. A. Stokes, 1906

Buster Brown Outcault Cartoon Lectures

"Come on Tige"	15 - 20	20 - 25
"Gee, What's Playing?"	15 - 20	20 - 25
"Give it to Mary Jane, Buddy"	15 - 20	20 - 25
"If Tige Would Only Go Away"	15 - 20	20 - 25
"Where Are You Going?"	15 - 20	20 - 25

H. H. Tammen, 1906

Buster Brown Series (Embossed) *

"Come and Join Us in a Blowout"	12 - 15	15 - 18
"I Ain't Got no Time..."	12 - 15	15 - 18
"Hurry Back with the Answer"	12 - 15	15 - 18
"It was de Dutch"	12 - 15	15 - 18
"Way Down in My Heart..."	12 - 15	15 - 18
* Reduced Series of Above Set, 1908	20 - 25	25 - 30

Raphael Tuck, 1903

Valentine Series (12)	10 - 12	12 - 15

Raphael Tuck, 1904

Valentine Scroll Series (6)	10 - 12	12 - 15
"Can you Guess the One...?"	10 - 12	12 - 15
"Don't Monkey with this Heart of Mine"	10 - 12	12 - 15
"Here's a Wireless Telegram..."	10 - 12	12 - 15
"I am Perfectly Willing..."	10 - 12	12 - 15
"Why Don't Someone Ask...?"	10 - 12	12 - 15
"Won't You be my Honey...?"	10 - 12	12 - 15
"There's a Certain Person..."	10 - 12	12 - 15
"Will you be my Valentine...?"	10 - 12	12 - 15

Raphael Tuck

New Outcault Series 7 Valentine Postcards	12 - 15	15 - 18

Buster Brown

Series 8 Valentine Postcards (10)

"Bear, Bear, Don't Go Away"	10 - 15	15 - 18
"Honey, How Your Eyes Do Shine"	10 - 15	15 - 18

"I Am Perfectly Willing..."	10 - 15	15 - 18
"I Dreams Erbout Yo' Eb'ry Night..."	10 - 15	15 - 18
"Laugh, Laugh and be Merry..."	10 - 15	15 - 18
"Love Me, and the World is Mine"	10 - 15	15 - 18
"Now How Do Little Birdies Know..."	10 - 15	15 - 18
"Of All the Days in the Year..."	10 - 15	15 - 18
"Oh, Maid, Take Pity..."	10 - 15	15 - 18
"Someone Has Asked Someone..."	10 - 15	15 - 18
Buster Brown Postcards	12 - 15	15 - 18
Love Tributes		
Series 5	10 - 12	12 - 15
Ullman Mfg. Co., 1906 *		
Series 76 "Darktown" (4)		
"Darktown Doctors"	25 - 30	30 - 35
"Darktown Dames"	25 - 30	30 - 35
"Deed, I Dun Eat No Chicken"	20 - 25	25 - 30
"Koontown Kids"	25 - 30	30 - 35
* **American Postcard Co.** also did **Series 76**		
Buster Brown Co., Chicago, 1906		
Buster Brown 1906 Calendars	15 - 20	20 - 25
Buster Brown 1907 Calendars	15 - 20	20 - 25
Outcault Adv. Co., Chicago, 1907		
Buster Brown 1908 Calendars	18 - 22	22 - 26
Buster Brown 1909 Calendars	18 - 22	22 - 26
Buster Brown 1910 Calendars	18 - 22	22 - 26
Buster Brown 1911 Calendars	18 - 22	22 - 26
R. F. Outcault, New York, 1907		
Little House Maid 1908 Calendars	15 - 20	20 - 25
Little House Maid 1909 Calendars	15 - 20	20 - 25
Little House Maid 1910 Calendars	15 - 20	20 - 25
Little House Maid 1911 Calendars	15 - 20	20 - 25
Mr. Swell Dresser 1908 Calendars	15 - 18	18 - 22
Mr. Swell Dresser 1909 Calendars	15 - 18	18 - 22
Mr. Swell Dresser 1910 Calendars	15 - 18	18 - 22
R. F. Outcault, N.Y., 1908-11		
Bank Series 1909-11 Calendars	12 - 15	15 - 20
R. F. Outcault, N.Y., 1909		
Bank Series 1912-13 Calendars	20 - 25	25 - 30
Rockford Watch 1909-10 Calendars	25 - 30	30 - 35
R. F. Outcault, N.Y., 1911		
Yellow Kid 1910 -12 Calendars	80 - 100	100 - 125
Yellow Kid 1913 Calendars	80 - 100	100 - 125
R. F. Outcault, Copyright		
Blue Boy 1912-14 Calendars	12 - 15	15 - 20
Buster Brown 1912-15 Calendars	12 - 15	15 - 20
Furniture 1912-15 Calendars	12 - 15	15 - 20
Mary Jane 1911-13 Calendars	12 - 15	15 - 20

Robt. Robinson, Edward Gross
No. 203

Robt. Robinson, Edward Gross
No. 202

Yellow Kid Look-a-Like 1914-15 Calendars	15 - 20	20 - 25
PARTLETT, HARRY (GB)		
Taylor's Orthochrome		
Series 2830 (6) Roller Skating	12 - 15	15 - 20
Others	4 - 7	7 - 9
PHIZ (**H.K. BROWNE**)	8 - 10	10 - 12
PIPPO (FR)		
Big Eyed Man Series		
Barber Blacksmith	10 - 12	12 - 16
Cook Doctor	10 - 12	12 - 16
Gambler Musician	10 - 12	12 - 16
Richman Sculptor	10 - 12	12 - 16
Blacks	15 - 20	20 - 25
POULBOT, F. (FR)	8 - 10	10 - 12
RAEMAKERS, LOUIS (NETH)	6 - 8	8 - 10
REYNOLDS, FRANK (US)	5 - 6	6 - 8
REZNICEK (DEN)	12 - 15	15 - 18
ROBERTS, VIOLET	8 - 10	10 - 12
ROBIDA (FR)	10 - 12	12 - 15
ROBINSON, ROBT. (US)		
Edward Gross, Nos. 202 and 203	15 - 20	20 - 30
ROBINSON, W. HEATH (US)	6 - 8	8 - 10
ROCKWELL, NORMAN (US)	30 - 40	40 - 50
ROWNTREE, HARRY (GB) See Teddy Bears	6 - 8	8 - 10

Fritz Schonflug, B.K.W.I., Series 278-6

SANDFORD, H. DIX (See Blacks)	6 - 7	7 - 8
SCHÖNPFLUG, FRITZ (AUS) (See Artist-Signed)	10 - 15	15 - 20
Boxing Sries 278	15 - 20	20 - 25
SCHULTZ, C. E. (Bunny)		
"Foxy Grandpa" Series	6 - 8	8 - 10
SHEPHEARD, GEORGE E.	5 - 6	6 - 7
SHINN, COBB and TOM YAD (US)	3 - 4	4 - 5
See Art Nouveau		
H. A. Waters Co.		
"Foolish Questions" Series	3 - 4	4 - 6
"Ford" Comics	8 - 10	10 - 12
"Charlie Chaplin" Cartoons	8 - 10	10 - 12
ZB & Co.		
"Buying Votes"	25 - 30	30 - 35
SPURGIN, FRED (LAT) See Blacks		
Series 956 "Leap Year"	8 - 10	10 - 12
Others	5 - 6	6 - 8
STUDDY, G. E. (GB)		
"Bonzo" Series	8 - 10	10 - 12
Golf	15 - 25	25 - 28
Tennis	12 - 15	15 - 20
Others	4 - 5	5 - 6
SWINNERTON		
American Journal Examiner	6 - 7	7 - 10
TAYLOR, A. (GB)		
Bamforth Comics (1950's)	2 - 3	3 - 4
TEMPEST, D. (GB) (See Blacks)		
Bamforth Co. "Kiddy Comics"	4 - 6	6 - 10

Arth. Thiele, G. Dietrich, No. 250/4 — "Frau Klempnermeister."

Golf	12 - 15	15 - 18
Tennis	10 - 12	12 - 15
Others	4 - 6	6 - 10

THACKERAY, LANCE (GB)
  Raphael Tuck

"At the Seaside" Series (6)	8 - 9	9 - 12
Series 1272 "Popular Plays" (6)	8 - 10	10 - 12
Series 9304, 9305 "The Game of Golf" (6)	25 - 30	30 - 35
Series 9088 "Weather Reports" (6)	7 - 8	8 - 10
Series 9499 Golf images	20 - 25	25 - 30

THIELE, ARTHUR (GER) See Blacks, Cats, Animals
  G. Dietrich

No. 250/4 "Frau Klempnermeister."	15 - 20	20 - 30

  Theo. Stroefer

Early Outhouse, Military, etc. Comics	15 - 20	20 - 30

  L & P

Fat Lady Series	10 - 12	12 - 15
Bathing Girls Series	12 - 15	15 - 20
Others	10 - 12	12 - 15

TWELVETREES, C. (See Artist-Signed Children

UPTON, FLORENCE (GB) (See Golliwoggs)	30 - 35	35 - 40

WAIN, LOUIS (GB) See Cats, Dog
WALL, BERNHARDT (US) (See Artist-Signed)

Many Sets and Series	5 - 6	6 - 10
WARD, DUDLEY	3 - 4	4 - 5

WEAVER, E. (US)

Ford Comics	8 - 10	10 - 12

Others	1 - 2	2 - 3
WELLMAN, WALTER (US)		
"Try Dan Cupid" Series (32)	5 - 7	7 - 10
"Merry Widow Wiles" (8)	6 - 8	8 - 10
"Last Will & Testament" Series (8)	6 - 8	8 - 10
"Weaker Sex" Series (12)	5 - 8	8 - 10
"Hand" Series (12)	5 - 6	6 - 8
"The Suffragette" Ser. (16) See Topics, Suffragettes		
"Life's Little Tragedies" (16)	5 - 6	6 - 8
Linen Comics (See Blacks)	1 - 1.50	1.50 - 2
WELLS, C.		
Lounsbury		
Series 2025 "Lovely Lilly"	6 - 8	8 - 10
WITT, MIA		
"Ford Booster" Comics (10)	7 - 8	8 - 10
WOOD, LAWSON (GB)		
Chimps, Parrots, etc.	6 - 8	8 - 10
Golf	12 - 15	15 - 18
S.H. & Co., Ltd. Comics	6 - 8	8 - 10
Valentine's See Suffragettes		
"Gran 'pop Series"	6 - 8	8 - 10
Golf	15 - 20	20 - 25
YAD, TOM (Also **COBB SHINN**)	1 - 2	2 - 3

PUBLISHERS

A H Co. (Undb)	4 - 6	6 - 8
Bauman (Uns.)		
Ugly Girls - Days of the Week (6)	6 - 8	8 - 10
Gartner & Bender		
Water Color Sets (6) Each (6)		
"Amy Bility"	6 - 8	8 - 10
"Antie Quate"	6 - 8	8 - 10
"Gee Whiz"	6 - 8	8 - 10
"Gee Willikins"	6 - 8	8 - 10
"Jimmy"	6 - 8	8 - 10
"Optimistic Miss"	6 - 8	8 - 10
"Phil Os Opher"	6 - 8	8 - 10
R. Hill (Edward Stern) (30+)	6 - 9	8 - 12
Irwin Kline (Unsigned)		
Masonic (No Numbers) (6)	6 - 7	7 - 9
E. Nash		
Series 1		
Valentine Comics (24)	5 - 7	7 - 10
P.F.B. (Unsigned)		
Series 5077 (6)	8 - 10	10 - 15
Series 5897 Mother-in-Law (6)	8 - 10	10 - 15
Series 6307 Comic Lovers (6)	8 - 10	10 - 12
Series 6538 Domestic Riot (6)	8 - 10	10 - 12
Series 6895 First of April (6)	10 - 12	12 - 15

Publisher P.F.B.
Series 9395

Publisher P.F.B.
Series 5077

Publisher P.F.B., Series
6895 – "1er Avril"

Series 9395 Big Headed Ladies (6)	8 - 10	10 - 12
Many Others	6 - 8	8 - 10
Rose Co.		
Copyright 1907 Scroll around images	4 - 5	5 - 8
Football player	8 - 10	10 - 12
Series 264		
Valentine Comics (10+) (1911)	4 - 5	5 - 8
Football player	8 - 10	10 - 12
Raphael Tuck		
Valentine "Penny Dreadful" types		
Series A, B, C (many, up to 24 in each series)	5 - 7	7 - 10
Series 5, 6, 7	5 - 7	7 - 10
Golf	15 - 18	18 - 22
Series 3600 "Golf Humor" (6)	25 - 30	30 - 35
Series 9641 "Humorous Golf" (6)	20 - 25	25 - 30

SILHOUETTES

ALLMAHER, JOSEFINE	6 - 8	8 - 10
BECKMAN, JOHANNA (GER)	8 - 10	10 - 12
BURKE, PAUL	5 - 7	7 - 8
BORRMEISTER, R. (GER)	8 - 10	10 - 12
BRENING, H.	10 - 12	12 - 15
CARUS (GER)		
Berliner Tierschutz-Verein Animals	12 - 15	15 - 18
DIEFENBACH, K.W. (GER)		
B. G. Teubner		
Fantasy Children	12 - 15	15 - 18
Animals	10 - 12	12 - 15
FIDUS (GER) Chidren and Sports	12 - 15	15 - 20
FORCK, ELSBETH (GER)	10 - 12	12 - 15
Herman A. Peters **Tales and Fairy Tales**	12 - 15	15 - 18

Elsbeth Forck *H. A. Peters, "Rapunzel"*	*Carus* *Berliner Tierschutz-Verein*	*K. W. Diefenbach* *B. G. Teubner*

GRAF, MARTE (GER)		
Art Deco Series 1, 2, 3, 4 (743-754)	8 - 10	10 - 15
GROSS, CH.	5 - 7	7 - 8
GROSZE, MANNI (GER)		
P.F.B. (In Diamond)		
Deco Series 2041 "After Bath"	12 - 15	15 - 20
Nude Series 2042	12 - 15	15 - 18
Series 2043	10 - 12	12 - 15
Nude Series 3339	12 - 15	15 - 20
Series 3341 & 3342	10 - 12	12 - 15
K.M.H.	8 - 10	10 - 12
KASKELINE (GER)		
Art Deco, Ladies/Children	10 - 12	12 - 16
Art Deco Nudes	12 - 15	15 - 22
Dancing	10 - 15	15 - 18
LAMP, H.		
Series 3, Deco Dancing	15 - 18	18 - 22
Series 4, Bathing	12 - 15	15 - 20
PHILIPP, FELICIEN	8 - 10	10 - 12
PEANITSCH, LEO	10 - 12	12 - 15
ROBA (Deco Fantasy)	12 - 15	15 - 20
SACHSE-SCHUBERT, M. (GER)	10 - 12	12 - 15
SCHIRMER (See Fairy Tales/Nursery Rhymes)	10 - 12	12 - 15
SCHÖNPFLUG, FRITZ (AUS)	12 - 15	15 - 20
SCHMIDT, GERDA LUISE (GER)		
Meissner & Buch	12 - 15	15 - 20
STUBNER, LOTTE (GER)	8 - 10	10 - 12
S.K.		
Meissner & Buch	8 - 10	10 - 12
SUSS, PAUL	10 - 12	12 - 15
TREBICKY (GER)		
Kleiner 3318 (Tennis)	20 - 25	25 - 30

BLACKS, SIGNED

AB (US)
    Roth & Langley Kids   8 - 10   10 - 12
AJO. (SWE)   10 - 12   12 - 15
ATTWELL, MABEL L. (GB)
    Valentine & Sons   22 - 25   25 - 30
      Golliwoggs   25 - 30   30 - 35
    Other Publishers
      Early Period, Pre-1915   22 - 25   25 - 28
      Golliwoggs   25 - 30   30 - 35
      Middle Period, 1915-30   16 - 18   18 - 22
      Late Period, 1930-50   10 - 12   12 - 15
B.
    E. Nister
      Series 71   30 - 35   35 - 45
      Series 72   30 - 35   35 - 45
      Series 73   30 - 35   35 - 45
      Series 74   30 - 35   35 - 45
    T.S.N. (Theo. Stroefer)
      Series 440 (N1-N20)   30 - 35   35 - 45
BENSON, HENRY (US)
    Ullman Mfg. Co.   6 - 8   8 - 10
BERTIGLIA, A. (IT)
    Series 518 (Blacks/Whites)   15 - 18   18 - 22
BISHOP (US)   8 - 10   10 - 12
BONTE
    E. Nister (Undb)
      Series 404
        386 Mammy with Iron   30 - 35   35 - 45
        389 The Cook, with bowl and spoon   30 - 35   35 - 45
      Others in Series   30 - 35   35 - 45
    Theo. Stroefer (T.S.N.)
      389 Same as #389 above   30 - 35   35 - 40
      Series 404
      N-2 Mammy with pan of biscuits   30 - 35   35 - 40
      Others in Series   30 - 35   35 - 40
BORISS, MARGRET (NETH)
    Amag Series 0322, 0397   15 - 18   18 - 22
BROWNE, TOM (GB)
    Davidson Bros.
      Black/White Series 2586, 2614   25 - 30   30 - 35
BRUNDAGE, FRANCES (US)
    Raphael Tuck
      Oilette Series "Christmas Greetings"
      "The Night Before Christmas"   25 - 28   28 - 32
      Series 100 "Valentine" (1) (Uns.)
      "Loving Thoughts"   22 - 25   25 - 28

Series 101 "Valentine" (3) *	25 - 28	28 - 32
* Same as **Series 106** and **French Series 941**	25 - 28	28 - 32
Series 102 "Valentine" (1)		
"To Ma Honey"	22 - 25	25 - 28
Series 103 "Valentine" (1) (Uns.)		
"Git a Move On..."	22 - 25	25 - 28
Series 107 "Valentine" (2) (Uns.)		
"To My Heart's Beloved"	22 - 25	25 - 28
"To My Loved One"	22 - 25	25 - 28
Series 108 Valentines (4) (Uns.)		
Girl - "Does yo' reckon I would do..."	22 - 25	25 - 28
Boy - "I'm cuttin up now..."	22 - 25	25 - 28
Boy - "I lubs yo' deah, and dats why... "	*22 - 25*	*25 - 28*
Girl - "I lubs yo' deah, wid my hearts..."	22 - 25	25 - 28
Series 115 "Little Wooers" Valentine (2) (Uns.)		
Boy Angel "To My Valentine"	22 - 25	25 - 30
Lovers - "My little love..."	22 - 25	25 - 30
Series 118 "Little Loves & Lovers" (2) (Uns.)		
Girl - "Waiting fo' Mah Sweetheart"	25 - 30	30 - 35
Boy - "To Greet Mah Valentine"	25 - 30	30 - 35
Series 165 (2) Valentine	22 - 25	25 - 28
No. R106 Valentine	22 - 25	25 - 28
Series 1035 (?) **Valentine**	22 - 25	25 - 30
Series 2723 "Colored Folks" (6)		
"The Christening," "Church Parade"	55 - 65	65 - 75
"De Proof of de Puddin"	55 - 65	65 - 75
"Don't took de las' piece"	55 - 65	65 - 75
"The Village Choir," "You is a Chicken"	55 - 65	65 - 75
Series 2816 The "Connoisseur" Series (6)		
Duplicates **Series 2723**	55 - 65	65 - 75
Series 4096 "Funny Folk" (5)		
"A Trial of Patience"	50 - 60	60 - 70
"I'se Just Been Married"	50 - 60	60 - 70
"The Pickaninnies Bedtime"	50 - 60	60 - 70
"Preparing for the Party"	50 - 60	60 - 70
"Tubbing Time in Darkie Land"	50 - 60	60 - 70
Series 6616 "Humorous" (1) (Uns.)		
"Get a move on..."	20 - 25	25 - 30
Series 8201 Black Angels (?)	20 - 25	25 - 30
T.S.N. (**Theo. Stroefer**, Nürnberg)		
Series 664 Girl looks through picket fence	18 - 22	22 - 26
Other Signed Brundage	18 - 22	22 - 26
Unsigned issues	18 - 20	20 - 22
BUCHANAN, FRED (GB)		
Raphael Tuck "Write Away" Comics		
Series 9309 (6)	25 - 30	30 - 35
Valentine & Sons		
2294 "Yo' sho' ain't expectin' dis one!"	20 - 25	25 - 30

Sofia Chiostri, Ballerini & Fratini
Series 349, No Caption

A. M. Cook, C. W. Faulkner & Co.
"Pack up your troubles and smile"

Others	20 - 25	25 - 30
CARTER, SYDNEY (GB)		
Hildesheimer & Co.	15 - 18	18 - 22
CHIOSTRI, SOFIA (IT)		
Ballerini & Fratini		
Series 242 (4)	40 - 50	50 - 60
Series 349 (4)	40 - 50	50 - 60
CHRISTIE, G.F. (GB)	18 - 22	22 - 26
CLAPSADDLE, ELLEN H. (US)		
Int. Art. Pub. Co.		
Mechanical Series 1236		
"A Jolly Halloween" Black Child	400 - 450	450 - 500
No Number Valentine, New Year, Christmas	22 - 25	25 - 28
Series 780 (6) **"Love's Fair Exchange"**		
1 - Boy offers ice cream to girl	22 - 25	25 - 30
"To My Valentine" (2)		
1 - Boy with Banjo	25 - 30	30 - 35
2 - Boy with top hat and cane	25 - 30	30 - 35
"With Love's Greeting" (3)		
1 - Boy with Straw Hat Walking Left	25 - 30	30 - 35
2 - Boy offers watermelon to girl	25 - 30	30 - 35
3 - Girl in blue dress sits on wooden box	25 - 30	30 - 35
Series 781 (4)		
"Affectionate Greetings"	25 - 30	30 - 35

"My Love to You"	25 - 30	30 - 35
"True Love"	25 - 30	30 - 35
"With Fondest Love"	25 - 30	30 - 35
Unsigned: Elegant boy/girl do cake walk	25 - 30	30 - 35
Kopal		
New Year Series (4)	30 - 35	35 - 40
No Captions (2)	30 - 35	35 - 40
Stewart & Woolf, London		
Series 696		
"A Happy Christmas" (2)		
"A Joyful Christmas"	25 - 28	28 - 32
"With Best Christmas Wishes"	25 - 28	28 - 32
Boy and girl with slice of watermelon	25 - 28	28 - 32
Anonymous, German		
Cotton background, Embossed (Uns.)		
Same images as Series 780 (6)		
"My Love to You"	30 - 35	35 - 40
"My Valentine Think of Me"	30 - 35	35 - 40
"To my Valentine"	30 - 35	35 - 40
"To the One I Love"	30 - 35	35 - 40
"With Fondest Love"	30 - 35	35 - 40
"To My Valentine" Boy offers girl watermelon	30 - 35	35 - 40
CLARK, ROSE (US)		
Ullman		
"Kute Koon Kids" Series 165 (4)	15 - 18	18 - 22
COCKRELL	10 - 12	12 - 15
COLOMBO, E. (IT)		
GAM "Ultra"		
Series 2048, 2219, 2224, 2245, 2254 (4)	15 - 20	20 - 25
CONELL, MARY (US)	12 - 15	15 - 18
COOK, A. M. (GB)		
C. W. Faulkner		
Series 1413 (6)	15 - 18	18 - 22
Series 1594 (6)	15 - 18	18 - 22
COWHAM, HILDA (GB)	15 - 18	18 - 22
CRANE	8 - 10	10 - 12
CURTIS, E. (US)		
Raphael Tuck		
Valentine Series 3, "From Many Lands" (2)	12 - 15	15 - 20
DAESTER, MARY (BEL)		
Coloprint B		
Series 4641 (6) (1940's)	8 - 10	10 - 12
DONADINI, JR. (IT)		
Anonymous		
Series 415 No captions		
Lady kicks man in the teeth	30 - 40	40 - 50
Man drinking bottle of ink	30 - 40	40 - 50
Sitting man plays accordion	30 - 40	40 - 50

Ellam, Anon. Pub., "Black Judge" Series
"Pathetic Speech by Defendant's Counsel."

Donadini, Jr., Anon. Publisher
Series 454, "Sleep Darling Sleep"

Fernel, Anonymous French Publisher
"Cake Walk"

Man and woman under red umbrella	30 - 40	40 - 50
Man pulls another man's tooth with rope	30 - 40	40 - 50
Series 454 (6)*		
"Bellamy the Magnificent" Man smoking cigar	30 - 40	40 - 50
"The Voice that breathed o'er Eden"	30 - 40	40 - 50
Tall Lady with hurt child walking behind	30 - 40	40 - 50
Lovers under red umbrella	30 - 40	40 - 50
Surprised man washes foot	30 - 40	40 - 50
Well dressed Dude with suitcase	30 - 40	40 - 50
Man singing from "Sleep, Darling Sleep"	30 - 40	40 - 50
* There is also an anonymous, unsigned series		
of series 454 – Each:	25 - 30	30 - 35
ELLAM, WILLIAM (GB)		
Anonymous "Black Judge" Series (6)	30 - 40	40 - 50
Hold-to-Light Transparency		
Minstrel Man with tambourine	40 - 50	50 - 75
ELLKA (GB)		
Valentine & Sons		
Black Santa "Bring your stockings"	150 - 175	175 - 200
FASCHE, HANS (AUS)		
"SECT" Black & White Dancers	20 - 25	25 - 28
F.E.M. (**F.E. Morgan**) (GB)		
R. Tuck		
Series 8497, 10002, 1062	15 - 18	18 - 22

Fych, Valentine's – "The Cake-Walk"

FERNEL (F in circle) (FR)

Cakewalks	60 - 70	70 - 80
FIALKOWSKA, WALLY (AUS)	12 - 15	15 - 18

FYCH, C. D. (GB)

Valentine & Sons (6)	35 - 40	40 - 45

GASSAWAY, KATHARINE

Rotograph Co.

105 "I Scared I'll Get Sunburned"	12 - 15	15 - 20
123 "I Wish I was in Dixie"	12 - 15	15 - 20

GILSON, T. (GB)

E. J. Hey & Co.

Series 151, 262, 378, 410, 473, 474	12 - 15	15 - 20

J. Salmon

Series 2571, 2580, 3256	12 - 15	15 - 18
British Manufacturer & Ludgate Series	12 - 15	15 - 18

GREINER, MAGNUS (US)

International Art

Series 701-710

701 "A Darktown Trip"	22 - 25	25 - 30
702 "The Serenade"	22 - 25	25 - 30
704 "A Lad and a Ladder"	22 - 25	25 - 30
707 "A Darktown Idyl"	22 - 25	25 - 30
708 "A Feast"	22 - 25	25 - 30
709 "A Darktown Lover"	22 - 25	25 - 30
710 "A Darktown Philosopher"	22 - 25	25 - 30
Series 780 Valentines (1?)	15 - 20	20 - 25

H.B.G. (H.B. GRIGGS) (US)

L & E

Series 2217 (6)	18 - 22	22 - 25

Series 2224	15 - 18	18 - 22
H.H. (**H. HERMAN**) (US)		
J. I. Austen Co. Sepia Series	15 - 18	18 - 22
Bamforth Co. Series 234	20 - 25	25 - 30
Ullman Mfg. Co.		
Series 85 Thanksgiving	15 - 18	18 - 22
Series 103 #2082 "Gin"	22 - 25	25 - 30
Series 106 "In the Colored Swim" (4)	20 - 25	25 - 35
Series 109 "The National Game" (4)	50 - 60	60 - 70
Series 113 "Thanksgiving" #1988	15 - 18	18 - 22
Series 116 Skaters (4)	25 - 30	30 - 35
White City Art Co. Series 234	15 - 18	18 - 22
HALLIDAY (GB)		
Alfred Stiebel & Sons "Modern Humor" Series (6)	18 - 22	22 - 26
HARLOW, GRACE (US)	10 - 12	12 - 15
HARTMAN, E. VON	18 - 22	22 - 26
HUTAF, AUGUST (US)		
Ullman		
Series 113 "Blacktown Babies" (4)	20 - 25	25 - 30
HYDE, GRAHAM (GB)		
Raphael Tuck		
Series 9094 "Coons Motoring" (6)	20 - 25	25 - 30
K.V.		
L.P.		
Series 205, 206 Black-White Kewpies	12 - 18	18 - 22
Series 210 Black Kewpies	12 - 18	18 - 22
Series 224, 227 Black-White Boxers (not Kewpies)	15 - 18	18 - 22
KVKV		
Series 340, 341 (6) Black-White Kewpies	12 - 15	15 - 20
KEMBLE, E.W. (US)		
Detroit Pub. Co.		
"Kemble's Coontown" (10) (B&W)	30 - 40	40 - 50
KEMBLE, E.B. (US)		
Fairman Co. (B&W)	12 - 15	15 - 20
Pink of Perfection (Fairman)		
Series 159 (6) Baseball	35 - 40	40 - 50
Gibson Art (B&W)	10 - 12	12 - 15
KENNEDY, T. R. or **TRK** (GB)		
A. M. Davis Co.		
Series 521 "Little Darkies" (6)	15 - 18	18 - 22
Gale & Polden Series 2143 (6)	15 - 18	18 - 22
Inter-Art Series 6129	15 - 18	18 - 22
Raphael Tuck		
Series 8470 "All For You" (6)	18 - 22	22 - 26
KINSELLA, E. P. (GB)		
Langsdorf & Co.		
Series 713 (6) "Diabolo"	25 - 30	30 - 38
KOBER, P.C. (AUS)		
B.K.W.I. Series 2966 Cake Walk	40 - 50	50 - 60

Uns. T. R. Kennedy, Inter-Art Co.
Series 6129, "You lika ukelele..."

F. Lewin, Moderner Kunst
No. 3030/5, "Cake Walk"

KOCH, LUDWIG "...2000 jahre karikatur"	50 - 60	60 - 70
LEVI, C. (US)		
Ullman Mfg. Co.		
Series 165 "Kute Koon" (4)	15 - 18	18 - 22
- **Series 210, 3308** "Suffragette"	30 - 35	35 - 40
LEWIN, F. G. (GB)		
Inter-Art Co.		
"Artisque" Series	12 - 15	15 - 20
Others	12 - 15	15 - 20
W. E. Mack	10 - 12	12 - 15
M. Munk (Signed/Unsigned **FGL**)		
Series 242, 244, 415, 416 (6)	35 - 40	40 - 45
J. Salmon	12 - 15	15 - 20
Bamforth Co.		
"Black Kid Comics"	10 - 12	12 - 15
"Nigger Kid" Series	10 - 12	12 - 15
"Pickaninny Comics"	10 - 12	12 - 15
Florence House "Artisque" Series	12 - 15	15 - 18
L.N.S. (Dutch Publisher)	10 - 12	12 - 15
Geo. Pulman "The Nigger Series" (6)	15 - 18	18 - 22
E.W. Savory, Bristol	15 - 18	18 - 22
F. W. Woolworth	10 - 12	12 - 15
LEWIN, F.		
Moderner Kunst No. 3030/5, "Cake Walk"	30 - 40	40 - 50

LEWIS (GB)
   Inter-Art   10 - 12   12 - 15

LEWIS (GB)		
Inter-Art	10 - 12	12 - 15
Ullman Mfg. Co. Series 165 "Cute Coon Kids"	15 - 18	18 - 22
LONG, F. G. (US)		
Kaufmann & Strauss, 1904		
49-57 (Undb)	25 - 30	30 - 35
49-57 With advertising overprints	50 - 60	60 - 75
Series 60 Valentines	18 - 20	20 - 25
Red Star Compressed Yeast Adv. Card	125 - 150	150 - 175
M.D.S.		
Ullman Mfg. Co. Series 81 "Happy Day"	12 - 15	15 - 18
American P.C. Co. Series 165 "Kute Koon Kids"	10 - 12	12 - 15
M.M.S.		
G.K. Prince & Co.	10 - 12	12 - 16
MALLET, BEATRICE (FR)	10 - 12	12 - 16
MARQUIS (FR)		
IMP		
American Series 14		
"Black and White" Nursing Black Baby	50 - 60	60 - 75
MAURICE, REG. (GB)		
Regent Series 501, 2499, 4137	12 - 15	15 - 20
McGILL, DONALD (GB)		
J. Asher & Co.	10 - 12	12 - 16
Bamforth Co.		
5 "If Dat Chile Doan Soon Change Color"	12 - 15	15 - 20
174 "We're Rather Crowded..."	8 - 10	10 - 12
D. Constance, Ltd.	6 - 8	8 - 10
Inter-Art Co.	10 - 12	12 - 16
MINNS, B. E. (GB/AUST)		
Carlton Publishing Co. "Glad Eye" Series (6)	20 - 25	25 - 30
MONT.		
Raphael Tuck		
"Christmas" Series		
C-280, C-281	20 - 25	25 - 28
C-28	20 - 25	25 - 28
MOUTON, G. (FR)		
Anonymous "Le Cake Walk" Series (6)	50 - 60	60 - 70
White Lady-Black Man in top hat and yellow coat		
MUNSON, WALT (US) Linens	5 - 6	6 - 8
Baseball "Let's Play Around" (Uns.)	8 - 10	10 - 15
O'NEILL, ROSE (US)		
Campbell Art Co. KleverKard		
218 Black Kewpie rickshaw boy	40 - 50	50 - 60
Raphael Tuck		
"Pickings from Puck" or		
"American Humor from Puck"		
Series 2482 or 9411		
"High Society in Coontown" (Uns.)		
"A Misunderstanding"	100 - 120	120 - 135

Rose O'Neill, R.Tuck, "Pickings from Puck" Series 9412 — "An Advantage"

Mont., Raphael Tuck, "Christmas" Series No. C-281, "The Compliments..."

R. F. Outcault, Raphael Tuck, "Valentine" Series—"I dreams erbout ..."

"A Provisional Fiancee"	100 - 120	120 - 135
"All That Was Necessary"	100 - 120	120 - 135
"His Limited Provisional Capacity"	100 - 120	120 - 135
"Finis"	100 - 120	120 - 135
"Taken"	100 - 120	120 - 135
Series 2483 or 9412 "Coontown Kids" (Uns.)		
"A Brain Worker"	80 - 90	90 - 100
"A Matrimonial Alliance"	80 - 90	90 - 100
"An Advantage"	80 - 90	90 - 100
"Better than a Sermon"	80 - 90	90 - 100
"Ne Plus Ultra"	80 - 90	90 - 100
"One View"	80 - 90	90 - 100
OUTCAULT, RICHARD F. (US)		
I. H. Blanchard Co.		
"Buster Brown & His Bubble" *		
3 "Black or White"	25 - 30	30 - 35
6 "A Good Bump"	25 - 30	30 - 35
8 "A Bit of Smooth Road"	25 - 30	30 - 35
* Same series also by **Souvenir P.C. Co.**		
J. Ottoman	12 - 15	15 - 20
R. F. Outcault Copyright		
"Swell Dresser" 1909 Calendar Series		
Black Man with broom	30 - 35	35 - 40
Black Waiter	30 - 35	35 - 40

Zwart en wit.

Noir et blanc.

Puvasio, A.R., Italy
Series "Musicisti"

Uns. Agnes Richardson, Anon. Publisher
German Caption (White & Black)

Ullman Mfg. Co.
  Series 76 "Darktown" *

1889 "Koontown Kids"	25 - 30	30 - 35
1890 "Deed, I dun eat no Chickun"	20 - 25	25 - 30
1891 "Darktown Doctors"	25 - 30	30 - 35
1892 "Darkytown Dames"	25 - 30	30 - 35

• **American P.C. Co.** also published this series.
H.H. Tammen

Buster Brown Series 1001 (Emb.)	15 - 20	20 - 25

Raphael Tuck

Valentines (Undb)	15 - 18	18 - 22

  Series 1001

Buster Brown and His Bubble (3, 6 & 8)	25 - 30	30 - 35

PARKINSON, ETHEL (GB)

B. Dondorf Series 517	15 - 20	20 - 25

PAT (US) **Colourpicture** (Linens)

3 - 4	4 - 7

PATERSON, VERA (GB)

B. Dondorf Series 517	15 - 18	18 - 22
Regent Publishing Co. Comical series	18 - 22	22 - 26

PETERSEN, HANNES (DEN)

12 - 15	15 - 18

PIPPO (FR)

20 - 25	25 - 30

PHIFER, L. C. (US)

Theo. Eismann Baseball Song Series 1820 (4)	40 - 50	50 - 60

De Witt C. Wheeler

Same with light blue borders (4)	40 - 50	50 - 60
Note: Also issued in strip form (4)	30 - 40	40 - 50
PUVASIO (IT) **Musical Series** (7)	20 - 25	25 - 30

RICHARDSON, AGNES (GB)

Cellaro "Dolly Series" (Uns.) (4)	18 - 22	22 - 26
Photochrome "Celesque" Series	18 - 22	22 - 25
Unsigned Children Series	15 - 18	18 - 22

RIGHT (FR)

Lapina, Paris Both English and French Captions	20 - 25	25 - 35
RYAN, C. (U.S.) **Winsch Backs** **A100 Series**	20 - 25	25 - 30

SANDFORD, H. DIX (or **H.D.** or **H.D.S.**)

Hildesheimer & Co.

Series 5268 "Negroes"	20 - 25	25 - 30

Raphael Tuck

Series 6891, 8457 "Happy Little Coons" (6)	18 - 22	22 - 26
Series 8457 "Happy Little Coons" (6)	18 - 22	22 - 26
Series 9003, 9048 "Happy Little Coons" (6)	18 - 22	22 - 26
Series 9049, 9050 "Happy Little Coons" (6)	18 - 22	22 - 26
Series 9093 "Curly Coons" (6)	20 - 25	25 - 28
Series 9227 "Happy Little Coons" (6)	18 - 22	22 - 25
Series 9228, 9229 "Happy Little Coons" (6)	18 - 22	22 - 26
Series 9299 "Happy Little Coons" (6)	18 - 22	22 - 26
Series 9818, 9819 "Seaside Coons" (6)	18 - 22	22 - 25
Series 9427 "More Coons" (6)	18 - 22	22 - 26
Series 9428, 9489 "Dark Girls & Black Boys" (6)	20 - 25	25 - 28
"Linked on the Links" Golf	30 - 35	35 - 40
Series 9457 "Happy Little Coons" (6)	18 - 22	22 - 26
Series 9761, 9791 (6)	18 - 22	22 - 26
Series 9819 "Seaside Coons" (6)	18 - 22	22 - 26
Series 9968, 9969 "Seaside Coons" (6)	18 - 22	22 - 26

SANFORD, M. (GB)

Raphael Tuck Black Series	12 - 15	15 - 18

SHEPHEARD, GEORGE E. (GB)

Raphael Tuck

Series 9068, 9536 "Coon's Cooning" (6)	22 - 25	25 - 30
Series 9297 "Among the Darkies" (6)	22 - 25	25 - 30
Series 9536 "Coons Cooning" (6)	22 - 25	25 - 30
Series 9940 "Beside the Seaside" (6)	22 - 25	25 - 30
Series 740 French Tucks (6)	22 - 25	25 - 30

SHINN, COBB (US)	8 - 10	10 - 12

SPARKUHL & SPARKY

AVM

Series 636 White/Black	15 - 20	20 - 25

SPURGIN, FRED (LAT/GB)

J & A Co. "Coon Series" 401-406 (6)

"Am My Nose Still Shiny?"	15 - 18	18 - 22
"Golly! You are Looking Pale"	15 - 18	18 - 22
"Things are Looking Black"	15 - 18	18 - 22

H. D. Sandford, Raphael Tuck
"Curly Coons" Series 9093

Fred Spurgin, J & A Co., "Coon" Series
No. 404, "Is I so black as I is painted"

Inter-Art		
Series "One-Four-Nine"	15 - 18	18 - 22
SUZE (FR)		
Cathelain & Bartrim		
Series 50	18 - 22	22 - 26
T.B. B.K.W.I. Series 753 (6)	25 - 30	30 - 35
T.R. A.M. Davis Co.	10 - 12	12 - 15
TAYLOR, A. or A.T.		
Bamforth "Kid Comics"	6 - 8	8 - 10
TEMPEST, DOUGLAS (GB)		
Bamforth Co.		
"Kiddy Comics"		
"Look me over, buddy ..."	10 - 12	12 - 15
"Oh, Honey! If ..."	10 - 12	12 - 15
"I'se Black all over ..."	8 - 10	10 - 12
"Full on top – cooler than riding inside!"	8 - 10	10 - 12
"Here's a Quaint Coon"	8 - 10	10 - 12
"Kiddy" Series		
101 "Let's Kiss and Be Friends"	10 - 12	12 - 15
Other Publishers & Series	8 - 10	10 - 12
THIELE, ARTHUR (GER)		
F.E.D.		
Series 306 Head Studies (6)	40 - 50	50 - 60
Series 386 Ladies-Men Head Studies (6)	40 - 50	50 - 60

D. Tempest, Bamforth & Co., "Kiddy"
Series 101, "Let's Kiss and Be Friends!"

G. H. Thompson, E. Nister, No. 299
"Golly, see dem chickens fly!"

Theo. Stroefer		
Series 871 Sports (6)	40 - 50	50 - 60
German-American Novelty Art Co.		
Series 871 duplication but less quality	40 - 45	45 - 50
THOMPSON, G.H. or G.T. (GB)		
Vivian A. Mansell & Co.		
Fry's Cocoa Adv. "A Source of Delight"	125 - 150	150 175
E. Nister (Uns.)		
294 "Golly, but I wish I could grow..."	50 - 60	60 - 70
295 "Me en leetle Pete seed de Circus Parade..."	40 - 50	50 - 60
297 "Why do folks call me Jim Crow..."	60 - 80	80 - 100
298 "Good-bye honey, I'se in a hurry..."	40 - 50	50 - 60
299 "Golly, see dem chickens fly!..."	40 - 50	50 - 60
303 "I see Mr Possum up de tree..."	40 - 50	50 - 60
304 "Watermillion's juicy, an de ham am sweet..."	40 - 50	50 - 60
TIMMONS, JR. (US) (Linens)	4 - 5	5 - 6
TWELVETREES, CHARLES (US)		
Bergman Co.	8 - 10	10 - 12
Edward Gross Co. *	10 - 12	12 - 15
* Add $2-3 for die-cut stand-up types.		
Reinthal & Newman Series 706 "Blackmail"	8 - 12	12 - 15
TYRRELL, E. R. (US) **S. S. Porter**	10 - 12	12 - 15
USABAL, LOTTE (GER)		
S.W.S.B. Series 1295-1300 Black-White Dancers	20 - 25	25 - 30

L. Usabal, SWSB, No. 1298
No Caption (Cake-Walk)

Uns. Walter Wellman, Manhattan
Post Card Pub. Co., No. C-45

WALL, BERNHARDT (US)

Bamforth Co. (Back) "I'm Your Melon Honey"	20 - 25	25 - 30
Bergman Co.	8 - 10	10 - 12
Ullman Mfg. Co.		
Series 59 "Little Coons"		
1660 "You all can hab de Rine"	12 - 15	15 - 18
1661 "Deed, I didn't steal um"	12 - 15	15 - 18
1662 "Who's dat say chicken?"	12 - 15	15 - 18
1663 "Just two Coons"	12 - 15	15 - 18
Series 70 "Cute Coons"		
1852 "A chip off the old Block"	12 - 15	15 - 15
1853 "Whose Baby is OO?"	10 - 12	12 - 15
1854 "He lubs me"	10 - 12	12 - 15
1855 "I's so happy" (Uns.)	10 - 12	12 - 15
Series 81 "Happy Day"	10 - 12	12 - 15
Series 143 Black Halloween		
2414 "Who is OO?"	50 - 60	60 - 70
Series 173		
2703 "Here is a Man Who Never Drinks"	10 - 12	12 - 15
Series 155 Thanksgiving	10 - 12	12 - 15
Series 155 Automobiles	10 - 12	12 - 15
Card Series "A Dangerous Club"	18 - 22	22 - 26

WELLMAN, WALTER (US)

Manhattan P.C. Co. Art Deco types (Uns.)	10 - 12	12 - 15

Colourpicture (Tichnor) (Linens)	8 - 10	10 - 12
WIEDERSEIM, GRACE (US)		
Handmade of Black & White kids	50 - 60	60 - 75
WHITE, E. L. (Linens)	3 - 4	4 - 5
WHITE, FLORA (GB)	10 - 12	12 - 15
WITT, MIA		
A.M.P. Series 2002 (8)	10 - 12	12 - 15
WUYTS, A. (AUS)		
A. Noyer Series 76 (6)	10 - 12	12 - 14
YOUNG, HAYWARD (GB)		
Photochrom Co. "Celesque Series" (6)	10 - 12	12 - 15
ZA, NINO (IT)		
A74 Josephine Baker (Continental)	120 - 130	130 - 140
ZAHL		
A.R. & C.i.B. Poster Series		
"Othello"	18 - 22	22 - 26
"Be's Jst Du?"	18 - 22	22 - 26

BLACKS, UNSIGNED

Albertype Co. PMC		
"Greetings from the Sunny South" (12)	30 - 35	35 - 40
AMAG		
Series 0260 Blacks courting white girls	15 - 18	18 - 22
A.M.P. Series 70 "Cute Coons"	12 - 15	15 - 18
Joseph Asher & Co.		
"Two Blacks don't make a White"	25 - 30	30 - 35
J. I. Austen	15 - 18	18 - 22
B.K.W.I. Series 634 Cake Walk Series	30 - 40	40 - 50
Bergman Co.		
Series 6343 and Series 6505 (Uns. **B. WALL**)	18 - 22	22 - 25
Julius Bien "Comic Series"	12 - 15	15 - 20
Series 930 Thanksgiving	12 - 15	15 - 20
E.S.D.		
"Serenade" **Series 8058** Chromolithographs (4)	70 - 80	80 - 100
Fairman Co. (Uns. **E.B. KEMBLE**)		
Series 159 Baseball Comics (8) (B&W)	30 - 35	35 - 38
G. B. Co.		
Series G Husband & Wife (6)	8 - 10	10 - 12
H.M.B. Series 2847	25 - 30	30 - 35
J. Raymond Howe Co. Series 713	10 - 12	12 - 15
Franz Huld Cake Walk, "Darkey Series" (PMC)	12 - 15	15 - 18
Ill. P.C. Co. Series 78 "Darkies"	8 - 10	10 - 12
E.C. Kropp, Milwaukee Comics	12 - 15	15 - 18
Langsdorf		
"Greetings from the Sunny South"	10 - 12	12 - 15
Livermore & Knight	20 - 25	25 - 30
Arthur Livingston		
Black Comics	12 - 15	15 - 18

Anon., E.S.D.,
"Serenade" Series 8058

Anon., E.S.D., Serenade Series 8058
Chromolithograph

Manhattan Postcard Co. (1920's-1930's)

Uns. **WALTER WELLMAN**	10 - 12	12 - 15

Moore & Gibson, New York

15 "Brushing up on Acquaintance"	30 - 35	35 - 40
26 "The Whole Black Family"	40 - 50	50 - 60
29 "Yo ain't no dude yo' self"	20 - 25	25 - 30
31 "A Souther Bird Fancier"	20 - 25	25 - 30
32 "I Take This Opportunity"	20 - 25	25 - 30
34 "The pearly gates ajar"	20 - 25	25 - 30
35 "It's the Little Things in Life..."	20 - 25	25 - 30
36 "A Sudden Rise in Wool"	20 - 25	25 - 30

Evolution Comic

2 "Evolution of a Coon"	100 - 125	125 - 150

E. Nash

Series 31 "Sporting Girl"   (Emb.) (6)

Baseball Girl, Football Girl	40 - 50	50 - 60
Chorus Girl, Yachting Girl, Cowboy Girl,	30 - 35	35 - 40
Bathing Girl	30 - 35	35 - 40
Nelly **Anonymous Caricatures**	15 - 20	20 - 25

E. Nister

Unsigned G.H.T. (See GEORGE H. THOMPSON)

O.P.F.

Cake Walkers on sack cloth B.G.	50 - 60	60 - 75
Others	40 - 50	50 - 60

Anonymous, Nelly
No. 219

Anonymous, Raphael Tuck
Series 970, "You'll hardly believe"

P.F.B.		
Series 7179, 7942	22 - 25	25 - 30
Black Gents & Ladies (6)	22 - 25	25 - 30
Series 7946 (6)	22 - 25	25 - 30
Charles Rose Co.		
Series 11 Song Cards	15 - 18	18 - 22
Roth & Langley		
Comical children	10 - 12	12 - 15
S in Diamond (Santway) Series 034	18 - 22	22 - 26
SB (Samson Bros.)		
Series 142, 495, CS528, Series 605	15 - 18	18 - 22
S&M Series 1515 (Uns. **DONADINI, JR**)	25 - 28	28 - 32

REPRODUCTION OF IMAGES IN THIS BOOK

All images in this book are the final results of using various computer programs where each card is scanned, photostyled to the best grayscale clarity, and placed into position in the text. Real photo and some black and white cards are usually the best for this process, and these images reproduce very well. However, the majority of original postcards were printed in many colors and shades, in sepia or, in many instances, were simply very poorly printed. Therefore, they are sometimes difficult to reproduce for books where only black and white copy is used. Because of their great historical value, their rarity, or great interest to collectors, we have intentionally used many of these cards even though they did not reproduce well.

Anonymous, Raphael Tuck – "Little Piccaninnies" Series 4153

Schlesinger Bros. Children Comics (B&W)	12 - 15	15 - 18
Theo. Stroefer, Nürnberg (T.S.N.)		
Series 440 (6) Classical Blacks	25 - 30	30 - 35
W. M. Taggart		
Red Background Series N-24 (6)	25 - 30	30 - 35
Thanksgiving Series 607, 608 (6)	12 - 15	15 - 18
Others	10 - 12	12 - 15
Curt Teich, Chicago		
Courting and Marriage Series (10) (Undb)	25 - 30	30 - 35
Linens		
CT "Jitterbug Comics" (10)	40 - 50	50 - 60
C.T. "Chocolate Drop" Comics C-241-C-250	5 - 8	8 - 10
"Chocolate Drop Comics" (10)	4 - 6	6 - 8
C.T. "Pickaninnies" Comics Series C-251-C-260	5 - 8	8 - 10
"Pickaninny Comics" (10)	4 - 6	6 - 8
Tichnor Bros. 1940's Linens	3 - 4	4 - 8
Raphael Tuck Most have 6-card sets.		
Series 100 "Love Songs"	22 - 25	25 - 28
Series 115 "Little Wooers"	15 - 18	18 - 22
Series 368M (French) "Cake Walk"	22 - 25	25 - 28
Series 970 "Write Away" Minstrels	25 - 30	30 - 40
Series 1043 "Calendar"	22 - 25	25 - 28
Series 1794 "Write Away" Cake Walk	25 - 28	28 - 32
Series 1819 "Cake Walk"	22 - 25	25 - 28
Series 4153 "Little Pickaninnies"	20 - 25	25 - 30
Series 6706 "Humorous Series" Cake Walk	25 - 28	28 - 32
Series 6813 Sophisticated, well dressed	18 - 22	22 - 25
Series 2398, 6909 Negro Melodies	20 - 25	25 - 28
Oilette Series 9297	20 - 25	25 - 28

Anonymous, Valentine's – "Coonville" Series
"The Coonville Fire Brigade."

"Coontown Kids" Series 2843, 9092, 9412	15 - 18	18 - 22
Series 9281, 9285 "Gentle Art of Making Love"	18 - 22	22 - 26
Series 9899 "Smartness in Coonland"	30 - 40	40 - 50
J. Tully	10 - 12	12 - 15
Ullman Mfg. Co.		
"Little Coons," Series 59 (6)	10 - 15	15 - 18
Series 81 Valentine "Happy Days"	12 - 15	15 - 20
"Kute Koon Kids," Series 165 (6)	15 - 20	20 - 25
Mechanical - "Pick the Pickaninnies"		
Puzzle	50 - 55	55 - 60
Suffrage Series 210		
3308 "De Suffre-Jet"	25 - 30	30 - 35
Valentine & Sons		
"Christmas in Coon Land"		
Kids making giant snowball	200 - 250	250 - 300
"A Merry Xmas to You"		
Boy dressed only in hat, scarf, booties, gloves		
"A Merry Xmas to You"	200 - 250	250 - 300
Santa on roof in red robe- kids in chimney		
"We've Come to Meet Yo' Massy Santy..."	300 - 400	400 - 500
Black Santa in white suit- with snowballs		
"I'se a waitin' for you!	250 - 300	300 - 400
Black Santa and five kids in bed		
"A Merry Christmas"	300 - 400	400 - 500
Family of seven at table ready for feast		
"A Merry Xmas"	200 - 250	250 - 300
Five well-dressed children appear to be posing		

"Christmas in Coonland" Series by Valentine's — (See Text Below)

"A Merry Christmas"	200 - 250	250 - 300
Children playing on ice & in snow *		
"Fun on the ice"	200 - 250	250 - 300
Children sledding in snow		
"Christmas in Coonland – Sport in the Snow"	200 - 250	250 - 300
Others in series	200 - 250	250 - 300
* May be from another set.		
"Little Nigger" Series (6)	30 - 35	35 - 40
"Coonville" Series (6)	35 - 40	40 - 50
Series 602		
Black Santa with black-white kids	175 - 200	200 - 225
"Uncle Tom's Cabin" (Undb) (6)	18 - 22	22 - 26
Watkins & Kracke, Ltd.		
The "Infantastic" Series Kids	18 - 22	22 - 26
WELLS, R. L.		
"Baseball Series" (6)	35 - 40	40 - 50
Non-Artist Types (1900-1915) Taken		
with a camera of real people, by publishers.	10 - 15	15 - 25
White Border (1915-1930)	5 - 8	8 - 15
Linen Cards (1930-1949)	2 - 4	4 - 10

For a more comprehensive listing of all blacks see *"Black Postcard Price Guide"* by J. L. Mashburn. It contains over 700 photos, has 400 pages, 6x9. ISBN: 1-885940-06-8 - $21.95. Can be obtained from bookstores or may be ordered from Colonial House, P.O. Box 609, Enka, NC 28728. Please add $3 postage.

COWBOYS & INDIANS

BETTS, HAROLD (US)
  Detroit Pub. Co. - Fred Harvey

New Mexico Indian scenes	6 - 9	9 - 12

BISCHOFF, E. H. (US)
  Eukabi Publishers

Pueblo Indian Series (16+)	6 - 8	8 - 10

CRAIG, CHARLES (US)

Williamson-Hafner Indian Series	8 - 10	10 - 12

CURTIS, E. S. (US)   Sepia
  Indian Series

"Hopi Girl"	40 - 50	50 - 60
"Red Thunder Nez-Perce"	40 - 50	50 - 60
"Zuni Water Carriers"	40 - 50	50 - 60
Others	40 - 50	50 - 60
DAVENPORT, R. A. (US) **Cowboys**	6 - 8	8 - 10

E. H. Bischoff, Eukabi Publishers
"Indian Mother–Taos Pueblo, N.M."

E. S. Curtis
"Red Thunder Nez-Perce"

Wolbon Fawcett, Anonymous
"Tall Man Dan, Sioux"

Wolbon Fawcett, Anonymous
"Hollow Horn Bear, Sioux Indian Chief"

FAWCETT, WOLBON (US)

"Hollow Horn Bear, Sioux Indian Chief"	10 - 12	12 - 15
"Tall Man Dan, Sioux"	10 - 12	12 - 15
FELLER, FRANK (US)	8 - 10	10 - 12
GOLLINS	8 - 10	10 - 12

GREGG, PAUL   (US)

H. H. Tammen Co. Cowboy Series	8 - 10	10 - 12

INNES, JOHN   (US)

Western Art Series (6)

"The Bad Man," "Pack Train"	10 - 12	12 - 15
"The Portage," "Prairie Schooner"	10 - 12	12 - 15
"Roping Bronco," "Warping the Fur Barge ..."	10 - 12	12 - 15

MacFarlane Pub. Co.

"Troilene" Series

"Cattle Girl," "Cowboys at Work on the Range"	10 - 12	12 - 15
"Indians in a Snow Storm," "Fur Canoe"	10 - 12	12 - 15
"Indian Pony Race," "Roping a Steer"	10 - 12	12 - 15
"The Town Marshal," "The War Canoe"	10 - 12	12 - 15
"The Forty-Niner"	10 - 12	12 - 15
"Warping the Air Barge Upstream"	10 - 12	12 - 15

G. de L.

Raphael Tuck

Series 8668, "Muscalero Apache"	12 - 15	15 - 20

John Innes, W. G. MacFarlane, "Troilene" Ranching Series—"Cowboys at Work..."

Harry Payne, Raphael Tuck, "Wild, Wild West," Series 9531, "A Prairie Belle"

Harry Payne, Raphael Tuck, "Wild, Wild West" Series 9531, "The Bucking..."

LARSEN, DUDE AND DOT (US)
    Linens of 30's and 40's   2 - 3   3 - 5
MAY, KARL (GER)
    Cowboys and Indians   12 - 15   15 - 20

PAXSON, E.S. (US) **(Indian portraits)**
Northwest Postcard and Souvenir Co.

"Apache," "Crow," "Curley," "Custer's Scout"	20 - 25	25 - 30
"Flathead," "Mis-sou-la"	20 - 25	25 - 30
"A Nez Perce," "Northern Indian"	20 - 25	25 - 30
"Sioux"	20 - 25	25 - 30

McKee Printing Co. (1940's)

Reprints of many of the above cards	2 - 3	3 - 5

PAYNE, HARRY (GB)
Raphael Tuck

Series 9530 **"The Wild, Wild West"** (6)	15 - 20	20 - 25
Series 9531 (I) **"The Wild, Wild West"** (6)		
"A Prairie Belle," "The Bucking Bronco"	15 - 20	20 - 25
"Cowboy Fun," "A Scamper Across the Prairie"	15 - 20	20 - 25
"Neck or Nothing" (Indians) "Throwing the Lariat"	15 - 20	20 - 25
"Sounding the 'Turn Out'"	15 - 20	20 - 25
Series 9532 (II) **"The Wild, Wild West"** (6)		
"The Abduction," "The Scout"	15 - 20	20 - 25

PETERSON, L. (US)
H. H. Tammen Co.
Indian Series

3420 "Chief Sitting Bull"	12 - 15	15 - 18
3421 "Chief Geronimo"	12 - 15	15 - 18
3422 "Chief Yellow Hawk"	10 - 12	12 - 15
3423 "Chief Eagle Feather"	12 - 15	15 - 18
3424 "Chief High Horse"	12 - 15	15 - 18
3425 "Starlight"	10 - 12	12 - 15
3426 "Chief Big Feather"	12 - 15	15 - 18
3427 "Sunshine"	12 - 15	15 - 18
3428 "Fighting Wolf"	12 - 15	15 - 18
3429 "Minnehaha"	12 - 15	15 - 18
3430 "Hiawatha"	12 - 15	15 - 18
3431 "Chief Red Cloud"	12 - 15	15 - 18
3432 "Eagle Feather & Squaw"	10 - 12	12 - 15
3433 "Chief Black Hawk"	12 - 15	15 - 18
Unsigned Series	8 - 10	10 - 12
H. H. Tammen Co. **"Cow Girl Series"**	6 - 8	8 - 10

REISS, WINOLD (GER-US)

"Angry Bull" Mighty Blackfoot Hunter	15 - 20	20 - 25
"Clears Up" Indian Brave	15 - 18	18 - 22
"Lazy Boy" Witch Doctor	15 - 20	20 - 25
"Middle Rider" Indian Brave	15 - 18	18 - 22
"Mountain Flower" Indian Maiden	15 - 20	20 - 25
"The Sign Talkers" Indian Brave and Chief	15 - 18	18 - 22
"Wades in the Water" Indian Chief	15 - 20	20 - 25

REMINGTON, FREDERIC (US)
Detroit Publishing Co.

14179 "Evening on a Canadian"	35 - 45	45 - 55
14180 "His First Lesson"	30 - 35	35 - 45

14181 "A Fight for the Water Hole"	35 - 45	45 - 55
14182 "An Argument with the Marshal"	35 - 45	45 - 55
14183 "Calling the Moose"	30 - 35	35 - 45
Taylor Publishing		
1012 "Pony War Dance"	80 - 90	90 - 100
1022 "The Sun Fisher"	80 - 90	90 - 100
1027 "The Punchers"	80 - 90	90 - 100
REYNOLDS		
Cowboy Series 4400	5 - 6	6 - 9
Cowgirl Series 4406	5 - 6	6 - 9
RINEHART, F.A. (US)		
Indian Series		
"Rain in the Face" (Sioux)	10 - 12	12 - 15
"Big Man"	10 - 12	12 - 15
"Chief Wolf Robe" (Cheyenne)	10 - 12	12 - 15
"Chief Red Cloud" (Sioux)	10 - 12	12 - 15
"Chief Sitting Bull" (Sioux)	10 - 12	12 - 15
"Wa-ta-Waso" (Sioux)	10 - 12	12 - 15
"Sioux Squaw and Papoose"	10 - 12	12 - 15
"Two Little Braves – Sac and Fox"	10 - 12	12 - 15
"Lost Bird" (Sioux)	10 - 12	12 - 15
"Annie Red Shirt" (Sioux)	10 - 12	12 - 15
"Eagle Feather & Papoose"	10 - 12	12 - 15
"Two Little Braves" (Sioux & Fox)	10 - 12	12 - 15
"Chase-in-the-Morning"	10 - 12	12 - 15
"Hattie Tom" (Chiricahua, Apache)	10 - 12	12 - 15
ROLLINS, W. E. (US)	6 -10	10 - 12
RUSSELL, CHARLES M. (US)		
Ridgley Calendar Co. (In Color)		
"All Who Know Me ..."	12 - 18	18 - 26
"Antelope Hunt"	12 - 18	18 - 26
"Are You the Real Thing?"	12 - 18	18 - 26
"A Bad Bronco"	12 - 18	18 - 26
"The Bear in the Park ..."	12 - 18	18 - 26
"Better than Bacon"	12 - 18	18 - 26
"Blackfeet Burning ..."	12 - 18	18 - 26
"Bold Hunters ..."	12 - 18	18 - 26
"Boss of the Herd"	12 - 18	18 - 26
"Cowboys Off for Town"	12 - 18	18 - 26
"Elk in Lake McDonald"	12 - 18	18 - 26
"The First Furrow"	12 - 18	18 - 26
"Have One on Me"	12 - 18	18 - 26
"I Savvy These Folks"	12 - 18	18 - 26
"Jerked Down"	12 - 18	18 - 26
"Lassoing a Wolf"	12 - 18	18 - 26
"Lone Wolf – Piegan"	12 - 18	18 - 26
"Powderface – Arapahoe"	12 - 18	18 - 26
"Rainy Morning in a..."	12 - 18	18 - 26
"Red Cloud"	12 - 18	18 - 26

"Roping a Grizzly"	12 - 18	18 - 26
"Roping a Wolf #2"	12 - 18	18 - 26
"The Round Up #1"	12 - 18	18 - 26
"The Round Up #2"	12 - 18	18 - 26
"Scattering the Riders"	12 - 18	18 - 26
"The Scouts"	12 - 18	18 - 26
"Stay With Him!"	12 - 18	18 - 26
"Sun Shine and Shadow"	12 - 18	18 - 26
"A Touch of Western..."	12 - 18	18 - 26
"Waiting for a Chinook"	12 - 18	18 - 26
"Where Ignorance is Bliss"	12 - 18	18 - 26
"White Man's Skunk..."	12 - 18	18 - 26
"Wild Horse Hunters #1"	12 - 18	18 - 26
"Wild Horse Hunters #2"	12 - 18	18 - 26
"Women of the Plains"	12 - 18	18 - 26
"Wound Up"	12 - 18	18 - 26
"A Wounded Grizzly"	12 - 18	18 - 26
(In Sepia or Black and White)		
"The Buffalo Hunt #28"	10 - 12	12 - 15
"Buffalo Protecting Calf"	10 - 12	12 - 16
"The Christmas Dinner" (B/W)	10 - 12	12 - 16
"Cowboys off for Town"	10 - 12	12 - 16
"Gnome with Lantern"	10 - 12	12 - 16
"Holding up the ... Stage" (B/W)	10 - 12	12 - 16
"Indian Dog Team"	10 - 12	12 - 16
"Initiated" (B/W)	10 - 12	12 - 16
"The Initiation of..." (B/W)	10 - 12	12 - 16
"The Last of the Buffalo" (B/W)	10 - 12	12 - 16
"Nez Perce"	10 - 12	12 - 16
"An Old Fashioned ..."	10 - 12	12 - 16
"Painting the Town" (B/W)	10 - 12	12 - 16
"Powderface – Arapahoe"	10 - 12	12 - 16
"A Roper"	10 - 12	12 - 16
"The Shell Game" (B/W)	10 - 12	12 - 16
"The Trail Boss" (B/W)	10 - 12	12 - 16
Printed Photograph (Head in Oval)		
(Black ink on pale green silk)		
a. "A Christmas Dinner"	100 - 150	150 - 200
b. "The Initiation of the Tenderfoot"	100 - 150	150 - 200
c. "The Last of the Buffalo"	100 - 150	150 - 200
d. "Painting the Town"	100 - 150	150 - 200
e. "The Shell Game"	100 - 150	150 - 200
f. "The Trail Boss"	100 - 150	150 - 200
C.A. Read & Co.		
"Hold her Zeb, I'm Coming"	30 - 40	40 - 50
Roberts, Helena, Montana		
"Waiting for a Chinook"	6 - 8	8 - 10
Souvenir of Circus & Wild West Show		
Southhampton, L.I., NY, July 2-4, 1910	40 - 50	50 - 60

Schlesinger Bros. – Indian Maiden Series

SCHULTZ, F. W. (US)
   Cowboy Series 1728-1746

1728 "The Outlaw"	10 - 15	15 - 18
1729 "Go It, You –!"	10 - 15	15 - 18
1730 "Alkalai Ike"	10 - 15	15 - 18
1741 "Roping the Bull"	10 - 15	15 - 18
1744 "Roping the Broncho"	10 - 15	15 - 18
"Shooting the Town"	10 - 15	15 - 18

PUBLISHERS
   Detroit Publishing Co.

13941 "Montera Cabezon (Apache)"	12 - 15	15 - 20
13943 "A Jicarilla Apache Chief, Arizona"	12 - 15	15 - 20
13943 "Buffalo Calf (Jicarilla Apache)"	12 - 15	15 - 20

   Fred Harvey, for Detroit Pub Co.

Hopi Indians, etc.	5 - 10	10 - 15

   Franz Huld
   Indian Chiefs, 1906

1 "George Standing Bear"	12 - 15	15 - 20
4 "Tsi-Loya-Greatest Chief"	12 - 15	15 - 20

   Illustrated Post Card Co.

Series 183 Cowboys and Indians	5 - 7	7 - 12

   E. C. Kropp

271 "Kicking Bear"	12 - 15	15 - 20
F. E. Moore "Hiawatha Series" (12) (B&W)	3 - 5	5 - 8

   Schlesinger Bros.

Indian Maiden Series (B&W)	8 - 10	10 - 12

   A. Selige, St. Louis
   Indian Chief Series

"Chief Black Hawk"	12 - 15	15 - 18
"Chief Afraid of Eagle"	12 - 15	15 - 18
"Chief Fleet of Foot"	12 - 15	15 - 18

"Chief Bear Goes Inwoods"	12 - 15	15 - 18
"Chief Yellow Hair"	12 - 15	15 - 18
Curt Teich　Seminole Indians	6 - 8	8 - 12

Raphael Tuck
Series 2171 "Indian Chiefs" (12)

"Chief Charging Bear"	12 - 15	15 - 18
"Chief Yellow Thunder"	12 - 15	15 - 18
"Chief Yellow Horn"	12 - 15	15 - 18
"Chief White Swan"	12 - 15	15 - 18
"Chief Shooting Hawk"	12 - 15	15 - 18
"Chief Black Thunder"	12 - 15	15 - 18
"Chief Eagle Track"	12 - 15	15 - 18
"Chief Red Owl"	12 - 15	15 - 18
"Chief Black Chicken"	12 - 15	15 - 18

Series 9131 (6)

"Chief Charging Bear"	12 - 15	15 - 18
"Chief Not Afraid of Pawnee"	12 - 15	15 - 18
"Chief Black Chicken"	12 - 15	15 - 18
"Chief Eagle Track"	12 - 15	15 - 18
"Chief Black Thunder"	12 - 15	15 - 18
"Chief White Swan"	12 - 15	15 - 18
Series 9011 "Hiawatha" (6) (II)	10 - 12	12 - 15
Series 1330 "Hiawatha" (6)	10 - 12	12 - 15
Series 3495 "Indian Chiefs" (6)	12 - 15	15 - 18
Cowboy Series 2499	5 - 6	6 - 8

Weiners, Ltd.

"Buffalo Bill's Wild West" (6)	20 - 25	25 - 30

Anonymous German UndB Chromolithos
Indian Chief (Hauptling) Series

"Apachen - Hauptling"	20 - 25	25 - 30

| *Anonymous Indian Chief Series "Apachen-Hauptling"* | *Anonymous Indian Chief Series "Cherokee-Hauptling"* | *Anonymous Indian Chief Series "Pueblo-Hauptling"* |

"Cherokee - Hauptling"	20 - 25	25 - 30
"Pueblo - Hauptling"	20 - 25	25 - 30
Others	20 - 25	25 - 30

ANIMALS

CATS

AINSLEY, ANNIE (GB)		
Regent Pub. Co. Comical Cats	8 - 10	10 - 12
ALDIN, CECIL (GB)	6 - 7	7 - 8
BARNES, G. L. (GB)		
Raphael Tuck Fairy Tales-Nursery Rhymes		
Series 5600 "Cat Studies (6)	10 - 12	12 - 15
Series 9301		
"Little Bo Peep," "Little Boy Blue"	15 - 18	18 - 22
"The Queen of Hearts," "Old King Cole"	15 - 18	18 - 22
"Red Riding Hood," "Tom, Tom, the Piper..."	15 - 18	18 - 22
Series 9402 "Pussy in Fairyland" (6)	15 - 20	20 - 25
Series 9477 "Pussy in Fairyland" (6)	15 - 20	20 - 25
Series 9504 "Pussy in Fairyland" (6)	15 - 20	20 - 25
BEBB, ROSA (GB) Photochrom "Celesque" (6)	8 - 10	10 - 15
BECKLKES, E.L.	5 - 7	7 - 10
BOULANGER, MAURICE (FR)		
H.M. & Co.		
Series 104 (12) (B&W)	5 - 8	8 - 12
International Art Publishing Co.		
Series 586 (6)	8 - 10	10 - 12
Series 472 Large Image (6)	15 - 18	18 - 25
Series 473 Large Image (6)	15 - 18	18 - 25
K. F. Editeurs Series 586, 897	18 - 20	22 - 25
Kopal Series 417	12 - 15	15 - 20
Raphael Tuck		
Series 122 "Humorous Cats" (6) (Uns.)	15 - 18	18 - 25
BROWNE, TOM (GB)		
Davidson Brothers		
Series 2509 "Funny Cats" (6)	10 - 12	12 - 15
Series 2528 "Comic Cats" (6)	10 - 12	12 - 15
CARTER, REG (GB)		
Valentine & Sons (6)	12 - 15	15 - 20
CLIVETTE	8 - 10	10 - 12
COBBE, B. (GB)		
Raphael Tuck		
Oilette Series 3054, 8883, 8884 9099, 9157		
9436, 9538, 9707 (6)	10 - 12	12 - 15
DAWSON, LUCY	5 - 6	6 - 8
ELLAM, WILLIAM H. (GB)		
A.G. & Co. Series 400 (6)	12 - 15	15 - 18

Alfred Mainzer, Inc.
No. 4879

Maurice Boulanger, Raphael Tuck
Series 122, "Merry Days"

Sperlich, German-American
Novelty Art, 768

FEIERTAG (AUS)	6 - 8	8 - 10
FREES, H. W.		
Rotograph Co.		
Real Photo Cat Comics	6 - 8	8 - 12
GEAR, MABEL (GB)		
Valentine & Sons	10 - 12	12 - 15
HOFFMAN, A. (GER)	5 - 8	8 - 10
KASKELINE (GER)		
S.W.S.B.		
Series 4370	5 - 8	8 - 10
LANDER, EDGAR (GB)		
Raphael Tuck		
Real Photo Studies		
Series 5088, 7006 (6)	4 - 5	5 - 10
LESTER, ADRIENNE		
C. W. Faulkner		
Series 738 (6)	8 - 10	10 - 12
MAC or HENRY SHEPHEARD (GB)		
Valentine & Sons		
Cat Studies	6 - 8	8 - 10
MAGUIRE, HELENA J. (GB)		
Raphael Tuck		
Animal Studies 6714 (Uns.)	10 - 12	12 - 15

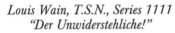

Louis Wain, T.S.N., Series 1111
"Der Unwiderstehliche!"

Louis Wain, C. W. Faulkner, No. 598E
"Awfully good joke that!"

NEILSON, HARRY B.	10 - 12	12 - 15
POPE, DOROTHY T. (GB)		
Misch & Co.		
Series 805, 807, 858 (6)	12 - 15	15 - 18
ROBERTS, VIOLET (GB)		
"Celesque" Series Cat soldier	10 - 12	12 - 15
Raphael Tuck No. 4201-4206 Seaside scenes	12 - 15	15 - 18
SCHWAR (GER)		
Many Cat Studies by various publishers	8 - 10	10 - 15
SPERLICH, T. (GB)		
German-American Novelty Co.		
Series 648, 768 (6)	10 - 12	12 - 15
Langsdorf Co. Series 3047	10 - 12	12 - 15
STOCKS, M.	6 - 8	8 - 10
H. K. Co.		
Series 217, 3237, 381 (6)	6 - 8	8 - 10
STOKES, VERNON G.		
"Celesque" Series Various breeds	8 - 10	10 - 12
THIELE, ARTHUR (GER)		
Many Cat Series by Theo. Stroefer (T.S.N.), Tucks, etc.		
Large Cats	25 - 30	30 - 45
Small Cats	20 - 25	25 - 35
THOMAS, PAUL (GB)		
Raphael Tuck Series 1196 (6)	8 - 10	10 - 12

WAIN, LOUIS

T.S.N. Series 1111 "Der Unwiderstehliche!"	60 - 70	70 - 80
Many by a great number of publishers	50 - 100	100 - 200
Raphael Tuck "Dressing Doll"		
Series 3385	300 - 350	350 - 400

UNSIGNED, BY PUBLISHERS

1900-1920 era	4 - 7	7 - 12
Post 1920	3 - 5	5 - 7
Alfred Mainzer issues by artist HARTUNG	3 - 5	5 - 7
Alfred Mainzer issues by Max Kunzli, ca. 1950	3 - 5	5 - 8
Alfred Mainzer issues printed in Belgium, 50's-70's	1 - 2	2 - 3

DOGS

BARTH, KATH (GER)	8 - 10	10 - 12
BUTONY		
B.K.W.I. Series 859 (6)	8 - 10	10 - 12
C.A.	6 - 8	8 - 10
C.E.B. (GB)		
Valentine's		
"Ready for Sport" Series (6)	12 - 15	15 - 18
CORBELLA, TITO (IT)		
Series 378 (6)	12 - 15	15 - 20
Others	10 - 12	12 - 15
DONADINI, JR. (IT)		
Dog Studies (6)	10 - 12	12 - 15
Series 235 (6)	12 - 14	14 - 16
DE DREUX, ALFRED (GER)	8 - 10	10 - 12
DRUMMOND, NORAH (GB)		
Raphael Tuck		
Series 3599 (6) "All Scotch"	8 - 10	10 - 12
Series 9105 (6)	8 - 10	10 - 12
"Sporting Dogs"	12 - 15	15 - 18
"Faithful Friends"	7 - 8	8 - 12
Series 772 Dachshunds	12 - 15	15 - 20
FREES, H.W.		
Rotograph Co.		
Comic Dog Photos	4 - 6	6 - 9
GAULIS, R. E.		
S.T.Z.F.		
111 Wire Haired Fox Terrier	8 - 10	10 - 12
GREINER, A.		
Series 726 (Dog Studies) (6)	8 - 10	10 - 12
Series 727 (6)	10 - 12	12 - 15
GROSSMAN, A.	6 - 8	8 - 10
GROSSMAN, M.	8 - 10	10 - 12
HANSTEIN, A. (GER)	10 - 12	12 - 15
Raphael Tuck		
Series 4092 "Favorite Dogs" (6)	10 - 12	12 - 15

C.E.B., Valentine's "Ready for Sport" Series — "Eager for Sport"

W & G, Berlin		
Series 437 (6)	10 - 12	12 - 15
HARTLEIN, W.	6 - 8	8 - 10
HERZ, E.W. (AUS)	7 - 8	8 - 10
KENNEDY, A. E. (GB)		
C. W. Faulkner		
Series 1424	10 - 12	12 - 15
KIENE	10 - 12	12 - 15
KIRMBE		
Raphael Tuck		
Series 3586 "Racing Greyhounds" (6)	12 - 15	15 - 20
KLUGMEYER (AUS)	8 - 10	10 - 12
MacGUIRE (GB)		
Head Studies (Pastels)	8 - 10	10 - 15
MAILICK, A. (GER)		
W.W.		
Series 5113 Dachshunds (UndB)	12 - 15	15 - 20
Series 5648 Dachshund Studies (6) (UndB)	12 - 15	15 - 18
MANSTEIN, A.		
Wohlgemuth & Sissner		
Series 437	10 - 12	12 - 15
MOODY, FANNIE (GB)	6 - 8	8 - 10
MÜLLER, A. (GER)		
Series 3956 (6) Dachshunds	12 - 15	15 - 20
MÜLLER, M. (GER)	8 - 10	10 - 14
REICHERT, CARL (AUS)		
T.S.N.		
Series 923, 1280, 1336, 1337, 1851 (6)	10 - 12	12 - 15
Series 1232 (6) Dog and Horse Studies	12 - 15	15 - 18

A. Manstein, Wohlgemuth & Sissner,
Series 437

Carl Reichert, T.S.N.
Series 1544

Series 1411, 1541, 1544, 1565 (6) Dog Studies	10 - 12	12 - 15
Series 1666 (4) Dog Studies	12 - 15	15 - 18
SCHONIAN (GER)		
German American Art		
Series 1961 (6)	8 - 10	10 - 14
T.S.N. Series 1961	8 - 10	10 - 14
SCOTT, AMY		
Anonymous, "Beauty"	10 - 12	12 - 15
SPECHT, AUG. (GER)	10 - 12	12 - 15
SPERLICH, SOFIE (GER)	8 - 10	10 - 12
STOLZ, A. (AUS)		
Series 772 Dachshunds	10 - 12	12 - 15
STUDDY (GB)		
"Bonzo" Issues	10 - 12	12 - 15
With Tennis or Golf	12 - 15	15 - 20
With Black Dolls	15 - 18	18 - 25
THOMAS, PAUL (GB)		
Raphael Tuck		
Series 6990 "French Poodles" (6)	10 - 12	12 - 15
Wohlgemuth & Sissner Series 270 (6)	10 - 12	12 - 15
WATSON, MAUDE WEST (GB)		
Raphael Tuck		
"Dog Sketches"		
Series 3346, 8682, E8837 (6)	8 - 10	10 - 15

| *Amy Scott, Anonymous*
"Beauty" | *Maud West Watson*
R. Tuck, Series 9977
"Blenheim Spaniel" | *A. Weczerzick*
Hanfstaengl's, No. 50
"Der Preisdackel" |

Series 3103 (6)	10 - 12	12 - 15
Series 9977 (6) "Sketches of Doggies"	12 - 15	15 - 20
WECZERZICK, A. Dachshunds	15 - 18	18 - 22
Hanfstaengl's, No. 50 "Der Preisdackel"	15 - 18	18 - 22
WILLMANN (GER)	10 - 12	12 - 15
WOMELE		
M. Munk, Vienna	10 - 12	12 - 15
WUNDERLICH, A.		
Dachshunds	12 - 15	15 - 20
UNSIGNED, BY PUBLISHER		
1900-1920 era	5 - 7	7 - 12
Post 1921-1940	3 - 5	5 - 7

HORSES

ADAMS, RICHARD B. (GER)		
Meissner & Buch		
Series 1880 Head Studies	15 - 20	20 - 25
BARTH, W. (GER)	12 - 15	15 - 18
BUNGARTZ, J. (GER) Full Studies	12 - 15	15 - 20
BRAUN, LOUIS (GER)	12 - 15	15 - 18
BURTON, C. (AUS)		
B.K.W.I.		
Series 892 (6) Head Studies	12 - 15	15 - 18
CASTALANZA		
Series 342	8 - 10	10 - 12
CORBELLA, TITO (IT)		
Series 316 (6)	15 - 18	18 - 22

COREAGGIO, JOS.
  B D (B. Dondorf)
    Series 833 Steeplechase   12 - 15   15 - 18
    Series 893 Fox Hunting   10 - 12   12 - 15
DINK (GB)
  Raphael Tuck
    "Popular Racing Colors" (6) Jockey/Horse   15 - 18   18 - 22
DONADINI, JR. (IT)
  SG&S
    Series 1495 Head Studies   12 - 15   15 - 20
    Star Series 237 Racing   12 - 15   15 - 18
DRUMMOND, NORAH (GB)
  Raphael Tuck
    Series 9065, 9138 (6)   10 - 12   12 - 15
    Series 9561 (6)   15 - 18   18 - 22
    Series 3109, 3194, 3603 (6)   10 - 12   12 - 15
ELIOTT, M. (FR)
  Anonymous
    Racing and Steeplechase   25 - 30   30 - 35
FENNI (Racing Series)   10 - 12   12 - 15
FRIEDRICH, H. (GER)
    Series 464 (6)   10 - 12   12 - 15
HANSTEIN, A. (GER)
  Raphael Tuck   Series 810 Steeple Chase (6)   10 - 12   12 - 15
HERMAN
  Raphael Tuck Oilettes
    "The Horse" (6)   10 - 12   12 - 15
JANK, ANGELO (GER) Fox Hunting   10 - 12   12 - 15
KOCH, LUDWIG (AUS)
  B.K.W.I.
    Series 372 "Wiener Fiaker" Series (6)   15 - 18   18 - 22
    Series 377 (6)   12 - 15   15 - 20
    Series 473 (6) Trotters   20 - 25   25 - 30
    Series 493 (6)   12 - 15   15 - 18
    Series 494 Steeplechase (6)   15 - 18   18 - 22
    Series 566 (6) Head Studies   15 - 18   18 - 22
    Series 660, 739, 865 (6)   15 - 18   18 - 22
    Series 830 (18?) Military Horses & Rider (Undb)   12 - 15   15 - 20
    Series 948 (6) Trotters   20 - 25   25 - 30
    Series 1447, 1470 (6)   12 - 15   15 - 18
    Series 966 Circus Studies (6)   12 - 15   15 - 20
  O.G.Z.-L
    Series 280-285   12 - 15   15 - 18
  Anonymous
    Military Horse & Rider Series   15 - 18   18 - 22
KOCH, PROF. G. (GER)
  Meissner & Buch
    Series 1415 (6) Fox Hunting   10 - 12   12 - 15

J. Bungartz, E.K.N., Series 312 − "Rassepferde"

Raphael Tuck **Series 588B** (6)	12 - 15	15 - 18
KOLB		
Raphael Tuck		
Series 4084 Oilette (6)	10 - 12	12 - 15
KROMBACK	10 - 12	12 - 15
LEHMANN, F. (GER)		
O.G.Z.-L		
Racing and Steeplechase Series	12 - 15	15 - 18
MATHEUSON	8 - 10	10 - 12
MAUZAN (IT) **Series 383** (6)	10 - 12	12 - 16
MERTÉ, O. (AUS)		
A.M.S.		
Series 589, 599, 660 (6)	10 - 15	15 - 18
Series 623 - Circus Horses (6)	8 - 10	10 - 15
Series 729 (6)	8 - 10	10 - 15
Raphael Tuck		
Series 9946 - Circus Horses (6)	10 - 12	12 - 15
MÜLLER, A. (GER)		
H.K. & Co.		
Series 411 Head Studies	12 - 15	15 - 20
Series 509 Head Studies	12 - 15	15 - 20
K.V.B.		
Series 909 Head Studies	12 - 15	15 - 20
S.W.S.B.		
Series 6919 (6)	8 - 10	10 - 12
T.S.N. (Theo. Stroefer, Nürnberg)		
Series 128, 133 (6)	8 - 10	10 - 12
Series 333 Head Studies, with Dogs	10 - 12	12 - 15

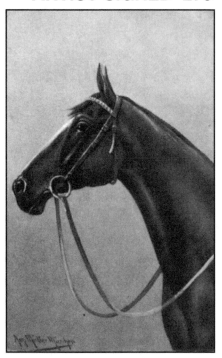

Donadini, Jr., S.G.&S.
Series 1495

A. Müller, H.K. & Co.
Series 509

Series 411, 509 (6)	10 - 12	12 - 15
NANNI, G. (IT)		
Series 257, 307 (6)	8 - 10	10 - 16
PAYNE, HARRY (GB)		
Raphael Tuck		
Series 550, 553 (6)	12 - 15	15 - 20
Series 544 "Animal Life" (6)	12 - 15	15 - 20
R.K.		
B.K.W.I.		
Series 350, 380, 386 (6)	10 - 12	12 - 15
RANKIN, GEORGE (GB)		
J. Salmon		
Head Studies 1351-1356	8 - 10	10 - 12
Head Studies 3350's Series	8 - 10	10 - 12
REICHERT, CARL (GER)		
T.S.N. (Theo. Stroefer, Nürnberg)		
Series 896, 934, with dogs (6)	12 - 15	15 - 20
Series 1359 (6)	10 - 12	12 - 15
Series 1422 (6) Head Studies	15 - 18	18 - 22
Series 1605, 1606, with dogs (6)	12 - 15	15 - 18
Series 1716 (Uns.) **1732, 1781,** with dogs (6)	12 - 15	15 - 18
Series 1782, 1870 (6)	10 - 12	12 - 15
Series 1422, Unsigned (6)	8 - 10	10 - 12

M. Munk, Vienna

Series 268, 771 (6)	10 - 12	12 - 15
Series 1162 (6) Heads Studies, with dogs	12 - 15	15 - 20
Series 1165 (6)	10 - 12	12 - 15

RICHTER, ALBERT (GER)

Racing and Steeplechase (Undb)	15 - 20	20 - 25

RIVST (SW) (1930's - 40's) — 5 - 7 — 7 - 10

SHILLING, F. (GER)

A.R. & C.i.B. Series 1136 (6)	8 - 10	10 - 12

SCHONIAN (GER)

T.S.N.

Series 1838, 5826 (6)	10 - 12	12 - 15
Series 1935, with dogs (6)	12 - 14	14 - 16
Series E1935 (6)	10 - 12	12 - 14

SCHÖNPFLUG, FRITZ (GER)

B.K.W.I.

Series 679 (6) Racing Comics	15 - 18	18 - 22
Series 723 (6) Fox Chase	15 - 18	18 - 22
Series 755 (6) Racing	15 - 20	20 - 25

SCHULTZ-DRATZIG, M. V.

Raphael Tuck

Series 972 "Saphir," "Ravensberg"	12 - 15	15 - 18

SCHUTZ

Series 972 (6)	8 - 10	10 - 12

Alfred Stiebel Co.

Series 430, 438 (6)	10 - 12	12 - 15

STOKES, VERNON

Photochrom Co. "Celesque" Series (6)	7 - 8	8 - 10

T.V.

L.P. Co. Comical Horse Race Series	12 - 15	15 - 18

TENNI

Harness Racing Series	10 - 12	12 - 16

TERZI, A. (IT)

Series 320 (6) Ladies/Horses	15 - 20	20 - 25

THAMES

Raphael Tuck	6 - 8	8 - 10

THOMAS, PAUL (GB)

Raphael Tuck

Series 353, 529 (6) Head Studies	12 - 15	15 - 20
Series 1182, 9254 (6)	12 - 15	15 - 20
Series 575-B - Trotters (6)	15 - 20	20 - 25
Series 579 - Steeplechase (6)	12 - 15	15 - 18
Racing Series	15 - 18	18 - 22
Series 9254 (6)	8 - 10	10 - 12

W&S, Berlin

Series 353 (6) Head Studies	12 - 15	15 - 20
Series 575 (6) Trotters	15 - 20	20 - 25
Series 1182	10 - 12	12 - 14

M. V. Schultz-Dratzig, Raphael Tuck
Series 972 – "Saphir"

Anonymous
T.S.N., Series 1716

TRACHE, R. (GER)
Hans Friedrich

Series 463-66 (4)	10 - 12	12 - 15
Series 464, 466, 788 (6)	10 - 12	12 - 15
Series E463, 1175 (4)	10 - 12	12 - 15

VEIT, M.

C.A.E.S. Series 2927	10 - 12	12 - 15

VELTEN

A.B.D. Series 775	8 - 10	10 - 12
W.F.A.	8 - 10	10 - 12

WALKER (GB)

Raphael Tuck Series 9544 (6) "Chargers"	8 - 10	10 - 12

WRIGHT, ALAN (GB)

Series 12219 (6)	10 - 12	12 - 15

WRIGHT, GEORGE (GB)

E. W. Savory, Ltd. Series 578 (6) Heads	10 - 12	12 - 15
E. W. Savory, Ltd. Series 2118 (6)	8 - 10	10 - 12

UNSIGNED, BY PUBLISHER

1900-1920 Era	5 - 7	7 - 12
1920-1940 Era	3 - 5	5 - 7

FAMOUS HORSES

Dan Patch

V. O. Hammon #155	20 - 25	25 - 30
T. P. & Co. Series	20 - 25	25 - 28
"Dan Patch at Great Allentown Fair"	30 - 40	40 - 50
Wright, Barnett & Stillwell	25 - 30	30 - 40
Real Photo # 155 ca. 1910	100 - 110	110 - 125
Other Real Photos	30 - 40	40 - 50
Other Printed (B&W)	25 - 30	30 - 35

Bold Ruler, Citation, Count Fleet, Native Dancer, Secretariat, Spectacular Bid & Whirlaway

Chromes	3 - 5	5 - 8

Linen or black & white	6 - 8	8 - 10
Real Photos	15 - 20	20 - 25
Goldsmith Maid		
Printed (B&W)	15 - 20	20 - 25
Real Photos	20 - 25	25 - 35
King LeGear - Giant Clydesdale (DB)	12 - 15	15 - 20
Lady Maud and Hedgewood Boy (B&W)		
Advertising Western Livestock Ins. Co.	20 - 25	25 - 30
Man O' War		
Linen or black & white	8 - 12	12 - 15
Real Photos	20 - 25	25 - 30
Needles		
Chrome	6 - 8	8 - 10

OTHER ANIMALS

CANTLE, J. M. (GB)	6 - 7	7 - 8
COBBS, B. (GB)		
Raphael Tuck		
Series 9539 (6) "Bunnies"	5 - 6	6 - 10
DONADINI, JR. (IT) Animal Studies	10 - 12	12 - 16
DRUMMOND, NORAH (GB)		
Raphael Tuck		
Series 9507 (6) "Famous British Cattle"	7 - 8	8 - 10
Series 3297 (6) "Faithful Friends"	7 - 8	8 - 12
EARNSHAW, HAROLD C. (GB)		
Millar & Lang (Comic Animals)	4 - 6	6 - 9
Gottschalk, Dreyfus & Davis	4 - 6	6 - 9
GEAR, MABEL (US)	8 - 10	10 - 12
GREEN, ROLAND (GB)	5 - 6	6 - 7
HARVEY		
Charles Reed Co. (18) "Nurse Guinnipen"	12 - 15	15 - 20
JAMES, FRANK (GB)	5 - 8	8 - 10
KEENE, MINNIE (GB)	5 - 8	8 - 10
KENNEDY, A. E. (GB)	10 - 12	12 - 15
LANDSEER, SIR EDWIN (GB)	8 - 10	10 - 15
MAGUIRE, HELENA (GB)	5 - 6	6 - 9
Raphael Tuck		
Series 6713, 6714 (6) **"Animal Studies"**	7 - 8	8 - 12
MÜLLER, A. (GER) Birds, Hunting Scenes	5 - 6	6 - 9
PERLBERG, F.		
Raphael Tuck		
Art Series 991 (6)	6 - 7	7 - 9
POPE, DOROTHY (GB)	4 - 5	5 - 7
RANKIN, GEORGE (GB)	4 - 5	5 - 7
SCRIVENER, MAUDE (GB)	6 - 7	7 - 10
VALTER, EUGENIE (GB)	5 - 6	6 - 9
WEST, A. L. (GB)	5 - 6	6 - 8

3

Fantasy

Fantasy postcards are now one of the most popular artist-drawn types in the hobby. Most of this interest is from the beautiful and desirable English, German and other European publishers of make-believe cards targeted for children. U.S. collectors of the 70' and 80's had little interest in fantasy types because good material was very limited. However, imported gems of beautiful and colorful Fairies, fairy tales, and nursery rhymes; delightfully dressed animals perceived for holiday greetings and storybook formats; Santas, Krampus, St. Nicholas, and mermaids, etc., became the rage. Now, it seems that everyone has discovered them. The values have accelerated and better material is becoming very hard to find.

To children and adults alike, fantasy is the result of their varied imaginations in everyday life. Whether wild or visionary, unnatural or bizarre, they can flourish in daydreaming or make believe. The imaginative qualities of artists have left collectors with a plethora of wonderful and colorful fantasy postcards.

Most fantasies bring back the treasured days of youth...of fairies and fairy tales, of nursery rhymes and teddy bears and dressed animals doing people things. Fantasy worlds change as youth grows to more mature heights, and it is notable that imagined fantasies, both good and bad, remain throughout life. All are chronicled and portrayed on postcards that make a wonderful fantasy world for us all!

FAIRIES

The Fairy family includes Brownies, Elves, Gnomes, Goblins, Fairies, Leprechauns, Pixies, Sprites and other diminutive, unnamed creatures.

	VG	EX
ANDERSON, FANNIE MAY (GB)		
Vivian A. Mansell & Co.		
Series 2115 (6)	$ 20 - 25	$ 25 - 30
ANICHINI, EZIO (IT)		
Ballerini & Fratini		
Series 351	18 - 22	22 - 26

Fritz Baumgarten, Opel & Hess
Series 5187, "Der Fillchtvergessene"

Fritz Baumgarten, Opel & Hess
Series 1486, "Der Gratulant"

A. Bertiglia, Butterfly Fairies, N. M. M.,
Milano

ATTWELL, MABEL L. (GB)		
Valentine & Sons	18 - 22	22 - 25
BARHAM, SYBIL (GB)		
C. W. Faulkner Series 1859 (6) "Fairies"	10 - 12	12 - 16
BAUMGARTEN, FRITZ (GER)		
Oppel & Hess, Jena		
Series 1486, 1502, 1509, 1514, 1534, 1535 (6)	12 - 15	15 - 20
Series 5179, 5187, 5192, 5195, 6182 (6)	12 - 15	15 - 20
Other Publishers	10 - 12	12 - 15
BERGER		
Series 116 (B&W)	15 - 20	20 - 25
BERTIGLIA, A.		
N.M.M., Milano Butterfly Fairies Series	20 - 25	25 - 30
BOWDEN, DORIS (GB)	18 - 22	22 - 26
BRISLEY, NINA		
Vivian A. Mansell & Co.		
Series 1059 "Wish I could do that."	15 - 20	20 - 25
CHECKLEY, GLADYS (GB)	12 - 15	15 - 20
CLOKE, RENE (GB)		
Valentine & Sons "Fairies"		
Series 1002, 1183, 1848, 1851 (6)	15 - 20	20 - 25
Series 5372-77 (6)	12 - 15	15 - 18
J. Salmon, Ltd.	6 - 8	8 - 10
COWHAM, HILDA (GB)		
C. W. Faulkner		
Series 1601 (6) **"Fairies"**	18 - 22	22 - 26

Nina Brisley, Vivian Mansell & Co.
Series 1059, "Wish I Could Do That."

THE DAISY FAIRY.

Rene Cloke, Valentine's 1848
"The Daisy Fairy"

Series 1918 "Fairies" (6)	18 - 22	22 - 26
"The Fairy Glen" Series (6)	18 - 22	22 - 26
DAUSTY		
C. P. & Co.		
Series 704 "Nymphs" (6)	8 - 10	10 - 15
DIELITZ "Alpen Fairy"	12 - 15	15 - 20
DUDDLE, JOSEPHINE (GB)	15 - 20	20 - 25
FORCK, ELSBETH (GER) Silhouettes	12 - 15	15 - 20
GIRIS, CESAR (IT)		
Raphael Tuck Series 2365 "Madame Butterfly"	25 - 30	30 - 35
GOVEY, A. (GB)	25 - 28	28 - 32
F.H. (GB)	15 - 18	18 - 22
HAIG, BERYL (GB)	12 - 15	15 - 20
HERRFURTH, O.		
UvaChrom Fairy Dance	20 - 25	25 - 28
HINE, L. M. (GB)	32 - 35	35 - 38
A. & C. Black, London		
"A Pixie made a chain of flowers..."	30 - 35	35 - 40
"A Pretty Fairy Mother..."	30 - 35	35 - 40
"Some Fairies found some Bubbles..."	30 - 35	35 - 40
"Some Fairies met a Butterfly..."	30 - 35	35 - 40
"When Fairies Dance at Twilight..."	30 - 35	35 - 40
"When Fairies find a Tiny Pool..."	30 - 35	35 - 40
KENNEDY, TOM or TK (GB)	15 - 18	18 - 22
KONEWKA, PAUL (GER)		
Series 110 "Titania" (12) Silhouettes	22 - 25	25 - 30

O. Herrfurth, UvaChrom
Fairy Dance – German Caption

Gaston Noury
Anonymous French Publisher

MARGOTSON, HESTER (GB)		
Series 2127, 2129 (6)	15 - 20	20 - 25
MARSH-LAMBERT, H.G.C. (GB)		
A. M. Davis & Co.		
Series 519 "Flower Fairies" (6)	15 - 20	20 - 25
C. W. Faulkner Series 1400, 1510 (6)	12 - 15	15 - 20
MARSHALL, ALICE (GB)		
Raphael Tuck		
Series 3489 "Fairyland Fancies" I (6)	30 - 35	35 - 40
Series 3489 "Fairyland Fancies" II (6)	30 - 35	35 - 40
MAUSER, PHYLLIS (GB)		
P. Salmon		
Series 5159 "Brownies & Fairies" (6)	8 - 10	10 - 12
MAYBANK, THOMAS (GB)		
Raphael Tuck		
Series 6683 "Midsummer Dreams" (6)	25 - 30	30 - 35
MILLER, HILDA T. (GB)		
C. W. Faulkner		
Series 1690, 1693 "Fairies" (6)	25 - 30	30 - 35
Series 1822 "Peter Pan" (6)	20 - 25	25 - 30
MÜLLER, PAUL LOTHAR (GER)		
Oscar Heierman, Berlin (Novitas)		
Series 550 "Gnomes"	10 - 15	15 - 20
Fingerle Co. Series 326	10 - 15	15 - 20
NOURY, GASTON (FR)		
Anonymous Fairy Nudes Series	40 - 45	45 - 55

OUTHWAITE, IDA R. (AUS)

Ida Sherbourne Rentoul was born in Melbourne, Australia in 1888. She and her older sister, Annie Rattray Rentoul, began writing books for children even before Ida finished school. Both girls composed the stories and verse and Ida did the illustrations. This early beginning led to greater things as Ida became the leading illustrator of fairy books throughout Australia and Great Britain.

The famous London publisher, A. & C. Black, Ltd., was the first to note her artistic talent and quickly contracted her to do future work for them. Her books, "The Enchanted Forest," "Elves and Fairies," "Fairyland," "Bunny and Brownie," and "Blossom" gained much acclaim and later led to their publishing several beautiful series of postcards that were adapted from illustrations.

Ida married Grenby Outhwaite in 1909 and he became the promoter of her work, both in Australia and in London. He co-authored some of her books and his initial "G." is included on many of the postcards as a part of the Ida R. Outhwaite signature.

A. & C. Black Ltd., London
  Series 71 "The Enchanted Forest" (6)
    by **I. R. & G. Outhwaite**

"The Butterfly Chariot"	25 - 28	28 - 32
"Good-bye to Patty"	25 - 28	28 - 32
Others	25 - 28	28 - 32

  Series 71-A "Elves & Fairies" (6)

"Fairy Frolic"	25 - 30	30 - 35
"The Glowlamp Fairy"	25 - 30	30 - 35
"The Nautilus Fairy"	25 - 30	30 - 35
"Serena's Wedding"	25 - 30	30 - 35
"They stood still in front of her"	25 - 30	30 - 35
"The Witch"	25 - 30	30 - 35

  Series 72 "Fairyland" (6)

"Butterfly Ferry"	25 - 30	30 - 35
"Catching the Moon"	25 - 30	30 - 35
"Listening to the Nightingale"	25 - 30	30 - 35
"Tossing up the Rainbow Bubbles"	25 - 30	30 - 35
Others	25 - 30	30 - 35

  Series 73 "Bunny and Brownie" (6)

"Driving the others with reins..."	30 - 35	35 - 40
"Fairies were dancing in and out."	30 - 35	35 - 40
"Playing with the bubbles" Mermaid	35 - 40	40 - 50
"Round the grass-tuft...a Pearly Shell"	30 - 35	35 - 40
"She was rather severe with George"	30 - 35	35 - 40

  Series 74 "Blossom" (6)

"A little mist played over the Pond"	30 - 35	35 - 40
"The frogs learn to jump..."	30 - 35	35 - 40
"One on a huge Dragon-Fly"	30 - 35	35 - 40
"She is a Spring Fairy"	30 - 35	35 - 40
* "Seated on the edge of a Mauve Crocus"	30 - 35	35 - 40
"What is time Bus?"	30 - 35	35 - 40
* Ad for Black's Postcards on back	35 - 40	40 - 45

  Series 75 "The Little Fairy Sister" (6)
    by **I. R. and G. Outhwaite**

"Bridget the Fairy Beauty"	30 - 35	35 - 38
"Fairy Beauty rocks a Babe"	30 - 35	35 - 38

"The Fairy Beauty"	30 - 35	35 - 40
* "The Fairy Bridget and Kookaburra"	35 - 40	40 - 45
"The Fairy Bridget and the Merman"	30 - 35	35 - 38
"Periwinkle painting the Petals"	30 - 35	35 - 38
* Ad for Black's Postcards on back	35 - 40	40 - 45
Series 76 "The Enchanted Forest" (6)		
by **I. R. and G. Outhwaite**		
"Anne plays the pipes"	30 - 35	35 - 38
"Drawn along by Fishes"	30 - 35	35 - 38
"Patty talks to forest creatures"	30 - 35	35 - 38
"The Witch's Sister on her broom"	30 - 35	35 - 38
"The Witch on her broom"	30 - 35	35 - 38
Series 79 "The Little Road to Fairyland" (6)		
by **A.R. Rentoul and I. R. Outhwaite**		
"Anne rides on a Nautilus Shell"	30 - 35	35 - 38
"The farthest one looked like..."	30 - 35	35 - 38
"The little one took it's paws..."	30 - 35	35 - 38
"She flew through the window..."	30 - 35	35 - 38
"What a fright she got"	30 - 35	35 - 38
PEYK, H. (GER) (Oversize)	10 - 12	12 - 15
PLUMSTEAD, JOYCE (GB)	10 - 12	12 - 15
PURSER, PHYLLIS M. (GB)	8 - 10	10 - 12
RICHARD, J. (GB)	22 - 25	25 - 30
RICHARDSON, AGNES		
Raphael Tuck		
Series 1649 "Fairies"	22 - 25	25 - 30
Series 1650, 1850, 3244 3447 (6)	22 - 25	25 - 30
ROSE, FREDA M. (GB)	12 - 15	15 - 20
SCHERMELE, WILLY (NETH)	10 - 12	12 - 15
SCHUTZ, E. (AUS)		
B.K.W.I.		
Series 165 "Fairy Nudes" (6)	28 - 32	32 - 35
Series 391 (6)	20 - 25	25 - 28
M. Munk, Vienna		
Series 1363, 1364, 1365 (6)	15 - 20	20 - 25
Series 435 (6) Uns. Andersen's Fairy Tales	18 - 22	22 - 26
SHAND, C. Z.		
Anonymous "Let's"	30 - 40	40 - 50
SHERBORNE, M. (GB)		
Salmon & Co.		
Series 4239 "Fairies of the Wood"	10 - 12	12 - 15
SOWERBY, A. M. (See Artist-Signed Children)		
Humphrey Milford "Flowers & Wings" Series		
"By Moonlight the Woodfairies Prance"	25 - 30	30 - 35
SPURGIN, FRED (LAT/GB)		
Inter-Art Co.		
Series 615 "Fairy" (6)	15 - 18	18 - 22
Raphael Tuck		
Series 3032 (6)	15 - 18	18 - 22
STEELE, L. R. (GB)		
Salmon & Co.		
Series 4964-4969 "Peeps at Pixies"	12 - 15	15 - 20
Series 5050-5055 "Famous Fairies"	12 - 15	15 - 20
Series 5172-77	10 - 12	12 - 15

C. Z. Shand, Anonymous Publisher
"Let's"

Margaret Tarrant, W&S, Series 3430
"Morgangrusse"

A. M. Sowerby, Humphrey Milford, "Flowers & Wings" Series
"By Moonlight the Woodfairies Prance: The Elf with the Flute is the Band..."

Valentine's "Fairy Series" 1847-1852	12 - 15	15 - 18

SYMONDS, CONSTANCE (GB)
  C. W. Faulkner & Co.

Series 1645 (6)		
"Do you love Butter?," "The Duet," "Fairy Piper"	15 - 18	18 - 22
"The Morning Walk," "The Punt," "Wake Up"	15 - 18	18 - 22
Series 1926, 1957 (6)	18 - 22	22 - 26
Series 1958 (6)		
American Starwort - "Welcome Stranger"	18 - 22	22 - 26
Blue Convolvuloua - "Night"	18 - 22	22 - 26
Bundles of Reeds - "Music"	18 - 22	22 - 26
Guelder Rose - "Snow"	18 - 22	22 - 26
Heather - "Solitude"	18 - 22	22 - 26
Michaelmas Daisies - "Farewell"	18 - 22	22 - 26

TARRANT, MARGARET (GB)
  Medici Society

PK 120 "The Fairy Troupe"	8 - 10	10 - 12
PK 184 "The Enchantress"	8 - 10	10 - 12
Others	8 - 10	10 - 12
W&S Series 3430 "Morgangrusse"	12 - 15	15 - 18

UNTERSBERGER, ANDREAS (GER)
  Emil Kohn, München

Fairy and Gnome Series (12)	12 - 15	15 - 20

WATKINS, DOROTHY (GB)
  Valentine & Sons

Series 6 "The Dance of the Elves"	8 - 12	12 - 15

WEIGAND, MARTIN (AUS)

Gnomes & Mushroom Series	15 - 20	20 - 25
Gnomes, Mushroom Series (12)	15 - 18	18 - 22

  Raphael Tuck

Oilette Series 6683 (6)	15 - 18	18 - 22
"Mid-Summer Dreams" (6)	15 - 20	20 - 25
Valentine & Sons Series 108 (6)	10 - 12	12 - 15

WHEELER, DOROTHY (GB) (See Fairy Tales)
  Bamforth & Co.

Series 1 "Fairy Secret" (6)	12 - 15	15 - 20

WHITE, FLORA (GB)
  P. Salmon

Series 4419 (6)	18 - 22	22 - 25

WIELANDT, MANUEL (GER)   12 - 15   15 - 20

WILLIAMS, MADGE (GB)

J. Salmon, Ltd.	12 - 15	15 - 20
Raphael Tuck Series 1160 (6)	8 - 12	12 - 15
Valentine & Sons "Fairy" Series 6044-6049	12 - 15	15 - 20

ANONYMOUS

Elves	5 - 8	8 - 15
Fairies	8 - 12	12 - 18
Gnomes	6 - 8	8 - 12
Goblins (Usually Halloween)	6 - 8	8 - 12
Leprechauns	5 - 7	7 - 12
Pixies	8 - 10	10 - 15
Sprites	7 - 8	8 - 10
Russian Real Photo Types	10 - 12	12 - 15

FAIRY TALES AND NURSERY RHYMES

ACKLEY, MABEL (US)
  Minneapolis Shirts Adv. **Nursery Rhymes** (6)   15 - 20   20 - 25
ATTWELL, MABEL LUCIE (GB) (Uns.)
  Raphael Tuck Series, 3328, 3376 (6)   20 - 25   25 - 30
BANKS, M. (GB)
  Raphael Tuck "Paper Dolls" & "Mechanical Dolls"
  Series 3381-I, 3382-II, 3383-III, 3384-IV (6/Ser.)   125 - 150   150 - 180
BARHAM, SYBIL (GB)
  Series 1734 "The Pied Piper of Hamelin"   10 - 12   12 - 15
BARNES, G. L. (GB)
  Raphael Tuck Cat Fairy Tales-Nursery Rhymes
  See Cats in Artist-Signed Section
BAUMGARTEN, FRITZ (FB)
  Oppel & Hess Series 1472, 1487, 1516   12 - 15   15 - 18
BILIBIN, IVAN (RUS)
  Russian Fairy Tales, Art Nouveau Style   75 - 100   100 - 125
BORISS, MARGRET (NETH)
  Amag
    Series 0347 "Hansel and Gretel" (6)   10 - 12   12 - 15
    Series 0349 "Pied Piper of Hamelin" (6)   10 - 12   12 - 15
    Series 0350, 0412 "Cinderella" (6)   10 - 12   12 - 15
    "Puss in Boots" (6)   10 - 12   12 - 15
    "Rotkäppchen" (6)   10 - 12   12 - 15
    "Schneewittchen" (Snow White) (6)   10 - 12   12 - 15
  PEB Netherlands Same tales as Amag, each   8 - 10   10 - 12
BOWLEY, A.L. (GB)
  Raphael Tuck
  Series 3386 "Father Tuck's Fairy Land
  Panorama" Perforated Punchouts stand-ups (6)
    "Cinderella," "Beauty and the Beast"   150 - 175   175 - 200
    "Jack and the Beanstalk," "Little Snow-White"   150 - 175   175 - 200
    "Red Riding Hood," "The Sleeping Beauty"   150 - 175   175 - 200
BRETT, MOLLY (GB)
  The Medici Society, Ltd., London
  Series 1, 145, 147, 155, 168, 179, 185   6 - 8   8 - 12
BRUNDAGE, FRANCES (US)
  Raphael Tuck
  Series 4095 "Little Sunbeams" (8)
    "Little Bo Peep," "Little Milk Maid"   35 - 45   45 - 55
    "Little Miss Muffet," "May Blossoms"   35 - 45   45 - 55
    "Polly and her Kettle," "Rosy Apples"   35 - 45   45 - 55
    "The Snow Maiden," "Summer at Sea"   35 - 45   45 - 55
BURD, C. M. (US)
  K & Co. Fralinger's Taffey
  Series 18 "Nursery Rhymes" (24?)
    "Little Tommy Tucker" With Santa Claus   200 - 250   250 - 300
    "A Friend in Need...," "Alice in Wonderland"   30 - 30   40 - 50
    "Hush-a-bye Baby...," "Little Boy Blue"   30 - 40   40 - 50
    "Little Jack Horner," "The Man in the Moon"   30 - 40   40 - 50
    "Peter, Peter Taffy Eater," "Rip Van Winkle"   30 - 40   40 - 50
    "Rock-a-bye Baby," "Save the Best for Last"   30 - 40   40 - 50
    "Sing a Song of Six Pence," "Sleeping Beauty"   30 - 40   40 - 50

"The Frog Prince," "The Three Bears"	30 - 40	40 - 50
"Tom, Tom the Pipers Son"	30 - 40	40 - 50
Others (?)	30 - 40	40 - 50
CALDECOTT, RANDOLPH (GB)		
F. Warne & Co. 48-card Set	8 - 10	10 - 12
1970's Reprint of the 48 card set	3 - 4	4 - 5
CARTER, SYDNEY (GB)		
"Hans Andersen's Fairy Tales" (6)	15 - 20	20 - 25
COMMIEHAU, A. Series 48	6 - 8	8 - 10
COOPER, PHYLLIS (GB)		
Raphael Tuck		
Series 3482 "Happy Land" V (6) *	25 - 30	30 - 35
Series 3487 "Happy Land" VI (6) *	25 - 30	30 - 35
Series 3486 I, II, III, IV, V, VI (6 each) *	25 - 30	30 - 35
Nursery Rhymes III Series 3488 (6) *	20 - 25	25 - 30
* Add $10 to cards with Golliwoggs.		
DOCKAL, H. (GER)		
UVACHROM Series 407	8 - 10	10 - 12
DRAYTON, GRACE (US)		
Reinthal & Newman Nursery Rhymes		
488 "O come and be my Lambey dear..."	40 - 45	45 - 50
489 "O dear me, what do I see..."	40 - 45	45 - 50
490 "It's nice to be a little boy..."	40 - 45	45 - 50
491 "Little maid neat and sweet..."	40 - 45	45 - 50
492 "Gee up Dobbin – tried and true..."	40 - 45	45 - 55
493 "The sun is shining warm and sweet..."	40 - 45	45 - 55
EDGERTON, LINDA (GB)		
Mansell & Company Series 1111 (6)	10 - 12	12 - 15
EINBECK, W. "Froschkönigs Tochterlein"	12 - 15	15 - 20
FORCK, E. (GER) (Silhouettes)		
Series 1230 Fairy Tales	12 - 15	15 - 20
GREENAWAY, KATE (GB)		

Postcards relating to the works of Kate Greenaway were published after her death in 1901, and were adapted from her images and rhymes in Rutledge & Sons' *Mother Goose* and *Old Nursery Rhymes* books which appeared before 1900. Two series have surfaced. One is black and white and the other colored, and both are signed KG. Each has a small verse along with the image. These are extremely rare, and few have been seen for sale or in auctions for many years. The cards have undivided backs, are not numbered, and can only be identified by the verse and Kate's easily recognized images and initialed signature. There are no publisher bylines.

Colored Series (Signed KG)		
German Undivided Back	150 - 200	200 - 300
Black & White Series (Signed KG)		
"A dillar, a dollar..."	90 - 100	100 - 125
"As Tommy Snooks, and Bessie Brooks..."	90 - 100	100 - 125
"Little Boy Blue..."	90 - 100	100 - 125
"Cross Patch, lift the latch..."	90 - 100	100 - 125
"Elsie Marley has grown so fine..."	90 - 100	100 - 125
"Girls and boys come out to plat..."	90 - 100	100 - 125
"Goosey, goosey, gander..."	90 - 100	100 - 125
"Hark! Hark! The dogs bark..."	90 - 100	100 - 125
"Here am I, little jumping Joan..."	90 - 100	100 - 125

Oscar Herrfurth, UvaChrom
Series 355 No. 5092, "Der
Froschkönig"

Oscar Herrfurth, UvaChrom
Series 140, No. 3801
"Dornröschen"

O. Herrfurth, Uvachrom
Series 242, No. 4390
"Der Rattenfänger von..."

"Humpty Dumpty sat on a wall..."	90 - 100	100 - 125
"Jack and Jill went up the hill..."	90 - 100	100 - 125
"Johnny shall have a new bonnet..."	90 - 100	100 - 125
"Little Betty Blue lost her..."	90 - 100	100 - 125
"Little Jack Horner sat in a corner..."	90 - 100	100 - 125
"Little lad, little lad..."	90 - 100	100 - 125
"Mary, Mary, quite contrary..."	90 - 100	100 - 125
"Polly put the kettle on..."	90 - 100	100 - 125
"Ride a cock-horse to Banbury-cross..."	90 - 100	100 - 125
"Ring-a-ring-a-roses..."	90 - 100	100 - 125
"Rock-a-bye baby..."	90 - 100	100 - 125
"There was an old woman..."	90 - 100	100 - 125
"Tom, Tom, the piper's son..."	90 - 100	100 - 125

HERRFURTH, OSCAR (GER) Several other
artists are presented in sets below.
UVAChrom, Stuttgart
Brothers Grimm Fairy Tales (6 per Series)

139	"Frau Holle" (Lady Hell)	4 - 5	5 - 6
140	"Dornröschen"	12 - 15	15 - 20
223	"Der Gestiefelte Kater" (Puss in Boots)	5 - 6	6 - 8
241	"Die Gansemagd" (The Goose Maid)	5 - 6	6 - 8
242	"Der Rattenfanger von Hameln" (Pied Piper)	8 - 10	10 - 12
252	"Der Schweinhirt" (The Pig Herdsman)	5 - 6	6 - 8
254	"Siebenschön" (Seven Lovelies)	5 - 6	6 - 8
264	"Der Tannenbäum" (The Fir Tree)	4 - 5	5 - 6
265	"Der Wolf und die Sieben Geisslein" (The Wolf and the Seven Goats)	5 - 6	6 - 8
266	"Marienkind"	4 - 5	5 - 6
267	"Tischlein deck dich"	4 - 5	5 - 6
268	"Die Sieben Schwaben"	5 - 6	6 - 8
269	"Bruderchein und Schwesterchen"	6 - 7	7 - 8
285	"Die Bremer Stadtmusikanten"	5 - 6	6 - 8
298	"Hans im Gluck" (The Lucky Hans)	5 - 6	6 - 8
299	"Das Tapfere Schneiderlein"	5 - 6	6 - 8

311 "Der Kleine Daumling" (Tom Thumb)	6 - 7	7 - 10
319 "Hase und Igel - Das Lumpengesindel"	5 - 6	6 - 7
320 "Die Sieben Raben" (The Seven Ravens)	6 - 7	7 - 8
324 "Münchhausen I"	4 - 5	5 - 6
325 "Münchhausen II"	4 - 5	5 - 6
354 "Das Schlaraffenland" (Milk & Honey Land)	4 - 5	5 - 6
355 "Der Frosch König" (The Frog King) (O.H.)	12 - 15	15 - 20
363 "Die Heinselmannchen"	5 - 6	6 - 8
369 "Till Eulenspiegel" (12 cards)	4 - 5	5 - 6
376 "Schneewittchen und Rosenrot – Die Sterntaler"	5 - 6	6 - 8
379 "König Drosselbart"	4 - 5	5 - 6
387 "Caliph Stork"	4 - 5	5 - 6
388 "Aus Flem deutschen Marchenwald I"	4 - 5	5 - 6
406 "Aus Flem deutschen Marchenwald II"	4 - 5	5 - 6
407 "Rumpelstilken"	6 - 8	8 - 10
413 "Marchen-Elfen"	5 - 6	6 - 8
Tales (Sagen) Other than Grimm (6-Card Series)		
Sage - A fantastic or incredible tale.		
127 "Die Nibelungen - Sage"	6 - 7	7 - 8
141 "Parsival" (Parsifal)	7 - 8	8 - 10
157 "Rubezahl I"	4 - 5	5 - 6
158 "Wilhelm Tell" (12)	4 - 5	5 - 6
161 "Rubezahl II"	4 - 5	5 - 6
239 "Die Tristan - Sage"	6 - 7	7 - 8
247 "Die Parsival - Sage I"	6 - 7	7 - 8
HESTER, LOTTE (GER) Silhouette Fairy Tales	12 - 15	15 - 18
HEY, PAUL (GER) Many Fairy Tales	6 - 9	9 - 12
HOCH, DANIEL (GER) "Der Froschkönig" (B&W)	15 - 18	18 - 22
DE HOOCH, PIETER (NETH)		
SVD 649 **"Aschenbrodel"** **(Cinderella)**	8 - 10	10 - 12
HUTAF, AUGUST W. (US)		
Series 105 (Little Bakers)		
2089 "Pat-a-Cake"	7 - 10	10 - 12
2090 "Make Me a Cake ..."	7 - 10	10 - 12
2091 "Criss It and Cross It ..."	7 - 10	10 - 12
2092 "Put It in the Oven ..."	7 - 10	10 - 12
2093 "Put on the Chocolate ..."	7 - 10	10 - 12
2094 "Icing and Candles ..."	7 - 10	10 - 12
JACKSON, HELEN		
Raphael Tuck		
Art Series 6749 (6)	18 - 22	22 - 25
JUCHTZER(GER)	7 - 8	8 - 10
KENNEDY, A. E. (GB)		
C. W. Faulkner Series 1633 (6)	12 - 15	15 - 20
KOCH, A. O. (GER)	15 - 18	18 - 22
KUBEL, OTTO (GER) See O. Herrfurth listing		
UVAChrom Brothers Grimm Tales	6 - 9	9 - 12
125 "Hansel & Gretel"	8 - 10	10 - 12
128 "Rotkäppchen" (Little Red Riding Hood)	8 - 10	10 - 12
140 "Dornröschen" (Sleeping Beauty)	8 - 10	10 - 12

E. Kutzer, Bund Der Deutschen, No. 382
"Das tapfere Schneiderlein"

H. Willibeek LeMair, Augener, Ltd.,
"Old Rhymes..." – "Three Blind Mice"

147 "Schneewittchen" (Snow White)	8 - 10	10 - 12
154 "Aschenbrödl" (Cinderella)	8 - 10	10 - 12
KUTZER, ERNST (AUS)		
Der. Sudmark Poster Series		
248 "Walther von der Vogelweide"	12 - 15	15 - 18
253 "Die Parsival - Sage II"	18 - 22	22 - 26
258 "Die Lohengrin - Sage"	18 - 22	22 - 26
259 "Die Tannehäuser - Sage"	18 - 22	22 - 26
263 "Aus der Zeit der Minnesanger"	12 - 15	15 - 18
361 "Der Lichtenstein" (12)	4 - 5	5 - 6
Bund Der Deutschen		
373 "Rotkäppchen" (Red Riding Hood)	15 - 18	18 - 22
382 "Das tapfere Schneiderlein"	15 - 18	18 - 22
Others	15 - 18	18 - 22
LANDSTROM, B. (FIN)	6 - 8	8 - 10
LEEKE, FERDINAND (GER)		
H.K. & M. Co.		
"Siegfried" Poster Cards (6)	12 - 15	15 - 18
MAILICK		
S.V.D. #880 The Frog King	15 - 20	20 - 25
MASSMAN, HANS (AUS)		
W.R.B. & Co., Wien "Froschkönig"	15 - 20	20 - 25
MAUZAN (IT)		
"Cendrillon" (Cinderella) (6)	10 - 12	12 - 15
LeMAIR, WILLIBEEK (GB)		
Augener, Ltd.		
Our Old Nursery Rhymes (12)		
"Baa Baa Black Sheep," "Hickory, Dickory, Dock"	15 - 18	18 - 22
"Georgy Porgy," "Here We Go Round the Mulb... "	15 - 18	18 - 22
"I Love Little Pussy," "Little Bo Peep"	15 - 18	18 - 22
"Mary Had a Little Lamb," "Oranges and Lemons"	15 - 18	18 - 22
"O Where is My Little Dog Gone," "Pata Cake"	15 - 18	18 - 22
"Pussy Cat, Pussy Cat," "Sing a Song of Sixpence"	15 - 18	18 - 22
Old Rhymes With New Pictures (12)		
"Humpty Dumpty," "Little Boy Blue"	12 - 15	15 - 20
"Little Miss Muffet," "Lucy Locket"	12 - 15	15 - 20
"Polly Put the Kettle on ...," "Twinkle Twinkle"	12 - 15	15 - 20
"Jack & Jill," "Little Jack Horner"	12 - 15	15 - 20
"Little Mother," "Mary, Mary Quite Contrary"	12 - 15	15 - 20
"Three Blind Mice," "Yankee Doodle"	12 - 15	15 - 20

Little Songs of Long Ago (12)

"Dame Get Up and Bake Your Pies"	10 - 12	12 - 15
"I Had a Little Nut Tree"	10 - 12	12 - 15
"I Saw Three Ships a Sailing"	10 - 12	12 - 15
"Little Polly Flinders," "Little Tom Tucker"	10 - 12	12 - 15
"London Bridge Has Broken Down," "Old King Cole"	10 - 12	12 - 15
"Over the Hills and Far Away"	10 - 12	12 - 15
"There Came to My Window"	10 - 12	12 - 15
"The North Wind Doth Blow"	10 - 12	12 - 15
"Young Lambs to Sell," "Simple Simon"	10 - 12	12 - 15

Little People (6)

"Evening Prayer," "In the Garden"	10 - 12	12 - 15
"Good Evening, Mr. Hare," "Little Culprit"	10 - 12	12 - 15
"In the Belfrey," "Time to Get Up"	10 - 12	12 - 15

More Old Nursery Rhymes (12)

"A Frog He Would a Wooing Go," "A Happy Family"	15 - 18	18 - 22
"Bed Time," "Curley Locks"	15 - 18	18 - 22
"Girls and Boys Come Out to Play," "Hush-a-by Baby"	15 - 18	18 - 22
"Ride a Cock Horse," "The Crooked Man"	15 - 18	18 - 22
"There Was a Little Man," "Three Little Kittens"	15 - 18	18 - 22
"Three Little Kittens"	15 - 18	18 - 22

Old Dutch Nursery Rhymes

"Follow the Leader," "Our Baby Prince"	12 - 15	15 - 18
"Polly Perkin," "The Little Sailor"	12 - 15	15 - 18
"The Marionettes," "The Tiny M͞"	12 - 15	15 - 18
"Turn Round, Turn Round"	12 - 15	15 - 18

Small Rhymes for Small People

"Dance-a-Baby Ditty," "Dance to Your Daddy"	12 - 15	15 - 18
"Goosey Gander," "Lavender Blue"	12 - 15	15 - 18
"Lazy Sheep," "Little Jumping Joan"	12 - 15	15 - 18
"Sleep, Baby, Sleep," "The Babes in the Woods"	12 - 15	15 - 18
"Three Mice Went to a Hole to Spin"	12 - 15	15 - 18

M.M.H. (GB)	10 - 12	12 - 15

MARSH-LAMBERT, H.G.C. (GB)

  A.M. Davis & Co.

Series 518, 550 Nursery Rhymes (6)	20 - 22	22 - 26

MILLER, HILDA T. (GB)

  C. W. Faulkner & Sons

Series 1746 Fairy Tales (6)	15 - 20	20 - 26
Series 1784 Nursery Rhymes (6)	15 - 20	20 - 26

MILLER, MARION

Ernest Nister Series 2032 Nursery Rhymes	10 - 15	15 - 20
MÜHLBERG, GEORG (GER)	8 - 10	10 - 14

MÜLLER, P. L. (GER)

  Hermann A. Wischmann

5002 "Schneewittchen und die Seiben Zwerge"	12 - 15	15 - 20

NIXON, K. (GB)

  C. W. Faulkner & Co.

"Alice in Wonderland" (6)	15 - 18	18 - 22

NOSWORTHY, FLORENCE E. (US)

  F. A. Owen   Series 160

	10 - 12	12 - 15

NYSTROM, JENNY (SWE)

  Axel Eliassons, Stockholm

	20 - 22	22 - 25

E. Schutz, Deutscher
Schulverein, No. 320
"Schneewittchen"

E. Schutz, Deutscher
Schulverein, No. 654
"Dorn Roschen"

E. Schutz, Deutscher
Schulverein, No. 905
"Der Rattenfanger"

Unsigned Issues	10 - 12	12 - 15
PAYER, E. (GER)	12 - 15	15 - 18
The Froschkönig (The Frog King)	15 - 20	20 - 25
PEZELLERZ, F. (GER) **Silhouette Fairy Tales**	15 - 18	18 - 22
PINGGERA, HEINZ (AUS)		
Posters		
239 "Sans Däumling" (Tom Thumb)	20 - 25	25 - 30
240 "Schneewittchen" (Snow White)	20 - 25	25 - 30
241 "Das Tapfere Schneiderlein und die Riefen"	20 - 25	25 - 30
242 "Siegfried"	20 - 25	25 - 30
243 "Frauhitt"	18 - 22	22 - 26
245 "Aschenpuitel" (Cinderella)	20 - 25	25 - 30
246 "Rübezahl"	18 - 22	22 - 26
248 "Herr Olof"	18 - 22	22 - 26
249 "Parsifal"	18 - 22	22 - 26
250 "Tannhäuser"	18 - 22	22 - 26
251 "Jung Frau"	18 - 22	22 - 26
Others	18 - 22	22 - 26
ROWLAND, FR. (GER)	12 - 15	15 - 20
RYAN, C. (US)	10 - 12	12 - 15
SCHIRMER, ANNA (GER)	8 - 10	10 - 12
SCHUTZ, E. (AUS)		
B.K.W.I.		
Poster Cards		
Series 435 Andersen's Fairy Tales (6)	15 - 20	20 - 25
Series 885 Poster cards of Fairy Tales (6)	25 - 30	30 - 35
Deutscher Schulverein		
Poster Cards		
319 "Rumpelstilzchen"	20 - 25	25 - 30
320 "Schneewittchen" (Snow White)	20 - 25	25 - 30
321 "Rotkäppchen" (Red Riding Hood)	20 - 25	25 - 30
322 "Die Sieben Raben" (Seven Ravens)	15 - 20	20 - 25
564 "Aschenbrödel" (Cinderella)	20 - 25	25 - 30
653 "Der Froschkönig" (The Frog King)	25 - 28	28 - 32
654 "Dorn Roschen" (Sleeping Beauty)	25 - 28	28 - 32

Little Miss Muffet
Sat on a tuffet,
Eating her curds and whey;
There came a big spider
And sat down beside her,
And frightened Miss Muffet away

Hazel Sirper, J. Arthur Dixon, Ltd., "Nursery Rhyme" Series 1 — "Little Miss Muffet"

862 "Dornröschen" (Sleeping Beauty)	20 - 25	25 - 30
905 "Der Rattenfanger" (The Pied Piper)	25 - 28	28 - 32
SIRPER, HAZEL (GB) 1940's - 1950's) Nursery Rhymes	3 - 5	5 - 10
J. Arthur Dixon, Ltd.		
"Nursery Rhyme" Series 1 — "Little Miss Muffet"	4 - 6	6 - 10
SOWERBY, AMY MILLICENT (GB)		
(See Artist-Signed Children)		
TARRANT, MARGARET (GB)		
T. P. & Company, N.Y.		
"Story Book Series"	6 - 8	8 - 10
TYPO, Boston		
"Tell Me a Story"	6 - 8	8 - 10
Valentine's Series (6)	6 - 8	8 - 10
THIELE, ARTH. (GER)		
Series 1180 (6)	20 - 25	25 - 28
WAIN, LOUIS (GB)		
Raphael Tuck		
Calendar Series 304 (6)	100 - 125	125 - 150
Series 3385 **(Cutouts)**		
"Fairy Tale Dressing Dolls" Cats		
"Aladdin, Princess & the Magician"	300 - 400	400 - 600
"Beauty and the Beast"	300 - 400	400 - 600
"Cinderella"	300 - 400	400 - 600
"Little Red-Riding Hood"	300 - 400	400 - 600
"Robinhood"	300 - 400	400 - 600
"Dick Whittington"	400 - 500	500 - 700
WALL, BERNHARDT (US)		
Ullman Mfg. Co.		
"Nursery Rhymes" Series 1664-1668		
"Red Riding Hood" Series		
1752 "Take Some Cakes..."	15 - 18	18 - 22

Dorothy Wheeler, A. & C. Black Ltd.
Ser. 45a, "A Frog he would a-wooing go"

Dorothy Wheeler, A. & C. Black Ltd.
Ser. 45a, "Sing a Song of Sixpence"

1753 "On the Way to Grandmother's..."	15 - 18	18 - 22
1754 "Arrives at Grandmother's..."	15 - 18	18 - 22
1755 "Comes to Bed..."	15 - 18	18 - 22
1756 "Innocently Lay Down in Bed..."	15 - 18	18 - 22
1757 "Hears the Wolf Say..."	15 - 18	18 - 22
"Mary and Her Lamb" Series 1759-1762	12 - 15	15 - 20
WHEELER, DOROTHY (GB) (See Fairies)		
A. & C. Black, Ltd.		
Series 45a (6)		
"Dame, get up, and bake your Pies"	12 - 15	15 - 20
"A Frog he would a-wooing go"	15 - 20	20 - 25
"Goosey, Goosey Gander"	12 - 15	15 - 20
"Lavender's Blue"	12 - 15	15 - 20
"Sing a Song of Sixpence"	12 - 15	15 - 20
"Where are you going to?"	12 - 15	15 - 18
Humphrey Milford		
"Snow Children" Series (6)	12 - 15	15 - 20
WHITE, FLORA (GB)		
Ilfracombe Mermaid, "Who are You?"	20 - 25	25 - 30
J. Salmon Poster Series		
"Cinderella"	12 - 15	15 - 18
"Dick Whittington"	12 - 15	15 - 18
"Goose Girl"	12 - 15	15 - 18
"Hop-O-My-Thumb"	12 - 15	15 - 18
"Peter Pan"	12 - 15	15 - 18
"Puss in Boots"	12 - 15	15 - 18
WINKLER, ROLF	7 - 8	8 - 10

Anonymous   Same images as those by
M. E. Banks and published by R. Tuck
Paper Doll Cutouts
Series 3382 "Little Bo-Peep"	150 - 175	175 - 200
Series 3383 "Little Boy Blue"	150 - 175	175 - 200

PUBLISHERS & ADVERTISING
Julius Bien Series 40 (6)	10 - 12	12 - 15
A. & C. Black		
Series 44, 45 "English Nursery Rhymes" (6) *	12 - 15	15 - 20
* Probably by artist Dorothy Wheeler, above.		
Series 80 "Alice in Wonderland"	20 - 25	25 - 28
C. S. Clark Series	6 - 8	8 - 10
F.A.S. Co. Series 9 (6)	8 - 10	10 - 12
Fairman Co. Series 625 (B&W)	8 - 10	10 - 12
F. Firth & Co. Rhymes	8 - 10	10 - 12
German-American Novelty Art		
Series 307, 397 (6)	8 - 10	10 - 15
Gottschalk & Dreyfuss (German)		
Series 2114 and 2115	10 - 12	12 - 15
Vivian A. Mansell, & Co., London		
Series 1067, 2105 (6)	8 - 10	10 - 12
Misch & Stock		
Series 120 "Fairy Tales & Pantomimes" (6)	12 - 15	15 - 18
National Art Company		
Series 308 - 314 (6)	10 - 12	12 - 15
Newman, Wolsey & Co.		
Nursery Rhymes, Signed MMH	10 - 12	12 - 15
F. A. Owen Series 160, 161 (6)	8 - 10	10 - 12
P.F.B. (Paul Finkenrath) (Emb)		
Series 3714 (6)		
"Cinderella," "The House of Sweets"	25 - 30	30 - 35
"Little Red Riding Hood," "Sleeping Beauty"	25 - 30	30 - 35
"Snow White," "Tom Thumb"	25 - 30	30 - 35
Series 6943 (6)	22 - 25	25 - 28
Series 8666 (6) Same as Series 8666, above.	25 - 30	30 - 35
Salmon & Company		
Fairy Tale Series	10 - 12	12 - 15
Dr. Swett's Root Beer Nursery Rhymes	25 - 30	30 - 35
Swift's Premium, 1918 Nursery Rhymes (6)		
"Jack Spratt," "Little Tommy Tucker"	15 - 18	18 - 22
"Old King Cole," "Little Jack Horner"	15 - 18	18 - 22
"Simple Simon," "Queen of Hearts"	15 - 18	18 - 22
Raphael Tuck		
Dressing Dolls		
Series 3383 "Nursery Rhymes" (6)		
"Little Boy Blue,"	150 - 175	175 - 200
"Handy Spandy...," "Simple Simon"	150 - 175	175 - 200
"The Queen of Hearts," "Tom, Tom, the Piper's..."	150 - 175	175 - 200
Series 3385 "Fairy Tale Dolls" (6)		
"Baby Bunting," "Little Miss Muffet"	125 - 150	150 - 180
Others	125 - 150	150 - 180
Series IX Glosso "Happy Childhood" (B/W)	6 - 8	8 - 10

Anonymous, No. 3513, "Aschenbrödel" (Cinderella)

Series 12 "Nursery Don'ts" (12)	12 - 15	15 - 18
Series 132 "Lovers in Nursery Land"	10 - 12	12 - 15
Series 3376 "Nursery Rhymes" (6)	10 - 12	12 - 18
Series 3328, 3379, 3488 (6)	10 - 12	12 - 15
Series 3470-3475 (6) (Chromolithos)		
"Cinderella," "Puss 'n' Boots"	20 - 25	25 - 30
"Red Riding Hood," "Sleeping Beauty"	20 - 25	25 - 30
"Snow White," "Tom Thumb"	20 - 25	25 - 30
Series 5579 "Happy Childhood"	10 - 12	12 - 15
Series 5600 "Cat Studies" (6) B/W	12 - 15	15 - 18
Series 5629 "Pussy in Fairyland"	10 - 12	12 - 15
Series 6496 "Landor's Cat Studies" (B/W)	6 - 8	8 - 10
Series 8484 Oilette "Aesop's Fables" (6)	15 - 18	18 - 22
T.P. & Co., New York		
"Story Book" Series	10 - 12	12 - 15
Tullar-Meredith		
"This Little Pig" (5)	10 - 12	12 - 15
Walk-Over Shoes Nursery Rhymes (11)		
"Alladin," "Baa Baa Black Sheep"	10 - 12	12 - 15
"Ding Dong Bell," "Hey Diddle Diddle"	10 - 12	12 - 15
"Humpty Dumpty," "Little Bo Peep"	10 - 12	12 - 15
"Little Miss Muffet," "Little Red Riding Hood"	10 - 12	12 - 15
"Simple Simon," "Sing a song of Sixpence"	10 - 12	12 - 15
"The Three Bears"	10 - 12	12 - 15
ANONYMOUS		
Eagle on back Series, Lacy Border (10) (Emb)		
"Cock-a doodle-doo," Little Bo Peep"	10 - 12	12 - 15
"Little Boy Blue," "Little Jack Horner"	10 - 12	12 - 15
"Mary, Mary, Quite Contrary,"	10 - 12	12 - 15
"Old Mother Hubbard" "Pussy Cat, Pussy Cat,"	10 - 12	12 - 15
"Little Miss Muffet," "Little Red Riding Hood"	10 - 12	12 - 15
"Simple Simon," "Sing a song of Sixpence"	10 - 12	12 - 15

Uns. Fritz Baumgarten, Meissner & Buch
Series 1903, "Botanikers Freude."

Rose Clark, Rotograph Co., F.L. 386
"Lilly-Pad Frog."

"The Three Bears"	10 - 12	12 - 15
"Aschenbrödel" Undivided Back No. 3513	15 - 18	18 - 22

DRESSED ANIMALS

(Animals, Non-Dressed, listed in Artist-Signed Animal Section)

BARNES, G. L. (GB) **Cats** **See Nursery Rhymes**		
BARNES-AUSTIN, EDGAR (GB)		
Raphael Tuck **"Piggie-Wiggie" Series** (6)	12 - 15	15 - 20
BAUMGARTEN, FRITZ (F.B.) (GER)		
Meissner & Buch		
Bunnies		
Series 2960, 3058, 3271	15 - 20	20 - 25
Series 2454 **Frogs/Chickens**	20 - 25	25 - 35
Series 1903 Frog "Botanikers Freude"	25 - 30	30 - 40
Dogs	12 - 15	15 - 20
Series 1457, 1458, 1486, 1511 (Bears) (6)	12 - 15	15 - 20
BOULANGER, MAURICE (FR) See Cats, Artist-Signed		
CADY, HARRISON (US)		
Quaddy Plaything Co.		
"Quaddy" Postcards (10)		
"Danny Meadow Mouse," "Grandfather Frog"	90 - 100	100 - 125
"Hooty the Owl," "Happy Jack Squirrel"	90 - 100	100 - 125
"Mrs. Peter Rabbit," "Peter Rabbit"	90 - 100	100 - 125
"Reddy Fox," "Spotty Turtle"	90 - 100	100 - 125
"Unc' Billy Possum"	90 - 100	100 - 125

CHARLIN, F. Bears	12 - 15	15 - 18
CLARK, ROSE (US)		
National Art Co. Chicks Series	12 - 15	15 - 18
Rotograph Co. Frogs Series		
F.L. 379 "Officer Stout Frog"	30 - 35	35 - 45
F.L. 380 "Dew-Drop Frog"	30 - 35	35 - 45
F.L. 381 "Will B. Stout Frog"	30 - 35	35 - 45
F.L. 382 "Mrs. Hoppin Frog"	30 - 35	35 - 45
F.L. 383 "Leap Frog"	30 - 35	35 - 45
F.L. 384 "Hammersly Frog, the Village.."	30 - 35	35 - 45
F.L. 385 "Grandmother Bullsie"	30 - 35	35 - 45
F.L. 386 "Lily-Pad Frog"	30 - 35	35 - 45
F.L. 387 "Professor Singer Frog"	30 - 35	35 - 45
F.L. 388 "Captain Skippin Frog..."	30 - 35	35 - 45
F.L. 389 "Brassie Frog"	30 - 35	35 - 45
F.L. 390 "I M. De Bull Frog"	40 - 45	45 - 50
Raphael Tuck		
Series 36, 4121, 4122 Chicks (6)	15 - 18	18 - 22
CLIVETTE		
Series 619 Dancing Cats (6)	12 - 15	15 - 20
CLOKE, RENE (GB)		
J. Salmon Co. Squirrel Series	8 - 10	10 - 12
COBBE, BERNHARD		
Raphael Tuck		
Series 9539 Bunnies (6)	8 - 10	10 - 12
Cats, Dogs	8 - 10	10 - 12
COWELL, CYRIL (GB)		
"Squirrilquins" (6)	8 - 10	10 - 12
CRANE, D. P.		
Baby Duckling Series (6)	18 - 22	22 - 26
CRITE		
HSV Litho Co.		
"Billy Possum Political Series" (12)		
"Are you Dead - or Just Playing Possum?"	20 - 25	25 - 30
"Aw don't play possum"	20 - 25	25 - 30
"The Boogie Man'll Get You..."	20 - 25	25 - 30
"Dear Friends, My Home Address..."	20 - 25	25 - 30
"Dear, Am unavoidably detained..."	20 - 25	25 - 30
"Do it Now! Don't Play Possum: But..."	20 - 25	25 - 30
"Give My Regards to Bill!"	25 - 30	30 - 35
"Good Eating Here!"	30 - 35	35 - 40
"I'm having a high old time..."	20 - 25	25 - 35
"It' a Great Game for Us Fat People..." Golf	30 - 35	35 - 40
"Oo's 'ittle' possum is 'oo?"	20 - 25	25 - 30
"Very Busy; Both Hands Full..."	20 - 25	25 - 30
DE WEES, ETHEL (US)		
A.M.P. Co. "Billy Possum" Series		
"Arrived here just at right time"	25 - 30	30 - 35
"I'll make another drive..."	25 - 30	30 - 35
"I'm going to make a record this trip"	25 - 30	30 - 35
"It's a bad thing to put off..."	25 - 30	30 - 35
"Just a few lines before game..."	30 - 35	35 - 38
"Yale's Favorite Son"	30 - 35	35 - 38

K. Hesse, A. Sch. & Co., No. 2112
"Wir gratulieren!"

Alfred Mainzer (Hartung), Max Künzli
No. 4731, No Caption

DOD, GIL (GB)		
S. Hildesheimer Series 5244 "Sports Meet" (6)	20 - 25	25 - 30
DOVIE, E. H. (GB) Squirrels	8 - 10	10 - 12
ELLAM, WILLIAM HENRY (GB)		
B. Dondorf Bear Series (6)	15 - 20	20 - 25
Raphael Tuck		
"Breakfast in Bed"		
Series 9321 I & II	18 - 22	22 - 25
Series 9953, 9784, 9793	18 - 22	22 - 25
Series 574B With German Captions	15 - 18	18 - 22
"Mrs. Caudle's Lectures"		
Series 8683, 8684	15 - 18	18 - 22
F.D.S. (Bears)	15 - 18	18 - 22
FEIERTAG, K. (AUS)		
B.K.W.I.		
Series 160 (Bears) (6)	12 - 15	15 - 18
Dogs	8 - 10	10 - 12
FIALKOWSKA, WALLY or **WF** (AUS)		
Cats, Dogs, Frogs	12 - 15	15 - 18
FREES, H. W.		
Rotograph Co. Real Photo Dress Dogs & Cats	8 - 10	10 - 12
GOVEY, L. A. (GB) The Little Mouse Family" (6)	22 - 25	25 - 28
GRATZ, THOMAS (GER)	10 - 12	12 - 15
GROSMANN, M.		
B.K.W.I. Series 797 Dogs (6)	10 - 12	12 - 15
GUGGENBERGER, I. G. (GER) Mice	20 - 25	25 - 30
HANKE, H. or **H.H.** (GER)		
Series 4056 Dressed Dachshunds (6)	15 -18	18 - 22
HESSE, K.		
A. Sch. & Co.		
No. 2112 Ducks "Wir gratulieren!"	12 - 15	15 - 20
HORINA, H. (US)		
Ullman Co.		
Series 91 "Jimmy Pig" (10)	15 - 18	18 - 22
HUDSON, G. M.		
Raphael Tuck Series 8648 "Guinnipens" (6)	30 - 35	35 - 40
JIRAS, A. (AUS?) **Dressed Donkeys**	25 - 30	30 - 35
HY-M (Henry Mayer) (GER)		
E. Nister "Jumbo" Elephant Series		
Series 186 "Jumbo" (6) (Uns.)	30 - 35	35 - 40

Series 187, 188, 189 (6)	30 - 35	35 - 40
MAINZER, ALFRED (Artist - **HARTUNG**) (40's - 60's)		
Max Künzli		
Cats, Dogs	4 - 5	5 - 6
Golf or Tennis Themes	8 - 10	10 - 12
MANASSE, A. Bears	10 - 12	12 - 15
MARTIN, L. (GB) **Bears**	10 - 12	12 - 15
MEGGENDORFER, L. (GER)		
H.K.C.M. Monkey Series		
Series 224, 263, 264, 265 (6)	18 - 22	22 - 25
MÜLLER, A. (GER) **Dog Series 3908**	15 - 20	20 - 25
MÜLLER, R. (AUS) **Frogs**	20 - 25	25 - 30
OHLER, C. (HUN)		
B.K.W.I. Series 4678 (6)	20 - 25	25 - 28
Birds Series, Duck Series, Comical Dogs (6)	6 - 8	8 - 10
OPSWALD, EUGEN (GER)		
"Animal Sports" (6)	35 - 50	50 - 75
ONSLOW, LOLA (GB)		
Mack Co. "Storybook" Series Bunnies	8 - 10	10 - 12
PANKRATZ Comical Dachshunds	10 - 12	12 - 15
PAYER, E. (AUS)		
B.K.W.I. Series 1748 Frogs (6)	20 - 25	25 - 30
Others (The Frog King)	18 - 22	22 - 26
P.O.E. (GER) **Dressed Dogs**	12 - 15	15 - 18
REICHERT, C. (GER) **Dressed Dogs**	12 - 15	15 - 20
ROGER (FR)		
K. F. Editeurs		
Series 590 **Elephants in Restaurant** (6)	15 - 20	20 - 25
ROGIND, CARL (DEN) Pig Sports Series	20 - 25	25 - 30
ROWNTREE, HARRY (GB)		
"Sporting Duckling" Series	15 - 18	18 - 22
SCHERMELE, WILLY		
De Muinck & Co. 490 Dressed Bunnies	8 - 10	10 - 12
SCHNOPLER, A. (AUS) Comical Dachshunds	12 - 15	15 - 20
A.S.M. Series 625 Dressed Cats (6)	15 - 18	18 - 22
SCHONIAN, ALFRED (GER)		
Elf and Frog Series	18 - 22	22 - 25
SCHUTZ, ERIC (AUS)		
B.K.W.I. Poster 41 "The Froschkönig"	25 - 30	30 - 35
STUDDY, GEORGE (GB)		
B.K.W.I. Bonzo Series	10 - 12	12 - 15
Golf & Tennis themes	15 - 20	20 - 25
Valentine's Bonzo Series	10 - 12	12 - 15
Golf & Tennis themes	15 - 20	20 - 25
TEMPEST, MARGARET		
Medici Society Series 61 (Bears)	6 - 8	8 - 10
THIELE, ARTH. (GER)		
F.E.D. Series 160, 474 (6)	25 - 30	30 - 35
German American Art		
Series 789 Dressed Hog Head Studies (6)	25 - 28	28 - 32
Series 806 Dressed Dog Head Studies (6)	25 - 28	28 - 32
T.S.N. (Theo. Stroefer)		
Series 710, 861, 947, 995, 1412, 1424 Cats (6)	30 - 35	35 - 40
Series 1468 (Cats) (6)	30 - 35	35 - 40

Three Wonderful Cats by Arth. Thiele, T.S.N., Series1412, German Captions

Series 962, 975, 1012, 1077, 1194 (Cats) (6)	15 - 20	20 - 25
Series 1326, 1423, 1403, 1405, 1423 (Cats) (6)	15 - 20	20 - 25
Series 1438, 1601, 1602, 1646, 1852 (Cats) (6)	15 - 20	20 - 25
Series 1880, 1881, 1882, 3575 (Cats) (6)	15 - 20	20 - 25
Series 1010, 1229 Cats (6)	20 - 25	25 - 30
Series 1020, 1021 Bunnies (6)	15 - 20	20 - 25
Series 1240, 1355, 1451 Bunnies (6)	20 - 25	25 - 28
Series 1021, 1165, 1352, 1452 Chicks (6)	15 - 18	18 - 25
Series 843, 946 Dogs (6)	18 - 22	22 - 25
Series 1215 Horse Head Studies (6)	35 - 45	45 - 55
Series 781, 844 Monkeys (6)	22 - 25	25 - 30
Series 1413 Animal Head Studies (6)	22 - 25	25 - 30

G.H.T. (THOMPSON, G. H.) (GB)

Ernest Nister, London Signed & Unsigned

Series 6 Hippo Series (6)	35 - 40	40 - 50
Series 179 "The Animals' Trip to the Sea" (6)	45 - 55	55 - 65
Series 180 "The Animals' Picnic" (6)	45 - 55	55 - 65
Series 181 "The Animals' Rebellion" (6)	45 - 50	50 - 60
Series 70 (6)	45 - 50	50 - 60
Series 172 Hippo Head Series (6) Signed	45 - 55	55 - 65
Series 354 "The Animals' School"	45 - 55	55 - 65

Note: Uns. large images were then made from the
small images on the above series into individual
series by **E. Nister & Theo. Stroefer** listed below.

Nister - Series 316, 328, 331, 333 (6)	40 - 45	45 - 55
Series 330 Bunny Series (6)	30 - 35	35 - 40

T.S.N. (Theo Stroefer)

Series 44, No. N-5 Hippo in School	45 - 55	55 - 65
Series 302, 319, 325, 330, 441 (6)	35 - 40	40 - 50
Series 757 (Same as Series 179)	45 - 55	55 - 65
Series 965 (6)	45 - 55	55 - 65

TWELVETREES, CHARLES H. (US)

National Art Co. Frog Series

136 "Matinee Idol"	20 - 25	25 - 30
137 "Paul and Virginia"	20 - 25	25 - 30

Unsigned G. H. Thompson, T.S.N., Series 965 (Animals' Trip to the Sea)

Unsigned G. H. Thompson	*Unsigned G. H. Thompson*	*Unsigned G. H. Thompson*
Ernest Nister, No. 318	*T.S.N., Series 319, No. 1*	*T.S.N., Series 44, N-5*

138 "Come in the Water's Fine"	20 - 25	25 - 30
139 "The Bride"	25 - 30	30 - 35
140 "The Groom"	25 - 30	30 - 35

WAIN, LOUIS (GB)

Max Ettlinger

Series 5376 Cat Santas	450 - 500	500 - 550
E. J. Hey Series 423	75 - 100	100 - 125

Raphael Tuck   Cats

Series 3551-Cats, 3552-Dogs "Mascots" (6)	150 - 175	175 - 200
Series 3553, 3554 "Mascots" (6)	150 - 175	175 - 200
Series 8612, 8615 "Taking the Waters" (6)	100 - 125	125 - 150
Series 8613, 8614 "Taking the Harrogate..." (6)	100 - 125	125 - 150

Louis Wain, E.J. Hey & Co.
Ser. 423, "Will you be...?"

Publisher E.A.S., No. 1032
"Fröliche Pfingsten"

Publisher Lith-Artist
Anstalt, Series 93

Series 9396 (6)	60 - 75	75 - 100
Charlie Chaplin Series (6)	250 - 275	275 - 300
Many others	60 - 75	75 - 150
WESSEL, E. (GER)		
B. Dondorf		
Series 28 "Sporting Frogs"	20 - 25	25 - 35
WEIGAND, MARTIN (GER)		
Emil Kohn "The Frog King"	25 - 30	30 - 35
Others	12 - 15	15 - 20
WINKLER, ROLF (GER) Dressed Dogs	20 - 22	22 - 25
WOOD, LAWSON (GB)		
Valentine Pub. Co. Monkey Series	10 - 12	12 - 15
Golf	15 - 20	20 - 25

PUBLISHERS

A. & M. B. Series 47 Chromolithos Fish	20 - 25	25 - 30
Series 113,170, 283 Frogs (6) Chromolithos	25 - 30	30 - 35
AMAG Series 2143 Bunnies (6)	12 - 15	15 - 20
A. R. Company Series 1394-1	20 - 22	22 - 26
Birn Brothers (B.B. London)		
Series E243 "We love Billy Possum..."	28 - 32	32 - 36
Frank J. Cohen & Son, Atlanta		
"Billy Possum" (B&W)	100 - 125	125 - 150
E.A.S.		
Series 1032 Frog "Fröliche Pfingsten"	20 - 25	25 - 35
Series 1044 "The Frog Gardener"	20 - 25	25 - 35
H.H.i.W. Dog Series 459 (6)	12 - 15	15 - 20
H.W.B. Pig Chimney Sweeps	15 - 18	18 - 22
Lester Book & Stationery, Atlanta		
Taft with Possum "Beat it Teddy Bear"	300 - 350	350 - 400
Lith-Artist Anstalt Series 93, Dressed Donkey	35 - 45	45 - 55
Fred C. Lounsbury		
"Billy Possum" Series 2515 (4) (Sepia)		
"The only Possum that escaped"	20 - 25	25 - 30

	Publisher P.F.B. *Series 8467*	*Publisher P.F.B.* *Series 8403*	*Publisher P.P.* *"Die Besten Bunsche..."*
"Billy Possum and Jimmy P. on the links"		28 - 32	32 - 35
"Good Bye Teddy"		20 - 25	25 - 30
"Moving day in Possum Town"		20 - 25	25 - 30
"Billy Possum" **Series 2517** (4) (Blue tone)			
"Billy Possum to the Front"		28 - 32	32 - 35
"Columbia's Latest 'Possum and Taters"		28 - 32	32 - 35
"Uncle Sam's New Toy"		28 - 32	32 - 35
"The Nation's Choice"		28 - 32	32 - 35
Meissner & Buch Series 2960 Bunnies (6)		15 - 18	18 - 22
Misch & Co.			
Series 420 "Fishy Customers" (6)		20 - 25	25 - 30
Series 403 Frogs (6) Chromolithos		20 - 25	25 - 30
M. Munk, Vienna Bear Series		12 - 15	15 - 18
Series 420 Frogs Dance Series (6)		22 - 25	25 - 30
Series 729 Bunnies (6)			
O.P.F. Dressed Frogs Very high quality		40 - 50	50 - 60
F. A. Owen Co. "Billy Possum" (B&W)			
"Hurrah for Bill and Old Eli"		40 - 50	50 - 60
P.F.B. Dog Series 5957, 8168 (6)		20 - 25	25 - 28
Series 3903 Animals do Cake Walk (6)		20 - 25	25 - 35
Easter Series 8403, 8467		15 - 20	20 - 25
P.P. Dressed Elephant		40 - 50	50 - 60
S.W.S.B. Series 8837 Bears		12 - 15	15 - 18
Novitas Series 80607 Courting Birds		6 - 8	8 - 10
Raphael Tuck			
Series 294, 4089 (6) **Frogs**		20 - 25	25 - 30
Series 1723 Chromolithos (6)		20 - 25	25 - 30
Series 2598 (6)		18 - 22	22 - 25
Ullman Mfg. Co.			
Series 72 "Jungle Sports" Various animals		15 - 18	18 - 22
Series 84 "Bunny Girl"		10 - 12	12 - 15
Series 112 "Br'er Rabbit"		12 - 15	15 - 18
Series 196 "Monkey Doodle"		8 - 10	10 - 12
Albert Hahn "Kaatskill Cats"		10 - 12	12 - 15
ADVERTISING			
Robeson Cutlery Co. Red Pig Knives (10)		50 - 75	75 - 100

Original Art, Undivided Back – See "Anonymous" in Text

ANONYMOUS
Bear with Honey Pot (Original Art, Undivided Back)	60 - 70	70 - 80
The Frog Proposal (Original Art, Undivided Back)	75 - 85	85 - 100
The Gentleman Pig (Original Art, Undivided Back)	50 - 60	60 - 70

OTHER ARTIST DRESSED ANIMALS, ETC.
Note: Average values. Values reflect the particular card and prominence of artist.

BIRDS	5 - 6	6 - 8
BUGS	8 - 10	10 - 15
CATS	6 - 8	8 - 12
COWS, BULLS, ETC.	10 - 12	12 - 15
DOGS	8 - 10	10 - 12
DUCKS, GEESE, CHICKENS	8 - 10	10 - 12
ELEPHANTS, GIRAFFES	12 - 15	15 - 22
FROGS	15 - 20	20 - 25
GOATS	12 - 15	15 - 18
GRASSHOPPERS	10 - 12	12 - 15
GROUNDHOGS, HIPPOPOTAMUS	15 - 20	20 - 25
HORSES, BURROS, DONKEYS, ZEBRAS	12 - 15	15 - 18
MAY BUGS (MAIKÄFERS), BEETLES, INSECTS	12 - 15	15 - 22
MONKEYS	8 - 10	10 - 12
OPOSSUMS	12 - 15	15 - 20
PARROTS, OWLS	8 - 10	10 - 12
PIGS	10 - 12	12 - 18
PIG CHIMNEY SWEEPS	12 - 15	15 - 20
RABBITS, SQUIRRELS	6 - 8	8 - 15
RATS/MICE	10 - 12	12 - 15

See Artist-Signed Chapter for Animals not Dressed.

MISCELLANEOUS FANTASY

AUTOS FLYING ABOVE CITY	8 - 10	10 - 12
BUSI, ADOLFO		
Series 3059 Women/Snowmen (6)	18 - 22	22 - 26

P/**Kaplan**
  Series 57 Women's Heads in Clouds (12) 12 - 15 15 - 20
CORBELLA, TITO
  Uff. Rev. Stampa, Milano
    Series 268   Death and Edith Cavell
      1 - "Cavell Standing over the Conquered
        Figure of Death ..." 15 - 20 20 - 25
      2 - "Death Offering Head of Cavell ..." 15 - 20 20 - 25
      3 - "Death and Arrogant German Officer ..." 15 - 20 20 - 25
      4 - "Cavell Standing Before Death ..." 15 - 20 20 - 25
      5 - "Death Hovers as Cavell Gives Water ..." 15 - 20 20 - 25
      6 - "Death Plays Piano as Cavell Lies ..." 15 - 20 20 - 25
ELVES, GNOMES 5 - 8 8 - 12
FACES IN MOUNTAINS 10 - 12 12 - 20
FLOWER FACES 6 - 8 8 - 12
  Ernest Nister, London 10 - 12 12 - 15
  The Standard, London (Multi-Baby) **Series 67** 6 - 8 8 - 10
GIANT PEOPLE 5 - 6 6 - 7

GOLLIWOGGS

ATTWELL, MABEL L. (GB)
  Valentine's
    Series A551 20 - 25 25 - 30
    Series A579 20 - 25 25 - 30
    689 "Golly, It's Nice!" 25 - 30 30 - 35
    "How Time Flies" 25 - 30 30 - 35
    "Oh! Golly! How I Love You!" 25 - 30 30 - 35
    Series 7346 20 - 25 25 - 30
BRISLEY, NINA
  "June, you're not listening." 15 - 20 20 - 25
GOVEY, A. (GB)
  Humphrey Milford
    "Dreams & Fairies" Series (6)
    "Jack and the Twins in Golliwogg's Boat" 25 - 30 30 - 35
KENNEDY, T. R. (GB) 15 - 20 20 - 25
MARSH-LAMBERT, H.G.C. (GB)
  A.M. Davis Co.
    Series 501 "Round the Clock"
    "I'll play, I think, with Sambo..." 20 - 25 25 - 30
    "At nine my breakfast is over..." 20 - 25 25 - 30
    "Oh Dear! How quickly six has come..." 20 - 25 25 - 30
PEARSE, S. B.
  M. Munk Series 856
    Little girl with Golliwogg & Dolls
    "A-B-C Schutsen" 25 - 30 30 - 40
RICHARDSON, AGNES (GB)
  Raphael Tuck
    Series 1232 "**Rescued**" (6) 25 - 30 30 - 35
    Series 1262 (6) 25 - 30 30 - 35
    Series 1397 (6) 25 - 30 30 - 35

M. L. Attwell, Valentine's Series A579, "How Time Flies"

M. L. Attwell, Valentine's Series A579 – "Oh! Golly! How I Love You!"

Nina Brisley, "June, you're not listening."

A. Govey Humphrey Milford ""Jack and the Twins in..."

Susan B. Pearse, M. Munk Series 856, "Die Kleine Tanzmeisterin."

Agnes Richardson R. Tuck Series 8688, "I'm down here with the..."

Card C1420 "Little Snowflakes..."	25 - 30	30 - 35
Card C1421 "My Greeting is Loving..."	25 - 30	30 - 35
Series C2005	25 - 30	30 - 35
Series 8688		
"I'm down here with the family"	30 - 35	35 - 38
Valentine & Sons		
Series C2006 (6)	20 - 25	25 - 30
STOCKS, M. (GB)		
H.K. & Co.		
"Jack-in-the Box" with Golliwogg	15 - 20	20 - 25
UPTON, FLORENCE (GB)		
Raphael Tuck "Golliwoggs"		
Series 1252	35 - 40	40 - 50

Florence Upton, Raphael Tuck Series 1785
"The 'Golliwogg' Introducing Himself"

Uns. Florence Upton, R. Tuck Series 1282
"The 'Golliwogg'"

Series 1281 "Art" Series (6)		
"Golliwogg's Auto-Go-Cart"	35 - 40	40 - 50
"Golliwogg & his Auto-Go-Cart"	35 - 40	40 - 50
"Golliwogg & his Auto-Go-Cart–Applying the Pump"	35 - 40	40 - 50
"Golliwogg Motoring"	35 - 40	40 - 50
"Golliwogg taken to Prison"	35 - 40	40 - 50
"Golliwogg and the Highwayman"	35 - 40	40 - 50
Series 1282 "Art" (6)		
"The Golliwogg"	30 - 40	40 - 50
"Golliwogg Introducing Himself"	35 - 40	40 - 50
"Golliwogg and the Highwayman"	35 - 40	40 - 50
"Golliwogg Rescued"	35 - 40	40 - 50
"Golliwogg Taken to Prison"	35 - 40	40 - 50
"Golliwogg Escapes from Prison"	35 - 40	40 - 50
Series 1397 "Golliwogg Art" Series		
"The Golliwogg Comes to Grief on the Ice"	35 - 40	40 - 50
Series 1785 "Christmas" (6)	35 - 40	40 - 50
Series 1791 (6)	35 - 40	40 - 50
"Golliwogg and His Auto Car"	35 - 40	40 - 50
Series 1792 Christmas, New Year (6)	35 - 40	40 - 50
"Golliwogg and the Highwayman"	35 - 40	40 - 50
Series 1793 (6)		
"Golliwogg in Prison"	35 - 40	40 - 50
Series 1794 (6) Signed	35 - 40	40 - 50
Series 6065 "Humorous" (6)	35 - 40	40 - 50
Series 6067 (6)		
"Golliwogg goes Crabbing"	35 - 40	40 - 50
"Golliwogg goes Fishing"	35 - 40	40 - 50
"Golliwogg in the Water"	35 - 40	40 - 50
Others	35 - 40	40 - 50
Series 8063 "Christmas" (6)	35 - 40	40 - 50
"Golliwogg" Skating	35 - 40	40 - 50
Davidson Bros. Series	22 - 25	25 - 30
Regent Publishing Co.	30 - 35	35 - 40
A. C. Redmon Co.	30 - 35	35 - 40
Others	30 - 35	35 - 40

B.B., London (Birn Brothers) (Anon. Artist) (Silver BG)

Series 10 Courtship-Marriage w/Stickgirl		
At the Beach, In a Row Boat, In Automobile	20 - 25	25 - 30
On Park Bench, Playing Cards, The Family Outing	20 - 25	25 - 30
Series X296	20 - 22	22 - 25
C. W. Faulkner		
Series 996	18 - 22	22 - 25
Series 1136 (6)	20 - 25	25 - 30
Raphael Tuck		
Series 507 (6)	15 - 20	20 - 25
John Winsch		
1910 Issue	15 - 20	20 - 25
1912 Issue (Santa)	20 - 25	25 - 35
1913 Issue (Santa) (2)	40 - 50	50 - 60
Anonymous Series 733	15 - 20	20 - 25
DEPICTING THE FUTURE	7 - 8	8 - 10
EGG OR FOOT PEOPLE	15 - 18	18 - 22
MAN IN THE MOON	8 - 10	10 - 12
METAMORPHICS See Topicals		
MUSHROOMS, GIANT	6 - 8	8 - 12
MUSHROOM PEOPLE	8 - 12	12 - 16
SKELETONS, DEPICTING DEATH	8 - 10	10 - 15
SNOWMEN	6 - 10	10 - 20
S/A. THIELE Snowman Series 1297 (6)	15 - 20	20 - 30
P.F.B. Series 11144	20 - 22	22 - 26
SOLOMKO		
UN		
1015 "Dream of Icarius"	12 - 15	15 - 20
1019 "Blue Bird"	15 - 18	18 - 22
STICK OR WOOD PEOPLE	12 - 15	15 - 20

WAGNER OPERA FIGURES

Many think Richard Wagner, the German composer, was the greatest composer who ever lived. In 1883 he died, leaving a legacy that will live forever. It is believed that he alone fundamentally changed European musical, literary, and theatrical life. To Europeans he was a great man, and at the turn of the century his operas continued to be a passion for all who loved music and the theatre.

Wagner's first opera was *Rienzi* and then *The Flying Dutchman.* Later came his famous *Tannhäuser* and *Löhengrin*, which were operas concerning the romantic views of medieval life. His greatest creation, however, was *The Ring of the Nibelungs*, which was four operas in one...*The Rhine Gold, The Valkyrie, Siegfried*, and *The Twilight of the Gods*.

The love story of *Tristan and Isolde* was one of his most popular, and *The Mastersingers of Nürnberg* was his only mature comedy. Wagner's final work was *Parsifal*, a religious story of early Spain and the Holy Grail.

German artists, because of their great love for the works of Wagner, painted many beautiful fantasy sets and series about the heroes and heroines of his operas. The great poster-type cards by Hanns Printz, Heinz Pinggera, and Eric Schutz are certainly of epic proportions. Also, the works by R. Tuck and ESD of paintings by Stassen are among the best in a very wide field.

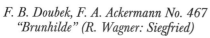

F. B. Doubek, F. A. Ackermann No. 467
"Brunhilde" (R. Wagner: Siegfried)

P. V. Erlang, HMM, No. 3221
"Siegfried und die Rheintöchter"

AIGNER		
Series 259 (6) 4490 "Tannhäuser"	8 - 10	10 - 12
AUBERT, PAUL (GER)		
27 "Tannhäuser" B&W	8 - 10	10 - 12
BAUFCHILD (GER) **"Löhengrin"** (6)	10 - 12	12 - 15
BERGMULLER, C. W. (GER) Nude – "Walküre"	12 - 15	15 - 22
BRAUNE, ERWIN (GER)		
Nude – "Walküre"	12 - 15	15 - 22
DOUBEK, F. (GER)		
F. A. Ackermann Ladies in Wagner Operas (Undb)		
"Brunhilde," "Gurtrune (Krimhilde)," "Senta," etc.	15 - 20	20 - 25
ERLANG, P. V. (GER)	8 - 10	10 - 12
HMM		
"Richard Wagner's Musikdramen"		
3214-3225 (12)	12 - 15	15 - 20
FAHRENKROG, LUDVIG (GER)		
298 "Parsifal"	8 - 10	10 - 12
520 "Parsifal"	8 - 10	10 - 12
FRÜNDT, H. (GER)		
M. Kimmelstiel & Co.		
"Lohengrin," "Walküre," "Fliegende Hollander"	18 - 22	22 - 26
Others	20 - 22	22 - 26
GEIGER, C. A. (GER)		
Marke J.S.C. 6108 "Tannhaüser"	12 - 15	15 - 18

GLOTZ, A. D. (GER)
   "Parsival" Series   12 - 15   15 - 18
   Series 22   8 - 10   10 - 12
GOETZ (GER)   8 - 10   10 - 12
HENDRICHS (GER)
   Poster "Siegfried's Tod"   15 - 18   18 - 22
HOFFMAN, H. (GER) "Siegfried" (6) 12 - 15   15 - 20
JANOWITSCH (AUS)
   B.K.W.I.
     3219 "Parsifal"   8 - 10   10 - 12
KLIMESOVA, M.   10 - 12   12 - 15
KUDERNY, F. (AUS)
   Deutsch. Dereines fur Osterreich
   "Die Nibelungen" Posters
     "Kriemfild," "Siegfried"   15 - 18   18 - 22
     Others   15 - 18   18 - 22
KUTZER, E. (AUS)
   B.K.W.I. Series 438 Poster Cards (6)
     1 "Tannhäuser"   20 - 25   25 - 28
     2 "Der Fliegende Holländers" 20 - 25   25 - 28
     3 "Meistersinger"   20 - 25   25 - 28
     4 "Parsifal"   20 - 25   25 - 28
     5 Wagner's "Rienzi"   20 - 25   25 - 28
     6 "Löhengrin"   20 - 25   25 - 28
   Vereines Sudmark
     245 "Die Meistersinger von Nürnberg" 20 - 25   25 - 28
     246 "Die Meistersinger von Nürnberg" 20 - 25   25 - 28
     247 "Die Meistersinger von Nürnberg" 20 - 25   25 - 28
     248 "Löhengrin"   20 - 25   25 - 28
     249 "Tristan und Isolde"   20 - 25   25 - 28
     252 "Tannhäuser"   20 - 25   25 - 28
     253 "Die Walküre"   20 - 25   25 - 28
     254 "Das Rheingold"   20 - 25   25 - 28
     255 "Siegfried"   20 - 25   25 - 28
     256 "Siegfried"   20 - 25   25 - 28
   Schulverein fur Osterreich
   "Die Nibelungen" Poster Cards (8)
     "Siegfried und der Trache" (Dragon) 18 - 22   22 - 26
   L.R.
     1096 "Parsifal"   10 - 12   12 - 15
     1097 "Siegfried"   10 - 12   12 - 15
     Others   10 - 12   12 - 15
LEEKE, FERDINAND (GER)
   M. Munk, Vienna
   Series 861 (12)
     "Die Feen"   8 - 10   10 - 12
     "Die Meistersinger" (The Master Singer from
       Nürnberg)   8 - 10   10 - 12
     "Die Walküre" (The Valkyrie)   8 - 10   10 - 12

F. Leeke, Hanfstaengl's No. 17
Series 72, "Lohengrin"

F. Leeke, L. Pernitzsch, No. 8
"Lohengrin

"Götterdämmerung" (Twilight of the Gods)	10 - 12	12 - 15
"Löhengrin"	8 - 10	10 - 12
"Parsifal"	10 - 12	12 - 14
"Rienzi"	8 - 10	10 - 12
"Rheingold"	10 - 12	12 - 15
"Siegfried"	8 - 10	10 - 12
"Tannhaüser"	8 - 10	10 - 12
"Tristan und Isolde"	10 - 12	12 - 14
"Tristan und Isolde"	10 - 12	12 - 14
Series 982 (12)		
Same images as **Series 861**	8 - 10	10 - 12
984 and E984 (12) Reprint of **Series 861**	6 - 8	8 - 10
Hanfstaengl's Kunstlerkarte or **H.K.M. Co.**		
Series 72 (6)		
"Die Walküre," "Götterdämmerung"	10 - 12	12 - 15
"Löhengrin," "Siegfried"	10 - 12	12 - 15
"Tannhäuser," "Tristan und Isolde"	10 - 12	12 - 15
H.K.M. Co.		
Series 12 Same as series 72	10 - 12	12 - 15
Poster Cards		
L. Pernitzch		
"Richard Wagner's Heldengestalten" (24)		
1 "Rienzi"	15 - 18	18 - 22
2 "Der Fliegende Holländer"		
(The Flying Dutchman)	15 - 18	18 - 22

3 "Der Fliegende Holländer"	15 - 18	18 - 22
4 "Tannhäuser"	15 - 18	18 - 22
5 "Tannhäuser"	15 - 18	18 - 22
6 "Tannhäuser"	15 - 18	18 - 22
7 "Löhengrin"	15 - 18	18 - 22
8 "Löhengrin"	15 - 18	18 - 22
9 "Tristan und Isolde"	15 - 18	18 - 22
10 "Tristan und Isolde"	15 - 18	18 - 22
11 "Tristan und Isolde"	15 - 18	18 - 22
14 "Die Walküre"	15 - 18	18 - 22
15 "Die Walküre"	15 - 18	18 - 22
16 "Die Walküre"	15 - 18	18 - 22
17 "Siegfried"	15 - 18	18 - 22
18 "Siegfried"	15 - 18	18 - 22
21 "Götterdämmerung"	15 - 18	18 - 22
22 "Götterdämmerung"	15 - 18	18 - 22
23 "Götterdämmerung"	15 - 18	18 - 22
24 "Götterdämmerung"	15 - 18	18 - 22

LEFLER, PROF. HEINRICH (AUS)
  M. Munk, Vienna
  Wagner's Frauengsetalten Series 1281 (6)

"Brünhilde" - Götterdämmerung	15 - 20	20 - 25
"Elisabeth" - Tannhäuser	15 - 20	20 - 25
"Elsa" - Löhengrin	15 - 20	20 - 25
"Eva" - Die Meistersinger	15 - 20	20 - 25
"Fricka" - Die Walküre	15 - 20	20 - 25
"Isolde" - Tristan and Isolde	15 - 20	20 - 25
"Ortrud" - Löhengrin	15 - 20	20 - 25

LUDVIG

Series 718 (6)	8 - 10	10 - 12

NOWAK, OTTO (AUS)
  B.K.W.I.

Series 1412 "Parsival"	8 - 10	10 - 12
Series 2352 "Wotan"	8 - 10	10 - 12
PEETE "Siegfried" and the Dragon	12 - 15	15 - 20

PETER, O. (GER)

Series 399 "Brünhilde"	12 - 15	15 - 20

PILGER

"Tannhaüser" (With Music)	10 - 12	12 - 15

PINGGERA, HEINZ (AUS)
  Bund der Deutchen in Niederösterrich
  Series 242-252   Poster cards

242 "Siegfried"	18 - 22	22 - 26
248 "Herr Olof"	18 - 22	22 - 26
250 "Tannhaüser im Sorfelberg"	18 - 22	22 - 26
750 "Götterdämmerung"	18 - 22	22 - 26
751 "Die Walküre"	18 - 22	22 - 26
752 "Tannhaüser"	18 - 22	22- 26

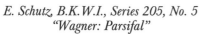

E. Schutz, B.K.W.I., Series 205, No. 5
"Wagner: Parsifal"

F. Stassen, R. Tuck, Series 1219
"Walküre"

PRINTZ, HANNS (AUS)
  T.S.N. (**Theo. Stroefer,** Nürnberg)
    Series 1370 (6) Chromolithographs

"Das Rheingold" Mermaid	30 - 35	35 - 40
"Die Meistersinger von Nürnberg"	25 - 30	30 - 35
"Die Walküre"	25 - 30	30 - 35
"Löhengrin"	25 - 30	30 - 35
"Parsival"	25 - 30	30 - 35
"Tannhäuser"	25 - 30	30 - 35

ROWLAND, FR. (GER)

Series 258 "Parsifal"	18 - 22	22 - 26

SCHLIMARSKI
  Series 420 (6)

1 "Parsifal"	10 - 12	12 - 15
Others	10 - 12	12 - 15

SCHUTZ, ERIC (Austria)
  B.K.W.I.
    Series 205 Musical Posters (6)

1 "Wagner - Parsifal"	20 - 25	25 - 30
4 "Wagner - Parsifal"	20 - 25	25 - 30
5 "Wagner - Parsifal"	20 - 25	25 - 30
6 "Wagner - Parsifal"	20 - 25	25 - 30

    Series 438 Posters

1 "Tannhäuser"	20 - 25	25 - 30
2 "Der Fliegende Holländers"	20 - 25	25 - 30

3 "Meistersinger"	20 - 25	25 - 30
4 "Tristan & Isolde"	20 - 25	25 - 30
5 "Rienzi"	20 - 25	25 - 30
6 "Löhengrin"	20 - 25	25 - 30
SINZ, MAX	8 - 10	10 - 12
SPIELZ, A. (GER)		
Series 247 (6)		
4423 "Parsival"	10 - 12	12 - 15
STASSEN, FRANZ (GER)		
H & A Bruning		
Richard Wagner Series (6)		
5990 11 "Elsa"	20 - 25	25 - 30
6991 III "Venusburg"	20 - 25	25 - 30
6992 IV	20 - 25	25 - 30
6993 V "Brünhild"	20 - 25	25 - 30
6994 XIV "Senta"	20 - 25	25 - 30
Raphael Tuck		
"Wagner" Series		
Series 690 "Siegfried"	22 - 25	25 - 30
Series 691 "Löhengrin"	22 - 25	25 - 30
Series 692 "Götterdämmerung"	22 - 25	25 - 30
Series 693 "Tristan and Isolde"	22 - 25	25 - 30
Series 694 "The Rheingold"	22 - 25	25 - 30
Series 695 "The Flying Dutchman"	22 - 25	25 - 30
German "Modern Meister" XX, 1219 (6)		
"Götterdämmerung," "Löhengrin"	20 - 25	25 - 30
"Walkure," "Rheingold"	20 - 25	25 - 30
"Siegfried," "Tristan und Isolde"	20 - 25	25 - 30
E.S.D. (Unsigned Stassen)*		
German and American Art Nouveau Series		
8157 "Die Walküre" (6)	18 - 22	22 - 25
8158 "Siegfried" (6) Add $5 for dragon images.	18 - 22	22 - 25
8159 "Das Rheingold" (6)	18 - 22	22 - 25
Add $15 for Mermaid Images		
8160 "Götterdämmerung" (6)	18 - 22	22 - 25
8161 "Die Meistersinger" (6)	18 - 22	22 - 25
8162 "Tristan und Isolde" (6)	18 - 22	22 - 25
8163 "Der Fliegende Holländer" (6)	18 - 22	22 - 25
8164 "Löhengrin" (6)	12 - 15	15 - 18
* Same caption number on both U.S. and German		
TOEPPER, HANS (GER)		
F. A. Ackerman, München (Continental size)		
Series 625 "Ring des Nibelungen" (12)	12 - 15	15 - 20
TOUSSAINT "Isolde"	8 - 10	10 - 12
WEISLEIN "Barbarossa" Poster	10 - 15	15 - 18
PUBLISHERS		
B. & W. 271 "Siegfried's Death"	12 - 15	15 - 20
B.K.W.I. Series 206, 438 (6)	12 - 15	15 - 20

Wilhelm Boehme		
"Altgermanische Gotter" 625-630 (6)	12 - 15	15 - 18
F.M.K.		
3153 "Löhengrin" (6)		
FRG		
Series 247 "Parsifal" (6)	12 - 15	15 - 18
Series 258 "Löhengrin" (6)	12 - 15	15 - 18
C. W. Faulkner 1401 "Die Feen"	12 - 15	15 - 18
M. Munk, Vienna		
Wagner's Series 28	15 - 18	18 - 22
Ricordi & Co.		
"Siegfried & the Dragon"	8 - 10	10 - 15
Ladies in Wagner's Operas	12 - 15	15 - 18
T.S.N. (Theo. Stroefer)		
Series 141 "Löhengrin" (6)	15 - 18	18 - 22
Raphael Tuck *		
"Wagner" Series See Franz Stassen		
* Same as E.S.D. Series Above		
Series XX, 1219 "Modern Meister" (6)	18 - 22	22 - 25
Same Captions as "Wagner" Series (6)	18 - 22	22 - 25
Stengel & Co.		
29132 "Die Walküre"	8 - 10	10 - 12
Ottmar Ziehr		
Wagner's Operas (6)	25 - 28	28 - 32

DEATH FANTASY

Death is a process of nature for all mankind and, in that vein, it certainly is not a fantasy. However, some of the events that precede it make it so. The fears and anguish of growing old, the thoughts of wars and pestilence, and the torment of dying with a deadly, lingering disease all bring fantastic thoughts and dreams which are indeed Death Fantasy.

Death, while feared by many, may be relatively calm and peaceful for some. Death, in myth and literature, has been portrayed by writers and artists as one of the greatest enemies of man. Picture the black-hooded Grim Reaper with his merciless scythe–a skeleton on a black horse with eyes of madness and nostrils flaring–a smiling death head so sure of his prey–and a cynical staring death head laughing at the foolish as they drink and revel. These are the epic images in a fantasy world.

BALUSCHECK		
"Ghost and Death"	10 - 12	12 - 15
BÖCKLIN, A. (GER)		
Julius Bard, Berlin		
"Der Kreig"	15 - 18	18 - 22
F. Bruckmann, München		
"Selfportrait mit Tod"	12 - 15	15 - 20
BÜRFEL, G. (GER)		
Death in Black	12 - 15	15 - 20

CIEZKIEWKZ, E.
"Girl in Red"	12 - 15	15 - 20
"Woman & Skull"	12 - 15	15 - 18
"Le Nocturne de Chopin"	15 - 18	18 - 20
Girl looks at death	12 - 15	15 - 18

CHOPIN, FR.
Series 116 "Playing Death"	10 - 12	12 - 15

CORBELLA, TITO (IT)
Uff. Rev. Stampa, Milano
Series 268 "Death and Edith Cavell"
1 - "Cavell Standing over the Conquered Figure of Death ..."	15 - 18	18 - 22
2 - "Death Offering Head of Cavell ..."	15 - 18	18 - 22
3 - "Death and Arrogant German Officer ..."	15 - 18	18 - 22
4 - "Cavell Standing Before Death ..."	15 - 18	18 - 22
5 - "Death Hovers as Cavell Gives Water ..."	15 - 18	18 - 22
6 - "Death Plays Piano as Cavell Lies ..."	15 - 18	18 - 22

ERLANG
"Die Vision," Nude and Death Head	15 - 20	20 - 25

FAHRENKROG, LUDVIG (GER)
Wilhelm Hartung 104 "Fate"	15 - 18	18 - 22

FISCHER, J. (CZ)
Minerva, Prague
40 "Spectre de la guerre"	15 - 18	18 - 22

GASSNER
Death on a Black Horse	12 - 15	15 - 20

GOLTZ, A. D. (GER)
"Illusion"	12 - 15	15 - 20

HERING, ADOLF (GER)
Arthur Rehn & Co.
"Der Tod and das Madchen"	18 - 22	22 - 25

KELLER, FERDINAND   (GER)
Franz Hanfstaengl "Finale"	12 - 15	15 - 20

JUNG, F.
Ghost in the swamp	8 - 10	10 - 12

KLAKARSCHEVA "Ikarus" | 10 - 12 | 12 - 15 |

KRAMSKOI, I.N. (RUS)
Granbergs #56 "Herodias"	15 - 20	20 - 25

KORPAK, T.
Ghost and Death	12 - 15	15 - 20

LAMM, ERICH (AUS)
B.K.W.I. 1521 Death in the Field	10 - 12	12 - 15
LEOPAROVA "Fable"	12 - 15	15 - 20

LIST, FR. (HUN)
Series 116/2
"Rhapsodie Hongroise"	10 - 12	12 - 15
MANDL, J. "The End"	12 - 15	15 - 18

E. Winkler, Goldfullfederkonig, Wien
"Die Figuren sind in Lebensgrosse"

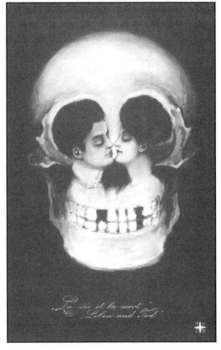

A.H.D., Novitas, #21-101
No Caption

Anonymous, Published by N.V.S.B.
"Lieben und Tod"

NEJEDLY
  Salon J.P.P. "Inspiration"   12 - 15   15 - 18
PETER, O. (GER)
  400 Burning Nudes   12 - 15   15 - 20
PODKOWINSKI (PO)
  Nude on Fiery Horse   15 - 18   18 - 22
REASTELLI "The Coming Storm"   12 - 15   15 - 18
WACHSMUTH, M. (GER)
  P.F.B. in diamond "Die Beute"   12 - 15   15 - 20
WILFE
  Poster "Der Walschrat"   15 - 18   18 - 22
WINKLER, E. (AUS)
  Goldfullfederkonig, Wien
    "Die Figuren sind..."   20 - 25   25 - 30
WOLFF, H. (GER)
  P.F.B. in diamond
  4480 Death Rides a Horse   12 - 15   15 - 20
WOLLNER, H. (GER)
  B.K.W.I.
    2402 "Seduction"   15 - 18   18 - 25
  P.F.B. Series 226   15 - 20   20 - 25
  Anonymous   12 - 15   15 - 18
    Death Fiddles while Clowns Dance (Und.)   20 - 25   25 - 30
ANONYMOUS
  Unidentified Russian Artist, #1753
    Nude & Death   15 - 20   20 - 25

DEATH HEADS

A.H.D.
  Novitas
    21-101 Death Head on car body   20 - 25   25 - 28
    21-102 Death Head with 2 Drinkers   20 - 25   25 - 28
WOLLNER, H. (AUS)
  B.K.W.I. 1101 "Sadismus" (Death Head)   12 - 15   15 - 18
PUBLISHERS
  Rotophot   20 - 25   25 - 30
  N.V.S.B.   Lovers, "Lieben und Tod" (R.P.)   20 - 25   25 - 28
  Ramer Publishers   35 - 50   50 100
  SB
    Death Head; Lovers Drinking (6)   18 - 22   22 - 25
  Schweizer
    129 Death Head - "All is Vanity"   20 - 22   22 - 25
Real Photos Types
    "L'amour de Pierrot"   25 - 30   30 - 35
  P.F.B.   226 "Lettre d'adieu"   25 - 30   30 - 35
    "Napoleon" (2)   25 - 30   30 - 35
    09-585 Death Head; Man-Woman cooking   22 - 25   25 - 28

NUDE FANTASY

BENDER, S.
   H.R. "La Femme" Series
      Reclining nude with animals (12)

1217 With parrot	20 - 25	25 - 30
1220 With monkey and spider	20 - 25	25 - 30
1222 With cat	20 - 25	25 - 30
Others	20 - 25	25 - 30

   Others

(Snakes)	12 - 15	15 - 20

BEROUD, L. (FR)
   Salon 1901

Series 201-20 "Fantasie" Tiger and nude	15 - 20	20 - 25

BÖCKLIN, A. (GER)
   Bruckmann A. G.

6 "Die Nereide"	12 - 15	15 - 18
16 "Im Meere" (Nude and Merman)	12 - 15	15 - 18
21 "Triton & Nereide" (Merman)	12 - 15	15 - 18
"Spiel der Wellen" Nudes and Horse-man	15 - 20	20 - 25

BRAUNE, E. (AUS)

Amag Kunst 63. "Walküre" (Horse)	12 - 15	15 - 22

CABANEL, A. (FR)
   Salon J.P.P.

2206 "Nymph & Faun" (Man-Goat)	15 - 18	18 - 22

CIKOS-SESIA, B. (YUGO)
   Edition Camoos

"Salome"	20 - 25	25 - 30

COURSELLES DUMONT, H. (FR)

Lapina 564. "In der Arena" (Lion)	12 - 15	15 - 20
Salon de 1912 47. "In the Arena" (Lion)		

DE BOUCHE, A. (GER)

Moderner Kunst, Berlin 2516 "Salambo"	15 - 20	20 - 25

DUSSEK, E. A. (AUS)

J.K. 69 "Froschkönigs Braut" (Frog)	22 - 25	25 - 30

FIDUS

Among the most beautiful fantasy real photo nudes on postcards are the graphic works of Hugo Hoppener (who used the pen name of Fidus). He did great drawings of nude and sometimes erotic young ladies and young boys, plus many others, for his books, posters and magazines. In most of his works he used very precise graphic border illustrations which greatly enhanced their beauty.

To advertise and sell these works he published real photo advertising postcards, describing each of them, and distributed the cards widely. It is not known just how successful he was in selling his works with the cards, but the cards themselves have become extremely popular with collectors. The series entitled "Tempeltanz der Seele" (Temple Dance of the Soul) of young maidens standing on fantasy petals, leaves, stems and the universe, is probably the most sought after by today's collector. However, Fidus did many others in the fantasy vein that are also in great demand.

B. Cikos-Sesia, Edition Camoos
"Salome"

Fidus, St. Georgs-Bundes 102
"Tempeltanz der Seele II"

FIDUS or **Hugo Hoppener**   (GER)
  N.B.C. (Real Photos)

2 "Drachen Kampfer" Nudes and Dragon	25 - 28	28 - 35
101 "Tempeltanz Der Seele I"	30 - 35	35 - 45
102 "Tempeltanz Der Seele II"	30 - 35	35 - 45
103 "Tempeltanz Der Seele III"	30 - 35	35 - 45
104 "Tempeltanz Der Seele IV"	30 - 35	35 - 45
105 "Tempeltanz Der Seele V"	30 - 35	35 - 45
106 "Tempeltanz Der Seele VI"	30 - 35	35 - 45
134 "Erwartung" Nude in white birch grove	20 - 25	25 - 35
135 "Sterntänzerin" Nude standing on globe	30 - 35	35 - 45
393 Nude and statue of Wagner	20 - 25	25 - 30
515 "Neapmierinatais Lucifers" Satan	20 - 25	25 - 30
Many other Fantasy types	20 - 25	25 - 30
Others – non-Fantasy	12 - 15	15 - 20

FISCHER-COERLINE (GER)
  M.K.B.   2475. "Salome" (Severed Head)   18 - 22   22 - 25

FRATINO, CESARE (IT)
  Rev. Stampa   Series 123, "Salambo"   20 - 25   25 - 30

GEBHARDT, CARL (GER)
  E.M.   132. "Loreley"   20 - 25   25 - 28

GEIGER, C. A. (HUN)
  Marke J.S.C.
    6109 "Liebeskampf" (Man-Sea Beast)   18 - 22   22 - 25

Cesare Fratino, Rev. Stampa, #123
"Salambo"

Ferd. Leete, Munchener Kunst, #3113
"Nidre und Wassermann"

6112 "Salome" (Severed Head)	20 - 25	25 - 28
GIOVANNI, A. (IT)		
ARS Minima 119. "Salome" (Severed Head)	12 - 15	15 - 20
GLOTZ, A. D. (GER)		
B.K.W.I. 1009 "Lebensluge" (Ghost of Dead)	12 - 15	15 - 20
HIRSCH	10 - 12	12 - 15
HOESSLIN, GEORGE		
NPG 491 "Die Schaumgebstene"		
(Nude in Oyster Shell)	15 - 18	18 - 22
HORST (GER)		
P.F.B. in Diamond		
4323 Semi Nude and Horse Drink	12 - 15	15 - 20
ICHNOWSKI, M. (PO)		
Series 90 16. Nude and Lion	18 - 22	22 - 25
KANDLER, V. (GER) Nude and Snake	15 - 20	20 - 25
KELLER, F. (GER)		
Russian Publisher 076. "Finale" (Death Head)	15 - 18	18 - 22
KOMINEL	15 - 18	18 - 22
KORPAL	15 - 18	18 - 22
LAMM	15 - 18	18 - 22
LANGENMANTEL Nude on Bull	12 - 15	15 - 20
LEETE, F. (GER)		
Münchener Kunst		
3113 "Nidre und Wasserman" (Water Creature)	12 - 15	15 - 20

3114 "Gefangene Nymphe" (Dwarfs)	12 - 15	15 - 18
3117 "Triton Belaufde Nereide" (Merman)	15 - 18	18 - 22
LENOIR, CH. (France)		
Lapina 5122 "Victory!!" (Octopus)	22 - 25	25 - 28
LEOPAROVA		
KV		
1183 "Salome" (Severed Head)	12 - 15	15 - 20
LINS, ADOLF (GER)		
EAS 607 "Faun and Nymphe"	12 - 15	15 - 18
MANDL, J.		
Minerva 177 "Printemps" (Wings)	10 - 12	12 - 15
MASTAGLIO (GER)		
Galerie Münchener Meister		
380 "Duell" (Nudes Fencing)	12 - 15	15 - 20
MASTROIANNI, C. (IT)		
198 "Fievre d'Amore" (Waterfall)	10 - 12	12 - 15
MEUNIER, SUZANNE (FR)		
MARQUE L. E.		
Series 64 (6) Nudes & big snakes	35 - 40	40 - 45
MICHAELIS, O.		
P.F.B. **Series 4416** "Centaur und Nymphe"	20 - 25	25 - 30
MÜHLBERG, GEORG (GER)		
Nude Riding a Seahorse	12 - 15	15 - 20
MÜLLER, PROF. RICH (AUS)		
251 Nude riding goldfish "Perlen"	20 - 22	22 - 25
252 Nude with red Ibis	20 - 25	25 - 28
MÜLLER-BAUMGARTEN (GER)		
FEM 161 "Faun & Nymphe" (Man-Goat)	10 - 12	12 - 15
MUTTICH, C. V. (CZ)		
V.K.K.V. 2077 "Sulejka" (Peacock)	12 - 15	15 - 20
OKON, T.		
Stella, Bochina 1233 Nude and black cat	15 - 18	18 - 22
PENOT, Albert (FR)		
Lapina		
1340 "Red Butterfly" (Red-Winged Nude)	15 - 18	18 - 22
PETER, O.		
S.V.D. #400 "Die lebenden Fackeln Neros"	20 - 25	25 - 30
PIOTROWSKI, A. (PO)		
Minerva		
505 Woman/Children/Serpent	15 - 20	20 - 25
1028 "Salome" (Severed Head)	18 - 22	22 - 25
Marke J.S.C.		
6082 "Charmeuse de Serpents" (Snake)	15 - 18	18 - 22
PODKOWINSKI (PO)		
Nude on wild Horse	18 - 22	22 - 25
RAVA, GIOVANNI (IT)		
Rev. Stampa		
515 "Salome"	25 - 30	30 - 35

O. Peter, S.V.D., #400
"Die lebenden Fackeln Neros"

Giovanni Rava, Rev. Stampa, #515
"Salome"

REINACKER, PROF. G. (GER)
  P.F.B.
    6082 "Schlangen-Bandigerin" (Snake)   15 - 20   20 - 25
  Marke J.S.C.
    6082 Same as above   15 - 20   20 - 25
ROTHAUG, ALEX (GER)
  LP   2815 "Pan and Psyche" (Man-Beast)   15 - 18   18 - 22
  W.R.B. & Company   No. 4 "Nymphe"   12 - 15   15 - 20
ROWLAND, FR. (GB)
  SVD   379 "Sirenen" (Snakes)   18 - 22   22 - 25
ROYER, L. (FR)
  Salon de Paris   374 "La Sirene" (Death Head)   15 - 18   18 - 22
RÜDISÜHLI, EDUARD
  K.E.B.   "The Demon of Love"   12 - 15   15 - 20
SAMSON, E. (FR)
  A.N., Paris
    243 "Diane" (Wolf Dogs)   15 - 18   18 - 22
SCALBRET, J.
  S.P.A.
    48 "Leda & the Swan"   10 - 12   12 - 15
SCHIFF, R. (GER)
  W.R.B. & Co.
    22-74 "Leda & the Swan"   15 - 18   18 - 22
    22-74 "Head in Clouds"   12 - 15   15 - 20

S. Schneider, Schonheit, Dresden, #A-24 – "Hercules and Omphale"

SCHIVERT, V. (GER)
    Arthur Rehn & Co. "Die Hexe"   20 - 25   25 - 30
SCHMUTZLER, L. (GER)
    Russian Publisher, Richard
      245 "Salome" (Severed Head)   15 - 18   18 - 22
SCHNEIDER, S. (GER) Real Photos *
      182 Nude adorned with thorny shoots   30 - 35   35 - 40
      1085 Flying man-bull and student   25 - 30   30 - 35
      1088 Supernatural animal, angel, corpse   25 - 30   30 - 35
      Death mourner and huge breasted beast   20 - 25   25 - 30
      1216 Nude with torch & eerie monster   30 - 35   35 - 40
      1235 Nude in chains & eerie monster   30 - 35   35 - 40
      1245 Nude bird-man with slave   20 - 25   25 - 30
    * Deduct $10 for printed cards
    Schönheit, Dresden
      A-24 "Hercules and Omphale"   30 - 35   35 - 40
SCHUTZ, ERIC (AUS)
    B.K.W.I. Poster Cards
      41 "The Frog King" (Big Frog)   20 - 25   25 - 30
      885 Goethe's "Der Fischer" (Mermaid)   35 - 40   40 - 50
      885 "Der Gott und Der Baiadere" Nude   20 - 25   25 - 30
      979 "Die Forelle" (Mermaid)   35 - 40   40 - 50
      205 Wagner's "Parsival"   15 - 20   20 - 25
      557 "Lotusblume" (Nude in flower)   25 - 30   30 - 40
      Series 165 (6) (Nudes on Giant Flowers)   25 - 30   30 - 35
SETKOWICZ
    Music, Harp and Snakes   18 - 22   22 - 25

SIMONSON-CASTELLI, PROF.
Hans Friedrich

565 Nude and big snake	15 - 20	20 - 25

SOLOMKO, S. (RUS)
T.S.N.

"The Blue Bird," "Circe," "Dream of Icarius,"	15 - 20	20 - 25
"Fortune Telling," "Glow Worm," "Phantasy"	15 - 20	20 - 25
Semi-Nude in Peacock Feathers	18 - 22	22 - 26
"The Tale"	15 - 20	20 - 25

STANKE, W. (GER)
S.W.S.B.

4776 "Das Marchen" Nude with horse	10 - 12	12 - 15
4777 "Das Geheimnis" Nude with horse	10 - 12	12 - 15

STELLA, EDUARD (GER)
B.R.W.

354 "Diana" (W/Dogs)	20 - 25	25 - 28

STRNAD, JOS. (GER)

Anonymous 255 "Nymphe"	12 - 15	15 - 20

STUCK, FRANZ VON (GER)

	10 - 12	12 - 15

STYKA, JAN (FR)

Lapina 810 "Good Friends" (Horse)	10 - 12	12 - 15

SZYNDIER, P. (PO)

Mal. Polske 22 "Éve" (Snakes)	20 - 25	25 - 30

TABARY, EMILE (FR)

Salon de Paris "The Lover Lion"	15 - 20	20 - 25
THOMAS "Leda" Nude and Swan	12 - 15	15 - 20

VEITH, E. (AUS)

B.K.W.I. 1101 "Teasing" (Man-Goat)	10 - 12	12 - 15
WACHSMUTH, M.	10 - 12	12 - 15
WARZENIECKI, M.	12 - 15	15 - 18

WILSA

90 "Une Nouvelle Esclave" (Death)	12 - 15	15 - 18

ZANDER (GER)
S.S.W.B.

4790 "Sieg der Schönheit" (Tiger)	12 - 15	15 - 18

ZATZKA, H. (NETH)

Panphot, Vienne 1284 "La Perle"		
(Nude in Large Oyster Shell)	15 - 18	18 - 22

ANONYMOUS

Russian

Real Photo 547 Nude and Moon	25 - 30	30 - 35
Real Photo 752 Nude with Snake	18 - 22	22 - 26
Real Photo No No. Centaur and Nude	18 - 22	22 - 26

MERMAIDS

The mermaid was a mythical creature that lived in the seas and streams. According to popular belief they had bodies that were half human and half fish.

Their beauty and mystique, as they sang and combed their long hair, was a great attraction for mortal men. A magical cap always lay beside them, and when the man they wanted appeared they would slip the cap on his head and take him away with them. A human being could live in the sea by wearing this cap. There were, on the other hand, mermen who also captured mortal maidens.

Through the years, mermaids and mermen have continued to be painted or dramatized in art and poetry. Certain sea animals–e.g., seals–look a little like humans from a distance. This similarity may explain the myths related to them.

The most beautiful mermaids on postcards are the works of Eric Schutz and Sofia Chiostri, "The Mermaid" series by Raphael Tuck, the Art Nouveau series by Gaston Noury, and the great early anonymous German chromolithographs. All are extremely scarce and are in great demand.

ABILLE (FR)		
French "Political"	75 - 100	100 - 135
ADOLF, T. (GER)	15 - 18	18 - 22
ATTWELL, MABEL LUCIE (GB)		
Valentine & Sons 951 (With Black Doll)	25 - 30	30 - 40
E.B. (GER)		
M. L. Cartlens, Hamburg		
Series 5508 "Ein Guter Fang"	15 - 20	20 - 25
BENEZUR "Der Kampf"	15 - 20	20 - 25
BERNHARD, L. (AUS)		
Karl H. Detlefsen		
Series 3156 B&W "Ein Stelldichen"	12 - 15	15 - 20
BÖCKLIN, A. (GER)		
F. Bruckmann AG		
"Play of Naiads"	12 - 15	15 - 20
"Im Spiel der Wellen"	12 - 15	15 - 20
BOISSELIER (FR)		
Salon de Paris 1143 "Les Nerides"	15 - 18	18 - 22
BRUNNER		
Art Moderne Series 715 (6)	12 - 15	15 - 20
BUXTON, DUDLEY (GB)		
Bamforth Co.		
"Ye Gods: It's the Missus!"	8 - 10	10 - 12
CARTER, REG. (G.B.)		
Max Ettlinger & Co.		
Series 4453 (Diver Series) (6)		
"A Diver walked along one day..."	18 - 22	22 - 26
"They fell in love..."	18 - 22	22 - 26
"Things cannot go on like this..."	18 - 22	22 - 26
"They went for a walk..."	18 - 22	22 - 26
"But true love not always runs smooth..."	18 - 22	22 - 26
"Her father passed by that way..."	18 - 22	22 - 26
CHIOSTRI, SOFIA (IT)		
Ballerini & Fratini		
Series 238 Cupid and Mermaid (4) Deco	50 - 60	60 - 80
Series 317 (4) Deco	50 - 60	60 - 80

CLAY, JOHN CECIL (US)
  Alfred Schweizer
    Gibson Karte 1018 No Caption, Sepia   15 - 18   18 - 22
COT, WILLIAM (FR)
  AN, Paris Real Photo #224   15 - 18   18 - 22
DUBOSCLARD, PAUL (US)
  M. A. Sheehan (Serigraphs)   10 - 12   12 - 15
FISCHER, SAMUEL (SW)
  "Boecklin Jubilaeum Basel" (Undb)   40 - 50   50 - 60
FITZPATRICK (GB)
  Bamforth & Co.   8 - 10   10 - 15
FULLER, EDMUND G. (GB)
  "Midsummer Nights Dream" Series   15 - 20   20 - 25
GEO. Valentine's "Mr. Popple sees a Mermaid"   15 - 20   20 - 25
GIBBS, MAY (AUST)
  Western Mail Postcards (B&W)
    "Pearling in the Norwest"   80 - 90   90 - 100
GIRARDOT, GEORGES (FR)
  Societe des Artistes Francais
    "Siren at the mirror" (R.P.)   12 - 15   15 - 20
GOHLER, H.
  "Rishar" Russian
    566 "Du Nixlein Wunderhold..."   30 - 35   35 - 40

H. Kley, E. von König, No. 118
"Rheingold, Rheingold!"

M. Liebenwein, B.K.W.I., 1028
"L'etang Decrie" (The Frog King)

Abille, French Political,"Le Vertige –
Nicolas au Bord de L'abime"

GRIMM (AUS)	12 - 15	15 - 20
GUILLAUME, ALBERT A. (FR)		
A.N., Paris "The Wreck"	20 - 25	25 - 30
Art Moderne Series 764 "Seetrift"	20 - 25	25 - 28
GUTMANN, BESSIE PEASE (See Children)		
Rishar (Russian) Russian Caption		
99 "Die Perle"	80 - 90	100 - 110
100 "Wasserlilie"	80 - 90	100 - 110
H.F.	10 - 12	12 - 15
H.N.		
Rud. Stolle 472 "Kuste bei Georgenwalde"	10 - 15	15 - 18
IRWIN	6 - 8	8 - 10
JACOBS, HELEN (GB)		
C. W. Faulkner		
Series 1764 (6)	18 - 22	22 - 25
KASPARIDES "Bath of Water Fairy"	15 - 20	20 - 25
KENNEDY, C. N. (GB)		
Leeds Gallery "The Mermaid"	5 - 6	6 - 8
KIRCHNER, RAPHAEL (AUS)		
Anonymous "Flussnixe"	150 - 200	200 - 250
Marque L-E "Ondine"	100 - 125	125 - 150
KLEY, H. (GER)		
EDM		
366 "Rheingold, Rheingold!" (B&W)	10 - 12	12 - 15
E. von König		
118 "Rheingold, Rheingold!" (C)	20 - 25	25 - 28
KUPFER, B.		
Klio		
#852 "Les Sirenes"	25 - 30	30 - 35
LA PIERRE-RENOUARD (FR)		
Lapina, Paris		
1312 "Idyll"	12 - 15	15 - 20
LEEKE, F. (GER)		
Münchener Kunst		
3116 "De Taufe des Fawn"	15 - 20	20 - 25
LIEBENWEIN, M. (AUS)		
B.K.W.I.		
1028 "L'etang Decrie"	40 - 45	45 - 55
LOWY, J.		
Anonymous (B&W) Baby Mermaids	20 - 25	25 - 30
LUPIAC, A. P. (FR)		
A.N., Paris		
79 "Centaur and sea-maid"	25 - 28	28 - 32
M. I.		
W. de Haan		
Series 1020 (6) (B&W)	10 - 12	12 - 15
MARAPAN		
Vetta "The Neptune Myth" (1945)	10 - 12	12 - 15

MILLER, HILDA T. (GB) (See Children}		
C. W. Faulkner **Series 1822** (6)	22 - 25	25 - 35
MUNSON, WALT (US)		
Tichnor (Linen) 70327 "Fresh Guy"	6 - 8	8 - 10
E. C. Kropp (Linen)		
C43 "Believe it or not"	6 - 8	8 - 10
NOURY, GASTON (FR)		
Anonymous Series (8) Chromolithos	125 - 150	150 - 175
O'NEILL, ROSE (US)		
Gibson Art Co.		
96014 "For the Rainy Day"	40 - 45	45 - 50
OUTHWAITE, IDA R. (AUST) (See Fairies)		
A. & C. Black, London		
Series 73 "Playing with Bubbles"	35 - 40	40 - 50
PAPPERITZ, G. (GER)		
Real Photos 151-12	10 - 12	12 - 15
M.E.P. (PRICE, MARGARET EVANS) (US)		
C.M. Klump		
Zodiac, Pisces (February & March)	12 - 15	12 - 20
PRINTZ, HANNS (AUS)		
T.S.N. Series 1370 "Das Rheingold"	40 - 45	45 - 50
R.B. Anonymous	25 - 30	30 - 40
RICHARDSON, AGNES (GB)		
Photochrom Co.		
2018 "Now I've caught you"	20 - 25	25 - 30
ROTHAUG, ALEX (GER)		
W. R. B. Co. No. 4 "Nymphe"	20 - 25	25 - 28
S.D. (GER)		
Doring-Kessler, Berlin		
"Das Sitzbad"	100 - 125	125 - 150
SADKO		
(Russian) "Canko" and Alexander III	20 - 25	25 - 30
SAGER, XAVIER (FR)		
Big Letter Card "Un Baiser D'Ostende"	25 - 30	30 - 35
SCHMUTZLER, L. (GER)		
Hanfstaengl Co.	18 - 22	22 - 25
SCHREKHASSE, P. (GER)		
S. Hildesheimer & Co. Series 5317 (6)	8 - 10	10 - 15
Hans Köhler Series 329 (6)	12 - 15	15 - 20
SCHUTZ, ERIC (AUS)		
B.K.W.I. Poster Cards		
203 "Flame of Love"	30 - 35	35 - 40
391-3 Heine - "Der Mond ist ..."	35 - 40	40 - 50
434-4 Andersen's Märchen	30 - 35	35 - 40
766-2 Schubert - "Das Wasser ..."	35 - 40	40 - 50
885-5 Goethe - "Der Fischer"	35 - 40	40 - 50
979-5 Schubert - "Die Forelle"	35 - 40	40 - 50
SHAPPIDIA (FR)		
Anonymous Poster card "La Sirene"	100 - 150	150 - 200

Gaston Noury
Anonymous Chromolithic

Gaston Noury
Anonymous Chromolithic

Hanns Printz, T.S.N. (Theo Stroefer), Series 1370 – "Das Rheingold"

SHINN, COBB and **YAD** (US)
   Anonymous (B&W)   10 - 12   12 - 15

S.D., Doring-Kessler, Berlin
"Das Sitzbad"

French Poster by Shappidia, Anonymous
Publisher, "La Sirene"

SOLOMKO, SERGE (RUS)
  T.S.N.

93 "The Tale"	15 - 18	18 - 25

STEINHAUSER (GER)

August Drosse, Berlin "Gruss aus Friedrichshafen"	30 - 35	35 - 40

STUDDY, GEORGE E. (GB)
  Bonzo Series by Valentine's

Series 2982 "I'm a poor fish..."	12 - 15	15 - 20

TM (US) (Linen)

U.S. Navy card "U.S.S. Pittsburgh"	15 - 20	20 - 25

TOLNAY (HUN)
  Rotophot, Budapest

"Die Quelle" (B&W)	18 - 22	22 - 26
WARNER, CHET (US) Linens	8 - 10	10 - 12

WEISS, R. (SW)

A.W.R., Zurich "Auf Der Meersgrund"	12 - 15	15 - 20

WELLMAN, WALTER (US)

1026 "Beauty isn't all on the surface"	10 - 12	12 - 15

WHITE, FLORA (GB)

W. E. Mack, Hampstead "The Little Mermaid"	18 - 22	22 - 26
Photochrom Co. "Who are You?"	18 - 22	22 - 26

  J. Salmon Co. (6) (Uns.)

3820 "My Hat"	18 - 22	22 - 26
WILKIN, BOB	6 - 8	8 - 10

WINK
L.P. 2772 "Auf Stiller Flut"	12 - 15	15 - 18

WIWEL, KIRSTEN (GER)
Eneret Series 5047 (6) 1950's	8 - 10	10 - 12

PUBLISHERS

American P. C. Co. Series 1319 (6)	10 - 12	12 - 15
E.S.D. "Wagner" Series (Uns. Stassen)		
Series 8158 Scenes from Opera "Seigfried"	25 - 30	30 - 40
Series 8159 From Opera "Das Rheingold"		
No captions	30 - 35	35 - 45
Series 8160 (Emb) (6)		
Scenes from "Das Rheingold"	30 - 35	35 - 45
Series 8164 Scenes from Opera "Löhengrin"	25 - 30	30 - 35
S. Hildeshimer & Co.		
Andersen's "The Little Mermaid"	20 - 25	25 - 30
L.M.M. Series 1010 "Auf Abwegen"	20 - 25	25 - 28
E. S., Lyon Series 122 (B&W)	8 - 10	10 - 12
M. N. Co., 1910		
Unsigned and Unnumbered (10)		
"Come around and play with me"	20 - 25	25 - 30
"Every Queen needs a King"	20 - 25	25 - 30
"I want you and I want you right away"	20 - 25	25 - 30
"If music be the food"	20 - 25	25 - 30
"I'm leading an easy life"	20 - 25	25 - 30
"I'll take another chance"	20 - 25	25 - 30
"I'm going some nowadays"	20 - 25	25 - 30
"I's Oo's little mermaid"	20 - 25	25 - 30
"I'm hooked at last"	20 - 25	25 - 30
"I'm looking for a partner"	20 - 25	25 - 30
"Just meet me at the same old place"	20 - 25	25 - 30
"Tag - You're it!"	20 - 25	25 - 30
M.&L.G.		
National Series, Untitled		
Art Nouveau – With Seashell	25 - 30	30 - 40
Mutoscope Co. Navy comics with mermaids	4 - 5	5 - 7
N.L.M. *		
Metamorphic Real Photo #510		
"Richard Wagner"	50 - 60	60 - 75
* Also published by **The Dutch Shop** #1276	50 - 60	60 - 75
O.Z.M.		
"Souvenir de _____" With Walrus	40 - 50	50 - 65
P.F.B. in Diamond		
S/R. KAMMERER		
Series 6097	12 - 15	15 - 20
Percy McG. Mann, Philadelphia (B&W)	10 - 12	12 - 15
S.W.S.B. Children Series	8 - 10	10 - 12
Salis, München (UndB) Chromolithos	40 - 50	50 - 60

Publisher E.S.D., Series 8159, "Das Rheingold"

Wagner Metamorphic − Mermaid by NLN, No. 510

Theo. Stroefer		
Series IV 314 Mermaid in shell	20 - 25	25 - 35
H. H. Tammen "Here's to the girl..."	8 - 10	10 - 12
Curt Teich Linens		
3C-H549 Ad for Shedd Aquarium	12 - 15	15 - 20
Tichnor Bros. Linens		
"What I saw at..."	8 - 10	10 - 12
Raphael Tuck		
Series 3027 "Fun at the Seaside" (6)	12 - 15	15 - 20
Series 6822 "Mermaid" Series (6)	30 - 40	40 - 50
Series 694 "Wagner" Series "Rhine Gold" (6)	30 - 40	40 - 50
Typo, Boston		
207 "There's something fishy"	6 - 8	8 - 10
Anonymous		
Art Nouveau (Undb) Chromolitho		
Series 643 "Wassernixen" (6)	60 - 70	70 - 80
Series 8160 Mermaid in Seashell	40 - 50	50 - 60
Copenhagen Statue (Early Real Photo)		
"La Petite Sirene"	4 - 5	5 - 6
1 er Avril (French April Fool) Montage	15 - 20	20 - 25
Japanese back, Unknown Artist	40 - 50	50 - 60
Montage (B&W)		
Series 12, #2, Girl's head/Mermaid body	15 - 18	18 - 22
Private Mailing Card (Chromolitho)		
Mermaid & Singing Frog	60 - 70	70 - 80

Embossed Art Nouveau
Anonymous Series 8160

Anonymous Series 643
"Wassernixen"

Real Photo Montage Borders (French)	18 - 22	22 - 25
357, 358, 359	30 - 40	40 - 50
Silhouette Poster "Die Rheintochter"	20 - 25	25 - 30

ADVERTISING

Ackers Chocolates	30 - 35	35 - 40
Fish & Chips (A California Dish)		
Longshaw Card Co. Linen	12 - 15	15 - 18
Hartman Litho	10 - 12	12 - 15

SUPERIOR WOMEN/LITTLE MEN FANTASY

COLLINS, SEWELL

Henderson & Sons		
"Humorous" Series B-8	10 - 12	12 - 15

FASCHE, TH. (GER)

M. Munk, Vienna		
"Diabolo" Series (6)	15 - 20	20 - 25

GIRIS, C. (FR)

ATV, Paris		
Series 135 (6) 2 "Domination"	20 - 25	25 - 28

KRANZLE

H & L, Wien Little Mushroom Men	15 - 20	20 - 25

KUDERNEY, F. (AUS)

M. Munk, Vienna Series 556, 606 (6)	15 - 18	18 - 22

Series 699 (6) Little men on strings	15 - 20	20 - 25
Series 792 "Glückliches Neujahr!" Little men	15 - 18	18 - 22

N.F.

Series 160-165 (6)	10 - 12	12 - 15

KYOPINSKI

Peter Triem Little Men (6)

162 "Der Schuchferne"	12 - 15	15 - 20
163 "Der Eifersuchfige	12 - 15	15 - 20

MAUZAN, L. (FR)

Series 83, Little Men (6)	12 - 15	15 - 18

PEANITSCH, LEO

L.P.

Series 105 "Ihr Spielzeug" Silhouettes	15 - 20	20 - 25

PENOT, A.

Lapina Little Men Series (6)	15 - 20	20 - 25

SAGER, XAVIER

Series 43 Soldiers/Little Women (6)	18 - 20	20 - 25

SCHEUERMANN, W. (GER)

S.W.S.B. **Series 6582** "Proving his hearts"	10 - 12	12 - 15

SCHÖNPFLUG (AUS)

B.K.W.I.

Series 4132 (6)	10 - 12	12 - 16

Kranzle, H&L Co.
"Ein Frohes Jahr"

Kuderny
M. Munk Series 699

TAM, JEAN (FR)
    Marque L.E.   70-4   20 - 25   25 - 30
VINCENTINI (IT)
    Deco Ladies in Spider Webs, Little Men   15 - 20   20 - 25

PUBLISHERS

B.G.W. Series 123/1233 (6)	8 - 10	10 - 12
J. Marks Series 155 "Summer Girl" (8)	10 - 12	12 - 15
B.K.W.I. Series 136 (6)	10 - 12	12 - 15
WBG Series 123 (6)	8 - 10	10 - 12

TEDDY BEARS

The lovable and ever-popular Teddy Bears are very much in demand by postcard collectors who search for both artist-signed, unsigned, and real-photo types. Many great sets and series were published during the 1905-1914 era, both in the U.S. and Europe, and are extremely popular with today's fantasy enthusiasts. A considerable number in this group are unsigned and, because of inadequate records by publishers, the artists have not been identified.

Collectors are indebted to Teddy Roosevelt and the U.S. press for the Teddy Bear. We are told that Mr. Roosevelt was invited to go bear hunting by some of his friends. After some period of time with no apparent success in finding bear meat, someone supposedly spotted one; however, it turned out to be a little cub. Roosevelt refused to shoot the bear, and afterwards the press picked up on this unusual story of "Teddy's Bear." Thus, the Teddy Bear legend was born and the fad grew worldwide.

Books were written about the adventures of Teddy Bear, and toys and novelties of all types were generated. Publishers of postcards also took advantage of the terrific interest in the new fad. The resulting output of collectible cards was enormous, and many remain for the collectors of today. The "Roosevelt Bears," named after the President, are perhaps the most recognized of the sets or series and "The Cracker Jack Bears" are perhaps the most popular.

BAUMGARTEN, FRITZ (FB) (GER)
    Meissner & Buch Series 1974   12 - 15   15 - 18
BEM, E. (RUS)
    Russian "Rishar"   20 - 25   25 - 30
    Russian Red Cross Soc. (St. Eugenia)   20 - 25   25 - 30
    Other Russian Publishers   20 - 25   25 - 28
    Lapina, Paris   15 - 20   20 - 25
BUSY BEARS (12)
    J. I. Austen Co.

427 Monday (Washing)	15 - 18	18 - 22
428 Tuesday (Ironing)	15 - 18	18 - 22
429 Wednesday (Cleaning)	15 - 18	18 - 22
430 Saturday (Mopping the Floor)	15 - 18	18 - 22
431 Thursday (Mending)	15 - 18	18 - 22
432 Saturday (Sewing)	15 - 18	18 - 22

Busy Bears, J. I. Austen Co.
No. 427, "Busy Bears on Monday"

Fred Cavally Bears, Thayer Pub. Co.
"Rain, rain go away..."

433 "Learning to Spell"	15 - 18	18 - 22
434 "Playing Leap Frog"	15 - 18	18 - 22
435 "Off to School"	15 - 18	18 - 22
436 "Getting it in the Usual Place"	15 - 18	18 - 22
437 "Something Doing"	15 - 18	18 - 22
438 "Vacation"	15 - 18	18 - 22

CAVALLY BEARS (Nursery Rhymes)
CAVALLY, FRED (US)
Thayer Publishing Co., Denver

"See-saw, Margery Daw"	18 - 22	22 - 26
"Rain, rain, go away"	18 - 22	22 - 26
"To make your candles last for aye"	18 - 22	22 - 26
"Cock crows in the morn"	18 - 22	22 - 26
"Little Red Snooks was fond ..."	18 - 22	22 - 26
"What are little Ted Boys made of?"	18 - 22	22 - 26
"As I went to Bonner"	18 - 22	22 - 26
"Nose, nose, jolly red nose"	18 - 22	22 - 26
"Dame Bear made a curtsy"	18 - 22	22 - 26
"Wash me, and comb me"	18 - 22	22 - 26
"Ding dong bell"	18 - 22	22 - 26
"Little Ted Grundy"	18 - 22	22 - 26
"Teddy be nimble"	18 - 22	22 - 26
"Multiplication is vexation"	18 - 22	22 - 26
"Tell Tale Tit!"	18 - 22	22 - 26

"Little Ted Horner"	18 - 22	22 - 26

ROSE CLARK BEARS
  CLARK, ROSE (US)
  Rotograph Co., N.Y. (12)

307 "Bear Town Cadet"	20 - 25	25 - 28
308 "Is That You Henry?"	20 - 25	25 - 28
309 "Henry"	20 - 25	25 - 28
310 "The Bride"	20 - 25	25 - 28
311 "The Groom"	20 - 25	25 - 28
312 "A Bear Town Sport"	20 - 25	25 - 28
313 "A Bear Town Dude"	20 - 25	25 - 28
314 "I'm Going a-Milking"	20 - 25	25 - 28
315 "I Won't be Home ..."	20 - 25	25 - 28
316 "C-c-come on in"	20 - 25	25 - 28
317 "Fifth Avenue"	20 - 25	25 - 28
318 "Hymn No. 23"	20 - 25	25 - 28

COLLINS BAKING CO. (4)   25 - 30   30 - 35

CRACKER JACK BEARS
  B. E. MORELAND (US)
  Rueckheim & Eckstein (16)

1 At the Lincoln Zoo	30 - 40	40 - 50
2 In Balloon	30 - 35	35 - 40
3 Over Niagara Falls	30 - 35	35 - 40
4 At Statue of Liberty	30 - 35	35 - 40
5 At Coney Island	30 - 35	35 - 40
6 In New York	30 - 35	35 - 40
7 Shaking Teddy's Hand (Roosevelt)	35 - 45	45 - 50
8 At Jamestown Fair	30 - 35	35 - 40
9 To the South	35 - 40	40 - 45
10 At Husking Bee	30 - 35	35 - 40
11 At the Circus	30 - 35	35 - 40
12 Playing Baseball	45 - 50	50 - 60
13 Cracker Jack Time	35 - 40	40 - 50
14 Making Cracker Jacks	30 - 35	35 - 40
15 At Yellowstone	30 - 35	35 - 40
16 Away to Mars	30 - 35	35 - 40

CRANE BEARS
  CRANE, D. P. (US)
  H.G.Z. & Co. (ZIM)

"Days of the Week" (7)	15 - 18	18 - 22
"Months of the Year" (12)	18 - 22	22 - 25

"TEDDY BEAR" BREAD, Kolbs Bakery (4)
  DENSLOW, W.W.

1 "Is there anything in it?"	35 - 45	45 - 60
2 "I'll See!"	35 - 45	45 - 60
3 "Why, It's 'Teddy Bear' Bread!"	35 - 45	45 - 60
4 I'll buy it!"	50 - 60	60 - 75

*Crane Bears, D. P. Crane, Zim
Publishing Co., "June"*

*Rose Clark Bears, Rotograph Co., No. 314
"I'm going a-milking Sir,–she said!"*

*Ellam Bears, R. Tuck Series 9793
"Teddy on the Beach"*

DOGGEREL DODGER BEARS
WHEELAN, A. R. (US)
Paul Elder Co. (6)

"This Bear's Witness..."	18 - 22	22 - 26
Others	18 - 22	22 - 26

ELLAM BEARS
B. Dondorf

Series 347 (6) No Captions	15 - 18	18 - 22
Series 370 (6)	18 - 22	22 - 25

Raphael Tuck

Series 9793 (6)	15 - 20	20 - 25
Series 9794 Rinking Teddy (6)	15 - 20	20 - 25

FEIERTAG, K. (AUS)
B.K.W.I.

Series 609	12 - 15	15 - 18

HAHN BEARS
SHEARER (US)
Albert Hahn Co. (A.H. in Trademark) (8)

"En Route"	"Just too Late"	10 - 12	12 - 15
"Happy"	"Look Pleasant"	10 - 12	12 - 15
"In Court"	"On Duty"	10 - 12	12 - 15
"In War"	"Painting the Town"	10 - 12	12 - 15

Heal Bears, "Days of the Week" – "Sunday" (Going to Church)

HEAL DAYS OF THE WEEK

William S. Heal (US)

"Sunday" Going to Church	10 - 12	12 - 15
"Monday" Washing Clothes	10 - 12	12 - 15
"Tuesday" Ironing	10 - 12	12 - 15
"Wednesday" Mending	10 - 12	12 - 15
"Thursday" Baking	10 - 12	12 - 15
"Friday" House Cleaning	10 - 12	12 - 15
"Saturday" Shopping	10 - 12	12 - 15
Same Series in Leather	12 - 15	15 - 20

HILDEBRANT (GB)

Raphael Tuck Series 9792

Teddy Bears (6)	15 - 18	18 - 22

HILLSON DAYS OF THE WEEK

D. Hillson

"Monday" Washday	10 - 12	12 - 15
"Tuesday" Ironing	10 - 12	12 - 15
"Wednesday" Mending	10 - 12	12 - 15
"Thursday" Baking	10 - 12	12 - 15
"Friday" Cleaning	10 - 12	12 - 15
"Saturday" Shopping	10 - 12	12 - 15
"Sunday" Church	10 - 12	12 - 15

KENNEDY, A. E.

C. W. Faulkner & Co., Ltd.

"Somebody's been sitting on my chair!"	15 - 18	18 - 22

LANGSDORFF BEARS

G. S.

Teddy Bear Orchestra, No. 4	15 - 20	20 - 25

D. Hillson Bears, "Days of the Week"
"Monday" (Wash Day)

D. Hilson Bears, "Days of the Week"
"Thursday" (Baking Day)

LITTLE BEARS
Raphael Tuck Series 118 (12)

"A Morning Dip"	"A Very Funny Song"	15 - 18	18 - 22
"Breaking the Record"	"Kept in at School"	15 - 18	18 - 22
"Missed Again"	"Oh! What a Shock"	15 - 18	18 - 22
"Once in the Eye"		15 - 20	20 - 25
"The Cake Walk"		15 - 20	20 - 25
"The Ice Bears Beautifully"		15 - 20	20 - 25
"The Jolly Anglers"		15 - 20	20 - 25
"Tobogganing in the Snow"		15 - 18	18 - 22
"Your Good Health"		15 - 18	18 - 22

MARY'S BEARS
C.L. (US)
Ullman Mfg. Co.   Series 119 (4)

"Mary had a little bear..."	10 - 12	12 - 15
"Everywhere that Mary went..."	10 - 12	12 - 15
"It followed her to school one day..."	10 - 12	12 - 15
"It made the children laugh..."	10 - 12	12 - 15

McLAUGHLIN BROS. BEARS
McLaughlin Bros.

	15 - 18	18 - 22

MOLLY & TEDDY BEARS
GREINER, M. (US)
International Art Co. Series 791 (6)

	15 - 20	20 - 25

OTTOMAN LITHOGRAPHING BEARS
Ottoman Lithographing Co., N.Y.

	15 - 18	18 - 22
"Come Birdie Come"	15 - 18	18 - 22
"Good Old Summertime"	15 - 18	18 - 22
"Is Marriage a Failure?"	15 - 18	18 - 22
"Many Happy Returns"	15 - 18	18 - 22
"Never Touched Me"	15 - 18	18 - 22
"Please Ask Pa"	15 - 18	18 - 22
"Right Up-To-Date"	15 - 18	18 - 22
"Well, Well, You never can Tell"	15 - 18	18 - 22
"Where am I at?"	15 - 18	18 - 22
"Will She Get the Lobster"	15 - 18	18 - 22

PILLARD (US)
S. Langsdorf & Co. Series 730

Teddy at Golf	22 - 25	25 - 30

Little Bears, Raphael Tuck, Series 118
"Breaking the Record"

Little Bears, Raphael Tuck, Series 118
"Oh What a Shock!"

Teddy at Soccer	18 - 22	22 - 26
S. S. PORTER BEARS (6)	8 - 10	10 - 12
ROMANTIC BEARS		
M.D.S. (US)		
Ullman		
Series 88 (4)		
1950 "Too Late"	15 - 18	18 - 22
1951 "Who Cares?"	15 - 18	18 - 22
1952 "The Lullaby"	15 - 18	18 - 22
1953 "A Letter to My Love"	15 - 18	18 - 22
ROOSEVELT BEARS		
E. Stern Co. (First Series, 1906)		
1 "At Home"	25 - 28	28 - 32
2 "Go Aboard the Train"	25 - 28	28 - 32
3 "In Sleeping Car"	25 - 28	28 - 32
4 "On A Farm"	25 - 28	28 - 32
5 "At a Country School"	25 - 28	28 - 32
6 "At the County Fair"	25 - 28	28 - 32
7 "Leaving the Balloon"	25 - 28	28 - 32
8 "At the Tailors"	25 - 28	28 - 32
9 "In the Department Store"	25 - 28	28 - 32
10 "At Niagara Falls"	25 - 28	28 - 32
11 "At Boston Public Library"	25 - 28	28 - 32
12 "Take an Auto Ride"	25 - 28	28 - 32

Romantic Bears, M.D.S., Ullman Ser. 88
No. 1953, "A Letter to My Love"

Roosevelt Bears, E. Stern Co., No. 30
"The Roosevelt Bears on a Pullman"

13 "At Harvard"	25 - 28	28 - 32
14 "On Iceberg"	25 - 28	28 - 32
15 "In New York City"	25 - 28	28 - 32
16 "At the Circus"	25 - 28	28 - 32
Second Series		
17 "Out West"	60 - 70	70 - 80
18 "Put out a fire"	60 - 70	70 - 80
19 "At the Wax Museum"	60 - 70	70 - 80
20 "At West Point"	60 - 70	70 - 80
21 "As Cadets"	60 - 70	70 - 80
22 "In New York"	60 - 70	70 - 80
23 "In Philadelphia"	60 - 70	70 - 80
24 "At the Theatre"	60 - 70	70 - 80
25 "Swimming"	60 - 70	70 - 80
26 "At Independence Hall"	60 - 70	70 - 80
27 "Celebrate the Fourth"	60 - 70	70 - 80
28 "At the Zoo"	60 - 70	70 - 80
29 "Go Fishing"	60 - 70	70 - 80
30 "Bears on a Pullman"	60 - 70	70 - 80
31 "Hunters"	80 - 90	90 - 100
32 "At Washington" (With Roosevelt)	35 - 40	40 - 50
Third Series (no captions)		
17 "Lighting Firecracker" (horizontal)	250 - 275	275 - 300
18 "Celebrating the Fourth" (horizontal)	250 - 275	275 - 300

19 "Waving Flags"	250 - 275	275 - 300
20 "Ringing Liberty Bell"	250 - 275	275 - 300
No No. Series		
Roosevelt Bears in Canada	250 - 275	275 - 300
Roosevelt Bears in England	250 - 275	275 - 300
Roosevelt Bears in Ireland	250 - 275	275 - 300
Roosevelt Bears in Scotland	250 - 275	275 - 300
Roosevelt Bears in Switzerland	250 - 275	275 - 300
The Roosevelt Bears "Return from abroad"	250 - 275	275 - 300
ROWNTREE, HARRY (GB)		
C. W. Faulkner & Co. Series 236 (6)		
"I am collecting"	20 - 25	25 - 30
"I am coming up to see you"	20 - 25	25 - 30
"I'm feeling a bit off color"	20 - 25	25 - 30
"The Weather is Perfect"	20 - 25	25 - 30
Williston Press		
Same images as Series 236	15 - 20	20 - 25
SPORTY BEARS		
M.D.S. (US)		
Ullman Mfg. Co.		
Series 83 (7)		
1923 "Love All"	12 - 15	15 - 20
1924 "Here's for a Home Run"	15 - 20	20 - 25
1925 "Out for Big Game"	10 - 12	12 - 15
1926 "King of the Alley"	12 - 15	15 - 18
1927 "A Dip in the Surf"	10 - 12	12 - 15
1928 "An Unexpected Bite"	10 - 12	12 - 15
ST. JOHN BEARS		
Western News Co.		
161 "Spring"	12 - 15	15 - 18
162 "Summer"	12 - 15	15 - 18
163 "Autumn"	12 - 15	15 - 18
164 "Winter"	12 - 15	15 - 18
V.O.H.P. Co.		
Series X40　Days of the Week (7)	10 - 12	12 - 15
H.H. TAMMEN CO. BEAR CUBS		
"A Boy and a Lass...," "Bear Up...," "A Little Bear..."	8 - 10	10 - 12
"Don't You Feel It in Your Toes...," No Caption (6 ?)	8 - 10	10 - 12
TEMPEST, MARGARET (GB)		
Medici Society		
Series 61 (6)	8 - 10	10 - 12
TOWER TEDDY BEARS		
Tower M. & N. Co. (30)	10 - 12	12 - 15
"Beary Well, Thank You"	10 - 12	12 - 15
"But We Are Civilized"	10 - 12	12 - 15
"Did You Ever Wear..."	10 - 12	12 - 15
"Don't Say a Word"	10 - 12	12 - 15
"Here's to the Stars and Stripes ..."	10 - 12	12 - 15

"Hurrah for - Eagle"	10 - 12	12 - 15
"Hurrah for the..."	10 - 12	12 - 15
"I'm Waiting For You"	10 - 12	12 - 15
"Our Birth, You Know"	10 - 12	12 - 15
"We Wear Pajamas"	10 - 12	12 - 15
"You Don't Say"	10 - 12	12 - 15

T. P. & CO. TEDDY BEARS

T. P. & Co.

	10 - 12	12 - 15
"Out for Airing"	10 - 12	12 - 15
"I Wonder if He Saw Me?"	10 - 12	12 - 15
"Isn't He a Darling"	10 - 12	12 - 15
"How Strong He Is"	10 - 12	12 - 15
"Oh! My! - He's Coming!"	10 - 12	12 - 15
"Off for the Honeymoon"	10 - 12	12 - 15
"Little Girl with Teddy"	10 - 12	12 - 15
"Dolly Gets an Inspiration"	10 - 12	12 - 15
"Lost, Strayed, or Stolen"	10 - 12	12 - 15
Others		

TWELVETREES BEARS

TWELVETREES, CHARLES or C.T.

National Art Co. (6)

206 "Little Bear Behind"	10 - 12	12 - 15
207 "Stung"	10 - 12	12 - 15
208 "The Bear on Dark Stairway"	10 - 12	12 - 15
209 "How can you Bear this Weather?"	10 - 12	12 - 15
210 "A Bear Impression"	10 - 12	12 - 15
211 "The Seashore Bear"	10 - 12	12 - 15

National Art Co.

271 "It's Up to You"	10 - 12	12 - 15

WALL, BERNHARDT

Ullman "Busy Bears"

Series 79

1905 Sunday	10 - 15	15 - 20
1906 Monday	10 - 15	15 - 20
1907 Tuesday	10 - 15	15 - 20
1908 Wednesday	10 - 15	15 - 20
1909 Thursday	10 - 15	15 - 20
1910 Friday	10 - 15	15 - 20
1911 Saturday	10 - 15	15 - 20

Ullman "Little Bears"

Series 92	12 - 15	15 - 18
WELLS BEARS (7)	8 - 10	10 - 12

ANONYMOUS (Vine Through Post Card) Flat Printed

241 "I am in a whirl"	6 - 8	8 - 10
242 "'I'm certainly enjoying myself"	6 - 8	8 - 10
243 "I never expected to meet you"	6 - 8	8 - 12
244 "Oh my but you are sweet"	6 - 8	8 - 12
245 "I have not had much luck so far"	6 - 8	8 - 12
246 "I am not going anywhere..."	6 - 8	8 - 12

247 "The joys of a bachelor's life"	6 - 8	8 - 12
248 "It was a touching scene"	6 - 8	8 - 12
249 "Stuck again"	6 - 8	8 - 12
250 "I have been hunting for you"	6 - 8	8 - 12

REAL PHOTO TEDDY BEARS

With Children (Large Bears)	25 - 35	35 - 45
With Children (Small Bears)	20 - 25	25 - 30
With Ladies (Large Bears)	18 - 22	22 - 28
With Ladies (Small Bears)	12 - 15	15 - 20
Bears Alone (Large)	15 - 20	20 - 25
Bears Alone (Small)	12 - 14	14 - 16
Bears and Movie Stars	10 - 12	12 - 15

OTHER ARTIST-SIGNED TEDDY BEARS

With Children or Ladies (Large Bears)	10 - 15	15 - 18
With Children or Ladies (Small Bears)	8 - 10	10 - 15

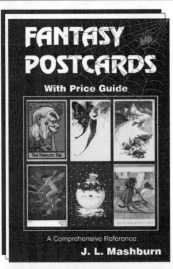

4

Nudes

COLOR NUDES

For many years color nudes were completely neglected by the American postcard collector. The only issues available, until recently, were those of the Great Masters' reproductions of paintings from big museums and art galleries throughout the world. Stengel Art Co. of Dresden, Germany and Misch & Co. of England were the major publishers.

These museum reproductions gave color nudes a bad impression and repressed their growth until it was finally realized that there were hundreds of other beautiful nudes and semi-nudes that were not museum reproductions. During postcards' Golden Years, European artists–especially the French and Germans–painted beautiful nudes relating to mythical, historical, Biblical, fairy tales, and fantasy motifs that were beautifully adapted to postcards. These cards have become highly collectible and are pursued by many American deltiologists.

Since there was no demand in the United States from 1900 to 1920, color nudes by American artists are very rare. Therefore, most all of the nudes listed here are from Europe. Many artists painted only a limited number of different nudes; therefore, very few sets or series are available. Nude Fantasy types of most all artists are very desirable.

		VG	EX
ADRIAN-DUSSEK, ED. (AUS)			
Kilophot Co.			
JK18	"Das Neue Modell"	$15 - 20	$20 - 25
JK25	"Modelpause"	12 - 15	15 - 20
JK51	"In Gedanken"	18 - 22	22 - 26
JK52	"Im Atelier"	20 - 22	22 - 26
JK53	"Studie"	18 - 22	22 - 26
JK54	"Das Model"	12 - 15	15 - 20
JK55	"The Hat"	15 - 18	18 - 22
JK56	"Studie"	18 - 20	20 - 26

JK57	"The Model"	15 - 18	18 - 22
JK58	"The Hat"	15 - 18	18 - 22
JK59	"In Gedanken"	18 - 22	22 - 26
JK60	"Schwuller Tag"	12 - 15	15 - 18
JK61	"Koketterie"	15 - 18	18 - 22
JK62	"Die Gold Gube"	15 - 18	18 - 22
JK63	"Vertraumt"	15 - 18	18 - 22
JK64	"Jugendstil Akstudie"	18 - 20	20 - 22
JK65	"Im Abendlicht"	25 - 28	28 - 32
JK66	"Halbakt"	25 - 28	28 - 32
JK67	"Erwachen"	18 - 22	22 - 25
JK68	"Blonder Akt"	22 - 25	25 - 28
JK69	"Frosch Koenigs Bride"	25 - 28	28 - 32
JK70	"Gross Toilette am Land"	12 - 15	15 - 18

ALLEAUME, L. (FR)
  Lapina, Paris

59	"In the Rose"	15 - 18	18 - 22
201	"Offering"	12 - 15	15 - 20

ASTI, ANGELO (IT)

JL & W 36/25, No Caption, Unsigned		15 - 20	20 - 25
Salon 1897, "Songeuse"		18 - 22	22 - 25
Salon de Paris (Sepia)			
5255 "Volupte"		18 - 22	22 - 26
Others		18 - 22	22 - 26

Ed. Adrian-Dussek, Kilophot Co.
JK-51, "In Gedanken"

Ed. Adrian-Dussek, Kilophot Co.
JK-65, "Im Abendlicht"

Angelo Asti, Salon de Paris
5255, "Volupte"

T. Axentowicz
Anczyc, #110, "Noc"

AUER, R.
  Salon J.C.Z. 4 "Tender Flower"   15 - 18   18 - 22
     1 "Delight"   12 - 15   15 - 18
AXENTOWICZ, T. (PO)
  ANCZYC
     10 "Noc"   25 - 30   30 - 35
     110 "Noc"   25 - 30   30 - 40
  D.N.   29 "Studjum"   18 - 20   20 - 25
BARBER, COURT (US)
  S. & G.S.i.B.
     1283 "Nach dem Bade"   12 - 15   15 - 20
     1284 "Der Goldene Schal"   12 - 15   15 - 18
BEAUFEREY, M. LOUISE (FR)
  A.N., Paris
     89 "The Rest"   12 - 15   15 - 20
  Salon de Paris
     292 "Young Woman at Her ..."   18 - 22   22 - 26
BECAGLI, P. (FR)
  Salon de Paris "Paressguse"   12 - 15   15 - 20
BENDER, S.
  H.M.
     "La Femme" Series (12)   18 - 22   22 - 26
MEYER-BERNBURG, A. (GER)
  O.G.Z-L
     1132 "Erwacht"   15 - 18   18 - 22
BERNHARD, LEO (GER)
     "Bachante"   12 - 15   15 - 20

M. Louise Beauferey, Salon de Paris
#292, "Young Woman at Her Dressing"

Max Bruning
E.W.E., #100c/1

F. Brisard
Lapina #5132, "Nude"

BIESSY, GABRIEL (FR)		
Salon de Paris "The Model"	15 - 18	18 - 22
BORRMEISTER, R. (GER)		
Herman Wolff		
1128 "Morgengruss"	12 - 15	15 - 20
1093 "Wald Marchen"	15 - 18	18 - 22
1094 "Versuchung"	18 - 22	22 - 26
BOTTINGER, H. (GER)		
J.P.P. 1074 "Marchen"	12 - 15	15 - 20
BOULAND, M. (FR)		
A.N., Paris 446 "Femme a l'echape"	15 - 18	18 - 22
BRICHARD, X. (FR)		
A.N., Paris 404 "After the Bath"	15 - 18	18 - 22
BRISARD, F.		
Lapina #5132 "Nude"	20 - 25	25 - 28
BRUNING, MAX (GER)		
E.W.E. 100c/1 (Sepia)	20 - 25	25 - 28
BRUNNER (GER)		
Art Moderne 717 "Wassernymphe"	15 - 20	20 - 25
BUBNA, G. (GER)		
Herman Wolff 1135 "Ein Neugierger"	10 - 12	12 - 15
BUKOVAC, V. (CZ)		
Minerva		
21 No Caption	12 - 15	15 - 18
28 "Koketa"	12 - 15	15 - 18
Lapina 825 "The Dream of Love"	15 - 18	18 - 22
BUSSIÈRE, GASTON (FR)		
Salon de Paris 744 "Salome"	15 - 18	18 - 22
CARRIER-BELLEUSE		
Salon de Paris 4055 "Etude"	15 - 18	18 - 22
CAYRON, J. (FR)		
Lapina 5433 "Repose"	12 - 15	15 - 20
CHANTRON, A. J. (FR)		
Salon de Paris 993 "The Bind Weed"	12 - 15	15 - 20
A.N., Paris 38 "Spring"	12 - 15	15 - 20
Lapina 5016 "Woman with a Parrot"	12 - 15	15 - 20
CHAPIN		
Stengel 29920 "Souvenirs"	8 - 10	10 - 12
CHERY "The Source"	12 - 15	15 - 20
COLLIN, R.		
Lapina 408 "Floreal"	8 - 10	10 - 12
COMERRE, LEON		
Palais des Beaux Arts "The Golden Rain"	10 - 12	12 - 15
A.N., Paris 164 "While the Artist..."	8 - 10	10 - 12
Musee de Luxembourg		
411 "The Spider"	12 - 15	15 - 18
CORABCEUF, J.		
A.N., Paris, "Awaking"	18 - 22	22 - 25
COURTEN (FR)		
Salon J.P.P. 1015 "La Source"	15 - 18	18 - 22
COURTOIS, G.		
Lapina 526 "La Lecture"	12 - 15	15 - 18
CREMIEU, A. (FR)		
L-E Series 44 "Blondes et Rousses"	25 - 30	30 - 35

Crozat, Galerie d'Art, #117
"Apres le Bal"

D. Enjolras, Lapina, #1696
"Pearls"

S. Des Essarts, Lapina, #913
"Annoying Accident"

A. Faugeron, Lapina, #5913
"Na Jade"

CROY, Mme. Th. (FR)		
Lapina 5289 "The model"	12 - 15	15 - 18
CROZAT		
Galerie d'Art 117 "Apres le bal"	12 - 15	15 - 20
CUNICEL, EDW.		
O.F.Z.-L "Coquetry"	12 - 15	15 - 18
CZECH, E. (BUL)		
"Apollon Sophia" 70 "Temptation"	12 - 15	15 - 18
DE BOUCHE, A.		
E.K.N. 1050 "The New Ornament"	8 - 10	10 - 15
DERVAUX, G. (FR)		
Lapina 5412 "Naughty"	12 - 15	15 - 18
DEWALD, A.		
Emgre-Sabn 229 "Eve"	12 - 15	15 - 20
DOLEZEL-EZEL, P. (FR)		
F.H. & S. 5221 No Caption	10 - 12	12 - 15
DOMERGUE, JEAN-GABRIEL (FR)		
A.N., Paris Real Photo Art Deco Nudes	30 - 35	35 - 40
(Also see Artist-Signed)		
DUPUIS, P.		
Hanfstaengel 199 "The Wave"	12 - 15	15 - 20
DU THOIT (FR)		
A.N., Paris		
334 "Dressing"	15 - 20	20 - 25
338 "Fair Haired Woman"	15 - 18	18 - 22
EICHLER, MAX		
O.G.Z-L 291 "Nach Dem Bade"	12 - 15	15 - 20
EINBECK "Nana"		
ENJOLRAS, D. (FR)		
Lapina		
718 "Repose"	12 - 15	15 - 20
"Ruth"	12 - 15	15 - 18
"Rest"	12 - 15	15 - 20
1401 "Nude"	12 - 15	15 - 20
1696 "Pearls"	12 - 15	15 - 20
DES ESSARTS, S.		
Lapina		
913 "Annoying Accident"	15 - 20	20 - 25
5913 "Na Jade"	15 - 20	20 - 25
EVERART, M.		
A.N., Paris 7 "The Woman With Ribbons"	15 - 20	20 - 25
E.S., Paris 37 "On the Telephone"	12 - 15	15 - 20
SPA		
4059 "The Woman With Lamp"	15 - 18	18 - 22
76 "Young Woman at the Mirror"	20 - 25	25 - 30
FAR-SI (FR)		
A.N., Paris "Oriental Perfume"	12 - 15	15 - 20
FAUGERON, A. (FR)		
Lapina, Paris		
5913 "Na Jade"	15 - 20	20 - 25
FEIKL, S. (GER)		
J.K.P. 236 "Akt"	12 - 15	15 - 18
FENNER-BEHMER, H.		
Hanfstaengl's 194 "Ysabel"	20 - 25	25 - 28

H. Fenner-Behmer
Hanfstaengl's, #194, "Ysabel"

E. Friand, Lapina, #5415
"Familiar Birds"

FERRARIS, A.V. (AUS)		
B.K.W.I. "Leda"	12 - 15	15 - 20
FOURNIER "Woman Bathing"	10 - 12	12 - 15
FRIAND, E. (FR)		
Lapina 5415 "Familiar Birds"	20 - 25	25 - 28
Salon de Paris 1911 "Forest's Echo"	12 - 15	15 - 18
FREISKE (FR)		
Lapina 546 "A Woman Sleeping"	12 - 15	15 - 20
FRIEDRICH, OTTO (AUS)		
B.K.W.I. 1541 "Eitelkeit"	12 - 15	15 - 18
FRONTE, M. (FR)		
Lapina "Woman Lying Down"	12 - 15	15 - 20
FUCHS, RUDOLPH (GER)		
W.R.B. & Co.		
738 "Blaue Augen"	12 - 15	15 - 18
GALAND, LEON		
Salon de Paris "A Sleeping Woman"	12 - 15	15 - 20
GALLELLI, M.		
P. Heckscher		
143 "The First Pose"	12 - 15	15 - 18
GEIGER, C. AUG.		
NPG 453 "Eva"	12 - 15	15 - 18
GERMAIN "First Session"	15 - 18	18 - 22
GERVEX, HENRI (FR)		
Palais des Beaux-Arts		
261 "Birth of Venus"	10 - 12	12 - 15

S. Glucklich, Hanfstaengl's, #202
"Sieste"

G. Herve, Lapina, #75
"My Model and My Dog"

G. Herve, Lapina, #1214
"Coquetry"

GITTER, H. (GER)
  Galerie München Meister

"Morgen"	10 - 12	12 - 15
"Tag"	8 - 10	10 - 12

GLUCKLEIN, S. (GER)
  Hanfstaengel's 202 "Reposing"

	12 - 15	15 - 18

GLUCKLICH, S. (GER)
  Hanfstaengl's #202 "Sieste"

	20 - 25	25 - 28

  Herman Wolff
  1188 "Quellnymphe"

	15 - 18	18 - 22

GODWARD, J.W.
  Rishar
  295 "A Fair Reflection"

	12 - 15	15 - 18

GOEPFART, FRANZ
  301 "Ruhender Akt"

	12 - 15	15 - 18

GOROKHOV
  N.P.G., Berlin "Wassernixe"

	12 - 15	15 - 20

GRENOUILLOUX, J. (FR)
  Lapina

"The Fair Summer Days"	12 - 15	15 - 20
"The Nymph with Flags"	12 - 15	15 - 20

  Apollon
  78 "Speil der Wellen"

	10 - 12	12 - 15

  Salon de Paris

"The Nymph with Flags"	12 - 15	15 - 20
206 "La Nymphe Aux Iris"	15 - 20	20 - 25

CROY, MME. TH. (FR)
   Lapina, Paris 5289 "The model"   20 - 25   25 - 28
GSELL, HENRY (FR)
   A.N., Paris 435 "Summer"   12 - 15   15 - 20
GUETIN, V.
   Lapina 799 "Das Bad"   10 - 12   12 - 15
GUILLAUME, R.M. (FR)
   Lapina
      1400 "The Repose of the Model"   15 - 18   18 - 15
      1083 "Rapid Change"   15 - 18   18 - 22
      1523 "Rubbing the Leg"   15 - 18   18 - 22
      5450 "The girl and the parrot"   15 - 18   18 - 22
   Soc. des Artistes 58 "The Fly"   8 - 10   10 - 12
A.H.
   K.th W.II 636 "Lybelle"   10 - 12   12 - 15
HERRFURTH, O. (GER)
   N.P.G. 489 "An der Quelle"   15 - 18   18 - 22
HERVÉ, GABRIEL (FR)
   Lapina
      44 "Resting"   12 - 15   15 - 20
      75 "My Model and My Dog"   15 - 20   20 - 25
      813 "Farniente"   12 - 15   15 - 20
      1214 "Coquetry"   20 - 25   25 - 30
   Heinrich Hoffman "Psyche"   10 - 12   12 - 15
HILSER (CZ)
   Minerva
      83 No Caption   10 - 12   12 - 15
      1130 "Siesta"   12 - 15   15 - 18
HOESSLIN
   NPG 491 "Die Schaumgeborene"   12 - 15   15 - 20
JANUSZEWSKI, J. (PO)
   ANCZYC
      185 "Akt"   15 - 18   18 - 22
      455 No Caption   15 - 18   18 - 22
JOANNON, E. (FR)
   Salon de Paris 5331 "Lassitude"   15 - 18   18 - 22
KÄMMERER, PAUL
   E.M.M. Poster 255 "Frühling"   25 - 28   28 - 32
KASPARIDES, E.
   B.K.W.I.
      161-4 "A Warm Summer Morning"   10 - 12   12 - 15
      164-3 "The Airbath"   12 - 15   15 - 18
      164-10 "Forest Silence"   10 - 12   12 - 15
   Others   10 - 12   12 - 15
KIESEL, C.
   A.R. & C.i.B. 463 "Salome"   12 - 15   15 - 18
KLIMES
   Minerva 1227 "Nymphe"   12 - 15   15 - 18
KNOBLOCH, J.R.
   O.G.Z.-L 1700 "Tired"   12 - 15   15 - 18
KNOEFEL (GER)
   Novitas
      668 (4) Illuminated Nudes   20 - 25   25 - 30

Ch. Lenoir, Lapina, Paris
#853, "Stream Song"

Otto Linger, Rishar
#121, "Walpurgis"

866 (4) Illuminated Nudes	20 - 25	25 - 30
KORPAL, T.		
ANCYZ 16 Bather "Au Ete"	10 - 12	12 - 15
KOSEL, H.C. (AUS)		
B.K.W.I.		
181-3 "Kungstgeschlchte"	10 - 12	12 - 15
181-8 "Nach im Bade"	10 - 12	12 - 15
181-9 "Lekture"	10 - 12	12 - 15
181-10 "Sklavin"	12 - 15	15 - 18
KRENNES, H. C1-12 "Danse"	10 - 12	12 - 15
KRIER, E.A. (FR)		
Salon de Paris 5379 "Folly at Home"	10 - 12	12 - 15
KUTEW, CH.		
Frist		
Series 90, 8 No Caption	12 - 15	15 - 20
Series 90, 10 No Caption	12 - 15	15 - 20
A.F.W.		
111-2 "Ondine"	12 - 15	15 - 20
"Nymph"	15 - 18	18 - 22
LANDAU, E.		
Lapina 979 "Putting things in order"	10 - 12	12 - 15
LANDROW, F. (GER)		
S.V.D. 416 "Meereslockung"	12 - 15	15 - 18
LANZDORF, R.		
R. & J.D. 501 "Young Bedouin Girl"	8 - 10	10 - 12
LAURENS, P.A. (FR)		
Lapina 2032 "Didon"	12 - 15	15 - 18

E. Meier, Edition SID, #1026/5
"Beflowered Beauty"

G. Papperitz, J. Plichta
#2181, "Aurora"

LEEKE, F. (GER)
Münchener Kunst

3114 "Bad de Bestalin"	15 - 18	18 - 22
Hans Koehler & Co. 76 "Bacchantalin"	15 - 18	18 - 22

LEFEBRE, J.

Salon J.P.P. 2215 "Es werde Licht!"	15 - 18	18 - 22

LEFFEBURE, J.
Musee de Luxembourg

500 "Woman Warming Herself"	8 - 10	10 - 12

LENDIR

P. Heckscher 366 "Die Sofe"	12 - 15	15 - 18

LENOIR, CH. (FR)

Lapina 853 "Stream Song"	20 - 25	25 - 28
A.N., Paris 19 "Tanzerin"	15 - 20	20 - 25

L'EVEIL (FR)

Salon 1914 304 "The Awakening"	12 - 15	15 - 20

LIEBERMAN, E. (GER)

Emil Kohn 890 "At the Window"	10 - 12	12 - 15

LINGER, O. (GER)
G. Liersch & Co.

537 "Susses Nichtshen"	12 - 15	15 - 18
Rishar (Russia) 121 "Walpurgis"	20 - 25	25 - 28

LOUP, EUF. (FR)

A.N., Paris 292 "Study"	22 - 25	25 - 30

LUCAS, H.

Lapina 890 "Happy Night"	10 - 12	12 - 15

MAKOVSKY, C. (RU)
  Russia 539 "Dans ie Boudoir"   12 - 15   15 - 20
MALIQUET, C. (FR)
  Lapina "Voluptuousness"   12 - 15   15 - 20
  Salon de Paris
    56 "At the Hairdresser"   12 - 15   15 - 20
MANDL, JOS.
  Salon J.P.P. 2056 "L'Innocence"   10 - 12   12 - 15
MARECEK
  KV 1335 "Nach dem Bade"   10 - 12   12 - 15
  VKKA 1201 "Toileta"   8 - 10   10 - 12
MARTIN, F. (GER)
  A.R. & C.i.B.
    395 "Vom dem Spiegel"   10 - 12   12 - 15
MARTIN-KAVEL
  Lapina
  "Nude on Tiger Rug"   10 - 12   12 - 15
  934 "Surprised"   12 - 15   15 - 18
MAX, G. (BUL)
  Apollon Sophia 68 "Bacchante"   12 - 15   15 - 18
MEIER, E. (GER)
  Edition SID #1925 (6)
    5 "Beflowered Beauty"   15 - 20   20 - 25
    Others   15 - 20   20 - 25
MENZLER, W. (GER)
  NPG 512 "Akt"   10 - 12   12 - 15
MERCIER
  Art Moderne
    748 "Nymphe Endormie"   12 - 15   15 - 18
    "Nymph Reclining"   15 - 18   18 - 22
MERLE, K.
  Moderner Kunst 2355 "After the Bath" 10 - 12   12 - 15
MIASSOJEDOW, J.
  224 Russian "Arabian Tanzerin"   12 - 15   15 - 20
MOHN, ROTER
  Moderner Kunst
    245 "Feuerlilien"   10 - 12   12 - 15
    246 No Caption   10 - 12   12 - 15
MORIN
  Salon J.P.P. 1124 "Feu Follet"   10 - 12   12 - 15
MÜLLER, A.
  Anon. Watercolor No. 6 "Le Peignoir-Chemise" 25 - 30   30 - 35
MÜLLER, RICH.
  Malke & Co.
    25 "My Models"   18 - 22   22 - 25
  SPGA
    251 "Gold Fish"   22 - 25   25 - 28
    252 "Der Rote Ibis"   22 - 25   25 - 28
    Others   18 - 22   22 - 26
NAKLADATEL, J.
  Salon J.P.P.
    440-445 (6) Semi-Nudes   18 - 22   22 - 26
NEJEDLY
  Salon J.P.P. "Erwachen"   10 - 12   12 - 15

A. Penot, L-E, #313
"Poisson Rouge"

Prof. G. Rienacker, P.F.B. #7007
"Die Favoritin des Sultans"

NEMEJC, AUG. (PO) "Tragedie"	10 - 12	12 - 15
NISSL, RUDOLF (GER)		
Novitas 388 "Akt im Mantel"	12 - 15	15 - 18
NONNENBRUCH, M. (GER)		
Salon J.P.P. 2187 "La Sculpture"	12 - 15	15 - 20
O.G.Z.-L 1174 "After Dancing"	12 - 15	15 - 20
Hanfstaengel's 49 "Flora"	12 - 15	15 - 20
OSTROWSKI, A.J. (RU)		
Russian, **Rishar** 2172 "The Model"	15 - 18	18 - 22
OTTOMAN **Lapina** "The Sleeping Courtesan"	10 - 12	12 - 15
PAPPERITZ, G. (BUL)		
Apollon		
84 "Boa Neuf"	15 - 18	18 - 22
237 "Bayadere"	18 - 22	22 - 26
Hanfstaengel's 197 "Chrysanthemums"	12 - 15	15 - 20
J. Plichta 2181 "Aurora"	22 - 25	25 - 30
PARYS, MME VON (FR)		
Lapina, Paris 5015 "Souvenir"	12 - 15	15 - 18
PAUSINGER Russian 063 "Salome"	15 - 20	20 - 25
PENOT, A.		
A.N., Paris		
27 "Frolicsome"	18 - 22	22 - 26
229 "Repose"	18 - 22	22 - 26
408 "Fariente"	18 - 22	22 - 26
Lapina		
"Water Flower"	18 - 22	22 - 26

"Bayadera"	20 - 25	25 - 28
"Libelle"	15 - 18	18 - 22
1223 "Repose"	18 - 22	22 - 26
1226 "The Charm of Spring"	12 - 15	15 - 20
1227 "A Young Girl"	25 - 30	30 - 35
1340 "Red Butterfly"	20 - 25	25 - 30
1345 "The Fur Stole"	15 - 18	18 - 22
L-E 313 "Poisson Rouge"	25 - 30	30 - 35
Salon de Paris		
727 "Der Erste Mai"	12 - 15	15 - 20
S.V.D.		
291 "Einheisser Sommertag"	12 - 15	15 - 20
292 "Das Kunstler Modell"	12 - 15	15 - 20
PIOTROWSKI, A.		
Minerva 1028 "Salome"	15 - 18	18 - 22
PRICE, J. M.		
Hanfstaengel's 117 "Odaliske"	12 - 15	15 - 20
R.R.		
M. Munk Series 684 (6)	18 - 22	22 - 26
RASCH, PROF. (GER)		
N.P.G. 42 "Akt"	12 - 15	15 - 18
Series 873 (6)	18 - 22	22 - 26
RAYNOLT, ANTOINE (FR)		
Lapina, Paris 1551 "Sleep"	15 - 18	18 - 22
REIFENSTEIN, LEO (GER)		
Galzburger Kunst 45 "Schönhut"	12 - 15	15 - 20
REINACKER, G. (GR)		
M.K.B.		
2517 "Triumphant Love"	12 - 15	15 - 20
Marke JSC		
6054 "Am Morgen"	12 - 15	15 - 20
6055 "Verkauft"	12 - 15	15 - 20
6083 "Der Neue Schmuck"	15 - 18	18 - 22
PFB 6034 "Die Favoritin des Sultans"	15 - 20	20 - 25
RETTIG, H. (GER)		
Munchener Meister 568 "Im Spiegel"	12 - 15	15 - 18
RIESEN, O. (GER)		
A. Sch. & Co. 7152 "Unschuld"	12 - 15	15 - 20
S. & G. S.i.B. 1471 "Am Morgen"	15 - 18	18 - 22
RITTER, C. **Novitas** 397 "Im Gotteskleid"	12 - 15	15 - 18
ROGER, LOUIS (FR)		
Lapina, Paris 543 "Awaking"	15 - 20	20 - 24
ROTMANNER, ALFRED (GER)		
Hans Kohler 71 "Beim Lampenschein"	12 - 15	15 - 20
ROUSSELET, E. (FR)		
Lapina		
1129 "Bathing"	12 - 15	15 - 20
"The Dream"	10 - 12	12 - 15
ROUSTEAUX-DARBOURD		
Salon 1912 571 "Am Feuer"	12 - 15	15 - 18
SAIZEDE		
Lapina "A Woman & Statuette"	8 - 10	10 - 12
SALIGER		
Haus der D. Kunst "Die Sinne"	10 - 12	12 - 15

Olga V. Riesen, S.&G. SiB, #1471
"Am Morgen"

L. Schmutzler, OGZ.-L
"Courtezan"

SCALBERT, J.
   A.N., Paris   422 "The Shift"   10 - 12   12 - 15
   Lapina
      795 "The Toilet"   12 - 15   15 - 18
      1329 "An Ugly Fellow"   10 - 12   12 - 15
      5158 "Hesitation"   12 - 15   15 - 18
   SPA 30 "Satisfaction"   10 - 12   12 - 15
   Salon de Paris
      1570 "Five O'Clock Tea"   12 - 15   15 - 18
      5085 "The Looking Glass"   12 - 15   15 - 20
SCIHLABITZ, A.   **NPGA** 30 "Akstudie"   12 - 15   15 - 18
SCHIVERT, V. (GER)
   TSN 801 "Der Liebestraube"   8 - 10   10 - 12
   NPG
      237 "Susanne"   12 - 15   15 - 18
      238 "Akt"   12 - 15   15 - 20
   Munchener Kunst
      193   No Caption   12 - 15   15 - 20
      199   No Caption   12 - 15   15 - 20
   PFB 42291 "Das Modell"   15 - 20   20 - 25
   Arthur Rehn & Co.
      "Die Quelle"   15 - 18   18 - 22
      "Die Rivalin"   12 - 15   15 - 20
SCHLEMO, E.
   TSN
      888 "Schonheit ist alles"   12 - 15   15 - 20

889 "Beauty"	12 - 15	15 - 18
SCHLIMARSKI, H.		
B.K.W.I. 1805 "Vanity"	12 - 15	15 - 18
SCHMUTZLER, L. (GER)		
O.G.Z-L 364 "Courtezan"	20 - 25	25 - 30
E.N. K. 810 "Passion"	20 - 25	25 - 30
SCHNEIDER, E.		
"Die Windsbraut"	10 - 12	12 - 12
NPGA 54 "Halbakt"	12 - 15	15 - 18
AMAG Kunst 51 "Bacchantin"	10 - 12	12 - 15
SCHUTZ, E. (AUS)		
B.K.W.I.		
Series 165 (4)	22 - 25	25 - 30
885-1 Gothe's "Der Got und Baidere" Poster	20 - 25	25 - 30
SCHWARZSCHILD, A.		
Munchener Kunst "Ball Spiel"	10 - 12	12 - 15
SEEBERGER, J.		
A.N., Paris		
368 "A Dragon-Fly"	18 - 22	22 - 26
466 "After the Bath"	12 - 15	15 - 18
470 "Smit with Love"	12 - 15	15 - 20
A.N., Paris		
"Gachucha"	10 - 12	12 - 15
470 "Smit with Love"	12 - 15	15 - 20
597 "A Sprightly Girl"	12 - 15	15 - 18
760 "Indolence"	12 - 15	15 - 20
Art Moderne 760 "Indolence"	12 - 15	15 - 20
Lapina "The Birth of Venus"	15 - 18	18 - 22
SEZILLE, D.E. (FR)		
Lapina 913 "Annoying Accident"	15 - 18	18 - 22
SIEFERT, PAUL (FR)		
A.N., Paris "Diana"	15 - 18	18 - 22
Salon de Paris 746, "Diana"	15 - 18	18 - 22
SKALA		
Minerva		
1069 "Susses Nichtstun"	10 - 12	12 - 15
1117 "Eva"	15 - 20	20 - 25
SOLOMKO, SERGE (RUS)		
TSN 153 "Circe"	15 - 20	20 - 25
SOUBBOTINE, A.		
NPGA #87 "Studie"	20 - 25	25 - 28
STACHIEWICZ, P. (PO)		
Wydann. Salon		
152/23 "Kwiat Olean"	15 - 18	18 - 22
152/24 "Zloty Zawoj"	12 - 15	15 - 20
STELLA, EDUARD		
BRW		
353 "Madame Sans Gene"	20 - 25	25 - 30
354 "Diana"	18 - 20	20 - 22
STEMBER, N.K.		
Rishar 1078 "Elegie"	18 - 20	20 - 25
Hanfstaengel's 56 "Jugend"	18 - 22	22 - 26
STYKA, JAN (FR)		
Lapina "Harmony in yellow"	15 - 18	18 - 22

L. Vallet, Lapina, #2499
"La Colere"

Fr. Zmurko, ANCZYC, #291
No Caption

STYKA, TADE (FR)
  Lapina 183 "Cinquecento" — 8 - 10   10 - 12

SUBBOTIN, A. (RU)
  NPG 87 "Studie" — 15 - 18   18 - 22
  Granbergs, Stockholm 577 "Im Harem" — 15 - 20   20 - 25

SUCHANKE
  VKKA 1336 "Fruhlingslied" — 8 - 10   10 - 12

SYKORA, G.
  G.Z. 032 "Der Necker" — 8 - 10   10 - 12

SZYNDLER
  J. Czerneckiego #901 "Eve" — 20 - 25   25 - 30

TABARY, E. (FR)
  A.N., Paris
    115 "An Actress in her box" — 15 - 20   20 - 25
    906 "The Pendant" — 12 - 15   15 - 20

TARDIEU, VICTOR (FR)
  Salon de Paris 168 "Study in Nude" — 12 - 15   15 - 20

TOLNAY (HUN)
  Rotophot, Budapest "Venus Anadyomene" — 12 - 15   15 - 20

URBAN, J.
  D.K. & Co. Series 678 (4) — 20 - 25   25 - 30
  J.P.P. 42 — 18 - 22   22 - 26

VACHA, L.
  Minerva 1170 "Suzanne" — 8 - 10   10 - 12

VALLET, L. (FR)
  Lapina
    2498 "The Gourmet" — 25 - 30   30 - 35

2499 "La Colere"	25 - 30	30 - 35
2506 "Luxury"	25 - 30	30 - 35
2507 "Pride"	25 - 30	30 - 35
VASNIER, E.		
Lapina 779 "The Toilet"	12 - 15	15 - 20
VASSELON, H. (FR)		
A. Noyer "The Spring"	20 - 25	25 - 30
Salon J.P.P. 1004 "Danse aux voiles"	15 - 18	18 - 22
VOLKER, ROB. (GER)		
Munchener Kunst		
385 "Eitkelkeit"	12 - 15	15 - 20
386 No Caption	12 - 15	15 - 20
VOWE, P.G.		
MBK 2546 No Caption	8 - 10	10 - 12
WALLIKOW, F.B.		
GK. v., Berlin 432 "Reifers Obst"	12 - 15	15 - 18
WEBER, E. (GER)		
B.K.W.I. 2363 "Akt"	12 - 15	15 - 20
WINCK, W.		
Otto Ploeger		
625 "Verlassen"	15 - 18	18 - 22
WITTING, W. (GER)		
S.V.D. 358 "Auf Freier Hohe"	12 - 15	15 - 20
Dresdner KK "Jugend"	12 - 15	15 - 18
WOBRING, F. (GER)		
S.W.S.B. 4771 "Morgentau"	12 - 15	15 - 18
ZIER, ED. (GER)		
Russian, **Rishar** "La Siesta"	12 - 15	15 - 20

Professionally Posed Real Photo by Salon J.A., Paris, Series 0141

ZMURKO, FR. (POL)
  ANCZYC

291, 297, 352, 355, 448, 516	15 - 18	18 - 22
280, 347, 449, 352, 510, 648, 705	12 - 15	15 - 18

ZOPF, C. (GER)

O.G.Z.-L 865 "Curious"	8 - 10	10 - 12

ZWILLER, A. (FR)

Salon de Paris "The Rest"	12 - 15	15 - 18

PUBLISHERS

STENGEL NUDES

Various Artists	6 - 9	9 - 12

REAL PHOTO NUDES

Real photo nude postcards were first made famous by French publishers who selected bountiful beauties of the day to pose sans clothes. The more important publishing Salons were **AN, Corona, Noyer, PC, SAPI,** and **Super.** Others such as **AG, BMV, CA, ER, GP, JA, JB, JOPA, J.R., Leo, Lydia, MAH, SDK, S.I.C., S.O.L., Star, VC,** and **WA** added to the many cards produced.

Although not always the norm, many publishers used airbrushing to obliterate any pubic or underarm hair from the photos and painted on lingerie for the prudish buyers in some markets. Tinting, especially those by **S.O.L., Paris,** enhanced the eye appeal and quality of selected series but, for today's collector, these are not quite as popular as the untouched material.

The cards were usually published and sold in sets of 6, 10 or 12, and from these many classical nudes exist. Various studio props were used for background affect. Chairs, tables, chests with mirrors, hanging tapestries, vases, and statues were among the favorites.

The most popular nudes, however, are those that were not professionally posed...where hair was not airbrushed away, and therefore nothing was left to the imagination. Although the French did their share, cards of this particular type were produced mainly in Germany and Austria, and normally do not have publisher by-lines. A small number of cards in this group may also have been done in the United States. Many cards do not have postcard backs as they were not usually sent through the mails. This apparently has not made a difference to collectors in relation to the pricing structure. It is becoming much harder to find good quality nudes and prices continue to rise.

Non-Professionally Posed

Full Frontal, with pubic hair	35 - 45	45 - 65
Semi-Nude, with underarm hair	30 - 40	40 - 60
Semi-Nude, no underarm hair in view	25 - 30	30 - 35
Rear View	25 - 30	30 - 35
Lesbian Types	30 - 35	35 - 40

Add $5 to $10 to above for nicely tinted cards.

Professionally Posed

Full Frontal, with pubic hair	30 - 35	35 - 45
Full Frontal, no pubic hair	25 - 30	30 - 40
Semi-Nude, with underarm hair	35 - 40	40 - 55
Semi-Nude, no underarm hair	20 - 25	25 - 35

*Non-Professionally Posed Real Photo
Nude, No Airbrushing, German PC Back*

*Professionally Posed Real Photo Nude, No
Airbrushing, by Salon ER, Series 207*

*Professionally Posed Real Photo
by Salon ER, Paris, Series 214*

*Professionally Posed Real Photo
by Salon Leo, Series 70*

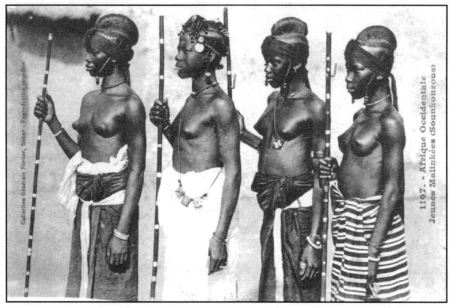

Afrique Occidentale, #1107, "Jeunes Malinkees (Sounkourous)

Rear View	20 - 25	25 - 30
Lesbian Types	25 - 30	30 - 35
Add $5 to $10 for nicely tinted images.		
Cheesecake Types, showing lingerie, etc.	10 - 15	15 - 20

AFRICAN AND ASIAN SEMI-NUDES

Ethnic African and Asian nude postcards continue to be very popular with collectors and there seems to be and abundant supply. Two quality groups entitled "Afrique Occidentale" and L & L appear to be most desirable to collectors.

L & L produced a colorful numbered series of Arabians, Algerians, Tunisians, etc. Others, titled "Scenes et Types," "Egyptian Types," and a group of "Deutsch Sud West Africa" natives by **Albert Aust**, are also commanding good prices from collectors interested in this type material. Black and white or sepia copies of many series were also produced. These are not as popular and prices are around 50% less than those produced in color. Real photo types, if original, are priced higher.

Afrique Occidentale		
Filles	12 - 15	15 - 20
Jeunes	12 - 15	15 - 18
Femmes	10 - 12	12 - 15
Others	8 - 10	10 - 12
L & L	10 - 12	12 - 15
Filles	12 - 15	15 - 18
Jeunes	12 - 15	15 - 18
Femmes	10 - 12	12 - 15
Others	8 - 10	10 - 12
Scenes et Types	8 - 10	10 - 14
Egyptian Types	8 - 10	10 - 14
P/Albert Aust	12 - 15	15 - 20
Other Nationalities	8 - 10	10 - 15

Publisher

OPF

5

Osnabrucker Papierwaaren Fabrik, of Berlin (better known to collectors as OPF), was the classical publisher of "top of the line" postcards of the 1900 to 1912 era. Their unusual methods of printing, unique image placement, and the varied assortment of paper stocks they used made their works totally different from other publishers.

Most collectors may be unfamiliar with OPF simply because it is hard to see and recognize their publisher byline. The letters OPF (with no periods) appear in a tiny three-leaf clover type logo with the "O" above the "P" and "F", that is located on the front near the image, or on the reverse side of the card. The byline "Ges. gesch- Depose" appears after the logo on some issues. There is a special "look" about the cards that others do not have. Many images are printed on tow-sack looking stock while others have a wallpaper or wood texture or other finishes, and some are etched around the edges and have borders of various colors. Many images are embossed or are die-cut paste-ons. There are cards of leather, aluminum, celluloid, wood and other materials and add-ons of many descriptions...the list goes on and on.

OPF maintained offices in Paris and London as well as Berlin, and did work for several other publishers and distributors. They published all types of postcards including greetings, holidays, comics, animals, transportation, sports, classics, ladies, children, ethnic, stamp and coin reproductions, city views, etc. However, those most adored by collectors are those of Blacks, Golliwoggs, Father Christmas, St. Nicholas, Krampus, and the ever-wonderful Fantasy types, of which many think there is no equal. The Easter Egg Lady above is valued $40-50 – 50-60. (Also note OPF logo.)

The OPF output was usually printed in sets of six or more, but without identification as to a series name or number. There are a few exceptions to this rule, but generally cards in a set will all have the same particular motif and will have the same look as to image, paper stock, border, etc. Artist signatures are rare because most images were cropped for their affect and placement on the card. Therefore, the signature, if the image originally had one, may have been deleted. In many instances, cards of a series will have the same image (usually in different size) appearing several times in a set–i.e., the Golliwoggs or the Black Cakewalk on tow-sack background.

(Continued on Page 377)

ANIMAL KINGDOM

Dog Series 1– Mouse eats hole in card.
$30-40 – 40-50

Dog Series 2 - Embossed
$25- 30 – 30-40

Mice Series 1
$20-25 – 25-35

Mice Series 2 – Mice eat hole in card.
$30-40 – 40-50

Frog and Pig Celluloid or Plastic Add-ons, various colors
$30-35 – 35-45

ANTHROPOMORPHIC CHARACTERS

Hairbrush Series
$45-50 - 50-55

Clock Series
$40-45 - 45-50

Bottle Series
$45-50 - 50-55

Clothes Series - $40-45 - 45-50

Umbrella Series - $40 -45 - 45-50

Moon Series 1 – $50-55 - 55-65

Moon Series 2 – $45-50 – 50-55

BLACKS...
GOLLIWOGGS, CAKEWALKS

Golliwogg Series 1
$50-60 — 60-70

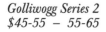

Golliwogg Series 2
$45-55 — 55-65

Caricature Heads, Uns. G. H. Thompson
$65-75 — 75-85

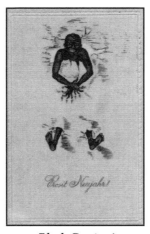

Cakewalk Series 1
$60-70 – 70-80

Black Comics 1
$50-55 – 55-60

Black Comics 2
$60-70 – 70-80

Cakewalk Series 1
$70-80 – 80-90

Blacks-Animals Cakewalk 2 (3 others are white dancers)
$50-60 – 60-70

CHILDREN

Greenaway-types
$40-50 – 50-55

Educational Comics
$40-50 – $50-55

Greenaway-types
$40-50 – 50-55

Dutch Kids – Die-cut
$40-50 – 50-55

Miscellaneous Children – $40-45 –45-50

COINS & STAMPS

National Coins Series — $35-40 — 40-45

National Stamps — $35-40 — 40-45   *National Stamps — $35-40 — 40-45*

Since there are problems with identification of OPF cards and sets, as related above, we are valuing them differently. The card(s) illustrated will contain values (VG and EX) below the image, as opposed to our regular format of placing values in the text. Since there are almost always six or more cards in each series, please assume that the value of the others not shown are most likely very close to the same value as the pictured image. The cards illustrated are just a very small sampling of the great output of this fine publisher. Collectors should search carefully for these quality cards, as many remain undetected in dealer stocks in the U.S. and in Europe. It may be noted that OPF used many images related to American themes and were, therefore, obtained from illustrators and artists here. These were distributed to European markets as well as being exported for distribution to the United States.

FANTASY

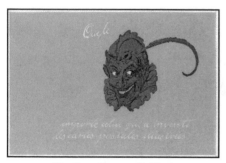

Devil or Demon Series 1
$45-50 – 50-60

Devil or Demon Series 2
$45-50 – 50-60

Umbrella Series
$40-45 – 45-50

Hat Series
$40-45 – 45-50

Stork Series
$40-45 – 45-50

Clown Series
$40-45 – 45-50

Shoes Series
$40-45 – 45-50

PEOPLE...
ALL TYPES & NATIONS

Dutch Series (B.S.L.) – $30-35 – 35-40

Egyptian Series – $30-35 – 35-40

Little "Pointed" People Series (B.S.L. Publishers)
$45-50 – 50-60

"Le Poet" – Vignette Series
$30-35 – 35-40

Fashionable Ladies Series
$40-45 – 45-55

Fashionable Men Series
$40-45 – 45-55

Street Beggar Series
$40-45 – 45-50

Street Beggar Ser. – Leather
$40-45 – 45-50

Street Beggar Ser.– Tow-
sack B.G., $40-45 – 45-55

Street Beggar Series
$40-45 – 45-50

Street Beggar Series
$40-45 – 45-55

Masters Paintings
30-35 – 35-40

Dancing Series 1
$35-40 – 40-50

Ethnic Pallet Series
$40-50 – 50-60

Comic "Gendarme" Series
$30-35 – 35-40

SPECIAL OCCASIONS

Easter Fantasy
$40-50 – 50-60

Christmas Joy
$30-35 – 35-40

Fertility Stork
$25-30 – 30-35

Dachshund Greetings
$35-40 – 40-50

Easter Chick Greetings
$20-25 – 25-30

Dancing Series 2
$35-40 – $40-50

Christmas Die-cut Add-on Doll Series
$50-60 – 60-70

SPORTS

Steeplechase Sports
$35-40 – 40-50

S/W. DeMay, Riding Series
$35-40 – 40-50

Silhouette – Hunting Series
$35-40 – 40-50

Chanticleer Series
$35-40 – 40-50

Skating Series 1
$35-45 – 45-55

Sports Skating Series 1
$35-45 – 45-55

MISCELLANEOUS

Auto Series 1
$35-40 – 40-45

Auto Series 2
$35-40 – 40-45

Smoking Series
$30-35– 35-40

Fantasy Fairy Head Series (BRW, 495)
$50 -60 – 60-70

Christmas Lovers Greeting
$25-30 – 30-40

May Bugs (Maikafirs)
$35-40 – 40-50

Vignettes Series (P.S.L., Paris)
$25-30 – 30-35

Fantasy face in clouds
$40-45 – 45-50

Revelers -Telegram Series
$25-30 – 30-35

Brussels, Belgium Statues, Bldgs. Series
$15-20 – 20-25

Uncle Sam & National Drinkers
$40-50 – 50-60

Sad Dog Comics
$20-25 – 25-35

Bathing Beauty Comic Series
$30-35 – 35-45

Hand-painted on Wood
$15-20 – 20-25

Santas are one of the most avidly collected postcards of all times. In greatest demand are the early chromolithographs and embossed issues of German origin where Santa is dressed in robes of colors other than red. Robes of white, yellow, orange, black, and gray are the most desired by collectors. The most outstanding cards are the early chromolithos by artist A. Mailick, the wonderful Hold-to-Light issues (including Uncle Sam Santas), and those of publishers PFB and John Winsch.

Santa Claus is the mythical old man who visits at Christmas and brings toys and goodies to children who have been good. American Santas are plump and jolly, wear red suits, and have a twinkle in their eye. Depending on the country, European Santas are called Father Christmas, St. Nicholas, or Nicolo. The German Father Christmas, or "Weihnachtensmanner," is thin, wears fur-trimmed robes of various colors, and sometimes has an angel to assist him on his many long journeys. He is also seen carrying the Christ Child. Most cards portray him as having a very stern countenance and he may be seen with a bundle of switches used to punish unruly children. In some instances, St. Nicholas and Nicolo have the impish devil Krampus as their helper.

It is impossible to identify the countless number of great Santas because many are unsigned and do not have a publisher byline. Others have only a series number or "Printed in Germany" as the only means of identification. This is especially true of those not published for American distribution.

SANTAS

ARTIST-SIGNED

	VG	EX
A		
French		
Lady Santa facing right - "Bonne Annee"	$70 - 80	$80 - 90
Lady Santa facing left - "Bonne Annee"	70 - 80	80 - 90
BAUMGARTEN, FRITZ or F.B. (GER)		
Comical Santas, various color robes	20 - 25	25 - 30
Art Deco type Robes	25 - 30	30 - 40

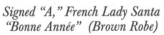

Signed "A," French Lady Santa
"Bonne Année" (Brown Robe)

Signed "A," French Lady Santa
"Bonne Année" (Brown Robe)

BOWLEY, A. L. (GB)
  Raphael Tuck
    Series 512 (6) (Unsigned)   25 - 30   30 - 35
    Series C1758 , C2099   25 - 30   30 - 35
    Series 8437, 8449   25 - 30   30 - 35
BRUNDAGE, FRANCES (US)
  Raphael Tuck
    Series 4 (12)   20 - 25   25 - 30
    Series 525, Santa Scroll Series (6)   15 - 18   18 - 22
    Series 1822 (6)   30 - 35   35 - 40
    Sam Gabriel   Series 200, 300   15 - 20   20 - 25
BEATY
  AH   8 - 10   10 - 12
CASPARI, S.
  Erika   No. 1694 Brown Robed Child Santa   25 - 30   30 - 35
CLAPSADDLE, ELLEN (US)
  International Art
    Signed   18 - 22   22 - 25
    Unsigned   15 - 18   18 - 22
  Anonymous German
    Child Santa with Switches (Very Rare)   50 - 60   60 - 75
    Other German unsigned issues   20 - 25   25 - 35
CHIOSTRI, SOFIA (IT)
  Ballerini & Fratini
    Series 220 Black Robed Santa   60 - 70   70 - 90
    Black Robed Father Time   40 - 50   50 - 60

*Rie Cramer, Months of the Year
December Santa (Brown Robe)*

*R. Ebner, Minerva, Art Deco
Series 733-3*

CRAMER, RIE (NETH)		
Months of the Year - December Santa	70 - 80	80 - 100
EBNER, PAULI (AUS)		
B. Dondorf & M. Munk issues	25 - 30	30 - 35
EBNER, R.		
Minerva		
Art Deco Series 733-3	40 - 45	45 - 50
FP Anonymous Publisher, Foreign Caption	175 - 200	200 - 225
GAILITIS, D.		
Anonymous Latvian-Russian Santa	20 - 25	25 - 30
GASSAWAY, KATHARINE (US)		
Raphael Tuck Series 501	20 - 25	25 - 40
HBG (H. B. GRIGGS) (US)		
L & E		
Series 2224, 2264, 2275 (6)		
Black Robe	30 - 35	35 - 40
Green or Brown Robe	25 - 30	30 - 35
Others	20 - 22	22 - 25
HARPER, R. FORD (US)		
Lady Santas (4)	30 - 35	35 - 45
HEY, PAUL (GER) Early German Santas		
Brown Robes	25 - 30	30 - 40
With Christ Child	30 - 35	35 - 45
HOGER, A. With Christ Child	30 - 35	35 - 40
HZONEY, CH. (CZ)		
Anonymous French Publisher (Black Santa)	110 - 120	120 - 140

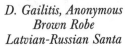

D. Gailitis, Anonymous
Brown Robe
Latvian-Russian Santa

J. Kranzle, BKWI
(Purple Robe)
Series 309-3

E. Kutzer, W.A., Dresden
No. 333, Art Deco

KIRCHNER, RAPHAEL (AUS)		
H & M Co. "Christmas" Series Santa	300 - 400	400 - 500
KÖHLER, MELA (WW) (AUS)	300 - 800	800 - 1000
KRANZLE, J. (AUS)		
B.K.W.I. **Series 3009** (6)	30 - 35	35 - 40
KUTZER, E. (GER) Art Deco Comic Santas	30 - 35	35 - 40
MBH		
Raphael Tuck		
Series 549 "Santa Claus" (6)	12 - 15	15 - 20
MEG		
Raphael Tuck		
Series 535 "Santa Claus" (6)	10 - 12	12 - 15
MAILICK, A. (GER)		
Hold-To-Light		
Red Robe	150 - 250	250 - 350
Robes of other Colors	250 - 300	300 - 400
Early Chromolithographs	25 - 50	50 - 100
W.W.		
Series 4914, 6308	65 - 75	75 - 90
Series 6670 (with Christ Child)	75 - 80	80 - 100
Red Robe	40 - 50	50 - 70
Robes of other Colors	65 - 75	75 - 100
St. Nicholas & Krampus Series	35 - 40	40 - 50
Others	65 - 75	75 - 90
MAUFF, RICH. (Stengel Art Nouveau)	200 - 225	225 - 275
NYSTROM, JENNY (SWE)		
Red Robes	15 - 20	20 - 25
Robes of other Colors	20 - 25	25 - 30
PHILLIPS, ART		
P. F. Volland & Co.	50 - 60	60 - 75
ROSMAN, AXEL (SWE)	25 - 30	30 - 35
SANDFORD, H. D. (GB)		
Raphael Tuck		
Series 8247, 8248 (6)	20 - 25	25 - 28

A. Mailick, Anonymous (Purple Robe)
"Fur die artigen Kinder"

A. Mailick, W.W. No. 4914 (Green Robe)
"Fröliche Weihnachten"

A. Mailick, Anonymous (Green Robe)
"Fröliche Weihnachten"

Axel Rosman, Brown
Fur-Trimmed Robe
(Swedish)

E. Sanger, PG-W.I., 651
Father Christmas &
Christ Child

Schentel, Richard Reutel,
Stuttgart, No. 131
"Der Weihnachtsmann"

SANGER, E.
  PG-W.I., 651 Father Christmas and Christ Child   40 - 50   50 - 60
SCHENTEL
  Richard Reutel No. 131, "Der Weihnachtsmann"   30 - 40   40 - 45
SCHONIAN (GER)
  T.S.N. Series 1090 Various Color Robes   30 - 35   35 - 45

SCHUBERT, H. (AUS) Various Color Robes	25 - 30	30 - 40
SHEPHEARD, E. (GB)		
Raphael Tuck Series 8415, 8421 (6)	15 - 20	20 - 25
WAIN, LOUIS (GB)		
M. Ettlinger		
Cat Santa Series 5226 (3)		
"Father Christmas disappointed"	300 - 350	350 - 450
"Father Christmas caught in snow"	300 - 350	350 - 450
"Father Christmas finds his way blocked"	300 - 350	350 - 450
Cat Santa Series 5376 (3) (Uns.)		
"A Jolly Christmas"	300 - 350	350 - 450
"A Merry Christmas"	300 - 350	350 - 450
"May Christmas Bring Good Luck"	300 - 350	350 - 450
Valentine & Sons		
"Santa Claus in Pussyland"	300 - 350	350 - 400
Wrench Cat Santa Series	250 - 300	300 - 350
Anonymous (1)		
"With Best Wishes for a Happy Christmas"	250 - 300	300 - 350
GERMAN SANTAS (Anonymous)		
LARGE FULL FIGURES		
(Old World, thin figures)		
Black Robe	60 - 75	75 - 95
Gray or White Robe	50 - 60	60 - 70
Blue, Tan or Purple Robe	35 - 40	40 - 50
Yellow or Orange Robe	50 - 60	60 - 70
Brown or Wine Robe	30 - 35	35 - 45
Striped, Two-color or Art Deco	45 - 50	50 - 60
Red Robe	15 - 20	20 - 30
HEADS, Upper Body or Small Image		
(Valued at 50%, or less, than Full Figures.)		
HOLD-TO-LIGHT (See Uncle Sam below)		
FULL FIGURES		
Red Robes	200 - 300	300 - 400
Robes colored other than red	300 - 450	450 - 550
HEADS, Upper Body or Small Image		
Red Robes	200 - 300	300 - 350
Robes colored other than red	300 - 350	350 - 450
TRANSPARENCIES	75 - 100	100 - 125
MECHANICALS		
Honeycomb Folders	60 - 70	70 - 80
Pop-outs	35 - 40	40 - 45
Pull-tabs	250 - 300	300 - 400
Stand-ups	50 - 75	75 - 100
Wheel-type	200 - 250	250 - 300
SILK APPLIQUE		
FULL FIGURES		
Langsdorf	40 - 50	50 - 60
AMB	35 - 40	40 - 45
Others	25 - 30	30 - 35
SMALL FIGURES	15 - 20	20 - 25
UNCLE SAM SANTAS		
(1) Flat-Printed (4)	600 - 650	650 - 800

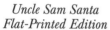

Uncle Sam Santa
Flat-Printed Edition

Publisher A.A., 3038 - NO F
"Loving Christmas Wishes"

(2) **Embossed** (4)	700 - 800	800 - 900
(3) **Squeakers** (4)	1600 - 1650	1650 - 1750
(4) **Hold-to-Light** (4)		
a. Santa Knocking on Door	2750 - 3200	3200 - 4000
b. Santa Trimming the Tree	2750 - 3200	3200 - 4000
c. Santa Standing on Step	2750 - 3200	3200 - 4000
d. Santa at Window (bag of toys)	3500 - 4000	4000 - 4400

PUBLISHERS

AA (Anglo American)		
Series 705, 708, 709 (6)	15 - 18	18 - 22
AMB Silks	35 - 40	40 - 50
AMP		
Modes of transportation	15 - 20	20 - 25
Others	8 - 10	10 - 15
ASB Series 87 Various color robes	30 - 35	35 - 40
B.W., Germany		
Series 291, 296, 305, 324	15 - 18	18 - 22
Series 297	20 - 25	25 - 30
MAB		
Series 15850 Chromolithos	25 - 30	30 - 40
Julius Bien		
Series 500	12 - 15	15 - 18
Series 5000	12 - 15	15 - 18
Bruning Santa Claus Snowman		
"Fröliche Weihnachten!"	12 - 15	15 - 18

White-Robed Santa by Publisher CeKo
No. 902-16, "Joyeux Noël"

German Blue-Robed Santa by
Publisher HWB, Series 6587

CeKo
No. 902-16 White-robed Santa, "Joyeux Noël"	40 - 50	50 - 60

Cellaro (Scandinavian)
Green-robed Santa (Drinking?)	25 - 30	30 - 35
R. L. Conwell	10 - 12	12 - 15
E.A.S.	20 - 25	25 - 30
Child Santas	30 - 35	35 - 40
Embossed German Santas	20 - 25	25 - 35
Gibson Art	6 - 8	8 - 10
Sepia	5 - 6	6 - 8

HWB
Series 6587 German Blue-Robed Santa	30 - 35	35 - 40

International Art
Signed Clapsaddle	18 - 22	22 - 25
Unsigned Clapsaddle	15 - 18	18 - 22

L&B
Series 16284 (Blue-Gray Robe)	25 - 30	30 - 35

Langsdorf
Series 1320	20 - 22	22 - 30
Silks	40 - 50	50 - 60

M.K.
Art Deco German Santa, "Am Ziel"	30 - 35	35 - 45
M.M.B.	15 - 18	18 - 22

J. Marks
Series 538 (6)	5 - 8	8 - 10
Meissner & Buch	15 - 20	20 - 30
S/F.B.	20 - 25	25 - 30

Art Deco German Santa Published by
M.K., "Am Ziel"

Embossed Brown-Robed Santa by
Publisher P.F.B., No. 7930

E. Nash
Series 3 Heads, Smoking pipe	12 - 15	15 - 18
Series 18	10 - 12	12 - 15

E. Nister
Series 2046 (6)	30 - 35	35 - 40
Series 2409 (6) Small images	20 - 25	25 - 30

OPF Paste on — 40 - 50 / 50 - 70

P.F.B. (Paul Finkenrath, Berlin) (Emb.)
Series 5431, 6227, 7933 (6)	40 - 45	45 - 50
Series 7312, 6481 (6)	25 - 30	30 - 40
Series 7930, 5434 (6)	20 - 25	25 - 30
Series 6434, 9593 (6)	35 - 40	40 - 45
Series 6439, 8935 St. Nicholas (6)	35 - 40	40 - 50
Other St. Nicholas Series	30 - 35	35 - 40
Other Santas	25 - 30	30 - 35

Robbins Bros.
Series 1163 Old Style (6) (Emb.)	25 - 30	30 - 35

Rotograph Co.
H3025 Black Robe	60 - 70	70 - 80

SB
Series 433, 7519 (6) Old Style	30 - 35	35 - 40

SB Logo (**Samson Bros.**) — 8 - 10 / 10 - 12

S&M
Series 36 (6)	20 - 25	25 - 30
Series 149 "Big Sack" Series (6)	20 - 25	25 - 30

Samson Bros.
Series 31, 705 (6)	12 - 15	15 - 20

Series 3102	25 - 28	28 - 32
P. Sander		
Lady Santas (4) – Signed **HARPER**	30 - 35	35 - 45
Black Santa – No No. Full Figure	100 - 125	125 - 150
No No. Full Figure	15 - 18	18 - 22
Large Images	20 - 25	25 - 28
Silk Santas	30 - 40	40 - 50
Santway		
Large Images, various color robes	30 - 35	35 - 40
Series 1251 Small Images	10 - 12	12 - 15
Souvenir P.C. Co.		
Series 426 (6)	8 - 10	10 - 12
Stecher Litho. Co.		
Series 55, 1555 (6)	8 - 10	10 - 12
Series 61, 203, 314, 504, 732, 737 (6)	10 - 12	12 - 15
Series 68 (6) Uns. **James E. Pitts**	12 - 15	15 - 20
Series 213 (6)	12 - 15	15 - 18
Series 227 (6)	15 - 18	18 - 22
Reprints of 1930's, 40's	3 - 4	4 - 5
Stengel & Co.		
Rich. Mauff		
Series 10-23	200 - 225	225 - 275
S.W.S.B.		
Red Robes	20 - 22	22 - 25
Other Color Robes	30 - 35	35 - 45
Transportation	20 - 22	22 - 25
Raphael Tuck* **		
Series 1, 102, 8000, 8619	30 - 35	35 - 40
Series 5, "Kris Kringle"	10 - 12	12 - 15
Series 55, 1029, 1744	25 - 30	30 - 35
Series 1766 Chromolithos	40 - 45	45 - 55
Series 136, 501	10 - 12	12 - 15
Series 512, 535, 806	12 - 15	15 - 20
Series 598 (6) Pine Cone Man Santa	20 - 25	25 - 30
Series 505, "The Christmas Series"	25 - 30	30 - 35
White Robes	40 - 50	50 - 60
Series 576B	25 - 30	30 - 35
Colors other than red	30 - 35	35 - 40
Series 1803, 8267, 8320	15 - 18	18 - 22
Series 8263	25 - 30	30 - 35
Series 8620 Various Color Robes	25 - 30	30 - 35
No No. Series "Christmas Postcards"	10 - 12	12 - 15
* Most series contain cards of children.		
** Most series contain 6 cards.		
Ullman Co.		
National Santa Claus Series 2000	25 - 30	30 - 35
Valentine and Sons		
"Christmas in Coonland" See Artist-Signed, Blacks		
WB Series 307	10 - 12	12 - 15
George C. Whitney		
Full Santas	15 - 18	18 - 22
Small Figure Santas	8 - 10	10 - 12

John Winsch, Copyright 1913, "A Joyful Christmas"

John Winsch*
Copyright 1912 – Vertical (4)
Red Robe, yellow/gold background

"A Joyful Christmas"	25 - 30	30 - 35

Red Robe, green background

"A Merry Christmas"	25 - 30	30 - 35

Santa on gold background

"I Wish You a Merry Christmas"	25 - 30	30 - 35

Orange Robe, blue background

"May Your Christmas be Bright..."	25 - 30	30 - 35

Copyright 1912 – Vertical (4)
Children watch Santa in plane

"A Merry Christmas"	20 - 25	25 - 30

Child watching Santa's shadow

"A Joyful Christmas"	20 - 25	25 - 30

Child watching Santa around chimney

"Best Christmas Wishes" (Horizontal)	20 - 25	25 - 30

Children see Santa coming from chimney

"A Joyful Christmas"	20 - 25	25 - 30

Copyright 1912 – Vertical (2)
Red-Robed Santa with Teddy Bear and
   Golliwogg at chimney

"Best Christmas Wishes"	35 - 45	45 - 55

Santa in red jacket, blue-striped pants flying bi-plane

"A Happy Christmastide"	20 - 25	25 - 30

Copyright 1913 – Horizontal (4)
Red Robe, Teddy Bear, Smokes pipe

"Best Christmas Wishes"	40 - 50	50 - 60

Red Robe, teddy bear, jack-in-box"

"Christmas Greetings"	40 - 50	50 - 60

Red Robe, with arm-load of dolls		
"Christmas Wishes"	35 - 40	40 - 45
Red/Pink Robe carrying bag of fruit		
"Merry Christmas"	30 - 35	35 - 40

Copyright 1913 – Horizontal (4)

Santa in airplane tosses toys to		
children on balcony		
"A Joyful Christmas"	25 - 30	30 - 40
Santa in airplane tosses toys to		
children on ground		
"A Joyous Christmas"	25 - 30	30 - 40
Children watch Santa in balloon basket		
"A Merry Christmas"	25 - 30	30 - 40
Children on balcony watch Santa with		
toys in airplane		
"A Christmas Greeting"	25 - 30	30 - 40

Copyright 1913 – Vertical (2)

Red Robe, driving car, big clock		
"Christmas Greetings"	25 - 30	30 - 40
Santa driving motor bus		
"A Christmas Greeting"	25 - 30	30 - 40
Red Robe, two Children...one on back		
"Best Christmas Wishes"	25 - 30	30 - 40
Red Robe, kissing one of two children		
"A Joyful Christmas"	25 - 30	30 - 40
Red Robe, one of two children whispers		
"A Merry Christmas"	25 - 30	30 - 40

Copyright 1914 – Vertical

Add-on, Santa and children on bell	30 - 35	35 - 45

No Copyright Date

Red & Gold Borders, Horizontal		
Children greet Red Robe Santa at door		
"Christmas Wishes" – No. 4164	50 - 55	55 - 60
Children greeting Santa from bed		
"A Merry Christmas"	30 - 35	35 - 45

* With Silk or Ribbon Inserts add $3-5.

REAL PHOTOS

French & European

Black & White	15 - 20	20 - 30
Tinted	15 - 25	25 - 35
St. Nicholas	10 - 15	15 - 20
U.S. Real Photos	15 - 25	25 - 30
Tinted	20 - 25	25 - 35

OTHER SANTAS

Child Santas	20 - 25	25 - 35
Lady Santas	25 - 30	30 - 45

Santa W/Christ Child - Add $10.
Santa W/Switches - Add $5 - $10.
Santa W/Angels - Add $5.00.
Santa Switching Child - Add $5 - $10.
Santa W/Odd Transportation - Add $5 - $10.
   Airplanes - Add $5.
   Autos - Add $5.00

Tinted Real Photo, Blue Robe
E.G., No. 1699/700

German Real Photo, E.A.S., No. 1041
"Ein frohes Weihnachtsfast"

S/J. Krasnowolski, Polish
St. Nicholas, Purple Robe

St. Nicholas Image by
Schönpflug, B.K.W.I.
Ser. 2586/6 (White Robe)

Yellow/White-Robed St.
Nicholas Published by
E.A.W., No. 8837

Balloons - Add $5.00
Boats, Canoes - Add $5.00
Donkey - Add $6.00
Motorcycle - Add $7.
Parachute - Add $8.

Santas in Zeppelins

25 - 100   100 - 200

Santa W/Golliwogg - Add $10.
Santa W/Teddy Bear - Add $5.
Santa W/Krampus - Add $10 - $15.
Santa Smoking Pipe - Add $5.
Santa and Mrs. Claus - Add $10.

SAINT NICHOLAS, NICOLO

KRASNOWOLSKI, J.		
Polish – Purple Robe	30 - 40	40 - 50
SCHÖNPFLUG		
B.K.W.I.		
Series 2586/6 White Robe	30 - 40	40 - 50
PFB Series 6439, 8935	35 - 40	40 - 50
Other PFB	30 - 35	35 - 40
Wearing Red/white Robe		
Full Figure	20 - 30	30 - 40
Small Figure, Head or Upper Body	10 - 15	15 - 20
Wearing Robes other than Red/White		
Full Figure	25 - 35	35 - 45
Small Figure, Head or Upper Body	15 - 20	20 - 25
Real Photo Types	15 - 25	25 - 30

KRAMPUS

Krampus was the impish devil with one cloven hoof who helped Saint Nicholas distribute toys, gifts, fruits, and nuts during the Christmas season, especially in Austria, Czechoslovakia and some other European countries. While traveling with Nicholas, he played with the children, and was good to those who had been good. However, he always carried chains and a big bundle of switches, and made use of a large basket on his back to help in the storage and later punishment of children and adults who had been bad.

Those who knew they had been bad in any way quickly scurried away to escape his wrath. Krampus, however, chased and always caught them and put them in his basket. This terrified them, thinking they were going to be switched or thrown into the flames. The crying children or adults were later released after promising Krampus they would be on their best behavior during the coming year.

He was also painted as being very suave and debonair around the pretty ladies, and many cards imply that they welcomed his passionate advances toward them. However, it was not so with the older and ugly ladies. He usually made fun of them or threw them into burning flames.

The cards of Krampus, being part of the fantasy world, are highly desirable and very collectible. The early 1900's images, especially those signed by artists and without the red backgrounds, command very high prices. Cards by artists of the highly regarded Wiener Werkstätte and any containing Art Nouveau renderings are especially in demand, as are those with both Krampus and St. Nicholas together on the same card.

On early Krampus cards, collectors will find that many artists signed only their initials or did not sign them at all. Most of the red background cards are unsigned, making them less desirable. Krampus cards are a continuing tradition, much like our Santas, and are still being produced for each Christmas season. Therefore, collectors must be wary and be sure of the era of the cards they plan to buy. All listings which follow are pre-1930.

BH, A. R. Nchf. K, Ser. 230
"Gruss vom Krampus!"

Josef Von Diveky, Wiener
Werkstatte No. 499

G.L., PG, Series 517/2
"Gruss vom Nikolaus!"

B.F.	12 - 15	15 - 20
BH		
A.R. Nchf. K, Wien		
Series 230 Girl Krampus	25 - 30	30 - 40
BOURGET (AUS) Lady Krampus	30 - 35	35 - 45
BRAUN, W. H. (AUS)		
W.R.B. & Co. Series 22 (32)	25 - 30	30 - 40
C.B.		
Georg Wagrandl, Wien		
Russian Krampus teased by soldiers	30 - 35	35 - 45
CR		
A.R., Wien Girl Krampus	25 - 30	30 - 40
DIVEKY, JOSEF VON (HUN)		
Wiener Werkstätte, 238, 499	300 - 500	500 - 750
DOCKER, E. (AUS)		
Series 45 (6) K. & Nicholas Series	25 - 30	30 - 35
Series 83 Krampus & Nicholas Series (6)	20 - 25	25 - 30
DYLER		
B.K.W.I.		
Krampus Series	18 - 22	22 - 25
EBERLE, JOSEF (AUS)		
Deutschen Schulverein, 122	30 - 35	35 - 38
EBNER, PAULI (AUS)		
M. Munk Krampus and children (6)	25 - 30	30 - 35
ENDRODI (AUS)		
Lady Krampus plays Diabolo	22 - 25	25 - 35
F.G. K. jumps through fire	22 - 25	25 - 30
FASCHE, TH. (GER)		
M. Munk Series 1086	20 - 22	22 - 25
G.L.		
Little Krampus looks down in basket	25 - 30	30 - 40
Little Krampus carries St. Nicholas' Staff	25 - 30	30 - 40
GEL, H. (AUS)		
Mean Krampus with kids (6)	25 - 30	30 - 35
Silhouettes (6)	20 - 25	25 - 30

GELLARO	20 - 25	25 - 30
H.		
Series 234 (6)		
Krampus with old ladies	25 - 30	30 - 35
Krampus wrestles old lady	25 - 30	30 - 35
H.B. Krampus & Nicholas Series (6)	25 - 30	30 - 35
H.G. H.H.i.W., Wien **Series 695**		
K. hands lady to Devil in furnace	30 - 35	35 - 40
Others	30 - 35	35 - 40
Series 568 Krampus with crying boy	25 - 30	30 - 35
H.W.	15 - 20	20 - 25
FEIERTAG, KARL (AUS)		
Child Krampus Series (6)	15 - 20	20 - 25
HARTMANN, A. (AUS)		
C.H.W. VIII		
Series 2460 (6)		
K. whips lovers; kids in basket	25 - 30	30 - 35
K. and kids above hot flames	25 - 30	30 - 35
K. and Nicholas. K. whips kids	25 - 30	30 - 35
Kids play ring-around K. with adults in basket	25 - 30	30 - 35
Series 2489, 2490 (6)	30 - 35	35 - 40
Series 2491 (6)	30 - 35	35 - 40
K. watches lovers. Kids in chains, basket.	30 - 35	35 - 40
HATZ, H. (AUS)		
Dachshund dressed as Krampus	25 - 28	28 - 32
Others	25 - 28	28 - 32
HETZEL (AUS)		
B.K.W.I.		
Series 2013 (6) K. dressed as a dandy	25 - 30	30 - 35
K.V. The Krampus Family	30 - 35	35 - 40
KUDERNY, F. (AUS)		
B.K.W.I.		
Series 2601 (6) Toy Krampus	15 - 18	18 - 22
KUTZER, ERNST (AUS)		
B.K.W.I.		
Series 3236 (6)		
Krampus listens to angel	20 - 22	22 - 25
Girl on skis with small Krampus	22 - 25	25 - 30
Krampus behind angel	20 - 22	22 - 25
Deutschen Schulverein		
Kids fight Krampus and Nicholas	30 - 35	35 - 40
Small Krampus and Nicholas on skis	30 - 35	35 - 40
Others	25 - 30	30 - 35
LIKARZ (AUS)		
Wiener Werkstätte (2)		
#889	800 - 1000	1000 - 1200
M.S.H. Little Krampuses	15 - 18	18 - 22
MAILICK, A. (GER)		
Krampus and St. Nicholas	25 - 30	30 - 35
Others	25 - 30	30 - 35
MORAUS		
St. Nicholas and Krampus	25 - 30	30 - 35

Fr. Rüster, C.H.W. VIII/2
"Gruss vom Krampus!"

Susi Singer, Pantophot, No. 22-161
"Krampusgrusse!"

O.W.
    Women as Krampus   25 - 30   30 - 35
OHLER, C. (HUN)
   B.K.W.I.   **Series 2565** (6)   25 - 28   28 - 32
P.R.
   F.K.G.
      Series 3480/1   15 - 20   20 - 25
PAL   Krampus and Nicholas in autos   5 - 18   18 - 22
PAYER, E. (GER)
   Krampus and St. Nicholas   25 - 30   30 - 35
R
   B.K.W.I.
      Series 2566 (6)   15 - 20   20 - 25
RUSTER, FR. (AUS)
   C.H.W.   **Series VIII/2**
   Krampus throws couple into flames   40 - 50   50 - 60
S.K.
   L.W.K.W.
      Series 9021-9032 (12) "Gruss vom Krampus"   12 - 15   15 - 20
SASULSKI, K. (PO)
   Pocztowski   269 Krampus and St. Nicholas   30 - 35   35 - 40
SCHEINER (CZ)
   K. leads rich man away from his money   25 - 30   30 - 35
SCHÖNPFLUG, FRITZ (AUS)
   B.K.W.I.
      Series 2586 Thinly built Krampus - red striped shorts   30 - 35   35 - 40
      Krampus carries officer on shoulders   30 - 35   35 - 40
      Krampus sits on stool, brushes hair   30 - 35   35 - 40

Krampus tweaks chin of ugly old lady	30 - 35	35 - 40
Krampus sits on mean bulldog's house	30 - 35	35 - 40
Krampus hates tennis players	40 - 45	45 - 55
Series 22 (6)	30 - 35	35 - 38
SCHUBERT, M. (AUS)		
F.R.B.P.		
Children play Krampus (6)	20 - 25	25 - 30
SINGER, SUSI (AUS)		
Wiener Werkstätte, 319, 320	750 - 900	900 - 1000
B.K.W.I. (6)	90 - 100	100 - 125
Pantophot		
22-161 Little girl holds Krampus in arms	90 - 100	100 - 120
Girl & Krampus pull St. Nicholas on toy wagon	80 - 90	90 - 110
Others	80 - 90	90 - 110
T.W.		
Girl Krampus and Nicholas	30 - 35	35 - 40
PUBLISHERS		
B.K.W.I.		
Series 2017, (6)	20 - 25	25 - 30
Series 2840/II (6) (Emb., Red B.G.)	25 - 30	30 - 35
Series 3041 (6)	15 - 20	20 - 25
Series 3263 (6)	25 - 30	30 - 40
C.H.W.		
Series 2461 (6) (Red B.G.)	20 - 25	25 - 30
Man-woman in basket, K. switches kids	28 - 32	32 - 35
Series 2498 (10)	15 - 20	20 - 25
Series 2500, 2503 (20?)	15 - 20	20 - 25
Series 2502 (6) Red B.G.	15 - 20	20 - 25
Series 2507 (6) Red B.G.	15 - 20	20 - 25
Deutscher Schulverein		
No. 122 & No. 185 Krampus and St. Nicholas	25 - 30	30 - 40
EAS		
Krampus and Well-Dressed Couple	30 - 35	35 - 45
Others	30 - 35	35 - 45
Erika		
No No. Series Red B.G.	15 - 18	18 - 22
Series 2 (6) K. and St. Nicholas	15 - 20	20 - 25
H.H.i.W.		
Series 989 Krampus scolding 2 children	25 - 30	30 - 40
Series 1608, 1626, 1628 (6)	25 - 30	30 - 35
Krampus chases beautiful lady	30 - 35	35 - 40
Karl Kuhne, Wien		
Odd looking Krampus	15 - 20	20 - 25
LP		
Series 3977 Krampus with mean kids	35 - 40	40 - 45
LWKW		
Series 9000 Red B.G. (10)	12 - 15	15 - 20
Series 1600+ (?)	10 - 15	15 - 18
M. Munk, Wien		
Series 1043 (6) Krampus & Nicholas Series	25 - 30	30 - 38
O.K.W.		
Series 1633 Krampus & Nicholas (6)	28 - 32	32 - 36
OPF Any Sets or Series, Plus Add-ons	60 - 75	75 - 125

Published by EAS, Embossed
"Gruss vom Krampus"

Published by H.H.I.W., No. 989
"Gruss vom Krampus"

Tinted Real Photo, G.P., Series 2647
"Gruss vom Krampus"

SB
  Series 3180

Crying girl in basket	25 - 30	30 - 35
Series 6185 - 86 ?	15 - 20	20 - 25

SBW
  Series 1179
"TEHO"

Giant Krampus head eating kids	28 - 32	32 - 35
Anonymous Polish Krampus	28 - 32	32 - 35
Anonymous Huge Fat Krampus (Red B.G.)	15 - 20	20 - 25

MISCELLANEOUS

Pre-1920 Artist drawn	15 - 20	20 - 30
Embossed, quality with red background	20 25	25 - 35
1920-1940 Artist drawn	12 - 15	15 - 20
Pre-1920 Black on red background	15 - 20	20 - 25
1940+ Black Krampus on red background	8 - 10	10 - 15
1940+ Artist drawn	5 - 8	8 - 12
With add-on switches	10 - 12	12 - 20
Felt of Krampus in tuxedo	40 - 50	50 - 60
Full-face large, embossed	40 - 50	50 - 100
Silk sack & switches on embossed card	25 - 30	30 - 35

Printed, Real-life, dressed as Krampus

Ladies	18 - 22	22 - 30
Children, Men	15 - 18	18 - 22

Real Photos

Children or Ladies as Krampus	25 - 30	30 - 40

7

Greetings

Greeting cards are those sent to friends and family on specific holidays, birthdays, or to simply say "Hello." These were, by far, the largest single type of early postcards printed for the American trade, and there are millions still available today.

Many were beautifully printed and very desirable, while others were poorly designed and bland, unwanted by collectors and destined today to postcard dealers' "25 cent" boxes. The majority of cards in huge accumulations or the remnants of a dealer's stock are represented in this group. Easter, Birthday, Thanksgiving, Christmas and common flowered greetings make up the greater proportion.

There were high quality and most desirable greeting cards by artists such as Ellen H. Clapsaddle, Rose O'Neill, Frances Brundage, S. L. Schmucker, H. B. Griggs, Dwig, Grace Drayton-Wiederseim and many others. Outstanding cards were also produced by publishers such as John Winsch, Paul Finkenrath (PFB), Raphael Tuck, Nash, Santway, and Gabriel. These will always be in great demand by collectors.

NEW YEAR

	VG	EX
Common	$ 0.50 - 1	$ 1 - 1.50
With Children, Father Time, unsigned	2 - 5	5 - 10
With Beautiful Ladies	2 - 5	5 - 10
With Pigs	4 - 6	6 - 10
With Dressed Pigs	8 - 12	12 - 25
With Chimney Sweeps	8 - 12	12 - 25
With Pigs/Chimney Sweeps	10 - 15	15 - 25
With Elves/Mushrooms/Gold, etc.	5 - 8	8 - 15
With Big Snowmen	8 - 12	12 - 25
With Year Date - See Year Dates		

C. Bunnell, Lounsbury *Series 2083, "A Happy..."*	*Pub. Santway, No. 1223* *"A Happy New Year"*	*H.B.G., L. & E., Ser. 2266* *"May the New-Years Key..."*

With Dressed Mushrooms, Gnomes	8 - 12	12 - 20
Ballerini & Fratini S/CHIOSTRI		
Series 220, Black-Robed Father Time	40 - 50	50 - 60
Sam Gabriel S/BRUNDAGE		
Series 300, 302, 316 (10)	10 - 12	12 - 15
International Art Pub. Co. S/CLAPSADDLE		
Common	5 - 8	8 - 10
With Children	8 - 12	12 - 30
L & E S/H.B.G.		
Series 2225, 2227, 2266, 2276 (6)	7 - 12	12 - 16
Lounsbury		
S/BUNNELL Series 2083	7 - 10	10 - 14
P.F.B. (Paul Finkenrath, Berlin)		
Series 9501 Children/Auto (6)	8 - 10	10 - 15
Others	6 - 8	8 - 15
Santway		
1223 "A Happy New Year"	8 - 10	10 - 12
Raphael Tuck Various Series		
Simple	0.50 - 1	1 - 2
With Children	2 - 4	4 - 8
(See **BRUNDAGE**)		
Raphael Tuck (American)		
Series 618, 619 (See **S. L. SCHMUCKER**)		
John Winsch, Copyright	1 - 3	3 - 6
(See **S. L. SCHMUCKER**)		
George C. Whitney	1 - 2	2 - 10
(See **S. L. SCHMUCKER**)		
Wolf Co. Signed and Unsigned **CLAPSADDLE**	8 - 12	12 - 25
Add $3-5 per card to **Int. Art Pub. Co.** prices.		
Anonymous		
Foreign Uns./**CLAPSADDLE**	15 - 20	20 - 30

EASTER

Common	0.50 - 1	1 - 1.50

E. Clapsaddle, Int. Art Ser.   Anonymous, No. 206   Pub. E.A.S., Series 1032
402, "Easter Greetings"   "He Is Risen"   "Frohliche Pfingsten"

With Children, Unsigned	3 - 5	5 - 8
With Chicks, Lambs, Bunnies	2 - 3	3 - 6
With Dressed Chicks	8 - 10	10 - 15
With Dressed Bunnies	8 - 12	12 - 16
With Transportation	3 - 6	6 - 10
Easter Witches (Scandinavian) Normal size	8 - 12	12 - 16
Easter Witches (Scandinavian) Small cards	10 - 14	14 - 18
International Art. Pub. Co. S/CLAPSADDLE		
Children	8 - 12	12 - 18
Series 402, 5837, 8270, 8684 (6)	8 - 12	12 - 18
John Winsch Uns./S. L. SCHMUCKER		
Copyright 1910 Flower Faces (6)	35 - 40	40 - 45
Wolf & Co. Signed and Unsigned CLAPSADDLE	10 - 12	12 - 18
Add $2-5 per card to Int. Art Pub. Co. prices.		
Foreign Uns./CLAPSADDLE	20 - 25	25 - 30
Anonymous		
Easter Angel	3 - 4	4 - 7

PFINGSTEN (WHITSUN) German Holiday

Common	3 - 5	5 - 8
With Children	6 - 8	8 - 12
With Miakafirs (May Bugs)	10 - 12	12 - 18
With Dressed Miakafirs	15 - 18	18 - 26
With Bugs, Insects	7 - 10	10 - 15
With Frogs	15 - 20	20 - 30
With Dressed Frogs	15 - 25	25 - 35

ST. PATRICK'S DAY

Common	1 - 1.50	1.50 - 2
With Children, Ladies	4 - 8	8 - 12
With Comics	2 - 3	3 - 6
With Uncle Sam or Ethnic Slurs	6 - 8	8 - 12
With Flags, Pipes	2 - 4	4 - 7

E. Clapsaddle, Wolf & Co.   *Pub. Raphael Tuck*   *Pub. Raphael Tuck*
"St. Patrick's Day Memories"   *"St. Patrick's Day–and I..."*   *Series 11, "Floral Missives"*

ASB	2 - 6	6 - 9
Series 340 (6)	4 - 6	6 - 10
Anglo American (AA)	2 - 6	6 - 9
Series 776, 815 (6)	4 - 6	6 - 10
Julius Bien	1 - 2	2 - 6
Series 740 (6)	4 - 6	6 - 9
Sam Gabriel	2 - 6	6 - 9
Series 140 Uns./**BRUNDAGE** (10)	10 - 15	15 - 20
Series 141 (10)	3 - 5	5 - 8
Gottschalk, Dreyfuss & Davis	1 - 2	2 - 3
Series 2040, 2092, 2190, 2410	4 - 6	6 - 9
International Art Pub. Co. S/CLAPSADDLE		
Children	10 - 15	15 - 22
Others	4 - 5	6 - 9
L & E S/H.B.G	8 - 10	10 - 16
Raphael Tuck Series	6 - 9	9 - 12
John Winsch, Copyright	**3 - 5**	**5 - 7**
See **SCHMUCKER** in Artist-Signed		
Winsch Backs, No Copyright	3 - 4	4 - 6
See **SCHMUCKER** in Artist-Signed		
Wolf & Co. Signed and Unsigned **CLAPSADDLE**	10 - 12	12 - 20
Add $2-3 per card to **Int. Art** prices.		

VALENTINE'S DAY

Common	1 - 1.50	1.50 - 2
With Children, Ladies, Cupids	5 - 7	7 - 12
With Blacks (See **BRUNDAGE**)		
With Comics	2 - 3	3 - 6
With Animals	3 - 5	5 - 8
A.S.B.	1 - 2	2 - 3
Series 227, 229, 267 (6)	2 - 3	3 - 7
B.B. London	1 - 2	2 - 3
Series 1501 (6)	2 - 3	3 - 7
B.W. Many Series (6)	2 - 3	3 - 7
S. Bergman Many Series (6)	1 - 2	2 - 3

Anonymous Raphael Tuck
"Comic Cupids," Series 15

Anonymous Embossed Valentine
"To my Valentine..."

F.B., Meissner & Buch, Series 3024
"Herzlichen Glückwunsch zum Namens..."

Julius Bien	1 - 2	2 - 3
Series 335 (6)	1 - 3	3 - 5
L. R. Conwell Series 329, 409 (6)	1 - 3	3 - 5
Sam Gabriel		
S/J. JOHNSON, Series 407 (6)	4 - 5	5 - 8
Series 413 (See **BRUNDAGE**)		
Others	1 - 2	2 - 4
International Art. Pub. Co. S/CLAPSADDLE		
Angels, Cherubs	6 - 8	8 - 12
Greetings	4 - 6	6 - 8
Children	10 - 15	15 - 22
E. Nash Many Series	1 - 2	2 - 5
P.F.B. (Emb)		
Series 7185 Cupids	6 - 9	9 - 12
Others	5 - 8	8 - 10
Samson Bros. Many Series	2 - 3	3 - 5
Raphael Tuck		
Series 11, 15, 20, 26, 100, 101, 102, 106, 107, 108	4 - 7	7 - 12
Series 111, 114, 115, 117, 118, 165, 941,1033, 1035	4 - 7	7 - 12
See **BRUNDAGE in Artist-Signed Children**		
Other Unsigned Brundage	8 - 10	10 - 15
Blacks	20 - 25	25 - 30
Leatherette Series 114, 116 (6)	3 - 5	5 - 8
Series 106, 111, 112 S/OUTCAULT	8 - 10	10 - 15
Series A, B, C, 5, 6 & 7	4 - 5	5 - 7
Series 231, "Poster Girls	25 - 30	30 - 35

Signed/CURTIS (36)	4 - 6	6 - 10
H. Wessler	1 - 2	2 - 3
Ladies Series	5 - 7	7 - 10
John Winsch, Copyright		
(See SCHMUCKER)		
Common	1 - 1.50	1.50 - 2
W/Children or Ladies	5 - 7	7 - 10
Booklet-types	6 - 7	7 - 10
Silk Inserts (Ladies)	10 - 15	15 - 20
Rose Co. Comic Series	2 - 3	3 - 5
Illustrated P.C. Co. Comics	2 - 3	3 - 4
S/HORINA Series 5004	3 - 4	4 - 6
Aurochrome Co. Comics		
S/MEYER	3 - 4	4 - 5
Wolf & Co. Signed and Unsigned **CLAPSADDLE**		
Add $3-5 per card to **Int. Art Pub. Co.** prices.		
Anonymous Embossed	2 - 4	4 - 7

BIRTHDAY

Common	0.50 - 1	1 - 1.50
With Children	2 - 3	3 - 6
BRC – Unsigned **LD**	6 - 8	8 - 10
International Art S/CLAPSADDLE	2 - 3	3 - 5
With Children	10 - 15	15 - 18
Meissner & Buch S/F.B.		
Series 3024	12 - 15	15 - 20
Raphael Tuck (American)	1 - 2	2 - 3
"Birthday Children" Series 102 (10)	2 - 3	3 - 5
Unsigned S. L. SCHMUCKER		
Series 198 "Quaint Dutch" (6)	70 - 80	80 - 90
Winsch, Copyright	1 - 2	2 - 3
W/Beautiful Ladies	8 - 12	12 - 20
Wolf & Co. Signed and Unsigned **Clapsaddle**		
Add $2-3 to **Int. Art Pub. Co.** prices.		

APRIL FOOL'S DAY

Henderson Litho Series 102	7 - 8	8 - 10
P.C.K. (Paul C. Kober)		
S/A. HUTAF	6 - 8	8 - 12
Ullman Mfg. Co. S/B. WALL		
Series 156 (6)	6 - 7	7 - 8
Winsch Backs Series 1	8 - 10	10 - 15
FRENCH 1st of Avril Fish	8 - 12	12 - 22
P.F.B.		
Series 553, 6505	10 - 12	12 - 16

LEAP YEAR

S/BRILL, B&W and Red (12)	3 - 4	4 - 8
S/P. CROSBY		
Anonymous Series 024, 1912 Leap Year	3 - 5	5 - 8
D. P. Crane S/ZIM	7 - 9	9 - 12

Dwig, Sam Gabriel, "Leap Year" Series 401, "Don't go round and round—leap..."

Sam Gabriel
Series 401 "It's Leap Year" (12) S/**DWIG**	10 - 12	12 - 16
Grollman, 1908	6 - 8	8 - 12
H.T.M. 1060-1071 (12)	8 - 10	10 - 12
Henderson Litho Series 102	8 - 10	10 - 12
Illustrated P.C. Co. Series 217	6 - 8	8 - 10
P.C.K.		
S/**HUTAF** Leap Year Series	8 - 10	10 - 12
B.B. London Series E44, E81	8 - 9	9 - 10
E. Nash		
"Lemon" Series 1 (12)	8 - 10	10 - 15
"Diamond Ring" Series, 1912		
"Captured him in his lair"	10 - 12	12 - 15
"Caught on the run"	10 - 12	12 - 15
"Don't give up the ship"	10 - 12	12 - 15
"Lay for him"	10 - 12	12 - 15
"On the Trail"	10 - 12	12 - 15
"Ring up the man you want"	10 - 12	12 - 15
Rose Co. S/**G. Brill** (6)	6 - 8	8 - 10
P. Sanders, 1908	8 - 10	10 - 15
Raphael Tuck Series 7, S/**CURTIS** (12)	8 - 9	9 - 11
S/**L. THACKERAY**	8 - 10	10 - 12
Ullman Series 156	6 - 8	8 - 10
Anonymous Series 1065	8 - 10	10 - 12
Other Common cards	3 - 4	4 - 5

GROUND-HOG DAY (See Dressed Animals)

Henderson Litho Co., Series 101 (4)		
"Come out and make a shadow"	160 - 180	180 - 200
"Don't get so chesty any old hog can see..."	160 - 180	180 - 200
"May the Shadow of your purse grow larger..."	160 - 180	180 - 200

Anglo American, Series 725
"Labor to keep alive in your breast..."

R. Veenfliet, Int. Art, Series 51766
"Three Cheers for the Red, White & ..."

Raphael Tuck , "Decoration Day"
Series158, "And never may they rest..."

"May Miss Fortunes shadow never cross your path"	160 - 180	180 - 200
Curt Teich Co. (Linen)		
87657"Mr. Groundhog – The Original..."	12 - 15	15 - 20

MOTHER'S DAY

Metro Litho Co. Series 446 (6)	10 - 12	12 - 15
Anonymous		
Lady & Soldier, "Mother's Day"	8 - 10	10 - 15
Mother holds Baby, "Mother's Day"	8 - 10	10 - 15
Mother holds baby at arm's length.	20 - 25	25 - 30
Silhouette Types	10 - 12	12 - 15

GEORGE WASHINGTON'S BIRTHDAY

Anglo American (AA)		
Open Book Series 725 (6)	15 - 18	18 - 22
Series 728 (6)	15 - 18	18 - 22
B.W.	8 - 10	10 - 12
Julius Bien Series 605 (6)	6 - 8	8 - 10
Series 760 (4)	6 - 8	8 - 10
Gottschalk, Dreyfuss and Davis Series 216 (12)	8 - 10	10 - 12
International Art Co.		
Series 51646 (8) S/**CLAPSADDLE**	8 - 10	10 - 15
Series 16208, 16209 (4)	7 - 8	8 - 10
Series 16250 (6) Uns./**CLAPSADDLE**	8 - 10	10 - 15

E. Nash, "Decoration Day," Series J-6
"In Memoriam..."

E. Clapsaddle, Int. Art, No Number
"Lest we forget..."

Series 51896 (6) S/**CLAPSADDLE**	8 - 10	10 - 15
Series 51766 (6) S/**VEENFLIET**	8 - 10	10 - 12
L & E S/**H.B.G.** Series 2242 (8)	10 - 12	12 - 15
Lounsbury Series 2020 (4)	8 - 10	10 - 12
Series 1, 2, 4 (6)	5 - 8	8 - 10
Series W5, W6, W7 (4)	5 - 8	8 - 10
Series W9, W11, 14, 15 (4)	5 - 8	8 - 10
H.I. Robbins Series 329 (8)	6 - 8	8 - 10
P. Sander Series 414 (6)	8 - 10	10 - 12
M.W. Taggart, NY Series 605 (6)	8 - 10	10 - 12
Raphael Tuck Series 124, 156, 171, 178 (6)	6 - 8	8 - 12
Anonymous (Printed in Saxony) (6)	8 - 10	10 - 15

DECORATION DAY/MEMORIAL DAY

A.S.B. Series 283 (6)	8 - 10	10 - 12
Conwell Series 376-381 (6)	8 - 10	10 - 12
S. Gabriel Series 150 (10) (See **BRUNDAGE**)	15 - 20	20 - 25
Illustrated P.C. Company		
Series 151 (8)	6 - 8	8 - 10
International Art Pub. Co.		
No No. Series S/**CLAPSADDLE**	15 - 18	18 - 22
Series 6 S/**CHAPMAN** (6)	12 - 15	15 - 18
Series 6 S/**CLAPSADDLE** (6)	12 - 15	15 - 20
Series 973, 2444 S/**CLAPSADDLE** (6)	12 - 15	15 - 20
Series 2935 S/**CLAPSADDLE** (6)	12 - 15	15 - 18

GAR Series S/**CLAPSADDLE** (6)	8 - 10	10 - 12
Series 4397 S/**CLAPSADDLE** (6)	12 - 15	15 - 18
Lounsbury		
Series 2083 (4) S/**BUNNELL**	10 - 12	12 - 16
E. Nash		
Series 1, 2, 3, D4 (6)	8 - 10	10 - 12
Series J-6 (6)	15 - 20	20 - 25
Series 21 (6)	8 - 10	10 - 12
Santway Series 157 (6)	8 - 10	10 - 12
Taggart Series 602 **and** 603 (6 each)		
Raphael Tuck "Decoration Day"		
No No. Series	8 - 10	10 - 12
Series 107 (12)	12 - 15	15 - 18
Series 158 (12)	12 - 15	15 - 20
Series 173, 179 (12)	12 - 15	15 - 20
Anonymous Series No. 1	5 - 7	7 - 10
Others	4 - 5	5 - 6

CONFEDERATE MEMORIAL DAY

Raphael Tuck		
"Confederate" Series Divided Backs (12)		
"For though Conquered..."	10 - 15	15 - 20
"Furl that Banner!"	10 - 15	15 - 20
General Joseph E. Johnson	15 - 20	20 - 25
General Robert E. Lee	25 - 30	30 - 40
General Stonewall Jackson	25 - 30	30 - 40
Headquarters, Army of N. Virginia	10 - 15	15 - 22
"In Memoriam..." 2 flags	10 - 15	15 - 22
"In Memoriam..." 3 flags	10 - 15	15 - 22
"The Hands that grasped..." 4 flags	10 - 15	15 - 22
"The Warriors Banner takes its Flight"	10 - 15	15 - 22
"Twill live in Song and Story..."	10 - 15	15 - 20
"United Daughters Confederacy..."	15 - 20	20 - 25
Raphael Tuck		
"Heroes of the South" Series 2510	20 - 25	25 - 35
Souvenir P.C. Co. With "Bee Brand" (6)	10 - 15	15 - 20
Jamestown A & V Co.		
Jamestown Expo Cards (11) See Expositions		
Veteran Art Co. "National Souvenir" Series	8 - 10	10 - 15
Winsch-back, No Publisher	10 - 12	12 - 15
Two Southern Generals Card	12 - 15	15 - 22

ABRAHAM LINCOLN'S BIRTHDAY

Anglo American (AA)		
Open Book Series 726 (6)	20 - 25	25 - 30
Series 727 (6)	20 - 25	25 - 30
Century Co.		
Sepia Series (6)	8 - 10	10 - 12
Int. Art Pub. Co. Series 51658 (6)		
"Lincoln and the Contrabands" (1)	15 - 18	18 - 22
Lounsbury Centennial (4)	8 - 10	10 - 12

E. Nash

Series 1 (6)	7 - 8	8 - 10
Gold or Silver 2 (6)	8 - 10	10 - 12
P.F.B. Series 9463 (6)	10 - 12	12 - 15
P. Sander Series 415 (6)	7 - 8	8 - 10
M. A. Sheehan No No. Series (18)	7 - 8	8 - 10
Raphael Tuck Series 155 (6)	10 - 12	12 - 15
Others, Common, Anonymous, B&W	5 - 9	9 - 15

FOURTH OF JULY

Common	2 - 3	3 - 6
With Children, Ladies	5 - 8	8 - 12
With Uncle Sam (See Uncle Sam below)	7 - 10	10 - 15
Julius Bien Series 700 (6)	8 - 10	10 - 15
Conwell Series 380 (6)	6 - 8	8 - 12
S. Garre Series 51668 (6)		
S/Chapman	8 - 10	10 - 15
Gottschalk, Dreyfuss & Davis		
Series 2172, 2099 (6)	8 - 10	10 - 15
Illustrated Postal Card Co. 151-8	12 - 15	15 - 20
Int. Art Pub Co. S/CLAPSADDLE		
Series 974, 2443, 2936, 4398 (6)	8 - 12	12 - 18
Series 51668 S/CHAPMAN (6)	8 - 10	10 - 15
Fred C. Lounsbury S/BUNNELL		
Series 2076 (6)	8 - 10	10 - 15

E. Nash, Series J-8
"Wishing You a Joyful Fourth"

P. Sander, Series 440
"Hurrah, Hurrah – Fourth of July"

Uncle Sam Series (4)	15 - 20	20 - 25
E. Nash		
Comic Series 1 (6)		
1 "How to prevent your boy..."	8 - 10	10 - 12
2 "Ye Spit-Devil is a wily..."	8 - 10	10 - 12
3 "The Giant Cracker..."	8 - 10	10 - 12
4 "Photograph your boy..."	8 - 10	10 - 12
5 "Where ignorance is bliss"	8 - 10	10 - 12
6 "The Dog..."	8 - 10	10 - 12
Series 4, 5 (6)	5 - 8	8 - 12
Series J-6 (6)	5 - 7	7 - 9
Series J-8 (6)	10 - 12	12 - 15
With Uncle Sam, Lady Liberty, etc.	15 - 20	20 - 25
P.F.B.		
Series 8252 (6)	12 - 15	15 - 20
Series 9507 S/BUNNELL (6)	15 - 20	20 - 25
Rotograph Co. S/CARR		
Series 219 (6)	7 - 9	9 - 12
P. Sander Series 440 (6)	8 - 10	10 - 15
Steiner Series 129 (6)	6 - 8	8 - 10
Tower Series 106 (6)	5 - 6	6 - 8
Raphael Tuck Series 109, 159 (12)	6 - 9	9 - 12
Ullman Co. Series 124 (6)	6 - 9	9 - 12
Wolf Signed and Unsigned CLAPSADDLE		
Add $2-3 per card to Int. Art Pub. Co. prices.		
Anonymous		
Series 312, 752	8 - 10	10 - 12

FLAG OF THE U.S.

Julius Bien Series 710, 716	6 - 8	8 - 10
Ill. P.C. Co. Series 207	5 - 7	7 - 9
Souvenir P.C. Co.	5 - 7	7 - 9

HALLOWEEN

Auburn Postcard Co.		
S/H.W.A. Series 2500	8 - 10	10 - 13
S/E. WEAVER Series 2339, 2399 (8)		
Unsigned	6 - 8	8 - 12
AA (Anglo American)		
Series 876 Witch Series (6)	12 - 15	15 - 20
AMP Co.	10 - 12	12 - 15
B.B., London (Birn Bros.) Series E-59 (6)	12 - 15	15 - 20
Bergman Co. Many Series	8 - 10	10 - 12
Series 6026, 6027 S/E. Von. H.	12 - 15	15 - 18
Series 9101 S/WALL		
No No. Cat Series	15 - 18	18 - 22
No. No. Children Series	12 - 15	15 - 20
A. C. Bosselman	12 - 15	15 - 20
Julius Bien & Co. Series 980 (6)	15 - 18	18 - 22
R. L. Conwell Co.	10 - 15	15 - 20
A. M. Davis Series 657 (12) S/AEH	18 - 22	22 - 25
Fairman Co. or "Pink of Perfection"	10 - 12	12 - 15

Frances Brundage, Gabriel & Sons
"Hallowe'en Greetings"

Dwig, J. Marks, Series 981
"Tis Hallowe'en and all girls know..."

J. Freixas, Copyright John Winch
"Hallow'en Greetings"

Sam Gabriel or Gabriel & Sons

Series 120, 121, 123 (10) S/**BRUNDAGE**	18 - 22	22 - 26
Series 124 (6) S/**M LaFa R** (Mary Russell)	10 - 12	12 - 15
Series 125, 174 (6) S/**BRUNDAGE**	20 - 25	25 - 30
Series 184 (10) S/**BRUNDAGE**	18 - 22	22 - 26

Gibson Art

Series 606 **Children**	12 - 15	15 - 18
S/**ELLIOTT** (Sepia) (12 or more)	8 - 10	10 - 12
S/**WALL** (Sepia) (12)	8 - 10	10 - 12
Many other unnumbered series.	6 - 8	8 - 10

Gottschalk, Dreyfuss & Davis

Series 2010A, 2097, 2171	12 - 15	15 - 20
Series 2243, 2279	12 - 15	15 - 20
Series 2339, 2401, 2402, 2470, 2471 (4)	15 - 18	18 - 22
Series 2504, 2516, 2525, 2526, 2662 (4)	15 - 18	18 - 22
Series 2693, 2696 (4)	15 - 18	18 - 22
Girl/Mailbox Symbol (possibly GD&S) issues	15 - 18	18 - 22
Some have **B. Hoffman** copyright, 1909.		

International Art Mfg. Co.

No No. S/**CLAPSADDLE** (12)	15 - 20	20 - 25
Series 501 S/**Clapsaddle** (4)	20 - 30	30 - 40
Series 978 S/**Clapsaddle** (6)	15 - 20	20 - 25
Series 1002 S/**HEINMULLER** (6)	12 - 15	15 - 20
Series 1236 S/**Clapsaddle** Mechanicals (4)		
White Children	200 - 250	250 - 275
Black Child	400 - 450	450 - 550
Series 1237, 1238 S/**Clapsaddle** (4)	15 - 18	18 - 22

Whitney Made (Ghosts & Skeletons)
No Caption

Rare Clapsaddle Mechanical
International Art Series 1236

Anonymous Artist, John Winsch
"Hallowe'en Greeting"

Series 1301 S/**Clapsaddle** (12)	50 - 60	60 - 75
Series 1393 S/**Clapsaddle** (6)	15 - 18	18 - 22
Series 1667 S/**Clapsaddle** (12)	12 - 15	15 - 20
Series 1815 Uns./**CLAPSADDLE** (6)	12 - 15	15 - 18
Series 4439 S/**Clapsaddle** (6)	15 - 18	18 - 22
Series 1002 S/**HEINMULLER** (6)	12 - 15	15 - 18
No No. S/**Bernhardt Wall** (12)	12 - 15	15 - 18
S/**M. L. JACKSON** **"Don't" Series**	18 - 20	20 - 22
L & E		
H.B.G. (H. B. Griggs)		
Series 2214, 2215 (4)	12 - 15	15 - 20
Series 2216 (Uns.) (4)	20 - 22	22 - 25
Series E2231, 2262, 2272, 4010 (12)	12 - 15	15 - 20
S. Langsdorf & Co.		
No No. Gel Finish (12)	10 - 12	12 - 15
S/**E.C. BANKS**	15 - 18	18 - 22
S/**R. H. Lord** (Robert H. Lord)	10 - 12	12 - 15
Fred Lounsbury Co.		
Series 2052 (6)	15 - 18	18 - 20
J. Marks		
Series 980 S/**DWIG** (12)	15 - 20	20 - 25
Series 981 Uns./**Dwig** (6)	25 - 30	30 - 35
Metropolitan News Co. (M in Bean Pot)	10 - 12	12 - 15
E. Nash		
Series 1, 2, 3, 4, 5, 6 (6)	12 - 15	15 - 20
Series 6, H-6 through 28, H-28	12 - 15	15 - 20
Series H-12, Series 29, H-29 through **H-49**	12 - 15	15 - 20

Anonymous Mechanical (Pumpkin on Spring Wire) – "Hallowe'en Greetings"

National Art Co. S/**GUNN**	22 - 25	25 - 30
National Art Publishing Co. **Series 70** (4)	12 - 15	15 - 20
F. A. Owen	8 - 10	10 - 12
S/**OUTCAULT** Buster Brown Calendar	40 - 50	50 - 60
P.F.B. (Paul Finkenrath, Berlin)		
Series 778 (6)	20 - 25	25 - 30
Series 9422 (6) Same as Series 778	20 - 25	25 - 30
G. K. Prince		
S/**M.M.S.** Series 421	10 - 12	12 - 15
H.I. Robbins		
Series 142 (12) **Series 363**	10 - 12	12 - 16
Series 383 (12?) Same as **Series 142**	10 - 12	12 - 16
The Rose Co.	8 - 10	10 - 15
Rustcraft Shop	10 - 12	12 - 15
SAS Co.	10 - 12	12 - 15
SB	10 - 12	12 - 15
Samson Bros.	10 - 12	12 - 15
P. Sander	10 - 12	12 - 15
Sanford Card Co.	10 - 12	12 - 15
S/**A.B.C.** and S/**A.M.C.**	8 - 10	10 - 12
Stecher Litho Co.	10 - 12	12 - 15
S/**M.E.P.** (Margaret E. Price)		
Series 400, 419 (6)	15 - 18	18 - 22
Series 1239 Flat printed (4)	10 - 12	12 - 15
Series 57, 63 (6) Uns./**J.E.P.** (**James E. Pitts**)	12 - 15	15 - 20
T. P. & Co. (Taylor-Platt) **Series 866**	8 - 10	10 - 12
M. W. Taggart		
Series 803, 804, 806 (8)	12 - 15	15 - 20
Taylor Art	15 - 18	18 - 20
Tower Co.		
Series 103S (6)	6 - 8	8 - 10
Raphael Tuck		
Series 100 (See **SCHMUCKER**)		

Series 150, 183 (12)	10 - 15	15 - 18
Series 160 (12) **190** (10)	15 - 18	18 - 22
Series 174 Uns./**BRUNDAGE** (6)	20 - 25	25 - 30
Series 184 Uns./**BRUNDAGE** (12)	18 - 22	22 - 26
Series 181 S/**C.B.T.** (10)	12 - 15	15 - 18
Series 188 (10)	15 - 18	18 - 22
Series 803, 816	10 - 12	12 - 15
Series 830, 831 (3)	10 - 12	12 - 15
Series 197 S/**E.M.H.**	20 - 22	22 - 25
Series 807 Uns./**WIEDERSEIM** (4)	80 - 100	100 - 120
Ullman Mfg. Co.		
No No. (B&W)	8 - 10	10 - 12
No No. (Color) (8)	10 - 12	12 - 15
Series 143, 182 (7)	10 - 12	12 - 15
S/**WALL**	15 - 20	20 - 30
Valentine & Sons	10 - 12	12 - 15
(Signed & Uns./**WALL**)	12 - 15	15 - 18
P.F. Volland & Co. (4041-4048)	15 - 18	18 - 22
S/**E. WEAVER**		
Series 2335, 2399 (8)	8 - 10	10 - 12
Series 556, Christmas (8)	30 - 35	35 - 40
George C. Whitney (Whitney Made)	12 - 15	15 - 20
Unsigned S.L. Schmucker Series (6)		
Halloween Fold-Outs	100 - 125	125 - 150
John Winsch, Copyright		
Copyright, 1911, 1912, 1913 and variations		
See S. L. SCHMUCKER in Artist-Signed		
Other Winsch Issues		
1912 German, Unsigned (6)	60 - 75	75 - 90
German, smaller variations	90 - 100	100 - 140
1913 German, Unsigned	70 - 90	90 - 110
Smaller variations	60 - 70	70 - 90
1914, Copyright, Children, Uns./**FREIXAS**	90 - 100	100 - 120
Variations	70 - 80	80 - 100
1914, Copyright, Unsigned Witches, owls	75 - 85	85 - 100
Variations	50 - 60	60 - 70
1915, Copyright, Children, Uns./**FREIXAS**		
and other artists	100 - 125	125 - 150
Black Checkered Border, no copyright,		
Uns./**Freixas**	125 - 150	150 - 175
Orange Border, Children, no copyright	125 - 150	150 - 175
Series 4975, No copyright, cats, goblins (4)	50 - 60	60 - 75
Wolf & Co.		
S/**CLAPSADDLE**		
Series 1	20 - 25	25 - 30
Series 31 (18?)	20 - 25	25 - 30
Series 501 (6) (Black & Orange Colored)	40 - 50	50 - 70
H.L. Wohler	15 - 18	18 - 25
A.A. Zwiebel, Wilkes-Barre		
Children frolics (2 known)	80 - 90	90 - 100
ANONYMOUS PUBLISHERS		
Series B37, 38, 142, 160	12 - 15	15 - 25
Series 303, 304, 308, 363, 374	12 - 15	15 - 25

MECHANICALS

Anonymous Spring Wire (J.O.L.)	30 - 35	35 - 40
Series 552 (6) (Emb.)	25 - 30	30 - 35
Series 0624, 876, 914, 1026, 1028	12 - 15	15 - 18
Series 1015, 1035	12 - 15	15 - 20

BLACKS ON HALLOWEEN

International Art Publishing Co. S/CLAPSADDLE		
Series 1286 "Halloween" Mechanical		
"A Jolly Halloween" Black boy with J.O.L.	400 - 450	450 - 500
Ullman Mfg. Co. S/BERNHARDT WALL		
Series 143 2414 "Who is oo?"	50 - 60	60 - 70
Whitney Made		
"The Goblins will get you if you don't watch out"	75 - 100	100 - 125
Anonymous		
Card No. 6505 "You would laugh too..."	100 - 125	125 - 150
Card No. 6508 "Strange sights are seen..."	100 - 125	125 - 150

THANKSGIVING

Common	0.50 - 1	1 - 1.50
W/Turkeys	1 - 1.50	1.50 - 2
W/Children, Ladies, etc.	2 - 4	4 - 7
A.S.B. Series 282, 290 (6)	0.50 - 1	1 - 3
AA (Anglo American) Series 875	0.50 - 1	1 - 3
B.B. London		
Series 2700, 2701 (6)	1 - 3	3 - 5
Conwell		
Series 637 (6)	0.50 - 1	1 - 2
Sam Gabriel	0.50	1 - 2
Series 130, 132, 133 (10) S/BRUNDAGE	10 - 12	12 - 15
Series 135 (6) S/BRUNDAGE	8 - 10	10 - 12
Illustrated P.C. Co.	0.50 - 1	1 - 2
International Art. Pub. Co.	1 - 2	2 - 3
S/CLAPSADDLE		
Series 1311, 1660, 1817	5 - 7	7 - 10
Series 2445, 4154, 4440, 51670	6 - 9	9 - 12
W/Children	5 - 6	6 - 9
W/Pilgrims, Turkeys, Corn	3 - 4	4 - 5
L. & E. S/H.B.G.		
Series 2212, 2213, 2233 (6)	6 - 9	9 - 12
Series 2263, 2273 (6)	6 - 9	9 - 12
P.F.B.		
Series 8429, 8857 (6)	6 - 7	7 - 9
Taggart Series 608 Blacks (6)	12 - 15	15 - 22
Raphael Tuck (American)		
Series 101	2 - 3	3 - 5
Whitney Made	5 - 6	6 - 8
Winsch, Copyright		
Common	1 - 1.50	1.50 - 2
Indians	3 - 4	4 - 7
Ladies	5 - 7	7 - 10
Wolf & Co. Signed & Unsigned **CLAPSADDLE** –		
Add $2-3 per card to **Int. Art Pub. Co.** prices.		

Whitney Made — Thanksgiving
"What am I thankful for to-day..."

Nash Labor Day, Series 1
"Service shall with steel and..."

ANONYMOUS
  Blacks   12 - 15   15 - 22

LABOR DAY

  Lounsbury
    Series 2046 (4)   250 - 300   300 - 350
    "Our Latest Holiday"   350 - 400   400 - 450
  E. Nash
    Labor Day Series 1
    1 "Service Shall With Steeled..."   80 - 100   100 - 125
    2 "Labor Conquers Everything"   80 - 100   100 - 125

CHRISTMAS

  Common   0.50 - 1   1 - 2
  W/Children, Animals   2 - 3   3 - 4
  W/Children, w/Toys   4 - 5   5 - 10
  Small Santas, Red Suit   4 - 5   5 - 7
  Large Santas, Red Suit (See Black Santas)   6 - 10   10 - 15
  Santas, Bas Relief Types   6 - 9   9 - 12
  Santa Transportation   10 - 15   15 - 20
  Lady Santa   10 - 20   20 - 40
    S/R. FORD HARPER (4)   30 - 35   35 - 45
  Sam Gabriel
    Series 200, 208, 219 (10)   **S/BRUNDAGE**   12 - 15   15 - 20

Pub. Raphael Tuck & Sons "Shadowgraph Series" #507 "A Merry Christmas..."	*Anonymous German* Series 606 "Christmas Greetings"	*Uns. S. L. Schmucker,* Raphael Tuck Series 556 "I like the Christmas..."

International Art Pub. Co.

Children S/**CLAPSADDLE**	7 - 10	10 - 15
Wolf & Co. S/**CLAPSADDLE**	10 - 15	15 - 18
P.F.B.		
Series 7143 Boy/Girl (6)	7 - 8	8 - 10
Series 7422 Children/Tree (6)	10 - 12	12 - 15
Series 9103 (24 ?)	6 - 8	8 - 12
Raphael Tuck (American)		
"Playtime" Series 550 (10)	6 - 8	8 - 10
"A Christmas Message" Series (10)	4 - 7	7 - 8
"Holly Landscape" Series (10)	3 - 4	4 - 5
"Glad Christmas" Series (10)	3 - 4	4 - 5
"Christmas Greetings" Series 555 (10)	3 - 4	4 - 5
(Identical to New Year Series 620)		
"Long Ago Children" Series 556 (6)		
Unsigned **S. L. SCHMUCKER**	30 - 35	35 - 45
"Joys of Youth" Series (10)	5 - 8	8 - 10
"Christmas Poinsettia" Series 558	3 - 4	4 - 5
"Muff Kiddies" Series 559	5 - 7	7 - 10
"Christmas Symbols" Series 560	3 - 4	4 - 5
S/E. von H. (Evelyn Von **HARTMAN**)	5 - 7	7 - 10
"Oilette" Series 866 (S/**A. L. BOWLEY**)	20 - 25	25 - 28
"Shadowgraph" Series 507	6 - 8	8 - 10
Winsch, Copyright See S. L. SCHMUCKER		
Common (Non-Schmucker)	1 - 1.50	1.50 - 2
W/Children	4 - 5	5 - 7
W/Ladies	8 - 10	10 - 12
W/Silk Inserts, Common	3 - 5	5 - 7
W/Silk Ladies	12 - 15	15 - 20
Booklets, Common	3 - 5	5 - 7
Booklets W/Ladies	5 - 7	7 - 10
Copyright, 1913 (4) (Non-Schmucker)	18 - 22	22 - 26
Copyright, 1914 (4) (Non-Schmucker)	18 - 22	22 - 26

A. L. Bowley, Raphael Tuck & Sons
"Oilette" Series 866, No Caption

Copyright John Winsch, 1912
"Best Christmas Wishes"

Political Uncle Sam Leather, W. S. Heal
"Hands Across the Sea..."

UNCLE SAM

W. S. Heal
Leather, Political "Hands Across the Sea"	30 - 35	35 - 40
Common	6 - 7	7 - 10
Better Publishers	10 - 15	15 - 20
Franz Huld Installment Set (each)	20 - 25	25 - 30
See Fourth of July		
Uncle Sam Santas (See Santas)		

YEAR DATES

1894-1895	80 - 90	90 - 110
1896	50 - 60	60 - 75
1897	40 - 50	50 - 65
1898	35 - 40	40 - 50
1899	30 - 35	35 - 45
1900 Common	20 - 25	25 - 30
W/Animals, People	25 - 30	30 - 35
Hold-To-Light	50 - 60	60 - 75
1901 Common	15 - 20	20 - 25
W/Animals, People	20 - 25	25 - 28
Hold-To-Light	50 - 60	60 - 70
1902 Common	10 - 12	12 - 15
W/Animals, People	15 - 18	18 - 22

Anonymous 1908 Year Date – "Die besten Glückwünsche, zum neuen Jahre"

Hold-To-Light	30 - 40	40 - 50
1903 Common	8 - 10	10 - 12
W/Animals, People	10 - 12	12 - 15
Hold-To-Light	30 - 35	35 - 45
1904 Common	7 - 9	9 - 12
W/Animals, People	9 - 12	12 - 14
Hold-To-Light	30 - 35	35 - 40
1905 Common	5 - 6	6 - 8
W/Animals, People	6 - 8	8 - 10
Hold-To-Light	25 - 30	30 - 35
1906-1911 Common	4 - 5	5 - 6
W/Animals, People	6 - 7	7 - 8
W/Snowmen	15 - 18	18 - 22
1912-1914 Common	8 - 10	10 - 12
W/Animals, People	12 - 14	14 - 16
1915-1918 Common	10 - 12	12 - 15
W/Animals, People	12 - 14	14 - 16
1919-1925	20 - 25	25 - 30
1926-1930	25 - 28	28 - 32

RELIGIOUS, VIRTUES, ETC.

CHILD'S PRAYER		
Cunningham (6)	8 - 10	10 - 14
Geo. F. Holbrook (4)	10 - 12	12 - 16
GUARDIAN ANGEL		
A.S.B. Series 250 (4)	8 - 10	10 - 15
Mark Emege Series 178 (4)	8 - 10	10 - 15
Birn Bros. Series 2109 (4)	8 - 10	10 - 12
PFB		
Series 8618, 8621 (4)	10 - 12	12 - 15

THE HOLY SCRIPTURE

S/LEINWEBER Old Testament	4 - 6	6 - 7

LORD'S PRAYER

A.S.B. Series 264, 350 (8)	5 - 7	7 - 10
DB Series 350 (8)	6 - 8	8 - 11
I. S. Co. No No. Series (8)	6 - 7	7 - 8
PFB		
Series 7064-7070, Series 8415 (8)	10 - 12	12 - 16
Unknown Publisher		
Series N-700 G (8)	6 - 9	9 - 12

TEN COMMANDMENTS

PFB		
Series 163, 8554 (10)	8 - 10	10 - 14
M. W. Taggart Series (10)		
Rose Co. Series (10)	10 - 12	12 - 16
Raphael Tuck Series 163 (10)	8 - 10	10 - 114

VIRTUES - FAITH, HOPE, CHARITY

A.S.B. Series 178 (6)	6 - 8	8 - 12
E.A.S. Series	7 - 8	8 - 12
G.B. Series (6)	8 - 10	10 - 12
Langsdorf Series	7 - 9	9 - 12
PFB		
Series 8797, 8798	10 - 12	12 - 15
Rotograph P.96	5 - 6	6 - 8

MISCELLANEOUS

Autos, Christmas Angels, Children w/Dolls, Toys	2 - 3	3 - 6
Easter Angels, other Transportation, Silk inserts	2 - 3	3 - 4
Fans, Swastikas, Wishbones, Mushrooms, Butterflies	1 - 2	2 - 3
Bells, Horseshoes, Chicks and Bunnies	1 - 1.50	1.50 - 2

G-A Novelty Art
Mushroom Good Luck
Series 1052

Anonymous Valentine
Transportation Greeting
"To my Valentine"

Anonymous
Christmas Angel
"Christmas Greetings"

Whether there were two, six, twelve or one hundred, early publishers saw the great sales benefit of producing cards in sets or series. They commissioned artists and photographers to submit their works in series, and then packaged them to appeal to their customers. This method, as history has proven, turned out to be a good merchandising scheme, and greatly enhanced the interest and collectibility of postcards at that time, as well as today. *What a thrill it is to finally find the sixth and final card to complete the set!* Collectors have been known to pay double or triple value just to obtain that last elusive card.

Because of the comprehensive listings in this price guide, this section lists only a small number of the more important sets and series that are not otherwise listed in the artist-signed or other sections. Over 2000 others are listed in other sections of the book.

PUBLISHER SETS & SERIES

	VG	EX
A.L.		
Alphabet Series 1099 (26)	$ 3 - 5	$ 5 - 7
Acmegraph Co. "Lovelights" (20)	3 - 4	4 - 5
American Colortype, 1909		
"American Beauty" Series 12	6 - 8	8 - 10
American Historical Art Co.		
"Colonial Heroes" (40)	5 - 7	7 - 10
American Souvenir Co.		
"Patriographics" Views 15 sets of 12 each	12 - 15	15 - 20
Boston Series, Alaska Series	15 - 20	20 - 25
Anti-Axis		
Colourpicture (Tichnor) "Morale Builders" (10)		
S/WALTER WELLMAN	8 - 12	12 - 16
D.R. & Co. (B&W slick-finish)		
"Slam the Axis" (6)	10 - 15	15 - 18

MWM AV Series (Linen)		6 - 8	8 - 12
Tichnor Bros. "Jap Comics" (10)		7 - 10	10 - 14
Many other publishers		6 - 9	9 - 12
J. I. Austen			
"Famous Americans" Series (24) (A325-A348)			
A325	John Greenleaf Whittier	6 - 8	8 - 10
A326	John Phillip Sousa	6 - 8	8 - 10
A327	Cyrus McCormick	6 - 8	8 - 10
A328	Alexander Graham Bell	6 - 8	8 - 10
A329	George Washington	7 - 10	10 - 12
A330	Thomas Jefferson	7 - 10	10 - 12
A331	Cyrus West Field	6 - 8	8 - 10
A332	Ulysses S. Grant	7 - 10	10 - 12
A333	Robert Perry	6 - 8	8 - 10
A334	Henry Wadsworth Longfellow	6 - 8	8 - 10
A335	Wright Brothers	12 - 15	15 - 18
A336	Andrew Carnegie	6 - 8	8 - 10
A337	George Dewey	6 - 8	8 - 10
A338	Henry M. Stanley	6 - 8	8 - 10
A339	Benjamin Franklin	7 - 10	10 - 12
A340	Thomas Alva Edison	6 - 8	8 - 10
A341	Luther Burbank	6 - 8	8 - 10
A342	Robert Edmund Lee	15 - 18	18 - 22
A343	Mark Twain	6 - 8	8 - 10
A344	Samuel F. B. Morse	6 - 8	8 - 10

Walter Wellman, Colourpicture, "Morale Builders" Series, "To My Brave..."

Publisher D. R. & Co., "Slam the Axis" Series, "Mine Fuehrer, How did you...?"

Tichnor Brothers, "Jap Comics" Series No. 73940, "Those Japs will soon be..."

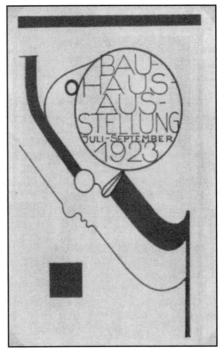

Wassily Kandinsky
3. "Bauhaus-Ausstellung Weimar"

Oskar Schlemmer
8. "Bauhaus-Ausstellung Weimar"

A345	Theodore Roosevelt	10 - 12	12 - 16
A346	Abraham Lincoln	10 - 12	12 - 16
A347	James McNeil Whistler	6 - 8	8 - 10
A348	Robert Fulton	6 - 8	8 - 10
A349	Mark Twain	6 - 8	8 - 10
Austin "Tours of the World" (100)		0.25 - 0.50	0.50 - 1
B.B., London Alphabet Series 3700 (26)		3 - 4	4 - 6
"Playing Card Series" E47 (6)		8 - 10	10 - 15
Bamforth Co.			
Song Series 063 "America's Mighty Army"		4 - 6	6 - 8

BAUHAUS EXHIBITION

A continental-size series of 20 cards was issued for **"The Bauhaus-Ausstellung"** of July-September, 1923 which was held in the German city of Weimar. These cards, drawn by 14 different artists, are among the most desired of all exhibition-type collectibles worldwide. Values are now in the $1500-5000 range, and seem to rise each time they are offered at auction. Values are for only the EX-Mint issues. Artists and the number of their cards and price in excellent condition are as follows:

FEININGER 1. "Stadt" 2. "Kirche"	4,000.00
W. KANDINSKY 3. "Komposition"	5,000.00
PAUL KLEE 4. "Die erhabene Seite"	
5. "Die heitere Seite"	5,000.00
GERHARD MARCKS 6. "Hande, Hausmodell haltend"	2,000.00
LASZLO MOHOLY-NAGY 7. "Geometrische Formen"	2,500.00

OSKAR SCHLEMMER 8. "Profile"		3,500.00
RUDOLF BASCHANT 9. "Häuser und Mästen"		
10. "Variation über Bauhaus-Signet"		5,000.00
HERBERT BAYER		
11. "Variation über Bauhaus-Signet"		3,000.00
12. "Geometrische Formen"		
P. HABERER 13. (Unknown)		1,500.00
D. HELM 14. "Variation über Bauhaus-Signet"		1,500.00
LUDWIG HORSCHFELD-MACK 15. "Figur mit		
Spruchbandern" 16. "Komposition mit Lettern"		3,500.00
W. F. MOLNAR 17. "Architektur."		1,500.00
KURT SCHMIDT 18. "Abstrakte Elemente"		
19. "Bäuhausler-Topografie"		1,500.00
GEORG TELTSCHER 20. "Männchen"		1,500.00
A. Bauman		
"Homely Girl" Series (6)	5 - 6	6 - 8
S. Bergman Co. "College Girls" Series	8 - 12	12 - 16
Julius Bien		
Series 155 "Summer Girls" (8) (Emb)	10 - 12	12 - 15
A. C. Bosselman State Capitals and Seals	6 - 8	8 - 10
Calcium Light Series P.J. Plant	4 - 6	6 - 8
Cromwell "Roosevelt in Africa" (16)	7 - 8	8 - 10
Cunningham College Girls	6 - 8	8 - 10
Daily Mail War Pictures "King at the Front" Cards of		
King of England at the Front. #81-88 (8)	8 - 10	10 - 14
Davidson Bros.		
S/Tom Browne		
Series 2569 "Adv. of a very young policeman" (6)	8 - 10	10 - 12
Series 2580 "Three Men in a Boat" (6)	8 - 10	10 - 12
H. M. Donaldson		
"American Heroes" (13)		
David Farragut	10 - 12	12 - 15
Sam Houston	10 - 12	12 - 15
Andrew Jackson	10 - 12	12 - 15
John Paul Jones	10 - 12	12 - 15
Gen. Robert E. Lee	20 - 25	25 - 28
Abraham Lincoln	15 - 18	18 - 22
William Penn	10 - 12	12 - 15
Oliver H. Perry	10 - 12	12 - 15
Israel Putnam	8 - 10	10 - 12
Paul Revere	10 - 12	12 - 15
Winfield Scott	8 - 10	10 - 12
Philip Sheridan	15 - 18	18 - 22
Capt. John Smith	10 - 12	12 - 15
George Washington	12 - 15	15 - 20
Douglas Postcard Co.		
"American Girl" (B&W)	3 - 4	4 - 6
L. Ferloni		
"Ferloni Popes" 1903	5 - 6	6 - 8
"Foolish Questions" S/COBB SHINN		
P/H.A. Waters (25?)	5 - 7	7 - 10
P. Gordon, 1908 Ladies (10)	6 - 8	8 - 10
Golf Girl, Tennis Girl	18 - 22	22 - 25

W. R. Gordon, Phila.
   Presidential Series (25) Unnumbered (B&W)   4 - 5   5 - 6
I. Grollman
   "Merry Widow Hat" Series (16)   4 - 5   5 - 6
E. Gross & Co.
   S/Hamilton King
     "Bathing Beauty" Series (12)   15 - 20   20 - 25
Hill   **University Girls, Series 8**   6 - 8   8 - 12
D. Hillson, 1907
   American Beauty Series 4100 (Red) (23)   6 - 8   8 - 12
   College Girls, Ivy League   10 - 12   12 - 15
Illustrated Post Card Co. State Capitols (47)   5 - 6   6 - 8
K-win, 1909 **"How Cook and Peary Discovered**
   the North Pole" Series (50) (B&W slick finish)   8 - 10   10 - 15
   Title card   15 - 20   20 - 25
Klein Alphabet Series (See **Topicals**)
P. C. Kober (PCK)
   "Advice to the Lovelorn" S/HUTAF   8 - 10   10 - 12
   Butterflies with Views in Wings   15 - 18   18 - 20
   "Diabolo" S/HUTAF   10 - 15   15 - 18
   Pansies with Views in Petals   12 - 15   15 - 20
   State Flags   8 - 10   10 - 12
J. Koehler
   "Hold-To-Light" Series
   New York City (24)   35 - 40   40 - 50

*Pub. K-win, "How Cook and Peary
Discovered The North Pole" Series*

"Daily Mail" War Pictures, No. 83
"The King at the Front"

Pub. K-win, "Cook and Peary" Series
"Aluminum sledge used by Dr. Cook ..."

Coney Island (12)	40 - 50	50 - 55
"Fighting the Flames"	1500 - 1800	1800 - 2200
Washington, D.C. (12)	30 - 35	35 - 45
Hudson River (12)	30 - 35	35 - 45
Philadelphia (12)	30 - 35	35 - 40
Boston (12)	30 - 35	35 - 40
Chicago (12)	35 - 40	40 - 50
Atlantic City (6)	35 - 40	40 - 50
Buffalo (6)	30 - 35	35 - 40
Niagara Falls (6)	30 - 35	35 - 40

K.V.i.B. National Flag Series
Woman in Flag Dress Series 80 200+	6 - 8	8 - 10

S. Langsdorf & Co.
Alligator Borders (165)		
Blacks	90 - 110	110 - 125
Views	30 - 35	35 - 40
Shell Border Views	10 - 15	15 - 20
State Capitals (5)	8 - 10	10 - 12
State Girls (30)	12 - 15	15 - 20
Embossed	15 - 18	18 - 22
Puzzles	30 - 35	35 - 40
Silk Applique	30 - 35	35 - 38
Military Uniform "L" Series	12 - 15	15 - 20
"Nonsense Rebus Series" Series 2047 (12?)	6 - 8	8 - 12

Large Letter Cards
Asheville Postcard Co.	2 - 3	3 - 5
W/Blacks	5 - 7	7 - 9
Colourpicture (Tichnor)	2 - 3	3 - 5
W/Blacks	5 - 7	7 - 9
E.C. Kropp Co.	2 - 3	3 - 5
W/Blacks	5 - 7	7 - 9
Other Publishers	2 - 3	3- 5
W/Blacks	5 - 7	7 - 10
Army, Marine, Air Force Training Bases		
Curt Teich & others	3 - 6	6 - 9

Hugh Leighton & Co.
Bathing Beauties Series (12)	8 - 10	10 - 15
State Capitols	6 - 8	8 - 10
Unnamed Presidential Series	6 - 8	8 - 10

Fred C. Lounsbury, 1908
American Flags & Betsy Ross	8 - 10	10 - 12
National Girls (4)	6 - 8	8 - 10
"The American Girl"	12 - 14	14 - 16

M. J. Mintz, Chicago
"African Safari" Series (24) (Sepia, Slick Finish)	8 - 10	10 - 12

E. H. Mitchell "Zodiac" S/AENZ (12)	8 - 10	10 - 12
Months of the Year, French (12) (Undb)	10 - 12	12 - 15

E. Nash
Months of the Year, Series 37 (12)	6 - 8	8 - 10
"National Song" Series (6)	8 - 12	12 - 15

Mutoscope-Exhibit Supply Pin-Ups (Non-P.C. Backs)
Group I (Note: Listed higher values are for NM-Mint)		
"Glamour Girls" (32) Various Artists *	12 - 16	18 - 24

S. Langsdorf & Co., "Alligator Borders"
Series, No. S-541, "On the Ocklawaha..."

S. Langsdorf & Co., "U. S. Military" L-
Series, "'Corporal,' U. S. Cavalry"

Colourpicture, "Large Letter States" Series
No. 16105, "Greetings from ARKANSAS"

Curt Teich, "Air Force Base" Series
"Greetings from VICTORVILLE"

Earl Moran, Mutoscope "Glamour Girls"
Series, "Do You Still Prefer Blondes?"

Pub. M. J. Mintz, "African Safari" Series
No. 15, No Caption

"All-American Girls" (33) Various Artists *	14 - 18	22 - 27
"Yankee Doodle Girls" (32) Various Artists *	14 - 18	18 - 27
"Up to Par" (Golf)	35 - 50	65 - 85
"Follies Girls" (32) Various Artists *	18 - 24	30 - 35
"Hotcha Girls" (65) Artist–**EARL MORAN**	14 - 18	22 - 27
"Golden Hours"	75 - 100	175 - 200
"My Drivers License"	180 - 200	200 - 220
"Up to Par" (Golf)	35 - 50	65 - 85
"Artist Pin-Up Girls" (64} Various Artists *	10 - 12	12 - 16

Group II–Exhibit Supply Co. Has "Litho USA," or "Litho in USA" but bylines of Exhibit Supply or Mutoscope does not appear on cards.

"Calendar Girls I" (32) Various Artists * **	85 - 120	120 - 185
"Calendar Girls II" (32) Various Artists * ***	65 - 100	100 - 165
"Slick Chicks" (Dipsy Doodle) (32) Var. Artists *		
W/Printed Poem	55 - 80	80 - 150
"Slick Chick Twins" (2/card) (32) Var. Artists *		
Slightly larger cards	55 - 80	80 - 120

*   ALDEN, ARMSTRONG, EARL CHRISTY
CONNALLY, D'ANCONA, DEVORSS
ELVGREN, FRAHM, GCA, HARRIS, LAYNE
LESLIE, DEL MASTERS, MORAN, MOZERT
MUNSON, RUSS, SHOWALTER & UNKNOWNS
** Identified by "Litho in USA"
*** Identified by "Litho USA"

National Art Co.

National Girls S/**ST. JOHN**	8 - 10	10 - 12
State Girls (46)	6 - 7	7 - 8
National Colortype Co. State Capitols	6 - 7	7 - 8

"National Dance" Series P/**W&A.K. Johnson**

Series 125	10 - 12	12 - 15
3 "U.S.A.–The Coon Dance"	20 - 25	25 - 30

P.F.B. (Paul Finkenrath, Berlin)

Series 3315 Cupids (6)	6 - 9	9 - 11
Series 5563 Girl and Cat (6)	8 - 10	10 - 12
Series 5897 Mother-in-Law Series (6)	10 - 12	12 - 15
Series 6012 "Punch and Judy" (6)	12 - 15	15 - 20
Series 6307 Comic Lovers (6)	6 - 8	8 - 10
Series 7143 Christmas Greetings (3) Children	8 - 10	10 - 12
Series 9327 "Diabolo" 6)	12 - 15	15 - 20
Series 6538 "Domestic Squabbles" (6)	8 - 10	10 - 12
Series 6800 Children and Roosters (6)	8 - 10	10 - 12
Series 6943 "Children's Games ..." (6)	10 - 12	12 - 15
Series 6949 Bride & Groom (6)	6 - 8	8 - 10
Series 7185 Cupids & Large Hearts (6)	6 - 8	8 - 10
Series 7318 Children in Vehicles (6)	10 - 12	12 - 15
Series 7608 Comic Lovers (6)	8 - 10	10 - 12
Series 8120 Nymph and Shell (6)	12 - 15	15 - 20
Series 8180 Two Mischievous Boys (6)	8 - 10	10 - 12
Series 8403 Dressed Rooster or Hen (6)	12 - 15	15 - 20

Platinachrome Co.

National Girls (23)	10 - 12	12 - 15
State Girls (45)	7 - 8	8 - 10

Pub. W. & A.K. Johnson
"National Dance" Series 125
"U.S.A., The Coon Dance"

Yves Diey, Publisher Adia
"Prostitute" Series 31-12

Yves Diey, Publisher Adia
"Prostitute" Series 31-13

Prohibition Comics S/**WEAVER** (10)	8 - 10	10 - 12
Prostitute Series 31, French P/**Adia,** S/**YVES DIEY**		
7 Lady with Red Rose	30 - 35	35 - 45
12 Lady with bare breasts	35 - 45	45 - 55
13 Lady smoking cigarette	30 - 35	35 - 45
Charles Rose, 1908		
Rose Song Cards (24)	6 - 8	8 - 10
"Maids" Series	5 - 6	6 - 9
"Ten Commandments" (10)	7 - 8	8 - 12
"Roosevelt's African Hunt"		
Underwood & Underwood (40)	5 - 8	8 - 12
"Roosevelt's Tour"		
Capper (24)	5 - 8	8 - 12
Rotograph Co. (Real Photos)		
Alphabet B-247 thru B-452 (26)	4 - 5	5 - 6
College Girls Series FL100 (6)	10 - 12	12 - 15
Large Letter Name Series B-848 thru B-879	6 - 8	8 - 10
Samson Brothers		
Series 86 "Vegetables" (12)	3 - 4	4 - 7
"Uneedn't" (12)	3 - 4	4 - 7
M. A. Sheehan (1940's)		
Serigraphs of Presidents by P. Dubosclard (32)	4 - 7	7 - 10
M. T. Sheehan "Your Fortune ...		
"If you were born in..." (12)	5 - 6	6 - 9
Souvenir Post Card Co., 1905		
College Girl, Series 4 (6)	8 - 10	10 - 15
M. W. Taggart Series 25 **Bathing Beauties** (6)	12 - 15	15 - 18
"Those Foolish Questions" Gartner & Bender (Sepia)	5 - 8	8 - 12
Raphael Tuck & Sons		
Advice to Scouts, Series 8745 (6)	15 - 20	20 - 25
Aeroplanes, Series 3101 (6)	15 - 20	20 - 25
Aeroplanes & Warships, Series 9857 (6)	12 - 15	15 - 18
Airships, Series 9495, 9998 (6)	10 - 15	15 - 20
All Sorts of Pets Series 5641, 8032 (6)	8 - 10	10 - 12
Allied Flags Series 872 (6)	10 - 12	12 - 15

Raphael Tuck, "Kings and Queens of England," Series 616 "William III"

Raphael Tuck "The Carnival" Series 363-B, No Caption

Raphael Tuck, "Fair Women" Series, No. 232, "A Valentine"

Among The Bunnies, Series 9539 (6)	6 - 8	8 - 10
Animal Expressions, Series 9249 (6)	6 - 8	8 - 10
Animal Life, Series 274, 1416, 1417, 1418, 1419	8 - 10	10 - 12
Animal Studies, Series 4453, 4454, 4455, 4461, 4462 (6)	8 - 12	12 - 15
Animal Studies S/McGUIRE Series 6713, 6714 (6)	10 - 12	12 - 15
"The Carnival," Glosso Series 363B (12) (B&W)	10 - 12	12 - 15
"At the Carnival," Series 117 (12)		
"A Gallant"	18 - 22	22 - 25
"Belle of the Ball"	18 - 22	22 - 25
"The Cake Walk"	20 - 25	25 - 28
"Confidants"	18 - 22	22 - 25
"Grace and Beauty"	18 - 22	22 - 25
"Harlequin and Columbine"	20 - 25	25 - 28
"Jolly Comrades"	18 - 22	22 - 25
"La Paloma"	18 - 22	22 - 25
"Music Hath Charms"	18 - 22	22 - 25
"Only Teasing"	18 - 22	22 - 25
"The Queen"	18 - 22	22 - 25
"Ticklish Situation"	18 - 22	22 - 25
"Celebrated Painters" Series 9404 (6)	8 - 10	10 - 12
"Characters from Dickens" S/KYD Series 540, 541, 856, 5441 (6)	10 - 12	12 - 15
College Girls "Football," Series 2344 (6)	20 - 25	25 - 28
"Diabolo," Series 102, Uns./Brundage (6)	18 - 22	22 - 25
"Greetings from the Seaside," Series 116 (12)	5 - 7	7 - 9
"Educational Series" 404 "U.S. Army" (12)	8 - 12	12 - 16
"Fair Women" Series 232 (6)	15 - 18	18 - 25
Heraldic Series, 3308-3331 (24)	15 - 18	18 - 22
Heraldic Series Boston #5010-5019 (Emb.)	15 - 18	18 - 22
"Heroes of the South" Raphael Tuck Series 2510	15 - 20	20 - 25
Hiawatha, Series 9011 (6)	10 - 12	12 - 15

R. Tuck, Series 8711, "Hurrah for the
Holidays!" – "On the Sands"

R. Tuck, Series 8711, "Hurrah for the
Holidays!" – "Would you like to join us?"

"Hurrah for the Holidays!" Series 8711 (6)	12 - 15	15 - 22
"Ideal Heads" Series 9392 (6)	15 - 20	20 - 25
"Indian Chiefs" Series 3495 (6)	12 - 15	15 - 20
"Leap Year" R. Tuck Series 7 (12)	7 - 10	10 - 12
"Little Men and Women" R. Tuck (24?)	8 - 10	10 - 12
"Name" Series 131 (50 or more)	7 - 10	10 - 12
"Oxford Pageant"		
By various artists throughout each set		
Series 2783, 2784, 2785 (6)	10 - 12	12 - 16
"Portraits of Presidents" Series 2328 (25)	10 - 12	12 - 15
"Presidents of the U.S." (26)	8 - 10	10 - 12
"Shakespeare" Series 472 (6)	6 - 8	8 - 10
"Shakespeare's Heroes & Heroines"		
Series 1277 (6)	12 - 15	15 - 20
"State Belles" Series 2669 (45)	10 - 12	12 - 15
"Zodiac" S/DWIG Series 128 (12) (See Dwig)		
Homes of U.S. Presidents, Series 2900 (25)	6 - 8	8 - 10
State Capitols & Seals, Series 2454 (45)	5 - 6	6 - 8
Kings & Queens of England		
Series 614 (12)	10 - 15	15 - 20
Series 615 (12), Series 616 (12)	10 - 15	15 - 20
Series 617 (6) – All of Edward VII	20 - 25	25 - 30
John Winsch Authors	6 - 7	7 - 8
"What Every Woman Knows" by A.P.F. Co. (12)	4 - 5	5 - 7

WIENER WERKSTÄTTE

The wonderful postcards of the Wiener Werkstätte were produced during the 1908-1912 era in Vienna while the "Secessionist" art movement was in vogue. A group of approximately 50 talented artists began producing extremely beautiful works differing in style from the Art Nouveau works of their predecessors.

The **WW** series consisted of almost 1100 different cards, and production runs varied from a low of 200 to as many as 6000-7000 per card. Therefore, the number produced, the particular artist, and the number believed to still be in existence influence the price structure.

Most have the WW trademark in a box on the reverse side and the card number just below. The most popular artists were O. Kokoshka, Egon Schiele, Rudolf Kalvich, Moritz Jung, Mela Köhler, and Joseph Hoffman. Some cards have reached values as high as $3000-4000 each. Other artists of importance, who are also well known for works by other publishers, are Mela Köhler, Susi Singer, and Walter Hampel. Values listed are only for cards in the very best condition.

Moriz Jung
Wiener Werkstätte, No. 52

Mela Köhler
Wiener Werkstätte, No. 426

Mela Köhler
Wiener Werkstätte, No. 595

WIENER WERKSTÄTTE (Vienna Workshops)

BERAN, OTTO Birthday, Easter (2)	400 - 500	500 - 600
BERGER, FRITZI Fashion (3)	350 - 450	450 - 550
BOHLER, HANS Japonism (6)	400 - 600	600 - 1000
CZESCHKA, CARL OTTO New Year (1)	800 - 1000	1000 - 1200
DELAVILA, FRANZ KARL		
Christmas, Easter, New Year (6)	400 - 500	500 - 700
DIVEKY, JOSEF		
City Sights (14)	200 - 500	300 - 700
Café Fledermaus (2)	1250 - 1500	1500 - 2000
1908 Kaiser Jubilee (6)	200 - 350	250 - 450
Christmas, Santa, Krampus (8)	250 - 600	400 - 800
Easter (1)	300 - 350	350 - 400
Fashion (8)	300 - 350	350 - 400
Dolls (7)	500 - 700	600 - 800
Fantasy (6)	400 - 1200	600 - 1500
DREXLER, LEOPOLD City Sights (2)	150 - 200	200 - 250
FRIEDMANN, MIZI		
Fantasy, Elves, Christmas (6)	300 - 400	400 - 500
GEYLING, REMIGIUS		
1908 Kaiser Jubilee (8)	150 - 350	200 - 400
Fashion (5)	150 - 350	200 - 400
HOFFMANN, JOSEF		
Easter (1)	800 - 1000	1000 - 1200
Café Fledermaus (1)	1500 - 2000	2000 - 2500
HOPPE, EMIL		
1908 Art Exhibition (4)	400 - 500	500 - 700
City Sights (7)	150 - 400	200 - 500
JANKE, URBAN		
Fantasy Jester (1)	300 - 400	400 - 500
Easter (1), Fashion (5), City Sights (9)	150 - 200	200 - 250
JESSER, HILDA Fashion (3)	400 - 500	500 - 700
JUNG, MORIS		
Christmas (1)	600 - 650	650 - 750
Social Satire (34)	500 - 1500	750 - 2000

E. Kuhn
Wiener Werkstätte, No. 449

Maria Likarz
Wiener Werkstätte. No. 769

Aviation Fantasy (5)	700 - 900	800 - 1000
City Sights (4)	300 - 500	400 - 700
Music, Phonographs (10))	700 - 1000	800 - 1200
At the Zoo (9))	400 - 800	600 - 1000
Satirical Caricatures (6)	700 - 900	800 - 1000
JUNGNICKEL, LUDWIG HEINRICH		
Fashion (6)	300 - 400	400 - 500
Fantasy Animals (5)	400 - 500	500 - 600
KALHAMMER, GUSTAV		
Decorative (2), City Sights (13)	150 - 300	200 - 350
KALMSTEINER, HANS Puppet Shows (7)	500 - 700	600 - 800
KALVACH, RUDOLF Birthday (1),		
Christening (2), Fantasy (19)	1200 - 2500	1500 - 3000
KÖHLER, MELA		
Children (24)	150 - 500	200 - 600
Easter (6)	200 - 250	250 - 300
Christmas (10)	150 - 800	200 - 1000
Santa, Krampus (6)	300 - 800	400 - 1000
New Year (5)	300 - 700	400 - 800
Fashion (89)	150 - 800	200 - 1000
KOKOSCHKA, OSKAR Fantasy (14),		
Christmas (1), Easter (1)	1000 - 2000	2000 - 3000
KOLBE, LEOPOLDINE Flower Baskets (6)	300 - 350	350 - 400
KRENEK, CARL		
City Sights (12)	150 - 400	200 - 500
Santa (1)	450 - 500	500 - 550

Fritzi Low
Wiener Werkstätte, No. 1003

Fritzi Low
Wiener Werkstätte. No. 1001

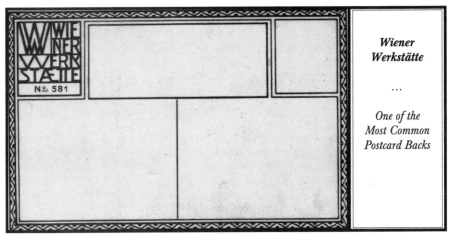

Wiener
Werkstätte

...

One of the
Most Common
Postcard Backs

KUHN, FRANZ

City Sights (33)	150 - 350	200 - 400
Easter (2), Fantasy (1)	800 - 1000	1000 - 1200
LEBISCH, FRANZ Decorative (10), Easter (1)	100 - 250	150 - 300
LENDECKE, OTTO		
Easter (2)	200 - 250	250 - 300
Fashion (12)	300 - 350	350 - 400
LEUPOLD-LOWENTHAL, ALOIS City Sights (3)	200 - 250	250 - 300

LIKARZ, MARIA
Easter (1), Christmas (1)	450 - 500	500 - 550
Krampus (2)	800 - 1000	1000 - 1200
New Year (5)	300 - 700	400 - 800
Decorative (1)	550 - 600	600 - 650
Woman w/Butterfly (1)	550 - 600	600 - 650
Woman w/Beetle (1)	500 - 550	550 - 600
Masked Costumers (13)	150 - 350	200 - 400
Fashion (34)	200 - 700	300 - 800

LOFFLER, BERTHOLD
Easter (1), Good Luck (1)	150 - 200	200 - 250
1908 Kaiser Jubilee (4)	150 - 350	200 - 400
Fantasy (17)	150 - 700	200 - 800
Fledermaus Cabaret Advertisement (2)	3000 - 3500	3000 - 4000

LÖW, FRITZI
Easter (3), New Year (1)	400 - 450	450 - 500
Months of the Year (12)	300 - 350	350 - 400
Fashion (28)	75 - 250	100 - 300

LOWENSOHN, F. New Year (1) — 750 - 800 — 800 - 850

LUKSCH-MAKOWSKA, ELENA
Social Satire of Russian Life (12)	400 - 700	500 - 800
Vienna Restaurant Interior (2)	400 - 450	450 - 500

MARISCH, GUSTAV New Year (1)
Sledding (1), Decorative (6)	300 - 350	350 - 400

NECHANSKY, ARNOLD
Easter (5)	600 - 800	800 - 1000
Christmas (1), Santa/Krampus (2),		
New Year (6)	500 - 800	600 - 1000

OSWALD, WENZEL
Easter (2)	350 - 400	400 - 450
Fantasy (1)	200 - 250	250 - 300

PECHE, DAGOBERT Harlequin (2) — 350 - 400 — 400 - 450
PETTER, VALERIE Easter (1) — 350 - 400 — 400 - 450
SCHIELE, EGON Women Portraits (3) — 3500 - 5000 — 4000 - 6000
SCHMALl, EMIL City Sights (8), Fashion (1) — 150 - 200 — 200 - 250
SCHWETZ, KARL City Sights (61) — 100- 250 — 150 - 300

SIKA, JUTTA
City Sights (5)	300 - 350	350 - 400
Krampus (1)	550 - 600	600 - 650

SINGER, SUSI
Fashion (5), Easter (1), Fantasy (1)	300 - 400	400 - 500
Christmas (3), Santa & Krampus (2)	500 - 1000	700 - 1200

SPEYER, AGNES Fantasy (1) — 900 - 1000 — 1000 - 1100

TESCHNER, RICHARD
Fantasy (2)	150 - 200	200 - 250
Children with Toys (5)	300 - 500	400 - 600

VELIM, ANTON Christmas (5) — 400 - 600 — 500 - 700

WIMMER-WISGRILL, EDUARD JOSEF
Fashion (10)	250 - 300	300 - 350

ZEYMER, FRITZ
Easter (1), Christmas (1)	350 - 400	400 - 450
Fledermaus Cabaret	700 - 750	750 - 800

ZWICKLE, HUBERT von 1908 Kaiser Jubilee (4) — 150 - 350 — 200 - 400

 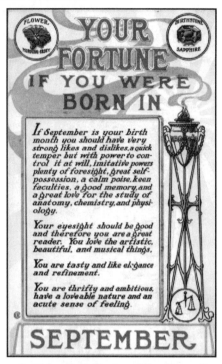

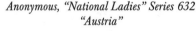

Anonymous, "National Ladies" Series 632
"Austria"

Publisher M. T. Sheehan, "Your Fortune"
Series, "September"

There are 100 additional Wiener Werkstätte postcards by anonymous artists. There are also 123 missing numbers which have not surfaced. The complete series runs from #1 through #1011. A few numbers have been used twice with different designs and artists. Much of the information here is taken from *Die Postkarten der Wiener Werkstätte* by Traude Hanse, which contains the most complete listing and illustrations of this series.

WOMEN'S WORLD

"Lover's Lane, St. Jo" Eugene Field (12)	2 - 3	3 - 5
ANONYMOUS		
"Adventures of Lovely Lilly" Series 2026	30 - 35	35 - 40
Flag & Eagle Presidents		
Millard Fillmore, U.S. Grant, B. Harrison	8 - 12	12 - 15
Thomas Jefferson, James Madison	8 - 12	12 - 15
Wm. McKinley, James Monroe, James Polk	8 - 12	12 - 15
T. Roosevelt, Zachary Taylor, John Tyler	8 - 12	12 - 15
George Washington	8 - 12	12 - 15
National Ladies Series 632	8 - 10	10 - 12
"Sheridan's Ride" (10)	8 - 10	10 - 12
Song Cards		
Series 1100, 1101 (18?)	4 - 5	5 - 7
"Your Fortune" (12) Birthstone, Zodiac,		
Fortune, etc., (Emb)	10 - 12	12 - 15

Advertising

The postcard as an advertising medium began in 1893 when cards were printed for vendors at the Columbian Exposition in Chicago. Those visiting the Exposition purchased these cards and sent them back home to friends as proof of their attendance at the gala event. Most of the cards issued showed buildings of the Expo. However, there were many issues by the exhibitors showing their products and telling of their services.

This first special trial was extremely successful and prompted manufacturers and service oriented businesses throughout the U.S. to "jump on the bandwagon." The great acceptance by the public and the reduced postage rates for postcards made the difference. Millions of advertising postcards, both color and black and white, were printed and mailed during the first year alone. Advertisers either mailed their own cards or gave them to customers to distribute.

High competition in all modes of product manufacturing and services prompted advertisers and merchants to publish high quality and beautiful sets and series by the artists of the day. As can be seen from the following listings, some of the companies are still in business and this alone makes them more collectible. The beauty and elusiveness of many of these cards have played a major role in making advertising postcards one of the favorites by many in the hobby.

	VG	EX
A.B.A. Travelers' Cheques	$ 10 - 12	$ 12 - 15
Absorbine Pain Killer	8 - 10	10 - 15
Acker's Swiss Chocolates	8 - 10	10 - 15
Acroline Dandruff Remover	8 - 12	12 - 16
Alamito Golden Guernsey Milk	6 - 8	8 - 10
Albert Hosiery Co. (12)	8 - 10	10 - 15
Alexander, M.H. Co., Molasses	8 - 10	10 - 12
Allentown Adpostals (7) Multiple ads	35 - 45	45 - 55
Amaro Gambarotta "Broken Leg" Bitters	300 - 350	350 - 400
American Enamel Co., 1906	5 - 7	7 - 10

American Thermos Bottle Company
"On the Beach"

"Amaro Gambarotta" – "Broken Leg"
Bitters Ad, ca. 1920

"American Souvenir Card Co."
Advertising Patriographic Ser. (Boston 3)

American Journal Examiner See Comics Section		
Comics, by many artists	8 - 10	10 - 15
American Fence Co.	5 - 7	7 - 10
American Lady Corsets	8 - 10	10 - 15
American Motor Co. (B&W)		
Motor Cycle Ad w/miles per gallon	30 - 35	35 - 40
American Souvenir Cards		
Advertising the Patriographic Card Series (Boston 3)	40 - 50	50 - 60
American Thermos Bottles (10)	5 - 7	7 - 10
"On The Beach"	10 - 12	12 - 15
American Woolen Co.	8 - 10	10 - 12
Anheuser-Busch Brewing Co. (Western)	6 - 8	8 - 12
Anheuser-Busch Brewery Scenes	8 - 10	10 - 15
Anheuser-Busch Beer Wagon/Horses	10 - 15	15 - 18
Argand Stoves	6 - 8	8 - 10
Armour & Co.		
American Girl Series (12)		
"The Karl Anderson Girl"	12 - 15	15 - 20
"The Walter A. Clark Girl"	12 - 15	15 - 20
"The John C. Clay Girl"	12 - 15	15 - 20
"The Howard C. Christy Girl"	15 - 20	20 - 25
"The Harrison Fisher Girl"	45 - 50	50 - 55
"The C. Allen Gilbert Girl"	15 - 20	20 - 25
"The Henry Hutt Girl"	12 - 15	15 - 20
"The Hamilton King Girl"	15 - 20	20 - 25
"The F. S. Manning Girl"	10 - 12	12 - 15

Baltic-Maxim Cream Separator
No. 249, "September"

"The Barnum & Bailey Greatest Show on
Earth" – "Famous Duryea Motor Wagon"

J. R. Wills, "Bouquet Romain"
Black Serving Ice Cream, Bruxelles

"The Thomas M. Pierce Girl"	10 - 12	12 - 15
"The W. T. Smedley Girl"	10 - 12	12 - 15
"The G. G. Wiederseim Girl"	30 - 35	35 - 45
German Published - Add $5-10 per card.		
Armour Star		
"The Ham What Am"	8 - 10	10 - 15
Arbuckle Coffee	5 - 7	7 - 10
Do-Wa-Jack Paintings, S/**SOULER**	18 - 22	22 - 25
Asbestos Century Shingles	6 - 8	8 - 10
Asbestos Sad Irons	10 - 12	12 - 15
Autopiano Player Pianos	8 - 10	10 - 15
5 A Horse Blankets		
"Athol" "Bouncer"	15 - 20	20 - 30
"Briar" "Buster"	15 - 20	20 - 30
"Essex" "Fashion"	15 - 20	20 - 30
"Myrtle" "Paris Faun"	15 - 20	20 - 30
"Stratton" "Plush Robe" 1300	15 - 20	20 - 30
"Plush Robe" 1652 "Plush Robe" 1853	15 - 20	20 - 30
Promotional Cards		
"Great For Wear"	15 - 20	20 - 25
"They Make Philadelphia Famous"	15 - 20	20 - 25
Bacardi Rum	10 - 15	15 - 20
Bakers Chocolate	6 - 7	7 - 10
Ballard's Obelisk Flour	8 - 10	10 - 15
Baltic-Maxim Cream Separator		
Months of the Year (12)	25 - 30	30 - 35

Bantam "60" Auto Linen by **Curt Teich**	100 - 125	125 - 150
Barnum & Bailey Greatest Show on Earth (Linen)		
Showing 1895 Duryea Motor Wagon (**Tichnor**)	15 - 20	20 - 25
Bauer Sisters Candy Delicatessen, Coney Island	10 - 12	12 - 15
Bear Brand Hosiery	15 - 20	20 - 25
Bell Telephone (12)		
R1 "Announces Unexpected Guests"	15 - 20	20 - 25
R2 "The Convenience of Marketing"	15 - 20	20 - 25
R3 "Keeps the Traveler in Touch"	15 - 20	20 - 25
R4 "Into the Heart of Shopping District"	15 - 20	20 - 25
R5 "When Servants Fail You"	15 - 20	20 - 25
R6 "The Social Call"	15 - 20	20 - 25
R7 "A Doctor Quick"	15 - 20	20 - 25
R8 "Guards the Home"	15 - 20	20 - 25
R9 "In Household Emergencies"	15 - 20	20 - 25
R10 "Relieves Anxieties"	15 - 20	20 - 25
R11 "Gives Instant Alarms"	15 - 20	20 - 25
R12 "When the Elements are Against You"	15 - 20	20 - 25
Ben-Hur Book	5 - 7	7 - 10
Ben-Hur Flour	6 - 8	8 - 12
Ben-Hur (Sears-Roebuck)	10 - 12	12 - 15
Bensdorp's Royal Dutch Cocoa (Dutch Life)	5 - 6	6 - 9
Costumed Children Series	15 - 18	18 - 22
Benjamin Suits	10 - 12	12 - 15
Berry Brothers Varnishes (18)	12 - 15	15 - 20
Bester Dairy Appliances	10 - 12	12 - 15
Bissel Carpet Sweepers		
Toledo Frogs (8)	40 - 45	45 - 50
Baseball Frog	50 - 60	60 - 70
Golf Frog	50 - 60	60 - 70
Bismark Beer	12 - 15	15 - 20
Black Beauty Axel Grease Black man on Donkey	40 - 50	50 - 60
Blair's Pencil Tablets	10 - 12	12 - 15
Blanke's Coffee		
Overprints on Louisiana Purchase Expo Views	18 - 22	22 - 27
Blatchford Calf Meal Co.	5 - 7	7 - 10
Blatz Beer	8 - 10	10 - 15
S/**GRACE DRAYTON**	80 - 90	90 - 100
Bloomingdale's S/**OUTCAULT**	90 - 100	100 - 120
Borden's (Elsie Says)	6 - 8	8 - 10
Dairy views	5 - 6	6 - 8
Boston Rubber Shoe Co. (10) (Historic Boston)	3 - 5	5 - 8
Bouquet Brand Rock Lobster	8 - 10	10 - 12
Bouquet Romain Ice Cream; S/**J. R. WILLS**	50 - 75	75 - 100
Boy's Newspaper	3 - 4	4 - 6
Brockton Shoe Industry	5 - 6	6 - 8
Brodrick Buggies	12 - 15	15 - 18
Brown's Bronchial Trochs	3 - 5	5 - 8
Brown & Bigelow Calendars		
Women by **STUART TRAVIS**	10 - 12	12 - 15
Women by **HAMILTON KING**	12 - 15	15 - 18
Couples by **WILL GREFE**	10 - 12	12 - 15
Children by **B. P. GUTMANN** (mis-spelled "Gutman")	75 - 85	85 - 100

Byrrh Tonic, Signed by Maurice Cleret
Tennis Lady

"Calpis" –Japanese Yogurt Drink
(From Poster Designed in 1923)

Brown Shoes		
Buster Brown Calendars, S/**OUTCAULT**(12)	20 - 25	25 - 35
Buchan's Soap (6)		
White Bears and Children	18 - 22	22 - 25
Buckbee's Seeds (6)	3 - 4	4 - 6
Budweiser Barley Malt Syrup	12 - 15	15 - 20
Budweiser Beer (early)	12 - 15	15 - 20
Budweiser Yeast	8 - 10	10 - 12
Buffalo Bill's Wild West (Posters) (6)	25 - 30	30 - 35
Buick Auto, 1939-41	10 - 12	12 - 15
Bull Durham (33 Countries)	75 - 85	85 - 100
Bulte's Best Flour (6) Kids	8 - 10	10 - 12
Burke's Medicine	6 - 8	8 - 12
Burke's Whiskey	10 - 15	15 - 20
Burlington Zephyr (Train Poster)	15 - 18	18 - 25
Burro Japs Patent Shoes	10 - 12	12 - 15
Busch Extra Dry Ginger Ale	20 - 25	25 - 30
Buster Brown Shoes, P/Curt Teich	10 - 12	12 - 15
Butter-Krust Bread	10 - 12	12 - 15
Butternut Bread S/LONG Black boy with razor	30 - 35	35 - 45
Byrr Tonique	40 - 50	50 - 75
S/**MAURICE CLERET** Tennis Lady	90 - 100	100 - 125
S/**RAPHAEL KIRCHNER** (1)	500 - 600	600 - 700
Cadbury's Cocoa	6 - 8	8 - 10
Calox Oxygen Tooth Powder	8 - 10	10 - 12
Calpis, Japanese Yogurt Drink	300 - 350	350 - 400
Calumet Baking Powder, S/OUTCAULT	20 - 25	25 - 30

Campbell Soup   Campbell Soup Kids
  GRACE WIEDERSEIM/DRAYTON (Uns.)

Horiz. issues - (4) (with variations) (1909)	35 - 40	40 - 50
Vertical issues - (10 cents a can) - 24 * **		
Series 1-12 with **No Series No**. (1912)	125 - 150	150 - 175
Series 1 Numbered 1 thru 6 (1912)	120 - 140	140 - 160
Series 2 Numbered 7 thru 12 (1912)	120 - 140	140 - 160
Card 7 with Suffragette jingles (2)	150 - 175	175 - 200
Series 3 Numbered 13 thru 18 (1913)	120 - 140	140 - 160
Series 4 Numbered 19 thru 24 (1913)	120 - 140	140 - 160

* The 24 images have from 3 to 4 different
jingles on each card...meaning there could be
as many as 80 to 96 different total cards.
** Grace Wiederseim remarried in 1911 so
any of these cards with copyright after that
would be by Grace Drayton. Nos. 1 thru 24
were copyright 1912-1913.

Cardui Woman's Tonic	8 - 10	10 - 12
Carnation Milk	6 - 8	8 - 10
Carnation Milk (A.Y.P. Expo)	12 - 15	15 - 18
Carswell Horse Shoe Nails	6 - 9	9 - 12
Canadian Club Whiskey	12 - 15	15 - 20
Candee Rubbers, by **Goodyear** Comics	12 - 15	15 - 18
Black Boy in water - "A Well Balanced Rubber"	100 - 125	125 - 150
Case Steam Engines	8 - 10	10 - 12
Case Ten-ton Roan Roller	20 - 25	25 - 30
Case Threshing Machines	10 - 12	12 - 15
Cauchois' Fulton Mills Coffee	6 - 8	8 - 10
Champion Spark Plugs (ad on auto)	15 - 20	20 - 25
A.B. Chase Co. Pianos	10 - 12	12 - 15
The Charles William Stores, New York City		
"Your Bargain Book"	5 - 7	7 - 10
Chase & Sanborn Co.	8 - 10	10 - 12
Cherry Blossom Calendar Cards (blacks) S/**REMY**	20 - 25	25 - 30
Cherry Ripe Ice Cream Gum	10 - 12	12 - 15
Cherry Smash		
(On Lawn at Mt. Vernon)	70 - 80	80 - 90
George Washington "The Nations Beverage"	100 - 125	125 - 150
Chesterfield Cigarettes		
Servicemen, Uns./**LEYENDECKER**	75 - 100	100 - 125
Chesterfield Cigarettes - Poster, Man Smoking	18 - 20	20 - 25
Chevrolet Auto, 1938-41	10 - 12	12 - 15
Chicago, Milwaukee, and St. Paul R.R.	8 - 10	10 - 12
Chicken in the Rough	6 - 8	8 - 10
Chi-Namel Varnish	10 - 12	12 - 15
Chocolate Lombart, Air Plane Series	15 - 18	18 - 22
Clark Candy Bar (D. L. Clark Company) - 40's	12 - 15	15 - 20
Clark's Teaberry Quality Gum	12 - 15	15 - 20
Cleveland Six Automobile	15 - 20	20 - 25
Clyde Steamship Lines Posters Color	25 - 30	30 - 35
Black & white advertising Ships Company	18 - 22	22 - 26
Coca Cola (Girl Driving)	1500 - 2000	2000 - 2500
Coca Cola (Girl's Head) S/**H. KING**	1200 - 1500	1500 - 2000

The Clyde Steamship Co.
"Shore View at Mrs. Mitchell's"

The Corno Mills Co.
"The Standard of Feed Excellence"

Cunard Line
"R.M.P. Aquitania" (Sectional View)

Community Silver	3 - 4	4 - 6
Community Silver Plate S/**COLES PHILLIPS**	40 - 50	50 - 60
Continental Pneumatic Tires	15 - 20	20 - 25
Continental Rubber Tires (Bike)	15 - 20	20 - 25
Continental Rubber Tires (Tennis)	25 - 30	30 - 35
Corbin Coaster Brakes (Bicycles) Famous Rides	20 - 25	25 - 30
Cook Beer	5 - 7	7 - 10
Coon Chicken Inn, Curt Teich		
3 diff. views of the Restaurant	175 - 200	200 - 250
Corno Mills Co. (East St. Louis Mills)		
"The Standard of Feed Excellence"	5 - 7	7 - 9
Cracker Jack Bears (16) By **B. E. MORELAND**		
See Teddy Bear Chapter for individual values		
Creamlac, Bicycle Cleaner (1898)	40 - 45	45 - 50
Crescent Flour	5 - 7	7 - 10
Crocker & Best Flour	5 - 7	7 - 10
Crown Millinery Co., 1910	5 - 7	7 - 10
Crown Flour	5 - 7	7 - 10
Cuddle Toys, Berea College, Kentucky		
Curt Teich Linen - 8A-H744	100 - 125	125 - 150
Cunard Line Sectional View of R.M.S. Aquitania	25 - 30	30 - 35
Curtis Publishing Co.	4 - 5	5 - 7
Daniel Webster Cigars	10 - 12	12 - 15
Daniel Webster Flour	4 - 7	7 - 10
Dannemiller's Royal Coffee	10 - 12	12 - 15
Denver Zephyrs (Train)	15 - 20	20 - 25

Derby's Croup Mix (w/Children)	6 - 9	9 - 12
Devars Whiskey	12 - 15	15 - 20
De Laval Cream Separator	10 - 15	15 - 18
Diamont Rubber Co., Akron	4 - 5	5 - 8
Dinah Black Enamel, Mechanical	45 - 55	55 - 75
Disinfectine Soap (Whole Dam Family) - 1905	12 - 15	15 - 20
Domino Sugar	6 - 8	8 - 10
Cubes in carton	6 - 8	8 - 12
Do-Wah-Jack, w/Indians - Months of Year Ser.	15 - 20	20 - 25
Round Oak Baseburner Stoves		
Dutch Boy Paints	8 - 10	10 - 12
Dunlop Tires (Inventor/Elves)	30 - 40	40 - 45
DuPont Bird & Wild Game (12) S/OSTHAUS		
"Blue Wing Teal" "Mallards"	35 - 40	40 - 50
"Canada Goose" "Prairie Chicken"	35 - 40	40 - 50
"Canvas Back" "Quail"	35 - 40	40 - 50
"Gray Squirrel" "Ruffled Grouse"	35 - 40	40 - 50
"Jack Rabbit" "Wild Turkey"	35 - 40	40 - 50
"Jack Snipe" "Woodcock"	35 - 40	40 - 50
Wyeth Painting Card	30 - 35	35 - 40
DuPont Dogs (13) By Osthaus		
"Joe Cummings" "Mohawk II"	95 - 105	105 - 140
"Allmabagh" "Monora"	95 - 105	105 - 140
"Count Gladstone IV" "Pioneer"	95 - 105	105 - 140
"Count Whitestone" "Tony's Gale"	95 - 105	105 - 140
"Prince-Whitestone" "Sioux"	95 - 105	105 - 140
Manitoba Rap" "Geneva"	95 - 105	105 - 140
"Lady's Count Gladstone"	95 - 105	105 - 140
Eastman Cameras	12 - 15	15 - 18
Eclipse Coaster Brakes (Bicycles) Cartoons	15 - 18	18 - 22
Champion Cyclists	20 - 25	25 - 30
Edison Phonograph (Famous Singers)	10 - 12	12 - 15
Egg Climax Incubator	6 - 8	8 - 10
Egg-O-See Cereals w/Children	8 - 10	10 - 12
Eiffel Hosiery	6 - 8	8 - 10
Eldredge Rotary Sewing Machines	10 - 12	12 - 15
Elgin Watch Co.	12 - 15	15 - 20
Emerson Foot-lift Plows	15 - 20	20 - 25
Emulsion Gripekoven, Brussels	20 - 25	25 - 35
Erasmic Soap - Beautiful Girl	6 - 8	8 - 10
EMF Auto (Glidden Tour)	12 - 15	15 - 18
Eskay's Foods	4 - 5	5 - 7
Evinrude Motor Girl, Real Photo	40 - 50	50 - 60
Excelsior Pneumatic Tires	15 - 20	20 - 25
Excelsior Stove & Mfg. Co.	6 - 8	8 - 10
F. A. Whitney Carriage Co.	8 - 10	10 - 12
Fall River Line		
Early Color Poster	25 - 30	30 - 35
B & W, with Ships	8 - 10	10 - 12
Falstaff Beer See Lemp Beer	8 - 10	10 - 12
Farm Journal Magazine	8 - 10	10 - 12
Faun Butters	4 - 5	5 - 7
Federal Cord Tires (3 1/2" x 6")	7 - 10	10 - 12

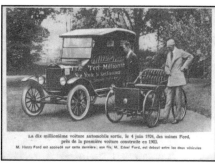

Ford Motor Company
(Henry Ford and Son, Edsel Ford)

Emulsion Gripekoven
"Pharmacie Gripekoven, Brussels"

Fry's Cocoa, Vivian Mansell & Co.
Signed by R.T., "A Source of Delight"

Firestone Tires (Calendars 1915 and 1916)	18 - 22	22 - 25
Fisk Tires	10 - 12	12 - 15
"Time to Re-Tire" Small Boy, various	20 - 25	25 - 30
S/ROCKWELL "Time to retire. Get a Fisk"	50 - 75	75 - 125
Fisk Red Top Tires	18 - 22	22 - 25
Fisk Removable Rims	12 - 15	15 - 20
Fitz Overalls	8 - 10	10 - 15
Flanders "20" Fore-Door Touring Cars	18 - 22	22 - 26
Flanders "30" Glidden Pathfinder Autos	15 - 20	20 - 25
Fleetwood Ltd. (Fashions)	7 - 9	9 - 12
Fleischmann Co. Yeast	3 - 4	4 - 6
Flexible Flyer Sleds	12 - 15	15 - 20
Flexible Flyer Sleds (Government Postal)	12 - 15	15 - 20
Flood & Conklin & Co., Varnish		
P. Boileau Ladies	100 - 110	110 - 125
Flower City Stoves and Ranges	8 - 10	10 - 15
Ford Motor Co.		
Early Union News color issues	15 - 18	18 - 22
1935 Ford V-8	22 - 25	25 - 28
Formosa Oolong Tea	4 - 5	5 - 8
Foss Orange Extract	8 - 10	10 - 12
Foss Pure Extract	6 - 8	8 - 10
Fowler's Cherry Smash (See Cherry Smash)		
Fox Head Lager Beer	5 - 8	8 - 12
Fralinger's Original Salt Water Taffy		
Beach Series	4 - 5	5 - 6

Series 18, Nursery Rhymes (24), S/**BURD**	30 - 40	40 - 50
Santa and "Tommy Tucker"	100 - 150	150 - 200
Others, S/**BURD**	10 - 15	15 - 18
Fralingers Salt Water Taffy - others	5 - 7	7 - 10
Franklin Davis Nursery Co.	2 - 3	3 - 5
Free Sewing Machine Co.	8 - 10	10 - 15
Frog in the Throat Lozenge Co.		
(PMC, 12, oversized)		
1 "A Social Success"	45 - 50	50 - 60
2 "A Universal Favorite"	45 - 50	50 - 60
3 "Don't Be Without It"	45 - 50	50 - 60
4 "Favorite at all Times"	45 - 50	50 - 60
5 "Fore Everybody" Golf	50 - 55	55 - 65
6 "For Singers"	45 - 50	50 - 60
7 "Innocent and Instantaneous"	45 - 50	50 - 60
8 "My Old Friend Dr. Frog"	45 - 50	50 - 60
9 "Needs No Introduction"	40 - 50	50 - 60
10 "Nothing Better"	40 - 50	50 - 60
11 "Pleasant to Take"	40 - 50	50 - 60
12 "Popular Everywhere"	40 - 50	50 - 60
"Frog in the Throat" Series (10) Oversized	40 - 45	45 - 55
Fry's Chocolates, S/**TOM BROWNE**	20 - 25	25 - 30
Fry's Cocoa	5 - 8	8 - 10
W/Black child "Cocoa Sah!" S/**EDGAR FILBY**	75 - 100	100 - 125
Fry's Pure Concentrated Cocoa		
S/**G.T.** (**G.H. THOMPSON**)	125 - 150	150 - 175
Fuller Brush Co.	3 - 5	5 - 7
Fuller Floor Wax	3 - 5	5 - 7
Gaar-Scott & Co. (Tractor)	12 - 15	15 - 20
Gales Chocolates (4" x 6")	4 - 6	6 - 9
Garland Stove		
Calvert Litho "The wonder of the age"	25 - 30	30 - 40
Gates Tires	10 - 15	15 - 18
G.E. Refrigerator Drowned in Water (30's)	20 - 25	25 - 30
German-American Coffee	10 - 12	12 - 15
Gilles Coffee	5 - 7	7 - 10
Gillette Safety Razor Co. (Child Shaving)	12 - 15	15 - 20
Gladwell's Lawn Mowers	12 - 15	15 - 20
Glidden Tour Autos See auto listings		
Globe-Wernicke Bookcases	6 - 8	8 - 10
Gold Dust Twins Cleanser (4) Uns/**E. W. KEMBLE**	40 - 50	50 - 60
Gold Dust Fairbanks Cleanser		
Gold Dust Twins Dressed as Black Santas	100 - 110	110 - 125
Thanksgiving	50 - 60	60 - 75
Real Photos of Black-Face Children w/products		
and costumes	150 - 175	175 - 225
Gold Label Beer	8 - 10	10 - 12
Golden Tree Syrup, New England Maple Syrup Co.	20 - 25	25 - 35
Gold Medal Flour	8 - 10	10 - 12
Good Luck Baking Powder (Jamestown Expo)	15 - 18	18 - 25
Goodrich Silvertown Tires	10 - 12	12 - 15
Gorham Silver Polish (1903)	8 - 10	10 - 15
Gosser Beer S/**FLEMAX**	20 - 25	25 - 30
Grande Ronde Meat Co., LaGrande, Oregon	6 - 8	8 - 10

Great Northern Railway	5 - 7	7 - 8
Interior Views	10 - 12	12 - 15
Green River Whiskey		
Black Man and horse with whiskey keg	60 - 70	70 - 80
Greenfield's Chocolate Sponge	5 - 8	8 - 12
Griswold Cast Ware	8 - 10	10 - 15
Grollman Hats, 1918	8 - 10	10 - 12
Gulf Refining Co. (Typical Filling Station)	15 - 20	20 - 25
Habler Bros. Brush Paint Remover	10 - 12	12 - 15
Hackett Carbart & Co. Clothing	3 - 5	5 - 7
Hamburg-Sudamerikanische Line		
Ship –"Monte Sarmiento" Menu (Speisenfolge)	20 - 25	25 - 35
Happy Day Washers	8 - 10	10 - 12
Happy Thought Chewing Tobacco (12)	15 - 18	18 - 22
Hamm Brewing Co.	12 - 15	15 - 20
Harburg-Wien Tennis-Balle Lady/man at courtside	30 - 40	40 - 50
Hart Hats, S/HOFFMAN	5 - 7	7 - 10
Harley Davidson Motorcycles (6) - Govt. Postals	22 - 26	26 - 32
Harvey Brothers Shirts & Ties	8 - 10	10 - 12
Hart-Parr Co. (Tractors)	10 - 12	12 - 15
Hartford Suspensions Shock Absorbers (Auto ads)	25 - 30	30 - 35
Hart Schaffner & Marx		
S/ED. PENFIELD	22 - 25	25 - 30
Hathaway's Bread	4 - 6	6 - 9
Havana Club Rum	8 - 10	10 - 15
Heather Bloom Petticoats (E. Barrymore)	6 - 9	9 - 12
Heinz Foods, 57 Varieties (w/Product on Front)	12 - 15	15 - 20
Heinz Foods - others	3 - 4	4 - 6
Hemostyl Tonic by Docteur Roussel		
Tennis	30 - 40	40 - 50
Tennis action	30 - 35	35 - 40
Golf	40 - 50	50 - 60
Canoeing	12 - 15	15 - 25
Hendel Motorcycles	12 - 15	15 - 20
Herman Reel Co. (Indians)	8 - 10	10 - 15
Hershey's Cocoa Views of cows/milking machines, etc.	3 - 5	5 - 8
High Life Beer	10 - 12	12 - 15
Hillsboro County Fair, Greenfield, N.H., 1923		
Tollman Printing Co. "Bridle Mates"	15 - 20	20 - 30
Himmel & Sons Furriers, P/Curt Teich	6 - 8	8 - 10
Hinds Honey and Almond Cream	6 - 8	8 - 10
Hiram Walker & Sons Liquors	8 - 10	10 - 15
Hires Root Bear	8 - 10	10 - 12
#4831 6-pack carton (Chrome)	4 - 6	6 - 9
Hispano-Suiza Autos French S/RENE TIMLENE	30 - 35	35 - 40
H-O Co. See Korn-Kinks		
Holsum Bread (Cartoons)	8 - 10	10 - 12
Holsum Bread, w/Billy Baker	10 - 12	12 - 15
Hoods Sarsaparilla Laboratory	6 - 8	8 - 10
Hoover Co., N. Canton, O. Electric Cleaners Factory	5 - 8	8 - 10
Horn & Hardart Co., New York Automat (B&W)	5 - 7	7 - 9
Hudson 1953 "Jet"	10 - 12	12 - 15
Humpty-Dumpty Stockings (Nursery Rhymes)	10 - 15	15 - 20
Humphrey's Witch Hazel Oil	6 - 9	9 - 12

Hillsboro County Fair, Greenfield, N.H.
"Bridle Mates"

Hispano-Suiza Automobiles (French)
S/Rene Timlene, "Profitez-en!..."

Hupmobile, 1911	20 - 25	25 - 30
Touring car	25 - 28	28 - 32
Huyler's Candy (w/Children)	8 - 10	10 - 15
S/Von Hartmann	12 - 15	15 - 20
ICA Cameras Illegible German artist signature		
Lady examining camera	30 - 35	35 - 45
I. X. L. Tamales	5 - 6	6 - 9
Imperial Auto (Pig cartoons) (4)	12 - 15	15 - 20
Imperial Diamond Needles	5 - 7	7 - 10
Independent Wall Paper Co.	3 - 4	4 - 7
India & Ceylon Tea	7 - 9	9 - 12
India Tea Growers	7 - 8	8 - 10
International Harvester, 1909 (12)	5 - 7	7 - 10
International Harvester, 1910 (12)	5 - 7	7 - 10
Inter-State Auto, Chilton		
Inter-State Forty Roadster, Model 32	20 - 25	25 - 30
Inter-State Bull Dog 40"	20 - 25	25 - 30
Iowa Seed Co.	2 - 3	3 - 5
Jack Sprat Oleomargarine	6 - 8	8 -12
Jackson Auto, Chilton		
Model #35 - $1250	20 - 25	25 - 30
Japan Tea	6 - 8	8 - 10
Job Cigarette Papers (30)		
Job Poster and Calendar designs, 1895-1914		
ASTI, A.	50 - 75	75 - 100
ATCHE, J.	50 - 75	75 - 100

Karang Coffee, Series 5469
No. 2, "The Mail in Morocco"

ICA Cameras
(Signed by German Artist, 1925)

Kellogg's Corn Flakes
"The Packing Room at Battle Creek..."

BOUISSET, F.	50 - 75	75 - 100
CAPPIELLO	50 - 75	75 - 100
CASAS	50 - 75	75 - 100
CHERET, J.	75 - 100	100 - 125
DU THOC, N.	50 - 75	75 - 10
DUVOCELLE (B&W)	35 - 50	50 - 75
GERVAIS, P. (7)	50 - 75	75 - 100
GRANER, L.	50 - 75	75 - 100
GRANIE	50 - 75	75 - 100
HERNANDEZ, D.	50 - 75	75 - 100
LEANDRE, C.	50 - 75	75 - 100
MAURICE, G.	50 - 75	75 - 100
MAXENCE (3)	50 - 75	75 - 100
MUCHA, A. (2)		
"Femme Blonde"	800 - 900	900 - 1000
RASSENFOSSE	50 - 75	75 - 100
ROCHEGROSSE, C. (2)	50 - 75	75 - 100
"Femme Brune"	800 - 900	900 - 1000
VILLA	50 - 75	75 - 100
Johnson Candies (with Santa)	20 - 25	25 - 35
Johnson's Corn Flower	8 - 10	10 - 12
Joplin Overalls (Girl)	6 - 8	8 - 10
Juniata Horse Shoes, w/Indian Girl	10 - 15	15 - 20
Kahn Tailors	6 - 8	8 - 10
Kalodont Toothpaste & Mouthwash (German)	20 - 25	25 - 30
Kansas City Casket & Furniture Co.	5 - 7	7 - 10

Karang Coffee Small Undersize cards		
Series 5469 Mail and Stamps of various countries		
2 "The Mail in Morocco"	10 - 15	15 - 20
Kaufman & Strauss F. G. LONG Black Cartoons	25 - 30	30 - 35
Kelloggs Corn Flakes (Allentown Adpostal)	35 - 40	40 - 45
Kelloggs Corn Flakes (Chrome)		
"Packing Room"	5 - 6	6 - 7
Kelso Laundry Co. Yellow delivery wagon	25 - 35	35 - 45
Kineto Clocks	15 - 18	18 - 22
King Bee Trimmed Hats	10 - 12	12 - 15
Kinsey Pure Rye Whiskey	6 - 9	9 - 12
Kippendorf Foot Rest Shoes	8 - 10	10 - 13
Klumbacher Beer (German Beer)	18 - 22	22 - 26
Knapp Calendars (See Artist-Signed Section)		
Frank Desch, Lester Ralph		
Kodak Cameras	20 - 25	25 - 28
Köhler Sewing Machine (German)	20 - 25	25 - 30
Kohn Brothers Fine Clothing	10 - 12	12 - 15
Kolb's Bakery S/W. W. DENSLOW	50 - 60	60 - 75
Korn-Kinks, H.O. Company		
The Jocular Jinks of Kornelia Kinks		
Series A (6)		
1 "Said Momma to Me..."	28 - 32	32 - 35
2 "Man, Whar's Your Politeness"	28 - 32	32 - 35
3 "Gran'pa done say dat..."	28 - 32	32 - 35
4 "I'se a going to be..."	28 - 32	32 - 35
5 "It ain't a bit o'use..."	28 - 32	32 - 35
6 "Susie done 'through'..."	28 - 32	32 - 35
The Korn-Kinks Advertising cards (2)		
Souvenir Card Back	30 - 35	35 - 40
Jocular Jinks of Kornelia Kinks"	30 - 32	32 - 35
Rare Variation (Kite in air; no 5 cents on building)	50 - 60	60 - 70
Korvin Ice Cream, Jersey Shore Creamery	6 - 9	9 - 12
Kulmbacher Export Beer, Gruss Aus	25 - 30	30 - 35
Kuppenheimer Suits, Uns./**LEYENDECKER**	15 - 20	20 - 25
Laco Lamps (Children/Bulbs)	12 - 15	15 - 20
Lady Like Shoes (Beautiful Girls' Heads)	15 - 20	20 - 25
Lash Bitters (Laxative) Drunks	15 - 18	18 - 22
Lehr Pianos	3 - 5	5 - 8
Lekko Hand Soap	8 - 10	10 - 12
Lemp Falstaff Beer Women Sportsmen Fadeways	15 - 20	20 - 25
Falstaff Bottled Beer	12 - 15	15 - 20
Lemp Beer, by Selige Co. (B&W)	6 - 8	8 - 10
Leonard's Bulk Seed	2 - 3	3 - 4
Lily White's Best Flour Lady cook at stove	25 - 30	30 - 40
Lindholm Piano Co.	5 - 6	6 - 9
Lindsay Gas Light Mantles	4 - 7	7 - 10
Lipton Tea (6)	5 - 6	6 - 7
Listerated Pepsin Gum (10) Bears	15 - 20	20 - 25
Lloyd Shipping Lines	20 - 25	25 - 30
Locomobile Auto, Chilton		
Model "3" Locomobile Roadster	20 - 25	25 - 30
Vanderbilt Cup Race, 1905 (7)	12 - 15	15 - 20
Vanderbilt Cup Race, 1908 (10)	12 - 15	15 - 20

Original Mauser Rifle
"Mauser-Wwerke A.G., Oberndorf"

Hotel Mount Washington, White Mts.
N.H., "Bretton Woods or Bust"

London & Northwestern R.R. Promotional Issues

Promotional Issues, 28 sets of 6 each (1905)	6 - 7	7 - 8
Love's Finer Candies, Rochester, NY	8 - 10	10 - 12
Lowney's Chocolates (Indians)	10 - 12	12 - 15
Girl Golfers, S/**ARCHIE GUNN**	25 - 30	30 - 40
Magic Curlers	3 - 4	4 - 7
Majestic Stove Ranges	10 - 12	12 - 15
Malt Breakfast Food	4 - 5	5 - 8
Malted Cereal Co.	4 - 7	7 - 10
Mammy's Pantry, Brooklyn, N.Y. (Sepia)	20 - 30	30 - 35
Mansville & Sons Pianos	6 - 8	8 - 10
Marathon Auto 1950's Checkey	12 - 15	15 - 18
Marionetten Theatre (Paul Brann's) Munich	35 - 40	40 - 50
Mason & Hanson Woolens, w/Pretty Girls	6 - 8	8 - 10
Men in mode of dress by century	8 - 10	10 - 12
Mason Auto	15 - 20	20 - 25
Mauser's Best Flour	8 - 10	10 - 12
Mauser Rifles German (Real Photo) (Continental)	25 - 30	30 - 35
Maytag Kitchen Washers, Automatic Washers	8 - 10	10 - 12
Maxwell Automobiles	30 - 35	35 - 45
Maxwell Exclusive Line Wall Paper	3 - 4	4 - 5
McCallum, D. & J. "Perfection" Scotch Whiskey	8 - 10	10 - 15
McPhail Pianos (Boston Views)	2 - 3	3 - 4
Mecca Cigarettes	18 - 22	22 - 25
Mecca Slippers Black man with guitar	20 - 25	25 - 30
Meco Kiln and Man Koolers (fans), P/Curt Teich	8 - 10	10 - 12
Meier & Frank Dept. Store (set of flags)		
Portland, Oregon	10 - 12	12 - 15
Men-tho-la-tum Salve	6 - 8	8 - 10
Metz Motorcycles	20 - 25	25 - 30
Michelin Tires	15 - 18	18 - 22
Anthropomorphic Tire Man	80 - 90	90 - 100
Michelin Tires, S/**VINCENT**	10 - 15	15 - 20
Middlebrook Razors	6 - 8	8 - 11
Miller High Life Beer - Kids in Auto	15 - 20	20 - 25
Minneapolis Knitting Works (Fairy Tales)	15 - 18	18 - 22
Mirroscope Postcard Projector	60 - 70	70 - 80
Mistletoe Margarine	12 - 15	15 - 18
Mitchell Mortuary Stretcher	8 - 10	10 - 15
Mogul Egyptian Cigarettes (La. Purchase Expo)	12 - 15	15 - 18

Monarch Typewriters	8 - 10	10 - 12
Mount Washington Hotel, Bretton Woods, N.H.	8 - 10	10 - 12
Moxie	40 - 50	50 - 60
20 Mule Team Borax	8 - 10	10 - 12
Mulford, H. K., Vaccine	5 - 6	6 - 7
Murad Cigarettes (Views)	6 - 8	8 - 10
National Girls	5 - 6	6 - 8
National Biscuit Co.	5 - 6	6 - 8
National Cash Register	5 - 7	7 - 10
National Cloak & Suit Co.	5 - 8	7 - 10
National Light Oil	5 - 6	6 - 9
National Lead Paint (Dutch Boy)	10 - 12	12 - 15
Others	4 - 5	5 - 7
Nestle's Baby Food	6 - 7	7 - 9
With Black child	18 - 22	22 - 25
Nestle's Chocolate	6 - 7	7 - 10
New Departure Brakes (Jack & Jill)	18 - 22	22 - 26
New Idea Manure Spreader	12 - 15	15 - 18
New Home Sewing Machine	8 - 10	10 - 12
Niagara Maid Silk Gloves	15 - 20	20 - 25
Northern Pacific R.R.	5 - 6	6 - 8
Northwestern Hide & Fur Co.	10 - 12	12 - 15
Nu-Life Cereal	5 - 6	6 - 8
Nuvida Springs, California (Indian Girl)	7 - 8	8 - 10
Nylo Chocolates	5 - 6	6 - 7
Oakland Auto, Chilton		
Model 35 - $1075	25 - 30	30 - 35
Model 42 - $1600	25 - 30	30 - 35
Ocherade Drink	6 - 8	8 - 10
Oil Pull Tractors	12 - 15	15 - 20
Old Style Lager	6 - 8	8 - 10
Oliver Farm Machinery	6 - 8	8 - 10
Old Prentice Whiskey	8 - 10	10 - 12
Oldsmobile Auto, 1907		
With celebrities	35 - 40	40 - 45
Model B Standard Runabout	30 - 35	35 - 40
Model S - Palace Touring Car	30 - 35	35 - 40
Hold-to-Lights	75 - 85	85 - 100
Omega Watch (French Poster)	35 - 40	40 - 45
Osborne Calendar Co.		
(See Artist-Signed section - Arthur, Boileau, Underwood, and Vernon)		
Oster "Stim-u-Lax" Massager	12 - 15	15 - 20
Outcault Calendars See R.F. Outcault in Comics section		
Overland Auto		
83B Touring Car	25 - 30	30 - 35
Ozark Pencil Company	6 - 8	8 - 10
Pabst Breweries (Views)	6 - 7	7 - 10
Pacific Mail Steamship Co.		
Color - ships	12 - 15	15 - 20
B & W	5 - 6	6 - 8
Pacific Tank & Pipe Co.	6 - 8	8 - 10
Palmolive Soap (Govt. Postal)	8 - 10	10 - 12

Pepsi Cola "Times Square Service Men's Center, Broadway at 47th St., N.Y.C." *Philips Projector (Russian) Dutch Children Encircling Projector*

Parisian Belle Perfume	7 - 8	8 - 10
Parker Guns	20 - 25	25 - 30
Parker Shot Guns	18 - 22	22 - 25
Pears Soap	6 - 7	7 - 9
Peerless Auto	10 - 12	12 - 15
On Glidden Tour	12 - 15	15 - 20
Penn Diner, New York City, Linen	50 - 75	75 - 100
Pepsi Cola		
"Times Square Service Men's Center," N.Y.C.	10 - 15	15 - 20
Peroxident Tooth Paste (Uns. MAUD HUMPHREY)		
Paintings of beautiful ladies	15 - 20	20 - 30
Peter's Weatherbird Shoes (Months of Year)	8 - 10	10 - 15
Seasons	8 - 10	10 - 12
Halloween	22 - 25	25 - 30
Philadelphia Lawn Mowers	8 - 10	10 - 15
Phillips Arga - Poster	20 - 25	25 - 30
Phillips Lamps, w/Dutch Girl (French)	25 - 30	30 - 35
Phillips Projector w/Dutch Children in ring-around	25- 30	30 - 40
Pillsbury Flour	5 - 8	8 - 12
W/Black twins dressed in flour sacks (B&W)		
"Economy is Wealth"	30 - 40	40 - 50
Pinkham, Lydia E., Medicine Co.	4 - 5	5 - 8
Piso's Cure for Colds	6 - 8	8 - 10
Plymouth Auto, 1939-41	10 - 12	12 - 15
Polarine Oil	6 - 9	9 - 12
Pontiac, 1933 Pontiac 8, 2-door Sedan	20 - 25	25 - 28
1937 Pontiac 8		
Post Toasties Cereal	6 - 8	8 - 10
Ponds Bitters	6 - 8	8 - 10
Post Toasties Corn Flakes	8 - 10	10 - 12
Postum Cereal	3 - 4	4 - 7
Powell's N.Y. Chocolates	3 - 4	4 - 7
Premier Bicycles	20 - 25	25 - 30
Prisco Lantern	6 - 9	9 - 12
Private Estate Coffee	6 - 7	7 - 9
Prudential Insurance Co.		
Battleships	8 - 10	10 - 12
Indians	10 - 12	12 - 15
Others	6 - 8	8 - 10
Purina Chick Chow	8 - 10	10 - 12

Puritan Blouses and Shirts	5 - 6	6 - 8
Purity Salt, PMC	15 - 18	18 - 20
Quaker Oats, w/B&W foreign views	8 - 10	10 - 12
Quaker Maid Brand	12 - 15	15 - 20
Comic Strip Characters	12 - 15	15 - 18
Movie Stars	12 - 15	15 - 20
Quick Meal Gas Stoves	12 - 15	15 - 18
R. B. Cigars	10 - 12	12 - 15
Ranier Beer, Seattle	12 - 15	15 - 20
RCA, Dog & Mule Calendars	5 - 8	8 - 12
Rat Bis-Kit (Dog/Cat)	6 - 9	9 - 12
Red Bird Coffee	10 - 12	12 - 15
Red Cross Cotton	6 - 8	8 - 10
Red Horse Tobacco	8 - 12	12 - 16
Red Pig Knives (Posters) See **Roberson Cutlery**		
Red Star Lines, S/Cassiers See Transportation	12 - 15	15 - 20
Regal Shoe Co. (Louisiana Purchase Expo)	12 - 15	15 - 20
Reliance Baking Powder	5 - 6	6 - 9
Remington Arms	8 - 10	10 - 15
Rexford Hotel, Boston, Mass.	12 - 15	15 - 20
Reynolds Tobacco Co.		
Pre-1920	10 - 12	12 - 15
Others	8 - 10	10 - 12
Richardson Skates	8 - 10	10 - 15
Ringling Bros. Animals	4 - 5	5 - 6
Ringling Bros. Circus Ads	12 - 15	15 - 20
Early Posters	35 - 40	40 - 45
Robeson Cutlery		
"Red Pig" Knives (12)	60 - 70	70 - 80
Rockford Watches - Calendars S/**OUTCAULT**	25 - 30	30 - 35
Round Up Cigars	8 - 10	10 - 12
Rumford Baking Powder	5 - 6	6 - 8
Rumley Tractors	10 - 12	12 - 15
Samoset Chocolates (8) Indians S/**ELWELL**	15 - 18	18 - 22
Sandeman Scotch Whiskey	10 - 15	15 - 18
San Felice Cigars	10 - 12	12 - 15
Sani-Tissue, Scott Paper Co., Phila.		
"Balsam Sanitissue Toilet Paper" (RP) with coupon	15 - 20	20 - 25
Sanitol Girl	8 - 10	10 - 15
Santa Fe R.R.	6 - 8	8 - 10
Sauermann's Kinder Nahrwurst	15 - 20	20 - 25
Savannah Line, Coast Steamers	10 - 12	12 - 15
Posters	20 - 25	25 - 30
Multiview w/Black cotton pickers	30 - 40	40 - 50
Sawyer Crystal Blue Laundry Soap	5 - 6	6 - 9
Schlitz Beer	8 - 10	10 - 12
Schraffts Chocolate	5 - 6	6 - 9
Schulze's Butter-Nut Bread	6 - 9	9 - 12
Scull, William S. Co., Coffee	6 - 9	9 - 12
Seattle Ice Co.	6 - 8	8 - 10
Selz Liberty Bell Shoes	5 - 7	7 - 10
Sen Sen Gum	10 - 12	12 - 15

Scott Paper Co., Philadelphia *"Sani-Tissue"*	*The Sharples Tubular Separator Co.* *"Helping Grandma"*

Sharples Cream Separator

The Sharples Co. (PMC)		
1 Boy and Girl	12 - 15	15 - 25
2 Cow and Ladies	12 - 15	15 - 25
3 Mother and Child	12 - 15	15 - 25
4 Farm Pleasures	12 - 15	15 - 25
5 Helping Grandma	12 - 15	15 - 25
6 Teddy	15 - 20	20 - 30
7 Modern Way	12 - 15	15 - 25
8 Dairyman's Choice		
Shredded Wheat Cereal	8 - 10	10 - 12
Shredded Wheat (Factory)	3 - 5	5 - 7
Simple Simon Oleo	6 - 9	9 - 12
Simplex Cream Separators	15 - 18	18 - 22
Simplex Typewriters	6 - 9	9 - 12
Singer Sewing Machines	6 - 9	9 - 12
Russian (Showing Machine)	15 - 20	20 - 25
Sleepy Eye Milling Co. (9) Indians	60 - 70	70 - 80
"A Mark of Quality"	60 - 70	70 - 80
"Chief Sleepy Eye Welcomes Whites"	90 - 100	100 - 120
"Indian Artist"	60 - 70	70 - 80
"Indian Canoeing"	60 - 70	70 - 80
"Indian Mode of Conveyance"	60 - 70	70 - 80
"Pipe of Peace"	60 - 70	70 - 80
"Sleepy Eye Mills"	60 - 70	70 - 80
"Sleepy Eye Monument"	60 - 70	70 - 80
"Sleepy Eye, The Meritorious Flour"	60 - 70	70 - 80

Monument	30 - 35	35 - 40
Snow Drift Cotton Oil Co.	5 - 6	6 - 9
Snow Drift Hogless Lard (Bunny & Pail of Lard)	15 - 18	18 - 22
Soapine Soap Powder	8 - 10	10 - 12
Socony Gasoline	5 - 7	7 -10
Le Soleil Foods (Italy)	15 - 18	18 - 22
Solis Cigar Co. Columbian Exposition, 1893	100 - 125	125 - 150
Sonora Phonographs	8 - 10	10 - 13
Solis Cigar Co. (Columbian Expo)	15 - 18	18 - 22
South Bend Lathes	5 - 7	7 - 10
Southern Cotton Oil Co. (Snowdrift)	5 - 7	7 - 10
Southern Pacific R.R	8 - 10	10 - 12
Interiors of trains	10 - 12	12 - 15
Southern Railway		
Pre 1907	15 - 18	18 - 22
1908-1915	10 - 12	12 - 15
Others	5 - 8	8 - 10
Sperry Flour Co. (sketch by Malloy, signed)	10 - 12	12 - 15
Spillers Victorian Dog Food	8 - 10	10 - 12
Stacey-Adams (shoe) Company	6 - 8	8 - 10
Standard Brewing Co.	8 - 10	10 - 12
Standard Harburg-Wien Tennis-Balle, Austria	40 - 45	45 - 55
Stanley Belting Corp. (B&W)	4 - 5	5 - 6
Sterling Ranges	6 - 8	8 - 10
Stern Bros., Market Square, Lewisburg, Pa.		
Steve's Cheese, Denmark, Wisconsin		
Stiletto Lawn Mowers	8 - 10	10 - 12
Storiettes-Books	6 - 8	8 - 10
Strauss Brothers Overcoats	6 - 8	8 - 10
Delivery Cars	30 - 35	35 - 38
Studebaker Corp.		
Pre-1915	30 - 35	35 - 40
1916-1940	20 - 25	25 - 35
Studebaker Jr. Wagons	25 - 30	30 - 35
Stukenbrok's Teutonia-Pneumatic Bicycles		
W/Golliwogg, Gruss aus with und/back	35 - 40	45 - 50
Suanito Writing Pens (Italy)	15 - 18	18 - 22
Suchard Cacao, Color Product, w/B&W views	10 - 12	12 - 15
Summit Shirts	5 - 6	6 - 9
Sunny Jim Whiskey	8 - 10	10 - 13
Swann "Pastel" Hats	8 - 10	10 - 13
Swift & Co., 6-Horse Team	8 - 10	10 - 13
Swift's Premium Butterine	6 - 9	9 - 12
Swift's Premium Nursery Rhymes		
"Jack Spratt"	18 - 22	22 - 26
"Little Jack Horner"	18 - 22	22 - 26
"Little Tommy Turner"	18 - 22	22 - 26
"Old King Cole"	18 - 22	22 - 26
"Queen of Hearts"	18 - 22	22 - 26
"Simple Simon"	18 - 22	22 - 26
Swift's Premium Oleomargarine		
"Children of World"	6 - 8	8 - 10
Swift's Pride, S/**GRACE WIEDERSEIM**		
Sunday's Child, Monday's Child, etc. (7)	35 - 40	40 - 50

Swift's Pride Soap (6) Shadows on Wall	10 - 12	12 - 15
Taylor's Headache Cologne	6 - 9	9 - 12
Templin's "Idea" Seeds	4 - 6	6 - 9
Teutonia-Pneumatic Bicycles (w/Golliwogg)	35 - 40	40 - 50
Texaco Axle Grease	8 - 10	10 - 12
Pre 1940 Local Gas Stations	10 - 15	15 - 20
Texaco Motor Oils	6 - 8	8 - 10
Tip Top Baking Goods Tip Top Boy	10 - 12	12 - 15
Thomas Brau Beer	15 - 20	20 - 25
Toledo Metal Wheel Co.	7 - 9	9 - 12
Toledo Scales	7 - 9	9 - 12
Trans World Airlines (1930's-40's)	12 - 15	15 - 20
Tredstep Shoes	8 - 10	10 - 12
Tropic Isle Restaurant, Embossed Breasts Nude	8 - 10	10 - 12
Troy Detachable Collars	4 - 6	6 - 9
True Fruit Flavors	5 - 6	6 - 9
Tudor Lights - Foreign Poster Style	15 - 18	18 - 22
Uhlen Baby Carriages	8 - 10	10 - 12
Uncle John's Syrup (Poster)	20 - 25	25 - 30
Underwood Typewriters	5 - 7	7 - 10
Union Pacific R.R.	5 - 6	6 - 8
Interior Views	10 - 12	12 - 15
United Air Lines (1940's)	10 - 12	12 - 15
Universal Regulators	5 - 6	6 - 9
USM City Collections	10 - 12	12 - 15
Utopia Yarns (Dutch Children)	5 - 6	6 - 8
Valentine's Varnishes (Auto)	10 - 12	12 - 15
Velvet Candy (Kissing on Joy Ride)	40 - 45	45 - 50
Velvetlawn Seeders	6 - 9	9 - 12
Verbeck & Lucas Stoves	6 - 9	9 - 12
Vick's Quality Seeds, Rochester	4 - 5	5 - 6
Voss Brothers Washing Machine	8 - 10	10 - 12
Wales-Goodyear Bear Brand Rubbers	10 - 15	15 - 18
Walker House, Toronto	5 - 6	6 - 9
Walk-Over Shoes, Famous Men (24)	6 - 8	8 - 10
Walk-Over Shoes, Dutch Children	4 - 5	5 - 7
Walk-Over Shoes, Pilgrim Series	4 - 5	5 - 7
Walk-Over Shoes, "Scenes from Shakespeare" (8)	8 - 10	10 - 12
Walk-Over Shoes, Topsy Hosiery Blacks (B&W)	15 - 18	18 - 22
Walk-Over Shoes, Western Series	4 - 6	6 - 9
Washington Airport (Sistership of the "Spirit of St. Louis")		
"The Most Scenic Ride in America"	15 - 20	20 - 25
Watkins, J. R. Medical	5 - 6	6 - 8
Watson-Plummer Shoe Co.	6 - 8	8 - 10
Weatherbird Shoes, Unsigned	8 - 10	10 - 12
Weather Shield for Autos - Wilson Company	6 - 8	8 - 10
Wellco House Slippers	6 - 8	8 - 10
Westinghouse Cooper Hewitt Mercury Rectifier	8 - 10	10 - 12
Westinghouse Electric Iron	6 - 9	9 - 12
Weyerheuser Lumber Co.	6 - 9	9 - 12
White Brothers Bread	6 - 9	9 - 12
White House Coffee & Tea	6 - 8	8 - 10
Whitney, F.A. Carriage Co.	10 - 12	12 - 15
Wilbur Chocolates, S/HENKELS (6)	10 - 12	12 - 14

Wilson & Co., Meat Packers *Wrigley's Spearmint Gum*
"World's Champion Six-Horse Clydesdale..." *"Wrigley's Spearmint Steadies the Nerves"*

Willys-Overland Autos		
Model 59T	22 - 25	25 - 30
Roadster	22 - 25	25 - 30
Wilson & Co., Meat Packers	6 - 8	8 - 10
"World's Champion Six-horse Clydesdale Team"	20 - 25	25 - 28
Winchester Arms & Ammo, Folding card, 1906	10 - 12	12 - 15
Wings American Cigarettes		
Blacks dancing	75 - 85	85 - 100
Witch Hazel Ointment	5 - 6	6 - 8
Woods Electric Autos	25 - 28	28 - 32
Woodstock Typewriters	6 - 7	7 - 9
Woonsocket Rubber Co. (10)		
Footwear of Nations	12 - 15	15 - 18
Wrigley's Spearmint Chewing Gum (Linen)		
Sign in New York City	6 - 8	8 - 10
Wyandotte Cleaner & Cleanser	5 - 6	6 - 8
Yale Tires		
Pure Oil Co. W/Maggie and Jiggs	50 - 60	60 -75
Youth's Companion Magazine	4 - 5	5 - 6
Zang's Beer	8 - 10	10 - 12
Zeiss Ikon Camera (20's)	15 - 18	18 - 20
Zeiss Ikon Film (20's)	15 - 18	18 - 20
Zenith Watches	5 - 8	8 - 10
Zeno Gum Co.	5 - 6	6 - 8

Although there are over 600 listings in our Advertising Postcards section, this by no means includes all that were issued. For a more comprehensive listing we suggest that you obtain a copy of Fred and Mary Megson's fine book, **American Advertising Postcards, Sets and Series, 1890-1920, Catalog and Price Guide.** Although it is out-of-date on values it is still the very best reference available.

Topicals

Topical postcards, as the name implies, are those of a particular place, a particular subject, and are any type not listed in a specific section of this publication. They are very special to the collecting fraternity, and make up a large part of every collection.

There were thousands of topics or motifs printed on postcards, and many are sure to appeal to any collector's fancy. As a general rule, collectors "specialize" in a particular subject or theme and try to obtain every card available, old or modern, until the collection is complete. Usually, because of their profound interest, they will also research the subject and become very knowledgeable about it and its history. This, in part, is one of the things that makes the collecting of postcards so interesting, and provides the momentum for the hobby to continue to grow and prosper.

Unless definite cards or sets are listed, values are for a generalized selection in each particular topic. There may be cards in each topic that will command higher, or even lower, prices.

ACTORS, ACTRESSES & PERFORMERS

	VG	EX
Astaire, Fred	$ 6 - 8	$ 8 - 10
Baker, Josephine See Artist-Signed and Blacks		
Bogart, H.	8 - 10	10 - 15
Bergman, I.	6 - 8	8 - 12
Bernhardt, Sarah	10 - 12	12 - 15
Cagney, J.	6 - 8	8 - 12
Chaplin, Charles	9 - 12	12 - 16
Crosby, Bing	8 - 10	10 - 12
Davis, Bette	6 - 8	8 - 10
Dean, James	12 - 16	16 - 22
Dietrich, Marlene	8 - 10	10 - 16

German W.W. II Fighters with Swastica Emblem, Real Photo by A. Klein

Sarah Bernhardt, "dans 'l'Aiglon'"
F.C.&Cie, No. 397 (Photo by A. Best)

U. S. Navy W.W. II Martin Patrol Bomber, Curt Teich, No. E-4914

Fields, W. C.	6 - 8	8 - 10
Flynn, Errol	8 - 10	10 - 12
Gable, Clark	8 - 12	12 - 15
Garbo, Greta	8 - 12	12 - 16
Garland, Judy	6 - 8	8 - 10
Harlow, Jean	8 - 10	10 - 14
Laurel & Hardy	10 - 12	12 - 15
Lloyd, Harold	6 - 8	8 - 10
Marx Brothers	8 - 10	10 - 12
Mix, Tom	10 - 12	12 - 15
Monroe, Marilyn	8 - 10	10 - 12
Rogers, Ginger	4 - 6	6 - 9
Temple, Shirley	8 - 10	10 - 12
Valentino, R.	10 - 12	12 - 16
Wayne, John	10 - 12	12 - 16
West, Mae	10 - 12	12 - 16
AESOP'S FABLES		
Raphael Tuck "Aesop's Fables Up to Date" (6)	20 - 25	25 - 28
AIRPLANES, Military	5 - 8	8 - 10
W/German Swastika	10 - 15	15 - 20
AIRPLANES (See Transportation)		
AIRPORTS (See Views)	3 - 5	5 - 8
ALLIGATORS, CROCODILES	2 - 3	3 - 4
ALLIGATOR BORDER CARDS (5500-5664)		
S. Langsdorf & Co. Views	30 - 35	35 - 40

Mailick Christmas Angel #4611, "Fröliche..."   *Anthropomorphic Spoon Man B. B. London, Series E-120*   *Stengel Art by Gleyre, #29095, "Charmeuse"*

Blacks on views "Greetings from the Sunny South" (30) S631-S660	90 - 110	110 - 130
ALPHABET		
Simple	2 - 3	3 - 6
W/Children, Ladies, Animals	4 - 6	6 - 10
C. KLEIN, Flower Series 148	12 - 15	15 - 20
Letters U,V,W,X,Y,Z	22 - 25	25 - 28
Rotograph Co. Series B428	4 - 5	5 - 7
AMISH PEOPLE, pre 1930	2 - 3	3 - 6
AMUSEMENT PARKS, Views	6 - 7	7 - 10
Ferris Wheels	5 - 8	8 - 12
Rides, Shows	10 - 12	12 - 16
Coney Island, Etc.	12 - 15	15 - 18
Real Photos, Views	15 - 18	18 - 22
Real Photos, Rides, Shows	25 - 35	35 - 45
Real Photos, Merry-Go-Rounds	35 - 45	45 - 55
ANGELS	3 - 6	6 - 12
S/ MAILICK	12 - 15	15 - 25
Others	5 - 8	8 - 15
ANIMALS, Domestic Also See Artist-Signed.	1 - 2	2 - 3
P.F.B. "Cake Walk" **Series 3903** (6)	15 - 20	20 - 30
Raphael Tuck Series 6989 "Russian Greyhounds"	12 - 15	15 - 20
ANIMALS, Wild	2 - 3	3 - 6
Official New York Zoo	2 - 3	3 - 4
ANIMALS, Prehistoric	2 - 3	3 - 6
ANTHROPOMORPHIC FIGURES (See Advertising)	15 - 20	20 - 25
Amag Series 2058		
Cork Men	12 - 15	15 - 20
B.B. London Series E120		
Spoon Man –"To Wish You Many a Spoon"	15 - 20	20 - 25
ANTI-CATHOLIC	5 - 10	10 - 12
APPLIQUE (Add-Ons) (See Novelties)		
ART MASTERPIECES (Reproductions)		
Publishers Stengel or Sborgi	1 - 2	2 - 3

Multiple Babies, R. P. by G.R. & Co.
No. W-566, No Caption

Bathing Beauties by Publisher M. Munk
Series 553, No Caption

Tinted French Bathing Beauty
Real Photo by Rex, No. 2449

Nudes	5 - 8	8 - 12
ASTROLOGY	3 - 5	5 - 8
ASYLUMS	5 - 8	8 - 12
AUTHORS	3 - 4	4 - 5
John Winsch (Author Series)	5 - 8	8 - 10
Others	3 - 5	5 - 6
AUTO RACING, Early	15 - 20	20 - 25
AUTO SERVICE STATIONS See Real Photos, Views and Roadside America		
BABIES (Multiple, or Babies by the Dozen types)	3 - 6	6 - 10
BALLET DANCING (Also see artist-signed)	4 - 5	5 - 10
BALLOONS, Flying, Early	10 - 15	15 - 20
Real Photo	20 - 25	25 - 35
BANDS, Musical	7 - 10	10 - 12
Military	6 - 9	9 - 11
BANDSTANDS	3 - 4	4 - 6
BANKS (See Views and Real Photos)		
BASEBALL PARKS, STADIUMS (See Baseball, Etc.)		
BASEBALL PLAYERS (See Baseball, Etc.)		
BASKETBALL PLAYERS, Home Teams, Schools	8 - 10	10 - 15
Real Photo	12 - 15	15 - 25
BATHING BEAUTIES		
French publishers' Real Photos	12 - 15	15 - 20
Hand Tinted	15 - 20	20 - 30
Illustrated P.C. Co. Series 80	9 - 12	12 - 15

Langsdorf & Co. (10)	9 - 12	12 - 15
Leighton & Co. (10)	8 - 10	10 - 12
J. Marks "Summer Girl" **Series 155**	9 - 12	12 - 15
M. Munk, Vienne **Series 205, 553** (6)	20 - 25	25 - 35
P.F.B. Series 6271 (6)	10 - 15	15 - 20
Souvenir Postcard Co. **Series 526** (6)	6 - 7	7 - 10
E. L. Theochrome **Series 1035**	5 - 6	6 - 9
W. M. Taggart **Series 25**	8 - 10	10 - 12
Raphael Tuck		
Ser. 116, 1363, 9414, E9466, 9494 (6)	10 - 12	12 - 16
Ullman Mfg. Co. "Seashore Girls" **Series 90**	7 - 8	8 - 10
Foreign Series **583** (6)	6 - 8	8 - 10
Chromolithographs		
Foreign Series **1070** (6)	6 - 8	8 - 10
Tinted Photos	10 - 12	12 - 15
Others	4 - 6	6 - 8
BATTLESHIPS (See Transportation)		
BEACH SCENES	1 - 2	2 - 5
W/Bathers	3 - 4	4 - 7
Real Photo	6 - 8	8 - 12
BEARS, Real (See Teddy Bear Section)	1 - 2	2 - 3
BICYCLES	3 - 4	4 - 6
Real Photo	8 - 10	10 - 15
Advertising	10 - 15	15 - 25
Advertising Real Photos	20 - 30	30 - 40
BILLIARDS	12 - 15	15 - 18
Artist-Signed	15 - 18	18 - 22
BIRDS	2 - 3	3 - 4
S/ C. KLEIN	5 - 8	8 - 12
Audubon Society	1 - 2	2 - 3
BIRTH ANNOUNCEMENTS	4 - 5	5 - 6
BIRTHSTONES		
E. Nash **Series 1**	6 - 9	9 - 12
E.P.C. Co. **Series 100, 200**	3 - 5	5 - 8
BLACKS, U.S. (See Artist-Signed, Uns. Blacks)		
Foreign	4 - 5	5 - 6
BOATS, Large Image	2 - 3	3 - 5
Small	1 - 1.50	1.50 - 2
BOER WAR	10 - 15	15 - 25
BOOKS	1 - 1.50	1.50 - 3
BOWLING	3 - 4	4 - 6
Artist-types	8 - 12	12 - 20
BOXING (See Sports, Etc.)		
BOY SCOUTS		
A. E. Marty, Hemostyl Adv. Scout Card	35 - 40	40 - 50
Colortype Co., Chicago Sepia	15 - 20	20 - 25
Gartner & Bender, Chicago	12 - 15	15 - 22
Henninger Co., N.Y.		
Scouts Law (12)	12 - 15	15 - 22
Scouts Gum Co. S/H. S. EDWARDS (12)		
1 "Bugle Calls"	18 - 22	22 - 26
2 "The Diving Board"	18 - 22	22 - 26

3	"Fire Without Matches"	18 - 22	22 - 26
4	"Blazing a Trail"	18 - 22	22 - 26
5		18 - 22	22 - 26
6	"Hiding a Trail"	18 - 22	22 - 26
7	"Vaulting a Stream"	18 - 22	22 - 26
8	"Loading a Canoe"	18 - 22	22 - 26
9	"Toting"	18 - 22	22 - 26
10	"First Aid"	18 - 22	22 - 26
11	"Flag of Salute"	20 - 25	25 - 30
12	"The Camp Fire"	18 - 22	22 - 26

Raphael Tuck Boy Scout Series 9950 (6)	125 - 150	150 - 175
Series 8745, S/SHEPHEARD		
"Advice to Scouts" (6)	18 - 22	22 - 26
BREWERIES - Exteriors	6 - 8	8 - 12
Interiors	10 - 12	12 - 15
BRIDGES	1 - 2	2 - 3
Covered Bridges	4 - 6	6 - 10
BROOKLYN EAGLE VIEWS	2 - 3	3 - 6
BULL FIGHTS	2 - 3	3 - 5
BUS DEPOTS	4 - 5	5 - 8
See Views and Real Photos.		
BUSES - 1900-1920	12 - 15	15 - 25
1920-1940	10 - 12	12 - 20
BUTTERFLIES	1 - 2	2 - 3
On Greetings	2 - 3	3 - 6
BUTTON FACES - BUTTON FAMILY		
GEORGE JERVIS	18 - 20	20 - 25
Blacks	30 - 40	40 - 50
CACTUS	1 - 2	2 - 3
CAKE WALK	10 - 15	15 - 25
See Blacks		
CALCIUM LIGHTS	3 - 4	4 - 5
J. Plant "Army-Navy Series"	3 - 4	4 - 5
CALENDARS, 1900	15 - 20	20 - 30
Pre-1904	8 - 10	10 - 12
1905-1910	4 - 7	7 - 10
1910-1915	3 - 5	5 - 8
1915-1940	2 - 3	3 - 5
CAMERAS		
Kodak Advertising	15 - 20	20 - 30
Other Advertising	15 - 20	20 - 25
Artist-Signed	7 - 10	10 - 20
Comics	2 - 3	3 - 6
CANALS	1 - 2	2 - 3
Panama Canal Construction Views	5 - 8	8 - 12
CANOEING	1 - 2	2 - 3
CAPITALS See Sets & Series		
State Capitols & Seals	5 - 7	7 - 10
CARNIVAL		
Raphael Tuck "Carnival" Series 117 (12)	15 - 20	20 - 25
Oilette Series 6435 (6)	12 - 15	15 - 20

Oilette "Mardi Gras" Series 2551 (6)	7 - 8	8 - 10
T. Gessner "Mardi Gras" Series	6 - 7	7 - 10
Foreign - Early Chromolithos	25 - 35	35 - 50
Real Carnivals		
Sideshows, Color	6 - 8	8 - 12
Sideshows, Real Photo	15 - 20	20 - 30
CAROUSELS Color	10 - 15	15 - 20
Real Photo	15 - 25	25 - 35
CARTS		
Goat, Pony	10 - 12	12 - 15
Horse, Oxen	8 - 10	10 - 12
See Real Photos		
CASTLES	1 - 2	2 - 3
Castles on the Rhine, etc.	3 - 5	5 - 8
CATHEDRALS	1 - 1.50	1.50 - 2
CATS See Artist-Signed Cats	1 - 2	2 - 3
CATTLE	1 - 2	2 - 3
CAVES and CAVERNS	1 - 2	2 - 4
CEMETERIES	1 - 1.50	1.50 - 2.00
CHESS/CHECKERS	5 - 7	7 - 12
Artist-signed	12 - 15	15 - 20
CHICKENS	1 - 3	3 - 6
Dressed like people.	8 - 10	10 - 15
CHILDREN, Foreign	1 - 2	2 - 4
Playing	2 - 3	3 - 5
W/Dolls, Toys	8 - 12	12 - 20
W/Animals	6 - 7	7 - 10
See Real Photos		
CHINESE PEOPLE	2 - 3	3 - 5
CHRISTMAS TREES		
Raphael Tuck Series 529 (6)	7 - 8	8 - 10
Real Photos with toys, gifts	10 - 15	15 - 20
CHURCHES (See Views)		
CIGARETTES, CIGARS (Also see Advertising)	4 - 5	5 - 8
CIRCUS		
Barnum & Bailey - 1900-1920	25 - 30	30 - 35
Posters	30 - 40	40 - 50
1920-1940	15 - 20	20 - 25
Other Circus	10 - 15	15 - 20
CLOCKS	1 - 2	2 - 3
CLOWNS - Barnum & Bailey	15 - 20	20 - 25
Barnum & Bailey early posters with clowns	30 - 40	40 - 50
Early Chromolithographs	30 - 35	35 - 40
Others	10 - 12	12 - 15
Linens	8 - 10	10 - 12
COACHES, CARRIAGES	5 - 6	6 - 8
COAT-OF-ARMS	3 - 5	5 - 7
COCA COLA SIGNS		
Small	4 - 7	7 - 10
Large	10 - 15	15 - 20
Linens	3 - 4	4 - 6

Carnival at Long Beach Resort, Panama City, FL, Curt Teich, No. 1B-H2665

Raphael Tuck, Series 2510, "Heroes of the South," "General Lee and ...Traveler"

Halley's Comet Signed K. Hesse 3090, Koch & Bitriol, "Komet 1910"

"Winnie Davis, Daughter of the Confederacy," 1909 by W. T. Terry

COIN CARDS, Embossed *

Walter Erhard	8 - 10	10 - 12
Flat Printed	7 - 9	9 - 12
H. Guggenheim (Emb.)	10 - 12	12 - 15
H.S.M.	10 - 12	12 - 15

   * Add $3-5 for U.S. Coin cards

COLISEUMS (See Views)

COLLEGES (See Views)

COMETS

Halley's, S/K. HESSE	10 - 12	12 - 20
Koch & Bitriol Series 3090 No. 2	15 - 18	18 - 22

COMIC STRIP CHARACTERS (See Comics)

COMPOSERS	2 - 3	3 - 5

CONFEDERACY, DAUGHTERS OF

W. T. Terry

"Winnie Davis, Daughter of the Confederacy"	40 - 50	50 - 75

CONFEDERATE STATES

CIVIL WAR

Raphael Tuck   Series 2510

"Heroes of the South"

1. General Lee & Traveler	25 - 30	30 - 35
2. General Robert E. Lee	25 - 30	30 - 35
3. Lee in Confederate Uniform	25 - 30	30 - 35
4. Gen. Thomas J. "Stonewall" Jackson	25 - 30	30 - 35
5. Lee and Jackson	25 - 30	30 - 35

6. Prayer in "Stonewall" Jackson's Camp	25 - 30	30 - 35
Jamestown A&V Co., 1907		
Jamestown Expo Series #50-59 & 67		
Confederate Cards (See Expositions)		
Others	10 - 12	12 - 15
"Sheridan's Ride" (10)	8 - 10	10 - 12
CONVENTS	2 - 3	3 - 6
CONVICTS	10 - 12	12 - 15
Black Men	60 - 75	75 - 90
Real Photos		
Black Men	400 - 450	450 - 500
Black Women	450 - 500	500 - 550
CORPSE, In Casket	3 - 5	5 - 7
Real Photo	6 - 9	9 - 12
COSTUMES, Native & Foreign	1 - 2	2 - 3
COURT HOUSES (See Views)		
COVERED BRIDGES	4 - 7	7 - 10
COWBOYS	3 - 5	5 - 8
Raphael Tuck "Among the Cowboys" Ser. 2499	8 - 10	10 - 12
Real Photos	12 - 15	15 - 25
COWGIRLS	6 - 7	7 - 8
Real Photos	12 - 15	15 - 25
CRADLES	2 - 3	3 - 4
CROSSES	1 - 1.50	1.50 - 2.00
CUPIDS	2 - 3	3 - 5
DAIRIES & CREAMERIES (See Views)		
DAMS	1 -1.50	1.50 - 2.00
Real Photo	5 - 7	7 - 10
DANCING	3 - 5	5 - 6
Artist-Signed See specific artists		
DAYS OF WEEK (Also see Teddy Bears, Sunbonnets)	2 - 3	3 - 6
DEATH (Also See Death Fantasy)	2 - 3	3 - 6
DEER	1 -1.50	1.50 - 2.00
DENTAL	12 - 15	15 - 18
Artist-Signed	12 - 15	15 - 20
Linens	5 - 6	6 - 8
DEPARTMENT STORES	4 - 5	5 - 8
Interiors	5 - 6	6 - 8
Interiors, Real Photos	8 - 10	10 - 15
DETROIT PUB. CO. VIEWS		
Early PMC Cards – Better Views	15 - 20	20 - 25
Common	5 - 6	6 - 8
Others - Better Views	6 - 8	8 - 10
Common	1 - 2	2 - 3
DEVIL or Satan	5 - 8	8 - 12
DIABOLO		
Davidson Series 2627 S/BROWNE (6)	12 - 15	15 - 20
Langsdorf Series 711 S/KINSELLA (6)	15 - 18	18 - 22
Raphael Tuck Series N49 S/SHEPHEARD (6)	15 - 18	18 - 22
LOUIS WAIN Series 9563, 9564 (6)	60 - 75	75 - 100
DICE	3 - 4	4 - 7
DIME STORES (Linens) (Newberry's, Kress, etc.)	3 - 5	5 - 7

Real Photo by W. H. Martin, ©1909
"How We Catch 'Em in Oklahoma"

Elf, Published by HWB, Series 2214
"Bonne Année"

"Cluett, Peabody & Co. ... Shirt Factory,
Troy, N.Y.," Valentine-Sou., #219209

DINERS (See Views, R. Photos, Roadside America)

DIONNE QUINTUPLETS	12 - 15	15 - 18
Real Photos	15 - 20	20 - 30
DIRIGIBLES, ZEPPELINS	10 - 12	12 - 20
(Also see Transportation & Real Photos)		
DISASTERS (**See Earthquakes**)		
Tornados & Hurricanes	5 - 8	8 - 15
Floods, Fire, etc.	6 - 8	8 - 12
(Also see Real Photos)		
DIVERS	2 - 3	3 - 5
DOG CARTS	6 - 8	8 - 12
Sleds	6 - 8	8 - 10
DOGS (Also see Artist-Signed Dogs)	2 - 3	3 - 5
A.S.B. Series 245	6 - 8	8 - 12
A. & M. B. Series 54	5 - 8	8 - 12
B.B. London Series E32	5 - 8	8 - 12
H.S.M. Series 719	5 - 8	8 - 12
P.F.B. Series 8163 (6) Large Image	15 - 17	17 - 22
Raphael Tuck "Art" Series 855 (6)	10 - 12	12 - 15
"Connoisseur" Series 2546 (6)	10 - 12	12 - 15
DOLLS (See Golliwoggs, Real Photos, Children)		
Gartner & Bender Rag Doll Series		
"A Wise Guy" (6)	6 - 9	9 - 12
"Amybility" (6)	6 - 9	9 - 12
"Antie Quate" (6)	6 - 9	9 - 12

"Dolly Dimple" (6)	6 - 9	9 - 12
"Epi Gram" (6)	6 - 9	9 - 12
"Gee Whiz" (6)	6 - 9	9 - 12
"Gee Willikens" (6)	6 - 9	9 - 12
"Heeza Korker" (6)	6 - 9	9 - 12
"Jiminy" (6)	6 - 9	9 - 12
"Optimistic Miss" (6)	6 - 9	9 - 12
"Phil Osopher" (6)	6 - 9	9 - 12
DONKEYS, MULES, BURROS	1 - 2	2 - 3
DOVES	0.50 - 1	1 - 1.50
DREAMING	2 - 3	3 - 6
DRINKING	1 - 2	2 - 5
(See SCHMUCKER)		
DRINKS Beer, Drunk Comics	2 - 3	3 - 5
Linens	1 - 1.50	1.50 - 2
DRUG STORES (See Views and Real Photos)		
DRUGS, ADDICTS, USING	8 - 10	10 - 12
DUCKS, GEESE (Also see Fantasy Dressed Animals)	1 - 2	2 - 3
DUTCH PEOPLE AND DUTCH CHILDREN	1 - 2	2 - 5
See Artists		
EARTHQUAKES	5 - 7	7 - 10
San Francisco	2 - 4	4 - 7
ELEPHANTS (Also see Fantasy Dressed Animals)	3 - 5	5 - 6
ELKS	2 - 3	3 - 4
Fraternal, Artist-Signed	6 - 7	7 - 10
ELVES, DWARFS (Also see Fantasy)	3 - 5	5 - 10
EVANGELISTS	2 - 4	4 - 7
Billy Sunday	6 - 9	9 - 12
Real Photos	9 - 12	12 - 16
EXAGGERATIONS		
Big Fish, Rabbits, Vegetables, Fruit, etc.	3 - 5	5 - 10
Big Grasshoppers	5 - 6	6 - 9
Add $8 -10 each to prices for Real Photos.		
EXECUTIONS	6 - 8	8 - 10
Chinese, Foreign	5 - 6	6 - 8
FAB PATCHWORK SILKS		
W. N. Sharpe		
Kings & Queens	25 - 30	30 - 40
Scenes	20 - 25	25 - 30
FACTORIES, PLANTS (See Views and Real Photos)	2 - 3	3 - 10
Linens	1 - 2	2 - 5
FAIRY TALES (See Fairy Tales)		
FAIRS, FESTIVALS	5 - 6	6 - 10
(See Views)		
FAMOUS PEOPLE'S HOMES		
Movie Stars	3 - 5	5 - 7
Linens	1 - 2	2 - 4
FANS (See Artist-Signed)	2 - 3	3 - 5
FARMING	2 - 3	3 - 5
FARMING EQUIPMENT		
Horse-Driven	6 - 8	8 - 10

"Grand Army of the Republic"
American Novelty Co.

Big Hat, Real Photo by G.L.
Co., Series 2074/6

Hitler, Real Photo by
O. Struck, Berlin

Motor-Driven	8 - 10	10 - 12
(See Real Photos)		
FASHIONS	3 - 5	5 - 10
FAT PEOPLE, Real	6 - 8	8 - 10
Circus Side Shows (See Real Photos)	7 - 9	9 - 12
Comics	1 - 1.50	1.50 - 2.00
FELIX THE CAT	15 - 20	20 - 25
FENCING	3 - 4	4 - 6
FERRY BOATS (Also see Real Photos)	6 - 7	7 - 10
FIRE ENGINES, Horse	8 - 10	10 - 16
Motor driven (Also see Real Photos)	15 - 18	18 - 22
FIRE HOUSES and/or Equipment (See Real Photos)	10 - 12	12 - 15
R. Wilkenson, Providence, R.I. (38)	10 - 12	12 - 15
FIRES (Disasters)	6 - 8	8 - 12
Named (Also see Real Photos)	6 - 8	8 - 15
FIREWORKS	4 - 5	5 - 6
FISH, FISHING (See Artist-Signed)	3 - 4	4 - 8
FLAGS, U.S.	4 - 5	5 - 6
Julius Bien Series 710	6 - 8	8 - 12
Ill. Post Card Co. Series 207	6 - 9	9 - 12
National Art Co. "Hands Across the Sea"	7 - 8	8 - 10
Real Photo	8 - 10	10 - 15
Foreign	2 - 3	3 - 4
FLOODS (Disasters)	5 - 7	7 - 10
Named (See Real Photos)	8 - 10	10 - 12
FLOWERS	1 - 1.50	1.50 - 2.00
S/C. KLEIN	3 - 5	5 - 8
FLOWER FACES	6 - 7	8 - 12
FOOTBALL Players (See Sports)		
FORTS	1 - 2	2 - 3
FOREIGN VIEWS See Views	0.50 - 1	1 - 1.50
FORTUNE TELLING	3 - 4	4 - 7
FRATERNAL		
Ullman Mfg. Co. Series 199	7 - 8	8 - 11

FREAKS, Animal	6 - 7	7 -10
People	8 - 10	10 - 15
FROGS (Also see Dressed Animals)	1 - 2	2 - 3
FUNERAL HOMES (See Views)		
GAMBLING, Casinos, Dice, etc.	4 - 5	5 - 6
GEISHA GIRLS (See Artist-Signed)	3 - 5	5 - 6
GEYSERS	1 - 2	2 - 3
GHOSTS (Also see Fantasy)	2 - 3	3 - 5
GIANTS, MIDGETS	5 - 8	8 - 10
GIRL SCOUTS		
BALLINGER, E.		
Girl Scout Laws Series M572	10 - 12	12 - 15
GILLESPIE, JESSIE		
Silhouettes of Scout Activities (6)	12 - 15	15 - 20
PRICE, EDITH B.		
The Four Seasons (4)	10 - 12	12 - 15
PRICE, MARGARET EVANS		
Girl Scout Laws Series M-578	12 - 15	15 - 20
GOATS	1 - 2	2 - 3
Bergman Series 1052 Billy Goat Comics (6)	5 - 6	6 - 9
GOLF Players in action	3 - 4	4 - 5
Courses	3 - 5	5 - 10
Golf Comics	10 - 15	15 - 25
Linens	4 - 7	7 - 10
See Artist-Signed Beautiful Ladies		
Raphael Tuck		
Ser. 697 "Golf Hints" (6)	18 - 22	22 - 26
Ser. 9499 "Humorous Golf" (6)	18 - 22	22 - 26
Ser. 3600 "Golf Humor" (6)	18 - 22	22 - 26
Ladies/Men Artist-Signed	15 - 20	20 - 30
Series 9427 Blacks, "More Coons" (1)	30 - 35	35 - 40
Advertising, product	15 - 25	25 - 40
GOOD LUCK SYMBOLS ON GREETINGS		
Horseshoes, Four-leaf Clover	1 - 2	2 - 3
Swastikas	4 - 5	5 - 6
GRAND ARMY OF THE REPUBLIC	5 - 8	8 - 12
GRUSS AUS (See Foreign Views)		
GYMNASIUMS (See Views)		
GYMNASTICS	3 - 4	4 - 6
GYPSIES	5 - 6	6 - 9
HANDBALL	4 - 6	6 - 8
HANDS ACROSS THE SEA (See Silks)	4 - 6	6 - 9
HARBORS	2 - 3	3 - 5
W/Ships, Busy	4 - 5	5 - 8
HATS (Also see Artist-Signed)		
Ladies Big Hats	3 - 4	4 - 6
Real Photos	4 - 6	6 - 10
HERALDIC	4 - 5	5 - 10
Paul Kohl (84)	8 - 10	10 - 12
Raphael Tuck		
"Boston"	8 - 10	10 - 12
"Philadelphia"	8 - 10	10 - 12

Unsigned F. Brundage Hold-to-Light
Easter Angels, WHB, "Gesegnete Ostern"

Hold-to-Light Christmas Angel	*Hold-to-Light Christmas Angel*	
C.R.G.M., 88077, "Frohe Weihnachten"	*"Fröliche Weihnachten"*	

"Washington, D.C." PMC's	10 - 12	12 - 15
HITLER		
Printed types	8 - 10	10 - 16
Real Photos		
Postmarked	15 - 20	20 - 25
Unused	12 - 15	15 - 20
Color, Continental size, Common	15 - 18	18 - 25
Color, Continental size, Rarer issues	50 - 75	75 - 125
HOLD-TO-LIGHT		
Fairy Tales Transparencies	40 - 50	50 - 60
Maikäfirs (May Bugs)	40 - 50	50 - 60
Transparencies	30 - 35	35 - 40
New Year		
Snowmen		
Large	50 - 60	60 - 75
Small	40 - 50	50 - 65
Signed by **MAILICK**	60 - 70	70 - 85
Year Dates	35 - 40	40 - 55
Figures made of children	40 - 50	50 - 65
Figures made of pigs	50 - 60	60 - 75
Figures made of snowmen	60 - 75	75 - 100
Unsigned **BRUNDAGE** Children	50 - 60	60 - 75
Scenic types	25 - 30	30 - 35
Valentine's Day		
Children, Cupids	50 - 60	60 - 75

Easter
Angels	30 - 40	40 - 55
Angels – Unsigned **BRUNDAGE**	50 - 75	75 - 90
Angels signed by **MAILICK**	70 - 80	80 - 95
Bunnies, Bunnies & Children	60 - 70	70 - 85
Chicks	40 - 50	50 - 60
Children in Easter Eggs	50 - 60	60 - 75
Crosses, Churches, Scenic	25 - 30	30 - 40

Thanksgiving
Turkeys	75 - 100	100 - 125
Children and Big Turkeys	150 - 175	175 - 200
Scenic, Vegetables, etc.	25 - 30	30 - 35

Christmas
Angels	50 - 60	60 - 75
Angels with Christmas Trees	65 - 70	70 - 75
Signed by **MAILICK**	70 - 80	80 - 100
Cherubs	40 - 50	50 - 65
Winter Scenes, Churches, etc.	25 - 30	30 - 40

Santas
Santas in red robes	150 - 175	175 - 250
Large Santas, Robes other than red	250 - 300	300 - 400
Small Santas	150 - 200	200 - 250
Santas signed by Mailick (See Santas)		
Santa Transparencies	75 - 100	100 - 125
Uncle Sam Santas (See Santas)		
Children	40 - 50	50 - 60
Transparencies	25 - 30	30 - 35
Artist-Signed See Specific Artist		
Koehler (See Sets & Series)		
Other Publishers, Views	25 - 30	30 - 40
Statue of Liberty	30 - 35	35 - 40
Trains, Ships	30 - 35	35 - 40
Other Views, Bldgs., etc.	25 - 30	30 - 35
Comics	15 - 20	20 - 25
Foreign Gruss Aus City Views	20 - 25	25 - 30
Paris Exposition (12)	30 - 35	35 - 40
Foreign War Issues (Belgian)	12 - 15	15 - 20
Other See-Through Issues (Transparencies)		
Comics	15 - 20	20 - 25
Other Foreign	12 - 15	15 - 20

HOROSCOPE
Dietrich & Co.	6 - 8	8 - 10
Williamson-Hafner Series 985		
Others	5 - 6	6 - 8
HORSE & BUGGIES, Large Image, Color	8 - 10	10 - 12
Small Image	5 - 6	6 - 8
See Real Photos.		
HORSES, Unsigned - Heads	5 - 7	7 - 10
Large Images	5 - 7	7 - 10
Small Images	2 - 3	3 - 4
See Artist-Signed Horses.		

Ku Klux Klan, Klan No. 2, Racine, Wisconsin – Real Photo by Wright, 1924

Ku Klux Klan, Marching in Washington D.C., 1926 – Real Photo by Hiram Evans

Dan Patch

Wright, Barnett & Stilwell Co.	20 - 25	25 - 30
V.O. Hammon 155	18 - 22	22 - 27
T.P. & Co.	15 - 20	20 - 25
Real Photos	40 - 50	50 - 50

HOSPITALS (See Views, Real Photos)
HOTELS (See Views, Real Photos)

HOURS OF THE DAY		
Rose Co.	3 - 4	4 - 7
Warwick Co.	3 - 4	4 - 6
HOUSEBOATS	4 - 5	5 - 6
HUNTING	1 - 2	2 - 5
Ladies Hunting (See Artist-Signed)	8 - 10	10 - 15
ILLUMINATED WINDOWS	5 - 6	6 - 8
ILLUSTRATED SONGS		
Bamforth Many different.	2 - 3	3 - 5
E. Nash "National Song" Series (6)	6 - 8	8 - 10
E. L. Theochromes	2 - 3	3 - 5
Blacks	15 - 20	20 - 25
INCLINE RAILWAYS (See Transportation)		
INDIANS, Chiefs See Cowboys and Indians.		
INDUSTRY, Exteriors	3 - 5	5 - 10
Interior	5 - 8	8 - 12
See Views and Real Photos.		
INSECTS (Also see Fantasy, Artist-Signed)	2 - 3	3 - 5
INSTALLMENT CARDS		
W. M. Beach		
Cow (4)	20 - 25	25 - 28
Others	20 - 25	25 - 28
Huld		
1 Alligator (4)	30 - 35	35 - 40
2 Dachshund (4)	30 - 35	35 - 40
3 Uncle Sam (4)	50 - 60	60 - 70
4 Fish (4)	25 - 30	30 - 35
5 Sea Serpent (4)	30 - 35	35 - 40
6 Mosquito (4)	30 - 35	35 - 40
7 Rip Van Winkle (4)	30 - 35	35 - 40
8 New York City (4)	25 - 30	30 - 35
9 Santa (4)	150 - 175	175 - 225
10 Christmas Tree (4)	35 - 40	40 - 45
11 Fisherwoman (4)	30 - 35	35 - 40
12 Fisherman (4)	25 - 30	30 - 35
14 Rabbit (4)	30 - 35	35 - 40
15 Teddy Bear (4)	70 - 75	75 - 85
N.Y. Journal-American Comic Characters	6 - 8	8 - 10
H.M. Rose	6 - 8	8 - 10
Wildwood Co.	6 - 8	8 - 10
Wrench & Co.	6 - 8	8 - 10
Ottmar Zieher	8 - 9	9 - 10
Standup Napoleon (10) Sepia	10 - 12	12 - 15
Albert of Belgium (10) B&W	8 - 10	10 - 12
Joan of Arc (10) B&W	10 - 15	15 - 18
JAILS	4 - 5	5 - 8
JAPANESE GIRLS P.C.K. Series	3 - 4	4 - 5
JAPANESE NAVY		
Raphael Tuck Oilette Series 9237 (6)	6 - 8	8 - 10
JERUSALEM		
Raphael Tuck Oilette Series 3355 (6)	6 - 8	8 - 10

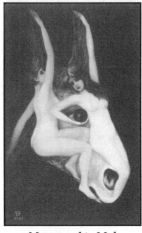  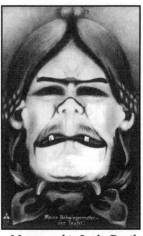

Metamorphic Mule   *Metamorphic "Phlegma als*   *Metamorphic Lady-Devil*
G. G. Co., No.5132   *Ehemann" – BNK, 33333*   *"Meine Schwiegermutter..."*

JEWISH NEW YEAR		
Hebrew Pub. Co.	6 - 9	9 - 12
Others	4 - 5	5 - 8
JEWISH PEOPLE	5 - 8	8 - 12
Comics	10 - 15	15 - 25
JEWISH SYNAGOGUES	15 - 20	20 - 30
Foreign	20 - 25	25 - 35
KU KLUX KLAN		
Printed	50 - 75	75 - 100
Real Photo	200 - 250	250 - 500
LAKES, Named	0.50 - 1	1 - 1.50
LANGUAGE OF FLOWERS	1 - 2	2 - 3
LARGE LETTERS, Cities, States (Early)	2 - 3	3 - 6
Linens	2 - 3	3 - 5
Names, Early	5 - 6	6 - 8
Letters of Alphabet	4 - 5	5 - 6
LEATHER (See Novelties)		
LESBIAN-RELATED	12 - 15	15 - 25
Real Photo Nudes	25 - 30	30 - 40
See specific Artists		
LIBRARIES (See Views)		
LIFE SAVING STATIONS	3 - 4	4 - 6
LIGHTHOUSES	2 - 4	4 - 6
Real Photos	5 - 8	8 - 12
LINENS (Postcards)		
Advertising, Product (See Advertising)		
Blacks (See Blacks)	3 - 5	5 - 10
Comics, Unsigned	0.50 - 1	1 - 1.50
Comics, Signed	1 - 2	2 - 3
Comics, WW2	3 - 4	4 - 6
Hitler, Anti-	2 - 5	5 - 10
Indians	1 - 2	2 - 3
Large Letters, States, Cities	2 - 3	3 - 5
Showing Blacks	5 - 7	7 - 9

Army Bases	3 - 4	4 - 5
Pin-up Girls	2 - 3	3 - 6
Political, Presidential	2 - 3	3 - 7
Court House, Post Office, etc.	1 -1.50	1.50 - 2
Depots, small town	2 - 3	3 - 5
Street Scenes, Small Town	1 - 2	2 - 5
See **Roadside America** for others.		
LIONS	1 - 2	2 - 3
LIONS CLUB	4 - 5	5 - 12
LITERARY CHARACTERS	2 - 3	3 - 6
LOVERS	1 - 2	2 - 3
MACABRE	5 - 6	6 - 10
MAGICIANS	5 - 6	6 - 9
MAIN STREETS See Views and Real Photos.		
MAPS	1 - 2	2 - 5
MASONIC	3 - 4	4 - 6
National Art Co.		
Series 679	5 - 7	7 - 10
Series 1444	5 - 7	7 - 10
MERRY WIDOW HATS		
Grollman	3 - 4	4 - 5
METAMORPHICS (Archiboldesque) Real Photos		
"Bléroit" Mermaids	50 - 60	60 - 75
"Richard Wagner" W/2 Mermaids on face and collar	50 - 60	60 - 75
"Francois Joseph"	40 - 50	50 - 60
"Graf Zeppelin"	65 - 70	70 - 80
Skulls, "Diabolo"	25 - 30	30 - 35
"Theodore Roosevelt"	175 - 200	200 - 250
"Bismarck," "Napoleon the great conqueror"	25 - 30	30 - 40
"A Sport," "Une Faune," "Rossini," "Bacchus"	25 - 30	30 - 40
"Edouard VII," "Alphonse XII," "Satyr"	25 - 30	30 - 40
"Cherchez le viveur," "Un bon vivant," "Abdul	25 - 30	30 - 40
"Aamid," "Beethoven," "Goethe," "Liszt"	25 - 30	30 - 40
"Gourmand," "Horse with Frauen," "Mephisto"	25 - 30	30 - 40
"Napoleon I," "Napoleon II," Jockey and Race	25 - 30	30 - 40
Horse, "Schiller," "Johann Strauss," "R. Wagner"	25 - 30	30 - 40
"Groten van Noordwijk," "Xantippe, "Tete de mort"	25 - 30	30 - 40
"Lamour de Pierrot," "Napoleon" (Le grand vainqeur)	40 - 45	45 - 50
G.G. Co. Mule, No. 5132	30 - 40	40 - 50
BNK, No. 33333 "Phlegma als Ehemann"	30 - 40	40 - 50
Lady-Devil, "Meine Schwiegermutter-Der Teufel!"	30 - 40	40 - 50
Many others	25 - 30	30 - 40
Black and White printed	10 - 15	15 - 25
MEXICAN REVOLUTION	5 - 6	6 - 8
Real Photos	10 - 15	15 - 25
Pancho Villa	22 - 25	25 - 30
W. H. Horne - Add $2-3 per card.		
MIDGETS, GIANTS	5 - 8	8 - 10
MILITARY		
Comics	3 - 4	4 - 5
Officers	3 - 5	5 - 8
Soldiers	2 - 3	3 - 4

Gale & Polden "Military Uniforms"	6 - 8	8 - 10
Langsdorf & Co. "Military Officers"	12 - 15	15 - 18
Raphael Tuck		
S/PAYNE		
Write Away Series 18, 19, 20, 21, 22,		
23, 24, 25, 26 (6 in each series)	12 - 15	15 - 20
"Our Fighting Regiments"		
Series 3105 "Royal Artillery" (6)	8 - 10	10 - 12
Series 3163 "Ist Life Guards" (6)	8 - 10	10 - 12
Series 3165 "First Dragoon Guards" (6)	8 - 10	10 - 12
Military in London		
Series 3546 "Military in London" (6)	10 - 12	12 - 15
Series 6412 "Military in London" I (6)	10 - 12	12 - 15
Series 9081 "Military in London" II (6)	10 - 12	12 - 15
Series 9587 "Military in London" III (6)	10 - 12	12 - 15
Series 3642 "Scots Pipers" (6)	8 - 10	10 - 12
Series 8637 "17th Lancers" (6)	10 - 12	12 - 15
Series 8762 "The Red Cross" (6)	10 - 12	12 - 15
Series 8807 "16th Lancers" (6)	10 - 12	12 - 15
Series 9884 "The Golden Highlanders" (6)	10 - 12	12 - 15
Series 9885 "Seaforth Highlanders" (6)	10 - 12	12 - 15
Series 9937 "Argyll & Southern Hilanders" (6)	10 - 12	12 - 15
Series 9994 "The Black Watch" (6)	10 - 12	12 - 15
Gale & Polden Issues	8 - 10	10 - 12
Valentine Co.	5 - 6	6 - 8
MILK CARTS	3 - 6	6 - 8
Real Photo	8 - 10	10 - 15
MILK WAGONS, TRUCKS　See Real Photo		
MILLS, Industry	3 - 4	4 - 6
Real Photo Interior	10 - 15	15 - 20
Real Photo Exterior	8 - 10	10 - 15
MINING	5 - 6	6 - 8
Real Photo	8 - 10	10 - 15
Add $3 to $5 for Gold Mining		
MINING DISASTERS	10 - 15	15 - 20
MIRRORS	1 - 2	2 - 3
MONKEYS, APES　(Also see Dressed Animals)	2 - 3	3 - 4
MONTHS OF YEAR	3 - 4	4 - 7
MONUMENTS	0.50 - 1	1 - 1.50
MOTHER & CHILD　(See Artist-Signed)	4 - 5	5 - 8
MOTORCYCLES	6 - 9	9 - 12
Named	10 - 15	15 - 20
Others	6 - 8	8 - 10
See Real Photos.		
MOTTOES	0.50 - 1	1 - 2
MOVIE STARS　(See Actors/Actresses)		
MUSHROOMS	1 - 2	2 - 3
MUSICAL INSTRUCTORS	2 - 3	3 - 5
MYTHOLOGY　(See Fantasy)	5 - 6	6 -10
NAMES		
Raphael Tuck　**Name Series 131**	5 - 6	6 - 9

"Revolving Pictures " – Ullman Mfg. Co. No. 2228, "A Merry-Go-Round"

Phonograph Record, Blacks' Song, "La Paloma" –LB, No. F1/2

Rotograph Co. Name Series (R.P.)	5 - 6	6 - 9
NATIONAL SOCIALISM	12 - 15	15 - 25
NATIVES	3 - 4	4 - 6
Semi-Nudes	8 - 10	10 - 15
NAVY		
Raphael Tuck U.S. Navy Series 2326	8 - 10	10 - 12
Illustrated P.C. Co.	6 - 8	8 - 10
NESBITT, EVELYN (Actress)	10 - 12	12 - 15
NEWSPAPER	3 - 4	4 - 6
NORTH POLE EXPEDITION	10 - 15	15 - 25
NOVELTIES		
Appliqued Materials *		
Feathered Birds, Feathered Hats	4 - 5	5 - 6
Flowers, Beads, Shells, Ribbons	1 - 2	2 - 3
Jewelry, Real Photos, Celluloid	3 - 4	4 - 5
Metal Models, Good Luck Charms, Horse Shoes, Bells, Hearts, etc.	7 - 8	8 - 10
Real Hair (On Beautiful Ladies)	15 - 20	20 - 30
Glitter (Distracting on most cards)		
Love letters, Notes - in envelopes	2 - 3	3 - 4
Felt (pennants, etc.)	3 - 4	4 - 10
Silk (See Santas, Langsdorf Ladies, E. Christy)	4 - 8	8 - 15
Miscellaneous	1 - 2	2 - 3

* Motif may make value of card higher but also can make value lower, eg., glitter added.

Valentine's, Mailing Novelty Pull-out, No. 832, "Lift the snowball and you will view..."

PAPER DOLL CUT-OUTS
Raphael Tuck

Series 3381, (I) (6) Paper Dolls, S/**BANKS**	125 - 150	150 - 180
Series 3382, (II) (6) Paper Dolls, S/**BANKS**	125 - 150	150 - 180
Series 3383 (III) (6) Paper Dolls, S/**BANKS**	125 - 150	150 - 175
Series 3384 (IV) (6) Paper Dolls, S/**BANKS**	125 - 150	150 - 180
Series 3385, (V) (6) S/**WAIN**	200 - 250	250 - 300
Series 3400 "Window Garden" (6)	50 - 75	75 - 100

MECHANICALS *
Special Types

Circle H Series 100	20 - 25	25 - 35
P.F.B. Series 9525 Day-Month-Date	35 - 45	45 - 50
Kaleidoscopes	20 - 30	30 - 50
Lever-pull	10 - 15	15 - 25
Rotating Wheels	20 - 25	25 - 35
Miscellaneous	8 - 10	10 - 15

See Clapsaddle Halloween, others.
* Prices relate to most common types. Other
specific and special types are valued to $200 ea.
Transparencies (See Hold-To-Lights)
MISCELLANEOUS
Motif or artist-signed may make value higher.

Aluminum	4 - 6	6 - 12
Bas Relief	3 - 4	4 - 5
Royalty	10 - 15	15 - 25
Book Marks	2 - 5	5 - 10
Common	1 - 2	2 - 3
Artist-Signed	5 - 10	10 - 18
Celluloid	5 - 6	6 - 10
Glass Eyes	2 - 3	3 - 5

Hold-to-Light (See Hold-To-Lights)

Jig Saw Puzzles	7 - 10	10 - 15
Leather		
Comics & Greetings	2 - 3	3 - 5
Blacks	10 - 15	15 - 20
Indians	8 - 10	10 - 12
Presidential or Political	15 - 20	20 - 30
Specials (Women, Golf, Bears, etc.)	6 - 10	10 - 20
Miniature Cards (Views, etc.)	4 - 5	5 - 8
Easter Witches of Scandinavia	12 - 15	15 - 20
Peat	6 - 8	8 - 12
Perfumed	3 - 4	4 - 5
Photo Inserts	1 - 2	2 - 3
Pull-outs (Views)	2 - 3	3 - 4
Valentine's		
Black Kids & Snowball, #832 "Lift the snowball..."	50 - 75	75 - 100
Records (Phonograph)	10 - 12	12 - 20
La Paloma (Blacks)	75 - 100	100 - 125
Satin Finish	4 - 5	5 - 6
Squeakers	2 - 3	3 - 4
Stamp Montage	6 - 7	7 - 10
Wire Tales	6 - 8	8 - 12
Wood, Bark	5 - 7	7 - 10
NUDES (See Nudes)		
NURSERY RHYMES (See Fantasy)		
NURSES (See specific artists)	5 - 6	6 - 8
OCEAN LINERS (See Transportation)		
OCCUPATIONS	6 - 8	8 - 12
Raphael Tuck – A. Selige		
S/E. CURTIS	8 - 10	10 - 12
"A cobbler sweetheart ..."	8 - 10	10 - 12
"All a-tiptoe ..."	8 - 10	10 - 12
"Be a baker ..."	8 - 10	10 - 12
"Come let me whisper ..."	8 - 10	10 - 12
"Cupid said you melted ..."	8 - 10	10 - 12
"Dear little teacher, ..."	8 - 10	10 - 12
"If I a sweetheart had ..."	8 - 10	10 - 12
"If you can heal a wounded ..."	8 - 10	10 - 12
"Just a line o'type ..."	8 - 10	10 - 12
"Links of love ..."	8 - 10	10 - 12
"My heart is nailed ..."	8 - 10	10 - 12
"O, queen of cooks, ..."	8 - 10	10 - 12
"O, would I were an artist ..."	8 - 10	10 - 12
"Pray if you love me, ..."	8 - 10	10 - 12
"Punch, punch, punch ..."	8 - 10	10 - 12
"The lark with notes ..."	8 - 10	10 - 12
"'Tis needless to try ..."	8 - 10	10 - 12
"What a bargain ..."	8 - 10	10 - 12
"When you're a grown-up ..."	8 - 10	10 - 12
"You may add to ..."	8 - 10	10 - 12
"You serve me kindly, ..."	8 - 10	10 - 12
"You'd keep the peace, ..."	8 - 10	10 - 12
"A little soldier ..."	8 - 10	10 - 12

"Miss Alice Roosevelt"
Rotograph, Series B789

"Der Duce Benito
Mussolini," A. Oemler #38

"De Heer Roosevelt"
Raphael Tuck & Sons

Others	3 - 5	5 - 7
OIL WELLS	3 - 4	4 - 6
OPERA SINGERS	4 - 6	6 - 10
OPIUM SMOKERS	4 - 6	6 - 10
ORANGES	1 - 2	2 - 3
ORCHESTRAS	5 - 6	6 - 8
ORGANS, MUSICAL	4 - 5	5 - 6
ORPHANAGES	4 - 5	5 - 8
OSTRICHES	2 - 3	3 - 4
PALACES	2 - 3	3 - 4
PAPER DOLL CUT-OUTS (See Novelties)		
PARADES, Color	4 - 5	5 - 6
Real Photo	8 - 10	10 - 12
PASSION PLAY		
Conwell Red Borders	5 - 6	6 - 8
Real Photo	6 - 8	8 - 10
Others	4 - 5	5 - 6
PATRIOTIC (See Greetings)		
National Song Series (6)	4 - 6	6 - 8
PENITENTIARIES	4 - 5	5 - 7
PENNANTS	1 - 2	2 - 3
PERSONALITIES		
Buffalo Bill	10 - 15	15 - 18
Poster Types	25 - 30	30 - 40
Calamity Jane	6 - 8	8 - 10
Winston Churchill	8 - 10	10 - 12
Elvis	8 - 12	12 - 16
Wild Bill Hickock	6 - 8	8 - 10
Hitler		
Printed photos	6 - 9	9 - 12
Real Photo	15 - 20	20 - 25
Elbert Hubbard	5 - 6	6 - 8
Charles Lindbergh	10 - 15	15 - 25
Lenin	10 - 12	12 - 15

Taft Caricature, Giris, "Le Plus Lourd Que L'Air"

Socialist Candidate Eugene Debs, 1908 Campaign

Billy Possum, F. A. Owen "Hurrah for Bill and ...!!"

Benito Mussolini	10 - 15	15 - 20
Wally Post	6 - 8	8 - 10
Will Rogers	8 - 10	10 - 15
Alice Roosevelt	8 - 10	10 - 12
Franklin D. Roosevelt	10 - 12	12 - 15
Billy Sunday	6 - 8	8 - 10
Real Photos	10 - 15	15 - 18
Joseph Stalin	12 - 15	15 - 20
PHONOGRAPHS	5 - 6	6 - 7
PHYSICIANS	3 - 5	5 - 7
Comics	6 - 8	8 - 10
PIANOS	3 - 4	4 - 5
PIGEONS	2 - 3	3 - 5
PIGS (Also See Dressed Animals)	3 - 4	4 - 5
PILGRIMS	2 - 3	3 - 4
PIN-UP GIRLS	3 - 4	4 - 8
PLAYING CARDS	4 - 6	6 - 8
POLICEMEN	4 - 5	5 - 8
POLITICAL		
"Billikens" (Bryan & Taft)	175 - 200	200 - 225
Others	8 - 10	10 - 12
AMP Co.		
ETHEL DeWEES		
"Billy Possum" Series (6)		
"Just a few lines before game..."	30 - 35	35 - 38
"It's a bad thing to put off..."	25 - 30	30 - 35
"Yale's Favorite Son"	30 - 35	35 - 38
"Arrived here just. at right time..."	25 - 30	30 - 35
"I'm going to make a record this trip..."	25 - 30	30 - 35
"I'll make another drive..."	25 - 30	30 - 35
Birn Brothers (B.B., London)		
Series E243 "We Love Billy Possum"	28 - 32	32 - 35
Frank J. Cohen & Son, Atlanta		
"Billy Possum"	200 - 250	250 - 300

T. Roosevelt as Peacemaker in Russian-Japanese War, "Roosevelt says enough!"

Hughes and Hearst, 1906 Gub.Campaign Pub. Alva Stern, "Heaven or Hell?"

Lester Book & Stationery, Atlanta

Taft with Possum "Beat it Teddy Bear"	300 - 350	350 - 400

HSV Litho Co.
   CRITE
   "Billy Possum" Series (12)

"Are You Dead - or Just Playing Possum?"	20 - 25	25 - 30
"Aw, don't play possum..."	20 - 25	25 - 30
"The Boogie Man'll Get You..."	20 - 25	25 - 30
"Dear Friends..."	20 - 25	25 - 30
"Dear, Am unavoidably detained..."	20 - 25	25 - 30
"Do it Now!"	20 - 25	25 - 30
"Give my regards to Bill!"	25 - 30	30 - 35
"Good eating here"	30 - 35	35 - 40
"I'm having a high old time..."	20 - 25	25 - 35
"It's a Great Game for Us Fat People ..." (Golf)	30 - 35	35 - 40
"Oo's 'ittle' possum is 'oo'?"	20 - 25	25 - 28
"Very Busy, Both Hands Full..."	20 - 25	25 - 30

Fred C. Lounsbury
   Billy Possum Series 2515, Emb., (4) (Sepia)

1. "The only Possums that escaped"	20 - 25	25 - 30
2. "Billy Possum and Jimmie P. on links.."	28 - 32	32 - 35
3. "Moving day in Possum Town"	20 - 25	25 - 30
4. "Good bye Teddy"	28 - 32	32 - 35

   Billy Possum Series 2517 (4) (Blue Tone)

1. "Uncle Sam's New Toy"	28 - 32	32 - 35
2. "Columbia's Latest 'Possum and Taters"	28 - 32	32 - 35
3. "Billy Possum to the front"	28 - 32	32 - 35
4. "The Nation's Choice"	28 - 32	32 - 35

F. A. Owen Co. (B&W)
   "Billy Possum"

"Hurrah for Old Eli"	50 - 60	60 - 75
Others	50 - 60	60 - 75

T. Bianco

T. Roosevelt and Japanese-Russo War	50 - 60	60 - 75

Alva Stern

Hughes and Hearst gubernatorial Race, 1906	50 - 75	75 - 100

Fuller & Fuller Co.
Grollman Political Set
   Bryan and Taft, 1908 (16) with Uncle Sam

Presidential Race, Baseball Game, Winners & Losers	50 - 60	60 - 75

MISCELLANEOUS

1896 Campaign

William McKinley-Hobart	50 - 55	55 - 60
William J. Bryan	40 - 50	50 - 60

1900 Campaign

Eugene V. Debs, Socialist Party	600 - 650	650 - 700
Roosevelt-Fairbanks	35 - 40	40 - 50
McKinley & Roosevelt Jugates, PMC	40 - 45	45 - 50

1904 Campaign

Eugene V. Debs, Socialist Party	600 - 650	650 - 700
Parker-Davis	100 - 150	150 - 200
P/**Huld,** "Teddy Roosevelt, He's Good Enough for Me,"	20 - 25	25 - 35
Roosevelt-Fairbanks	20 - 25	25 - 35

1908 Campaign

Eugene V. Debs, Socialist Party	500 - 550	550 - 600
Taft-Sherman Jugates	15 - 20	20 - 25
William H. Taft	15 - 20	20 - 25
William Jennings Bryan	15 - 20	20 - 25
I. Grollman "Willie B. and Willie T. ..."	25 - 30	30 - 35
E.D.L. Taft Stamp Montage	25 - 30	30 - 35

1912 Campaign

Eugene V. Debs, Socialist Party	500 - 550	550 - 600
Champ Clark	35 - 40	45 - 50
Woodrow Wilson-Marshall	15 - 20	20 - 25
Democratic Wire Tail Donkey-Wilson	30 - 40	40 - 50
Republican Wire Tail Donkey-Taft	30 - 40	40 - 50
T. Roosevelt-Johnson (Progressive Party)	40 - 50	50 - 60
Taft-Roosevelt Mechanical	50 - 55	55 - 65
Prohibition Candidates Eugene Chafin/Aaron Watkins	80 - 90	90 - 100

1916 Campaign

Eugene V. Debs, Socialist Party	300 - 350	350 - 400
Progressive party (Roosevelt)	35 - 40	40 - 50
Charles E. Hughes (Republican)	30 - 35	35 - 40
Wilson-Taft	18 - 22	22 - 26
Lapina, President Wilson	20 - 25	25 - 28
Wire-tail Political (Roosevelt)	75 - 85	85 - 100

1920 Campaign

Eugene V. Debs, Socialist Party	100 - 125	125 - 150
Harding-Coolidge	20 - 25	25 - 30
Cox-Roosevelt	20 - 25	25 - 30

1924 Campaign

Coolidge-Dawes (w/borders), post election	20 - 25	25 - 30
John W. Davis	15 - 20	20 - 25
LaFollette-Wheeler (Progressive)	50 - 60	60 - 75

1928 Campaign

Hoover-Curtis	12 - 15	15 - 20
Al Smith	20 - 25	25 - 28

1932 Campaign

Roosevelt-Garner	12 - 15	15 - 20
Herbert Hoover	15 - 20	20 - 25

1936 Campaign

Landon-Knox	20 - 25	25 - 30
Roosevelt	15 - 18	18 - 22

1940 Campaign

Wilkie-McNary	15 - 18	18 - 22
Roosevelt-Wallace		
"Franklin Roosevelt, Our Next President"	20 - 25	25 - 30

1944 Campaign

Thomas Dewey, "Vote Republican Nov. 7"	15 - 18	18 - 22
Roosevelt-Truman	10 - 12	12 - 15

1948 Campaign

Truman-Barkley	12 - 15	15 - 18
Thomas E. Dewey	10 - 12	12 - 15
Wallace-Taylor (Progressive)	20 - 25	25 - 30

1952 Campaign

Eisenhower-Nixon	12 - 15	15 - 18
Adlai Stevenson	10 - 12	12 - 15

1956 Campaign

Eisenhower-Nixon	6 - 8	8 - 10
Stevenson	6 - 8	8 - 10

1960 Campaign

Nixon-Lodge	6 - 8	8 - 10
Kennedy-Johnson	6 - 8	8 - 10

1964 Campaign

Johnson-Humphrey	5 - 6	6 - 8
Barry Goldwater	4 - 5	5 - 6

1968 Campaign

Nixon-Agnew-Humphrey	5 - 6	6 - 8

1972 Campaign

McGovern-Eagleton	8 - 10	10 - 12
Nixon-Ford	4 - 5	5 - 6

1976 Campaign

Jimmy Carter	6 - 8	8 - 10

1980 Campaign

Carter-Mondale	4 - 5	5 - 6
Reagan	2 - 3	3 - 4

POSTCARD SHOPS	15 - 20	20 - 25
Foreign	15 - 18	18 - 22
Advertising Postcards	15 - 20	20 - 25
Leather	20 - 25	25 - 35
POSTMEN	6 - 7	7 - 10
POULTRY	1 - 2	2 - 3
H.K. & Co., Series 356	4 - 5	5 - 7

PRESIDENTS, also see SETS/SERIES

Cromwell "Roosevelt in Africa" (16)	7 - 8	8 - 10
Hugh C. Leighton		
Unnamed Series	6 - 8	8 - 10
Similar to **Tuck's** below. (25)	6 - 7	7 - 9

J. W. Heide, Red Cross German Police
Dog, Publisher G. Stalling

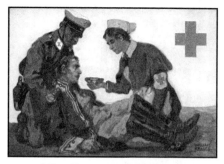

Wm. Krause, Red Cross Nurse
Published for "Rotes Kreuz" (Red Cross)

W. R. Gordon, Phila. Unnumbered (25) B&W	4 - 5	5 - 6
M. A. Sheehan (1940's) (32)		
Serigraphs by PAUL DUBOSCLARD (32)	4 - 5	5 - 8
Raphael Tuck Series 2328		
S/L. SPINNER		
"Presidents of the United States" (24)	6 - 8	8 - 10
President Taft - Added Later	12 - 15	15 - 20
"President Theodore Roosevelt" Series 2333	15 - 18	18 - 22
Underwood & Underwood		
"Roosevelt's African Hunt" (40)	5 - 6	6 - 7
ANONYMOUS		
"Flag & Eagle" Presidents (Emb.)	8 - 12	12 - 15
PRISONS	5 - 6	6 - 7
PROPAGANDA	7 - 9	9 - 12
German	10 - 15	15 - 20
Russian	15 - 20	20 - 30
PUZZLES	4 - 6	6 - 7
QUEEN'S DOLL HOUSE		
Raphael Tuck		
Series 4500 Set 1 (8)	6 - 8	8 - 10
Series 4501 Set 2 (8)	6 - 8	8 - 10
Series 4502 Set 3 (8)	6 - 8	8 - 10
Series 4503 Set 3 (8)	6 - 8	8 - 10
Series 4504 Set 4 (8)	6 - 8	8 - 10
Series 4505 Set 5 (8)	6 - 8	8 - 10
QUOTATIONS	1 - 2	2 - 3
RABBITS	1 - 2	2 - 3
Dressed (Also see Fantasy Dressed Animals)	5 - 8	8 - 20
RACING, Auto	8 - 10	10 - 12
Dog (Also see Dogs)	8 - 10	10 - 15
Horse (Also see Horses)	8 - 10	10 - 15
RADIO STARS, Early Years	6 - 7	7 - 9
RAINBOWS	3 - 4	4 - 6
REBUS CARDS	5 - 6	6 - 9
RED CROSS	5 - 7	7 - 9
Red Cross Dog, S/**HEIDE**	15 - 20	20 - 25
Red Cross Nurse, S/**KRAUSE**	18 - 22	22 - 26
See Artist-Signed Nurses		
REGIMENTAL BADGES	4 - 6	6 - 8

REGIMENTAL AND MILITARY UNIFORMS	4 - 6	6 - 9
RELIGIOUS	1 - 3	3 - 5
REPTILES (Also See Fantasy)	2 - 3	3 - 4
Linens	1 - 2	2 - 3
RESTAURANTS (See Views and Real Photos)		
RETIREMENT HOMES	2 - 3	3 - 5
RIVERS	0.50 - 1	1 - 1.50
RODEOS	3 - 4	4 - 6
Real Photos	6 - 9	9 - 12
ROWING	3 - 4	4 - 5

ROYALTY, EUROPEAN

GREAT BRITAIN

QUEEN VICTORIA		
1897 DIAMOND JUBILEE		
Postally Used, 1897	200 - 220	220 - 235
Unused	100 - 110	110 - 125
Raphael Tuck & Sons		
Portraits	20 - 22	22 - 28
Family Groups	8 - 10	10 - 12
Foreign Issues	12 - 15	15 - 18
Mourning Issues	15 - 20	20 - 25
KING EDWARD VII		
1901 ROYAL TOUR		
Wrench "Links of Empire" (20)		
Postally Used from Tour Cities	30 - 35	35 - 40
Unused	20 - 25	25 - 30
1902 CORONATION SERIES		
Raphael Tuck & Sons		
Series 239 (Color/Embossed)	15 - 20	20 - 25
Series 655, B&W	10 - 12	12 - 15
Stewart & Woolf Series 105 (10)	12 - 15	15 - 20
S/H. Cassiers, Views	8 - 10	10 - 15
Other Publishers	6 - 8	8 - 12
Views of Coronation Procession	3 - 6	4 - 6
Royal Visits to Foreign Countries	12 - 15	15 - 20
Royal Visits ot Great Britain	10 - 12	12 - 15
Mourning Cards	5 - 6	6 - 8
Portraits	5 - 6	6 - 8
Family Groups	4 - 5	5 - 6
Children	4 - 5	5 - 6
KING GEORGE V		
Souvenir Cards	10 - 12	12 - 15
Coronation Procession	2 - 3	3 - 5
J. Beagles, Real Photo of "HRH Prince of Wales"	8 - 10	10 - 15
Rotary Photo, Real Photos	8 - 10	10 - 12
Others	6 - 8	8 - 10
1935 SILVER JUBILEE		
Souvenir Cards	6 - 8	8 - 10

J. Beagles & Co., R.P. of
"HRH Prince of Wales"

Rapid Photo Co., R.P. of
"The Czarina of Russia"

French Caricature of
"Nicolas II" of Russia

Russian Czar, Czarina and Duchess Olga
at "Visit to Paris, Octobre 1896"

Russian Royal Family, R.P. by Russian
Publisher, No. 027, Russian Caption

Portraits & Family Groups	2 - 3	3 - 5
Visits	10 - 12	12 - 15
Mourning & Funeral Cards	2 - 4	4 - 7
KING EDWARD VIII		
Wedding Souvenir	30 - 35	35 - 40
Coronation Souvenir	6 - 8	8 - 10
Portraits	3 - 5	5 - 7
King Edward w/Mrs. Simpson	30 - 35	35 - 40
Abdicated Edward and Mrs. Simpson	12 - 15	15 - 18
Visits	10 - 12	12 - 18
KING GEORGE VI		
1937 Coronation Souvenir Card	4 - 5	5 - 7
Visits	8 - 10	10 - 15
Mourning Cards, 1952	5 - 6	6 - 8
Others	2 - 3	3 - 6
QUEEN ELIZABETH II		
Wedding, 1947 Souvenir Cards	5 - 6	6 - 9
Coronation Souvenir Cards	3 - 4	4 - 7
Raphael Tuck & Sons	5 - 6	6 - 8
Children	2 - 3	3 - 5

Portraits	2 - 3	3 - 5
Visits	7 - 8	8 - 10
MISCELLANEOUS BRITISH		
Raphael Tuck & Sons		
Kings & Queens of England		
Series 614, 615, 616 (12)	10 - 15	15 - 20
Series 617 (6)	20 - 25	25 - 30
Faulkner Series	8 - 10	10 - 12
RUSSIA		
Czar Nicholas & Family *		
Color Portraits of Nicholas or/and Alexandria	35 - 40	40 - 45
B&W Portraits of Nicholas or/and Alexandria	25 - 30	30 - 35
Family Groups	35 - 40	40 - 50
Real Photos	40 - 50	50 - 60
Children of the Czar	40 - 50	50 - 60
Real Photos	50 - 60	60 - 80
Alexandra	25 - 30	30 - 35
Real Photos	30 - 35	35 - 45
Rasputin	60 - 70	70 - 85
Real Photos	80 - 100	100 - 150
Czar Nicholas, 1896 Visit to France	40 - 45	45 - 50
Czar Nicholas, Comical Caricatures & Propaganda	30 - 35	35 - 45
Other Russian Nobility and Children	25 - 30	30 - 40
* Russian published. Others around 20% lower.		
Others	8 - 10	10 - 12
GERMANY		
Portraits	8 - 10	10 - 15
Family Groups	6 - 8	8 - 10
Comical/Propaganda	10 - 12	12 - 15
OTHER EUROPEAN	4 - 7	7 - 10
EASTERN EUROPE	5 - 8	8 - 10
P/AULT		
"RULERS OF THE WORLD" Series	8 - 10	10 - 12
Tsar Nicholas	30 - 35	35 - 40
OTHER RULERS	3 - 4	4 - 6
SAILORS	2 - 3	3 - 5
SAILBOATS	1 - 2	2 - 3
SALVATION ARMY	3 - 4	4 - 10
SAN FRANCISCO EARTHQUAKE	3 - 4	4 - 10
SANTA CLAUS (See Santas Chapter)		
SCHOOLS (See Views)		
23 SKIDDO	3 - 6	6 - 9
SCULPTURE	0.50 - 1	1 - 1.50
SCOUTS (See Boy Scouts)		
SEA SHELLS	1 - 2	2 - 3
SEPTEMBER MORN		
Various Cards	2 - 3	3 - 10
SHAKESPEARE	3 - 4	4 - 6
C. W. Faulkner Series	6 - 7	7 - 10
SHEEP	1 - 1.50	1.50 - 2
SHIP WRECKS (See specials, Titanic, etc.)	5 - 8	8 - 15

SHIP YARDS	3 - 4	4 - 6
SHOES	2 - 3	3 - 4
SHOPS, Industry Exteriors	4 - 7	7 - 10
Interiors Real Photo	8 - 10	10 - 15
SILKS (Also see Santas and Langsdorf Ladies)		
Beautiful Ladies, Children	15 - 18	18 - 25
Cats, other animals	10 - 12	12 - 15
Greetings	5 - 6	6 - 8
Woven Silks		
Glasgow Exhibition, 1911	45 - 50	50 - 60
"Hands Across the Sea" (19)	40 - 45	45 - 50
The Million Dollar Pier, Atlantic City	45 - 50	50 - 60
Presidential - Taft, Roosevelt, Wilson	150 - 175	175 - 200
St. Louis 1904 World's Fair (14)	300 - 325	325 - 350
Ships - RMS Arabic," "Baltic," "Ivernia,"		
"Mauretania," " Saxonia,"Others	60 - 70	70 - 85
See Transportation		
See **"P. Boileau"** for most expensive silk card.		
SINGERS	2 - 3	3 - 6
SKATING, Ice (See Artist-Signed)	3 - 6	6 - 9
Roller	4 - 6	6 - 10
SKELETONS, SKULLS (Also see Metamorphic)	4 - 6	6 - 10
SKIING	3 - 5	5 - 7
SLEDDING	3 - 4	4 - 5
SMOKING	1 - 2	2 - 5
See SCHMUCKER		
SNAKES (See Fantasy)	3 - 4	4 - 6
SNOWMEN (See Fantasy)		
SONGS Charles Rose Series #11 (24)	6 - 8	8 - 10
Bamforth Song Series (Many)	2 - 3	3 - 5
Many Others	2 - 3	3 - 5
SPOONS	3 - 4	4 - 5
STADIUMS, Football, Early	6 - 7	8 - 15
Others (See Baseball, Etc.)	3 - 4	4 - 8
STAGE		
Maude Adams	8 - 10	10 - 12
Lillian Russell	12 - 14	14 - 18
Others	4 - 5	5 - 8
SPANISH AMERICAN WAR	5 - 8	8 - 10
STAMP CARDS		
Kunzli Bros., Paris Series	12 - 15	15 - 20
Maduro, Jr., Panama Series	7 - 9	9 - 12
Menke-Huber Series	12 - 15	15 - 20
P/Piero, Luigi, Italy Series	7 - 8	8 - 10
P/Stengel Series (12)	7 - 9	9 - 12
P/VSM Series	7 - 8	8 - 10
Zieher, Ottmar (Add $2-3 if embossed)	10 - 12	12 - 15
S/Muller	12 - 15	15 - 18
Others	7 - 8	8 - 10
STAMP MONTAGE	5 - 6	6 - 10
Russian Real Photo Types	20 - 25	25 - 30

Bamforth Co., Song Card
"When the Great Red..."

C. H. Twelvetrees, R&N,
#716, "I'll get that vote..."

Cobb Shinn, T. P. & Co.
"Buying Votes."

STATE GIRLS (See Sets & Series)		
STATE CAPITALS & Seals (See Sets & Series)		
STATUE OF LIBERTY	2 - 4	4 - 8
Hold-To-Light	40 - 50	50 - 60
STATUES	0.50 - 1	1 - 1.50
STILL-LIFE PAINTINGS	1 - 2	2 - 3
S/M. Billing	3 - 4	4 - 6
S/Mary Golay	2 - 3	3 - 6
S/A. Gammis-Boecker	2 - 3	3 - 6
S/C. Klein	3 - 5	5 - 10
See Alphabet		
STORKS	2 - 3	3 - 5
STREET SCENES (See Views and Real Photos)		
STRIKES, Labor	8 - 10	10 - 15
Real Photos	10 - 15	15 - 25
STUDENTS	2 - 3	3 - 5
STUNTMEN	4 - 5	5 - 10
SUBMARINES	4 - 6	6 - 10
SUBWAYS	3 - 5	5 - 10
SUFFRAGETTES		
AA Pub. Co.		
698/12 "Stumping For Votes"	12 - 15	15 - 25
B.K.W.I.		
ATTWELL, MABEL L.		
257/4 Little Girl, "Now! Where's My Vote?"	25 - 30	30 - 40
H.B.G. George Washington "Votes for Women"	70 - 75	75 - 90
LEVI, C.		
"Komical Koons" Series 210, 3308	20 - 25	35 - 35
Bergman Co.		
Series 6342, S/B. WALL	30 - 35	35 - 45
Cargill Co., Michigan		
Series 103-129	12 - 15	15 - 25
Campbell Art Co. S/**CHAMBERLAIN** (6)	20 - 25	25 - 35

Still Life by M. Billing
T.S.N., Series 410

Still Life by C. Klein
Meissner & Buch, Series 1823

CLAPSADDLE (See Clapsaddle in Artist-Signed)
Dunston-Weiler Litho Co.

1 "Suffragette Madonna"	20 - 25	25 - 28
2 "Electioneering"	20 - 25	25 - 28
3 "Pantalette Suffragette"	20 - 25	25 - 28
4 "Suffragette Vote-Getter"	20 - 25	25 - 28
5 "Suffragette-Coppette"	20 - 25	25 - 28
6 "Uncle Sam-Suffragette...Easiest Way"	25 - 30	30 - 35
7 "Election Day"	20 - 25	25 - 28
8 "I Don't Care"	20 - 25	25 - 28
9 "Queen of the Poll"	20 - 25	25 - 28
10 "Where, Oh Where is My ..."	20 - 25	25 - 28
11 "I Want to Vote ..."	20 - 25	25 - 28
12 "I Love My Husband, But Oh You Vote"	20 - 25	25 - 28

E. Nash "Suffragette Madonna"

"Crop of 1910"	15 - 20	20 - 30

O'NEILL, ROSE
  Campbell Art Klever Card

228 "Votes for Women-Do I get your...?"	150 - 175	175 - 200

  National Suffrage Pub. Co.

"Votes for Women - Spirit of '76"	300 - 400	400 - 500
"Votes for our Mothers" (not Kewpies)	450 - 600	600 - 750

SHINN, COBB
  T. P. & Co.

"Buying Votes" (B&W)	15 - 20	20 - 30
Roth & Langley, 1909 Issues	12 - 15	15 - 18

TWELVETREES, C., Unsigned
  Reinthal & Newman

716 "I'll get that vote yet!!!"	20 - 25	25 - 30

WELLMAN, WALTER, Artist & Publisher
  The Suffragette Series

"Bar"	20 - 25	25 - 30
"Copess"	20 - 25	25 - 30
"Every Year Will be Leap Year"	20 - 25	25 - 30
"For Speaker of the House"	20 - 25	25 - 30
"Generaless of the Army"	20 - 25	25 - 30
"I Can Heartily Recommend My Wife"	20 - 25	25 - 30
"Judgess"	20 - 25	25 - 30
"Just Politics"	20 - 25	25 - 30

"Letter Carrier"	20 - 25	25 - 30
"Morning Suffragette Bulletin"	20 - 25	25 - 30
"Our Choice, Miss Taffy"	20 - 25	25 - 30
"Secretaryess of Treasury"	20 - 25	25 - 30
"Should Women Mix in Politics"	20 - 25	25 - 30
"Studentess"	20 - 25	25 - 30
"To Whom It May Concern"	20 - 25	25 - 30

SUNBONNET BABIES
  CORBETT, B.

Days of the Week 258-264 (7)	10 - 12	12 - 15
Series 119-124 (Uns.)	10 - 12	12 - 15
Beckworth Series	12 - 15	15 - 20

  DIXON, DOROTHY
    Ullman Mfg. Co.

Sunbonnets Series 503-512 (10)	10 - 12	12 - 15
Sunbonnet Girls 1385-1390 (6)	10 - 12	12 - 15

  WALL, B. (See B. Wall in Children Artists)

T.P. & Co. Issues	10 - 12	12 - 15

  Anonymous

Bergman Co.	8 - 10	10 - 12
H. I. Robbins Co. Series 897 (7)	12 - 15	15 - 18
Advertising Majestic Range Series	18 - 22	22 - 25
SUPERLATIVES - Largest-Smallest	2 - 3	3 - 6
SWANS	1 - 2	2 - 3
SYNAGOGUES	20 - 25	25 - 35
TARTANS	3 - 4	4 - 5
TELEGRAMS	1 - 2	2 - 3
TELEPHONES	5 - 7	7 - 12
TEMPERANCE	4 - 7	7 - 12

SHIRLEY TEMPLE

Black & White, Color, Real Photos	10 - 12	12 - 15
TENNIS, Courts	5 - 6	6 - 8
Matches in progress	6 - 7	7 - 10
Advertising Tennis Product	15 - 20	20 - 35

  See Artist-Signed for Others.
THEATRES   (See Views and Real Photos)
THEATRICAL

Maude Adams	6 - 8	8 - 10
Sarah Bernhardt (See A. Mucha)	10 - 15	15 - 20
Enrico Caruso	8 - 10	10 - 12
Zena Dare	6 - 8	8 - 10
Evelyn Nesbitt	8 - 10	10 - 12
TIGERS	2 - 3	3 - 5
TOLL GATES	3 - 4	4 - 7
TORNADOES	6 - 8	8 - 12

TRAINS AND TROLLEYS
  (See Transportation and Real Photos)

TRAMPS	2 - 3	3 - 4
TUNNELS	2 - 3	3 - 4
TURKEYS (See Greetings)	1 - 2	2 - 3
TYPEWRITERS (See Advertising)	3 - 4	4 - 6

Artist Type Anonymous Witch, SWSB, No. 1274

Real Photos	10 - 12	12 - 15
UMBRELLAS	2 - 3	3 - 4
UNCLE SAM (See Greetings and Real Photos))		
U.S. NAVY (See Transportation)		
Raphael Tuck Series 2326	5 - 8	8 - 12
Illustrated P.C. Co.	4 - 7	7 - 10
U.S. NAVY LIFE & MISCELLANEOUS		
Edw. H. Mitchell		
No. 1316 - 1329 (Color)	3 - 5	5 - 7
No. 4314 - 4318 (Black & White)	2 - 3	3 - 5
VIEWS (See Views and Real Photos)		
VOLCANOS	2 - 3	3 - 5
WANTED POSTERS	12 - 15	15 - 20
WAR BOND CAMPAIGNS POSTERS	12 - 15	15 - 20
Russian	30 - 35	35 - 45
WEDDINGS	3 - 5	5 - 6
Real Photos, Bride and Groom	8 - 10	10 - 12
Jewish	6 - 9	9 - 12
WHALES	10 - 12	12 - 15
Real Photos	15 - 20	20 - 25
WHOLE DAM FAMILY (Many)	4 - 7	7 - 12
WELLMAN, W. (Linens)	4 - 6	6 - 9
WINDMILLS	2 - 4	4 - 6
WINERIES	3 - 5	5 - 8
WITCHES	6 - 8	8 - 10
Artist-Signed	10 - 15	15 - 30
Easter Witches, Scandinavian	12 - 15	15 - 25
Miniature cards	15 - 20	20 - 25
WORLD WAR I	3 - 5	5 - 10

Walt Munson, Colourpicture No. 247
"Oh How I Hate to Get Up in the..."

Anonymous, Colourpicture No. 16115
"Greetings from Gulfport Field, Ms."

Daily Mail Series I thru XX (100)	4 - 7	7 - 12
Kavanaugh War Postals	3 - 5	5 - 7
Comics, Common	3 - 4	4 - 6
Comics, Bamforth	6 - 8	8 - 12
Camp Scenes	3 - 5	5 - 8
U.S.O./Salvation Army	5 - 6	6 - 9
W.C.A. Series 145-146	3 - 5	5 - 10
WORLD WAR I		
Camps, camp scenes	3 - 5	5 - 8
Service Men	3 - 4	4 - 7
Men in action	3 - 4	4 - 7
Ruins and destruction views	0.50 - 1	1 - 1.50
In French booklets	0.25 - 0.50	0.50 - 0.75
Posters	10 - 15	15 - 25
Propaganda	8 - 10	10 - 15
WORLD WAR II		
Comics, Linen	1 - 3	3 - 6
Anti-Hitler, Tojo, Mussolini Comics	4 - 7	7 - 15
Private Breger Comics	5 - 6	6 - 8
Camp Scenes	2 - 3	3 - 5
Army/Navy Air Force Bases	2 - 3	3 - 7
Large Letters	3 - 5	5 - 8
Third Reich Photos, with Swastika	12 - 15	15 - 25
Black & White	8 - 10	10 - 15
Propaganda	8 - 10	10 - 15
WRESTLING	5 - 7	7 - 10
YACHTING	2 - 3	3 - 5
YMCA	3 - 5	5 - 7
YWCA	4 - 5	6 - 8
ZODIAC		
S/**AENZ**	5 - 6	6 - 8
Julius Bien		
"Your Fortune" Series 37 (12)	8 - 10	10 - 12
Edw. H. Mitchell	12 - 15	15 - 19
Raphael Tuck,		
"Zodiac" Series 128 (12) S/**DWIG**	12 - 15	15 - 18
P/Paris Expo, 1900	100 - 125	125 - 150
P/Anon. 1970 Zodiac Series (12)	5 - 6	6 - 7
ZOOS	2 - 3	3 - 4

Transportation

Spiralling values of postcards of the ocean liner "Titanic" continue and apparently have had a positive effect on the sales of other ocean liners as well as other sea-going vessels. The big market in Railway and Trolley depots, especially the Real Photo types, has also activated good movement in the rails and rail-related issues.

Early aviation material of the Wright brothers and other pilots, Aviation Meets, and World War 1 "lighter than air" balloons and dirigibles also continue to gain interest, not only in the U.S., but throughout the world.

There was a wealth of great material published in these fields and collectors are now beginning to take advantage of it's current low evaluations. Transportation collectors are extremely fortunate that this material was very highly collected in the late 70's and 80's. Although rather dormant since that time, the cycle has now regained it's former momentum. This action has helped to return many good quality collections to the market and interest is currently very high, especially for better material.

RAIL TRANSPORTATION

ENGINES	VG	EX
Identified Close-up Images *		
Real Photos	$ 25 - 30	$ 30 - 40
Color	8 - 12	12 - 18
Black & White	6 - 8	8 - 12
Advertising issues	15 - 20	20 - 30
Linens	2 - 3	3 - 6
Chromes or Reproductions	0.50 - 1	1 - 1.50
Foreign, pre-1930	3 - 5	5 - 8
Real Photos	10 - 12	12 - 15
* Unidentified - deduct 25-50%.		
Engines with Cars		
Identified Real Photos	15 - 20	20 - 30

Engine and Train of Union Pacific System Ltd., Echo Canyon, Utah, ca. 1920

Real Photo, German Made Engine ca. 1912, "Hans Gasser"

Real Photo by AZO of "Portola–W.P. RY Yards, Oroville, Ca." (Hogan Photo)

"Lackawanna Station, Binghamton, N.Y." C. T. American Art No. A-79390

Color	6 - 8	8 - 12
Black & White	5 - 6	6 - 8
Advertising	10 - 15	15 - 20
Interiors, Advertising	10 - 15	15 - 20
Linens	1 - 2	2 - 4
Chromes or Reproductions	0.50 - 1	1 - 1.50
Foreign, pre-1930	3 - 5	5 - 7
*Unidentified - deduct 25-50%.		
Small, far away images have very little value.		
Wrecks		
Identified Real Photos	15 - 20	20 - 30
Unidentified Real Photos	5 - 10	10 - 15
Identified Color, or B&W	5 - 10	10 - 12
RAIL YARDS, REPAIR AREAS		
Identified		
Real Photo	10 - 15	15 - 25
Color	3 - 5	5 - 10
Black & White	2 - 3	3 - 6
Linens	1 - 2	2 - 3
Chromes	0.50 - 1	1 - 1.50
TRAIN STATIONS, DEPOTS		
SMALL TOWNS		
Real Photos *	15 - 25	25 - 40
Real Photos, W/Train in station *	20 - 30	30 - 45

"G. R. & I. Depot, Oden, Mich." – Alton G. Cook, No. 329

Color	10 - 15	15 - 20
Color, W/Train in station	8 - 12	12 - 20
B&W	5 - 8	8 - 12
Linens	4 - 6	6 - 10
Chromes	1 - 2	2 - 4
Foreign, pre-1930	5 - 8	8 - 12

* These are average values. Auction results have reached $100-150 in selected issues.

Large Cities

Real Photo	10 - 12	12 - 16
Real Photo W/Train in Station	10 - 12	12 - 18
Color, B&W	2 - 3	3 - 6
Linens	1 - 1.50	1.50 - 2
Chromes	0.50 - 0.75	0.75 - 1
Foreign, pre-1930	1 - 2	2 - 3

ELEVATED RAILWAYS

Large Cities (N.Y., Chicago, etc.)

Real Photos, Identified	10 - 15	15 - 20
Close-up Images, Color, B&W	2 - 4	4 - 7
Small Images, Color, B&W	1 - 2	2 - 3
Linens	1 - 1.50	1.50 - 2
Chromes	.50 - 1	1 - 1.50

Smaller Cities

Real Photos, Identified	15 - 20	20 - 25
Close-up Images, Color	3 - 5	5 - 10
Small Images	2 - 3	3 - 5
Linens	1.50 - 2	2 - 2.50
Chromes	0.75 - 1	1 - 1.50

INCLINE RAILWAYS

Identified Close-up Images*

Mauch Chunk, Pikes Peak, Mt. Washington	3 - 5	5 - 8

The Trolley at "Theatre, Plum Island, Mass." – Curt Teich, W38587

Real Photo by Cline, 1V-221, "The Incline at Lookout Mtn., Chattanooga, Tenn."

Real Photo by AZO, "Incline at Summit of Mt. Manitou, Colorado"

Mt. Tom, Un-Ca-Noo-Nuc Mt., Lookout Mt.	3 - 5	5 - 8
Mt. Manitou, Colorado	3 - 5	5 - 8
Real Photos	5 - 8	8 - 10
Angel's Flight, Mt. Penn, Mt. Beacon	3 - 5	5 - 8
Other, lesser known	3 - 4	4 - 6
Identified Small Images*		
Most well known inclines	1 - 2	2 - 3
Other, lesser known	2 - 3	3 - 5
Real Photos, Identified - Add 50%		
*Unidentified - deduct 25-50%.		
SUBWAYS, IDENTIFIED *		
Large Car Images	6 - 8	8 - 10
Cars at Loading Platform	4 - 6	6 - 8
Linens	3 - 5	5 - 8
Chromes	1 - 2	3 - 4
Real Photos, Identified - Add 50%.		
* Unidentified - deduct 25-50%.		
ELECTRIC TROLLEYS		
Identified Close-up Images*		
Real Photo **	25 - 35	35 - 45
Color	8 - 10	10 - 20
B&W	6 - 8	8 - 12
Linens	3 - 4	4 - 6
Chromes and Reproductions	1 - 1.50	1.50 - 2

Foreign	3 - 4	4 - 7

* Unidentified - deduct 25-50%.
** These are average values. Auction values have been as high as $100-125 on selected images.

Medium-sized, in Street Scenes

Real Photos	10 - 20	20 - 30
Color	5 - 8	8 - 12
B&W	2 - 4	4 - 6
Linens	2 - 3	3 - 4
Chromes and Reproductions	0.50 - 1	1 - 1.50
Foreign	1 - 2	2 - 3
Real Photos	8 - 10	10 - 12

Wrecks

Identified	12 - 15	15 - 25
Unidentified	6 - 8	8 - 12

TROLLEY STATIONS

Small Towns

Real Photo	15 - 20	20 - 35
Real Photo W/Trolley in Station	15 - 20	20 - 35
Color	8 - 10	10 - 15
Color, W/Trolley in Station	10 - 12	12 - 18
B&W	5 - 7	7 - 10
Linens	3 - 4	4 - 6
Chromes	1 - 2	2 - 3
Foreign, pre-1930	3 - 4	4 - 6
Real Photos	5 - 7	7 - 10

Large Cities

Real Photo	6 - 8	8 - 12
Real Photo, W/Trolley in Station	6 - 8	8 - 12
Color	1 - 2	2 - 3
Color, W/Trolley in Station	2 - 3	3 - 5
Linens	0.75 - 1	1 - 1.50
Chromes	0.50 - 0.75	0.75 - 1
Foreign, pre-1930	0.50 - 0.75	0.75 - 1

HORSE-DRAWN TROLLEYS

Real Photos	15 - 20	20 - 30
Color	10 - 12	12 - 15
Black & White	6 - 8	8 - 10
Linens, Chromes, Reproductions	1 - 2	2 - 3
Foreign, pre-1930	3 - 4	4 - 6

Unidentified - deduct 25-50%.

AIR TRANSPORTATION

AIRPLANES, PILOTS

Pioneers, Named (1896-1910)	20 - 25	25 - 40
Early 1910-1914	12 - 25	25 - 35
Langley Plane (Real Photos)	30 - 40	40 - 60
Wright Flyers (Real Photos)	20 - 30	30 - 50
Color & B&W	15 - 20	20 - 30
1910 Los Angeles Meet	20 - 25	25 - 35
Aeroplane Meet, Venice, CA	25 - 30	30 - 35

French Caricature by Giris, AN, Paris
"W. Wright, Un Jol á l'americaine"

The Wright Aeroplane, "La Conquéte De
L'Air" – Cliché Branger No. 43

Hans R. Schulze, No. 3, "Die Luftflotte..."
WWI Fighting Zeppelin

"Hoxsey Death Flight, Dec. 31, 1910"	20 - 30	30 - 40
"Louis Paulman making record flight altitude"	15 - 20	20 - 30
"Graham-White starting engine, 1910"	15 - 20	20 - 30
MAX RIGOT, Chicago		
1911 Chicago Aviation Meet	25 - 30	30 - 40
NC-4	30 - 40	40 - 60
"Spirit of St. Louis"	15 - 20	20 - 30
With Lindbergh	20 - 30	30 - 50
Air Meet, Compton, CA - 1910	20 - 25	25 - 35
Identified Accidents	30 - 40	40 - 50
Air Meet, Reims, France - 1909	20 - 25	25 - 30
MISCELLANEOUS		
French Aviation Set		
"Glenn Curtis"	30 - 35	35 - 45
"De la Grange"	25 - 30	30 - 35
"Henri Demanest"	25 - 30	30 - 35
"Hubert Latham"	30 - 35	35 - 45
"Orville Wright"	30 - 35	35 - 45
"Blériot"	25 - 30	30 - 35
"Voisin"	25 - 30	30 - 35
"Roger Sommer"	25 - 30	30 - 35
"Santo Dumont"	25 - 30	30 - 35
"Robert E. Pelterie"	25 - 30	30 - 35
Anonymous Sepia Series 39424		
"Glenn H. Curtis"	25 - 30	30 - 40

German WWII Fighter Plane (Urado
Ur-95) With Swastika Insignia

1940s "Delta Air Lines"
Litho by Foote & Davis

Others	20 - 25	25 - 30
Raphael Tuck & Sons		
Series 9 "Aviation" (12)		
"The Antoinette Monoplane"	15 - 20	20 - 25
"The Blériot Monoplane"	15 - 20	20 - 25
"The Farman Biplane"	15 - 20	20 - 25
"La Republic" Airship	15 - 20	20 - 25
"M. de Lesseps' Channel Flight"	15 - 20	20 - 25
"Nulli Secundus" Zeppelin type	15 - 20	20 - 25
"A.V. Roe Biplane"	15 - 20	20 - 25
"R.P.E. Monoplane"	15 - 20	20 - 25
"Spherical Balloons"	15 - 20	20 - 25
"The Voisin Biplane"	15 - 20	20 - 25
"Wright Brothers Biplane"	20 - 25	25 - 30
"Zeppelin"	20 - 25	25 - 30
Series 9943 **"Famous Aeroplanes"** (6)	18 - 22	22 - 26
Series 3101, 3103 (6)	12 - 18	18 - 22
Series 3144 (6)	15 - 20	20 - 26
DIRIGIBLES		
Pioneers, Named	20 - 30	30 - 50
La France Airship	20 - 40	40 - 60
Early 1898-1924	15 - 25	25 - 40
"Akron"	15 - 20	20 - 25
Real Photos	15 - 20	20 - 30
"Hindenberg"	20 - 30	30 - 40
Real Photos	25 - 35	35 - 45
Los Angeles (R.P.)	15 - 20	20 - 35
Macon	12 - 18	18 - 25
R-34	20 - 30	30 - 40
R101	20 - 30	30 - 40
"Shenandoah"	15 - 20	20 - 30
Goodyear (Early)	15 - 20	20 - 28
Goodyear (Linen)	6 - 10	10 - 15
"Astra Torres" P/John Drew (R.P.)	15 - 20	20 - 30
"Baby" P/John Drew (B&W)	15 - 20	20 - 25
"Beta II" and "Gamma II" P/Mays (R.P.)	20 - 25	25 - 35
"LeViolle de Paris, 1908" (R.P.)	15 - 20	20 - 25
ZEPPELINS		
Experimental Era 1898-1910	18 - 25	25 - 40

1910-1934 Era	15 - 20	20 - 30
"Graf Zeppelin"	20 - 25	25 - 35
Real Photos	25 - 35	35 - 50
WAR PLANES		
Pre-WWI	10 - 15	15 - 25
WWI	8 - 12	12 - 20
1918-1939 Era	5 - 10	10 - 15
WWII	3 - 5	5 - 10
German with Swastika insignia (R.P.)	12 - 15	15 - 20
Post 1945 and Linens	3 - 5	5 - 10
Post 1945 (R.P.)	5 - 8	8 - 12
COMMERCIAL AIRLINES (Usually Advertising)		
Identified, Pre-1930		
Western Airlines (earliest - 1929)	15 - 25	25 - 35
Others	12 - 15	15 - 25
1930's-1940's Linens, Black & White		
Penn Central	10 - 15	15 - 20
Central Airlines	10 - 15	15 - 20
Midwest Airlines	10 - 15	15 - 20
Pan Am, Delta, Continental, TWA, United	4 - 7	7 - 12
Pacific Southwest, Braniff, Catalina	4 - 7	7 - 12
Eastern, Northwest, Mohawk, North American	4 - 7	7 - 12
National, Island Air, American	4 - 7	7 - 12
Northwest Orient, Texas, International	4 - 7	7 - 12
Trans-Ocean, and Others	6 - 8	8 - 12
Real Photos – Add 25-50%.		
Chromes	1 - 2	2 - 5
Airfields	5 - 8	8 - 12
Linens	2 - 3	3 - 5
Advertising, without plane image	3 - 5	5 - 8
Advertising Interiors	4 - 5	5 - 10

WATER TRANSPORTATION

OCEAN LINERS

During the 1890-1940 era immigrants from all over Europe, Asia, Scandinavia and the British Isles embarked for the Americas in search of a better life. They were the predominant passengers and leading cause of the tremendous growth of ocean liner trade on the Atlantic Routes.

The return voyages to Europe were filled with rich and famous Americans...the Rockefellers, Astors, and other industrialists of the times...for luxury vacations to fashionable cities of their choice. To accommodate this elite class, owners commissioned shipbuilders to build the fastest, finest, most comfortable, and most luxurious first class accommodations that money could buy.

Industrial advances in America and British Colony expansion buoyed the growth of British lines, while interests in East and Central Africa and commercial interests in South America led to great growth by the German shipping lines. America and other countries, viewing this great prosperity, began building ships so that they too could take advantage of the immigration to America.

The British shipper, Cunard Lines, was the first and foremost in the industry. Their "Mauretania," became the fastest ship to cross the Atlantic, and held that record for 22 years. White Star Lines' "Titanic," was destined to be the world's most famous ship after hitting an iceberg and sinking on its maiden voyage.

The advent of two World Wars was a great detriment to the growth of the shipping and passenger lines. During World War 1, when the "Lusitania" was sunk by German submarines in 1914, shipping came to a standstill. Many liners became troop ships and were sunk on the open seas as well as in port. After the war, new ships were built and business prospered as before.

The same was true at the start of World War II. When war was declared, shipping ceased, and many of the great liners, such as "The Queen Mary" and "The Queen Elizabeth," became ships for troops. As in the first war, the casualty rate was tremendous on the ocean liners of the world. Those that escaped were placed back in service, new ones were built, and the liner trade again prospered until the late 1950's when immigration to North America came to a standstill and the rich and famous began flying to Europe. The liners began losing money, and one by one they were scuttled and sold for scrap. Only a few of the famous ships still exist.

Postcard collectors have benefited greatly as the Liners advertised their services to the utmost. Beautiful cards, showing magnificent ships at the docks and sailing on the open seas, have survived and are available for today's collector.

AMERICAN EXPORT LINES (1950's-1960's)   2 - 3   3 - 6

AMERICAN LINE
"Haverford," "Kroonland," "Merian," "New York"
"Philadelphia," "St. Louis," "Westernland"

Color	10 - 15	15 - 20
Black & White	5 - 8	8 - 10
Interiors	10 - 15	15 - 20
Real Photos and Advertising types	15 - 20	20 - 25

ANCHOR LINE*
"Athenia," "Bolivia," "Caledonia,"
"City of Rome," "Columbia," "Olympia,"
"Transylvania," "Tuscania"

Color	12 - 15	15 - 20
Black & White	6 - 8	8 - 10
Interiors	12 - 15	15 - 20
Real Photos	15 - 20	20 - 30

Canadian Pacific Line, "C.P.S. Montclare" – Gross Tonnage 16400

Cunard Line, "R.M.S. Carpathia Passing Gibraltar"

Cunard Line, "R.M.S. Caronia"
Tonnage 20,000

French Line, "S.S. Ile de France"
New York–Plymouth–Havre Service

Artist-Signed by **W.T.N.**	12 - 15	15 - 25
Advertising	15 - 20	20 - 30
*Purchased by **CUNARD LINE** in 1912.		
BERGEN LINE (Norway)	2 - 3	3 -6
CANADIAN PACIFIC		
Color	8 - 10	10 - 15
Black & White	4 - 5	5 - 8
Real Photos	15 - 20	20 - 25
"Empress of Ireland" - Disaster	15 - 25	25 - 30
Advertising	15 - 20	20 - 25

CUNARD LINES *
"Adriatic," "Alaunia" 1925, "Andavia"
"Andonia," "Ansonia," "Antonia"
"Aquiatania"1907, "Arabic," "Ascania"
"Athenia" first ship torpedoed in WW2
"Berengaria" 1918, "Britannic" 1934
"Bothnia," "Campania" 1893, "Canopic"
"Caronia" 1948 "Carpathia" 1903, "Catalonia"
"Cedric," "Celtic," "Cephalonia," "Corinthia"
"Coronia," "Cymbric," "Etruria," "Folia"
"Franconia," "Gaelic," "Ivirnia," "Lancastria"
"Laurentic," "Luciana" 1893, "Lusitania" 1907
"Majestic," Mauretania" 1907, "Media" 1947
"Meganic," "Olympia," "Orduna"
"Parthia" 1948, "Pavonia," "Persic"
"Pittsburgh," "Republic," "Royal George"
"Russia," "Saxonia," "Scythia," "Servia"
"Teutonic," "Umbria," Others
*Artist-Signed cards by MANN, TURNER,
O. ROSENVENGE, W. THOMAS - add $3-5/card.

Pre-1920 issues		
Color	10 - 15	15 - 20
Black & White	5 - 8	8 - 12
Real Photo	12 - 15	15 - 25
Interior Views	10 - 12	12 - 15
Poster Advertising	20 - 25	25 - 35
Sunk in WWI		
"Aurania," "Campania," "Franconia"		
Color	15 - 20	20 - 25

Black & White	5 - 7	7 - 12
Real Photo	20 - 25	25 - 28
Interiors	10 - 15	15 - 20
"Lusitania" – Sunk by German Submarines		
Color	20 - 25	25 - 35
Black & White	8 - 10	10 - 15
Real Photos	25 - 30	30 - 40
Interiors	10 - 15	15 - 20
Interior Real Photos	15 - 20	20 - 25
Memorial Issues	15 - 20	20 - 30
Disaster Sketches	12 - 15	15 - 25
"Carpathia" 1903 – Rescuer of Titanic		
Color, telling of rescue	20 - 25	25 - 30
Real Photo, telling of rescue	30 - 40	40 - 50
CUNARD-WHITE STAR LINE, 1934-1948		
New "Mauretania," "Queen Elizabeth" 1938,		
Queen Mary" 1936, "Georgic" 1934, Others		
Color	5 - 8	8 - 12
Black & White	2 - 3	3 -6
Interiors	6 - 8	8 - 10
Advertising	10 - 12	12 - 15
CUNARD LINE, after 1948		
"Caronia" 1948, "Queen E. II" 1969	2 - 3	3 - 5
DOMINION LINE (Hands Across the Sea)	8 - 10	10 - 15
FRENCH LINE		
Color	10 - 12	12 - 16
Black & White	5 - 7	8 - 10
Advertising	15 - 20	20 - 25
GDYNIA AMERICA LINE (Poland)	3 - 6	6 - 10
THE GRACE LINE		
GREAT WESTERN ("Grand Trunk" R.R. Ferry)	4 - 5	5 - 10
GREEK LINE (1940-1970's)	2 - 3	3 - 6
HAMBURG-AMERICA LINE		
"Alb. Ballin," "Amerika," "Belgravia"		
"Bismarck" 1914, "Blucher," "Caribia"		
"Cleveland," "Columbia" 1889		
"Cordillera," "Deutchland" 1898		
"Furst Bismarck," "Graf," "Hamburg"		
"Hansa," "Iberia," "Imperator" 1913		
"Kaiser Friedrich," "Kaiserin Auguste		
Victoria" 1889, "Milwaukee" 1929		
"Moltke," "New York," "Oceana"		
"Orinco," "Palatia," "Patricia"		
"Phoenicia," "Pres. Grant," "Princess		
Victoria Luise," "Reliance," "Pres. Lincoln"		
"Pennsylvania," "St. Louis" 1929		
"Vaterland" 1914, "Waldersee," Others		
Early Chromolithos, by S/**W. STOWER** &		
H. BUZRDT, P/**Muhlmeister & Johler**	20 - 25	25 - 30
Black & White Steel Engravings,		
S/**W. STOWER,** P/**Kutzner & Berger**	15 - 20	20 - 25
Color	15 - 18	18 - 22

Hamburg-Amerika Linie, S/Hans Bohrdt
Muhlmeister & Johler, "President Grant"

Hamburg-Amerika Linie, Elb-Feuerschiff
No. 1, "Fürst Bismarck" (1890s)

Hamburg-Amerika Linie, "Amerika"
A. J. Schultz, The "Speisesaal"

Black & White	6 - 8	8 - 10
Real Photos	20 - 25	25 - 30
Early Menus w/postcard attached	20 - 25	25 - 30
Poster Advertising	25 - 30	30 - 35
Views of Piers and Ships in Port	12 - 15	15 - 20
Pier, Hoboken, N.J.	12 - 15	15 - 20

HAMBURG-SOUTH AMERICA LINE 10 - 15 15 - 20
   With Menu 15 - 20 20 - 25

HOLLAND-AMERICA LINE
   "Edam" 1921, "Maasdam" 1952, "Niew
   Amsterdam" 1906,"Nieuw Amsterdam II"
   1938, "Potsdam" 1900, "Rotterdam,"
   1908, "Rotterdam II" 1959,"Ryndam"
   "Statendam" 1914, "Statendam II" 1929 -
   Bombed in 1940, "Statendam IV" 1957
   "Veendam" 1923, "Volendam" 1920
   "Werkendam," "Westdam" 1946
   "Zaandam" 1938 – Torpedoed in war; Others

Early Chromolithos by		
S/**C. DIXON** and **F. PARSING**	15 - 20	20 - 25
Color	10 - 15	15 - 20
Black & White	5 - 8	8 - 10
Real Photos	15 - 20	20 - 25
Poster Advertising	15 - 25	25 - 35

"The Hamburg-American Line Piers Hoboken, N.J."

Hamburg-Sudamerikanische Line
"Monte Sarmiento" with Menu

"Mallory Liner," Seawall Specialty Co.
(Entering Harbor at Galveston, Texas)

After 1935	3 - 5	5 - 8
HOME LINES (1939-1970's)	2 - 3	3 -7
ITALIAN LINE		
Color	10 - 12	12 - 20
Black & White	3 - 5	5 - 8
Poster Advertising	20 - 25	25 - 35
After 1935	2 - 3	3 - 5
MALLORY LINE	8 - 10	10 - 12
MATSON LINE (1920-1930's)		
Color	8 - 10	10 - 15
Black & White	3 - 5	5 - 8
MOORE-McCORMICK LINES, INC.		
"Brazil" and "Argentina"	4 - 5	5 - 10

NORDDEUTSCHER LLOYD, Bremen
(North German Lloyd Lines)
"Amerika," 1903, "Alb. Ballin" 1923, "Elbe," 1900
was sunk in collision, "Imperator" 1913, "Aller"
"Barbarossa," "Berlin" 1955, "Bremen" 1928
"Bulow," "Coblenz," "Columbus" 1922, "Dresden"
"Eider," "Ems," "Europa" 1929, "Eitel Friedrich"
"Fried. der Grosse," "Fulda," "Gen. v. Steuben"
"George Washington," "Goeben," "Grosser Kurfurst"
"Havel," "Kaiser Wilhelm II," "Kleist," "Konig Albert"
"Kronprinz Wilhelm," "Kronprinze. Cecille" 1904

Pacific Coast Steamship Co. – Alaska Excursion, "S. S. Spokane"

"Muenchen," "Orotava" "Prinzess Alice," "Roon"
"PrinzessIrene," "Prinz Regent Luitpold," "Saale"
"Scharnhorst," "Spree," "Trave," "Werra"
"Wilh. Gostloff" was torpedoed in 1945 (6,096 died)
"York," Others

Early Chromoliths, S/**T.v.E.**	20 - 25	25 - 35
Black & White vignettes, S/**T.v.E.**	15 - 18	18 - 22
Black & White Engravings	15 - 18	18 - 22
Color	12 - 15	15 - 18
Black & White	6 - 8	8 - 10
Real Photos	18 - 22	22 - 26
Early Menus with postcard attached	20 - 25	25 - 35
Post 30's Menus with postcard attached	15 - 18	18 - 22
Poster Advertising	20 - 25	25 - 35
St. Louis Exposition	15 - 25	25 - 35
Became HAPAG-LLOYD LINE IN 1932	6 - 10	10 - 15
And BREMEN-AMERICAN LINE IN 1954	2 - 3	3 - 6
N.Y.K. LINE		
Color	8 - 10	10 -15
Black & White	4 - 6	6 - 8
NORWEGIAN-AMERICAN LINE (1940-1980's)	2 - 5	5 - 8
O.S.K. LINE		
Color	8 - 10	10 - 15
Black & White	4 - 6	6 - 8
ORIENT LINE (Britain)	5 - 8	8 - 10
P & O LINE		
Color	6 - 8	8 - 10
Black & White	3 - 4	4 - 5
PACIFIC COAST STEAMSHIP CO. (B&W, Undb)		
Alaska Excursion, "S. S. Spokane"	15 - 20	20 - 25
PANAMA-PACIFIC LINE	5 - 6	6 - 10

Red Star Line, Steamer "Lapland"
Signed by Charles

Savannah Line
"S. S. City of St. Louis"

RED STAR LINE
  "Belgenland," "Finland," "Friesland"
  "Kensington," "Kroonland," "Lapland"
  "Marquette," "Noordland," "Pennland"
  "Westernland," "Vaderland," "Zeeland"

P/American Litho Co. PMC's	15 - 20	20 - 25
Chromolitho Posters, S/**H. CASSIERS**		
A Series, B&W, of Ships & Dutch People	15 - 20	20 - 25
B Series, Color, of Ships & Dutch People	20 - 25	25 - 30
C Series, Color	15 - 20	20 - 25
H Series, Color, of Ships in Harbor	15 - 20	20 - 25
L Series, Views and people of Antwerp	10 - 12	12 - 15
Others S/**H. CASSIERS, S/C. DIXON**	12 - 15	15 - 18
Posters, S/**V. GRETEN, K Series**	15 - 20	20 - 25
Wood Engravings, S/EDWARD PELLENS	12 - 15	15 - 20
Art Deco O & P Series, P/**J. L. Goffart**	30 - 35	35 - 40
Poster Advertising	20 - 25	25 - 35
ROYAL MAIL LINE Britain-South America	5 - 8	8 - 12
SAVANNAH LINE – "S. S. City of St. Louis"	5 - 8	8 - 12
SUD-ATLANTIQUE LINE		
"L'Atlantique"		
Color	10 - 15	15 - 18
Black & White	5 - 7	7 - 10
The **L'Atlantique** disaster	12 - 15	15 - 20
Others	6 - 7	7 - 10
SVENSKA (SWEDISH) AMERICA LINE		
Color	6 - 8	8 - 10
Black & White	4 - 5	5 - 6
Advertising	12 - 15	15 - 18

UNITED STATES LINE
  "Geo. Washington," "Leviathan"
  "Manhattan," "Pres. Harding"
  "Pres.Roosevelt," "Republic, "United States," 1952
  "The America" 1940

S/WILLY STOWER	10 - 12	12 - 18
Color	8 - 10	10 - 15
Black & White	4 - 6	6 - 8
Real Photos	10 - 15	15 - 20
Advertising	10 - 15	15 - 20

White Star Line, "The R.M.S. Olympic"
(Signed Walter Thomas)

White Star Line, "R.M.S. Titanic"
"Hands Across the Sea" Woven Silk

UNITED FRUIT CO. (Great White Fleet)	1 - 2	2 - 3
WHITE STAR LINES*		
"Adriatic" 1902, "Albertic," "Baltic" 1902		
"Britannic" 1914–lost in WWI, "Britannic II" 1930		
"Canopic," "Cedric" 1902, "Celtic" 1901, "Ceramic"		
"Cretic," "Doric" 1923, "Georgic," "Germanic"		
"Homeric," "Lapland," "Laurentic," "Majestic"		
"Megantic," "Oceanic" 1899, "Olympic" 1911		
"Republic" – Rammed and sunk 1909, "Runic"		
"Suevic," "Vedic," Others		
Color	10 - 15	15 - 20
Black & White	5 - 8	8 - 12
Real Photos	15 - 18	18 - 22
S/N. WILKENSON or M. BLACK	10 - 15	15 - 20
Poster Advertising	20 - 30	30 - 40
"Titanic" - 1912		
Postally Used before 4/15/12	1500 - 2000	2000 - 3000
Woven Silk	1500 - 2000	2000 - 2500
Hands-Across-The-Sea Woven Silk	900 - 1000	1000 - 150
Sea Trials - Belfast, Austrian R.P.	500 - 600	600 - 700
Pre-Sinking, Printed Photos	400 - 500	500 - 600
Pre-Sinking Real Photos	500 - 600	600 - 800
Post-Sinking, Real Photos	75 - 100	100 - 150
Real Photo Memorial Cards	100 - 125	125 - 150
Raphael Tuck & Sons	65 - 75	75 - 100
"Among the Icebergs," **Valentine** Pub.	85 - 100	100 - 120
"Steamer Titanic," **Tichnor Bros.** Pub.	75 - 85	85 - 100
"Nearer My God to Thee," **Bamforth Co.** (6)	40 - 50	50 - 80
Australian, French, Misc. Publishers	100 - 150	150 - 200
S.S. Titanic, **Success Post Card Co.**	50 - 60	60 - 75
"Titanic/Olympic" (White Star Line) (Color)	500 - 600	600 - 750
"Olympic"	35 - 40	40 - 50
After 1934	5 - 8	8 - 12
*****White Star** and **Cunard** merged in 1934.		
CELEBRATED LINERS SERIES		
Raphael Tuck (Oilette 6-Card sets)		
Series 3378, 3379, 6228 "White Star Lines"	15 - 22	22 - 30
Series 3592	10 - 12	12 - 15
Series 6229 "Orient-Pacific Line"	15 - 20	20 - 25

Series 6230, 8960, 8961	15 - 20	20 - 25
Series 9106 "The Cunard Line"	20 - 25	25 - 35
Series 9121, "Canadian-Pacific Line"	15 - 20	20 - 28
Series 9112, 9124, 9125	15 - 20	20 - 25
Series 9126 "Atlantic Transport Line"	15 - 20	20 - 25
Series 9133 "Union Castle Line"	15 - 20	20 - 25
Series 914 "American Line"	20 - 25	25 - 35
Series 9151, 9155, 9213	15 - 20	20 - 25
Series 9215 "White Star Line"	20 - 25	25 - 35
Series 9268 "Cunard Line"		
"Mauretania" (Image 1)	15 - 20	20 - 30
"Lusitania" (Image 1)	25 - 30	30 - 40
"Carmania"	15 - 20	20 - 25
"Lusitania" (Image 2)	25 - 30	30 - 40
"Mauretania" (Image 2)	15 - 20	20 - 30
"Carpathia"	25 - 30	30 - 35
Series 9503 "White Star Line"	20 - 25	25 - 30
Series 9625 "Canadian Pacific," Series II	20 - 25	25 - 30
Series 9808 "White Star Line"		
"Titanic" (2)	100 - 125	125 - 150
Others	20 - 25	25 - 30

OTHER LINERS

Pre -1930		
Color	6 - 8	8 - 10
Black & White	4 - 5	5 - 7
Interiors, Real Photos	8 - 10	10 - 12
After 1930	2 - 3	3 - 4

OCEAN COAST LINERS
CANADIAN PACIFIC RAILROAD

"Princess Charlotte"	8 - 10	10 - 15
"Princess Charlene"	8 - 10	10 - 15
"Princess Victoria"	8 - 10	10 - 15

CLYDE STEAMSHIP LINE

E. Coast, NY - Miami		
Early Vignettes, Black & White	12 - 15	15 - 25
Color	8 - 10	12 - 15
Real Photo	12 - 15	15 - 25

EASTERN STEAMSHIP LINES

"Boston," "New York"		
Color	4 - 6	6 - 10
Black & White	3 - 4	4 - 5
Real Photo	8 - 10	10 - 15

FURNESS-BERMUDA LINE	2 - 3	3 - 5

MAINE STEAMSHIP CO.

Color	4 - 6	6 - 10
Black & White	3 - 4	4 - 7
Real Photos	8 - 10	10 - 12

MATSON NAVIGATION CO. (San Francisco)	3 - 4	4 - 6

MERCHANTS & MINERS LINE (Atlantic Coast)

Color	4 - 6	6 - 10
Black & White	3 - 4	4 - 5

Real Photos	8 - 10	10 - 12
Old Dominion Line	6 - 8	8 - 12
PACIFIC MAIL CO. LINE (Pacific Coast)		
Color	4 - 6	6 - 10
Black & White	3 - 4	4 - 5
Real Photo	8 - 10	10 - 12
PANAMA PACIFIC LINE		
"City of Baltimore," "Newport News," "Norfolk"		
"L.A.," "S.F.," "Calif.," "Penna." "Virginia"		
Color	5 - 8	8 - 12
Black & White	3 - 5	5 - 7
Real Photos	8 - 10	10 - 15
SAVANNAH LINE (NY-Boston-Miami)		
"City of Birmingham," "City of Chattanooga"		
"City of Savannah," Others		
Color	5 - 8	8 - 12
Black & White	3 - 5	5 - 8
Real Photos	6 - 8	8 - 10
WARDS LINE New York-Havana		
Color	6 - 8	8 - 10
Black & White	4 - 5	5 - 6
Real Photo of **"Morro Castle"** Wreck	10 - 12	12 - 15
WOVEN SILKS OF SHIPS		
Stevensgraphs		
"S. S. Haverford" and "R.M.S. Baltic"	70 - 80	80 - 90
"R.M.S. Mauretania," "Arabic"	80 - 90	90 - 100
"Baltic," "Ivernia," "Lucania," "Saxonia"	70 - 80	80 - 90
Hands Across the Sea/With Flags		
"R.M.S. Victorian," "Ivernia" "Romanic"	40 - 45	45 - 50

GREAT LAKES AND RIVER STEAMERS

HUDSON RIVER DAY LINE	4 - 6	6 - 8
"Robt. Fulton," "New York" "Hend. Hudson"		
Color	3 - 5	5 - 7
Black & White	2 - 3	3 - 4
Real Photos	8 - 10	10 - 12
D & C LINE		
"City of Cleveland," Others		
Color	5 - 6	6 - 8
Black & White	1 - 2	2 - 5

BATTLESHIPS/CRUISERS/NAVAL VESSELS

Arthur Livingston PMC's "Maine"	12 - 15	15 - 20
Others	8 - 10	10 - 13
H.A. Rost, Pioneers & PMC's	15 - 20	20 - 30
American News Co.	4 - 5	5 - 8
American Souvenir Card Co.		
The White Squadron (12) "Patriographic"	12 - 15	15 - 25
A. C. Bosselman	5 - 7	7 - 12

U.S. Dreadnought "Delaware" – Valentines No. 217711

Boston P.C. Co. (Brown-tint)	4 - 5	5 - 9
Britton & Rey	4 - 5	5 - 9
Brooklyn Eagle, Black & White	3 - 4	4 - 6
E. P. Charlton	5 - 7	7 - 10
Detroit Photographic Co.	5 - 8	8 - 12
Allen Fanjoy	3 - 4	4 -6
Henderson Litho S/E. MULLER	5 - 7	7 - 10
Illustrated P.C. Co.	5 - 7	7 - 10
L. Kaufmann & Sons	4 - 6	6 - 8
Hugh C. Leighton	5 - 7	7 - 10
Lowman & Hanford	5 - 7	7 - 10
Metropolitan News Co.	4 - 6	6 - 8
Edward H. Mitchell	5 - 7	7 - 10
Rotograph Co. S/E. MULLER		
Real Photos, 1904, 1910	6 - 8	8 - 10
Prudential Insurance Co. (U.S. & Foreign)	4 - 6	6 - 9
Souvenir Postcard Co.	5 - 8	8 - 10
State of Washington, Puget Sound Ferries	5 - 7	7 - 9
Tichnor Bros. S/E. MULLER	5 - 8	8 - 12
Raphael Tuck		
1076 "U.S. Navy"	7 - 9	9 - 12
1223 "U.S. Navy Cruisers"	7 - 9	9 - 12
2324 "U.S. Navy-Battleships"	7 - 9	9 - 12
4484 "U.S. Ironclads"	7 - 9	9 - 12
Valentine Series S/ WATERMAN, 1909	4 - 5	5 - 8
Valentines Series U. S. Battleships		
U.S. Dreadnought "Delaware"	8 - 10	10 - 12
U. S. Battleship "Kansas"	8 - 10	10 - 12
Others	8 - 10	10 - 12

Sports

BASEBALL

Baseball will always be "America's Game." It enjoys the distinction of having two major groups–postcards and sports collectors–who continually vie for a great shortage of material. Therefore, any cards that surface are quickly purchased and, just as quickly, taken out of circulation again. Values vary widely, especially in some of the early 1900-1935 issues, and it is extremely difficult to value individual cards when so few are available.

Newer issues, especially those of Hall of Famers and those published by Perez Galleries, are enjoying much success because of the sports autograph craze. The cards are purchased by collectors and are signed by the players at sports card and autograph shows.

Values listed here are rather conservative and should be used only as a "ballpark" guide, as prices realized on some issues may be somewhat higher, especially on rare boxing and baseball real photos. Hopefully, more of these cards will surface so that an accurate listing can be made in future editions.

	VG	EX
American League Pub. Co., Cleveland, 1908 (B&W)		
Action + Oval Photo	$ 75 - 85	$ 85 - 100
Tyrus R. Cobb	200 - 250	250 - 300
Nap Lajoie	100 - 150	150 - 200
Honus Wagner	200 - 250	250 - 300
H.H. Bregstone, 1909-11 (45 + Unnumbered)		
Real Photos with AZO Postcard Backs		
St. Louis Browns & St. Louis Cardinals	80 - 90	90 - 110
Rube Waddell	125 - 150	150 - 175
Roger Bresnahan	100 - 125	125 - 150
Miller Huggins	125 - 140	140 - 160
Boston American Series, 1912		
Red Sox, Cream with Sepia Photos	70 - 80	80 - 90

American League Publishing Co.
"Elmer Flick, Outfielder"

H. H. Bregstone
"McAleer, Mgr. – St. Louis Browns"

Tris Speaker	100 - 125	125 - 140
Boston Daily American, 1912		
Red Sox (B&W)	70 - 80	80 - 90
F. P. Burke, 1907 (Bluetone)		
Detroit Tigers Team Picture	600 - 700	700 - 800
Chicago Cubs Team Picture	600 - 700	700 - 800
George Burke, Chicago Photographer		
Hundreds of issues 1948-1959 era		
Stars	10 - 15	15 - 20
Others	3 - 5	5 - 10
Cincinnati Reds		
Championship Postcards, 1920 (B&W)		
"World Champions" or National League		
Champions"	40 - 50	50 - 60
Edd Roush	80 - 90	90 - 100
Colourpicture Publishers (Chromes)		
P62008 "Baseball Greats – Mays, Koufax, Chance..."	20 - 25	25 - 30
Coral-Lee, 1982-1985	2- 4	4 - 7
H. S. Crocker, 1959		
Johnny Podres	15 - 20	20 - 25
Duke Snider	25 - 30	30 - 35
Denby Cigars, 1932 Chicago Cubs	50 - 75	75 - 100
Rogers Hornsby	125 - 150	150 - 175
Warneke	75 - 100	100 - 125
Dexter Press, 1968	6 - 8	8 - 10
Henry Aaron	15 - 20	20 - 25
Clemente	30 - 40	40 - 50

A. C. Dietche
Sam Crawford

Louis Dormand
Mickey Mantle, Jumbo

Mays	15 - 20	20 - 25
A. C. Dietsche, 1907 (B&W)		
Chicago Cubs		
Tinker, Evers, Chance, Brown	80 - 100	100 - 125
Others	60 - 70	70 - 80
A. C. Dietsche, 1907-09, (B&W)		
Series I, 1907, Title "Hughie Jennings and his		
Great 1907 Detroit Tigers"		
Tyrus Cobb (2)	100 - 150	150 - 200
Sam Crawford, Hughie Jennings	90 - 100	100 - 120
Others	60 - 70	70 - 80
Series II, 1908-09		
Tyrus Cobb	100 - 150	150 - 200
Hughie Jennings	70 - 80	80 - 90
Team Picture	100 - 120	120 - 140
Others	60 - 70	70 - 80
Detroit Free Press, 1908 (Cream w/green B.G.)		
Tigers	90 - 100	100 - 110
Cobb	200 - 250	250 - 300
Jennings	125 - 150	150 - 175
Louis Dormand 1954-55		
Premiums for Mason Candy (Color)		
Common Players	10 - 15	15 - 20
Mantle, batting stance	50 - 60	60 - 80
Mantle, bat on shoulder	75 - 100	100 - 150
Mantle, Oversized, 6 x 9	150 - 175	175 - 225
Mantle, Oversized. 9 x 12	450 - 500	500 - 550

Exhibit Supply Co.	*Exhibit Supply Co.*	*Morgan Stationery Co.*
"Lou Gehrig, Yankees A.L."	*"Babe Ruth, O.F., N.Y."*	*"Huggins, 2nd Baseman..."*

Gil Hodges	300 - 350	350 400
Casey Strengel	80 - 90	90 - 100
Berra, Rizzuto, Mize, Erskine, Campanella		
Reese, Furillo, Martin, Slaughter	30 - 40	40 - 50
Exhibit Supply Co., Chicago, 1921-66		
Postcard Backs only		
1929 Issues "Not to be used in exhibit machines"		
Ty Cobb	150 - 175	175 - 200
Lou Gehrig	125 - 150	150 - 200
Babe Ruth	600 - 650	650 - 700
Other Hall of Famers	40 - 50	50 - 60
Others players	15 - 20	20 - 25
1950's Issues (32?)		
Mantle, Mays	60 - 70	70 - 80
Musial, Campanella, Berra	25 - 30	30 - 40
Feller, Lemon, Kaline, Snider	15 - 20	20 - 25
Others	10 - 15	15 - 18
G. F. Grignon Co., 1907, Green Chicago Cubs		
Player Inset & Big Teddy Bear & Caption		
Tinker (2), Evers, Chance	150 - 175	175 - 200
Others	75 - 85	85 - 100
V. O. Hammon		
1906 Chicago Cubs Team	150 - 175	175 - 200
1906 Champion White Sox Team	125 - 150	150 - 175
George W. Hull, 1907, Black & White, (13)		
World Champs Chicago White Sox players		
in ovals on socks on clothesline	100 - 125	125 - 150
Eddie Walsh, Doc White	150 - 175	175 - 200
Masterpiece Jockey Club		
Pirates Team Players, Sepia (At Auction)	1000-1100	1100-1200
Morgan Stationery Co., Cincinnati, 1907		
Photos in Red's Palace of Stars Stadium (10)	65 - 75	75 - 90
Miller Huggins, Second Baseman Par Ex."	300 - 350	350 400
Variation with diff B.G.	150 - 200	200 - 250
"Opening of the Season 1907..."	350 - 400	400 - 500

The Rose Company
Tenney, New York, N.L.

Sepia, Anonymous Series
Ty "Cobb"

Novelty Cutlery Co., 1910, Sepia (25) *
  Players in gray, enclosed in frame

Birdwell, Devlin, Dooin, Flock	100 - 125	125 - 150
Gibson, Hoffman, Lord, Overall	125 - 150	150 - 175
Bresnahan, Brown, Chance, E. Collins	125 - 150	150 - 175
Street, Evers/Schaefer, Crawford	140 - 160	160 - 180
Chase, Lajoie, Plank, Walsh, Speaker	150 - 175	175 - 200
Wagner, Cobb	300 - 400	400 - 500
Johnson, Mathewson	175 - 200	200 - 225
Cobb-Wagner together	500 - 600	600 - 700

  * Same but smaller images as the anonymous
    "Sepia Baseball Players" Series

E. J. Offerman, 1908, Buffalo Players (20)

Action shot & photo inset	75 - 85	85 - 100

Pastime Novelty Co.

"Our Matty, Chris Mathewson..." (B&W Printed)	70 - 80	80 - 100

The Rose Co., 1909
  Players in Gold Frame above Diamond
    on yellow/green field (200+)

National League	80 - 90	90 - 100
Brown, Chicago	150 - 175	175 - 200
Tinker, Evers, Chance, Mathewson	200 - 225	225 - 250
Wagner	900 - 1000	1000 - 1100
Delahanty	110 - 120	120 - 140
American League	80 - 90	90 - 100
Lajoie	200 - 225	225 - 250
Cobb	900 - 1000	1000 - 1100

Bender, Chase, Waddell	140 - 160	160 - 180
Chesbro, F. Delahanty, Keeler	120 - 140	140 - 160
Scranton Players	80 - 90	90 - 100
The Rotograph Co., 1905, Real Photos	100 - 125	125 - 150
McGraw, Chesbro, Clark Griffith	150 - 175	175 - 200
Sepia - Anonymous		
Ty Cobb	500 - 600	600 - 800
"Sepia Baseball Players" 1910 *		
Anonymous, Sepia color	125 - 150	150 - 175
Cobb	700 - 800	800 - 900
Wagner	600 - 650	650 - 700
Ty Cobb-Honus Wagner	550 - 600	600 - 700
Johnson, Mathewson	200 - 250	250 - 300
* Same images as Novelty Cutlery Co. but larger.		
Souvenir Postcard Shop of Cleveland (17+)		
Cleveland Players (RP)		
Lajoie	150 - 175	175 - 200
Others	100 - 125	125 - 150
A. W. Spargo, 1908, Black & White		
Hartford Players (4?)	80 - 90	90 - 100
The Sporting Life, 1906 Collage of players (16) (Sepia)	150 - 200	200 - 250
Sporting News, 1915, Color (6)		
Ty Cobb	2000 - 2250	2250 - 2500
Walter Johnson-Gabby Street	300 - 350	350 - 400
Eddie Collins, Rube Marquard	200 - 225	225 - 250
Bresnahan	100 - 125	125 - 150
Vean Gregg	75 - 100	100 - 125
Max Stein, P/U.S. Pub. House, 1909-16		
35 Unnumbered, "Noted People" (Sepia)		
Cobb, Wagner	300 - 350	350 - 400
Mathewson, McGraw, Thorpe	150 - 175	175 - 200
Speaker, Marquard, Tinker, Evers, Chance	100 - 125	125 - 150
Teams	150 - 175	175 - 200
Other Players	90 - 100	100 - 120
H. M. Taylor, 1909-11, Tigers (7) (B&W)		
Ty Cobb (batting)	250 - 275	275 - 300
Jennings	150 - 175	175 - 200
Team	150 - 200	200 - 250
Others	100 - 125	125 - 150
St. Louis Cards "Dear Friends" Series		
Musial	25 - 30	30 - 35
Haddix, Hemus, Staley & others	15 - 18	18 - 22
Topping & Co., 1909, "Tiger Stars" (20)		
Black & yellow - Head in big star.		
Ty Cobb	300 - 350	350 - 400
Jennings, Crawford, Delahanty, Donavan	150 - 175	175 - 200
Others	90 - 100	100 - 110
Ullman Mfg. Co.		
World Champion Series		
Chicago Cub Team	200 - 300	300 - 400
Others	50 - 70	70 - 90
Wolverine News Co., 1909, Tiger Players (B&W)		
Ty Cobb (2)	200 - 250	250 - 300

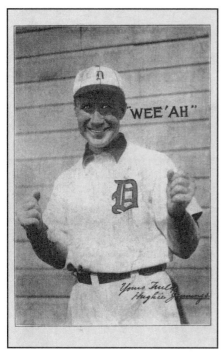

H. M. Taylor
Hughie Jennings, "WEE'AH"

Topping & Co., "Tiger Stars"
Ty Cobb, Right Field

Hughey Jennings	100 - 125	125 - 150
Others	80 - 90	90 - 100
MISCELLANEOUS		
Boston Red Sox, P/Furlong 1908		
Mechanical, Cobb/Wagner	3000 - 3250	3250 - 3700
Boston Red Sox, 1915		
Team, Real Photo (including Babe Ruth)	6000 - 6250	6250 - 6750
Chicago Cubs, 1911 Schedule and Players	200 - 225	225 - 250
Art P.C. Company		
Fold-out Cards, 1907-1910	2000 - 2500	2500 - 3000
Team Issues		
Baltimore Orioles (1954-75) (B&W, Color)	8 - 12	12 - 20
Cincinnati Reds Yearly Issues (1954-66)	8 - 12	12 - 20
Cleveland Indians (1948-75) (B&W)	8 - 12	12 - 20
L.A. Dodgers (1959-73)	8 - 12	12 - 20
St. Louis Cardinals (1950-74)	8 - 12	12 - 20
Team Photos		
Chicago White Sox, 1906, P/F. P. Burke	150 - 175	175 - 200
Chicago National League Ball Club, 1906		
P/V. O. Hammon	150 - 175	175 - 200
Philadelphia American League Team, 1905	200 - 250	250 - 300
St. Louis Cardinals, 1926 – R.P. by Block Bros.	60 - 75	75 - 100
Hall of Fame Issues		
Albertype Co.		
1936-1952 Inductees B&W, Plaques (62)		
Ruth, Cobb, Gehrig	25 - 30	30 - 40
Others	10 - 15	15 - 20

Chicago White Sox, 1906 Team
©1906 by F. P. Burke

Chicago National League Ball Club,
1906, V. O. Hammon Pub. Co.

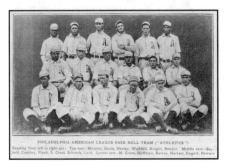

Philadelphia American League Team,
1905 ("Athletics")

The St. Louis Cardinals (1926)
Real Photo by Block Brothers

Artvue Co. Hall of Fame (94)
1953-1963 Inductees

J. DiMaggio, J. Robinson	15 - 20	20 - 30
Others	3 - 5	5 - 8

Curt Teich

1964- (Yellow-Brown)	1 - 2	2 - 3

Perez-Steele By Artist **George Perez**
1981- Color, Issued in Sets

Cards of living Hall of Famers by Perez-Steele reached astronomical values in 1990-93 because of the sports autograph scenario. Issues of DiMaggio, Williams, Musial, and Mantle were sold at values of $150-200 each and many others in the $50-100 range. Collectors and dealers purchased them, and the players autographed them by mail or at card shows. These high prices have somewhat abated in the last few years. Cards of early inductees (those deceased) are valued at $5-50. Those of Ruth, Gehrig, and other most prominent are becoming more collectible as time goes on. Since the deaths of DiMaggio and Mantle, images of living inductees are ranging from $20-50 each. Advertising issues are rare and are valued at $30-50.

BASEBALL COMICS

ARTIST-SIGNED

BROWNE, TOM (GB)
Davidson Bros.

Series 2618 (6)	20 - 25	25 - 30
Series 2619 (6)	20 - 25	25 - 30

T. Browne, Davidson Bros.
2618-1, "I am sorry I..."

K. Gassaway, Rotograph
151 "The Base-ball player"

M. Grimball, Gutmann &
Gutmann, "The Champion"

E. B. Kemble, Fairman Co., Series 159
"I'se jes makin' er short stop here."

L. C. Phifer, E. L. Co., Series 1820
"Goliath was struck out by David..."

CROSBY, P. (US)
   Anonymous (Sepia) 10)   12 - 15   15 - 18
DENNISTON (US)
   Gartner & Bender (6) *   18 - 22   22 - 26
   * Series also published by A.H. Katz   18 - 22   22 - 26
DEWEY, ALFRED JAMES (US)
   Frederickson & Co.
      Lovers Baseball Series 222 (12)
      No. 3 "A Hit" Rare!   30 - 35   35 - 38
      Others   12 - 15   15 - 18
   Boston Sunday Post (6) Issued with paper.   15 - 18   18 - 22
GASSAWAY, K.
   Rotograph Series 151 "The Base-ball player"   18 - 22   22 - 25
GIBSON, CHARLES DANA (See Artist-Signed)
GRIMBALL, META
   Gutmann & Gutmann "The Champion"   40 - 45   45 - 50
H.H. (H. HERMAN) (See Blacks, Artist-Signed)
K in box logo
   Raphael Tuck
      Series 2339 (6)   22 - 25   25 - 30

O. Naughty, Empire Art
769 – "Batter–up!"

C. A. Voight, ©C. A. Voight
No. 1, "Left Fielder"

Pub. O. D. Williams,106
"Say–Who's Boss of this..."

NAUGHTY, O. (US)
  Empire Art Co.

Series 769 (4) **Glamorous Baseball Ladies**	30 - 40	40 - 50

PHIFER, L.C. (US) **(See Blacks, Artist-Signed)**
ROBERSON, ROBERT (US)
  Edward Gross

208 Boy Ready to pitch	20 - 25	25 - 30
209 Player squaring to bunt	20 - 25	25 - 30
210 Catcher doffing mask	20 - 25	25 - 30
211 Three Fans cheering	20 - 25	25 - 30

SHINN, COBB X. (US)

H.W.P. Co. Children (12)	12 - 15	15 - 18

TWELVETREES, C. (US)
  Edward Gross   **Various Children**

Color issues	15 - 20	20 - 25
B&W issues	12 - 15	15 - 20

VOIGHT, C.A. (US)
  C.A. Voight Children (12)

1 "Left Fielder"	25 - 30	30 - 35
4 "First Baseman"	25 - 30	30 - 35
12 "The Water Boy"	30 - 35	35 - 40
Others	15 - 18	18 - 22

WALL, BERNHARDT (US)
  S. Bergman

Series 6501 (12)	12 - 15	15 - 20

PUBLISHERS

AA in circle logo **(Anglo-American)**

Series 32 **"Baseball Notes"** (8) (B&W)	35 - 40	40 - 45

A H Co. *

Baseball Humor (6)	15 - 18	18 - 22

AMP. Co. in a shield

Series 504 **"To My Valentine"** (6) (Emb)		
Series 809 **"The National Game"** (6) *	20 - 25	25 - 30

Same without titles (6) (Emb)	20 - 25	25 - 30
* Same as 504 except title		
F. von Bardelban (7)	22 - 25	25 - 28
S. Bergman		
Series 8811 **"Good Old Summertime"** (12)	15 - 18	18 - 22
Series 8812 **"Fill in the City Series"** (11 known)	10 - 12	12 - 16
Colonial Art Publishing Co.		
Printed Photos (9) (Sepia)	6 - 8	8 - 12
Eagle & Shield logo		
Heavily Embossed "Airbrushed Series"	20 - 25	25 - 28
The Fairman Co.		
Series 159 Blacks (8) (Color)	30 - 35	35 - 38
B&W issues	25 - 30	30 - 35
G.D. & D.		
Children Series 5017 (12)	22 - 25	25 - 28
I. Grollman		
Political Baseball "Presidential Camp" (4)	150 - 175	175 - 200
H in circle logo (8 known)	18 - 20	20 - 25
H.I.R. around circle logo (B&W)		
Girl and player photo (10)	15 - 18	18 - 22
F. Haas		
"Baseball Series" 66 (B&W) (6)	15 - 18	18 - 22
O.E. Hasselman (6)	20 - 25	25 - 28
J. Raymond Howe Co.		
Series 2715 (4 known)	18 - 22	22 - 26
A.H. Katz		
Children (B&W) (6)	18 - 22	22 - 26
Kosmos Art Co.		
"The Richard Carle" Baseball Series 1090 (17+)	20 - 25	25 - 30
L&R, New York		
"Fan-ie Series 100" Kewpies (12)	15 - 20	20 - 25
Leather Postcards	20 - 25	25 - 30
Pink of Perfection		
Series 159 Blacks (6)	35 - 40	40 - 50
C. J. Rose (20)	18 - 22	22 - 26
H.M. Rose		
Ball and Crossed Bats (Emb) with Verse (8)	20 - 25	25 - 30
Roth & Langley		
Printed Photo type (Sepia) (Glossy Finish) (26+)	10 - 12	12 - 16
SB in circle logo (**Samson Bros.**)		
Series 91	12 - 15	15 - 20
Series S114	12 - 15	15 - 20
Series A115	12 - 15	15 - 20
Series S125 Little boys in overalls (12) (B&W)	15 - 18	18 - 22
Series S129 Little Boy – Blue-striped Border (12 ?)	15 - 18	18 - 22
Series S256	12 - 15	15 - 18
Series CS459 Children	12 - 15	15 - 18
Series CS507 Boy & Girl (12)	15 - 18	18 - 22
Ullman Mfg. Co.		
Baseball Kidlets Series 195 (8)	22 - 26	26 - 32
Maurice Wells (A.T.F. Co., Chicago)		
"Baseball Series" Blacks	35 - 40	40 - 50
O.D. Williams		
"Boston Baseball" Series (12)	20 - 25	25 - 28

ANONYMOUS SERIES

"Balligan"
Similar to "Billikens" (12)   25 - 30   30 - 35
"Baseball Series"
Red Borders - Top has 13 baseballs (B&W) (12)   15 - 20   20 - 23
Blacks (1)   25 - 30   30 - 35
Black Border Series
Wide Black Border (Girl and Player) (B&W) (8)   15 - 18   18 - 22
Embossed Edges Series
Sepia and Creme (15 +)
Printed photo-types of Girls and Players   15 - 18   18 - 22
Series 113   (Sepia)   (Slightly oversized)
Shows Girls and Player (9 +)   15 - 18   18 - 22
Series 312   White around Brown Border   (12)
Small Baseball Scene at bottom   12 - 15   15 - 18
Blacks (1)   20 - 25   25 - 30
Series 529   (B&W)
Printed Photo-type - Player & Girls (8)   18 - 22   22 - 25
Photo Montage Series 720   (Printed Photo-types)
Men/Girls on Baseball Diamond (12)   15 - 18   18 - 22
No Identification #1   (4)   20 - 25   25 - 28
No Identification #2   Boy with Bat   20 - 25   25 - 30
No Identification # 3   (12) (B&W)
Baseball & Position on Pennant   18 - 20   20 - 25

MAJOR LEAGUE STADIUMS
1900-1910   (Average)   40 - 60   60 - 80
Real Photos   80 - 100   100 - 150
1910-1920   20 - 35   35 - 50
Real Photos   50 - 60   60 - 80
1920-1940   15 - 20   20 - 30
Real Photos   30 - 40   40 - 50
Linens, 1940-1949   5 - 15   15 - 25
Chromes   2 - 4   4 - 10

MINOR LEAGUE PARKS & STADIUMS
1900-1935   10 - 12   12 - 15
Others   5 - 8   8 - 10

Crosley Field, Cincinnati, Ohio   *Wrigley Field, Chicago, Illinois*
"Home of the Cincinnati Reds"   *"Home of the Chicago Cubs"*

BOXING

Early 1900-1930

Abe Attell	30 - 40	40 - 50
Real Photos	50 - 60	60 - 75
Al Brown (RP)	30 - 40	40 - 50
Frankie Burns (RP)	30 - 40	40 - 50
Tommy Burns	30 - 40	40 - 50
Real Photos	100 - 150	150 - 200
Georges Carpentier (RP)	20 - 25	25 - 30
James J. Corbett (RP)	80 - 100	100 - 125
Johnny Coulon	20 - 30	30 - 45
Jack Dempsey	25 - 30	30 - 40
Real Photos (Willard-Dempsey Fight)	40 - 50	50 - 70
Jack Dillon (RP)	45 - 55	55 - 65
Bob Fitzsimmons (Real Photo by Weidner)	70 - 80	80 - 90
Jim Flynn (Real Photo by C.E.J.C.)	70 - 80	80 - 90
Joe Gans (Real Photo by Weidner)	75 - 125	125 - 200
Joe Jeannette (RP)	30 - 40	40 - 50
Jim Jeffries	25 - 30	30 - 40
Real Photos by Dana Studios	50 - 60	60 - 80
Jefferies-Johnson Fight	80 - 100	100 - 150
Jack Johnson, Heavyweight Champ, 1908-1915	35 - 40	40 - 50
Real Photos		
With U.S. Flag as Belt	125 - 150	150 - 175
Birmingham Smallwares (5 known)	400 - 500	500 - 600
C.E.J.C. Photo (RP)	125 - 150	150 - 175
Johnson and white wife at dinner table	750 - 900	900 - 1100
Conn and Cann Photo		
Johnson and Cotton with white wife at ringside.	600 - 700	700 - 800
Dana Studios or Dana Photo, San Francisco (RP)		
Dana was official photographer of Johnson		
and Jeffries Fight. Over 30 cards exist		
with logo.	125 - 150	150 - 175

Jack Dempsey
Real Photo by Dix

Jim Jeffries
EDL Photo, French

Jack Johnson, Birmingham
Small Wares, Australia, 2

*C.E.J.C. Photo, Jack Johnson and His
Wife, Las Vegas, NM (July 4, 1912)*

*C.E.J.C. Photo, Jack Johnson with Party &
Wife, Las Vegas, NM (May 2, 1918?)*

*"Jack Johnson"
Rotary Photo, No. 7169-A*

*Stanley Ketchel–Johnson Pre-Fight
Oct.16, 1909, Dana Photo*

*"Jess Willard & Trainers, Havana, Cuba"
Anonymous Real Photo, 1915*

D.W.A. Photo		
Johnson arrives in Las Vegas, N.M.		
with white wife.	400 - 500	500 - 600
"Mirror of Life" Series	125 - 150	150 - 200
Rotary Photo Co. (RP)	100 - 125	125 - 150
Sport & General (Printed Photos)	70 - 80	80 - 100
Weidner Photo, San Francisco (RP)	100 - 125	125 - 150
Anonymous (RP)		
Johnson and his white wife standing with others	650 - 850	850 - 1000
Johnson shaking hands with John L. Sullivan	400 - 500	500 - 600
Stanley Ketchel		
Dana Photo (RP)		
Johnson-Ketchel Contest	150 - 175	175 - 230

93. Ketchel-Papke Contest	70 - 80	80 - 100
Weidner Photo (RP)	100 - 125	125 - 200
Johnny Kilbane (RP)	30 - 40	40 - 50
Sam Langford	25 - 30	30 - 40
Dana Photo	70 - 80	80 - 90
Ted "Kid" Lewis (RP)	40 - 50	50 - 60
Sam Mac Vea	30 - 40	40 - 50
Real Photos	40 - 50	50 - 65
Luther McCarty (Died in Ring, 1913)	50 - 60	60 - 75
Billy Papke (RP)	50 - 60	60 - 70
Paddy Ryan Dana Photo Reproduction, 1908	50 - 60	60 - 70
Tom Sharkey (RP)	40 - 50	50 - 60
John L. Sullivan Dana Photo Reproduction, 1908	75 - 100	100 - 150
Gene Tunney	20 - 25	25 - 35
Real Photos	30 - 40	40 - 50
Freddie Welsh (RP)	50 - 60	60 - 70
Jess Willard		
Training for Johnson fight (RP)	50 - 60	60 - 70
Johnson-Willard fight, 1915 (RP)	70 - 80	80 - 90
1930-1960 ERA		
Georges Carpentier (RP)	15 - 20	20 - 25
Billy Conn	15 - 20	20 - 25
Jack Dempsey		
Eagle Postcard Co. Dempsey and Restaurant	15 - 20	20 - 25
Real Photos	25 - 30	30 - 40
Linen Postcards	10 - 12	12 - 15
Dempsey-Carpentier Fight	30 - 35	35 - 40
Dempsey-Willard Fight		
I.F.S. from N. Moser Real Photos AZO backs		
"Willard & Dempsey-World Champ. Bout"	30 - 40	40 - 50
The Ring and surrounding Crowd	25 - 30	30 - 35
"Willard takes some heavy punishment"	40 - 45	45 - 55
"Willard Counted Out"		
Jack Dempsey, Real Photos by "Ross," Berlin	20 - 25	25 - 30
Zora Folley Advertising Card	20 - 25	25 - 30
Harry Jeffra (B&W)	15 - 20	20 - 25
Joe Louis		
Real Photos	25 - 30	30 - 40
Printed or color	15 - 20	20 - 25
Orcajo Photo Art (RP) (...Joe and Marva)	125 - 150	150 - 175
Advertising	30 - 40	40 - 60
Chrome	10 - 12	12 - 15
Rocky Marciano	20 - 25	25 - 28
Real Photos	30 - 40	40 - 50
Muhammed Ali	8 - 10	10 - 20
Cassius Clay	15 - 20	20 - 25
"Sugar Ray" Robinson	15 - 20	20 - 30
Real Photos	30 - 35	35 - 45
Advertising, Restaurant, etc.	30 - 35	35 - 40
Max Schmeling (RP)	20 - 25	25 - 30
Other Heavyweight Champions	10 - 20	20 - 30
Other Weight Champions	5 - 10	10 - 15
Exhibit Supply Company Issues	5 - 10	10 - 15
Champions	15 - 25	25 - 50

"Blanchertown Ind. Basket Ball Team,
Blanchertown, Mass." Pub./D. W. Short

Anonymous Real Photo, ca. 1908-09
Female Basketball Player

"Navy Football Team, 1905, Annap.,
Md." – Pub. by Charles G. Feldmever

HIGH SCHOOL & COLLEGE		
Boxers and Teams, Identified	10 - 15	15 - 25
ARTIST-SIGNED		
1900-1920	15 - 20	20 - 35
Blacks	20 - 25	25 - 40
1920-1940	10 - 12	12 - 15
Blacks	15 - 20	20 - 25

BASKETBALL

Identified Players and Teams, Printed	12 - 15	15 - 18
Blanchertown Ind. Team, Blanchertown, MA	15 - 20	20- 25
Unidentified	8 - 10	10 - 12
Real Photos, Identified	20 - 25	25 - 30
Unidentified	10 - 12	12 - 15

FOOTBALL

Exhibit Supply Co. B&W, Tints (32)		
Postcard Backs only		
Baugh, Graham, Connerly, Waterfield	30 - 40	40 - 50
Hirsch, Matson, Layne, Ratterman,	20 - 25	25 - 30
Fears, Motley, Matson, Trippi	20 - 25	25 - 30
Others	10 - 15	15 - 20
Red Grange	25 - 30	30 - 40
Jim Thorpe	30 - 40	40 - 50
Real Photo	50 - 70	70 - 90

Black Golf Caddies, 1905
Real Photo by AZO

Famous Player, W. T.
Tilden, Anon. R.P. #32

Real Photo of Glamourous
Young Girl

Professional Stars, early	15 - 20	20 - 30
College Players, early	10 - 15	15 - 20
Navy Team, 1905	20 - 25	25 - 30
High School Players, early	8 - 10	10 - 12

GOLF

Pre-1930 Stars	40 - 50	50 - 60
1930-1960 Stars	30 - 35	35 - 50
Artist-Signed (See Artist-Signed Chapter)	15 - 20	20 - 40
Caddies, Real Photos	20 - 25	25 - 30
Real Photos	12 - 15	15 - 25
Black Caddies		
Large Images	90 - 110	110 - 150
Small Images	50 - 60	60 - 70
Real Photos	12 - 15	15 - 25
Ladies with clubs, bag, etc.	20 - 25	25 - 35
Children, Men with clubs, bag, etc.	15 - 20	20 - 25
Movie Stars	15 - 20	20 - 25
Courses or famous Holes	10 - 12	12 - 16
Golf Advertising, Artist-Signed	35 - 45	45 - 75
Golf Courses, Famous Holes	5 - 8	8 - 12
with players in action	5 - 8	8 - 12

TENNIS

Artist-Signed (See Artist-Signed Chapter)	15 - 20	20 - 30
Tennis Advertising	25 - 35	35 - 50
Courts and players in action	4 - 6	6 - 10
Real Photos		
Pre-1930		
Famous Players	25 - 30	30 - 40
Movie Stars	15 - 20	20 - 30
Players with racket	15 - 18	18 - 22
Children with racket	15 - 18	18 - 22
Unidentified players	10 - 15	15 - 20

Real Photo by NBC, Series 8822/1
Unidentified Tennis Couple

Jesse Owens, Real Photo, No. 61 (Official
Carte) – 1936 Olympics

Jim Thorpe, Granbergs, 238
R.P., 1912 Olympics

Courts and players in action	4 - 6	6 - 10
Post-1930		
Players	8 - 10	10 - 12
Famous Players	15 - 20	20 - 30
Movie Stars	15 - 20	20 - 25
Courts	3 - 5	5 - 7

TRACK AND FIELD

Jesse Owens	20 - 25	25 - 30
Real Photo 1936 Olympics (2)	40 - 50	50 - 60
Jim Thorpe	30 - 40	40 - 50
1912 Stockholm Olympics Official Cards (RP)		
238 "Winner of the Penthalon and Decathalon"	90 - 100	100 - 120
Other 1912 US Olympian Track/Field participants	40 - 50	50 - 60
108 Ralph Craig, 100 meters winner	50 - 60	60 - 70
Others	40 - 50	50 - 60

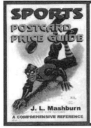

U.S. VIEWS

From their beginning as the "Pioneers" in the 1890's through the "chromes" of today, view cards have been the dominant collectible motif in the entire postcard hobby. Other types have periods of high interest only to level off and even lose popularity at times. Not so with view cards. A large majority of collectors get their start by collecting views of their home town. They have this great interest because of their familiarity with the city, town, or community as it is today, and the desire to know what it was like in earlier years.

This desire prompts each collector-historian to search every possible avenue to obtain all collectible gems of earlier years. The more views they find of the court house, post office, etc., the more they wonder if there was also one of the depot, the barber shop, meat market, and others. As the search continues, the interest expands to other views, possibly of a nearby town, a once visited memorable city, and finally for those from all over their state. The fever elevates until the home town collector has become a full-blown postcard collector who will travel hundreds of miles and spend countless hours to enhance his collection.

Although small town views are the most popular and command the highest prices, the collector has now started searching for other views of busy main streets, trolleys, depots, banks, etc., and does not care whether the town is large or small, whether in Missouri or North Carolina...it just doesn't really matter. This trend elevates the price of topicals and makes all small town views much dearer.

On the negative side, however, views of large cities such as New York, Washington, D.C., Philadelphia, etc., and tourist attractions such as Niagara Falls, Mount Vernon, Watkins Glen, Grand Canyon, Yellowstone Park and others, have very little value because of the millions produced for the people who visit and buy them as proof of being there. These are known in the hobby as "tourist trap"cards, and no collector or dealer will buy them. Only very special views in these areas have any value at all. Unnamed views and scenic views of mountains, rivers, lakes, etc., are also shunned by collectors.

THE VIEW PUBLISHER

Among the great early Pioneer publishers were **The Albertype Co., American Souvenir Co., E.C. Kropp, Arthur Livingston, Ed. Lowey, H.A. Rost, Souvenir Postal Card Co.,** and **Walter Wirth**. Views by these, plus those by anonymous publishers pre-1900, are extremely scarce and are rarely found.

More familiar to today's view collector are names like **American Souvenir Co., A.C. Bosselman, Detroit Publishing Co., Illustrated Postcard Co., Kraemer Art, Hugh Leighton, Rotograph Co., Edw. H. Mitchell, Curt Teich, Raphael Tuck,** and **Valentine & Sons**. These are among the most prolific of the era and are bylines most noted on cards that remain today. They usually sent representatives to all areas several times each year to take photos of the principal street scenes, statues, schools, and buildings. On the return trip, the representative would bring the photos and printing proofs and take orders from the drugstores and other postcard sellers. Photos were retouched (power lines, obstructions, etc., removed) and colored to conform with the natural shade as nearly as possible. Resulting orders were returned to the merchant by mail. File copies were retained by merchants for future orders.

Basically, this is how the tremendous view card business was handled throughout the U.S. Thanks to these photographers, publishers and distributors, histories of small town America have been recorded for future generations and have made it possible for the postcard hobby to attain unbelievable heights.

VIEWS

View cards are classified as to Era for this listing.

    1 = **Postcard Era** - 1900-1915
    2 = **White Border Era** - 1915-1930
    3 = **Linen Era** - 1930's-1940's

Values listed are for general views of the particular motif. Outstanding views, or special subject matter, may be valued higher. On the other hand, a poorly printed image would lessen the value.

According to the majority of dealers and collectors, the actual selling prices of view cards have basically the same value structure in most all states of the U.S. It all depends on the particular view and how much the collector is willing to pay. For instance, a collector in North Carolina will pay much more for a North Carolina view than a collector from Florida would pay for the same view. See Real Photo Section for higher valued views.

	VG	EX
U.S. PIONEER VIEWS, 1893-1898		
"Patriographics" by American Souv. Card Co.		
Alaska 6	$ 25 - 30	$ 30 - 40
Baltimore 12	15 - 20	20 - 25
Various Publishers	12 - 15	15 - 25
U.S. PRIVATE MAILING CARDS, 1898-1901		
Various Publishers	5 - 10	10 - 15
U.S. VIEWS		
Airports-1	5 - 10	10 - 15

Airports-2	5 - 8	8 - 12
Airports-3 (Add $2-4 for R.P.)	1 - 2	2 - 5
Amusement Parks-1 (Add $5-8 for R.P.)	8 - 12	12 - 20
Amusement Parks-2 (Add $4-7 for R.P.)	7 - 10	10 - 15
Amusement Parks-3 (Add $3-5 for R.P.)	2 - 3	3 - 5
Banks-1 (Add $3-5 for R.P.)	3 - 5	5 - 8
Banks-2 (Add $2-4 for R.P)	1 - 2	2 - 4
Banks-3 (Add $1-2 for R.P.)	0.50 - 1	1 - 1.50
Birds Eye View-1 (Add $4-7 for R.P.)	3 - 5	5 - 8
Birds Eye View-2 (Add $3-5 for R.P.)	2 - 3	3 - 5
Birds Eye View-3 (Add $1-2 for R.P.)	1 - 1.50	1 .50 - 2
Bridges-1 (Add $1-2 for R.P.)	1 - 2	2 - 3
Bridges-2 (Add $1 for R.P.)	1.50 - 2	2 - 2.50
Bridges-3	0.50 - 1	1 - 1.50
Bus Stations-1	N/A	N/A
Bus Stations-2 (Add $3-5 for R.P.)	5 - 8	8 - 12
Bus Stations-3 (Add $1-2 for R.P.)	2 - 3	3 - 5
Cemetery-1 (Add $2-3 for R.P.)	5 - 6	6 - 8
Cemetery-2 (Add $1-2 for R.P.)	4 - 5	5 - 6
Cemetery-3 (Add $1 for R.P.)	2 - 3	3 - 4
Churches-1 (Add $3-4 for R.P.)	3 - 4	4 - 6
Churches-2 (Add $1-2 for R.P.)	1 - 2	2 - 4
Churches-3 (Add $1 for R.P.)	1 - 1.50	1.50 - 2
Colleges-1 (Add $3-4 for R.P.)	2 - 4	4 - 7

Pioneer "Patriographic," Alaska 6
American Souvenir-Card Co., 1897

Pioneer "Patriographic," Baltimore 12
American Souvenir-Card Co., 1897

P.M.C. of "Soldiers' & Sailors' Monument"
Indianapolis, Ind. by E. C. Kropp, No. 159

Colleges-2	(Add $2-3 for R.P.)	1 - 2	2 - 5
Colleges-3	(Add $1-2 for R.P.)	1 - 1.50	1.50 - 2
County Fair-1	(Add $5-8 for R.P.)	8 - 12	12 - 16
County Fair-2	(Add $3-4 for R.P.)	5 - 7	7 - 10
County Fair-3	(Add $2 for R.P.)	3 - 5	5 - 8
Court House-1	(Add $3-4 for R.P.)	3 - 4	4 - 7
Court House-2	(Add $2-3 for R.P.)	2 - 3	3 - 5
Court House-3	(Add $1 for R.P.)	1 - 1.50	1.50 - 2
Depots-1	(Add $5-10 for R.P.)	7 - 10	10 - 20
Depots-2	(Add $4-7 for R.P.)	3 - 7	7 - 12
Depots-3	(Add $3-4 for R.P.)	2 - 3	3 - 5
Diners-1		N/A	N/A
Diners-2	(Add $20-25 for R.P.)	30 - 50	50 - 85
Diners-3	(Add $15-20 for R.P.)	20 - 40	40 - 75
Drug Stores-1	(Add $10-12 for R.P.)	10 - 15	15 - 20
Drug Stores-2	(Add $6-9 for R.P.)	8 - 10	10 - 12
Drug Stores-3	(Add $2-3 for R.P.)	3 - 4	3 - 6
Fire Department-1	(Add $7-10 for R.P.)	10 - 12	12 - 16
Fire Department-2	(Add $4-7 for R.P.)	5 - 8	8 - 12
Fire Department-3	(Add $2-3 for R.P.)	3 - 4	4 - 6
Funeral Homes-1	(Add $3-5 for R.P.)	7 - 10	10 - 14
Funeral Homes-2	(Add $2-3 for R.P.)	6 - 8	9 - 11
Funeral Homes-3	(Add $1-2 for R.P.)	4 - 5	5 - 7
Garages/Gas Stations-1	(Add $7-10 for R.P.)	10 - 15	15 - 20

Ess & Ess Photo Co., Lutheran Church
Maiden, N. C. – ca. 1920

Ess & Ess Photo Co., R. R. Depot
Maiden, N. C. – ca. 1920

Ess & Ess Photo Co., Victor Hotel
Maiden, N. C. – ca. 1920

Souvenir Post Card Co., 12075
Public Library, Laconia, N. H.

Hugh Leighton & Sons, No. 6935
Main Street, St. Albans, Vermont

Garages/Gas Stations-2 (Add $5-7 for R.P.	7 - 12	12 - 15
Garages/Gas Stations-3 (Add $3-4 for R.P.)	8 - 12	12 - 15
General Stores-1 (Add $7-10 for R.P.)	5 - 8	8 - 12
General Stores-2 (Add $5-8 for R.P.)	4 - 6	6 - 8
General Stores-3 (Add $3-4 for R.P.)	2 - 3	3 - 5
Gymnasiums-1 (Add $4-5 for R.P.)	4 - 7	7 - 10
Gymnasiums-2 (Add $3-4 for R.P.)	3 - 5	5 - 8
Gymnasiums-3 (Add $1-2 for R.P.)	1 - 2	2 - 3
Home for Aged; Deaf & Dumb; Insane-1 (+ $3-5 for R.P.)	5 - 7	7 - 10
Home for Aged; Deaf & Dumb; Insane-2 (+ $2-3 for R.P.)	4 - 6	6 - 8
Home for Aged; Deaf & Dumb; Insane-3 (+ 1-2 for R.P.)	3 - 4	4 - 6
Hospitals-1 (Add $3-5 for R.P.)	3 - 5	5 - 10
Hospitals-2 (Add $2-3 for R.P.)	2 - 3	3 - 6
Hospitals-3 (Add $1-2 for R.P.)	1 - 1.50	1.50 - 2
Hotels-1 (Add $3-5 for R.P.)	3 - 5	5 - 8
Hotels-2 (Add $2-3 for R.P.)	2 - 3	3 - 5
Hotels-3 (Add $1-2 for R.P.)	1 - 2	2 - 3
Library-1 (Add $3-4 for R.P.)	3 - 5	5 - 7
Library-2 (Add $2-3 for R.P.)	2 - 3	3 - 5
Library-3 (Add $1-2 for R.P.	1 - 2	2 - 3
Main Streets-1 (Add $5-10 for R.P.)	5 - 8	8 - 12
Main Streets-2 (Add $3-7 for R.P.)	4 - 5	5 - 8
Main Streets-3 (Add $2-3 for R.P.	1 - 2	2 - 4
Mills/Mfg. Plants-1 (Add $5-8 for R.P.)	4 - 7	7 - 12
Mills/Mfg. Plants-2 (Add $4-6 for R.P.)	3 - 5	5 - 8
Mills/Mfg. Plants-3 (Add $1-2 for R.P.)	1 - 2	2 - 4
Motels-1	N/A	N/A
Motels-2 (Add $7-10 for R.P.)	4 - 7	7 - 9
Motels-3 (Add $4-6 for R.P.)	2 - 3	3 - 5
Opera-1 (Add $7-9 for R.P.)	7 -10	10 - 15
Opera-2 (Add $4-6 for R.P.)	5 - 7	7 - 10
Opera-3 (Add $2-3 for R.P.)	2 - 3	3 - 6
Parks-1 (Add $2-3 for R.P.)	2 - 3	3 - 6
Parks-2 (Add $1-2 for R.P.)	1 - 1.50	1.50 - 2
Parks-3 (Add $1 for R.P.)	0.50 - 1	1 - 1.50
Post Office-1 (Add $4-6 for R.P.)	3 - 5	5 - 8
Post Office-2 (Add $2-3 for R.P.)	2 - 3	3 - 5
Post Office-3 (Add $1-2 for R.P.)	1 - 1.50	1.50 - 2
Prisons-1 (Add $4-7 for R.P.)	6 - 9	9 - 12

Curt Teich Linen, No. 7A-H3252
Kilby Prison, Montgomery, Alabama

G. W. Morris, No. 119435
Bethlehem Street, Bethlehem, N.H.

Prisons-2 (Add $3-4 for R.P.)	3 - 5	5 - 8
Prisons-3 (Add $1-2 for R.P.)	2-3	3 - 4
Restaurants-1 (Add $5-7 for R.P.)	9 - 12	12 - 15
Restaurants-2 (Add $4-6 for R.P.)	5 - 7	7 - 10
Restaurants-3 (Add $3-4 for R.P.)	2 - 3	3 - 5
Rivers, Creeks-1 (Add $1-2 for R.P.)	1 - 2	2 - 3
Rivers, Creeks-2 (Add $1 for R.P.)	1 - 1.50	1.50 - 2
Rivers, Creeks-3 (Add $0.50 for R.P.)	0.50 - 1	1 - 1.50
Roadside Stands-1	N/A	N/A
Roadside Stands-2 (Add $7-10 for R.P.)	7 - 12	12 - 16
Roadside Stands-3 (Add $5-7 for R.P.)	3 - 5	5 - 8
Schools-1 (Add $4-7 for R.P.)	3 - 5	5 - 7
Schools-2 (Add $3-5 for R.P.)	2 - 3	3 - 4
Schools-3 (Add $1-2 for R.P.)	1 - 1.50	1.50 - 2
Soldiers' Home-1 (Add $4-7 for R.P.)	5 - 7	7 - 12
Soldiers' Home-2 (Add $3-5 for R.P.)	4 - 6	6 - 8
Soldiers' Home-3 (Add $2-3 for R.P.)	3-4	4 - 6
Statues-1 (Add $1-2 for R.P.)	1 - 2	2 - 3
Statues-2 (Add $1 for R.P.)	1.50 - 2	2 - 2.50
Statues-3 (Add $0.50-1 for R.P.)	0.50 - 1	1 - 1.50
Street Scenes-1 (Add $6-9 for R.P.)	5 - 10	10 - 15
Street Scenes-2 (Add $4-6 for R.P.)	3 - 5	5 - 8
Street Scenes-3 (Add $2-3 for R.P.)	1 - 2	2 - 4
Busy-1 (Add $4-6 for R.P.)	7 - 12	12 - 16
Busy-2 (Add $3-4 for R.P.)	4 - 7	7 - 10
Busy-3 (Add $1-2 for R.P.)	2 - 3	3 - 5
W/Parades-1 (Add $8-10 for R.P.)	10 - 15	15 - 18
W/Parades-2 (Add $5-7 for R.P.)	5 - 8	8 - 12
W/Parades-3 (Add $3-5 for R.P.)	2 - 3	3 - 5
W/Large Identified Store Fronts-1 (Add $4-7 for R.P.)	7 - 12	12 - 16
W/Large Identified Store Fronts-2 (Add $3-4 for R.P.)	4 - 7	7 - 12
W/Large Identified Store Fronts-3 (Add $2-3 for R.P.)	3 - 4	4 - 7
Tennis Courts-1 (Add $4-7 for R.P.)	6 - 10	10 - 16
Tennis Courts-2 (Add $3-5 for R.P.)	5 - 7	7 - 10
Tennis Courts-3 (Add $2-3 for R.P.)	3 - 4	4 - 6
Theatres-1 (Add $5-8 for R.P.)	8 - 10	10 - 16
Theatres-2 (Add 3-5 for R.P.)	7 - 8	8 - 12
Theatres-3 (Add 2-3 for R.P.)	4 - 5	5 - 7
YMCA or YWCA-1 (Add $4-6 for R.P.)	7 - 10	10 - 15

Anonymous, Y.M.C.A.
Adrian, Michigan

Souvenir Post Card Co., No. 13300
Beach & Ocean Front, Atlantic City, N.J.

YMCA or YWCA-2	(Add $3-4 for R.P.)	5 - 8	8 - 12
YMCA or YWCA-3	(Add $2-3 for R.P.)	3- 4	4 - 6
MISCELLANEOUS			
Views or multiview in Pansies, Fish-types, Butterfly Wings, etc.		7 - 10	10 - 20

FOREIGN VIEWS

While the hobby in the U.S. grows by leaps and bounds, postcard collecting also thrives in other countries of the world. Great Britain, France, Germany and Italy are the leaders in Europe, but others are not far behind. What do they collect? They collect Topographicals, which are simply view cards showing all the various motifs of almost every description, and they are the rage.

Foreigners also collect cards of their home towns and soon expand to views of other towns, cities, and countries searching for motifs of their choice. Therefore, the search for good material now includes most all countries throughout the world. Collectors should reevaluate the contents of those boxes and albums of old foreign cards they believed worthless. Of special interest are early pre-1905 Chromolithographic Gruss Aus and vignette views of all countries. These early chromolithographs, usually multi-views, were printed by a special process where the design was etched on soft stone and printed in the various colors. Large irregular dots can be seen, usually with a magnifying glass, throughout the image surface as opposed to dots all the same size in the regularly printed lithograph cards.

After the chromolithograph cards, the most desired are identified topographicals...of people doing things, occupations, events, happenings, disasters, store and business fronts, exceptional busy street scenes, etc. These types, of course, are also those most desired by like collectors in the U.S., and the values are comparable in most instances. Therefore, the collector value of a small town depot in England or Germany would have a relative value to an American collector of a depot in a small town in the U.S.

The rarest and most highly valued foreign views are those of the tiny and thinly populated countries, colony possessions, and islands. Rarer still, with even higher valuations, are "postally used in country of origin" views of these cards. The philatelic value can be many times that of the image or scene. An unused view of tiny Bhutan is valued at around $6, but the same card stamped and postmarked in Bhutan commands $40 or more.

Special events make many cards more valuable. For instance, the Royal Visit to Ascension brings $40-45 unused, but up to $250 if postmarked in Ascension during that visit. As can be seen from these examples, a thorough examination of

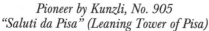

Pioneer by Kunzli, No. 905
"Saluti da Pisa" (Leaning Tower of Pisa)

Pioneer by F.S., Multiple View of
"Gruss aus Mainz"

seemingly "worthless" foreign views could prove to be most rewarding. Foreign dealers who appear at postcard shows in the U.S. are very happy to purchase worthwhile views.

Most views taken in larger cities, especiallyanygenerated for the tourist trade, have little value. The hordes of visitors to Paris, Rome, London, Brussels, Venice, Vienna, and other cities during postcards' golden years purchased tons of views of museums, churches, statues, buildings, landmarks, etc., so that millions still exist today. Many of these were the poorly printed black and white or sepia tones. However, many were also beautifully printed with radiant colors and can often be purchased for under $1.00 each by the patient collector.

The listings below should only be used as a guide to average values of views. It must be realized that views of various images could be valued much higher or lower, depending on the motif, the publisher, whether it is black and white, in color, a real photo, or other factors. Also, the demand by collectors in the city, town, or country of origin would determine whether the value is higher or lower.

EARLY CHROMOLITHOGRAPHS, Pre-1910
ALL COUNTRIES

Gruss Aus/Vignettes Single & Multi-views	5 - 10	10 - 15
Named Landscapes	4 - 5	5 - 7
Exhibitions	12 - 15	15 - 25
Festivals	15 - 20	20 - 30
Heraldic	8 - 12	12 - 16
Royalty Commeratives	12 - 15	15 - 30
Town/City Views, Color	5 - 8	8 - 12
Town/City Views, B&W or Sepia	3 - 4	4 - 7
Views in Shells, Fish, Leaves, etc.	5 - 8	8 - 12

PRINTED, Color, B&W and Real Photo, 1900-1920
EUROPEAN COUNTRIES

Costumes	1 - 2	2 - 4
Disasters	2 - 5	5 - 10
Industrial	2 - 4	4 - 9
Occupations	3 - 5	5 - 10
Small Town Street Scenes	3 - 5	5 - 10
Large City Views, Street Scenes	0.50 - 1	1 - 1.50
Synagogues	10 - 20	20 - 30

Exceptional views can be much higher.
French Occupational views are valued higher.

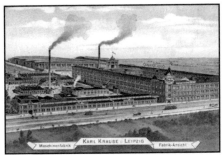

Pioneer by Julius Mocker
"Gruss aus Bremerhaven"

Emil Manner (München)
"...Kgl. Hofbrauhaus"

Anonymous, The Karl Krause Factory
Leipzig, Germany

AFRICAN NATIONS

Early Cards	2 - 5	5 - 10
Ethnic	2 - 4	4 - 7

AUSTRALIA

Early Cards	8 - 10	10 - 15
Aborigines	5 - 8	8 - 12
Animal Carts, Teams, Etc.	4 - 7	7 - 10
Gold Mining	4 - 7	7 - 12
Railway Stations, Works	6 - 9	9 - 12
Street Scenes	2 - 5	5 - 10

CANADA

Most values compare to those in U.S., Central and
South America, Cuba, Costa Rica, Bahamas, Barbados,
Bermuda, Puerto Rico, Dominican Republic, etc.

Early Cards	4 - 6	6 - 9
Costumes	1 - 2	2 - 2.50
Cities	1 - 1.50	1.50 - 2
Small Towns, Street Scenes, etc.	3 - 5	5 - 10
Industrial, Occupations	2 - 4	4 - 7
Railways, Stations	4 - 7	7 - 12
Ethnic	3 - 5	5 - 7

Exceptional views can be much higher.

RUSSIA & EASTERN EUROPE

Early Cards, Gruss Aus, etc.	4 - 7	7 - 12
Costumes	2 - 3	3 - 4

Cities	1 - 2	2 - 3
Small Towns, Street Scenes, etc.	4 - 5	5 - 7
Industrial	3 - 5	5 - 8
Occupations	4 - 6	6 - 9
Railways & Other Transportation	4 - 5	5 - 10
Ethnic	3 - 4	4 - 7

Exceptional views can be much higher.

FAR EASTERN COUNTRIES	Range	1 - 10

ISLANDS AND COLONIES, ETC., Early Cards*
   Price Range Only is listed

Aldabra	10 - 15
Andaman	8 - 10
Canary	3 - 7
Caroline	8 - 10
Cayman	20 - 25
Christmas	25 - 30
Coscos Keeling	25 - 30
Cook	12 - 15
Eastern	12 - 15
Falkland	10 - 35
Fanning	15 - 20
Faroe	12 - 15
Gilbert Isle and Lord Howe Isle	12 - 15
Mafia	8 - 12
New Guinea	8 - 12
Norfolk	20 - 25
Ocean	10 - 15
Perim	8 - 12
Pitcairn	15 - 20
Solomon	10 - 15
Thursday	15 - 20
Turks	15 - 20
Virgin	15 - 20
Others	1 - 10

* Cards stamped & postmarked in country of origin
  can have much higher values.

BRITISH, FRENCH, GERMAN, ETC., COLONIES

Early Cards	Range	4 - 15

To The Collectors and Readers of This Publication:

This reference has been a tremendous undertaking, and would have been impossible without the great effort and contributions of many collectors, dealers and postcard historians. We hope this book will fill the need for everyone in the hobby. However, we know that even though this fourth edition has hundreds of additional listings, there are more that we have not been able to find and, therefore, it is still incomplete. In order to make future editions even more comprehensive, we request that collectors send us any additions to checklists or publishers' listings that we may have missed.

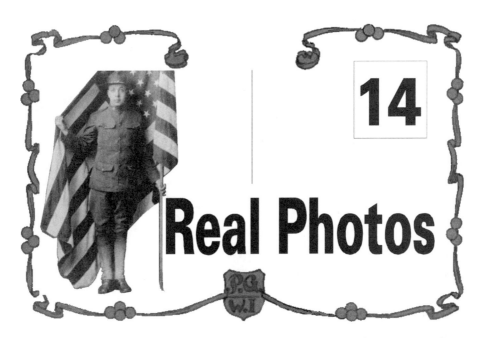

Real Photos

Real-Photo cards are still among the most popular groups as they continue their long climb from obscurity to the top of the view and topical fields. Their authenticity and portrayal of life and living as it actually was, plus the fact that many are one-of-a-kind, are determining factors to collectors.

It is important, in most instances, that the image be identified. Clarity and sharpness in the photo image is also extremely important so that all detail can be seen and the era can be determined. This is very important on unidentified photos. Each card must be judged on its own qualities, which makes it difficult to base values on the auction price of a similar card. For instance, an ice delivery wagon which is close-up, has sharp and clear features with legible name of the ice company and the city location could bring (to a person who really wanted it) up to $300. If another collector "really wanted it" then it could be bid up to $500. This euphoria does not make all ice delivery wagons worth $500...the image, location and desire make the price.

The most desired are those by amateur photographers of everyday life and "happenings," such as accidents, disasters, etc. However, those taken and signed by professionals, and distributed to the wholesale and retail trade are also widely collected. Real-photo collectors seek cards by these photographers just as avidly as a "beautiful lady"collector would seek cards of Fisher or Boileau.

Collectors must be wary of reproductions, especially in the transportation-related fields. Although easily spotted by the seasoned collector, some are actually being sold as originals to those who cannot spot the difference.

Various processes were used to produce real photo cards. AZO and VELOX were most used, with EKC, KRUXO, KODAK, CYKO, DARKO, and DOPS following (see chart on page 562).The process is notated in the stamp box area on the reverse, although many are not listed. Most European real photos have no byline.

	VG	EX
Automobiles		
Identified as to make -- Large Image	$ 20 - 25	$ 25 - 40

Anonymous 1911 Era Touring Automobile

Greyhound Bus at Depot in Keener, AL By EKC, ca. 1945

Small Image	10 - 15	15 - 20
Unidentified -- Large Image	12 - 15	15 - 20
Small Image	5 - 7	7 - 10
Buses		
Greyhound Bus at Depot, Keener, AL, ca 1945 (EKC)	20 - 25	25 - 35
Trucks		
Identified as to make – Large Image	20 - 25	25 - 35
Small Image	10 - 15	15 - 20
Unidentified – Large Image	10 - 12	12 - 15
Small Image	6 - 8	8 - 10
Auto Stage	35 - 40	40 - 45
Delivery Trucks		
Large Image, with Advertising	40 - 50	50 - 75
Small Image, with Advertising	30 - 35	35 - 45
Farm Trucks		
Large Image	15 - 20	20 - 25
Small Image	10 - 12	12 - 15
Service Vehicles		
Dump Trucks, etc., Large Image	25 - 30	30 - 40
Small Image	15 - 18	18 - 22
Mail Trucks – Large Image	20 - 25	25 - 35
Small Image	10 - 15	15 - 25
Fire Engines – Large Image	35 - 40	40 - 45
Small Image	12 - 15	15 - 25
Paddy Wagons	25 - 35	35 - 50
Farm Tractors		
Identified – Large Image	25 - 30	30 - 40
Small Image	10 - 15	15 - 25
Unidentified – Large Image	12 - 16	16 - 20
Small Image	8 - 12	12 - 15
Race Cars		
Large Image	20 - 30	30 - 50
Small Image	10 - 15	15 - 25
With Driver Identified – **Large Image**	30 - 35	35 - 55
Small Image	15 - 18	18 - 25
Motorcycles		
Identified – **Large Image**	25 - 30	30 - 40
BMW with side car	30 - 35	35 - 45
Small Image	15 - 20	20 - 25
Unidentified – **Large Image**	15 - 18	18 - 22
Small Image	8 - 10	10 - 12

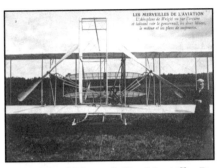

French Real Photo of "Les Merveilles De L'Aviation" – A Wright Airplane

Southern Pacific's Daylight Passenger Train, L.A. to San Francisco (by DOPS)

Bicycles
   Identified – Large Image   25 - 30   30 - 40
       Small Image   15 - 18   18 - 25
   Unidentified – Large Image   15 - 18   18 - 20
       Small Image   10 - 12   12 - 15
Airplanes   **(Also see Transportation)**
   Identified – **Large Image** (1896-1910)   20 - 30   30 - 45
       French "Les Merveilles..." (Wright Plane)   30 - 40   40 - 50
       Small Image   12 - 15   15 - 20
   With Pilot   20 - 30   30 - 40
Balloons
   Identified – **Large Image**   20 - 25   25 - 35
       Small Image   15 - 20   20 - 25
   Unidentified – **Large Image**   15 - 20   20 - 25
       Small Image   10 - 12   12 - 15
Dirigibles (Also see Zeppelins)
   Identified – **Large Image** (1898-1924)   20 - 30   30 - 50
       Small Image   15 - 20   20 - 30
   Unidentified – **Large Image**   15 - 20   20 - 25
       Small Image   10 - 12   12 - 15
Ships, Interior Views (Also see Transportation)   10 - 15   15 - 25
Trains, With Engine
   Identified – **Large Image**   15 - 25   25 - 40
   Unidentified – **Large Image**   10 - 15   15 - 20
   Identified – **Small Image; e.g. Southern Pacific**   12 - 15   15 - 18
   Passenger Car Interiors   20 - 25   25 - 35
   Repair Shops, Yards   15 - 20   20 - 25
   Repair Shop Interiors   15 - 20   20 - 25
Train Wrecks
   Identified – **Large Image**   10 - 20   20 - 30
       Small Image   8 - 10   10 - 20
   Unidentified -- **Large Image**   10 - 12   12 - 15
       Small Image   6 - 8   8 - 10
Train Depots
   Small Town, East *   10 - 15   15 - 30
       With Train in Station   15 - 20   20 - 35
   Large Town, East   5 - 8   8 - 15
   Small Town, West *   15 - 20   20 - 35
       With Train in Station   20 - 25   25 - 35
   Large Town, West   10 - 12   12 - 15
*   Special cards have auctioned from $100 to $150 each.

Trolley Car No. 620 of the Harper Center-Line – ca. 1912

Horse-Drawn Wagon Advertising Pabst Beer, Newark, N.J., ca. 1908

Trolley Cars		
Identified – Large Image	30 - 40	40 - 50
Small Image	15 - 20	20 - 30
Unidentified – Large Image	12 - 15	15 - 25
Small Image	8 - 10	10 - 12
Animal Drawn Transportation		
Horse & Buggy – Large Image	12 - 15	15 - 25
Small Image	8 - 10	10 - 15
Horse & Wagon, Carts – Large Image	12 - 15	15 - 25
Small Image	8 - 10	10 - 12
Goat Carts, With Children – Large Image	20 - 25	25 - 35
Small Image	10 - 12	12 - 15
Oxen-Driven Wagons	15 - 20	20 - 30
Horse-Drawn Delivery Wagons, Identified		
Beer – Large Image	75 - 100	100 - 125
Pabst Advertising Wagon	150 - 200	200 - 250
Small Image	40 - 50	50 - 65
Bread – Town Bakery		
Large Image	40 - 50	50 - 65
Small Image	25 - 35	35 - 40
Famous Name Bread -- Large Image	100 - 200	200 - 300
Small image	50 - 100	100 - 150
Ice – Large Image	50 - 60	60 - 85
Small Image	20 - 25	25 - 45
Mail – Large Image	50 - 60	60 - 85
Small Image	20 - 25	25 - 35
Coal – Large Image	50 - 60	60 - 75
Small Image	20 - 25	25 - 35
Others – Large Image	40 - 50	50 - 65
Small Image	20 - 25	25 - 35
Moving Vans/Freight Wagons – Large Image	40 - 50	50 - 65
Small Image	20 - 25	25 - 35
Horse-Drawn Sales Wagons		
Ice Cream – Large Image	60 - 80	80 - 110
Small Image	35 - 40	40 - 65
Bakery – Large Image	60 - 70	70 - 90
Small Image	30 - 35	35 - 50
Dairy – Large Image	25 - 35	35 - 50
Small Image	20 - 25	25 - 30
Grocery – Large	50 - 60	60 - 85
Small Image	30 - 35	35 - 45

Interior, Sparks Drug Store, ca. 1910
Greenville, Texas – By KRUXO

Interior of Dairy Lunch Bar, ca.1909
By AZO

Bakery Shop, Minneapolis, MN, ca. 1908
By AZO

St. A. & Dak. Elev. Co. Lumber Office
Minneapolis, MN Area, ca. 1909

Laundry – Large Image	30 - 35	35 - 40
Small Image	25 - 30	30 - 35
Others – Large Image	30 - 35	35 - 40
Small Image	25 - 30	30 - 35
Motorized Delivery Trucks		
Grocery	50 - 75	75 - 100
Ice Cream	75 - 100	100 - 150
Ice and Coal	50 - 75	75 - 100
Soft Drinks	75 -100	100 - 125
W/Drink Type	200 - 300	300 - 400
Fire Engines		
Hose Trucks	25 - 30	30 - 35
Horse-Driven Fire Engines	25 - 35	35 - 45
Horse-Driven Equipment	25 - 30	30 - 40
Small Business Buildings, **Identified**		
Auto Dealerships – Store Fronts	40 - 50	50 - 75
W/identified Auto in front	50 - 60	60 - 80
Bakeries – Store Fronts	20 - 25	25 - 40
Interiors	20 - 25	25 - 35
Banks – Exteriors	12 - 15	15 - 20
Interiors	15 - 20	20 - 25
Barber Shops	30 - 35	35 - 40
Interiors	35 - 40	40 - 50
W/Black Shoeshine boys	60 - 70	70 - 90
Billiard Parlors, Pool Halls	20 - 30	30 - 40
Interiors	25 - 35	35 - 45
Bowling Alleys – Exteriors	20 - 25	25 - 35

Antigo, Wisconsin, Clermont Street Near
Butterfield Hotel, ca. 1912, By SSSS

Guerneville, Calif., ca. 1950
Street Scene, By Kodak

Interiors	30 - 40	40 - 50
Cigar/Tobacco Stores	30 - 40	40 - 50
Interiors	50 - 55	55 - 60
Dairies	10 - 20	20 - 30
Interiors	10 - 15	15 - 20
Drug Stores – Store Front	15 - 20	20 - 30
Interiors	20 - 30	30 - 40
Fish/Meat Markets – Store Front	25 - 30	30 - 40
Interiors	30 - 35	35 - 45
General/Grocery Stores – Store Front	20 - 30	30 - 35
Interiors	25 - 35	35 - 45
Ice Cream Parlors – Store Front	35 - 45	45 - 55
Interiors	40 - 50	50 - 60
Post Office – Exteriors	10 - 15	15 - 20
Interiors	50 - 75	75 - 90
Restaurants – Store Front	15 - 20	20 - 25
Interiors	15 - 25	25 - 35
Service Stations – Exteriors	15 - 25	25 - 35
W/Gas Pumps	20 - 30	30 - 40
Shoe Repair Shops – Store Front	25 - 30	30 - 40
Interiors	30 - 35	35 - 45
Soda Fountains	25 - 35	35 - 45
With Ice Cream or Coca Cola Signs	30 - 40	40 - 50
Taverns – Store Front	15 - 20	20 - 25
Interiors	20 - 25	25 - 35
Theaters – Showing marque	20 - 25	25 - 35
Toy Store – Exteriors	20 - 25	25 - 35
Interiors, Showing Toys	35 - 40	40 - 50
Street Scenes		
Small Towns	8 - 15	15 - 25
Busy Street Scenes	15 - 20	20 - 30
W/Readable Signs of Stores, Hotels, etc.	30 - 40	40 - 55
1950 Guerneville, Calif.	10 - 15	15 - 18
Large Towns	8 - 10	10 - 15
Busy Street Scenes	8 - 12	12 - 15

MISCELLANEOUS

Barbers	30 - 35	35 - 45
Barbershop Interiors	35 - 40	40 - 50
Baseball Players, Identified (See Sports, Baseball)	25 - 35	35 - 45

Bathing Girls of 1910 era   *1927 Halloween Costume*   *Red Cross Nuns, Belton and*
Anonymous   *Baptist Dorm., LaPaz (AZO)*   *Ruth – ca. 1917 (AZO)*

Unidentified	15 - 20	20 - 25
Baseball Teams, Identified	30 - 40	40 - 50
Unidentified	15 - 20	20 - 30
Baseball Players, Professional (See Sports, Baseball)		
Baseball Teams, Professional (See Sports, Baseball) *	100 - 125	125 - 150
Bathing		
Attractive Ladies	8 - 10	10 - 15
Groups	7 - 8	8 - 12
Blacks		
Children	10 - 12	12 - 15
In School or Class Photos	100 - 125	125 - 150
Men/Women	6 - 8	8 - 10
Bands	35 - 45	45 - 55
Baseball Teams *	50 - 60	60 - 80
Identified	200 - 300	300 - 400
* Several have auctioned as high as $1000-2000.		
Caddies	125 -150	150 - 200
Blacks Working in Fields, etc.	10 - 12	12 - 15
Musical Groups	10 - 15	15 - 25
Halloween Costumes	200 - 250	250 - 300
Valentine's Day costume	150 - 200	200 - 250
Black-Face Minstrels	40 - 50	50 - 60
Other Entertainers, Dancing	30 - 40	40 - 50
Red Cross Nuns	100 - 125	125 - 150
Salesmen	150 - 200	200 - 250
Staged Studio Photos	75 - 100	100 - 125
Blacks by E.C. EDDY, Southern Pines, NC		
"A Fruitful Long Leaf Pine" Man and possum	150 - 175	175 - 200
"By the Sand Road" – 1914	100 - 125	125 - 150
"Cotton Picking Time" – 1914	100 - 125	125 - 150
"From Grand-daddy Down"	150 - 175	175 - 200
"Laundry–Special Delivery"	150 - 175	175 - 200
"The Life Saving Crew at 10th Hole..." (Golf)	200 - 250	250 - 300
"Meals at all Hours" (Eatery with Cola Sign)	200 - 250	250 - 300
"Ned's Cabin"	125 - 150	150 - 175

Anonymous 1911 Era Black School Children and Teacher, Photo by AZO

E. C. Eddy, "From Grand-daddy Down" Near So. Pines, N.C. – ca. 1915 (AZO)

Black Millinery Salesman, Florida ca. 1910 , Photo by VELOX

"Ned's Family, Southern Pines"	125 - 150	150 - 175
"No. Three Course, Pinehurst" (Golf)	200 - 250	250 - 300
"So. Pines, N.C." (Boy rides bull wagon, etc.)	125 - 150	150 - 175
"Southern Pines, N.C." (Man and possum in tree)	175 - 200	200 - 225
"Sunny South"	150 - 175	175 - 200
"Two Coons & One Possum"	150 - 175	175 - 200
"Uncle Gaddy"	150 - 175	175 - 200
"Uncle Billy"	150 - 175	175 - 200
"Uncle Joe's Express" (Oxcart)	125 - 150	150 - 175
"Uncle John"	150 - 175	175 - 200
"Uncle Tom's Cabin"	150 - 175	175 - 200
"Women's Exchange, Pinehurst, N.C."	125 - 150	150 - 175
"Working Hours" (Children asleep on cotton pile)	100 - 125	125 - 150

Blacks by Photographer F. MARCHANT, Hamlet, N.C.

"A Southern Darky & His 'Possum"	175 - 200	200 - 250
"Rufus and Rastus"	175 - 200	200 - 250
"Mammy's in de Cotton Patch"	150 - 175	175 - 225
"Hamlet, N.C. Seaboard Transfer"	150 - 175	175 - 225
"Come Down, Mr. Possum"	175 - 200	200 - 250

Convicts or Chain Gang

Men	75 - 100	100 - 150
Women	250 - 300	300 - 400

Blacksmiths — 30 - 40 / 40 - 50
 Shops — 35 - 45 / 45 - 55
Boxing (See Sports, Boxing Section)
Children – Common — 3 - 4 / 4 - 7

Photo by E. C. Eddy, AZO
"Meals at all Hours"

Photo by E. C. Eddy, AZO
"Uncle Gaddy"

Photo by E. C. Eddy, AZO
"Uncle Joe's Express"

Photo by F. Marchant, Hamlet, N.C.
"Seaboard Transfer"

Photo by F. Marchant, Hamlet, N.C.
"A Southern Darky & His 'Possum"

Photo by F. Marchant, Hamlet, N.C.
"Mammy's in de Cotton Patch"

With Animals	7 - 8	8 - 12
With Dolls	15 - 20	20 - 30
With Dolls in Doll Carriage	20 - 25	25 - 30
With Toys	10 - 15	15 - 25
With Large Teddy Bears	25 - 30	30 - 40
With Small Teddy Bears	15 - 20	20 - 25
In Costumes	15 - 18	18 - 25
Halloween Costumes	40 - 60	60 - 80
Christmas Trees	15 - 20	20 - 25
With Gifts Under Tree	20 - 25	25 - 30
Circus-Related		
Trapeze Artist, Identified	15 - 20	20 - 25
Other Performers	10 - 15	15 - 20
Fat Ladies, Freaks	15 - 20	20 - 25
Giants, Midgets, Strongmen, etc.	12 - 15	15 - 20
Advertising Circus	20 - 25	25 - 35
Animals -- Elephants, etc.	20 - 25	25 - 30
Add $5-8 for Barnum & Bailey Circus.		
Conductors		
Train and Trolly	25 - 30	30 - 35
Convicts or Chain Gang	20 - 25	25 - 40
Cooks, Bakers	20 - 25	25 - 30
Dentists or Doctors, at work	50 - 75	75 - 100
Exaggerated		
Photos by W.H. MARTIN		
Big Fish	10 - 15	15 - 20
Grasshoppers, Onions, Watermelons	15 - 18	18 - 22
Farm Products, Farm Animals	10 - 15	15 - 20
Watermelons, with Blacks	22 - 25	25 - 35
Big Fruit	10 - 15	15 - 20
Big Animals (Rabbits, etc.)	18 - 22	22 - 25
Buick Roadster chasing rabbit, other autos	20 - 25	25 - 28
Photos by A.S. JOHNSON, JR.	Range	30 - 100
Fire Departments	20 - 25	25 - 35
Hangings/Lynchings	25 - 30	30 - 50
Blacks	600 - 1000	1000 - 2000
See Mashburn's "Black Postcard Price Guide," 2nd.		
Adolf Hitler		
(By Hoffman)		
Used, With Postmark	15 - 18	18 - 25
Unused, No Postmark	12 - 15	15 - 20
Other Publishers		
Used, With Postmark	16 - 20	20 - 25
Unused, No Postmark	12 - 15	15 - 20
Indians		
Identified Chiefs	40 - 50	50 - 150
Alaska Indian Chiefs	50 - 75	75 - 100
Others, Identified	30 - 40	40 - 60
Unidentified	8 - 10	10 - 20
Potlacher Indian Maiden	30 - 40	40 - 50
School Bands	40 - 50	50 - 65
Ku Klux Klan	100 - 150	150 - 250
Mailman	25 - 30	30 - 40
Rural Mail Delivery Wagon	40 - 50	50 - 75

Anonymous Lady Conductor   *Adolph Hitler, Photo by*   *Potlacher Indian Maiden*
Ca. 1910   *Hoffman, No. 28*   *Ca. 1907, Juneau, Alaska*

Town Delivery Carts	30 - 40	40 - 50
City Delivery Trucks	40 - 50	50 - 60
Mining		
Coal Miners	20 - 25	25 - 30
Gold Miners	15 - 20	20 - 25
Alaska	15 - 20	20 - 25
Nudes (See "Real Photo Nudes")		
Plants, Mills		
Small Town – Exteriors	20 - 25	25 - 35
Large Town – Exteriors	10 - 15	15 - 20
Policemen	20 - 25	25 - 30
Political		
Presidents	10 - 20	20 - 25
President and Running Mate	30 - 40	40 - 50
Losing Candidates	15 - 20	20 - 35
Governors	20 - 25	25 - 30
Pony Express	20 - 25	25 - 35
Last Ride	35 - 45	45 - 60
Prisons	12 - 15	15 - 18
State Prison, Deer Lodge, Montana, ca. 1920	20 - 25	25 - 30
River Ferries	20 - 25	25 - 30
School House	10 - 15	15 - 20
One Room	40 - 50	50 - 60
School Children	10 - 15	15 - 20
Shakers		
At Work	75 - 100	100 - 125
Shakers Group, Mt. Lebanon, etc.	50 - 75	75 - 100
Stenographers		
With Typewriter	25 - 30	30 - 35
Street Vendors	35 - 45	45 - 60
With Vending Wagons	45 - 55	55 - 65
Popcorn, Ice Cream wagons or carts	75 - 100	100 - 150
Billy Sunday	10 - 12	12 - 18
Telephone Switchboard Operators	25 - 30	30 - 40
U.S. Flag		
People Dressed or Wrapped in Flag	35 - 40	40 - 60

State Prison, Deer Lodge, Montana
1920 Era, Photo by AZO

Public School, Bishop, Tex., Donated by
F.Z. Bishop, 1912 Era, Photo by AZO

1910 Era, Warren, N.H. School
Children and Teachers, Photo by AZO

1911 Era Stenographer with Typewriter
Photo by ARTURA

Uncle Sam in Flag	40 - 50	50 - 60
Rallies, Showing Flag, or Flag Day	30 - 40	40 - 50
Orations or Debates, Showing Flag	20 - 25	25 - 35
Patriotic Children	25 - 30	30 - 40
Zeppelins	20 - 25	25 - 40

REAL PHOTO DATING GUIDE

PROCESS	DATES	NOTES	PROCESS	DATES
AGFA ANSCO	1930-1940s		DOPS	1925-1942
ANSCO	1940-1960	Two stars at top and bottom.	EKC	1945-1950
			EKKP	1904-1950
ARGO	1905-1920		EKO	1942-1970
ARTURA	1910-1924		KODAK	1950-
AZO SQUARE	1927-1940s	Squares in corners.	KRUXO	1907-1920s
AZO DIA	1907-1908	Diamonds in corners.	NOKO	1907-1920s
AZO TRI 1	1904-1918	Four triangles pointed up.	PMO	1907-1915
			Sailboat	1905-1908
AZO TRI 2	1918-1930	Triangles; 2 up, 2 down.	SOLIO	1903-1920s
CYKO	1904-1920s	Hollow Letters.	VELOX 1	1901-1914
CYKO 2	1906-1908	Solid letters.	Squares in corners.	
DEFENDER 1	1910-1920	Diamond above and below.	VELOX 2	1907-1914
			Diamonds in corners.	
DEFENDER 2	1920-1940	Diamond inside.	VITAVA	1925-1934

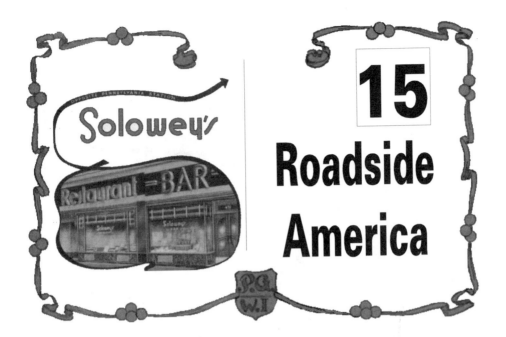

15 Roadside America

Roadside America consists of cards that were published to advertise a place of business on or near a busy highway during the 30's, 40's, and 50's. Cards were usually given to travelers stopping by, or were mailed to prospective customers. Most Roadside America cards were issued in the Linen and early Chrome Eras. There has, however, been some overlapping from the White Border Era, especially with cards of filling stations and restaurants. Real-photo views, and any views of diners, are always in great demand and command the highest prices.

The collecting of Roadside America material has continued to grow as collectors have become aware of the outstanding cards available. They like the possibility of getting into postcard groups where prices are still reasonable. Diners, gas stations, and drive-in restaurants are the most sought after, but they are becoming scarce. Chromes, as many dealers attest, have also become popular. Those new to the hobby, usually the 30-40 age group, can identify with cards of the 50's and are seeking them for their collections. Chrome prices on many topics are not too much below those of linens. In the final analysis, however, the particular view, its location, and the person buying it will always determine the value.

Values listed are for general cards of the particular motif. Subject matter and outstanding examples, plus supply and demand, would generate a higher value and very common cards could be much lower. Values for this listing are classified as to type as follows :

1   **Linens**
2   **Real Photos**
3   **Chromes**

	VG	EX
AUTOMOBILE DEALERSHIPS		
1	$ 6 - 9	$ 9 - 12
2	10 - 15	15 - 20
3	2 - 3	3 - 5

Winga's Cafe, Washing, Iowa
Standard Printing Co.

The Diamonds – "The Eating Place"
Near St. Louis, Missouri, S&K Co.

Patrick' Diner, Highland, New York
Curt Teich – No. 8B-H839

BAR & GRILL

1	5 - 7	7 - 10
2	7 - 10	10 - 15
3	2 - 3	3 - 5

CAFES

1	6 - 9	9 - 12
2	10 - 12	12 - 16
3	2 - 3	3 - 5

COFFEE POT CAFE TYPES

1	9 - 12	12 - 15
2	12 - 15	15 - 20
3	3 - 5	5 - 6

DINERS

1	20 - 40	40 - 75
2	40 - 50	50 - 100
3	5 - 10	10 - 15

*Reed's Corner Station, Shell Products,
Moberly, Missouri (Black and White)*

*Shadrick's Candy and Gift Shoppe
Jennings, Florida, R.P. by W. M. Cline*

*Fort View Court (with Gas Pumps) Near Chatsworth, Georgia
Curt Teich – No. E-10271*

DRIVE-IN RESTAURANTS

1	10 - 12	12 - 15
2	12 - 15	15 - 20
3	2 - 3	3 - 6

DRIVE-IN THEATERS

1	10 - 15	15 - 20
2	15 - 20	20 - 25
3	6 - 8	8 - 10

EXAGGERATED BUILDINGS

1	8 - 10	10 - 15
2	10 - 15	15 - 20
3	2 - 3	3 - 6

FILLING STATIONS/SERVICE STATIONS

1	10 - 15	15 - 20
2	15 - 20	20 - 25
3	3 - 4	4 - 7

*Riverview Hotel (with Gas Pumps)
Jacksonville, N.C., Tichnor, 71586*

*Frances Jewel Cabins, Wells, Maine
R.P., No. 256, by DOPS*

*Frick's Maple Beach Lodge, Pelican Lake,
Wisconsin – R.P. ca. 1938*

*Greystone Lodge, Dillsboro, N.C.
R.P. by Kodak*

FOOD AND GIFT MARKETS

1	5 - 8	8 - 12
2	10 - 15	15 - 20
3	2 - 3	3 - 6

FRUIT, VEGETABLE STANDS

1	8 - 12	12 - 16
2	10 - 15	15 - 20
3	2 - 3	3 - 6

GAS PUMPS

1	8 - 10	10 - 12
2	12 - 15	15 - 20
3	3 - 4	4 - 7

HOTELS

1	1 - 2	2 - 3
2	3 - 4	4 - 7
3	0.50 - 1	1 - 1.50

ICE CREAM SHOPS

1	8 - 12	12 - 15
2	15 - 20	20 - 25
3	3 - 4	4 - 6

LODGES AND INNS

1	5 - 7	7 - 10
2	7 - 9	9 - 12
3	3 - 4	4 - 6

Evelyn's Sea Food, Belmar, New Jersey
Andres Product Corporation, E-10730

Stockholm Restaurant, Near Summerville,
New Jersey, Tichnor, No. 77863

Interstate Glass House Restaurant, Chattanooga, Tenn. — "Good Food and Good
Service"

MINIATURE GOLF

1	6 - 9	9 - 12
2	10 - 15	15 - 18
3	2 - 3	3 - 6

MOTELS, MOTOR COURTS, Single View

1	1 - 3	3 - 5
2	4 - 7	7 - 10
3	0.50 - 1	1 - 2

MOTELS, MOTOR COURTS, Multiple Views

1	4 - 7	7 - 9
2	5 - 8	8 - 12
3	2 - 3	3 - 5

PECAN STANDS

1	6 - 9	9 - 12
2	10 - 15	15 - 18
3	3 - 5	5 - 8

Swimming Pool, 4-H Camp Caesar, Webster County, West Virginia
Real Photo by Kodak

RESTAURANTS

1	4 - 7	7 - 9
2	5 - 8	8 - 12
3	1 - 2	2 - 4

SANDWICH SHOPS

1	6 - 9	9 - 12
2	9 - 12	12 - 15
3	2 - 3	3 - 6

SKATING RINKS

1	4 - 7	7 - 10
2	8 - 12	12 - 16
3	2 - 3	3 - 5

SOUVENIR SHOPS, TRADING POSTS

1	4 - 7	7 - 10
2	8 - 12	12 - 15
3	1 - 2	2 - 4

SWIMMING POOLS, COMMERCIAL (Not Motels)

1	6 - 9	9 - 12
2	8 - 12	12 - 15
3	2 - 3	3 - 5

TAXI STANDS

1	8 - 12	12 - 15
2	12 - 15	15 - 20
3	3 - 5	5 - 8

TRAILER PARKS, COMMERCIAL

1	6 - 9	9 - 12
2	8 - 12	12 - 16
3	2 - 3	3 - 5

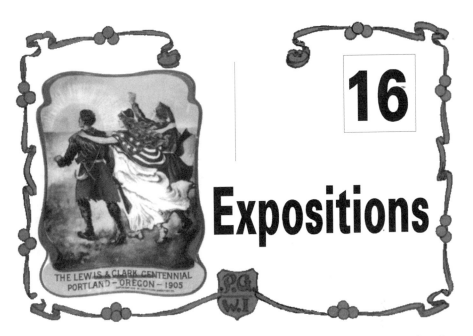

Exposition cards continue to generate interest but prices have been rather flat. Some of the better quality material is beginning to appear in auctions and dealer stocks that were heavily collected in the 1970-80 era. Continuing to lead the way are early hold-to-lights and woven silk issues. Interest should continue to grow as more of these fine collectibles re-appear. As of now, there appears to be some great bargains in all but the most expensive and rare expositions.

	VG	EX
1893 COLUMBIAN EXPOSITION		
Goldsmith Pre-Official, no Seal	$100 - 125	$125 - 150
Officials, Series 1	15 - 20	20 - 30
J. Koehler B&W Issues	35 - 45	45 - 55
PMC or Post Card Backs	15 - 25	25 - 35
Puck Magazine Advertising Cards	135 - 140	140 - 150
Other Advertising Cards	100 - 120	120 - 150
Signed **R. SELINGER**	100 - 115	115 - 145
Anonymous Publishers	100 - 150	150 - 180
1894 CALIFORNIA MID-WINTER EXPO	300 - 350	350 - 400
1895 COTTON STATES & INT. EXPO	160 - 190	190 - 220
Negro Building	350 - 375	375 - 400
1896 BERLINER GEWERBE-AUSSTELLUNG		
No. 1 "Haupt-Ausstellungsgebäude"	30 - 35	35 - 50
1897 LEIPZIG INDUSTRIE-U. GEWERBE-AUSST.		
Emil Pinkau Locomobilhalle von R. Wolf	25 - 30	30 - 35
1897 TENNESSEE CENTENNIAL EXPO	160 - 175	175 - 210
1898 TRANS-MISSISSIPPI EXPO		
Trans-Mississippi Official Cards	50 - 60	60 - 70
Albertype Co. Views	90 - 100	100 - 120
1898 WORCESTER SEMI-CENTENNIAL	80 - 90	90 - 100
1900 PARIS EXPOSITION		
Scenes	10 - 12	12 - 15
Hold-To-Light	20 - 25	25 - 35

*Berliner Gewerbe-Ausstellung 1896
No. 1, "Haupt-Ausstellungsgebäude"*

*Leipzig 1897, "Sächsisch-Thüringische
Industrie-u. Gewerbe-Ausstellung"*

*St. Louis World's Fair, 1904
Official Souvenir H-T-L Card of the Machinery Building*

1901 PAN AMERICAN EXPOSITION

Niagara Envelope Co. B&W	8 - 10	10 - 15
Color	10 - 15	15 - 20
Oversized	70 - 80	80 - 100

1902 SOUTH CAROLINA INTER-STATE

Albertype Co. Issues	125 - 150	150 - 175
Others	80 - 90	90 - 120

1903 20TH TRIENNIAL NAT. SANGERFEST

Franz Huld	15 - 20	20 - 30

1904 ST. LOUIS WORLD'S FAIR

Buxton & Skinner	8 - 10	10 - 15
Chisholm Bros.		
Samuel Cupples	8 - 12	12 - 15
Jumbo 6 x 9" H-T-L	200 - 225	225 - 250
Transparencies	8 - 10	10 - 15

Blanke's Coffee Adv. at 1904 St. Louis World's Fair – Machinery Building

1905 Lewis & Clark Expo., E. P. Charlton & Co., The Sunken Gardens..."

Fourth Annual Rose Festival, Portland, Oregon, 1910 – Portland Post Card Co.

Hold-To-Light	35 - 40	40 - 50
V.O. Hammon	6 - 8	8 - 10
The Inside Inn H-T-L	200 - 250	250 - 300
E. C. Kropp	5 - 10	10 - 12
Rotograph	10 - 12	12 - 15
Selige	10 - 12	12 - 15
Raphael Tuck	5 - 10	10 - 15
Woven Silks (14)	250 - 400	400 - 500
Advertising Cards	10 - 15	15 - 20
Blanke's Coffee "Machinery Building"	20 - 25	25 - 35
1905 LEWIS & CLARK EXPOSITION		
E.P. Charlton	9 - 12	12 - 15
Edw. H. Mitchell	9 - 12	12 - 15
B.B. Rich (10)	9 - 12	12 - 15
A. Selige (10)	9 - 12	12 - 15
Advertising Cards	15 - 18	18 - 22
1907 JAMESTOWN EXPOSITION		
A.C. Bosselman	7 - 8	8 - 10
Illustrated Post Card Co.	25 - 30	35 - 40
Jamestown A&V	7 - 10	10 - 12
Confederate		
50 Portrait of Jeff Davis	25 - 30	30 - 40
51 Beauvoir, Home of Jefferson Davis	20 - 25	25 - 30
52 White House of the Confederacy	20 - 25	25 - 30
53 Statue of Winnie Davis, Daughter of the Confederacy	20 - 25	25 - 30

54 Portrait of General Robert E. Lee	40 - 45	45 - 55
55 General Robert E. Lee and Officers	40 - 45	45 - 55
56 Last Meeting of Lee and Jackson	40 - 45	45 - 55
57 Surrender of Lee	40 - 45	45 - 55
58 "Arlington" Home of Gen. Lee..."	20 - 25	25 - 30
59 Statue of General Lee and Coat of Arms	20 - 25	25 - 30
67 Leading Statesmen of the Confederacy	30 - 35	35 - 40
Battleships	12 - 15	15 - 20
H.C. CHRISTY		
Army Girl	200 - 230	230 - 260
Navy Girl	200 - 230	230 - 260
Raphael Tuck Oilettes	6 - 9	9 - 12
Silver Issues (10)	12 -15	15 - 20
1908 PHILADELPHIA FOUNDERS WEEK		
Illustrated Post Card Co. (10)	6 - 8	8 - 10
Fred Lounsbury (10)	8 - 10	10 - 12
1908 APPALACHIAN EXPO, Knoxville, TN	10 - 15	15 - 20
1909 ALASKA YUKON-PACIFIC EXPOSITION		
Edw. H. Mitchell	5 - 6	6 - 10
Portland Post Card Co.	5 - 7	7 - 10
Advertising Postcards	7 - 10	10 - 15
1909 HUDSON-FULTON CELEBRATION		
J. Koehler	5 - 7	7 - 10
Fred Lounsbury	7 - 9	9 - 12
Redfield Floats (72)	5 - 6	6 - 9
Raphael Tuck, Series 164 (6)	5 - 9	9 - 12
Valentine & Co., S/Wall (6)	6 - 9	9 - 12
1909 PORTOLA FESTIVAL		
Pacific Novelty	8 - 10	10 - 12
Posters	10 - 12	12 - 16
Others	6 - 7	7 - 10
1910 APPALACHIAN EXPO, Knoxville	5 - 7	7 - 10
Advertising	7 - 9	9 - 12
Edw. H. Mitchell (Sepia)	18 - 22	22 - 26
1910 ROSE FESTIVAL, Portland, Oregon		
Portland Post Card Co.		
Poster Cards	12 - 15	15 - 20
1915 PANAMA-PACIFIC EXPOSITION	3 - 5	5 - 7
Advertising Poster Cards	10 - 12	12 - 16
1915 PANAMA-CALIFORNIA EXPOSITION	3 - 5	5 - 8
Pre-Issues	5 - 7	7 - 10
Advertising Poster Cards	20 - 25	25 - 30
1933 CENTURY OF PROGRESS		
Exhibits	1 - 2	2 - 4
Advertising	3 - 5	5 - 7
Comics		
1936 TEXAS CENTENNIAL	3 - 5	5 - 8
1939 NEW YORK WORLD'S FAIR	1 - 3	3 - 6
1939 SAN FRANCISCO EXPOSITION	1 - 3	3 - 6

Appendix

BIBLIOGRAPHY

The following publications, all related to the collection and study of postcards, are highly recommended for further reading.

All About Dwig, Bonnie P. Miller, Palm Bay, FL, 1976

American Advertising Postcards, Sets and Series, 1890-1920, Fred and Mary Megson, 1985

American & European Postcards of Harrison Fisher Illustrator. Naomi Welch, 1999, $34.95 + $4 P/H. Images of the Past, 309 Playa Blvd., La Selva Beach, CA 95076

The American Postcard Guide to Tuck, Sally Carver, Brookline, MA, 1979

The American Postcard Journal, Roy and Marilyn Nuhn, New Haven, CT

The Artist-Signed Postcard Price Guide, J. L. Mashburn, Colonial House, 1993

Art Nouveau Post Cards, Alan Weill, Image Graphics, NY, 1977

Bessie Pease Gutmann, Published Works Catalog, Victor J.W. Christie, 1986

Black Americana Postcard Price Guide, J.L. Mashburn, Enka, NC, 1996

Black Postcard Price Guide, J. L. Mashburn, Colonial House, Enka, NC, 1999

Coles Phillips: A Collector's Guide, Norman Platnick, 50 Brentwood Rd., Bay Shore, New York 11706 ($16.00 plus $4.00 for Priority Mail)

The Collector's Guide to Post Cards, Jane Wood, Gas City, IN

Directory of Postcard Artists, Publishers & Trademarks, Barbara Andrews, 1975

Encyclopedia of Antique Postcards, Susan Nicholson, Wallace-Homestead, 1994

Larger Than Life: The American Tall-Tale Postcard 1905-1915. Exaggeration Real Photo Postcards, Morgan Williams and Cynthia Rubins

Guide to Artists' Signatures & Monograms on Postcards, Nouhad A. Saleh., 1993 Minerva Press, Boca Raton, FL   33429-0969

Fantasy Postcards With Price Guide, J. L. Mashburn, Colonial House, Enka, NC, 1996

Halloween Postcards Published by John Winsch, Hazel Leler, Houston, 1994
Neudin Cartes Postales de Collection, 1991, 35 rue G. St-Hilaire, 75005 Paris
Official Postcard Price Guide, D. Allmen, House of Collectibles, NY, 1990
Philip Boileau, Painter of Fair Women, D. Ryan, Gotham Book Mart, NY, 1981
Picture Postcards in the U.S., 1893-1918, Dorothy Ryan
   Prairie Fires & Paper Moons: The American Photographic Postcard, 1902-1920, Hal Morgan, Andreas Brown, Boston, 1981
Real Photo Postcards, Robert Ward, Bellevue, 1994
The Postcard Price Guide, **1st Ed.** (1992), **2nd Ed.** (1995), & **3rd Ed.** (1997), J.L.Mashburn, Colonial House, Enka, NC
The Postcards of Alphonse Mucha, Q. David Bowers, Mary Martin, 1980
Samuel L. Schmucker: The Discovery of His Lost Art, Jack Davis and Dorothy Ryan, 2001, Softcover - $49.95 + $5 S/H; Hardcover - $100 + $6 S/P. Jack and Susan Davis, 501 E. Peach, Bozeman, MT 59715.
Sports Postcard Price Guide, J.L. Mashburn, Colonial House, Enka, NC, 1998
Standard Postcard Catalog, 1982, James L. Lowe, PA
The Super Rare Postcards of Harrison Fisher, J. L. Mashburn, 1992
Vintage View of Christmas Past, Jim Morrison, York, PA, 1995
What Cheer News, Mrs. E.K. Austin, Editor, R. Island Postcard Club

PERIODICALS

The following trade publications all contain articles, auctions, and advertisements concerning postcards. They may be contacted for subscription rates or cost of sample copies.

The Antique Trader Weekly, P.O. Box 1050, Dubuque, IA 52004
Antiques & Auction News, Monthly, P.O. Box 500, Mt. Joy, PA 17552
Barr's Post Card News, Bi-Weekly, 70 S. 6th St., Lansing, IA 52151
Collector News & Antique Reporter, Monthly, P.O. Box 156, Grundy Center, IA 50638
New England Antiques Journal, Monthly, 4 Church St., Ware, MA 01082
Paper Collectors Marketplace, Monthly, P.O. Box 128, Scandinavia, WI 54977
Picture Post Card Monthly, 15 Debdale Ln., Keyworth, Nottingham NG12 5HT, U.K. The leading Postcard Magazine in Europe.
   Subscription – $60 per year, via Airmail, at present exchange rates.
Postcard Collector, Monthly, P.O. Box 1050, Dubuque, IA 52004

MAJOR POSTCARD AUCTION HOUSES

The following firms have occasional postcard auctions and are all very reliable. Write or call for updated information on how to obtain copies of their catalogs. Some will send free of charge while others charge a small fee.

Antique Paper Guild, P.O. Box 5742, Belleview, WA 98006 (425) 643-5701
   Real Photo Specialists
Bennett's, Pickering Road, Dover, NH 03820

Butterfield & Butterfield, 220 San Bruno Ave., San Francisco, CA 90046

George C. Gibbs, 601 New Loudon Rd., #219, Latham, NY 12110
(518) 786-3292. (Usually in Barr's Post Card News)

Memory Lane Antique Postcards, P.O. Box 66, Keymar, MD 21757
(410) 775-0188

Richard Novick, 17 Abbey Lane, Marlboro, NJ 07746 (732) 536-2532
(Usually in Barr's Post Card News)

Swann Galleries, Inc., 104 East 25th St., New York, NY 10010

Code for Index:

Artists .... All Caps
Publishers ..... Lower Case
Topics .... Lower Case Bold

Index

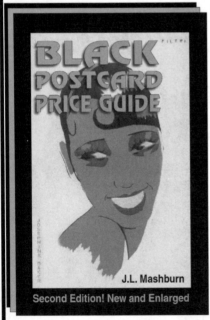